RETURN OF THE INFIDEL

VIRENDRA PANDIT

Vitasta
LET KNOWLEDGE SPREAD
www.vitastapublishing.com

Published by
Renu Kaul Verma
Vitasta Publishing Pvt Ltd
2/15, Ansari Road, Daryaganj
New Delhi - 110 002
info@vitastapublishing.com

ISBN 978-93-86473-07-3

Reprint 2018

Cover and layout by Vits Press
Printed by Vikas Computer and Printers

Dedicated to

Those Who Are Yet To Arrive

Contents

Acknowledgements

Sir Issac Newton once famously said: 'If I have seen further, it is by standing on the shoulders of giants.' And Osho Rajneesh believed that only lunatics could be the most original! Few people can, therefore, really be original; I am no exception.

This was planned to be a part of my first book, *The Biology of History: Ascent of Women*, published in 2013, but has come out as a sequel. It is based on a mountain of literature available in history books, monographs, theses, research papers, articles, and news items etc I have come across over the last 40 years, and with which eminent historians and discerning readers are acquainted. It is not designed as an academic or scholarly work but expects the patient reader to have a fair knowledge of world and Indian history and religions. Basically, I have aggregated and pieced together these nuggets of information to spot a trend in global civilisational progress. I thank all these known, unknown and forgotten authors and am immensely grateful to them.

To make this book a reality, sincere thanks are due to my friends:

Renu Kaul Verma, Managing Director, Vitasta Publishing.

Abhilash Khandekar, old journalist-author friend, for introducing me to Renu.

Papri Sen Sri Raman, my first reader and editor, for believing in the book and then doing an arduous job exceptionally well, and patiently.

M M Dahima, former IAS officer, Madhya Pradesh, for enlightening me to the intricacies of India's caste system, when I was posted in Bhopal.

Mukesh Vyas, my late journalist friend in Rajkot, for assisting me with the background of Mahatma Gandhi, M A Jinnah, their families, castes, religions and traditions

Mukesh Thakkar, a veteran banker, for introducing me to the *Pranami Sampraday* of the Mahatma.

R K Pugalia, for introducing me to the Jain saint Acharya Mahapragya in 2003 for an interview.

And my beloved wife, Kalpana, for tolerating me since 1985!

Thank you all, again.

Virendra Pandit
Ahmedabad
14 May 2017

Publisher's Note

What will you do if you have a manuscript which says 'Jinnah was, perhaps, Father of the Indian subcontinent'? Will you not publish the book? We will. We decided to because Vitasta began her life with a book titled, *Brahmacharya Gandhi & His Women Associates*. At that time some ten years ago, it was blasphemous to look at Gandhi critically, as a part of history. He could only be discussed as a Mahatma. It is in the same spirit that we bring you this new book, *Return of the Infidel*.

As a publisher, it is easy to say, 'Opinions expressed in it are the author's own. The publisher is in no way responsible for these'. We don't just want to say that. Virendra Pandit is a veteran journalist and avid reader of theology, philosophy and biology… and the thesis he puts forward can be likened to one by Richard Dawkins or Daniel Dennett or Paul Davies or even Paul Levi. What Pandit has done is lugged all the ingredients to the top of Mount Vesuvius and set up a fire on the brink of the volcano, and on it placed a witch's cauldron and has prepared his brew. How could we not let the world taste it? Elixir or poison, whatever it may be, our readers must sip it.

At the end of it, we are sure, you will ponder over all that has been said, and think, perhaps there is some truth in it. The author not only presents another perspective on Mahatma Gandhi, he also looks at Krishna as critically as he does at the Christ and Mohammed and makes fine distinctions between the atheist, agnostic, heretic and finally concludes that the AGE OF THE INFIDEL has arrived, when the Asian giants, all disbelievers, China, Japan, India are roaring and spitting fire in an orchard of cherry blossoms.

Prologue

The 21st century has unleashed two extraordinary globalising torrential currents: technology-enabled economy and theology-based terror. Interestingly, theology itself was our ancient 'technology', something that empowered our ancestors to achieve 'connectivity', making local and global groupings possible and providing survival benefits in our Darwinian evolution. Theology and its new avatar, technology, have often been great aggregators, enablers and levelers. And like technology now, even theology slowly suffered obsolescence, making its replacement necessary. In our times, what we know as 'technology' is itself being gradually upstaged by 'applications' or Apps, in which existing machines, programmes and services are increasingly mothering new ones, each with a shorter shelf-life.

While the 20th century saw emergence of great 'functional' powers, particularly during the World Wars, our century is witnessing a strange phenomenon: increasing dysfunctionality of hyper-powers. Obese, neither loved nor feared, both the USA and its possible successor China, at least in Asia, are paradoxically emerging as increasingly lonely powers, unable to convince and carry the world with them, the ones not trusted even by their temporary 'friends'. Globally, they are even seen as 'non-producing assets' (NPAs) as they abdicate leadership. For instance, if America undertakes the task of 'cleaning up' the Middle East, it will have to exercise power, which the world will not accept; not cleaning up makes Washington seen as 'weak'. Also, even in the West, America could no longer hope to create a 'Coalition of the Willing' against Islamists' terrorism, unlike the way it once forged NATO against the former USSR. Post-World War-II America's track record shows that it has mastered the art of cultivating tomorrow's Frankensteins today.

Until Barack Obama, few scarcely trusted sweet-talking Washington, and saw in it a necessary evil; Donald Trump's dilemma is that if he makes friends abroad, he loses his core constituency at home!

Similarly, China, despite its impressive economic progress over the last four decades, finds it difficult to convert its power into enduring influence as it has serious disputes with major Asian neighbours like India, Japan and Vietnam—both China and its neighbours view each other with suspicion. Bereft of any NATO-type security alliance, China has had relatively 'cordial' relations *only* with 'rogue states' like Pakistan, global nursery of terrorism, and North Korea, Beijing's client! Also, in the absence of democracy at home, China has never been seen as a role model in an increasingly democratising world. In South Asia, the very word 'China' has emerged as an unpopular acronym for 'fake' due to the cheap and 'substandard' products the users say the Dragon dumps in the region.

In such a global vacuum of unifying ideas, cults attract lonely minds and replace systems as unsuccessful people surrender before someone they believe would bring about Change; this Change is brought about by elimination of surplus population through wars and diseases, that ruthlessly clear the clutter and eases evolutionary flow of Life.

Islam, the most influential and biggest cult of all times, has been mutating itself each decade with its latest mutant being more lethal than the preceding one: so, the Taliban was 'milder' than the al-Qaeda which turned 'moderate' vis-à-vis its successor, the Islamic State (IS)! More terror-enrichment may be on the way...The Muslim world is now imploding and collapsing from within, studded as it is with some 1,500 militant groups—all Islamists, all anti-democratic, all nihilists—as technology comes in a fatal embrace of, and silently exterminates, theology. Within 'democratic' Islamic nations, there often emerge sub-mutants under various garbs, with shorter shelf-life—Mohamed Morsi in Egypt, Imran Khan and Muhammad Tahir-ul-Qadri in Pakistan, for instance—as the Muslim world struggles to experiment with democracy and technology in an attempt to somehow fit it into the overall architecture of Islam. The Muslim world has never ever seen a truly democratic leader since Mustafa Kemal Ataturk who abolished the Caliphate in 1924.

But other faiths are also in the same shaky boat. Even in democratic nations, hyper-nationalists, conservatives and de-globalisers are coming to power thanks to revivification of faith-based political alliances in new garbs—India, the USA and Turkey are recent examples. Coming to power is easier; once in power, the new rulers turn relatively 'normal' as they realise complexities of retaining power.

Since the 1990s, in India, the Bharatiya Janata Party leader Atal Behari Vajpayee emerged 'moderate' and his deputy L K Advani 'hardliner'; then, Advani turned 'moderate' and his successor Narendra Modi the 'hardliner'; as Prime Minister, Modi is seen as 'moderate' and his party chief Amit Shah as 'hardliner'! Recently, Yogi Adiyanath, as Chief Minister of the most populous State of Uttar Pradesh replaced Shah as hardliner. In the Buddhist countries like Sri Lanka and Myanmar, similar leaders are emerging.

In this interplay of globalising forces, even an atheist China is beset with emergence of cults. The Communist Party tolerates only those organised religions whose shrines are registered with the government; it is intolerant towards foreign and unregistered religious groups. As Fenggang Yang of Purdue University says, this reflects the emergence of 'militant atheism' in the Communist Party. In an 'irreligious' China, popular cults have been emerging periodically. In particular, in the 19th century, a cult called Taiping was founded by a 'younger brother of Jesus Christ'. In the 20th century, the Mao cult was crushed; it was followed by Falun Gong, which, too, was crushed when it acquired a threateningly popular appeal and offered an alternative system of belief and authority. Another important cult that flourished briefly in China in the 1990s was the Church of the Almighty God, founded by another 'brother' of Jesus Christ. But the Communist Party, itself the biggest cult, has crushed all rivals; recently, Chinese President Xi Jinping, who also heads the military and the party, has emerged as Mao-II and crushed all opposition. In the 21st century, an atheist China will emerge as the biggest antidote to monotheist Christianity and Islam.

So, our 21st century is watching the interplay of a 'militant Christianity' led by the USA, 'militant Islam' led by Saudi Arabia and Iran, a militant Jewry of Israel, a 'militant' Hinduism of India and a 'militant atheism' of China. Interplay of these self-righteous militancies will determine the fate of Homo sapiens in our next generations. The emerging scenario hints towards a possible big-picture evolution of global affairs.

This book is about the response of Asia to emergence of West Asia (Middle East) and the West in the last 2,000 years. It reinterprets history along Darwinian principles and explains emergence of India, China and Japan as an interplay of their evolution vis-à-vis the rise of Christianity and Islam, the biggest proselytisers. It is necessary to understand how Asia would shape up in the 21st century as these great unifying and mobilising faiths decline under the crushing impact of acceleration of technology.

With the fourth generation (4-G) of Muslim extremism (the Islamic State) emerging in the Middle East, and the West getting sunk and sucked into it, the three ancient Asian civilisations, revivified in the 20th century, will reshape the 21st century world. The 20th century has seen decline of Christianity as well as Islam through wars, decolonisation, terror, and revival of Asia, Africa and South America. In particular, 'infidel' nations like India, China and Japan behaved similarly. Their top leaders—Gandhi, Mao and Tojo—without ever meeting each other, often unconsciously worked with the same common purpose: *abolishing the monotheists' hegemony.* In this civilisational systolic and diastolic movement, it was a struggle for existence between the overstaying monotheist guests on one side and the native, revivified atheist/polytheists hosts on the other.

This book focuses on India's history in greater detail because this civilisation, representing Nature's bio-diversity, multicultural assimilation and polytheistic eco-system blended into one, was the closest to the Source of catalysts from West Asia and she had, therefore, to struggle the hardest to shape herself back by 1947. It sees Gandhi and Jinnah in a whole new light, as great game-changers and personification of a long process of change leading to transformation of their moribund societies and retreat of monotheists.

In this big picture of slow metamorphosis, it explains how China and Japan also followed a similar health regime and trajectory, evolving Mao and Tojo as natural offshoots and the best representatives of their respective contemporary societies.

Old Kids on the Block Return

IN 1954, A L Basham began to 'decolonise' the Indian mind, indirectly, with his famous book, *The Wonder That Was India*, in what was a survey of the culture of the Indian subcontinent before the arrival of Muslims. In fact, soon after the Second World War, similar books about other ancient civilisations—Greece, Rome, Egypt and Babylon—were published. It was an era of global decolonisation as the Western and West Asia's eastern empires slowly dissolved back into the vast ocean of Time, while ancient nations re-emerged. The three great Abrahamic religions (Judaism, Christianity and Islam), that had played a catalytic role in revivification of ancient civilisations, had, apparently, run their course in these settings: the contemporary rise of the BRICS nations is part of this evolutionary inevitability.

Incidentally, while Greece and Rome were almost fully converted by and underwent societal mutation due to Christianity, and Egypt and Babylon due to Islam, India not only steadfastly remained largely Hindu but also managed to reverse the tide of both the Abrahamic streams by 1947. China and Japan, too, did similarly since the 19th century.

In the 1960s, the then American Ambassador to India, Daniel Patrick Moynihan, famously observed that India was a 'functional anarchy'. Indira Gandhi, unlearning from her father Jawaharlal Nehru's *The Discovery of India*, forgot this apt observation in 1975, and erred into making it a 'dysfunctional monarchy'; the Indians punished her for trying to put India to Order and then also rewarded her in 1980 for restoring her inherent chaos! Her son, Rajiv, immensely contributed to the modernisation of India until he was assassinated. His successor, P V Narasimha Rao led the drive for economic liberalisation and globalisation before slipping into political oblivion. The fate of Narendra Modi, who is trying to emerge as an all-season leader, remains to be seen. Mother India ruthlessly exterminates its leaders after they deliver the next dose of semen, the way many non-chordate females swallow their male partners after sex.

Revisiting the country his forefathers emerged from, V S Naipaul slowly corrected himself, between 1964 and 1990, from *An Area of Darkness*, through *India: A Wounded Civilization* to *India: A Million Mutinies Now*; after thus trying to rediscover his own roots, he attempted to understand the life of others who had migrated from their faiths, as in *Among the Believers: An Islamic Journey*, and *Beyond Belief: Islamic Excursions among the Converted Peoples*.

Historian Romila Thapar, in her 1966 book *A History of India*, observed on the very first page that 'The fundamental sanity of Indian civilisation has been due to an absence of Satan'. Despite centuries of rule, Christianity and Islam could not make most Indians believe in a Satan; this Great Barrier Reef equivalent of coral colonies could not be fully converted to these alien faiths, unlike the other ancient civilisations to her west, —Iran, the Mesopotamia, Syria or Egypt— or in Europe like Greece or Rome.

Like India, other Asian civilisations also reacted similarly. That is why we find 'hybrid' nations like Indonesia and Singapore slowly rediscovering their pre-Islamic or pre-Christian past. In particular, the revivification of China and Japan in the 20th and 21st centuries has been astonishingly fast, as compared to the slow revival of India. Of all these Asian civilisations, India, due to her geographical proximity to the Source of Christian and Islamic powers-of-the-day, had been most affected by the arrival of alien rule after the Crusades, which left both these great religions weaker. However, India reacted to regain her evolutionary energy like no other nation had done in history.

How did this chaotic, polytheist, multicultural and diverse people manage to retain their inherent unity and sanity? Understanding India's history is like the proverbial seven blind men trying to explain how an elephant 'looked' like—all explanations seem partial. There must be something unique that has made this strange—even anarchic—country retain its character uninterruptedly for some 5,000 years. It emerges that India is a polytheist and pluralist culture that set out to rediscover order out of Nature's inherent chaos, and even, at times, gloated as a civilisation. And that when a culture metamorphoses into a civilisation, it gets afflicted with lifestyle diseases; it must, then, go through a thorough health regime, shed the flab through war, and become 'normal' again.

On a wider canvas, India's is the macro-history of a warm-weathered people who got exhausted whenever gargantuan social evolutionary Waves began to shift, globally, from the First (Agriculture) to the Second (Industry) to the Third (Knowledge), and needed energy drinks to remain in the marathon. Like a strongly-knit alien community that has replaced a tired *desi* leadership temporarily. All the countries in the world have seen migrations from other places; no country can claim otherwise. Immigrants often become strong enough to gain political power for some time; then the 'natives' return to power. The same was the case with India, too. In succession, the 'Aryans' replaced the Harappans around 1,500 BC, the Muslims replaced the Aryans in the 11th century, and the British replaced the Muslims in the 18th century: they all came as great game-changers, contributed and catalysed the native Hindu culture by ending its self-imposed isolation and reconnecting it with the world. Ironically, the urban Harappans were more 'connected' with the outside world than the re-ruralising Aryans, who put India on a back-foot but laid a solid foundation for its self-defense from alien influence. On the other hand, most of the Muslims and Christians, unlike other preceding immigrants, remained largely unassimilated due mainly to their holy places being *outside* India, and checked out of this guesthouse in 1947; they left behind the 'converted' people whose descendants may eventually return to the Hindu fold via their *caste-tunnel*—for instance, over 80 per cent of Indian Christians and Muslims, whose forefathers converted, now demand parity with the Hindus' 'lower' castes to derive social benefits.

It was difficult for the colonisers to remain in India for long unless they assimilated with the host country. Essentially a chaotic culture, in which *caste* emerged as the only long-term constant; India, while receiving the Abrahamic catalysts of Christianity and Islam, also began to slowly elbow these alien faiths out once they had served their limited purpose of revivifying the Hindu society. India has accumulated more than 6,000 major castes over the last 30-odd centuries—they are now its fulcrums and the country works somewhat like the shape-changing creature in the Hollywood film *The Transformer*. Only a minority of the sub-continental people—of all faiths—are beyond the pale of casteism.

If we humans are social organisms, well, our society, too, is like a living organism, evolving, multiplying and decaying. Far from being static or isolationist, our dynamic society also follows the Darwinian organic evolution through a food-web, with mutations thrown in, cocooned in its own ecosystem but also interacting with those outside; while doing so, it interacts with the world beyond, and reacts to the newer situations, the basic instincts, for food, mating or self-defense. In this competitive social world, only the fittest survive by adaptation, the ones who successfully react to external stimulus. Like any other country's, therefore, India's history cannot be fully comprehended in isolation from other neighbouring countries' history, not even with static references only to the Muslims or Christians or their belief systems vis-à-vis India's own. Familiarity with the *basics* of Christianity and Islam helps us understand how and why India reacted to these two external stimuli. Each country's history carries the elements of give-and-take in relation to other active neighbours of the time and the extent of interplay with them. For instance, Israel's history and evolution of Judaism, or even of Christianity, cannot be understood without taking into account the imperial interplay between contemporary Egypt and Mesopotamia which uprooted the Jews time and again centuries before Jesus was born. If India were a melting pot, then it must have been heated from outside.

Like other dynamic societies, India, too, followed these principles of organic evolution. During this incremental, Darwinian evolution, she reacted to the world around the way an organism reacts to an external stimulus or situation. Thus, with the theocratic evolution of West Asia, which fast-tracked the Fertile Crescent from polytheism to monotheism from the seventh century BC onwards, India had begun to adapt herself through the Vedic era for this *change-of-gods* that impacted her own people. This was how her long struggle involving both receiving the catalyst for adaptation and then rejecting its leftovers began. The evolution of the *Shrimad Bhagwad Gita*, possibly in the eighth century as a reaction to growing monotheism, followed by the 'cleansing' process culminating in the emergence of the Gandhi-Jinnah duo, and the arrival of 1947 was part of this big-picture evolving scenario.

The rest of the contemporary world, too, followed this pattern. China and Japan, two major 'infidel' Asian cultures, behaved similarly using their native ecosystem, although, unlike India, they were relatively less affected by the Abrahamic catalysts. For instance, while the Christians and Muslims, together, account for just four per cent of the total population in China and two per cent in Japan, they constitute over 15 per cent in India at present. Clearly, India's struggle against being absorbed by Abrahamist catalysts, through religious conversion, has been fiercer than that of China or Japan.

How did the three Semitic sister religions—Judaism, Christianity and Islam which all regarded Abraham as their Patriarch—behave vis-à-vis the host cultures they sought to convert? Judaism was not as focused on religious conversion, evangelisation and proselytisation and, as a result, the Jews, like the Parsis (Zoroastrians), found a safe haven in India for centuries after being forced out of their homelands; but Islam and Christianity, which regarded evangelisation and proselytisation as *cornerstones* of their Book-based Faiths, tried to process India into changing her gods. They did succeed for some time and to some extent, but were eventually rolled back by 1947.

Unlike India or China, other civilisations and cultures counted their days in terms of decades or, at best, centuries. These two peoples have always fancied themselves as mega-marathoners—India the *Jagadguru* (World Teacher), China the Middle Kingdom or Celestial Empire—who, turtle-like, thought in terms of geological times and spatial distances, unlike rabbits of the Occident. The various yugas, or eras of the *Vedic* and *Puranic* antiquity, for instance, are measured in hundreds of thousands of years. Contrast this with the Biblical eras—God could dispatch Satan to Hell *only* for a thousand years before Armageddon because much of the Fertile Crescent (except Egypt and the Mesopotamia) had not learnt to think beyond three zeros until the seventh century! That is why devout Christians, at every turn of the millennium, believe an Armageddon is round-the-corner: at the turn of their first millennium, they launched the bloody Crusades against the Muslims and at the turn of the second, in 2001, they tried to convert the 'infidels', including the Muslims, for an all-out emancipation of humanity. That is why, India and China have seen many a civilisation bubble up and burst while they went on with their normal business; for them Christianity and Islam were merely catalysts, even a passing phase.

Why did India, China or Japan evolve the peculiar way they did? Unlike the Fertile Crescent, these ancient Asian cultures, created largely around agriculture, mostly remained either polytheist or atheist, and the pace of their evolution as loosely connected societies was slow—culture, not faith, bound them. On the other hand, the Crescent evolved faster after monotheism converted and hyper-connected its populations. Christianity integrated Europe beyond the domains of Greece and Rome, the way Islam did beyond Egypt or Iran. Organic evolution of humans must take into account the masses beyond the classes because actual survival rate is low and leaves behind a lot of waste; as Alvin Toffler observed in *The Third Wave*, our social decay is the compost bed of a new civilisation. The proselytising Abrahamic religions played a great role in converting loose epicurean classes into hard-wired ecclesiastical masses. We, the *Homo sapiens*, can survive any possible mass extinction only by tightly wiring ourselves into a Wave-like architectural mass, which monotheism offered. At the same time, monotheism also intensified a struggle for existence within human societies, including the monotheists themselves, as we have seen during the Crusades, the two World Wars and now in the 'War on Terror'. This is akin to apoptosis within monotheism wherein it slowly disintegrates itself to make way for the next Set of Change. In other words, the way the post-Crusades Christianity decayed, our contemporary Islam has also entered into a theology-triggered, self-destruct mode wherein Muslims are killing even more Muslims—mostly males! A prolonged terror environment, or a major war, may eliminate large number of Muslim males and make their womenfolk break free or even lead the Islamic world!

If monotheism were such a catalytic and transformational agent, why could not it convert the entire world? Herein lay the second most important requirement for organic evolution: diversity and variation. Monotheism did 'massify' the people into tightly-knit societies but more-of-the-same could also lead to extinction, the way asexuality or incest does. Only through variation and mutation could the humans survive *and* evolve. This variation came from India, China, Japan and other countries not fully converted by Christianity and Islam. Apparently, Nature parceled out our survival to the converted West Asia and Europe and variation to the unconverted areas; in the 21st century, we are witnessing integration of this survival-cum-variation process through globalisation.

To India, China and Japan, among others, monotheism largely came as a catalyst to spur evolution, as an accelerator to upload these slowly-evolving societies onto a fast-forward train and make them change-ready for the next stage. The way a referee cannot be a player himself, a catalyst cannot *participate* in bio-chemical reaction, or get absorbed in the process. But monotheism got absorbed in West Asia and Europe; its theologies made the devout rather 'permanently' war-enabled; the Christian belief in Armageddon, ironically, has been a major catalyst for the growth of science and technology in the West. Interestingly, even Abrahamic monotheism had evolved from solar monotheism (Sumer, Egypt, Babylon and Iran) to lunar monotheism (Israel, Arabia) until the latter variety edged out the former. But cultures worshipping the Sun continued to react against those worshipping the Moon.

In Sun-worshipping India, China or Japan, lunar monotheism, which promoted evangelisation and proselytisation, was found incompatible with local Sun-centric cultures, and, therefore, incongruent beyond its referee/catalyst role. When Christianity and Islam decided to stay on in these host cultures, they faced resistance and were forced to exit—as in Spain of 1497 or India of 1947, when they checked Islam out, or as in the Sun worshipping Europe which is now slowly phasing out Christianity. The two great faiths had almost completely replaced their earlier civilisations but native cultures re-sprouted slowly, as the contemporary rebirth of paganism in Europe shows now.

Since China and Japan were not as afflicted due to Christianity or Islam, these two societies did not evolve matching holy books. India did, as she had to create a psychological barrier and shelter and theological hedging against this perceived alien invasion. Both the *Bible* and the *Qur'an* are the Books of Insistence, seeking to change the world according to *their weltanshauung* or world-view; to counter these monotheisms, India evolved the *Shrimad Bhagwad Gita* as the Book of Resistance. The two Abrahamic Books are also foreign policy instruments—the Declarations from Jerusalem/Bethlehem-Rome, and al Medina-Mecca—of the respective West Asian expansionist faiths. Both Christianity and Islam, while trying to wire and unite diverse communities, sought to make the believer adopt the Christian/Muslim cultures instead of his native one; it was medieval consumerism, spiritual monopoly, the way modern colas try to replace native beverages. Since the three faiths shared theologies and had much in common, one could convert from Christianity to Islam and vice-versa, and still survive, but his conversion to the 'infidel' religions often invited death. The market forces slowly protested against this restrictive trade practice; so, monotheism, after its *raison d'etre* of uniting and connecting the people from diverse cultures, began to weaken further with the arrival of modern communication. With the evolution of science and democracy, its decay became faster: in particular, the medieval empires built by Christianity and Islam began to totter in the late 18th century with the discovery of telegraphy (literally, 'writing at a distance'). After this, telephony (talking at a distance) and television (watching at a distance) also came to dominate human senses, *the things they once thought only God or a prophet could do*. If we can write, talk or watch from a *distance*, we don't really need a medium/prophet to transfer message from God! Haven't computers and mobile phones replaced stenographers and photographers? Many believers thought their inherited beliefs were an extra-baggage they could do better without. Travel light and enjoy reduced fare!

This technology-enabled self-empowerment of *Homo sapiens* in the last two centuries interconnected them like never before, with technology increasingly replacing theology, or at least shortening the latter's shelf-life for an individual. Because of this shift in the mode of connectivity, science and democracy gradually softened and weakened all faiths to the core, particularly Christianity, as state-patronage which had made it so strong, waned; it was due to this weakening that many among monotheists would no longer be ready to accept their inherited faith as a gospel which sought to kill their private belief, made imperial demands, and tried to convert their world-view.

How did Islam or Christianity contribute to Indian evolution, before they waned and largely exited in 1947? Why and how did India subconsciously 'plot' their exit?

Islam, despite its inability to replace the old Indian societal connector called the 'caste system', bequeathed to these people some unique features: social egalitarianism, at least in prayers, interplay between monotheism and monism, an anti-dote to the Aryan belief of India being a *Jagadguru* (World Teacher), and the importance of global connectivity. The Muslims ruthlessly made the Hindus rather level-headed, rubbing off the sharp-edges of their idiosyncrasy when their decaying, over-saturated and sexed-up 'religion' began to reflect in the likes of Khajuraho and Konark as signs of decadence, the way the West's porn industry is seen now in a negative light. Islam's victory in a post- 'Golden Age' India signified the civilisational humus the Hindus had fallen into and they actually needed an external rescue team to rejuvenate them, which Islam provided. But the aggressive faith gradually lost drive, energy and direction, based as it became on local caste-conscious converts at a time when Sunni replenishments from abroad waned due to Shia Iran's emergence across the Indus. Eventually, Islam could not fully convert India—some parts of the subcontinent always behaved differently and kept rebellion alive—unlike the way the complete Roman decay had led to the take-over of their Empire by Christianity. Cultures mature this way into a self-defeating civilisation, forcing their societies to return to Seed, and make way for the next game-changer.

Christianity, which came to India within decades of Jesus' 'Crucifixion', remained dormant for nearly 1,500 years before the Portuguese dusted it off and made it rather unpopular in places like Goa; then came its 'bad' phase with the Dutch, French and the British, roughly in that order, who all colonised India partly and exploited it fully for raw materials required for their Industrial Revolution back home in Europe. This was followed by the 'good' phase post-1857 when the British lifted the Hindus from the mud of the First Wave (Agriculture), launched it on to the Second Wave (Industry) and commenced the Third Wave as well. Intellectually, Rabindra Nath Tagore, C V Raman, S Chandrashekhar, Jagadish Chandra Bose and Satyendra Nath Bose integrated India with the modernising West, the way Gandhi and Jinnah did it politically. Then, their role up, Gandhi ejected the British catalyst but not before they, together, pushed out Pakistan into a corner, with back to the Hindukush. In the 19th and 20th centuries, the Chinese and Japanese societies, too, evolved intellectuals and thought-leaders much the same way.

Like all monopolistic tendencies, even monotheism would have competition, from without and then from within. Nature made India the softest culture and China the hardest civilisation that would not only resist but also slowly turn away the tide of monotheism. If Arabia was born in summer, Nature sculpted India in monsoon, China in winter and Japan in spring. Monsoon gave India an annual hope to survive yet another year; winter gave China the patient belief that she is the Middle Kingdom, a Celestial Empire, its King the Son of Heaven, and all others were the new kids-on-the-block. In the long run, only two major ancient cultures, India and China, have stood off, challenged and folded back monotheism while other contemporary civilisations—Egypt, Babylon, Persia, Rome—succumbed to the referees' whistle. But these nations, too, realised later, off and on, that they could reclaim their pre-Abrahamic legacy: in the 20th century, Anwar Saadat (Egypt), Saddam Hussein (the Mesopotamia), Ayatollah Khomeini (Iran), and Benito Mussolini (Italy), for instance, represented the subconscious unease of their respective proud peoples trying to rediscover their countries' pre-Islamic/pre-Christian past. Their next rounds may be overdue now.

Many other countries had also welcomed the guest Abrahamic religions as game-changing catalysts. And, like India, they are slowly checking out the guests. Thus, if Spain checked out Islam in 1497, Turkey did so—almost—in 1924 by abolishing the Caliphate; Pakistan and Afghanistan, Syria and Egypt are aping this now. Most countries now afflicted with Sunni-led Islamic terrorism, in Muslim-majority as well as Muslim-minority nations have mushroomed on the mucus of the former Ottoman and Mughal Empires where the pressure-from-within of democratisation of ideas and pollination of technology is, apparently, pushing out Islam in a slow motion; similarly, Israel is checking out Judaism, India her 'Hindutva', and the West its Christianity…This has happened in the past—the way Syria, Egypt or Byzantium (Turkey) converted from Christianity to Islam or Spain from Christianity-to-Islam-to-Christianity—and would happen in the future also as Nature chisels out the real humans from our humus.

To understand this amazing, cyclical phenomenon of how mega-picture Change occurs, we can go back to the great medieval Tunisian historiographer Ibn Khaldun who propounded that there was always a *rhythm* to the rise and fall of dynasties, which can be extended to even cultures and civilisations. Thought to be of Berber descent but claiming to be of an Arab lineage from Yemen, his family had emigrated, rather returned, from Seville to Tunisia after its fall to the *Reconquista* campaign in the Iberian Peninsula. Analysing history, he argued that desert tribesmen like the Arabs have been more courageous with greater social cohesion than the settled, civilised people whose rulers tended to decay into corrupt, complacent and incompetent dinosaurs. This enabled the tribes to conquer such inviting lands, creating new dynasties which, too, over time, decayed, ready to be overthrown by a new set of barbarians. In 2014, Lebanese intellectual Rami Khoury said the deeply religious societies in the Middle East are currently passing through the biggest transformation due to emergence of democratic aspirations for the first time in their 9,000 years of history; and, after a terror-attack in June 2015, Tunisia, harbinger of the 'Arab Spring', closed down a hundred mosques that nursed terror, a first in the Muslim world.

Sometimes, when societies found it difficult to remove their own rulers or beget a new sperm from abroad, barbarians are 'invited' by a domestic faction seeking a shake-up—so each society evolves its own 'traitors' like Quislings, Jaichands or Mir Jafars, from time to time, to facilitate entry of new game-changers. These are the breakout and disruptive events in the sleepy caravan of cultures and civilisations.

In this scenario, what we see today as global terrorism is indicative of a rhythmic phenomenon of incremental disappearance of the Old Order and emergence of the New. This violence is a reaction-cum-response-cum-readjustment, in that order, of diverse cultures that evolved under the common Abrahamic Tree, or their branches, to the impact of an accelerating pace of zigzagging technology and democracy of ideas; many of them now rediscover their roots and readjust themselves with the new technology that levels all contradictions. In other words, the way many nations in West Asia and Europe had adopted Christianity and Islam as catalysts when their own native pre-Christian or pre-Islamic religions suffered obsolescence in the medieval era, they are now offloading what they feel is an increasingly irrelevant

Christianity and Islam, as well, in the face of the challenges thrown by modernity. They look for a new set of catalysts. We all enable the world, in our own ways, to eliminate the waste that we become; all intake passes through the same evolutionary alimentary canal, and societies work like kidneys.

Why are our religions facing obsolescence? Modernity has injected a heavy dose of uncertainties in all of us, and our religions, brimming with certainties, find it difficult to stay strong in this deluge of information. In particular, the largest religious Brotherhoods, Christianity and Islam, both evangelising and proselytising, find the ground beneath slippery. Due to their unchangeable *core* certitudes—Jesus the Only Son of God and Muhammed the Last Prophet of Allah—these exclusivist Abrahamic faiths no longer appeal as the great change-makers they once were. As in any social revolution, they began as rebel pro-changers, before acquiescing as conformists and then decaying into fanaticism, thus setting the stage for ushering in the next set of Change-making-Catalysts, or *Changlysts*. But it was [illegible] of our own biological Evolution, always looking for the next-best. So, instead of being mere catalysts in a reaction for a longer duration, they slowly decayed into becoming participating reagents themselves. Predictably, the societies that once welcomed these Changlysts, began to brace themselves to get rid of them when they made imperial demands and tried to invade the native mythologies and traditions, the bed rock of a society's inherited and layered Mind.

It is due to this reason that Christianity and Islam are now in the throes of an existential dilemma. Their global reach is waning in the face of pressure-from-below—their numbers might be seen as increasing, their beliefs are getting diluted as they water down their past to accommodate the present—particularly in the most non-Christian and non-Muslim countries. The two great faiths find it increasingly difficult to get into the change-mode due to their inherited 'certainties'. They both seem to be imploding and bursting at the seams due to a collision between their obsolete theologies and the empowering new technologies, in what is a veritable fight-to-finish between irrelevance and irreverence. These religions often expanded and survived due to state-patronage; with this patronage waning due to the onslaught of irresistible democracy, they now face a mortal dilemma.

The resultant decline of a de-spiritualised West is now leading to the resurgence of the East, freshly menstruated with its fecundity restored.

That is why the USA, the world's biggest Changlyst since 1917, is slowly losing its leveraging capability to dictate the world into 'democracy' and, increasingly technology, whereas China, seen as the world's biggest no-changer from 1948 to 1980, is now the leading pro-changer; similarly, India, ridiculed until two decades ago, has emerged as the world's service station. What has brought about this apparent decline of the West in 100 years, and emergence of the BRIC nations?

To understand the West's predicament, we should first know about the existential crisis of Christianity, our largest stake-holder in human survival sweepstakes. With the failure of all eight Crusades against the intrepid Muslims in the 11th-14th centuries, Europe slowly rejected the 'invincibility' claims of the Vatican, and then of Christianity itself. In fact, Europe was so tired of Christianity and its many wars that, by 1945, it actually outsourced the *active arm* of the Faith (Protestantism) and the Continent's security to its foster-child, the USA. Fascism, Nazism and Communism, all, had a strong anti-Christianity ideological core to them. In fact, post-1945, Europe felt relieved when America virtually shouldered the responsibility of protecting the Faith. The USA camouflaged Protestantism with 'democracy' and 'human rights' abroad and virtually made these its foreign policy instruments. Protestant fundamentalists began to dictate terms in Washington. Also, the West, by reloading the Matrix called Israel in 1948, actually outsourced safety of the Holy Churches in Bethlehem and Jerusalem to the very Jews it had been denouncing for 2,000 years: remember, the twin objectives of the Crusades were wresting Jerusalem from the Muslim 'infidels', and a restoration of Europe's imperial 'Alexandrian Order' in West Asia. Europe found itself slowly revivifying paganism in the increasing *absence* of Christianity, as demonstrated by the post-Crusade eras of Enlightenment and Renaissance, and all that went with Harry Potter and *The Da Vinci Code*. The Muslim world, too, is passing through a similar painful phase of upheavals in belief system and societal reconstruction. All societies undergo such birth pangs during the big picture 'Wave-shift', from agriculture to industry to knowledge.

But the Abrahamic religions are not the only victims of modernity. Other religions, too, are facing similar existential crises due to their increasing obsolescence—despite the apparent 'popularity' of seasonal tele-evangelisation and the shrines increasingly crowded by the youth, as in India. This was reflected in the Tamil militancy of LTTE in Sri Lanka and the Sikh terrorism in India since the 1980s when those societies tried to anchor themselves in the midst of a flood of accelerating Change brought about by the invading technologies ejecting outdated traditions. One may sympathise with the Buddhist Tibetans and the Myanmarese, but they once had a paramountcy in China! Across the world, religion is, even by using modern technology, trying to remain relevant. The founders of various man-centric cults that later metamorphosed into 'religions' were the best representatives and reformers of *their* era who understood the mesmerising impact that their 'revelations' and interviews with God would make on the common people, the way our 'elected' leaders now try to do in indirect, representative democracies; the revelation-receiver-prophets evolved those contemporary pager-like theologies as connectors of the people, the way our politicians and their manifestoes do now. But religions, too, must move on, as their believers do. Since some believers cannot fight modern technology, which is essentially a wide-ranging next generation connecting tool, they have joined it in a desperate attempt to remain relevant and hang on to their old theologies; that is why terrorists of all hues are technologically far more advanced and initiative-takers than the police that fights them. In the real world, there is no 'sustainable technology' *per se*—Change is the First Law of Nature.

Technologies slowly shatter theologies and other inherited belief systems across all human societies. It is due to these gigantic changes being swept in by the silent tsunamis of technology and democratisation of ideas that Hinduism, too, is facing the onslaught of Change. People unable to absorb so many changes in such a short time are getting overwhelmed with the sheer pressure from within—and they seek answers from Lord Ganesh for their computer problems! We now have not millions but billions of Change-afflicted masses the world-over, trying to comprehend an expanding universe from inside their tiny, 1,400 cc cranium. But few would admit they are patients afflicted by the disease called Change.

Indeed, the number of 'religious-minded' people is seen as growing along with the global population; in the beginning, they are often no-changers heavily outnumbering the pro-changers, but slowly the ratio reverses. The economists call this '80:20 principle in which 20% people work and change and 80% reject an idea or project, before the ratio slowly reverses—no society is, therefore, ever free of its *core* idlers, the critical mass of fuel that goes into the making of Change possible. These numbers mushroom on a mangled spirituality and reflect the swarms of the Change-afflicted masses amidst us, who dread the new, incomprehensible realities and keep rushing into the comfort zones of their familiar psychological diapers, however dirty and stinking.

Global Islamic terrorism is rooted in this disorientation of the Muslim mind, the way the two World Wars were rooted in disorientation of the Christian mind reeling under the onslaughts of the punishing, irresistible forces of science and democracy. Terrorism as a disease afflicts non-Muslims as well whose minds slowly get disoriented due to their inability to absorb exponential global-level changes in a short time and they are burdened with information overload: the Naxalites in India, the Maoists in Nepal, the LTTE in Sri Lanka, the ETA in Spain, the IRA in the UK... they all used modern weapons to stall the inexorable emergence of modernity and even networked with Christian or Islamic extremist-enemy groups wherever possible as co-patients in the same ward of mental asylum. In other words, we all are like ship-wrecked Titanic passengers trying to find a toehold in a flood of Change.

Even the idler-idolater Hindus are not free of this disease of change. Senior BJP leader L K Advani, who, like a Hindu Moses, once led the masses to Mount Ayodhya in 1992, journeyed back to his roots in an Islamist Pakistan in 2005, and applauded its founder Muhammad Ali Jinnah at the latter's mausoleum in Karachi. He called the Partition of India 'making of history', when interestingly, Sardar Vallabh Bhai Patel, whom Advani apparently fashioned himself after, had, in 1947, termed Pakistan's birth a good riddance of 'poison'.

Even Israel is facing such dilemmas; Ariel Sharon, who led the Jewish victory in the Palestine in 1967, reclaiming the 'Promised Land', later favoured a trade off in this land-for-peace, something abhorred by the devout Jew: one can't simply give away to the 'infidels' the Land Promised by God to the Jews, as it were. If the Sharons and Advanis swallowed this poison, their faiths must be really passing through veritable internal psychological disorientation and convulsions of gigantic proportions as their societies restructure themselves. Interestingly, Advani, accused of being one of those masterminding the demolition of a medieval mosque in India in 1992, also laid the foundation stone for reconstruction of an ancient temple in Pakistan at the 'invitation' of Islamabad, calling the mosque demolition act the 'saddest day in life' although he was physically present amongst those who actively presided over the great act! Later, his party also threw the veteran Jaswant Singh into political oblivion for writing a book on the same *Baba-e-Qaum,* Jinnah.

With them, the five-century-old rightist undercurrent to give Hinduism an Abrahamist face, by making Lord Rama express *Satvik Krodh* (Divine Anger) as a Holy Warrior, may have come to an end. India has been spared the after-shocks of monotheism due to the failure of Hindutva to evolve Lord Rama into what the founder-philosopher of Pakistan, Allama Muhammad Iqbal, once called 'Imam-e-Hind'. Another important Hindu God, Krishna, is being increasingly relegated to the background by scores of those cults that mushroomed on the *Shrimad Bhagwad Gita*, as the cult-founder *gurus* became more 'valuable' than the Lord Himself. In the USA, too, the

Southern Baptist leaders virtually replaced Jesus in the USA, as former President Jimmy Carter complained in a book. The Wahhabis are also dismantling Muhammed's heritage in Arabia. Homo sapiens, having eliminated many a life form in the universal food web, may now be eyeing God Himself as their next meal!

The whole world seems to be crashing down on these faiths due to the theo-shift in these once-great unifying and connecting religions that, as the first global technologies, connected diverse people. These shocks, indeed the monotheistic religions, have been the product of the shifting patterns of the Three Waves that have brought about theo-shift and psychological disorientation of the faithful as they grope for new answers for their old questions and refashion their response in the world that they feel has changed beyond recognition—and is fast changing, forcing them to do likewise and, at the same time, protect themselves against the constantly emerging challenge of the incessant, interminable onslaught of that ultimate mind-disorienting, ever-accelerating and exponential disease called Change, observed by Toffler.

This Change is the Daughter of Chaos. And we are talking in terms of not decades but centuries. The way climate changes occur over centuries and subterranean activities like under-sea volcanoes and tectonic movements make the emergence or disappearance of islands possible, mega-Change also emerges over long periods of time. This churning was what gave birth to Mahatma Gandhi, Mao Zedong and Hideki Tojo in India, China and Japan, respectively, as the ***net gain*** of these nations' subterranean long-drawn-out process of Change that included invasion and evasion of alien religions. These great sons of their respective soils visited us in the 20th century that shaped the 21st.

In fact, beginning with the 20th century, our world has seen two main steams of changes: increasing decolonisation of ancient cultures that rejuvenated themselves thanks to Christianity and Islam which came to them as catalysts, and mutually-assured destruction of those cultures that became career of these great catalysts.

Christianity and Islam derisively called believers of those ancient religions as infidels, those whom the two faiths unsuccessfully tried to either convert or eliminate over the last 2,000 years. Ours is an era of Return of those rejuvenated Infidels on the world scene. This era began with Japan defeating Russia in 1904, and subsequent decolonisation of Asia, Africa and South America...as the world became increasingly free of Christianity and Islam. In this quest of modernity, the three nations were led by Brothers-in-Arms: Gandhi, Mao and Tojo.

This book is about the reasons behind colonisation and decolonisation of India, China and Japan. India, being the next door neighbour to medieval Changlysts, received the alien catalyst to the maximum extent. She had, therefore, to struggle the hardest to regain her character and get rid of the aliens. That is why we focus more on the Indian transformation in greater detail.

The Land and the Lords

IMAGINE 17 per cent human population of the Earth packed in just 0.6 per cent of landmass! India is the chaos of a society with a man's birth, *caste*, being a moderator, like deuterium (heavy water) in a nuclear reactor generating power; in each age, chaos has been a new normal here. Caste is the axle of the wheel called India; those who shun or fail to understand the caste system would never understand India, least of all Gandhi and Jinnah. A chaos of 6,000-plus castes, 2,000 languages (17 of them recognised by the Constitution), all under one roof—of a joint Hindu Undivided Family (HUF) which witnessed only a few of the 15,000-odd religious wars the rest of the world has fought since the dawn of agriculture. India is an organic unity, a biological culture, and most people do not know when it, like an omnivorous vulture, devours them. It is a controlled, even regimented, chaos; but caste, the biggest leveller, prevents any Indian ruler from being too ambitious, smart or adventurous.

Caste, selective inter-breeding, has preserved the Indian breed over the centuries while egalitarian organised faiths produced low-resistant, high-yielding genetically-modified human variety. Caste is India's UPS (Uninterrupted Power Supply), even Unique Selling Proposition (USP); it produces energy uninterruptedly. Due to the caste system, India kept decaying here and regenerating there, simultaneously, as it does even now.

Caste being central to India, what neutron is to an atom, each Hindu is a potential trigger of a chain reaction. Among the original River-Valley Civilisations of the First Wave (Agriculture), only India and China survived uninterruptedly; all other nations are ephemeral with low shelf-life, one-time flukes.

India has come to control elephantine creeds through ant-like castes, to preserve biological diversity, variety, multiculturalism and multi-ethnicity by integrating them into a great caste machine, polytheism and democracy. It is a strange country in which even poverty and beggary is a lucrative profession for some, an artefact: a Satyajit Ray earned an Oscar here or an Amartya Sen a Nobel Prize in Economics there, simply by portraying abject poverty in different colours. Many a Communist, too, earned their millions by investing in India's poverty. Poverty is precious like gold, a saleable commodity; nobody knew it better than Indira Gandhi! Beggars have often been the 'social face' of India, abroad; they easily confuse the newcomer tourist-turning-trader-turning-coloniser about his perceived permanence, power and prosperity and India's supposed vulnerability. Begging is a fine art, even business for some. A profession, as the Maharashtra government informed lawmakers, in which the beggars 'earned' Rs 1,800 million in the year 2005 in Mumbai alone, where some of them were millionaires and sent their children abroad for study; a survey in Bihar, in 2014, found that many educated beggars earned up to Rs 600 a day. No other country can boast of so many professional and even part-time beggars for whom it is a side-business to make a quick buck—Indian politicians, when they beg for votes, rob these beggars! India has guarded herself, her identity, behind so thick curtains that invaders and evaders could never really penetrate her heart and, exhausted, faded away like unknown corporals of history.

Chaos, therefore, is the first 'rule', *Rta*, the Upanishadic Cosmic Order, moral law or principle of righteousness Nature perhaps wrote for India and Pakistan, which unwillingly shares Indian culture and history and is an emporium of terrorists of all shades because it shares India's caste system to date and, therefore, Islam failed to tame Islamabad. This cultural emporium has always thrown to the dustbin those who tried to put it in order. We begin to understand India only by shunning our personal, inherited 'intellectual assets'.

And survival, through chaos, is the second rule. In monsoon, India found both chaos and its survival tactics.

No other culture waits for and worships monsoon the way India does; no other culture depends on rain waters for so much; no other country has a million folk songs on rains; no other culture ignores so many deaths in the monsoon floods each year because it also keeps so many, many others alive. India's monsoon is a celebration of chaos, of Life itself. With the first showers begin its very many classical *ragas*—India's potential 36,000 *raga*s emerged this way! It is also the beginning of the temporary order; 'holy' men suspend their dry business of religion in these four wet months, and take rest during the rainy season, like the polar bear hibernating for the winter after packing himself with fat and carbohydrates. Politicians and bureaucrats wait for the monsoon anxiously; floods and famines line their pockets and grease their careers. We cannot imagine India without her monsoon, the way we cannot imagine Arabia without her summer, China without winter or Japan without spring. For, these are not mere countries; their rise and fall represents Nature's cycle of seasons. Monsoon enters India in Kerala, *the Land of the Coconut*, or 'God's Own Country', alternately ruled by more-of-the-same: it was here that both Christianity and Islam came first, anywhere outside Israel and Arabia—and the *Shrimad Bhagwad Gita* began to emerge as India's response to the *westerly winds*, as we will see. Kerala demonstrates why Christianity and Islam failed to convert India fully; the Moplah Massacre of the early 1920s may have pushed India towards creation of Pakistan two decades later.

Early on, a survivalist India internalised her many a survival tactic, the way a chameleon or a squid escapes from their enemies.

That was how this Turtle of the Long Race was born, to defeat those rabbits of contemporary destiny. In the face of the Islamic torrent, post-Harshavardhana India beat herself to pulp, like a thin foil of mica, and insulated herself to occupy the minimum space in the comity of monotheistic mega-nations assembled by Christianity and Islam. Just to survive another day. Kings and emperors, crowns and towns, saints and scents, philosophers and Lords, books and religions—anything created by temporarily moral and eventually mortal humans—never really mattered to India; she suffered them all with equanimity, zigzagging like a pseudopod amoeba, along uneven surfaces, and chucked them to age, decay, degenerate, destroy and dissolve themselves in the vast ocean of Time.

No other culture offers us as many varieties of lifestyles and suicides to choose from; India smiles at the speed of innocent rabbits and velocity of docile horses whose strength lies in their legs, not heads. Life remains hidden in those invisible, indestructible seeds that lie dormant, regerminate after soaking the rain and carry forward the caravan. Adaptation is a great survival mantra India adopted long ago. Most Indians live in the worst-polluted country, society, economy, history, and yet they have calmly managed to survive, at the lowest possible level of existence. Some mendicants, on continuous fast, slow down their biological processes to the extreme and survive only on *nine* calories a day; modern medical surveys show the Indians are amongst the most disease-resistant people in the world, given the abysmal circumstances they live in. Millions of Hindus, rich and poor alike, willingly and faithfully starve themselves for nine days every year as they worship nine incarnations of the Mother Goddess, twice a year—many a devout and prosperous Jain actually starve themselves to death in what they say is *santhara*, embracing slow, voluntary death; countless others have practised the art of plain fasting since time immemorial, from the Buddha to Gandhi, and evolved an in-born, inherited immunity system in their body against external attacks of viruses; by thus moulding themselves to resist all sorts of enemies Nature threw at them in order to shape them, Indians turned out to be among the fittest human species for survival. No other people on the globe are as immune and resistant to external attacks—like defoliating trees in a hostile summer, India simply sheds her old leaves and withdraws in her shell until the day's enemy plays its role out, and a new spring heralds. She lies so low that the enemy has often cut itself to India's size! She has lived and strived like an ant, learnt to run like an antelope, think like an elephant. She begins her auspicious work by worshipping the Lord of Wisdom, Ganesh, the Elephant God. Nothing really perturbs India for long—even professional media has often found its self-important issues having the shelf-life of a milk product—24 hours!

Due to the unpredictable monsoon, India learnt how to save for the rainy day, receive stoically whatever the rains and the stormy, temporary rivulets of her many hills offered to seeds that would wash away to world shores. Each 'thought-monsoon' produced a new hero. India is a warm country inhabited by a rather cold-blooded people who are, like polar bear, born with an inherent capacity to hibernate or aestivate when the going gets tough. From this strange land would blossom those *nine* Flowers of Life, the greatest Indians: the silencer Gautam the Buddha, the planner sage Manu, the vaccinator Adi Shankaracharya, the mediator Guru Nanak, the organiser Goswami Tulsidas, the communicator Swami Vivekanand, the tactician Gandhi, the liberator Bheemrao Ambedkar and the incubator Rajneesh. None of them would be a King but each of them would unleash a great torrent of forces that would mould their day's India for tomorrow, to face the challenge of continuous change; besides, there would be hundreds of other greats to run this vast machine of *Rta*.

For most human beings, in each era, life merely remains a postponed death. In the desert cultures, uncertainties of life turned humans into death-addicts. Nature ordained India to philosophise about Death—called *Nirvana*, *Moksha*, or *Kaivalya*, by the Buddhists, Hindus and Jains, respectively—in the long, hot summer when she counted the stars under the clear sky; to ring in and then wait passively for the monsoon to pass away; to celebrate the new crops and mourn the old mud that the rains swept out with regular irregularity; to gather around the hearth in cold winters and marvel about the Nature of Things. India produces mud in the monsoon, philosophy in winter and children in summer. Nature made India utterly malleable; you ask her to bow, she will crawl until you realise she actually sneaked into your pants. A hundred thousand Muslim or European marauders, who had mushroomed on their own war-torn decaying societies, and who once ruled a thousand times as many Indians so easily, gradually returned to the lands of *their* origins; now their societies frantically discover potency drugs to save their civilisations from the virus of social segregation they carried back from their once-Hindu colony. India has been the punching bag of these civilisations around. But such is her tenacity and elasticity that each time she bounces back to regain her original shape as soon as the impact of the fist weakens. Alexander the Great refrained from entering the Indian heartland. The Greek word *amoebae* means continuous change; it was foolish to hope that the sands of the Indus could be moulded into a lasting Aristotelian bust. Perhaps he did not know that the Sanskrit word *Brahm* originated in *Brah,* that is continuous expansion and change. Physically, India has never been quite able to defend herself from enemies—who is the enemy after all? It is yesterday's 'enemies' who got assimilated and became the multi-layered India of today! Like many other countries, India shaped up as a pigeonholed and layered society of immigrants and converts of various hues. The only decisive victory she registered in her five-millennia-long history against the *real challenger*, monotheism, was in the 1971 Indo-Pak War, in which her infantry forcibly delivered an infant Bangladesh from the womb of a rather 'relieved' mother, Pakistan.

India has evolved a rare genius to turn a tragedy into opportunity, even entertainment. She does not believe in licking wounds for a long time and has a rare capacity to forget even a major bloody war in a matter of weeks. Even her gods are utterly human and weak; her people are headstrong, unlike in the Abrahamic faiths whose strong God, apparently, left the people weak. Nature grants us humans a limited strength: the stronger our God, the weaker we are, for He, like Voldemort, saps our power and enjoys His strength at our expense. The European Aryans, who had embraced Christianity, slowly realised that the Christ was sapping their Caesar's strength; they, therefore, cut their God to size after the Crusades. Contrary to common belief,

India has never been a democracy in the contemporary Western sense, thanks to her caste combinations-of-the-day: it has mostly been an oligarchy run by a few dynasties as contemporary political rulers, with whom they manage to 'adjust' as they come and go. Even in the 21st century, a dozen-odd families each in politics, business, media, bureaucracy, and other sectors control Indian 'democracy' at the Union level; similarly, the States have their own oligarchies. The interplay of these oligarchies is what India is all about, wheels-within-wheels—but even these oligarchies are not permanent as their members are often replaced by newcomers, mostly after three to four generations.

Who are Indians, after all? All those invaders and immigrants who adopted the *Hindu* way of life and polytheism, became Hindus and founded a caste of their own like each bird's family having its own nest on a great tree. Caravans became the heterogeneous and multi-cultural, multi-layered polyglot India of today. As Urdu poet Raghupati Sahai 'Firaq Gorakhpuri' said: *Sarzamin-e-Hind Par, Avam-e-Alam Ke Firaq, Kafile Basate Gaye, Hindustan Banta Gaya* (From all over the world, caravans of people came and settled down, making the India of today). India will remain a Great Caravan. Some Christian and Muslim zealots tried to rob it and, therefore, had to be repulsed; others, the converted ones, realised this and are slowly returning to their roots.

Like Arjuna between the two armies, India knows she belongs to all; like Krishna, she also knows she belongs to no one. The *Mahabharata* is not a mere literary epic: the five Pandava brothers are like the five senses in the human body which are constantly under attack by a hundred Kaurava diseases and unless you have a Krishna for your mind, you cannot win the struggle of Life; in the Great War, you stand to lose 180 million nerves, your soldiers. The *Mahabharata* is the real war each human will have to fight for survival and revival in each age, within oneself and in the world; the *Ramayana* is the ideal battle one should go through. India survives in the *Mahabharata* and strives for the *Ramayana*. Even these epics have different versions as different sub-cultures in the subcontinent evolved their own versions to reflect their aspirations. The *Mahabharata* and Bharat are coexistent; the latter is the former's reflection. A continuous, easy war to achieve a momentary, uneasy peace, the mirage of the mental desert: the fond hope of humans surpassing themselves and metamorphosing into super-humans. Man's evolution in God; and God's disintegration into men! India has survived all odds with equanimity because of its fundamental unity theme: nothing in Nature is evil or permanent. Accept the fragrance of food and foulness of faeces with equanimity. She has been fundamentally sane enough to accept evil merely as not-good for now; Satan, the Absolute Evil, has never existed in India, nor did she ever take her Good Gods too seriously—they are parts of a transient 'technology'. India is a merciless eliminator; many of her gods have not survived for long. So utilitarian she is that even reincarnations of mythological gods lived by miracles but 'died' like humans: Rama by drowning in the River Sarayu, Krishna by falling prey to the arrow of an ordinary tribal hunter. Her mythical arch-villains—Ravana, Kansa, Duryodhana—were all wayward under-trials, not hardened or unreformable Satan-type sinners; they were relative devils rather than Absolute Evil. The Indian wrong-doers languish in temporary and open jails unlike the monotheistic Satan who, as the sinner-in-chief, would be convicted to rot away in the fire of Hell until 'eternity'. India does not believe in the blacks and whites because the former is temporary and the latter a mere mirage of seven colours. One can still come across temples of her Aryan arch-villains, like Ravana or Mahishasur. India has survived the vicissitudes of history because of her basic wisdom in not inventing a Satan, as life, like politics, cannot afford to have a Permanent Villain. She knows that written, or dammed, history breeds hysteria and terrorism the way logged rainy water breeds insects—our dedication to 'history' shows our capacity to lick wounds, the way our devotion to God demonstrates our hedging against a perceived greed-and-sin-driven-guilt or just an inherent, cultivated desire to become slave without realising it. We may often measure the extent of potential guilt or sin in a person by knowing the extent of his inclination to God; the colder the weather, the thicker the wool you need to protect yourselves. Those who invented Satan would, therefore, be forced to have an absolutist and 'immortal' God—if you buy one you *must* get the other for free! And, like her work-charge demons, India's gods and their incarnations are also work-charge humanoid resources who vanish from the scene once their role is up. Even her great leaders have a shelf-life, a use-by date. For, being humans after all, they are as vulnerable also. Life is a long-chain of chemical reactions between biological reagents amid physical conditions and gets cleansed with Natural detergents from time to time. Peace is love. War is duty.

India did not need to write and, therefore, revise her history; all history is one-sided, seven blind men's incomplete sensory perception of the elephant. History is merely *his story*, the boast of the victor or apology of the loser. She has learnt it well; those who write theirs, are eventually forced to revise it and those who forget, revisit. That's why India never had to suffer her Hitlers or Stalins. That was why Gandhi realised how to take on the all-powerful British who dreaded mortal morals as much as they were frightened of the immortal Dracula, and that they were ultimately vulnerable to argument. Later, like the 'invincible British', even Indira Gandhi was made to believe that she was 'India' (1975), indispensable (1980) and indestructible (1984). India lets her friends and foes alike to expose and drag themselves to the dustbin of history; they roll in dust, as she plays the *been* (pied-pipe)…Muhammed Ali Jinnah luring the 'half-Muslims' to Pakistan in 1947 by promising them a 'paradise'; the Mandalites now luring the 'half-Hindus' back into their castes within the umbrella Hinduism by assuring them 'privileges'. Give her your most acclaimed product and India could de-engineer to prove it the worst and utterly digestible. Like Nature, she has no favourites. To most Hindus, each opportunity is a festival. Even death. When widows could no longer cry in the western provinces after a series of wars against the Muslims, a professional class of *rudalees* (hired women mourners) cropped up so that no death went un-mourned. No other people mourn their dead so loudly and then begin to virtually celebrate it patiently year after year. After each monsoon season, they solemnly observe even an inauspicious day-time *Pitra Paksha*, a fortnight-long period when they venerate their forefathers, take no new assets or business, and commemorate the dead flowers of the family tree, as if a snake were shedding its hide year after year and finding a new birth; thereafter, they celebrate the night-time auspicious *Navaratri* to worship nine incarnations of the Mother Goddess to eliminate evil. Hindu India has often been a matriarchate, the first major country to give voting rights to women at par with men, where the female is the Fertile Creator and male merely the sustainer, vis-à-vis the Abrahamic patriarchates of the Fertile Crescent, where women were treated like a farm for God's crop. Like her holy cow, India has been grazing the foreign grass at one go and then slowly regurgitating, digesting it at leisure.

The Hindus evolved a rare capacity to curse, even punish, their gods. They punished Brahma, Creator of the Universe, by dethroning Him because He 'raped' His daughter Saraswati in an incestuous relationship; they also punish Vishnu, Sustainer of the world, to be turned into a stone by a woman's curse. In Central India, the devout Hindu villager, even now, keeps a Shivalinga sunk in water, as a punishment to the Lord for having failed to cure his ailing son! The incarnations fared no better: Rama suffers separation from His sons because He got his enemy Ravana's son killed, and He continues to be despised even today by some Brahmins for killing a fellow Brahmin (Ravana); Krishna was cursed by the Kaurava's mother to witness a similar Yadavcide and that He would Himself die like an ordinary bird because Gandhari condemns Him for masterminding the killing of her 100 sons. India alone has had accursed gods!

Clearly, it is the unsafest place for gods; *They* must follow the morals of human beings, not the other way round as in monotheism, or risk oblivion. India does not respect those gods who try to become tyrant and knows how to make them behave. Religion and God are for the humans, *not* the other way round. Humans cannot be held to ransom by God or religion. She has been constantly hiring, benching and firing gods. No other country is a greater utilitarian. India is the mother of *real* human beings. Bharat Mata, the Mother India.

In the beginning, India's gods of the Harappan times yielded place to the Aryan gods; but, with the westerly winds entering from Western Asia, the Fertile Crescent, even these Aryan gods were found wanting. The way we use umbrella to protect ourselves from sun or rain, India slowly evolved and designed her gods to suit Her needs. Her new gods will be responses to the gods spawned by the Sons of Abraham.

The Reluctant Gods

THE Great Sage, Brihaspati-II, 'god' of the godless Lokayats or Charvakas, the early Indian epicurians, taught that all phenomena were reducible to Nature and Its elements; it is only the nincompoops who try to trace these back to *Sur*s or *Asur*s (ie. those deserving either the nectar of immortality, or death, later known as gods or devils). There is only one reality, matter, a permutation and combination of atoms; when matter evolves and develops thinking capacity, we call it 'mind'. There is no soul that senses: eyes see, nose smells, ears hear, tongue tastes, skin feels the touch. Where is the soul, or the need for it, then? It does not exist. Therefore, there is no question of its immortality or its being separate from the body. There is no rebirth either. Enjoy this life here; there is no hereafter. No afterlife. *Yaavajjeevet sukham jeevet, rinamkritva ghritam peevet; Bhasmibhootasya dehasya punaragamanam kutah?* (So long as you are alive, enjoy every pleasure, even if you have to borrow money; remember that your mortal body would be consumed in flames and you will never be born again.) Down the line, India's many notorious swindlers and fugitives, as 'religious' as anyone else, took this ancient teaching seriously.

These Lokayats of sixth century BC taught that the so-called 'religion' is a herding instinct, a state of mind, caused by its inability to understand the Nature of Things, or, at best, a fraud; no one can understand the world, what to talk of explaining it, on the basis of the hypothesis that God did it all—yes, moral science, the ethics, must be there but do not confuse or fuse morality with religion. Indeed, Life evolved in water but it also moved out of it to the drying land and cannot, therefore, sustain more than 70 per cent water; you can swim in religion but fools would drown themselves in it. The more real knowledge you have, the less faith you need; religion is intoxication, a drug, whose overdose makes you addict and you find solace only in it, even after knowing well that it eats you hollow and hastens your death. Since there is no immortality, there is no immorality either; all morals are natural, relative, and evolve with the society out of its convenience and not because of any divine order. Nature is indifferent to differences; its only quality is that of a transcendental chaos you call immorality and scientists now know as entropy; it beckons you, even entices, to indulge in love, hate, passion, instincts, even death. So forget cerebral nonsense, deem each virtue as an avoidable error. Just live happily for that is what you were born for; the very *raison d'etre* of your existence is happiness. That alone is Wisdom. Only hippies are happy.

This crass materialistic idea was revolutionary. The Aryans' *Vedas* and *Upanishads* were silent, matching and parallel responses to the evolution of Semitic-Hamitic-Iranian monotheism in India's contemporary neighbourhood—that created many a Sun God in West Asia (Fertile Crescent), such as Amon-Ra (Egypt), Marduk (Babylon) and Ashur (Assyria). In the same sixth century BC, also known for the *god-less* faiths in the East, such as that of Confucius, India was evolving a god-less response as well. With the heterodox Indian schools like Charvakas', this response came to the fore. For a time, it challenged the existing Brahminical order, but eventually the god-like varieties won the day. The bigger and serious challenge came from the *Old Testament*, now taking roots, around 536 BC, amongst the Jews of the Babylonian Captivity. At a time when the storm was gathering in the Fertile Crescent, India discovered that her weakened societal dykes needed to be replaced, especially when the remaining Harappans were yet to merge into the emerging Aryan *weltanshauung*. The Fertile Crescent was now getting fertile for messiahs. India needed a home-spun, umbrella-like *proselytising* religion to protect herself from a potential messianic Christianity that would be evangelising in the name of a Son of God: already, the First or Deutero Isaiah, a Buddha contemporary, was 'predicting' arrival of Jesus Christ! By that time, the Aryans had succeeded the Harappans in the Indus Valley and expanded to the Gangetic Valley across North India. In that heterodox *Naastik* (atheistic) or nihilist-hedonist society, the hold of the traditional Brahmins had gradually waned on the Indian mind; in a way, with the end of the Vedic and Upanishadic eras, the Indus Valley's cultural decay threatened to return. The 'Indian' Aryans, in other words, were following the same Indus footsteps they had so far studiously avoided: a self-destructive over-indulgence, the contemporary 'Romano-Americanisation'. The silent *Gyaankaandi*s were all gone; the boisterous *Karmakaandi*s were all there, mesmerising, pirating the gullible society like the contemporary Magis in neighbouring Iran. There was no enemy at the Indian borders; yet India trembled in fear. Fear of God. Of godlessness. India scared Indians. The Brahmins had lost drive in India, and the Vaishyas abroad. The so-called Shudras looked askance. The Kshatriyas, this time, came forward; some of them were descendents of those of the republican Indus people who had got almost assimilated in the Aryan society; they subsequently became powerful and created kingdoms in the Himalayan regions. Vishwamitra, the Brahminised Kshatriya sage, became almost a parallel 'Creator' but could not construct an Alternate Universe and hanged forever in limbo (as Trishanku); another Kshatriya, Siddharth Gautam, The Buddha, did. The Buddhists, and their cousins, the Jains, fought with two swords in their hands against the cultures of aliens as well as the Brahaminical order. But, eventually, they both caught the Aryans' viruses and slowly lost their positions when the real challenge came in the form of Christianity and Islam; India would then be forced to reinvent Krishna and the *Gita*. Still rooted firmly in the traditions of the far-away Indus Valley, these non-Aryan Kshatriyas believed not in any lofty religion but a business-like, practical one and many of them, in fact left weapons to become businessmen and Jains; following the *Naastikas*, they evolved atheistic and 'godless' cults—but India being what it has always been, both Siddhartha Gautam and Vardhaman Mahavira were, when superannuated, declared 'Bhagwan' and bestowed with godhood by their believers who did not realise this was poison to their potion—wherein devotion was made possible even without believing in a god. They said there was no need for sacerdotal ceremonies or Brahminical theology. The two Kshatriya warriors, Gautam the Buddha and Vardhaman the Mahavira, evolved active 'religions' in a passive India, fought an altogether different battle this time on an altogether different plane with an altogether different weapon. In the end, they acted like a moderator in a nuclear power plant, absorbing some of the ferocity of the alien attack: they saved India from Indians as well 'non-Indians' until India re-learnt the art of survival with the advent of Adi Shankaracharya in the eighth century.

In that fateful sixth century BC, Indian philosophical speculation ranged from one extreme of determinism to another of materialism. Those who believed in complete pre-determination, even monkhood, were called *Ajivikas*, who often lived like parasites on the society and gave India the unique idea that passivity leading to poverty, even beggary, could be a chosen livelihood, even lucrative profession—something that united all of India, the biggest recruiter being beggary of various hues; this idea later became an 'ideal' for almost all religions in India. In fact, the very word *ajivika* became synonymous with livelihood—and continues in government records even now! On the other extreme were the Lokayats or Charvakas preaching total materialism. Mahavira (599-527 BC), the pre-Einsteinian relativist, taught that the Universe was infinite, eternal, not created by any god who is simply non-existent; all knowledge is relative and temporal; even truth is relative and true only from one angle and it may even be false when looked at from another. All judgements of the common people, based on this partial knowledge and relative truth are, therefore, conditional and strictly limited; what we call 'absolute truth' comes only to the periodically appearing *Jins*, or Redeemers; there were, in all, 24 such High Souls or *Teerthankars*, Mahavira being the last one, the *Seal* of the Jain Prophets—these Enlightened Ones are those who had, through their pious deeds and acts of self-denial in numerous past lives had a zero-sum in their *Karma* debt account, overcome all worldly possessions, liberated themselves forever from the unending cycle of rebirths and attained the Ultimate Release, *Kaivalya*. The world follows an eternal law and continuously passes through a series of cosmic ways of progress and decline, crests and troughs, what we now call 'creative destruction'. Everything in the universe, whether animate or inanimate, has a soul whose purification is the highest purpose of a living being, the very purpose of Life; but this purification is not possible through knowledge which is always a relative quality. After unloading the baggage called god, Jainism also rejected the god-given *Veda*s, their interpreters, ie. the Brahminical priestly orders, and their pyramidal, increasingly structured caste system.

Since there is no God, the early Jains thought, the *Veda*s cannot be claimed to have been inspired by Him and are, therefore, quite useless. And since there is no God, the Brahminical 'Big Bang' theory of the Creation of the Universe, the *Hiranyagarbha*, was false. Mahavira gave a new meaning to Causation. There is no need to believe that a Creator or the First, Primeval Cause ever existed; for, it is impossible to know and prove absolutely that a causeless Cause or uncreated Creator ever existed; similarly, and equally, it was impossible to disprove that the world is uncaused or uncreated. The best thing to come out of this primordial quagmire is to assume that the Universe exists because of (what modern cosmogonists like Fred Hoyle, Hermann Bondi, Thomas Gold and Jayant Narlikar said) Continuous Creation and has been here, there, everywhere from all eternity—the Steady State Theory. Everything, whether *jarh* (inanimate) or *chetan* (animate), the Great Hero said, has *jeeva* or *atma* (Life Force, Soul) and the worst crime a man could indulge in was to take this life—indeed all Life in the Continuous Universe is sacred, inter-linked, and killing of any living creature amounted to killing of oneself—equivalent of hacking one's own computer. Human beings must exhaust their account of Karma and deliver themselves through *triratna*s or the three rules of social behaviour: right faith, right knowledge and right conduct. Right conduct means extreme and total non-violence, complete chastity, perfect belief and adherence to truth and total renunciation of all worldly possessions. The world continuously undergoes changes because of the inherent motions of Nature, and not because of any intervention from God. The inherent motions of Nature are due to the extremes playing upon one another and each action resulting into a Newtonian reaction. Therefore, the more violent your enemy is, the more non-violent you (must) become. Monotheism encouraged human beings to *possess* and *claim* things—progressively, the Jews claimed to possess the 'Promised Land', the Christians 'Son of God', and Muslims 'the Last Prophet', *apart from* their respective One God(s): *without knowing it, they all were dualists.* Therefore, Jainism shunned all worldly possessions. Declaration of *aparigraha* (non-possession) and *ahimsa* (non-violence) were a direct reaction to the Semitic theories of possession and violence. Like Islam, Jainism was, basically, an urban religion, mainly of traders, and shunned agriculture; unlike Islam, it got obsessed with non-violence.

Having said its bit, now was the time for Jainism to get embroiled in some of its own logical cobwebs. Since there was no God to create or rule the world, the sky appeared empty, at least theoretically; practically, it was not as heavenly bodies were there for all to see. The common souls cannot occupy such high mansions unless they followed the new religion; but the saints of the new faith, now deified, could and did go there, although even they were subject to decay and transmigration. The soul, or spirit, is an objective reality, characterised by 'consciousness' and is different from matter which lacks this consciousness. The bondage of Karma results in transmigration of the soul (ie. the cycle of birth and death). In order to emancipate the soul from this cycle, human beings must be free from the bondage of Karma, a steady state attainable only through one's own endeavours by practising self-discipline, eternal vigilance and equanimity; for this, Mahavira prescribed the four-fold path of *Sadhna.* And, any *atma* purifying itself to perfection could emerge as *Paramatma*, the unblemished Supreme Soul, spared of reincarnation for a while.

Jainism said the world composed of dualistic entities of mind and matter; the soul, *atma*, was all-pervasive, omnipresent, even in stone and iron, which continuously struggled to achieve *Paramatma*hood, or Supreme Soulness, through good deeds and unblemished record in a series of lives (like Mao Zedong's belief in a 'perpetual bath in the stream of revolution' for creation of a perfect, communist society); when the *atma* evolves into *Paramatma*, it would be spared reincarnation for some time (not forever, for that would negate continuous creation and might even overpopulate the world!) and would be born again when the scales of reward levelled up with that of merit. In contemporary Zoroastrian terms, it would mean Evil slowly dissolving into and itself becoming Good! For some time. That is, there is no absolute Evil or Good and, therefore, they do not engage in any perpetual struggle against one another and, again, human beings need not join this camp or that—neither with George W Bush nor with Osama bin-Laden! Moreover, since the world never began, it will never come to an end either; you are merely part of an endless process of continuous creation and dissolution and need no Messiah for your emancipation because there will not be any Last Day or Final Judgement (Hitler's 'Final Solution' was a logical evolution of the Final Judgement theory, beginning with Zoroastrianism and culminating in Islam via Judaism and Christianity). Those who need a 'theory' to prove anything and everything, should be ready to witness its practical manifestation as well. Was there any possibility of bringing to an end this chain of births? Souls passing through a perpetual bath in the endless stream of pure revolutions, words, deeds, would be eventually cleansed of their potency and tendency to be born and die; they would no longer affect the affairs of human beings, having sacrificed their urge for life and death at the altar of eternal bliss and happiness and having warded off all chances of rebirth, and therefore death. As such, only the highest, supreme and perfect spirits could alone achieve complete release and are known as *Arhat*s, Supreme Lords, who lived like 'Kings of Gods' in a remote realm. While monotheism propounded prolific population, struggle between Good and Evil and man's support to the former so as to reap the fruits in the end, and in another world, Jainism decided upon *brahmacharya* (complete celibacy), shunning violence of all kinds, even sex, as the price one would have to pay for *Kaivalya,* the Ultimate Release. In other words, while Zoroastrianism would have its believers struggle in this world for a reservation of comfortable berth in another, Jainism asked its adherents to shun birth and avoid rebirth altogether so that the other world was not overcrowded. Mahavira was the first demographer and civic planner—it is another thing that while the Great Hero emptied the sky of God, his followers soon peopled it again with deified saints; but even they were subject to decay, degeneration and transmigration and not regarded as the creators, managers or rulers of the world. The lasting, highest and complete release was possible only for the *Arhats*, the Supreme Lords living in an unknown, blissful realm, who never returned to the cycle of birth and death.

This road to release passed through the Five Commandments: *Ahimsa*, *Aparigriha*, *Satya*, *Brahmacharya* and *Tyaga*—non-violence, non-possession, truth, chastity and renunciation. Jainism approved voluntary end of life by slow starvation, saying it is the 'biggest' victory of the soul, spirit, over the blind desire and the will to live—even now, *santhara*, or voluntary fast-unto-death, so popularised by Gandhi to press his demands, is an honourable exit practice in some sub-sects of Jainism. In short, Jainism denied life, as against Abrahamism which extolled it, necessitating the 'existence' of God and all that follows: No life, No God; therefore, Jainism sought to nullify Abrahamism right in the womb.

In that same sixth century BC, Babylonian Emperor Nebuchadnezzar, a role model for Saddam Hussein of Iraq in the 1980s-90s, had enslaved the Jews and destroyed whatever agriculture they had developed in Judea and Israel; in Babylonia, the Jews were forced to make trade their main occupation. When they returned to their Fatherland with Iranian help, they had almost conceived their Yahvistic religion and were forced to remain traders as they were not allowed now to take back their land; the Jews, having lost land, chose to become lords of trade thereafter. Monotheism spread with their trade and later Iranian, Roman and Arab trade and this was followed up by all proselytisers subsequently—monotheism and trade gradually became fellow-travellers: although, earlier, only the poor could afford One God, the traders now found in Him their monopolistic dream. Jainism, on the other hand, imposed total ahimsa and a series of bans, including on vehicular travel, and even agriculture because it tore up the soil and killed innocent insects and worms. Adherent farmers gave up agriculture and took to trade; they concentrated in the western provinces to meet the intruding monotheistic trade with their own pseudo-atheistic trade. The monotheistic trade explosion of the Fertile Crescent was matched by an atheistic trade implosion in India. Jainism's stress on the two scales of merits and rewards attracted traders to this sect in large numbers and it ended up virtually as a traders' faith—it culminated in Rajneesh who completely inverted the faith and, unlike the founders of Jainism, became Messiah of the Moolah.

It was beginning of the Age of Trade in real terms; God, even godlessness, was the biggest commodity to be traded. Jainism proved that the fanatic violence of monotheism could be met by an equally fanatic non-violence of atheism; Gandhi, a Hindu *Vaishya* trader, followed this path as a ***policy*** with the tenacity of a fundamentalist, making the bullish British to punch him until they fatigued and retreated—not for nothing is Gandhi regarded by some as the 25th *Teerthankar* of Jainism! Jainism gave India its biggest 'weapon': non-violence, pacifism. Modern India's elements of foreign policy—*Panchsheel,* Non-Aligned Movement and no-first-use of nuclear weapons—flows directly from this. India can afford it because she knows the inherent capability of her age-old enemies to honourably pass away unsung. Such is the influence of 'non-violence and peace' on the Indian mind that many of even those who converted to alien faiths remained cowards: the only major difference between the Hindus and the Muslims of the Indian subcontinent is that while the former were mostly cowards until 1947, barring exceptions, the latter remained cowards even afterwards; that was why Pakistan continued to make tall claims of victory in 1971 even as its 93,000 soldiers were surrendering before the Indian Army in Dhaka; its 'holy warriors' (*Jehadis*), hot-air balloons, fled back from Afghanistan to the safety of Islamabad, their boasts and bravado melted away, once the Taliban lost to the USA in 2001—only some Pakistanis made Pakistan the hotbed of terrorism.

Jainism made India recognise the lowest and highest limits of violence; since you cannot fight for long a stronger enemy, hang on, therefore, to the highest limit of non-violence and withdraw within your shell like a tortoise so as to outlive the enemy—the only thing you could do without offending others—so that you could groom yourselves to absorb the highest limit of violence. If left undisturbed, violence is like ember which extinguishes itself. Non-violence became India's best deterrent, for the one extreme of monotheistic violence was matched by the other extreme of atheistic non-violence of the Jains: Muslim general Nasir-ud-din Qubacha was tired of letting the blood of the nude Jain saints in Bihar, because they 'offered no resistance' and it was 'unmanly' to kill such people; Gandhi exploited to the hilt the relatively 'civilised' British restraint and fear of crushing unarmed people, vis-à-vis other 'barbarian' European colonisers who did not hesitate to exterminate in large numbers, or herding their colonial subjects like cattle for slave trade in Africa and elsewhere.

Both the Mahavira and the Mahatma were great psychoanalysts. The two extremes matched one another; each would absorb the other. Non-violence would neutralise any attack; even refuse to acknowledge any attack at all! See how America and Britain were jittered after 9/11 or 7/7 and how India, attacked by terrorists so many times, began to take these in her stride—no other country could afford to produce jokes about serious Islamic terrorists. The enemy would be frustrated if you do not recognise his 'valour'; you can defeat any enemy in the long run by simply ignoring his short-term victory. The Zoroastrians and Jews came to India not as victors of India but as vanquished of West Asia. The Muslims did eliminate a large number of *Digambar* (sky-clad) Jain saints in Bihar, ridiculing their nudity, and found themselves being crushed subsequently under the weight of the many clothes they wore themselves. Jainism made India supple, a marshy land, like the Rann of Kutch, where the enemy could intrude at will but would not escape alive—they always left their footprints in the sands of Time. To this day, the *puggis* (footprint identifiers) easily trace Pakistanis trying to infiltrate into India through the desert route.

If monotheism extolled life to unnatural limits, Jainism based its faith on a profound doubt about life itself and even denied it. Monotheism extolled God, Jainism denied His very existence. Nine years after the Romans destroyed the Temple of Solomon in Jerusalem, circa 70 AD, the Jains split into two sects, the new one being the *Shwetambar*, which, questioning the wisdom of 'wearing' the sky, decided to cover themselves; the earliest sect of Jains remained in their birthday suit, *Digambar* (*Dik*, the sky, and *Ambar*, clad), who, their rivals claimed, were disturbing the emancipated *Arhats* Up There! In turn, the Digambars declared that not only Shwetambars but even the Digambar nuns, who do not practise nudity and thus indulge in possession, cannot attain liberation. Today, the five million population of the Jains, divided in several sub-sects of Digambars and Shwetambars, often sell ancient wares to each other. They mostly 'convert' from one sub-sect to another, thus retaining their population low as few outsiders convert to Jainism; they also marvel how the half-clad Mahatma Gandhi stole a march over them to become the Jainest-of-Jains, even without himself becoming one, and whether to enrol him as one of their own Jins, another incarnation of the great soul that appears in flesh-and-blood to redeem the world from time-to-time.

Such a strict code of conduct for its adherents could not have attracted many converts to Jainism. Its historic role was mainly to kick-start reaction of Indian culture and psychologically quarantine, season and condition the Hindu mind against the Abrahamic possession and violence. Having done that, India now needed to push the accelerator with the other foot—an actively proselytising creed which could create a supple, marshy fortress around Aryavarta, a trap for the descendents of Abraham. Buddhism was precisely this creed, the first arm of Hinduism against proselytising Abrahamic monotheism. As an insurance and protection to shield Hinduism, it created fortresses, or shock absorbers, in what is now Pakistan and Afghanistan in the west and Bangladesh and Burma (Myanmar) in the east, Tibet in the north and Sri Lanka in the south. The Abrahamic pinnacle, Islam, was to be absorbed in the first two of these areas. The birth of Pakistan and then Bangladesh, was, in a way, a case of Buddhist suffering.

For, the Lord taught that suffering is matter's primeval motion, which has a cause, which should be overcome and there is a way to accomplish this. In just four simple key-words we can explain Buddhism thus: the world is full of *suffering*, which is caused by human *desire*, whose *renunciation* is the path to *salvation*. These are the four Noble Truths, the *Arya Satyas*. Salvation is possible through an Eight-Fold Path. As in *Genesis*, The Buddha said the universe had originally been an abode of bliss but man's surrender to extremes and desires had reduced it into a place of suffering. Avoid the (Abrahamic) violence as well as the (Jain) non-violence as these are extremes and follow the *Mazzim Magga*, the Middle Path, through the Eight-Fold Way: Right kind of view, intention, speech, action, livelihood, effort, mindfulness and concentration. You may indulge in possession but cessation of pain, of suffering, comes with non-attachment. Buddhism accepted the dogmas of Karma and rebirth and was silent on the caste system even while opposing the Brahminical 'holy' tyranny—since salvation lay in achieving *Nirvana*, or extinction from all desire, freedom from the Wheel of Rebirth, the doctrine of Karma was necessary for this salvation. But The Buddha did not use Karma to simply explain away the caste status; he dismissed all that is 'supernatural' and claimed no 'revealed' truths. Since there was no God, there could be no prayer to Him—subsequently, when The Buddha himself was evolved into a God and his iconography became one of the most enduring in the world, elaborate rituals were also evolved to worship Him. God was simply not essential to the early Buddhist universe as there was an automatic, natural, cosmic rise and decline. Abrahamism was essentially a state of mind fashioned by a set of axioms. Buddhism's subconscious job was, therefore, to fashion an anti-dote to Abrahamism: The Teacher's was basically the path of liberation of human mind, of mental discipline, of psychological analysis. He never promised any Abrahamic heaven nor a Hindu *anand*, bliss. *Nibbana* (Nirvana), he said, was release, the 'extinguishing' of the wick called Life. The decline of Buddhism in India lay in its export-oriented Special Economic Zones which exported cheaper, more than they produced, and did not mind revenue loss at home, which eventually made the Faith unviable—until the 20th century. Adi Shankaracharya virtually bought off the Buddhist suffering, desire, renunciation, salvation, casteism, rebirth and other stock-in-trade for sale under the *Gita*'s banner, and emptied the Lord's warehouse.

Siddharth's republican and 'Kshatriyaised' ancestors had apparently come from the Indus Valley to settle down in Southern Nepal. Religion does not prosper in prosperity which brings in loose morals and tight schedules as its own anti-dote. The sixth and seventh century BC riches of India had made her people hedonist, epicurean and materialist that led to the evolution of a dozen heterodox sects, the 'godless religions'. Prosperity had released senses from the clutches of restraints and free-wheeling-philosophy was order of the day. Each man wanted to have his personalised liberation, like today's Permanent Account Number (PAN). Not only India, some other contemporary countries produced their own Mahaviras and Buddhas in that fateful sixth century BC: Zarathushtra in Iran, the Second or Deutero Isaiah in Judia, Confucius and Lao-tze in China. This was the time when maturing First Wave civilisations were causing disaffection among the have-nots the way the emerging Second (Industry) and the Third Wave (Knowledge) later unleashed the terrors of Christianity and Islam in the form of the Crusades and Jihad. Like Muhammed, The Buddha was supposed to remove the veil of 'ignorance'.

While Abrahamism extolled human birth, Jainism would deny birth altogether through brahmacharya; Buddhism, however, saw a succession of deaths and births, and scorned human life. The Lord found birth to be the origin of all evil—even born gods are, therefore, evil. Despite this, birth continues endlessly, thus replenishing the stream of human grief. But birth cannot be stopped because, as per the Law of Karma, the soul must atone for evils done in past existences via new incarnations. Rebirth can be spared if one could live a life of perfect judgement, eternal patience and mercy to all; by leading such a perfect life could alone one dry up his stream of desire, evil. Yes, desire is evil; and, Abrahamism originates in desire, of God and Paradise.

Siddharth could have, like Deutero Isaiah, claimed that a God was speaking through him, that his doctrine was a 'revelation'; but he described his own state of mind only as an 'enlightenment', not even an inspiration and never pretended any divinity. His doctrine was compressed in the Noble Truths: life is suffering, which is due to selfish desire and the wise are those who still all such desire. He behaved more like Confucius, a moral teacher rather than as a grim-faced saint; he also had a sense of humour and, in China, statues of Laughing Buddha were made. All pleasures, to him, were ephemeral in nature; only suffering was permanent. But he was not against all desire; selfish desire that led to advantage of the part, rather than good of the whole, was undesirable. Even sexual desire should be overcome because it stretches out the chain of life and death into new tributaries of suffering. Unlike Jainism, however, he did not favour self-annihilation as it could not stop the chain of life and death; the soul would have to be transmigrated for fulfilment of unfulfilled works.

Buddhism, in concept, was ethical and strongly based on an adherent's right conduct, not on his right belief, ritual, worship, theology or metaphysics. The Buddha was never interested in any philosophical disputations or discussions which, to him, were nothing but hair-splitting; he never discussed with anybody immortality, eternity or infinity, nor even God. All he would say was that an atom could never understand the universe and refrained from saying anything on the beginning or end of the world; even gods, if at all they existed, could not answer such questions, he would remark in his characteristic humour. Although his movement was apparently against Brahminism and caste system, he never openly condemned the latter, merely telling his students that all castes united in Buddhism. His faith has since been enjoying an honourable grandfatherly status in India which keeps the recalcitrant next generation of faiths in check although the grandchildren no longer obey their Patriarch, just tolerate him. He denounced all religious sacrifices, cults and worship of supernatural beings, mantras and incantations, prayers and asceticism. Early Buddhism was free of all dogma or priestcraft and even infidels could find salvation in it. There was no hell or heaven nor even a purgatory in the doctrine. The most interesting feature of Buddhism was, however, the fact that *religion can exist even without god*, that the universe was not designed by a divine personality nor the moral law as his will: in it, there is a theology but no deity, a psychology but no soul.

Here Buddhism encountered its weakest point: if there was no soul, how could it transmigrate to atone for sins of this life into the next. The Buddha, again in his characteristic silence, did not reply to it. The contradiction between rationalistic psychology and unconditional acceptance of reincarnation was too glaring to be ignored. Even the Lord took the theory of Karma and Rebirth for granted: it was on this *axiom* that his entire thought superstructure was based, as was Abrahamism based on the axiomatic unity of God. The Wheels of

Karma and Rebirth weighed upon his mind and he wanted to escape from these, achieve Nirvana, the ultimate annihilation, the blissfulness. Never to be born is the ultimate reward! The Noblest Prize. For the first time, he injected India with axiom, in order to inoculate her from the axioms that would rush in on sprinting horses in the coming centuries. Together, Jainism and Buddhism gave India her first weather reports about the theo-cyclones building up in the Arabian Sea and trans-Indus.

A contemporary with the emerging *Old Testament*, The Buddha (563-483 BC) almost anticipated the *New Testament* morality: Christianity borrowed for its Jesus Christ Buddhism's missionary zeal and the Order, proselytisation and evangelisation, seeking official patronage from Kings and converting them. Some of the Biblical stories of the 'morals' of Jesus, too, were copied wholesale from Buddhist literature—return good for evil, love for hate, kindness etc. Mercifully, there was no *Book of Revelation* in Buddhism! But, unlike Buddhism, a self-righteous Christianity that came to India could never learn to remain silent under misunderstanding and abuse nor could it even absorb The Buddha's humour. They utilised The Buddha's Sermon to his disciples to carry the New Message to all the lands and the people. Like the Buddhist enthusiasts weaving a hundred tales about the Master's Birth, Jesus' disciples, too, manufactured similar tales, as also about the 'marvels' he wrought—most such tales were based on ancient sun myths. Brahminical priestcraft sneaked into the Buddhist Order soon after the Lord's death, turning His disciples into neo-Brahmins, and incorporated women as nuns, magic, polytheism and superstitions that all ate into the vitals of this vibrant faith.

Once its role was up, it was time for Buddhism to split: within two centuries of the Lord, His Message had disintegrated into as many as 18 varieties of the doctrine, each claiming the Master's heritage. Buddhism in Burma alone remained the relatively purest form of the Faith; the Buddhists of South India, Sri Lanka and some in the South-East Asia held fast to the Lesser Vehicle (*Hinayana*), a relatively purer and simpler creed worshipping The Buddha not as God but as a Great Teacher. In North India, China, Mongolia, Tibet and Japan, the Greater Vehicle (*Mahayana*) prevailed after Kanishka's Council; the Teacher was morphed into a God, with assorted divinity, angels, saints, the Patanjali Yoga asceticism and Sanskrit canons; Mahayana was the embellished, people-friendly and market-savvy, popular, Brahminised version of Buddhism, rather than the austere pessimism of the Shakyamuni's faith.

This proselytising Buddhism provided an early escape route, an alternative, to those of the 'lower' castes, whom the mores of Brahminical Hinduism could potentially force into the approaching westerly winds of Abrahamism, to get a protective shield against it—it turned out so when Christianity and Islam came. In a way, it was pre-Christian Christianity: It had a Heaven with many Buddhas, the most popular being Amitabh Buddha, the Redeemer, and also a corresponding Hell for receiving rewards or punishments of good or evil done on the Earth. In this new theology, the greatest saints were called the *Bodhisattva*s, the future Buddhas, who could, like Bheeshma of the *Mahabharata*, defy death at will and refrain from achieving the Nirvana or freedom from rebirth, in order to be reborn again and again, until their very purpose of birth, to help others find the Great Way, was achieved.

Buddhism was the first proselytising religion in the world that saw no distinction between human beings on the basis of their physical or psychological origins. It sought to link all Homo sapiens in One Whole by winnowing out their inherited animal 'desires' and, therefore, killed their animal instincts, ie. the desire to remain alive during a struggle for existence. In fact, it made the Hindus the first batch amongst human societies who crossed the threshold of their native cultures into the world of Homo sapiens by making them tolerant of each other's presence and opinions, so much so that 'peaceful coexistence' became a bane for them. In this genetic change, they mostly lost their fighting spirit, got infested with immigrants and fortune-seekers from all over the world time and again, and were enslaved for more than a millennium. Fanatically adhering to peace and non-violence, they did not realise that ostriches cannot save their lives by sinking their heads in the sand as the carnivores still saw in them their food. The not-so-evolved people around the Indian peace-hawkers were still unfortunate creatures trapped in human skin; Gandhi finally eradicated this ancient Indian disease, as we will see.

Buddhism did fast-track India on the evolutionary path but also made it suffer in the animal kingdom around where concepts like peace and tolerance were alien; it made India aware that human peace could encourage animals' war against you. In that respect, India would have to learn about and evolve newer weaponry, even if by going back to Hinduism. This India did with the Gupta Empire. Both Buddhism and Jainism came as an anti-casteist and anti-Brahminical movements and, for a time, succeeded in churning and frothing up the Vaishya castes to the top of the social echelon—the Mauryans and the Guptas were supportive of these 'heterodox' sects as was Ashoka (also known also as *Devanampiya,* Beloved of the Gods and *Piyadassi,*The Ideal King), in what was an attempt to create a social system parallel to the Brahminical one.

After Siddharth Gautam, Buddhism achieved its zenith in Ashoka's era. Denounced in the beginning as 'Chandashoka' (Ashoka, The Terrible), due to his cruel ways, he became the Emperor at Patliputra after a bloody struggle for the throne. Soon, he won the war against the Republic of Kalinga in what is now Odisha. His pyrrhic victory was temporary as the Empire got infested with the disastrous after-effects on the Mauryan society itself. That was when he discovered in Buddhism the means to control the chaotic and seething realm and almost made it the state religion. His slow change of heart made him now known as 'Dharmashoka' (Ashoka, The Pious), although he did not himself convert to the new faith for nearly three years. He made two important contributions: one, by sending his son Mahendra and daughter Sanghamitra to Lanka and other places for popularising Buddhism he launched the first-ever Indian attempt to commission a religion to proselytise outside the soil of its origin and two, he almost replaced the concept of state with *Dhamma* (the Law of Righteousness). This made Buddhism inoculate India against the gathering storm from across the Indus. India realised that kings and empires would come and go; it was only by sticking to the Dharma and the Social Order that the nation could be saved and rejuvenated.

The Mediterranean Christianity absorbed in wholesale the Buddhist marketing strategy: saints crowding the pantheon of art and worship, forms and ceremonies from earlier faiths like veneration of 'holy water' and relics, incense, the rosary, candles, a dead language for liturgy, monasteries complete with monks and nuns, celibacy and tonsure, fasting and confessions, canonisation of saints, purgatory and popular masses for the dead. Mahayana won the world but lost India where the Brahmins returned and offered all these plus more. Mahayana was destined to match first the Mediterranean Christianity and then Roman Catholicism so completely in India that the number of faithful of these two Christian sects has remained almost constant: one per cent of the total population! Not only this, when about 50,000 Dalit ('low' caste) Hindus embraced Buddhism amid much fanfare in New Delhi in October 2001, they did so in the 'august' presence of Christian priests! Mahayana offered a home-made alternative to Christianity. The Buddha became a quarter-way house between Moses and Manu and monotheism became merely a wrapper of the gift-packed polytheism. By the time the Arabs knocked India's door, the Buddhists had, in their 1,000 years, spent all their steam, rendering India a supple, soft state, armed heavily with her beggars in various shapes and colours, a vast land of marshes and humus waiting for Abrahamism to sink.

Buddhism cautioned India with a last message, which would come echoing from the Fertile Crescent: the *Bhikkhu*s (monks) saluted each other and others with 'Peace to All Beings'; the Jews were already chanting *Shalom Aleichem* (Peace Be With You); a thousand years later, the Muslims would be appending it to Prophet Mohammed's name whenever they recalled him, Peace Be Upon Him (PBUH). India learnt the harder way: beware, therefore, of peace; it is preparation for war. Gandhi, too, learnt from it when he preached peace. So, despite hawking peace for over 2,500 years, India remained cautious: when Maulana Fazl-ur-Rehman of Pakistan paraded peace in India, his armed boys were being trained to attack India. Peace is a local anaesthetic to benumb you so that your neck becomes butter for the war-monger's sword.

To India, The Buddha advised: *Atmadeepo Bhav* (Be a Lamp unto Yourselves).

That's what India did.

Resultant Gods: Their Echoes

HERE, we will focus on how the Hindus gradually responded to the emergence of Judaism, Christianity and Islam (500 BC-800 AD) and created psychological defence mechanism against potential religious conversion of the masses under alien influence, how the 'inadequacies' of Buddhism and Jainism, in doing so, were overcome during the 'Golden Age' of Hinduism, from the fourth to the eighth centuries AD.

The Buddha's atheism did not satisfy many in a contemporary, still-on-the-drawing-board India where the population of gods, too, multiplied with each child's birth. 'How many Gods are There' was the moot question. Yajnavalkya, the greatest philosopher of India's Upanishadic era, apparently warned of the emerging theocratic danger from across the Indus. The *Upanishads* had been stressing upon the inadequacy of the human intellect as a mere transitory, miniscule fragment unable to comprehend the immense complexity of the complex immensity called Nature; you cannot compare logic with direct perception, immediate insight—which the West claimed was 'revelation', the 'divine directive'; the former is merely the package, the latter the real consignment. Logic is only as trustworthy as a politician's promises.

A monist, Yajnavalkya described Atma (Brahma) as the King of all living beings; everything else is embedded in it the way the spokes of a wheel are in the axle of a chariot. That showed how human intellect could be forced to be *finite*, logically: tired of their struggles, ordinary people often succumb to falsehood.

By the time of The Buddha's birth, monotheistic winds had begun to cross over into India; the monism of the *Chhandogya Upanishad* slowly morphed into the monotheism of *Brihadaranyak Upanishad*, literally meaning 'sitting near one vast dense forest'. The *Vedas* and *Upanishads* were India's psychological responses to the solar monotheism of West Asia; they were now superannuated and revered. With the Aryans' Achaemenid takeover of the vast Persian Empire, which replaced the Semitic race as the rulers of the Fertile Crescent, for a thousand years from the sixth century BC to the sixth century in AD, the intellectual and economic leadership of the contemporary inhabited world, from India to Europe, had come into the Aryan hands; although they were unable to stop the tide of the simmering Hamitic-Semitic monotheistic undercurrent, which culminated in Muhammed as a 'Semitic' reaction of collective human attitude, enforcing moral certitude; they did fortify their minds. The Buddha, Confucius, Socrates and some others represented the non-Semitic thought-trends.

The 'Aryan' tribes—threatened in Central Asia by the demographically burgeoning barbarians and geologically by the recurring natural disasters like earthquakes and the possible return of the Tenth Ice Age (for the first time in the 40,000-year history of *Homo sapiens'* dominance)—had migrated to many lands, including India, which, the way the Jews did in the Palestine, they would claim as their own country. Being immigrants, like others elsewhere all through human history, they were fast learners and adapters ready to struggle for existence. It was, after all, a question of survival and one could survive only when one had food; since food was scarce, one had to struggle against friends and foes alike and kill them if they turned enemy in an unending food web as part of their organic evolution. Only the fittest could survive in this struggle for existence and natural selection. Everyday.

A warm India was emerging as a magnet to the relatively docile and unwarlike tribes of Asia (and then of Europe, culminating in the British), while the Fertile Crescent was attracting martial races. India attracted those who were shedding their animal past of meat-eating-meat habit of the Zero Wave food web. With agricultural evolution, vegetarianism got a fillip; with this change of food habits, new survival patterns also emerged in India vis-à-vis aliens who largely stuck to the habit of flesh-as-food. This strange process shaped India as a land of peace-loving, even docile, people given more to boisterous emotions than silent ambitions.

But, in a world inhabited by an intrepid warrior atheist China to her East and warrior Iran and the Middle East to her West, how would this docile India survive?

Why did the Indians make their docile cow the holiest animal? Why did Gandhi have the docile goat for pet? Because these mulch cattle evolved species-specific survival tactics, in numbers for instance, against the Big Cats who subsequently became an endangered species cornered into circuses or protected enclosures across the world. The cow and the goat still roam around across India freely while Big Cats are facing extinction!

The Aryans were essentially nomadic shepherds, who carried their living and throbbing village on the back of their cows and horses, before transplanting their habitat upon dying towns and cities of the Indus Valley Civilisation and then migrating towards the more fertile Gangetic plain; many Indian sub-continental politicians still practice it by having pet cattle in their ministerial bungalows in the urban capitals, including New Delhi.

The Dravidians inherited Bull worship from their ancestors of possible Taurean origins in Anatolia, before they migrated to the Indian subcontinent and down south. Later, they integrated the animal, as Nandi, representing the male creative principle with the South Indian

God of Lightening, *Rudra*, who, like the Jewish Yahveh, had human weaknesses and was given to emotions. He later metamorphosed into Shiva, still inheriting weaknesses (therefore his nickname, *Bholenath*, the Innocent God, particularly in North India). In parts of North India and Nepal, He became Pashupatinath ('Lord of the Beasts') and was further integrated with female creative principle of *Shakti* in contact with the Aryans; when He spread across India, particularly to the Himalayas, He even more integrated with Parvati, Daughter of the Mountains.

The pre-Aryans had crossed the three great river systems, the Tigris, Euphrates and the Indus, before settling down to participate in the evolution of the Indus Valley civilisation. The Aryans had entered India from the three mountain passes of the Himalayas, called Khaibar, Bolan and Gomal; they had crossed three great valleys before settling down in the 'Aryavarta', the Kabul-Swat, the Indus-plus-five and the Ganges-Yamuna-Saraswati. They had crossed three mountain ranges—the Hindukush, the Aravallis and the Vindhyas as well. These passes, river valleys and the mountain ranges remained embedded in their psyche forever and shaped their destiny—that was how the map of 'Bharat Mata' emerged. After fanning out over large tracts in the Sindh and Punjab areas, they slowly internalised the ultimate survival tactics of mammals the way the 'fallen' hero switches on his emergency battery, as in Hollywood flicks like *Terminator* and *The Matrix*.

The Aryan shepherd's Cow began to move eastward and graze in the dense forests of a nearly empty land they later called 'Aryavarta', the Land of the Noble. The Exodus Jews returning from Egypt, circa 1250 BC, had massacred their way into the already inhabited Levant and faithfully recorded these events in the *Old Testament*; the Aryan nomads settled down in a nearly empty North India they would later call *their* homeland. The Jews opposed any other people's settlement in their 'Promised Land' they claimed was gifted by God; the Aryans welcomed immigrants like themselves as yet another layer on the cake, although they also maintained their distance until the new immigrants merged their identities with the locals.

The three mountain passes, like valves of the heart, regulated human traffic. Control the passes and you control your culture and civilisation. The Aryans internalised the habit of *not* checking intruders, and let them form yet another layer on the Indian social cake; they would then absorb the digestible and *adsorb* the indigestible among them; they would forgive, not forget, the enemy and always outsource the battles to the uppermost layer in the cake, the latest immigrant. In India's today walked her tomorrow. It was no coincidence, for instance, that the Taliban, many of whom were Aryan sub-tribes, unveiled the *fundamental* face of Islam, thus pushing the *adsorbed* Muslims further towards the land of their origins, from South Asia towards Arabia. In fact, Afghanistan and Pakistan are fighting India's delayed and outsourced battles against the Fertile Crescent's monotheism the way Israel is fighting the West's outsourced battles against Islam and America is fighting Europe's outsourced battle against Mecca.

All history in the Indian subcontinent, even the retreat of monotheism and deIslamisation, flows from the last batch of the Aryans' pre-historic attempts to survive the Tenth Ice Age: they have had nowhere else to go as all other lands had been occupied and inhabited by warrior races while the Indian Aryans were happy creating martial epics like the *Mahabharata* as a *psychological recompense* to their inherent weaknesses. Since they had to survive only in India, they were forced to evolve psychological defences and quarantine themselves against the long-term psychological warfare unleashed by the Fertile Crescent, particularly by the Jews, who were equally afraid to return to their home in the inhospitable deserts of Arabia.

The Jews had by now (seventh century BC) captured the Canaan from where they would not budge and do all they could to claim this *Promised Land* as the *Chosen People* of Yahveh, the Lord of their Hosts, the Canaanites—it was like the early Aryans claiming that India was gifted to them by their gods! Like the Jews adopting the God of the vanquished, the Aryans, too, adopted gods of the Indus people they had succeeded after natural disasters extinguished the Harappan Civilisation: the Sea God, the phallus, the Bull, the Mother Goddess and, finally, when they reached South India, their rural Lord Rudra, the Indus Lord of Lightening, a la Yahveh of Canaan. While retaining the Yahvistic simplicity and short-temper in Rudra, the Aryans and Dravidians modified His attributes to serve their own needs and the resultant Shiva turned out to be a hybrid of the Indus and Aryan traditions. Indeed, the Aryans evolved a whole retinue of other gods and assimilated even those from rival tribes which, theocratised, merged into and eventually crystallised in the post-Gupta era into the all-powerful triumvirate of Brahma, Vishnu and Shiva. Among these, the only pan-Indian God was Shiva whose temples could be found in every nook and corner of India; Brahma has had only one major temple to Him, in the desert state of Rajasthan, while Vishnu has often been worshipped only as a stone, not as an idol, because of a woman's 'curse' to this God—in no other culture would an all-powerful God, who sustained the world, be 'sentenced' like this by an ordinary woman! It was Vishnu's anthropomorphic Rama and Krishna incarnations that have mostly been worshipped in human forms, mainly in urban areas. Thus, the 'national' chief deity of India has been Rudra-Shiva, also the Lord of Destruction, whom the Indians adopted from the Indus people, just as the Jews adopted the Canaanites's Lord of Lightening, Yahveh, for their own purpose. Much of written history of our human race is the story of struggle of the Jews and the Aryans to somehow survive in their last refuges called Israel and India, respectively, as they did not want to return to their hostile hot and cold deserts respectively, and bowed before and adopted the frightening gods of the peoples they succeeded as neo-natives of their adopted lands.

The Aryans made the cow holy because it yielded bullock for the field, milk for the family, dung-cake for the hearth and beef for the occasional social heretic. If the horse was the Aryan's speed, the cow was his brake that would check his unbridled advance when it assumed suicidal dimensions. To this day, it is not the often absent traffic policeman but the cow that 'regulates' traffic on many an Indian road! The Aryans made the cow inviolable and the horse 'killable' after reaching the imperial limits, as in the *Ashwamedha yajna*: you cannot step into the same river twice and you cannot use the same horse in the series of battles. Life is a war for existence against the rest of the world; it is a series of battles some of which are won by both the sides.

Therefore, do not hesitate to change your horse. Even mid-stream. In mid-term elections.

For every battle, therefore, you need a new horse, as the famous phrase in Hindi goes: *nayi ghodi, naya daon* (A new mare/dice for a new groom/game). India has produced a new horse whenever intruders from the three passes threatened her identity. That was how her nine greatest sons, from The Buddha to Osho Rajneesh, descended. Nature issued this stream, like anti-bodies, to digest the impact left, respectively, by Zarathushtra, Jeremiah and Second Isaiah, Muhammed, the Sufi sects, Babar and others. Imperialists coming to India lamented that this strange land was never a 'nation' and that it was *they*, the intruders, who 'unified' it. Why did not India become 'one nation' by the Semitic yardsticks? It did not need to. The West did not know that light comprised seven colours, VIBGYOR, until Newton told them; Indians always knew that. They were like those colours and called the rainbow *Indradhanush*, The Bow of the Lord of Gods, ie. the biggest weapon was unity. The Hindus so loved their freedom that their guiding principles became *Aham Brahmasmi* (I Am The Universe), *Ekam Brahmam, Dwitiyo Naasti* (There Is Only One Universe, None Other) and *Brahmam Satyam, Jaganmithya* (The Universe Alone Is The Truth, Material World Is Not). It was not denial of others but acceptance of the Self. These strings bound Indians with India and, more recently, made Gandhi and Jayaprakash Narayan release silent force multipliers few could comprehend then.

The Indian Aryans evolved elaborate social rules for endogamy and exogamy in this country, unlike their Aryan cousins descending upon West Asia and Europe. They called the tall, black natives as *Daitya*s or *Danav*s, and those prohibited from partaking the holy liquor (*Somras*) because of their wayward behaviour, as *Asur*s; thus, the words '*Daitya*s' and '*Asur*s' did not carry any abusive meaning initially as they assumed later. For instance, the word *Raaksha*s merely meant 'defender of the forts' but when, like the German and Turk warriors, originally enrolled like our contemporary bouncers to guard VIPs, eventually overpowered the Papacy and the Caliphate, these same defenders became offenders. Their professional identity became a form of abuse, the way the word *bhai* (brother) now means a gangster in Mumbai and elsewhere. While assimilating the Indus people, the Vindhyan tribals and their monkey god Hanuman, the easterly Nagas and others, the Aryans included their progenitors in the pantheon of their own family trees, to make it a system of nine major *Gotras*, or the bloodline issued forth from a 'founding saint': many of the work-charge arch-villains of the evolving Hindu mindset would originate either in these non-Aryan incorporated gotras as in Mahishasur, or in cross-Aryan setting as in the case of Ravana which, too, were later Brahmanised and elaborate mythological ancestry and achievements were added to them, as in the case of their original seven gotras. Since the newly-incorporated gotras like the Daityas and Nagas were now part of the Aryan mould and fold, with occasional inter-marriage also, there were no permanent, Satan-type arch-villains; the Indian 'evil' men would be one-film wonders, to be invented off and on and then absolved of their sins by the hero produced in the original Aryan household; the pre-Aryan Dravidians and Nagas worshipped buffalo who, as Mahishasur, was vanquished by Goddess Durga, astride a lion. From Europe to India, the Aryan cousins had evolved different systems to incorporate those they defeated. The Greeks kept the vanquished at bay by excluding them from their 'democracy' of city-states while the dictatorship of their Draconian Law bequeathed to Europe the burden of 'white' or racial supremacy, culminating in Hitler. The Romans, on the other hand, indiscriminately inter-married with the brave amongst the slaves, and ended up planting their seed in the weakest wombs, while adopting their subcultures. They laughed their way out of the 'Holy' Roman Empires, leaving the Vatican behind as a relic of its former self. The Persian Aryans killed most of native male slaves and sold or married females when they descended upon Iran; their cousins coming to India virtually assimilated, in concentric circles, those they replaced.

Thus, there was a chain of 'looking-down-upon': the Greeks despising the Romans and both despising the Iranians, the latter too hating the former two—and eventually their foster child, the USA—and keeping aloof from the Indian Aryans, who, barring exceptions, were seen as docile and soft even amongst the sword-happy Aryan lot; even if docile, the Indians turned out to be long-race horses. This peculiar Indian survival tactic of using the weakest as a human shield against the strong, gave birth to the legend of the weakling Shikhandi, a eunuch, who became the strongest sheath for Arjuna against the Kaurava patriarch Bheeshma, in the *Mahabharata* war. Terrorists and politicians alike still use the poor and the weak as human shield to attack their enemies and protect themselves.

The links that joined the Indo-Iranian-European Aryans was their common ancestry in race, culture and languages. They shared common astral belief systems, particularly sun worship owing to their common origins in the Caucasian cold, evolved similar mythologies, immunities and reflexive response systems to the native counter-attacks that came from within before and through the arrival of alien monotheism: the Aryan Greeks and Romans gradually deconstructed the unity of Semitic Christianity and the Iranians did the same with the Semitic Islam. On the other hand, the Indian Aryans, who were physically the weakest but matured tribes among the Aryan Diaspora, were like a people made desperate after being driven to the wall by their fate and population pressures from within and without—they realised that India was, perhaps, their last post in Asia as they could not migrate beyond this shelter. To survive in India, they adopted a cow-like policy of rumination and regurgitation: let the assault sink in…and subside; then slowly digest it at leisure, and excrete the undesirable. Bio-diversity and food-chain keep the animate world going. One's poison being another's medicine, one's religion being another's superstition, one's hero being another's villain, there could not be any universally-accepted absolute whites and blacks or gods and devils. Even faeces manure a crop. To come into being is a strange thing; to procreate even stranger; and to survive is the strangest of all. If polytheism was to survive in India, it must create several insulated layers in the cake of the society, each as one more road-block to the enemy, each with its own taste. The lowest layer in a multi-layered cake melts first. India reckoned that the monotheists would attack it from below. She, therefore, insulated each caste from the rest in the cake by reserving their occupations and customs, their very livelihood, so as to slow-down and minimise the pace and impact of alien proselytisation. That was how India survived in its contemporary monotheistic, friendless world. Bravehearts solve problems with the stroke of the sword, in one moment; since the Indian Aryans were mainly warriors of the mind, all they could do was to solve their problems with the stroke of a genius, in a millennium. They defeated the Semitic brawn with Aryan brain. That was how India came to acquire more TV studio warriors than in her armed forces!

But, India discovered that, more than mere survival, there was an even more astonishing thing: to think. Not like a think-tank, which eventually decays into septic tank, due to mutually assured mental pollution. But like a *Thing*. Think like a Thing: the world is *Vasudhaiva Kutumbakam* (Global Family) whose goal it is to establish *Sanatan Dharma* (Eternal World Order); in this world, India's perceived role was that of the *Jagadguru* (World Teacher). India evolved these myths about the world around. Sometimes, these have even been a typical Indian psychological ailment, particularly in her international relations, although, internally, this Brahaminical policy was quite successful. Post-1947, India's entry into the First and Second Worlds having been stonewalled, she sought to lead the Third by recycling these myths, refurbished as the *Panchsheel*, serving these on a platter of the Non-Alignment Movement (NAM); after a few romanticist headlines, an ocean of ink replacing forests, and brouhaha, its hollowness was demonstrated with China rudely arousing India from her dogmatic slumber in 1962 and preparing her for 1965 and 1971, with Nehru correcting himself, posthumously, in his daughter. Other countries laughed at India's strange claims of 'superiority' in a Darwinian world, particularly when she was begging from the same countries she was seeking to sermonise. Sometimes cowards strive to become teachers, as a recompense to their inherent inability to rule others, especially the adults; they thus evolve an ambition to lord it over at least children. But, overall, Indians traditionally respected the teacher as much as they respected their parents as a tribute to their contribution to the next generation and began observing the Teachers' Day on 5 September in memory of the second President, Sarvepalli Radhakrishnan a teacher-philosopher, whose erudition often gave Nehru and Indira an inferiority complex; the country found another great teacher in her eleventh President, A P J Abdul Kalam.

These great teachers taught India to respect pluralism. Since there could be many facets of truth, and many paths leading to the same destination, humans should not depend on any one idea for their emancipation, for each idea that is born may die. Uncompromising belief in an idea would close mind and intellectual inquiry; it created fanaticism which could putrefy the individual and the society. By adhering to just one idea, cleansing is impossible in one go: let the society be a garden of many blooming flowers, even if they wilt the next day. All one can do is to pass through a series of *karma* (selfless deeds) and all a society can do is to evolve like a giant organism, slowly, securely; its leaders, even its gods and their *Avatar*s (Reincarnations) should not fall prey to the greed of personal immortality. Do not write history as it is merely 'his story' and often leads to hysteria.

India's cyclical history often shielded her from irreversibility. As populations of different layers of the society changed, she constantly shuffled her dominant Hindu social ruling classes: Kshatriyas (from 1500 BC to 500 BC), Kshudras or Shudras (from 500 BC to 200 BC), Brahmins (200 BC to 500 AD),Vaishyas (500 to 800 AD), Rajputs (800 to 1500 AD), and Brahmins (1500 to 1950 AD). After 1950, with accelerating urbanisation, the 'upper castes' increasingly adopted family planning and turned into nuclear families, thus leaving the field open for the lower castes to proportionately increase their numbers and the perceived 'demographic dividend'. That was how, in the next five decades, the era of the so-called Shudras returned and, in the post-Mandal churning, the under-privileged triumphed, culminating in the rise of an Other Backward Caste (OBC) supreme leader. With newer means of production and livelihood mushrooming, while the once-ruling Brahmins and other upper castes are exiting the era of domination that reserved their traditional jobs to the privatising economy and outreach levels of education and society now, the once-deprived classes and castes are capturing or controlling the government, Parliament and judiciary. The latter are doing so, of course, after a crash-course in what sociologist M N Sriniwas once called 'Brahminisation' and 'Sanskritisation', ie. learning the age-old Brahaminical ropes after replacing Brahmins, and assimilating the obsolete 'cultural technology' they left behind, thus upgrading themselves at least into the pager age. In the hope that it would make them cell-phone-ready: officially, however, it is known variously as 'percolation of benefits', 'trickle-down effect', 'financial inclusion', etc. Each class cut across religio-political divide and ruled like a monolith vis-à-vis the rest of India. The word 'Shudra' (a derivative of the original word 'Kshudra') merely meant 'small' as many of the pre-Aryan natives were shorter in stature; it had nothing to do with colour, race or caste. Post-1947, all those who followed Hinduism but were not from the *dwij* (twice-born) Aryans (ie. those not the Brahmins, Kshtriyas or Vaishyas) were incorporated into the umbrella nomenclature of the Scheduled Castes and Scheduled Tribes, and some others subsequently as Other Backward Classes or Most Backward Classes (OBCs and MBCs), in the Constitution of India; a new category, Extremely Backward Classes (EBCs), is currently emerging. The derogatory words defining these castes, like Harijans or 'Children of the Lord Vishnu' (a word coined by Gandhi) and the Dalits or the 'Oppressed', were subsequently removed from official literature, demonstrating their increasing socio-political clout.

The Aryans seldom actually ruled India; the minority Brahmins, like the Iranian Magis and Chinese Mandarins, seen as socially top-notch and 'repository of wisdom', were often social hegemonist, self-supremacist and opinion-makers as power-behind-the-throne, but they rarely became a directly ruling political force in the *central* governance of India, except in the pre-Christian Shung Dynasty and the Nehru-Gandhi dynasty after 1947. The only Brahmin dynasty that could briefly rule from the imperial seat of the subcontinent was that of Pushyamitra Shung who killed his Master, the last Maurya King, Brahadritha, in 184 BC; it was only after 22 centuries that another Brahmin, Jawaharlal Nehru, could found his dynasty to rule from the political capital of India, which has been swinging between Peshawar and Kolkata. The Brahmins, like cork, were the lightest in weight, and selectively shared 'knowledge' the way our nuclear experts do; only since the 1990s did they begin to slide in the Indian trough. They even caused the eclipse of their non-Brahmin masters, as Pushyamitra did unto Brahadritha and Nehru unto Gandhi. Outwardly, the *Karmakaandi* Brahmins have seldom been a unifying force in India as they believed in segregation—most castes had their own designated Brahmin priests from generation to generation—but wielded force disproportionate to their own population by claiming proximity to gods as repository of 'divine' knowledge. But it is not they who ruled India like a great machine. They were only the machine operators; the engineers and technologists were the *Gyankaandi*s most of whom had left the workshop after installing this great machine by the time of Ashoka.

Trade currents from across the Indus had imported monotheistic ideas also. Your god is a reflection of your population-prosperity ratio; poverty—of mind, money or both—promotes monotheism as they can afford only as many gods as their number of meals.In each case, the have-nots evolved a 'gold magnate' (Jerusalem, Mecca, Rome and Moscow) to attract pilgrims; subsequently, the Jews, the Christians and the Muslims turned prosperous. But this apparently global scenario did not really apply to India. Due to reserved caste-based occupations and social customs, many Hindus could afford at least two square meals and did not fall prey to monotheism, and, for the same reason, despite 'belief' that India was ripe for a Communist revolution, she never really turned red hot; on the contrary, the Communists emasculated themselves time and again while boasting of emancipation. The latest steps India took against hunger in a capitalist era—the biggest potential enemy that could make the country vulnerable to external attacks or internal revolution—are the 100-day employment guarantee scheme for rural labourers and the Food Security Policy.

Between 700 and 100 BC, when monotheism crystallised in the Fertile Crescent, different sects and sub-sects of the Aryans authored a hundred and a score *Upanishad*s to support their sub-beliefs. In the Mughal era, they even talked of the so-called *Allahopanishad,* 'so-called' because it meant an *infidel* Hindu would sit next to Allah—the Sanskrit word '*upanishad'* meant 'sitting closer'! Incidentally, in the Abrahamic belief system, only Jesus or Muhammed could sit next to God! Only a dozen of these *upanishad*s were original. This at a time when Judaism was being processed and transformed by its Judges and prophets into uncompromising monotheism, geography and demography. Like the Jews in the Fertile Crescent, the Indian Aryans, too, wanted to survive at any cost in a country they had adopted out of desperation and from where they were unable to go anywhere else; unlike the Jews, they would not increase their population exclusively by intra-marriage, although they also wanted to preserve their racial 'purity'. Therefore, they followed the coalition politics: the ways they devised to protect themselves were akin to the trees developing a ring of hard bark each year to face hostile weather, or the marine squids or octopuses jetting ink-like colour to hoodwink the enemy: Nature equips attackers with weapons in a food-chain and, at the same time, provides each creature the means to ward off dangers.

Unlike the Jews, the Aryans were horse-borne; unlike Israel, the Aryavarta was a scattered habitation. Trade did exist but was not popular in a largely subsistent economy; in fact, the early Aryans saw in trade a lowly profession. The Vaishyas remained the third of the four Varnas and, down the line, the word *Bania/Vania*, despite this business community's prosperity, evoked derision; till now, most successful traders and accountants come from this community. The Aryans were a race apart, warring only for peace: many Brahmins chose to wield the sword, but a few Kshatriyas would also take to the scriptures. The Brahmins, cutting across their ancient *Gotra*s belonged to two classes: *Gyankaandi*s and *Karmakaandi*s, ie. those dwelling the forests, mountains and other remote places to philosophise, and those earning a livelihood in the hamlets or towns by performing social rituals from pre-birth to post-death. The Gyankaandis, engineers and architects of the Indian psyche who wrote countless volumes of and commentaries on scriptures, have always ruled the mind of India while the Karmakaandis, the masons and artisans who laid the bricks to create the great edifice of about 430-odd Hindu rituals to be followed from womb to tomb, the bonds that bind India, have controlled the heart of the people.

No other country has had so many nameless authors, timeless scriptures and selfless workers who laboured to make their race survive; even now, print-lines and copyrights are considered avoidable fads and proprietors of most English and vernacular newspapers and periodicals either double up as editors or employ auditors as editors. Ved Vyas, the 'author' of the *Mahabharata*, was not a person but name of a *chair* occupied by those who edited the *Veda*s (the word *vyas* simply meant editor), much like the 'story department' of a Bollywood film company. The world's biggest epic was put together by the 28th Ved Vyas, whose predecessors had edited various *Veda*s and other scripture. Essentially rooted in the soil of their own village, the Aryan settlers chose not to huddle together to form well-knit rural communities, unlike the Semitic people in the Fertile Crescent, but spread thin, far and wide; always on the move, the more their population grew, the more they spread and expanded until they reached all corners of India; by the time of Jesus, they had spread almost all over the subcontinent. They lived with the native population and, being fair-complexioned, claimed 'superiority', even 'divinity'; the short-statured, dark-complexioned natives, later known as Adivasis/Vanvasis, often addressed them as *Deva*, divine people. This was somewhat akin to the Europeans in India; the 'Gora Sahibs', in fact, re-Aryanised India by reviving the questions of ethnicity, complexion and racial superiority. The Aryans were not other-worldly; they sought to establish hegemony in this very world even while uniting with other Indians. Around the 15th century BC, when the Fertile Crescent was being deforested and urbanised at a break-neck speed, India's Sindh and Punjab provinces were being re-ruralised due to the downfall of the Indus Civilization; its successor Aryans did not take much interest in urbanisation or carving any great empires in India until the sixth century BC. Unlike other races, the Aryans' priority in India was not to level out or destroy the local cultures and impose their own or create their empires but to stay and survive and, at the same time, retain their perceived 'racial purity', much like the Jews of Diaspora, or, later, the Parsis in India. You cannot build an empire unless you produce less or more than you need and thrust your hunger or surplus produce on others; when your religion outweighs your needs, you become proselytisers. Greed is the driving force of 'greatness'. India has often been a subsistence economy-polity-society-theogony; it produced just for its needs and did not need to turn a war-like imperialist.... She moved slowly like a tortoise and patiently waited to find foothold in the world, often watching from the sidelines the rabbits and horses who sped like future. Into the past. Despite being essentially villagers, the Aryans did not much believe in physical labour or farm production beyond their needs; they were classed into three *interchangeable* Varnas of warriors (Kshatriyas), teachers (Brahmins) and traders (Vaishyas), in *that order* of importance—and these Varnas, till the caste system became rigid, were merely based on complexions, not birth: the Brahmins were the fairest because they merely taught, the Kshtriyas were copper-coloured because they were professional militia who worked out and laboured to prepare for war and the Vaishyas, due to constant travel, turned sun-baked. For the physical labour, the Aryans depended on the natives who marvelled at the 'benevolence' of their off-white masters; till now, many of India's rulers have 'servants' from these classes, often paid for by the exchequer.

The Aryans and natives could not often assimilate at the level of *roti-beti* (eating together and marrying into each other's clans) due to racial segregation; they have always revolved in their respective cultural orbits, although they did jump from one orbit to another and often formed alliances, as in the Aryans adopting Lord Shiva and the Dravids venerating Vishnu, His incarnations and a few inter-marriages here and there. The Aryan traditions that evolved down the ages were a product of their primitive mode of production, dependence on natives for physical labour and geographical isolation in that hitherto rather un-integrated society with infrequent communication of settlements with each other in the vast Indian subcontinent. Unlike their warlike Iranian or European counterparts, the Indian Aryans were generally a submissive people who spun dreams of their perceived heroes; their lore offset their characteristic shortcomings, compensated their real weakness with the apparent strength of their mythological hero who constantly waged battles against their 'enemies' on *their* behalf. Their heroes had all that which they themselves could not have, like the fugitive Parsis, the last batch of Aryan settlers from Iran in India, who weaved tales of Rustom and Sohrab as an ointment to their psyche injured by Islam in the seventh century. Great story-tellers, the Aryans were day-dreamers and, despite odds, kept alive those dreams: the 'Battle of Ten Kings' from the Vedic era, when the Aryans had not yet set up the 16 republics, later expanded into the script of *Jay* when they founded their kingships, and then into the epic of *Mahabharata* as they founded the first empires and the Aryans spread throughout the subcontinent; the final major act of this Aryan was to compress all his scriptures into a 'natural gas', the *Gita*, downloaded directly by Lord Krishna into Arjuna, and incorporate it into the great epic when Christianity and then Islam eventually arrived in India.

But mythology, like true democracy, is a mirage. In real life, the few Aryans had to maintain their hegemony over the many natives. In the beginning, like the Hebrew tribal villages in Israel, the Aryan villages were *gotra*-based (they still do, as in Haryana, and caste-based settlements, townships and condominiums are the norm at many places across India); great distances made it difficult for them to communicate with each other in times of need. In such a community, force could not be used directly or frequently. The locals, after all, outnumbered the Aryan settlers, the way the Muslims and then the British were always outnumbered by the Hindus. No Canaan-like massacres took place in India due to Aryan 'intrusion' chiefly because neither the immigrants nor the natives were principally war-mongers and often managed to tolerate each other; that was, also, why no Revolution of French, Russian or the Chinese kind could ever rock India. It was because the means of livelihoods were different, reserved from generation to generation, and no 'outsider' could poach on jobs or bread—see how those enjoying the benefits of reservation policy now guard their turf. First the *Varna* system and then the caste system strictly segregated the means of livelihood—the 21st century Communists, supporting the caste-based reservation policy, could be forgiven for further making a Communist Revolution in India impossible! India has survived in the long run not because of its high-tech, IIT-IIM-type 'intellectuals' who often chased gold and migrated but because of the low-tech mediocre who stayed back! She never raced in a scheduled Marathon, once in a while, but jogged a little every day. Throughout history.

Racial hegemony was, however, always there to maintain, not by direct domination or coercion but by ingraining in the psyche of the rulers and the ruled the elements that would ensure an organised and permanent consent to perpetuate social hierarchy, traditions and customs laid down by the peers of the nine, mainly Brahmin, *gotras*. It was self-indoctrination, akin to the modern system of generation, transmission and usage of hydroelectricity: most consumers would not know the basics but only how to switch on or off an argument; the few who controlled the switchyard and transformers, lived in remote areas. Thus originated an 'ideology' that would be interiorised as a force by private initiative and, at the same time, appear 'voluntarily accepted'; as Jean Jacques Rousseau would call it in the 18th century, each individual would be 'forced to be free' to follow the General Will, because that alone would ensure liberty, equality and fraternity before *Rta*, the Natural or Cosmic Law. The Aryans were wise enough to know that a law not originating in native culture and tradition would be violated sooner or later if imposed, but a law transmigrating into the very human psyche would become tradition, and finally a human nature; they did not try to destroy the local culture and replace it with their own for they knew, as in the father-son dialogue in the *Chhandogya Upanishad*, veritable forces originate in vacuum. Moreover, they did not often evolve anything copyrighted to any individual, unlike the Semitic practice of a particular 'prophet' claiming to be inspired by God to reveal something. Most of the Aryan ideology, '*Shastrokt*', or *Shaastron mein likha hai* (thus-said-our-scriptures), was the handiwork of the Gyankaandis, the recluses in the isolated forests, which was operationalised into rituals by the Karmakaandis in the settlements. The more the forests disappeared, the more the Gyankaandis did, until, the 'land of philosophers' found that it would produce none after the eighth century AD—all 'philosophers' India produced after Adi Shankaracharya, after the eighth century, have, in fact, been recycling ancient parchment paper to make greeting cards for each other—all sects and cults originated in India thereafter have merely been multiple reflections of the *Gita* that almost replaced all earlier scripture. But these recluses had left behind them, by 500 BC, a mechanism of perpetuating a general theory of Aryan solar hegemony, and, within it, the special theory of Brahminical nuclear hegemony, that was hard to break until the 20th century. Nowhere else in the world did so many people self-hypnotise and enslave themselves of their own free will and for such a long time.

The Aryan world-view in the local populace—which had little of it—got as dissolved as sugar in water, so as to acquire a categorically imperative character to make unity-in-diversity and university-in-adversity a material force immune to foreign aggression; countless grim faces and empty bellies defeated the robust invader many a time. Social upheavals, disorders and revolutions take place when humans begin to think beyond themselves and take up causes. You cannot suppress them psychologically for long if you deprive them of their birth-right, that is birth and right: the Varna system of the Aryans, being reconstructed into the evolving hard-to-crack caste system of Aryavarta, ensured that each got according to his/her birth and had a right to derive fruits out of it. The 'lower' castes could never organise any major revolt because society did not allow others, even upper castes, to poach into their reserved means of livelihood; even today, 'lowly-born' scavengers, beggars and eunuchs have a birth-right to demand and get gifts from the higher castes on festivals or special occasions like marriage and birth and the Master happily and knowingly agrees to be fleeced by the slave. No other country has so many people who allow themselves to be religiously fleeced by a social system they inherited. In India, each man and woman is a self-hypnotiser, represses and suppresses oneself and does unto oneself what the ruler would have done, to ward off any social revolution, ie. something that would disturb the structural foundations of the society. Here you have a quicksilver society that would scatter into droplets at the first blow of the hammer and dissolve back as quickly into one another.

How did the Aryans, particularly those Gyankaandi recluses, like the Magis of Iran, achieve this long-term objective that had actually begun as a short-term survival strategy? They were not exactly astrologers claiming premonition, but learned sages with a rare capacity and patience to spend hours watching in amazement the extremely slow unfolding of a flower, the gentle breeze, the spread of its fragrance, the gliding of a gazelle through the wind, the dawn and the dusk, the twilight and the night, the silent melting of the snow catapulted into the roar and waves of the river; their pleasures were not a derivative of their desires. They marvelled at and enjoyed being one with Nature not because they wanted to be, out of their needs, but because they viewed in Nature their Goal; they knew their gods are *their* creations, in the image of their desires, so the heaven could not be their goal—their ultimate Goal was to get, like the Arctic glaciers they came from, dissolved in Nature, not *swarga* (Heaven/Paradise) but *moksha* (liberation). In India, the ephemeral nature of aggressors was due also to their short-term inability in imposing and perpetuating their *weltanshauung*, or world-view, vis-à-vis the society under their boot. Unlike the Aryans, all other free-incoming immigrants failed to manipulate the Indian's view about Nature, about the society and about himself. India always despised her present rulers, thought the bygones were better-off and expected little better from the future ones. The real rulers of Indian psyche were those not on a throne or in a temple but the unknown ones teaching under a tree, in a cave, or on the mountains. During the Kumbh Mela, every 12 years, they would suddenly appear in their thousands, as if from nowhere, take a holy dip on the *ghat*s of the Ganges, sermonise 20 million people in a fortnight and disappear in their hideouts for the next 12 years. It is they who have run the great Indian Circus, not Ashokas, Akbars or Mountbattens, from behind their loincloth. They have been the Hindus' emergency battery that kept these diverse people united and survive. In them is the Chaos called India controlled.

The societal response of the Aryans towards a theocratising thought process seeping into India from the trans-Indus region evolved slowly; no particular person did it but the society itself gradually responded. Great game-changers are not just the offspring of their biological parents; they are, basically, revolutions crystallised in their churning society. The emerging monotheist trends abroad moulded mass opinion at home as traders moved across the Indus. They apparently realised the difference between alien monotheism and home-spun monism, that monotheism could be a menace, a civilisational 'poison' produced by the forces of human civilisational evolution, but something that could be used as a catalyst. Uncompromising monotheism, although it unites, integrates, aggregates and connects the human society like nothing else, also kills evolution of private thought; in this respect, it is, *per se*, anti-evolutionary and anti-democratic—if you do not have a choice in the selection of your God up there, you cannot have choice in the election of your government either, down here; democracy means acceptance of more than one opinion or party. So, you cannot really be both a monotheist and a democrat, simultaneously, the way you cannot both be fascist and an anarchist, or lion and the lamb, at the same time. That is why many of the Christian and Muslim countries have had to pass through elimination of surplus populations in war—and currently in a time-warped elimination called 'War on Terror'—before they could become democratic; the 'democratised' Christian and Muslim countries, as also Israel, are so because they are well ahead on the path of deAbrahamisation. God, the Celestial Government, and Government, the Terrestrial God, reflect each other. That is why no country adhering to uncompromising monotheism could really be democratic. Democracy is a measure of the country's pace of deChristianisation or deIslamisation: so, the USA, despite its *Bible* Belt and Protestant fever, is half-deChristianised, Turkey deIslamised half-way and Indonesia nearly deIslamised. The more democracy you have, the more you drive away the demons from the past that ruled human society. Off and on, the Hindus realised the wiring capability of Abrahamism, about how their 'religions' united the Christians and the Muslims; a section of the Hindus, therefore, tried to emulate it in India also, as in the Arya Samaj movement. The last such effort was in the last two decades of the 20th century to make Lord Rama somewhat of a warrior Yahveh or revengeful Allah and turn Hinduism into Hindutva, a principle into practice. India experimented with it for a while, and rejected. It did not really gel with the psyche in a tradition-steeped Indian society where even the Third Wave enthusiasts match their horoscopes for weddings, like the First Wave simpletons did several thousand years ago! Astrologers replaced astronomers—and both now use computers. India is teeming with spurious 'intellectuals' and demonic 'democrats'—awaiting a major elimination round.

The very existence of an enemy is a Law of Nature that makes natural selection possible. Simple elimination through war is how this complex natural selection occurs. But you can eliminate an enemy physically only when it is an individual, not when it is an 'idea'; the Kshatriyas could deal with the advancing enemy at the border but what about the idea that comes mounted with the foe and slowly infects you? The Brahmins would quarantine the masses against this so that the Hindus, as a whole, remained safe even when the Kshatriyas succumbed to foreign might. The ongoing assimilation of the Aryan and Dravidian cultures was nearly halted with the 'theo-nuclear' process of emergence of Christianity and Islam, followed by repeated invasions of the Indian mind from across the Fertile Crescent. Two parallel streams of ideologies were at work then, *simultaneously*—the intra-Abrahamic currents crystallising into Islam trans-Indus Fertile Crescent, while intra-Aryan streams were frothing up the *Gita* in India. From the sixth century BC, India's cultural response vis-à-vis Abrahamism had begun to unfold with Buddhism which, being essentially casteless, godless and egalitarian, did not prove much effective—you cannot choose between two products of the same genre as Christianity and Islam, too, were like proselytising Buddhism minus atheism. Buddhism was India's earliest response to the gathering Abrahamic avalanche; but the Jews were non-proselytisers and conversion of infidels to Judaism, the way conversion of aliens to mainstream Hinduism, was difficult. With Jesus asking his successors to spread the Word of God far and wide, India needed to protect her flock by further vaccinating the society, with new layers. The response, therefore, swung to the other end, *Manu Smriti,* somewhat like the restrictive Homeland Laws in the post-9/11 America, which became a categorical imperative when the Aryans found that India too was, like the contemporary Fertile Crescent and Europe, being flooded by aliens and the Aryans needed to take steps to maintain 'purity' of their blood. Casteism, as the cast-iron response, incorporated racial segregation coupled with gradual theism.

If humans, like other members of animal and plant kingdoms are organic in nature, their societies, cultures and civilisations, too, behave likewise; they have similar reflexive responses to external stimulation, be it sex, food or enemy. The process of evolution of a reflexive Indian collective response continued the way an organism senses a situation in the neighbourhood and begins to move. With an exponential crystallisation of Abrahamism, until Islam, as the Aryans felt that only '*A* God' could shield the subcontinent against '*The* God' from across the Indus, the country created a psychological wall around itself. The thousand-year-long protective response fully crystallised in *Advaita* and the *Gita* when Islam finally exploded upon the Indian scene in the year 711, by when both Muhammed and his contemporary King Harsha had passed away. The first mosque anywhere outside Arabia had already been set up in Kerala in 629, a year before Muhammed won even Mecca; the Aryans' apprehension came true when Muhammad Ghori set up shop in Sindh in 711. The desert Arabs, who prided in racial purity and succeeded in converting the ruling classes in many other countries, had to be content with conversions in India mainly from 'lower' castes in India—and many among even these castes had only one foot in Islam, the other being still firmly in Hinduism—as they were yet to be fully assimilated in the overall Aryan universe. That is why militant organisations like Ahl-e-Hadis and Dawat-ul-Islam have been fervently trying to 'reIslamise' the Indian Muslims by cleansing them of 'infidel accretions'. Not that any one, or any Aryan group, created this reflexive response consciously; but the social eco-system, or the Matrix, over the centuries, had evolved and internalised such survival tactics among the Indians and they instinctively did it the way creatures smell their enemy or food from afar that triggers their responses. The way China raised a Wall against Mongols and other intruders, India, too, raised an invisible wall against Christianity and Islam—she would fight their Books with her own Book.

Why would the Aryans think like that? The tribes fleeing the scary Caspian Ice Age, who had joined the India-ward caravan of the Aryan nomads, were relatively peace-loving, vis-à-vis those reaching Greece, Rome or Iran: unlike their counterparts in these countries, the 'Indian' Aryans had packed all their valour in their mythological heroes and drew sustenance from them; they largely avoided wars because they could not win—but they did learn the fine art of identifying the enemy's footprint and worked to acquire mental processes as protective gear for their own survival. It is a strange world: man's valour is inversely proportional to his imaginary god's; in no other country's mythology have gods fought so many battles; no other country has lost in so many actual wars with foreigners—barring the Muslims and Christian aggressors, all invaders got assimilated and became Indians in India. Seen this way, India was a country of losers—but, on the long timeline, survival is more important than victory. And India has survived. She never aged; she always survived to see yet another day. In India, the Aryan's war was virtually reserved to be led and fought by gods and Kshatriyas. The Indian Aryans, being generally docile, manufactured great gods, until Krishna emerged as their first multiverse spiritual godhead downloading the *Gita*; they packed Him with all that they aspired for but did not and could not have. Man is, after all, a reflection of his representative god, not the adopted god; his left is His Right. That was why the martial Aryan Christians of Europe, instead of emulating a 'peace-loving' Jesus of the *New Testament*, would wage wars like the Jesus of the *Book of Revelation*; that is why the 'Muslims' of India would not violently and collectively resist their inexorable dissolution back into the Hindu ocean.

If you learn to ignore existence of the world, you can internalise a trait to ignore the very existence of the enemy as well. Maya is the switch any Hindu would use to shut off all arguments, his own thinking process. But, again, this switch was not discovered by any individual; the Aryan peers, many of them official philosophers and ideologues, deduced this unique switch from day-to-day life of the society around, its problems, its responses, its ways to skirt the problem itself or, when forced, to adopt and find a solution, to make generalisations and abstractions into what they called 'philosophy' and then *Sanatan Dharma*. This was ingrained into the very personality of men and women from their birth so that no one could challenge it. Responses thus matured into 'religion'; each new sect or religion in India was a response to and product of an enemy lurking at the door of Hinduism; the more the number, quality and category of enemies, the more the Hindu sects multiplied as response to each of these, until the enemy scattered in this confusion. Notice how Sikhism, as the sword-wielding arm of the Hindus of Punjab, emerged as a response to an alien, aggressive Islam.

In the evolution of this common consciousness, the rulers had only a little role: they had largely relegated the thinking process to their think tanks or thought police, the Brahmin *Rajgurus* (Masters of the Reign) who ensured that the people outsourced thinking and willingly supplicated to their circuitous arguments; leaders of political parties in contemporary India continue to relegate 'thinking' and choose for themselves the foot-soldier's subsidiary role—the fact that Indian political parties often have 'Intellectuals' Cells' suggests that others in the party are neither supposed nor empowered to think! These 'cells' are the modern versions of the twin ancient switches that put off all arguments: *Maya* and the *Shastra*s.

The Indian Aryan response slowly crystallised as a sequel to the Iranian Aryan response to the developments in the Hamitic and Semitic worlds in the Fertile Crescent. Both the Indian and Iranian Aryans had inherited the proto-*Veda*s, astral beliefs, Nature worship, and similar mythology and could, therefore, sense what the other could be thinking like. Iran's proximity to the Hamitic-Semitic, solar monotheists of West Asia, and the internecine warfare between them had metabolised the Iranian Aryan psyche into an organised response incorporating not the rejection of one world (as the Indian Aryan was doing) but acceptance of two, Good and Evil, both absolute, and man's duty to support the former in their supposedly endless struggle. This very Zoroastrian nebula would, in the next thousand years, gravitate to emerge as Islam. From the potions of contemporary Egypt and Babylonia, Zarathushtra tried to distil an organised response in what was the world's first prophetic faith. His successors and believers did create a strong army as well in the Achemenid and Sassanid Empires. But Iran could still not ward off Islam, because an idea can be countered only by an idea, not by an army; by the time of Islam, Zoroastrianism itself had decayed into what its enemy actually was: a God-intoxicated army. So, a superior and younger God-intoxicated army, Islam, could easily overpower it, although Iran succeeded in splitting the enemy ranks by encountering it on a forward front, Shiaism, thus averting a full Arab-takeover of the Aryan nation.

The Indian response, on the other hand, was to galvanise and quarantine her people's psyche, consciousness and mental processes against an increasing 'infection' of monotheism by deciding to evangelise selectively and not to proselytise in the Aryan mainstream. Only heterodox sects like Buddhism and Jainism did so, mainly on the Aryan periphery, and formed the first protective shield; the second shield was provided by the 'Hinduised' irreligious Central Asian immigrant clans, who flooded the Aryavarta in the thousand years preceding King Harsha—like Shakas (Scythians), Huns (Jats), Kushans, and other 'intermediate castes' like the Ahirs (Yadavs), Gurjars, Kurmis, Rajputs, among others—again on the *dwij* social periphery, who slowly got assimilated, evolved their own caste nests and meshed their respective imported godheads into the Hindu curry; they slowed down the enemy's march into the Aryan heartland to ensure, even making them walk into a trap and slowly sink into India's labyrinthine mental world. Buddhism, Jainism, Sikhism and scores of other sects, born like adventitious offshoots on the great banyan tree of *Chhandogya Upanishad*, did 'proselytise', acted like shields of Hinduism, and successfully kept hidden the soft tissues of Life and their varieties in the main trunk of the tree. Shutting off the scriptures (written mostly in Sanskrit, taught only to a select few) from the common people, unlike in the monotheistic creeds making reading of the Book compulsory for all believers, and simply making the Hindus believe that 'all this is there in the scriptures', enabled the wily Brahmins to deduce any and every argument from these hitherto largely unread, or even unwritten books; the common man would not question them because *they* thought for him, on his behalf, what he was unable to do for himself.

Each argument convenient to the Brahmins thus became 'deducible' from the little-read and virtually prohibited scriptures of the people, who could switch on or switch off an argument simply by pressing the *Shastra* or *Maya* button, meaning you do not have to argue about this 'truth', that is, just shut up and follow. Hinduism was moulded in such a framework that each Hindu felt he was free to do anything so long as he declared himself a Hindu; his today's response became tomorrow's 'philosophy' and the day after's internalised attitude, the very 'divine' law, as in the case of the Jew, but without the interference of a Yahveh. The Brahmins, too, had already incorporated the local Lord of the Hosts (ie. Lord of Lightening, Rudra, as Shiva, Lord of Blessings) in their own pantheon as Mahadev (Great God) but later stripped Him of the prime responsibilities of the Universe, Creation and Sustenance, bestowed exclusively on the Aryan Gods Brahma or Prajapati and Vishnu, respectively; Shiva, in His anthropomorphic form of Shankar, also came to be associated with Death and *Pralay* (Apocalyptic Dissolution of the Material World), until the backward reintegration of Shiva with *Shakti* (Primeval Energy) gave rise to ReCreation (*Prakriti*, Nature). Shiva, the simple but ferocious native God of India, mainly rural and folk in character, found an all-India expression in the 12 *Jyotirlingams* whose pilgrimage made a Hindu criss-cross the nation, providing an inherent cultural reconnect and religious unity to a diverse people; since each stone could be shaped as a *lingam*, the Muslim marauders could never destroy Shiva nor invade many of the inaccessible Jyotirligams—although they destroyed thousands of Hindu temples, the only major damage they could do in their 800 years of dominance was to the Somnath and Kashi shrines of Shiva, the Krishna shrine at Mathura and the Rama temple at Ayodhya: this damage made the fanatic Muslims permanently outcaste villains in majority Hindu views.

By the time of Muhammed, Hinduism had transformed into a pseudo-monotheism of the Brahmins and a pseudo-polytheism of the people, to the bewilderment of the Abrahamic forces. India's six major philosophical schools were the official Aryan ideologies generated at different places at different times as different responses to the different assaults from without and not as something mystical or divine that erupted spontaneously in reclusive, working minds. Indian philosophy has mostly been derived from the common man's basic problem, survival, culminating into the *Gita*, as his own means to solve the problems he confronted, the word he was forced by circumstances to invent vis-à-vis the decidedly superior sword perpetually charging at him from the West. India was fortunate not to have conceived any 'religion' at all; all it did, down the ages, was to temporarily respond to the monsoon winds and fold the umbrella back after the showers. The *Rigveda* was the first unorganised response. Most of this book was a product of the work done by the sages who lived between 1500 and 1300 BC. In the initial stages of social stratification and segregation, the *Varna* system had begun to crystallise into castes but it will remain in a hazy, liquid state for the next thousand years; the Varna system was based on one's importance on the basis of his occupation, not birth. From Iran to the Ganges in India, via *Ashwaganstban* (the Land or Republic of the Horses, Afghanistan), there was a chain of Aryan communes, which were successively lesser and lesser bigoted, depending upon their distance from that powerhouse, the Fertile Crescent; the Aryans of non-Aryavarta areas were more hot-headed while the Aryavartis were more flexible and evolved defence mechanisms to shield their race not only from the Abrahamites of West Asia but also from some of the Dravids, the 'Adivasis' and the Nagas from within. The Aryans who occupied large tracts outside the Aryavarta, were relatively more hardy, inflexible and purists, being the first and last batches to enter the Indian subcontinent. Ironically, as the end-product of this theo-chemical process, Islam, in India, slowly came to provide the last frontline of defence for Hinduism, as Pakistan and Bangladesh now act as buffer states to absorb cultural shocks from the powerless-monotheist Arabia and the powerful-atheist China. The Indus has been the two-way great mirror between West Asia and India; one could see reflections of events of one side into the other, so much so that the Indian subcontinent reflected the Fertile Crescent as its own Infertile Crescent extending from today's Sri Lanka to Bangladesh via the Indian states of the east coast, up to Bengal, the Rice Belt, where poverty and rice grew together.

The *Rigveda* is a compilation of Aryan eulogies for different natural phenomena, their gods; but, towards its Tenth Book (*Dasham Mandal*), composed in the prime of the contemporary solar monotheism of the Assyrian and the Second Babylonian Empires (eighth to sixth century BC), polytheism gravitated into monism, even hinting at monotheism. The Brahmins had merged all fiery gods—Surya, Agni, Yama—into one and promoted a unitary and monopolist Varun, who later acquired some of the attributes of Yahveh, the Lord of the Lightening. With the importance of the Kshatriyas waning, an ordinary god of traders, Brahm, became Brahma, the omnipotent, omniscient Creator, the God of the emerging all-powerful traders' guild—the way Mata Vaishno Devi emerged as the goddess of music industry, and then of the common people in the 1980s and 1990s.

Prajapati, in the last stages of evolution of the Rigveda, became the greatest god, and later even these two merged to become Prajapati Brahma. That was the height of theocrasia in Aryavarta at a time when the Jews were declaring their King Solomon as the 'wisest' man ever born. Brahma, literally meaning 'continuously expanding', like the traders' wealth, as it turned out, seemed to be the Indian response to the Fertile Crescent's A-braham!

In West Asia, the Egyptian idea of an after-life and the hereafter had caught on and influenced all religions, including those in India; the Great Pyramids had dwarfed man's desire for this life and the societal chaos had forced and intoxicated him towards the inexorable idea of Oneness of God because he could not afford to feed more than One. Eventually, in this theo-biological refinement, Islam was reached at the bottom of man's 'spiritual' poverty (although Muslim apologists claim that the Taliban/al-Qaeda/ISIS did not represent the 'true' face of Islam). They actually reflected Muhammed's *Medinese* phase of Islam at Yathrib in its purest form—the shifting of *Qibla* from Jerusalem to Mecca in 624 AD, the brutal massacre of 700-odd Jews (627) that silenced Muhammed's critics forever, for example—*the* main reason why many Muslims silently surrender to them.

The monotheistic idea had infected some Vedic sages also who came to believe that those doing good deeds went to enjoy heaven after death and the others were herded off to the netherworld to pay for their follies; the word *Atma* meant self, one's mind, that would merge with *Paramatma*, the Universal Self, at the time of death. That was a typical Aryan hereafter but after-life, the idea of rebirth, came only in the era of *Upanishads* when social inequality had taken roots—'social inequality exists so that you could pay for your misdeeds of previous life into this life' was the Brahminical justification—and critics were challenging the now-crystallised caste system; Adi Shankaracharya, erecting the last mental defence in the eighth century through the *Gita*, India's spiritual Maginot/Siegfried line, against Islam's attempt to invade the Indian mind, would make full use of this concept to shape up the country's mass psyche, the common ethos, for the next thousand years. The *Chhandogya Upanishad* proclaimed that sin cannot touch a wise man; it was later reversed by vested interests to mean that the wise men do not commit any sin. As Goswami Tulsidas said, *Samrath ko nahin dosh Gusain* (The mighty cannot be faulted!)—many criminal-turned-Indian politicians used this to shield themselves until the Supreme Court, in July 2013, stripped them of immunity in the wake of conviction in court.

Emancipation is not possible without true knowledge and the latter cannot be had without a true Master. This *Upanishad* was the first to put forth the theory of rebirth, ie. each living being, whether in this world or the hereafter, is born as a consequence of his deeds, Karma; no other idea in the whole of Indian philosophy has ever been more important than this one and it proved to be the deadliest psychological weapon against monotheism: even today, most Hindus believe their present is a reflection of their past life and, despite abject poverty and utter ignorance, India could neither be Christianised nor Islamised fully because of the masses reconciling to their wretched present in anticipation of a better after-life and next birth—the landslide victory of Narendra Modi's *achche din* (better days ahead) promise in parliamentary polls of May 2014 is an indicator of this age-old aspiration of the Hindu masses, a majority of whom now come from the non-Aryan stock of the 'low castes'. Millions of Hindus, barely surviving on the fringes of the society which refused even to being touched by their shadows, did not willingly convert to monotheistic creeds *because* of their strong belief in Karma. Some of them did, for reasons ranging from shielding community, settling personal scores, lure of the lucre, the hope to board the winning bandwagon, or simple alien terror; most converts never believed in Islam (or Christianity) whole-heartedly, a reason why Islamic militant outfits like Tablighi Jamaat and Dawat ul-Islam have been trying to 'reIslamise' them. The concept of Karma gave the people eternal hope for a better tomorrow and ignore their unfortunate present as they believed their past deeds 'justified' their present plight. The *Gita* exploited this belief to nail on the Hindu mind the psychological barbed wire defence that protected him from converting to Islam and Christianity by the hordes. By backward integration, today's needs were retrospectively incorporated in yesterday's 'law' to make it effective and up-to-date, the way modern constitutions are amended to incorporate emerging exigencies.

The *Upanishads* taught that the *dwij*, or twice-born (ie. the original Aryans, Brahmins, Kshatriyas and Vaishyas) belonged to independent *yonis*. They were not ordinary, mortal humans, not equal to one-another or anyone else; this was done to justify and defend the individual power and prosperity of these communities and strengthen the state, protector of this property, through Dharma. With backward integration, again, the inherent inequality of human beings, was promoted by the *Manu Smriti*, which emerged alongside the *New Testament* and put up a psychological defence against the perceived Christian 'equality'. This *Dharmashastra* was incorporated into the *Purush Sookta* of the Rigveda to accommodate the interests of the then ruling cliques. It was later turned into an immutable 'holy cow', ie the changes once introduced were unchangeable henceforth, as in the case of the *Bible* and the *Qur'an*, which, too, were declared completed by the official establishment but surreptitiously manipulated time and again by those who could. The more the *Bible* and the *Qur'an* were manipulated to meet the needs of the times, the more the Hindu scriptures were re-written to meet the emerging situations. The Brahminical hold on society also ensured primogeniture and a patriarchal pattern of society, as in the Fertile Crescent; monotheism distilled aristocracy and oligarchy into fascism not based on birth, while Brahminism transformed their psycho-aristocracy into a kind of fascism by birth. While monotheism reduced deeds to words, Brahminism reduced these to mere birth. Two of the four great building blocks or *Mahavakyas* (mega-formulae), around which the Hindu mind has revolved for 3,000 years to twist nails into screws—*Sarva Khalvidam Brahm* (It Is All Brahm), *Tat Tvam Asi* (That Art Thou), both employed by Adi Shankarachaya in his Advaita-led backward integration, and *Pragyanaam Brahm* (The Greatest Knowledge Is Brahm) and *Aham Brahmasmi* (I Am The Brahm)—were the culmination of the Vedic-Upanishadic era.

The *Brihadaranyaka Upanishad* believed, like the Jewish Judges did, that all knowledge should first be acquired by the Brahmins for their continuing predominance. It said Brahm had two forms: *Sagun* and *Saakaar*, or attributable, morphous and mortal, and *Nirgun* and *Niraakaar*, or unattributable, amorphous and immortal; the lesser mortals believed in the former, the emancipated in the latter. (In politics, the alternate BJP and Congress-led regimes represented these!). The Niraakaar Brahm was akin to God of the *Old Testament*, and later to Allah of the *Qur'an,* whose attributes were unknowable, unquantifiable and unqualifiable. Muhammed, like Krishna, on the other hand was Sagun and Sakar! Smoothly, thus, the Hindus, without sacrificing their inherent polytheism in any manner, found an underground tunnel to flit in from monotheism to polytheism and vice-versa and later confused Muhammad Ghori into believing that the Hindus also were *People of the Book*. Anticipating Muhammed who, if he knew Sanskrit, would have said *Iti, Iti,* (This is the end, this is the end—of religion), the *Brihadaranyaka Upanishad* declared *Neti Neti* (Neither This, Nor That), that is, the Supreme Self is unattributable, none of the attributes man imagined in God belonged to Him. A thousand years later, Adi Shankaracharya, in his effort for forward integration this time, incorporated this concept into the *Gita* and his apparent refutations of Buddhism to 're-establish' the Sanatan Dharma.

The *Mundakopnishad*, which foresaw monotheism, identified *Jeevatma* and *Paramatma* (souls of ordinary creatures and Supreme God) as two similar but separate entities—*Dvaita*—and contributed an important word, *Vedanta* (Culmination of the *Veda*s), for use by Adi Shankaracharya a millennium later, when another 'Culmination of the Holy Word', the *Qur'an,* would enter the Aryavarta. Brahm, it said, was the cause, effect and end-product of this world. The hundred-odd *Upanishads*, as also the *Veda*s earlier, reflected the ongoing theo-refining process, the different schools of thought prevailing among the different sects of the polytheistic Aryan society; the Advaita (Non-Dualism) school, consummated by Adi Shankaracharya, that, being a reaction, even a Hindu rejoinder, to Islam, virtually stamped out all others' influence. It was the culmination of a responsive process that came to fruition vis-à-vis the simultaneous culmination of monotheism in Islam's societal Dualism: Krishna, literally meaning black, is akin to the Hindus' Allah. Krishna-in-Arjuna is their Muhammed, Adi Shankaracharya their Caliph Abu Bakr and the *Gita* their *Qur'an*:

the Vedanta is the Hindu version of the Last Prophethood of Islam, but with retail messiahs ('Whenever the World Order is disturbed, O' Son of the Earth [Parth], I Create Myself to set it Right', assured the Lord to Arjuna). The fratricidal *Mahabharata* War was akin to the Last Judgement.

Krishna and Arjuna distributed between themselves the attributes of Allah and Muhammed: like Allah, Krishna was Omnipresent, Omniscient and Omnipotent but like Muhammed, He was polygamous, a fugitive from His birthplace when enemies struck at Him, lived an extraordinary life and died an ordinary death while Arjuna, like the Almighty, was hermaphrodite, unconquerable but, like Muhammed, he was also recipient of the Divine Message, although at one go. Indian philosophy and religion stopped evolving after thus quarantining and inoculating the Hindu mind against Islam and India has not produced any original philosopher since the seventh century the way the Fertile Crescent, too, became infertile after appearance of the Crescent; the 'philosophers' born in India and Islam afterwards have had nothing new to offer, as they were mostly apologists and defenders of their respective faiths, adventitious roots of these two great banyan trees which only strengthened the main trunk and nothing original has actually grown under them since. The monotheistic school of Krishna alone, among the different still surviving ones, like Christianity and Islam, has proselytised and crossed the Indian shores, although some other sects also tried to proselytise like their predecessor Abrahamic globalisers. But, being co-terminus, the Sanatan Dharma, Brahmin-centric school of Adi Shankaracharya, is now folding back as Islam, too, is retreating. The four seats of Shankaracharyas have multiplied into 44 and the *Gita* is awaiting the fate of Sita (which means a 'Furrow' in the Earth, ie. Daughter of the Earth).

The literal meaning of the words *Rama* and *Sita* is similar to that of Eve and Adam, ie Life and the Earth, but with the sequence reversed—while Abrahamism stressed that Life (Eve) exists because of and as part of the Earth (Adam), India said just the opposite. Krishna was an edited version of Rama (opposite of which is *mara*, 'I die') and had double the number of attributes (16 *kala*s) than the Prince of Ayodhya (from the words *A' Yudhya*, where no war shall or can be waged, the Land of No-War)—vis-à-vis Jerusalem and al-Baghdad, meaning the *City of Peace* and *City of God*, respectively. Their better halves were Radha (Upstream, Source, opposite of *Dhaara*, Downstream) and Sita. If Rama and Sita were questions of India, Krishna and Radha were the answers; Rama was theory of war-for-peace, Krishna was the continuous practice of war, as Sita was the depth of the Earth and Radha the immensity of the heaven, the very source of Divine Consciousness.

No other culture has ever lived as fully. And as dangerously. At war with itself and yet the winner. Quitters cannot be winners nor are winners quitters: Egypt was a quitter as she was much too mummified to fight off Islam; Syria, as now, was much too Ashur-baked to fight off the Arabs; Iran was much too magic-struck to fight off Mecca—earlier, so were Greece and Rome and succumbed to Golgotha. They all got almost completely assimilated in the alien victorious religions and lost their roots. India survived, largely unproselytised: at first amused with cricket, she would play it in her own, *Lagaan*-style, to emerge victorious. 'You frame the rules, we evolve our style', as it were. India invented little since her Golden Age; but she mastered the art of backward integration, innovative copying and *jugaad*! Innocent Indians continue to 'discover' modern marvels in ancient texts! No wonder some of the world's best computer programmers, even 'ethical hackers' assisting security regimes against cyber terrorists, came from India—without inventing computer, for instance, India sought to teach the world how to use it!

The essential, inherent unity of Atma with Brahm was internalised into the mass psyche of ancient India, vis-à-vis the separateness of man from God in the Fertile Crescent; the former liberated Indian mind from God-fixation as humans themselves were allowed to emerge as gods; the latter turned West Asia into a God-intoxicated domain because of man's natural hunger but inability to attain godhood. In no other culture, least of all in the Abrahamic world, anyone with the prefix of 'Bhagwan' (God) would have survived; in India, they come dime a dozen and disappear like bubbles. No God ever terrorised a Hindu—he would simply dump Him and pick another *Hindu* God! The more monotheism evolved, the more it extolled and exalted the human body but proliferating polytheism made India take the reverse course. Although the *Upanishads*, by proclaiming the unity of Atma and Brahm, exalted the individual human, the latter was not empirical being of flesh-and-blood but an abstract one. Human body was seen as 'dirty' and death-ward, forcing the Atman to leave it and join the Brahm—the Brahmins conceived of 28 *naraks*, or levels of hell, wherein eligibility to enter depended on demerits and accumulated sins—even now, in Bahasa, Indonesia, the word for heaven is *surga* (from the Sanskrit root, *swarga*) and that for hell *neraka* (*narak*)—and many there call their country *Hindesia*! As part of their evolving response to monotheism, they began to deny life so they could brave death anticipated from across the Indus.

Gradual reductionism—that, absolute reality is one, which gives us an indivisible Brahm beyond which nothing exists, and which, in turn, leads us to conclude that material world does not absolutely exist. It is a mere illusion of our mind, thus an effective weapon of virtual unity of polytheism against the seeming diversity of the two- world theory (believers versus non-believers) propounded by monotheism; it filters out the perceived *uniqueness* of the latter. By extending the argument, even the unique Oneness of Brahm or God would ultimately be perceived only as virtual and monotheistic dualism of society is no different from polytheistic unity. Extend it further to the sixth century AD, 16th century, or the 20th: therefore, it makes no difference to you and me if we force each other to convert to our respective persuasion: I remain what my environment has shaped me into and you remain what yours has done unto you. For, we all are culture creatures. Eternal Tribals! In the end, there would be no Christian or Muslim Indians but only *Indian* Christians or Muslims: as blissfully caste-conscious now as their forefathers were when they converted. They would not mind returning to the Hindu fold if similar survival benefits became available to them. After all, their forefathers had converted to alien faiths for similar reasons under the influence of Christian or Muslim zealots; why should they now mind returning to the fold with Hindu zealots' protection? Aren't they already belittling their adopted religions by demanding reservations in job etc just like the 'low caste' Hindus, ignoring 'egalitarianism' of Christianity and Islam. Or why did Goa Deputy Chief Minister Francis D'Souza, in July 2014, say that India was a Hindu nation and he a '*Hindu* Christian'; why did some of the Goan Christians threaten, in recent past, to convert to Hinduism if their demands are not met?. That was exactly what Hinduism aimed at! Even an *Allahopanishad* was envisaged during the Mughal rule; and India would, probably, have assimilated the Founders of Christianity and Islam had the Papacy and the Caliphate been headquartered in the subcontinent. Some zealots in Pakistan have been trying to revive the Caliphate in Islamabad, without realising that there could eventually arrive a 'Hindu Caliph'; after all, Jinnah was half-Hindu and it is the Hindu politicians and 'intellectuals' who are now leading the Muslims in India! For, didn't the sages say that all distinctions, when seen from different angles of Truth, end up as false: *the Cup returns to Clay, for there is nothing beyond Brahm*!

Mark the words 'angle of Truth': looked at from the point of view of police, all others are criminals and preachers believe everyone else, but them, are sinners...the distinctions will extend to the Crusades and the al-Jihads...to the Sunnis now deIslamising the Ahmedias in Pakistan and then heading for a similar treatment to the Shias (even Pervez Musharraf once bemoaned that Pakistan has seen more Muslims converting fellow Muslims into infidels rather than the other way round!)...to the 'Dalit' Christians and Muslims re-identifying themselves with their own castes among the Hindus in India.....*until the Cup returns to the Clay*. So, we have a 21st century Indian subcontinent in which the Hindus are becoming inclusivist, proclaiming that whosoever says so is a Hindu, and the exclusivist Christians and Muslims who decide who amongst them is *not* an adequate Christian or Muslim! All proselytisation shall be negated by an equal and opposite deproselytising action, at a distance, like theodesics. Logic weakens all distinctions and yet nurtures them to the hilt. India did not waste her time inventing weapons; she used yours against you. Wisdom lay not in invention or construction but in using others' for, didn't you know that idiots make houses for the wise to live in; that's why India produced more computer programmers and information technologists than computers, information or technologies.

When everything returns to the origins, even Life to Death, Brahm, like zero-end, is the residual entity left after all phenomenal world's existence and entities have been denied: it is, after all, the indestructible seed. The world is, therefore, like the journey of the seed from seed to seed: seed, root, stem, branches, foliage, flower, fruit, seed. No rubber is more stretchable than Brahm. Even before Arthur Stanley Eddington said so in the 1920s, India knew that the Universe was expanding! Such an unsurpassable Brahm tunnels us into Maya, like the black into white hole in astronomy, or from total existence into total non-existence. Monotheism, while hard-wiring diverse people in a human connective to launch or resist the next Wave, also led to psychological bondage by stripping men of their creative genius; only great human bloodshed could cleanse their blocked blood vessels, the way the Crusades and World Wars eliminated surplus Christian population, and now the Jihads are doing the same among Muslims, leading to their respective Renaissance.

Monotheists inexorably got sucked into a great warfare within and without in their existential dilemma faced similarly by modern corporate world—expand to survive, but expansion means diversification, adjusting divergent work cultures in different time zones, and risking your *core competence* which itself leads to contraction, forcing you back to square one! And, of course, there are market forces and cyclical 'consolidations' and 'corrections', like white-collar job lovers returning to yellow-collared, passion-driven jobs! Even polytheism was a like force but at local level. The two, together, played upon each other like the alternate clockwise and anti-clockwise motion of clothes in the tub of a washing machine. In order to counter this imperialising argument from the top, ie. from the God of *Genesis*, India began at the counter-argument, at the bottom: you insist that the material dualistic world does exist because of God but I say that it does not exist at all, that God, too, does not exist either as a person or as a thing, and is indescribable either as He or She. What, however, does seem to exist is the Brahm, neither a person nor a thing— or may be even 'It' does not exist. That is, all material world we experience is merely an illusion, Maya, non-existence of existence. Total non-existence. Your God is meaningless without His Creation; our Brahm is meaningful only because of absolute non-creation.

Together with Karma, Maya gave India its most effective psychological vaccination, the absorber of the Abrahamic shock. In other words, India totally denied the existence of and recognition to the God of monotheism, what to talk of His People(s). No other culture had the guts to continuously denounce its victors as *mlechchhas* (impure, untouchables), forcing them, too, to believe in this description (even now, many an Indian Muslim, believing he was a *mlechchha*, would often have meals prepared separately for a Brahmin guest invited to attend a marriage!). India is a snake-and-ladder in which no one ever reaches the destination. None has been a topper.

Ever since, the Indian classics—from the *Vedas* and *Upanishads* to the *Gita*—have been described as unauthored and revealed, like the *Bible* and the *Qur'an,* downloaded from the Cloud. By revealing one thing to India and quite the opposite to the others, God thus created an anti-dote of Himself. The more monotheism hypnotised the world, the more India self-hypnotised against it. The whole idea of the Abrahamic God was a pure abstraction, a postulate, woven like a woollen sweater, tied up at the end by the Knot of the Book to prevent it from being unspooled; India simply cut away the Knot by undoing the uniqueness of 'revelation' and, pulling just one thread of *Neti, Neti,* vis-à-vis the Abrahamic 'This Is It', left the garment to gently come apart. The very concepts of 'synthesis' 'assimilation', 'comparative religions' and 'syncretic cultures', proved poison to alien faiths which prided no end on their own perceived superiority, self-righteousness and *uniqueness*; post-1947, the Indian Constitution's stress on 'secularism', *Sarvadharma Sambhav* (Equality of All Religions) completely watered down the perceived 'exclusivity' and 'supremacy' of Christianity and Islam: an eraser is not necessary as you can shorten a line just by drawing another, a bigger one!

To counter the silence of monotheistic prayers, India invented loud chants of *Naamsiddhanta*: from the pre-Christian *Om* to the post-Gandhian *Vaishnav jan*...and *Hare Rama Hare Krishna,* via the Bhakti Movement and innumerable *Kirtan Mandals,* India's chaotic and boisterous exterior popular religiosity has constantly poured into the unwilling ears of Indian Christians and Muslims—you are unlikely to come across a Hindu presiding over Christian or Muslim religious bodies or shrines but can easily meet a Christian or Muslim happily heading Hindu festival bodies, or even praying at a temple. It was as if a home-grown Goebbels was protecting India from Hitler! The agony of monotheism found its remedy in the ecstasy of polytheism. Unwittingly, Islam, too, fell for this during the Sufi movement in India: the *Qawwalis*, Islamic variant of the Hindu *Kirtans* and *Bhajans*, devised to attract the Hindus through devotional surrender, got infected with the idea cf 'unity' of all religions, robbing Islam of its 'uniqueness'; on the contrary, the Hindus would regularly visit a Sufi shrine, like those having no stake in a bank but allowed to withdraw money at will. It slowly bankrupted the alien faiths.

After abolition of the Caliphate and the resultant ejection of Pakistan as Islam's retreat from India, the three major but exhausted Sufi sects called the *Chishti, Naqshabandi* and *Suharawardi*, also folded up business in much of the Indian subcontinent like the receding shadows after an eclipse. Since Allah had a thousand names, some of the warrior Indians gods and goddesses, too, like Vishnu and Durga, were given similar attributes and people of different regions adopted them the way they liked. With a huge domestic demand, India, like a retail hyper-market, evolved so many flourishing choices and alternatives to choose from, at such low prices and end-of-season sales and set up such a fierce in-house competition, that the theo-customer would not go elsewhere, making Wal-Marts retreat in this democratic crowd and chaos. Indian economy, not much export-oriented, weathered the global slowdown in 2008 because of this huge domestic demand that kept their soul and hearth together—some newspapers survived merely by scaling down up to 95% discount in advertisement rates! And a large number of Indians simply cut down their needs, as they have done all through history, instead of going to war against themselves or others.

So effective has been the *Naamsiddhanta* that many among the Christians and Muslims in India wonder how to counter noisy Hindu chants from striking a raw nerve in their minds: as a result, the Hindu would not know a word of *theoretical* Christianity or Islam but a fatigued Christian or a Muslim would understand what *practical* Hinduism is and get slowly sucked back to the fold:

through the 'shared' classical music, films, cultural ingress, cuisines, and increasing religious salinity through the Hindus' excessive theo-irrigation to counter monotheistic desertification. No wonder, the exhausted Kashmiri Muslim would rather have his daughter marry a Hindu and settle outside this 'Valley of Death' rather than entertain Muslim extremist. *Naamsiddhanta* became a one-way valve, allowing only the Christians and Muslims to hear Hindu chants and making them believe where their future might really lay. India's cacophony was the answer to silent prayers of Christianity and Islam, even after destruction of her many idols; God's unity paled before India's diversity.

God's unity was a product of man's inability to safeguard his diversity and failure in preventing his being dragged into Him. The ancient Aryan tradition was that unity itself could be an illusion and produce diversity—the case of an elephant being felt differently by blindfolded men—or that diversity could eventually mean unity—the blindfolds removed—and so human beings shall be allowed to go the way they chose to. The invading Abrahamic tradition, however, forced them to adopt new ways to guard their thinking processes. Now, the new challenge was from a bitter unity being forced down their throats and how to untie it. The Aryans, therefore, returned to their time-tested empty box, Brahm, in which to repackage the enemy and roll it back. Since there was only one reality, man could also have only one aim in life: attainment of that which you call is your reality, to perceive it, to dissolve in it, to be one with That One. But, why should man realise That One? The Abrahamite would say: because you have no one else to follow, there is nothing else to pursue, because He Alone Is There, because He is the Only and All Knowledge and key to everything else, without Whose Knowledge all your life is null and void. The Aryan opened his own mall in his trusted carton of Brahm: he invented hundreds of rituals as the means to attain That One End, to realise Brahm, for he felt that man's emphasis on correct rituals, the means *a la* Abrahamism, and not conduct, would eventually render That One redundant and unimportant (for, monotheism, after all, boils down to the ritual, unlike polytheism which at least attempts to arrive at the actual from the choices). It left Brahm empty again, recyclable and reusable. Even otherwise, the sixth century BC Aryan society in India was getting devoid of knowledge-seekers and infested with ritualists; the few Gyankaandis that still remained in the wild woods knew, from their experience of the first globalising, force-multiplying, game-changing Wave-maker, ie. Buddhism, that god-intoxicated man's hangover could end only with a little morning peg as a counter. In due course, a theocratising, parallel God would emerge in India as well. But, until then, India needed mental defences. They, therefore, wove intricate logic, a meshwork, in which would be lost the intruders; like the Iranian Magis, they created magic but it was in their logic few could really comprehend and fewer still ever knew why this gigantic *thought machine* evolved; again, evolution of this machine was not a conscious single-handed or even institutional effort but a semi-conscious, collective societal effort that took on the form of a response in an all-India reference.They spread the seeds that awaited the rains; they spread the oil that awaited the spark; they, in short, infested India with psychological mines and booby-traps that awaited the enemy. They taught that your miseries are merely a reflection of your failure to know the nature of Brahm; this failure is *avidya* (ignorance, unawareness) whose end should now be the aim of your life. India monkeyed around monotheism for three millennia and called its Monkey God, Hanuman, a *sankatmochak*, problem-solver and the Elephant God, Ganesh, with elephantine memory, the solution-provider—even now, a new Indian computer often starts only after its Hindu owner worships Ganesh. By evolving a rare capacity to laugh at itself, India turned everything upside down in this long-drawn psychological warfare. India is a serious joke.

You are not happy with your present conditions (only pigs have the rare capacity to be satisfied!) and want to rid yourself with the unending cycle of birth and death? That is because you have failed to attain That One Reality. Your *avidya* would end only when you dissolve yourself in That Brahm, for perpetual bliss. How to do it? Come to our Great Carnival that is India, the Land of Festivals, where even death could be a festivity to be 'celebrated' in a mournful mood. Hundreds of choices. Festival discounts. Special offers. Thus, while monotheists of the Fertile Crescent evolved similar prayers, liturgies and theologies to make the West Asian God's Juggernaut, the Indian Aryan, by offering multiple choices, even abuses, created so many encroachments and obstacles that God found it difficult to plough His bulldozer through the subcontinent's cultural hinterland: no other country provided as many choices to her people to pick and choose their gods and goods from; so many that they did not have to look beyond for alternatives. You are forced to slow down on a footpath infested with vendors, as it were. Many Hindus continued to live in houses that tripled as temples, schools and workplace, unlike separate ones in the Abrahamic societies; for the Hindus, their god was like a family member. Like their Hindu counterparts, therefore, for many of converted Indian Christians and Muslims, Jesus and Muhammed were not messiahs to lead them to Paradise but yet other sectarian gurus who gave them their new names while they zealously retained their old ones, inherited habits and caste identities—'conversion' of the Hindus to Christianity or Islam was seldom due to their desire for spiritual emancipation; the 'converted', who was, in fact merely inverted, was prone to revert when the impact of the cause of change no longer existed. Many among the Christians or Muslims in India have largely been Hindus standing upside down, on *sheershasana*. The Hindu saints, who stood on head everyday, knew this.

The Indian Christians' or Muslims' continuing caste consciousness kept open the hidden tunnel to their 'Hindu' origins. So powerful has this caste system been in India that the whole society revolved around this fulcrum. The Aryan system of *gotras* and gurus kept alive this tunnel for the flitting 'converted' people. To the gotra they traced their origins—there are millions of Indian Christians and Muslims who proudly remember this fact and often emphasise it in their names, traditions, marriages etc even if they have migrated to other countries; their guru, the Teacher, as in China, was their arbiter in the world. Whereas Jesus and Muhammed tried to abolish the priestly middleman between man and God, the Aryans emphasised that *vidya*, knowledge, cannot be achieved without an intermediary guru. Thus, while Abrahamism encouraged belief in The Invisible One through the today visible-tomorrow invisible messiah, the embattled Aryans, per force, promoted belief in Your Invisible One, through our visible manys, through the 24x7x365 available middleman. Due to the theoretical absence of middlemen, which made their practical presence controversial, faith and belief were, therefore, gradually lost during transmission of faith from man to the Abrahamic God; in India, faith and belief continued to be generated, transmitted and retransmitted through that theoretically and practically present and vigilant transformer: *the guru*, the local solar power cell, and *the panchayat*, the local god. For the Hindus, faith has always been a power-grid in which the gods of antiquity and contemporary gurus contributed their share equally, every time increasing it more than the installed capacity to meet the growing demand, while in monotheism faith was produced and transmitted by just one mega-theo-power station. The Hindus evolved individual, personalised and designer gurus, like their permanent account number (PAN) now. Millions of Buddhists and Jains—even Parsis and Sikhs, and also Christians and Muslims—continued to worship Hindu gods and gurus covertly or overtly: who knows which one of them would click to sort out your woes! The Hindus did not have to repose their faith in an invisible god but could go to enjoy their siesta after outsourcing their woes to their visible guru who would think *for them*. Christianity and Islam failed to click in India, in the long term, primarily because they mostly failed to convert clan leaders and community teachers and were content enrolling the ineffective fringe to their respective faiths. Unlike the Hebrew Judges who herded their folk into monotheism, the gurus, including the Ten Gurus of the Sikhs, guarded India against the invasion of an alien God.

No other culture gave as much importance to the teacher: even today, the simple villager would urge the school teacher not to be lenient to his child: 'his bones are ours, but his skin is yours.' Even Confucius bemoaned that no ruler in China would take him for a teacher; in India, even a wily Chanakya continues to be respected as the ideal Master because he not only masterminded the creation of the first great Indian Empire but also selflessly worked *under* his disciple, Chandragupta Maurya. Many *dwij* parents would leave their toddler at the *Gurukul* (Family of the Guru) and not see him for the next 12 years until he graduated as a *Brahmachaari* (Bachelor); princes would perform all the chores as a pauper disciple would do in the Gurukul. How could the teachers, having such a hold on the Hindu society, fail? They taught India to grow humbly like low-lying grass, not as a tall tree, to patiently wait until the storms uprooting the trees and forests passed, swallow the poisons of history and civilisation like Shiva, the *Neelkanth*, regurgitate the dirt, and vomit it out again. Christianity and Islam, which drew strength between the four walls of a shrine, could never invade India's sprawling open spaces where these little schools functioned: under the trees, in the cowsheds, in the caves, in the snow-capped mountains. Like a snake shedding hide and renewing youth every year, in the great Kumbh fairs, India would renew her youth every 12 years, as if recharging its battery for the next mile. Meanwhile, the 'central' governments would come and go, barging in with bangs and committing suicide with whimpers. The gurus, not gods, gave India her undying hope. Gandhi was her last great guru. Rajneesh relieved India of her spiritual-socialist constipation by injecting her with a materialist enema—without Osho and Dhirubhai Ambani, who created the soil for reforms, P V Narasimha Rao and Manmohan Singh would not have been possible. But remember, despite all this reverence, the guru was not the caste or community leader, although many castes had their own gurus; and he was certainly not like the inviolable Hebrew Judges, who virtually blind-folded and herded off the Jews into the *Old Testament*, the *Torah*, the Diaspora, and the Holocaust; the Hindus had a right to disobey, or even kill, their guru: Nehru's differences with Gandhi were public and Yudhishthira did not sin even after lying and ensuring that Arjuna killed their teacher, Dronacharya in the *Mahabharata* War, as the latter was seen siding with evil. India has never seen cult leaders like those of the Heaven's Gate, Jonestown or the Taliban who lead their disciples to mass suicide. Charlatans masquerading as 'holy men' have often found themselves behind bars and forgotten. Abrahamism created God; the Hindus, and the Chinese, created Man.

What did these gurus do, after all? How did they shape, control human minds? Monotheism, despite its unique connecting and integrating mass production and assembling capacity, turned out, in the long run, an affliction of the unsteady and relatively less developed mind stripped of innovation and natural genius; since a monotheist human mind gradually lost creativity, it was unable to comprehend the Nature of Things, their immense complexity and utter simplicity, and its resultant surrender to something non-existent, God, to explain those Things. The Hindu guru, on the other hand, quarantined his disciple's mind not by forcing him to shun something but by extolling or even imposing his own product: like the modern consumer product advertiser, he refrained from openly criticising the rival's product but dropped enough hints what he was against (Hindus do not like anyone criticising others in matters religious—they are the best self-critics, proud of not inventing the word 'blasphemy'—but Christian and Islamist zealots, unwittingly, continued to criticise Hindu gods and culture, and ended up banished like Zakir Naik). Gandhi, fierce Hindu as he was, had experienced this himself in his early years in Gujarat and South Africa; later, he stressed *unity* of all religions because he knew no true Christian or Muslim zealot could ever be secular or accept his religion being *equated* to anybody else's. As a result, Abrahamic medicines exposed themselves more and more to Indian weather reports and, with expiry dates, slowly went out of the market; on the other hand, Ayurvedic medicines had no use-before-dates! Competition, not rivalry, has been the buzz-word for the Hindu who never liked monopolistic practices practised by any collectives like Abrahamism and remained fiercely individualistic.

After planting the seed, the guru waited for its germination, sometimes even challenging the disciple to defeat him, as in the case of Parashuram and Bheeshma and Dronacharya and Arjuna, to ensure that education has reached the deserving candidate; the ideal Hindu guru was one who made sure his disciple surpassed and defeated him. They then taught him that mind was the cause of bondage, but it could also liberate him, and asked him to transcend this bondage. But the mind, being extremely sensitive to the external stimuli (that is why it is seat of ideation, response to these stimuli), is mercurial like Nature and it was necessary to control it: the *Upanishads* compared human mind with a monkey for its fickleness, with a vagabond woman for its proneness to fall for anyone, with a street-dog for polluting itself and then others. Such a mind needed to be slowly, progressively attenuated so as to prepare it for total dissolution: folklores like those of Valmiki and Angulimals, wherein criminals turned into saints, were used as examples for this. *The gurus controlled the Hindu mind not by shaping it for their own use, but by rendering it supple and unusable by others.* They taught the disciple that s/he would become what s/he thought and since s/he wanted to dissolve herself/himself, s/he must quieten, still and steel her/his mind to such a degree that it was left with no choice but to dissolve itself, like salt or sugar into water, and be one with the world which is not a universe but the aggregate of countless illusions. Such a non-existence of mind is transcendence in which one's capacity to wonder is extinguished. When the mind, like power station, is shut down, there would be no complaint whatsoever: even darkness is a state of mind, a stimulus due to your eyes. By thus shutting down mind as well as ignorance, you would get rid of *avidya*, ignorance, and by giving up fancying you would give up differentiation as well. Nirvana, or annihilation of mind, is basically a total absence of interest, *vasana*. Therefore, roll up all your faculties, shut down all your senses, go in a deep slumber. To this day, no other people are as fond of enjoying their afternoon siesta: And thus saith Uddalaka Aruni to his son, Shwetketu: 'Understand from me, my dear, the ultimate in the state of sleep. *When a person here sleeps, he has verily reached the Being, to his own.*'

In one go, the *Upanishad*, thus, surreptitiously packs off That One God to passivity, to sleep, to inaction, to unCreation (because creation requires awakening, activity). That is, 'realising' God means statelessness or annihilation of human mind; the more awakened you are, the distant you are from Him. In sleep, deep slumber, meditation, you tend to be closer to God, to unCreation. Contrast this: in Abrahamism, God means Creation, Supreme Activity, and His true disciples are in a state of perpetual Crusade/al-Jihad against non-believers; in Hinduism, God means unCreation, Supreme Passivity, that is, the former says God created this world and the latter maintains He cannot because He sleeps. That is, if you believe God exists, then the world doesn't because He is inactive. But since the world is there for all to see, and it is active, verily, it proves that God doesn't exist at all!

If you still argue: Who, then, created this world? The counter-question is, where is the world, after all?? It's all Maya, illusion, fickleness of human mind, a haphazard conglomeration of temporary events, and you'd agree bubbles don't mean water; the absolute world doesn't exist, only a relative one does. These countless Hindu sages were, by propagating this circuitous argument, teaching irreligion!

How to arrive at this statelessness of the mind? Well, the choices, again, are countless; your guru will guide you... and thus emerged the plethora of rituals today's Hindus inherited. No other country was guided by its peers to indulge in worthless rituals on such a vast scale, with such a wide choice, to keep the largest possible number of fickle-minded masses so engrossed with inanities, with themselves and within their overall fold, to keep them busy in nothingness. It was to vaccinate them from the onslaughts of a hostile outside world, so that most of them could not be herded off by rival cultures or alien religions: this 'busy' culture gave rise to the popular Hindi/Urdu phrase, *Kaam kaudi ka nahin, fursat ghadi ki nahin* (Without an iota of work, s/he remains extremely busy!). Individually, again, this attempt was not conscious but collectively it took the form of a societal response, a resistance, from the bits and pieces at local levels, to the explosion of the *Gita*, parallel to the *Bible* and the *Qur'an,* gradually leading to ejection of Pakistan.

Because of its vast, conscious illiteracy and zenith-levels of non-knowledge, but *not* ignorance, India stayed polytheistic and Hindu and did not convert wholly to monotheism: areas like Kerala, where literacy was traditionally higher, had a high percentage of Christians and Muslims; indeed the missionaries entering India from the South focused on literacy, unlike Islamists who mostly entered from the North, and were soon lost in the vast ocean of Maya. Pakistan, a colony carved out within the subcontinent by illiterate, relocated millions of and from India, for and under the leadership of a highly-literate pied piper, M A Jinnah, himself a *muhajir* (refugee) in the nation of his own creation, was typically Indian in virtually, though unofficially, banning its own 'official' language, Urdu. No other culture prohibited use of its own 'sacred' language and cultivated ignorance virtually as a state policy. While monotheism made the Books, its permanent manuals, a compulsory reading so as to *process* human minds in a particular way, India nearly banned her scriptures from reaching many people and freed the mind to draw its own conclusions and also to conceal her mind-control technology from falling in possibly wrong hands; for the 'intellectuals', the inquisitive few, there were those mind-numbing fads to keep them preoccupied, free from asking uncomfortable questions at an inopportune time—something practised now by many a nation, the way the West does through the failed CTBT, Intellectual Property Rights etc, but without understanding the functioning of human mind. Preventing knowledge from falling into dangerous and rogue hands is as important as creation of new information; each penny saved is a penny earned.

India grew haphazard forests of logic, not manicured gardens, parks and orchards of a well-architectured Abrahamic God, and then allowed her people to negotiate their way through the apples, oranges and snakes alike. Due to this 'spiritual' afforestation, she was able to put up a thick fencing against monotheism as the intruder could not decide which the real India was, and after failing to brave the marshes and beasts, retreated; the last Mughal Emperor Aurangzeb's last and fatal mistake was to send a great army to Kamrup (Assam) to expand imperial limits. Only one soldier survived, as all others died of malaria without fighting any war, to tell the Alamgir (Emperor of the World!) how Nature defeated the 'ideal' Muslim ruler; this considerably weakened his realm, leading to its steep decline. Most Indians do not flaunt their wisdom or strength; rather they encourage others to flaunt theirs and expose themselves. This is how the pauper and illiterate Indian voter, equipped only with raw intellect, time and again, foxes the western and westernized media to make a fool of themselves in each election. If monotheism was eventually reduced to correct ritual rather than the right conduct to create a domain for God, polytheism, too, stooped to this level to meet the enemy at its own level. With the arrival of Christianity and Islam and emergence of the Vaishnavite schools and *Upanishads* in the vast landmass between the Indus and Brahmaputra, India evolved a counter-proselytising symbolism: symbolic gestures, ranging from self-mesmeric mantras (formulae), yantras (diagrams) and to tantras (magic and erotic-esoteric hallucinations), to mere utterance of these, or of a particular city or name, came to the fore and crystallised in the erotic temples of Khajuraho and Konark: they transport you from sex and animal instincts on the periphery to the Sun God in the *sanctum sanctorum.* Apart from this fencing and protective hedging, India also evolved a spiritual hypermarket by allowing different communities and castes to evolve their own, personal, designer godlets, making the subcontinent a vast fashion ramp to incrementally absorb alien Gods, the way tiny ants and termites collectively defeat far larger creatures. Egypt also had so many gods but these were virtually stamped out by Islam because the un-hedged Hamitic society itself had decayed. In contrast, the vibrant, polytheist India never degenerated up to the societal core—the degeneration was, basically, in its political-security regimes—and preserved her soft and living tissues protected by hard bark. Different sects continued to interpolate and extrapolate in their own 'scriptures' and *Upanishads* to adjust to challenges of the changing times; they often competed with each other to fish in the murky spiritual waters, to hoodwink themselves and hook-in customers and consumers (disciples) but never organised pogroms or launched the likes of the Crusades and Jihads against rivals for not believing in their persuasions. Outsized dinosaurs go extinct but not the lizard and the cockroach as they manage to sneak into crevices. And, not by struggling to live, but by feigning death.

As a direct response to the trade-routes of Christianity and Islam, Devotional Vaishnavism was basically evolved by the Vaishyas (traders) among the North Indian Hindus in urban areas. Krishna, like Muhammed, was the culmination of this theodynamics and the *Gita*, like the *Qur'an*, the trade directory. It was due to these spiritual market forces that the Krishna cult and the Vaishnavite sect turned proselytisers, like the rival Christianity and Islam, and their franchisees continued to multiply like outlets of a fast-food chain owned by a million gurus: Krishna came to be worshipped as a fugitive, *Ranchhod*, in Gujarat, where a large number of refugees had settled down after Islam evicted them, as *Shrinathji*, the Black Stone deity, *a la* the Kaa'ba's, in Rajasthan where the desert province was fighting the Muslims with sword. Traders of different areas evolved their own versions of Krishna and even the *Gita* to suit to their needs, for, didn't He declare that all routes led to Him! The interpolation of the *Gita* into the *Bheeshmaparva* of the *Mahabharata* was significant: it demonstrated that while the Old World of Bheeshma, the Kuru Patriarch, struggled merely to keep the word he gave his father to protect the latter's progeny, unlike Abraham's readiness to sacrifice his son to keep his word with God, the New World of Krishna demanded peace and order at any cost, even risking a fratricidal war, so as to uphold 'social values', and, in doing so, no relations were important, *a la* Islam, in the contemporary feudal society. If you know knitting, you'd understand it: intertwined forward and backward loops, as in a sweater, tie up and incorporate designs. Krishna, like Muhammed, crossed all social bonds to impose His own version of ethics and attempted to evolve a world community based not on society but, as the Second Wave (industry and trade) variables demanded, on economy, on gains, bargains. The Vaishnavite Mohandas (ie. Devotee of Krishna) Gandhi, was a typical example, and culmination, of this psyche, as was his rival Muhammed Ali Jinnah. The cults of both Mohammed and Madanmohan were, basically, supported by urban traders; while modest Shiva temples dominated the rural scene, the cash-rich Krishna temples did so in urban areas.

No, the ancient Hindus did not extol death but *jeevanmukti*, liberation from the cycle of life *while still alive*—the enlightened Brahmins could even perform *ghatshraddha*, their own last rites when still alive. It was only with advent of Islam that India prepared herself in a completely new *avatar*: now, the gurus extolled just the opposite when they taught that the human mind should have the sensitivity of a newly-born babe, of a blind-deaf-dumb man, stilling the sense organs, yet retaining that primordial capacity for inquisitiveness, to marvel, child-like, about the Nature of Things, so that the doting mother Yashoda could see the Universe in the soiled mouth of her toddler Krishna, who has swallowed earth. The Krishna of *Gita*, due to His very nature of being *Madanmohan* (One without Ego or Attachment), just the reverse of Mohammed (Sanskritisation of this Quraish name meant one with *moh* and *mad*, attachment and ego), having emphasised liberation from all bondage through *nishkam karmayoga* (selfless duty) in this very life, propounded evolution of the spiritual from the material, *a la* Rajneesh, vis-à-vis the evolution of the 'material from the spiritual' concept of monotheism. Since Krishna's unstated purpose was to produce a foil to the *Bible* and *Qur'an,* the *Gita* is as contradictory as its rival Books: it simultaneously encourages all work-all play (desire-less duty, but, *a la*, Zoroastrianism, one can't shun the world), no work-no play (you don't really work and never get any fruits either because you all—Good and Evil—are merely My reflections which emanate from and dissolve in Me), all work-no play (the world works according to My desire but essentially remains unchanged because of Maya) and no work-all play (nothing really changes, all change being merely illusory and temporary, as all apparent changes are part of Maya)!

When India discovered zero and the decimal, she logically took on a monotheistic God, who had, despite His supposedly proclaimed attributelessness, surreptitiously acquired attributes, like being 'Compassionate, Merciful'. Without realising that their Almighty, too, had attributes like them—indeed all matter, God and man, are accompanied by attributes and by killing attributed gods, you cannot outgrow your own unattributable God—monotheism fought within itself for 2,000 years over whether *their* Almighty was Male or Female, or had any relations. Islam, believing in One God, evolved attributes for a *masculine* Allah, 'Compassionate and Merciful', 'All-knowing and forgiving', while *feminine* Christianity personified these attributes to evolve as a disguised polytheism by evolving the family and office of Jesus, who ended up being the Only Son of Father, and a Mother, Mary, for many. Christianity, besides having God and Jesus and also the Holy Spirit, acquired hundreds of 'national churches' and thousands of local, national, international, or even inter-stellar saints (like Santa Claus). Most of these were, of course, acquired wholesale from the vanquished 'infidel': Jesus may have been a modest 'Christ' but his Church has historically often been a cartel of fraudsters, right from the alleged 'Donation of Rome'. The Jesus Cult robbed the heathen of his land and culture in the 'benevolent' exchange of the *Bible,* through a well-organised corporate office; not only this, by granting affiliations and franchisees, the 'teachings' of Jesus were transformed into the propaganda of a well-organised multinational corporation. Indeed, Christianity, which evolved from a Hebrew loaf into the Italian pizza, was the first MNC selling Jesus as a commodity, as the USP: Christianity evolved exclusive patron saints even for 'hopeless causes' (St Jude), body piercers (St Sebastian), television (St Clare), hairdressers (St Martin de Porres), animal lovers (St Francis), race car drivers (St Richard) etc. Of these, Jude and Francis are, alas, called 'super-saints'. God save Jesus from this stampede of saints! The Vatican emerged as the saint-manufacturing monopolist corporation, using Jesus as the common soda in all brands of soap with different fragrances thrown in for effect—Pope John Paul II, alone, manufactured nearly 80 'saints' in his two decades at the Vatican, putting himself and Mother Teresa etc in the same league! Clearly, India had to put up trade barriers and impose higher custom duty to protect her domestic spiritual market from aliens dumping their products.

With the advent of Islam in the seventh century, monotheism had crystallised God's Word, finally, to an absolutist time and space. In the lineage of lunar monotheism, Zoroastrianism had all but fossilised, Judaism dispersed, Christianity was uprooted from West Asia and only Islam, as the logical outcome, the residual asphalt, of a log-drawn-out theo-refining process had remained in the Crucible. Islam, like a theo-cyclone, arose from the low pressure deserts of Arabia where had gathered strong winds blowing in from Israel and Persia over the thousand years preceding Muhammed. The resultant anti-cyclone emerged in India, a high-pressure polytheistic centre. Like other varieties of monotheism, Islam, literally meaning 'Surrender', claimed to be the pinnacle of Knowledge, proclaimed that with its arrival the Era of Jahiliah (Ignorance) had ended.

This the *Ishopanishad* had foreseen: *Those worshipping Ignorance, enter a blinding darkness. But Those delighting in Knowledge, enter in an even greater darkness Than this.*

Rapid expansion of Islam indicated this inexorable trend; in a couple of centuries, *the* Knowledge had crossed the geographical limits of what it believed was Ignorance, the Iberian Peninsula in the west and the Indian Peninsula in the east. In the next two centuries,

Spain evolved its extrovert carnivorous responses to divest Islam of its claims of invincibility as India evolved her own introvert herbivorous responses to digest Knowledge itself, slowly. Europe gradually started pushing away monotheism—Islam towards Arabia, Christianity towards America—India pulled it in, the way amoeba absorbs food by allowing it to enter, encircling it and digesting most of it.

By the sixth century, while Islam was emerging trans-Indus, India was designing a fully responsive God: Krishna.

The Designer God

THE *Upanishads* ensured that the Indian response would be inward-moving, asking man to turn his back on the outside world, roll up his senses and enter his own self. In particular, *Kathopanishad*, which the *Gita* derived upon so much, proclaimed that the wise man was one who could look into his own Self, one who thus realised Brahm. Since Islam claimed to be the End of All Knowledge, trying to eliminate all external forms of ignorance demonstrated by the seemingly unnecessary rituals, the *Gita*, too, proclaimed likewise; both ended up replacing old ignorance with the new. They provided all answers but permitted no questions!

From the beginning, the *Upanishads* had, as reactions to the emerging Abrahamic ideology across the Indus River, Crucible of Monotheism, advised that men should shun all empirical knowledge gathered by the senses and end all ideation to bring to an absolute inertness, turning within and forgetting the outside world. A major difference between monotheists and polytheists was that the former never attempted a 'discovery' of God, for they *axiomatically* believed they already had One. The more the monotheists exploded upon the world, the more India imploded upon herself; the *Brahmasootra* even explored the *architecture* of God. Some *Upanishads*, even the *Gita*, recommended a revolt against rituals of the Vedic religion, saying the real *Gyanis* and *Sannyasis* were those who transcended this abracadabra. However, India was not ruled by the books or bookworms. Rituals were like coastal weeds that reduced the impact of a cyclone—see how the US, or its UN Security Council brothers, pass ritual resolutions to reduce impact of sanction/action against a nation *they* decide is 'rogue'! Since the monotheistic cyclone was knocking at the doors, India ignored the anti-ritualistic exhortations of all 'reformers', including Adi Shankaracharya—no god or Hindu reformer ever grew too big for his boots—came to a naught. By the time of Aurangzeb in the 17th century, the Hindus had evolved nearly 430 personal and hundreds of family or community rituals that guided their course in the world from womb to pyre. Since these rituals were basically adventitious extensions of culture and rooted in the original caste or pedigree of an individual (irrespective of the sect or 'religion' s/he followed), even those who 'converted' to alien proselytisers like Christianity or Islam continued to adhere to many of these roots; most Indian 'Christians' and 'Muslims' still follow some of the customs their Hindu forefathers followed. Like puppets hanging by the strings, not surprisingly, they are now 'rediscovering' their caste. Rituals are, therefore, reflection of *Rta*. The Hindus knew that one could change everything, including faith, but not parents or caste; by stoutly adhering to their caste, the Indian converts ensured their gradual rebirth in the future Hindu society of today.

Parallel to the crystallisation of the *Old Testament*, India was, in fact, launching a two-pronged protective shield against monotheism. On the intellectual plane, it was preparing to meet the challenge of a feminine Christianity by evolving Rama as a nice guy community messiah who would adhere to good words and deeds, but carrying arrows coated with sweet poison—to kill, for instance, Baali, in a battle of the brothers, or to eliminate, on Vibhishan's advice, targeting the rival brother Ravan's belly, although, in both cases, the traditional Kshatriya rules of war prohibited attack beneath thorax. On the popular plane, it met the masculine Islam with Krishna who taught that faith decided the conduct and the ends justified the means. The Hindus' militant sect, Sikhism, would arise in the Punjab where the *Mahabharata* evolved over several thousand years preceding Muhammed. Sikhism was the next stage of the evolving Krishna cult—half of the Sikh Gurus derived their names from the *Ramayana* or *Mahabharata*—which emphasised the importance of a Guru (the word Sikh is a derivative of *shishya*, disciple). Guru Gobind Singh, founder of the Khalsa Panth within Sikhism, shared a name of Krishna, the way Mohan Das (Mahatma) Gandhi did—the former weakened Islam, the latter pushed it back, across the Indus.

Both Christianity and Islam, when they entered, gave food for thought to India and were gradually subjected to a slow digestive process—digestion is different from assimilation as there is no egestion (defecation) in the latter. Christianity, having failed to gain more souls in the Indian soil despite a stay longer than Islam, did not claim separateness in mainland India, except in the North East. Christianity slowly got digested, as in the case of 'converted' Christians (although, some millennial, apocalyptic Protestant sects, hurrying to book their berth in Heaven before the 'Second Coming' of Jesus as the year 2000 approached, attempted to 'harvest' Indians). A large number of 'Christians' in India are only nominally so.

Pakistan, too, could not sleep for long with its Eastern wing and had to let go of Bangladesh in 1971 the way India had to let Pakistan happen in 1947. Both of these 'nations' may be on their way to return to the India fold, the Cup returning to the Clay, *sans* Islam. Clearly, the two alien faiths, which did catalyse Indian civilisation, got only visitor's visa, not permanent residence, in the country, because their holiest motherboard shrines were overseas, their local places of franchisee worship had no *garbhagriha* (sanctum sanctorum)—and their God was not under the *control* of those who created Him.

It is a reality. For, reality, the *Upanishads* said, is a strange thing: it is something indescribable and inconceivable, even pure consciousness, which cannot be sensed with our sense organs. Whatever we sense is unreal! Abrahamism tried to crush the real individual at the altar of an unreal God; Hinduism exalted the individual to the level of God, the Absolute Itself. But it was a conditional exaltation: if you want to achieve godhood, you must disembody and dissolve yourself in a non-corporeal Atma. India thus reduced man to an abstraction, to the level of another abstraction called God, one reflecting the other, the size depending upon whether you hold a convex or a concave mirror. By this abstraction, India found fault in herself, continuously flogged and flayed herself, the best example being Gandhi's famous fasts. This therapeutic policy has continued unabated as an insurance against colonised minds dominating the national scene, until their destiny caught up with them. That is why the five per cent English-speaking, self-flagellating, self-appointed 'secular' conscience-keepers slowly turned into cultural diabetics now facing extinction: insulated from reality, harbouring messiahnic dreams they borrowed from Abrahamic traditions, they supported minorities to the hilt, *a la* Gandhi, and unwittingly triggered the revival of majority Hindu reaction, making Modi possible.

India has always been like this. Her Kauravas and Pandavas belong to the same Kuru clan and they are merely virtual enemies. Krishna realised that the Pandavas' real but hidden 'enemy' was not Duryodhan but Bheeshma who refused to outgrow and evolve out of his unnatural vow, come what may, to protect the progeny of a retrogressive, humanoid species spawned by his younger brother, *Vichitraveerya* (Strange Creature) from step-mother Satyavati, the mermaid. It is not for nothing that the *Gita* forms part of *Bheeshmaparva* in the *Mahabharata*—as the Gujaratis say, your enemy is born in your mother's womb! That was why Krishna aimed at removing from the scene, *first of all* in that fratricidal war, the Grand Sire and Patriarch, the Enemy General, from the latter's fossilised past, an obstacle to the growth of the Pandavas, the future. The peculiar nature of Indian culture allowing growth of an 'enemy' within, like the resistant leucocytes and anti-bodies that inoculate our body, made its people rather immune to pain of failure or pleasure of success. But it also killed the very human nature of holding others responsible for one's own woes—unlike what the monotheists did—so as to embalm and heal her ailments, the wounds inflicted on her psyche by the trampling, ruthless march of own history and alien civilisations. In order to restrain herself and protect her mind, she fossilised herself, hid her children in a thick, inaccessible forest of junk ideas to defend herself from an advancing abstraction called God. Since she aimed at denying a non-corporeal God, she had to sacrifice a corporeal Man as well: there will be no provable God if there were no provable Man! Self-flagellation enabled India to overcome the horrors of an imaginary hell or the riches of a perceived heaven of the monotheist; she learnt to have it all here, on this very earth. No customer ever returned empty-handed from the super-mall called Hinduism: even those obsessed with hell, have a variety of 28 hells to choose from! She even made Heaven rather unattractive—the King of Heaven, Indra, has himself been seeking refuge here and there all through Indian mythological history. Nobody could ever scare a Hindu with the dark visions of hell or entice him with the lure of heaven—clearly, Christianity and Islam, which ran their proselytisation business marketing Heaven and Hell, were bound to fold up shop.

Even the *Gita*, which evolved as the Hindu response to the *Bible* and the *Qur'an*, did not quite terrorise the people with the horrors of a Hell or entice them with the bliss of a material Heaven. The Divine Song's orchestra merely enchants and titillates them with multiple voices and choices to choose from—a reason why so many, even contradictory, 'commentaries' on the *Gita* emerged over the centuries—so that by the time you finish the Book with 700-plus Verses, you are overwhelmed with the sheer dimensions and loads of alternatives it offers in the spiritual hypermarket, unlike the uni-dimensional, single-commodity (One God) offered by the aliens' Books. While monotheism offers you a standard God and cuts *you* according to His Size, the monism of *Gita* offers you a zillion varieties and sizes to choose from; you are allowed to cut God according to your own size and grind Him, make a paste, or a chutney, even add spices to suit your taste: devotional poetess Meerabai would 'marry' Lord Krishna Who could even be made to run from the battlefield or a Shiva could be forced to run away from His own disciple, Bhasmasur. Those who ruled India for a thousand years were often confused that the Hindus' staple crop was religion and philosophy; no, her food intake changes seasonally as she looks for amusement even in a tragedy and turns crisis into opportunity—many Hindus routinely share jokes or discuss cuisines or business even during funerals. They have always been bearded children playing with their gods as friends and partners; they changed gods seasonally or even retired them. For your god is basically in your senses and India turned them into actors to dance to man's tunes, not the other way round. India never cut a corpse to be fitted in a readymade coffin but had a separate coffin for each dead. The Hindu would not keep them dead for long in a grave but quickly dispose off the body before sunset. Monotheism, like group insurance, is a community religion where you are forced to be free by joining the Common Will; in your personal bondage, therefore, is your social freedom! In India, polytheism has always been an individual belief; an individual is free to follow any or many gods, even deny, reject, misuse or abuse Them; a Hindu can rebel even against God, provided he does not violate His fundamental rule, caste, in which case not only he but his family would be socially ostracised. Casting out of the caste for an individual 'sin' was worse than a private punishment. Even now, in 'honour killing' cases across South Asia, parents agree to the society handing down capital punishment to their children. In his individual freedom is rooted the Hindu's social slavery which itself is rooted in his caste. As a result, he is allowed to defy any or every god but not the society.

For man is, after all, a social animal. No other culture freed the individual to such an extent and tied up social man so fast to the origins. By learning the art of *sheershasana* (standing on the head), India learnt the fine art of turning the world upside down and understanding its functioning from the 'other' side. Few *Indian* Islamic scholars, still following strict caste or clan rules of their forefathers, could ever cross over to the full-blooded Islamism of the Taliban, al-Qaeda or the ISIS variety even as they tried to fit ageing Islam into a youthful Hindu India. Tele-evangelist and proselytiser-preacher Zakir Naik claimed from hundreds of platforms that Muhammed was the Tenth (Kalkin) *avatar* of Lord Vishhu the Hindus are waiting for, and that the *Qur'an* was an updated version of the *Veda*s; few, however, followed him. On the contrary, like his Prophet fleeing Mecca for

Medina, a fleeing Naik found himself 'wanted' by India. Clearly, Islam was not a replacement for Hinduism; or why would low-caste Muslims demand parity with the low-caste Hindus? The *re-Islamising* attempts of Ahl-e-Hadis and some other Wahhabi Sunni organisations prove that their Faith has been unable to keep the Indian Muslims within the Islamic fold. The practice of *sheershasan* enabled a Hindu to see through his enemies better than others.

While in Christianity and Islam, religion was sheltered in a shrine, the Hindu's gods were part of his household, shared his trials and tribulations. Their birth, marriage etc. would be celebrated like festivals and They would even be sacked when the house could not offer them enough space, or He 'failed' to solve the man's personal problems, or replaced when he needed new gods—even in the 21st century, some Hindus 'punish' gods by keeping their idols in water if They fail to bring rains, or cure the ailing son! An 'inadequacy' in his god would, at best, make him acquire another *Hindu* god with similar job profile, rather than adopting an alien God about whom he knew nothing. Contrast this with the Romans (fourth century) and the Meccans (sixth century) adopting in wholesale the gods of the very rebels they were warring against until yesterday when they suddenly discovered that the New God on offer would bring them New Gold. Temples did not really matter to a Hindu where he often went to offer prayers and on pilgrimage; unlike the Jew's, his actual temple was not even in a Book. It was in the corner of his own small house where his several gods vied with each other for space as did members of the host family. No other culture lets you unfold a box, give a quick bath to and worship your godlets and close the box thereafter as if it, too, were a routine after your own bath. Muslim marauders destroyed countless temples across India and erected mosques using their rubble, little realising that the same rubble could again be used to rebuild temples: bricks of an ancient Rama temple at Ayodhya, destroyed in 1526 by Babar, were taken away by Hindu revivalists in 1992 after demolishing a controversial, disused mosque, for this purpose. *The Cup returns to the Clay*, again and again. On a popular plane, the Krishna temples were mainly an urban phenomenon because the Lord was mass-manufactured as a trading community's reaction to the urban Islam; the Shiva temples, on the other hand, were often located in the villages and remote areas where the urban-dweller Christians or Muslims, even their missionaries, could never reach. Thus, while Krishna fought monotheism in the plains of urban India through the *Gita*, Shiva kept polytheism thriving in the hinterland. Shiva, not Krishna, has been the national Soul of Spiritual India: with the 'birthday' of Shiva in spring, winter crops begin to mature while grasslands and forests grow with Krishna's 'birthday' in the monsoon. Both Rama and Krishna, however, have been only reincarnations, specific *project-based* or work-charge recruits, who would lose their powers and disappear like ordinary mortals once their Missions ended; Shiva, on the other hand, is the Great God, Mahadev, whose intercession is sought by both Rama and Arjuna-Krishna during the wars they fought against demons. Clearly, the devout believed, it is Shiva who would deliver even Ayodhya to the Hindus: *Kahe Ayodhya Aas Tumhari. Jaani Sakal Dukh Harhu Hamari* (Ayodhya Looks to You with Hope, O Lord, for Deliverance and Freedom from Sorrows), says Ayodhyadas in the extremely popular *Shiva Chalisa*.

Even amongst the gods, the Hindus instilled nine *rasas* to describe their very human-like moods; the wrath of Shiva in his *Tandav* dance was a warning that the simple underdog, if pushed to the wall and taken for granted, would revolt and bring about apocalyptic changes. But the same angry Shiva would be tamed by an even fiercer goddess Kaali. No Hindu god has ever claimed to be the greatest of all or with round-the-year importance: they all have been seasonal, like fluctuating share prices on the stock market. And all Hindu gods scratch each other's back in a peaceful coexistence and mutual admiration club as no Hindu god ever tried to eliminate another. Those who converted to Christianity and Islam belonged mainly to the Shiva constituency, the underdog segment of the Hindus. Change of season impacted this change of god; but seasons, too, return and so did the gods! Each season flowers a god in India, the way each hour has a *raga*; but the same god must reappear next year the same season, the way the same raga must be sung next morning, the same time. Clearly, the *same* all-weather, 24x7x365 Gods of Christianity and Islam could not click in the Indian market.

Post-Vedic Age, the Hindus evolved a dual strategy: rebirth of man as a 'curse', and reincarnation of god as a blessing. Man's cycle of rebirths was due to his past deeds, Karma. That is, his real worth in the market was reflected in his assets/liabilities/debt-worthiness. God's reincarnation was, however, like an auditor or tax official's periodical review visits to decide rewards or penalties one deserved. He would not terrorise you with a Hell nor kill a golden egg provider like you; He would punish only the individual defaulters, not the whole society of 'infidels'—provided, of course, the suspect is not accused of offending his own parents (caste). Thus, while in monotheism you have a God who balances your joint account only at the time of your collective retirement from life, in one go, in polytheism you have a god visiting you individually and periodically. Monotheists, therefore, enjoyed *this* life to the full and turned more and more materialist in the actual sense—God was after all far away! And, they believed in letting their neighbour do good deeds for them, they both being members of a Brotherhood; after all, their faiths promised them omnibus, collective emancipation not based on conduct but on belief. The polytheist, on the other hand, would always be wary of the sudden visitor—the guest was welcome (*Atithi Devo Bhava*, the Visitor is God), until he did not overstay—and in an attempt to keep the accounts clear, be more and more 'other-worldly'. Karma provided the shell or the safe vault to the tortoise called Hindu to duck into securely to defend himself from external assaults. The Abrahamic Satan was an immortal, fallen angel, to be condemned by God for ever, but the Hindu villains were merely fallen, mortal, even if exalted, human beings who are emancipated the moment they repented and turned debt-worthy again. No other country has had open jails for surrendered dreaded dacoits; a heritage prison in Andhra Pradesh even offers a fee-based prison-experience to tourists! In fact, India has had only confused anti-heroes rather than confirmed villains—and, as a corollary, transient gods and gurus. No other Parliament has accommodated so many criminals amongst 'lawmakers'. This was how Hinduism regularly flushed out its civilisational faeces to remain healthy rather than being forced to periodically take enema to get rid of cultural constipation, represented by Hitlers.

The very denial of human existence and physical man being seen as part of a mere mega-illusion, *Maya*, vaccinated most of the Hindus against catching the 'infection' of monotheism: how can you really convert somebody who believes he doesn't *exist* at all! That is, his faith, and, therefore his gods are non-existent *per se*; since he himself does not really exist, in his world-view, no other humans could exist either: there could, therefore, be no Gentiles, no Dar-ul-Harb, no Christians/Muslims nor Hindus. And, logically, No God. Remove man and you remove the object, God, whose image he is supposed to be in the Mirror of Life. The Hindu, master of his spiritual kingdom having the power to select or reject god(s), denied man because he was unwilling to accept the *kind* of God *who was beyond his control.* For instance, Indira Gandhi, admired as Goddess Durga for killing the demon (Pakistan) to deliver Bangladesh in 1971, would be toppled in 1977 when found uncontrollable; chastened, she returned to power in 1980. The Hindus house *only* those gods they can control, not the other way round. To a contemporary Hindu, election is the social god he controls. No other Parliament has amended its holy cow-like Constitution over a hundred times in 60 years. Pakistan and Bangladesh, sharing the same Indian culture and civilisation, are also churning their politics along similar lines.

The new, post-Jesus challenges, culminating in Islam, called for evolution of *business-like* god-wooing men, One Who could hold and sustain the two panes of balance of trade, *a la* The God of Abraham. It was this desire that made Vaishnavism complicated like tax laws and the predominant public sector sect with commanding heights, especially in North India (and particularly among the influential traders) where Islam invaded the deepest; the South, relatively free of the huge bloodshed the North witnessed in the desert attacks, continued to repose faith in the simplicity of Shiva. With Islam expanding to South Asia in the eighth century, India was, for the first time, facing a newer, stronger enemy that could *impose an uncontrollable God* and crush this chaotic multicultural, polytheistic and pluralist society into a mangled Orwellian Order. To avoid its imminent collapse like that of Rome and Mecca due to Christianity and Islam in the medieval era, or that of the Soviet Union in the 1990s, India now needed to evolve not merely a reaction but *resistance.*

Between the 25th century BC and the seventh century AD, the *nirgun* and *nirakar* (Attributeless and Shapeless) Aryan Brahm gradually refined theo-chemically into a *sagun* and *saakar* (Attributed and Crystallised) Madanmohan (Krishna), as inexorably as the Sun Gods like Shamash of Sumer, Amon-Ra of Egypt, Ashur of Assyria and Marduk of Babylonia collectively evolved into the Moon God of Allah, ie. Muhammed, of Arabia in the long theocratising process. After Muhammed, the Fertile Crescent evolved no one else on a theological-social psychological plane; India, too, evolved none since Krishna and Adi Shankaracharya's advent; both the *Bible* and *Qur'an* are co-terminus with the *Shrimad Bhagwad Gita*. The major difference between the *Qur'an* and the *Gita* is that while the former has a linear time, the latter has a cyclical one: so, you do not know whether God or Allah would create the world again after the Armageddon/ *Qayamat*, but you do know that Vishnu is scheduled to Reappear as the Tenth Reincarnation, Kalki, the Eighth and Ninth being Krishna and The Buddha, respectively, at the end of the 432,000-year-long *Kaliyuga*; after Kalki, the present world would be dissolved and the Universe will begin anew for yet another round…the Cycle goes on, the Cup returns to Clay.

But all this was the stuff for intellectuals as it provided them a Matrix to theorise and lay the foundation of a Faith, understood by only a few. At a more mundane level, comprehensible to the layman, it was the immaculate ritual that gave the Hindu common man the mental framework for making the Brahm brick for his personal use. Hundreds of rituals that formed the larger network served yet another purpose: the 'creativity' of Brahm was deftly shifted to the inanities of these rituals, aiming at making man turn into a mere puppet of Fate and keeping him busy in an as pure and undifferentiated inanity as Brahm itself. All men are born as children; most of them never grow into mental adulthood and pack off as ignorantly as when they were born. Therefore, give them toys to play with, leave them in a wonderland and do not let them feel the terror of spiritual loneliness and vacuum. Give them as many shoulders to weep on as they need. If you do not, they would find themselves in the darkness of ignorance. This might lead them into believing that they were surviving in a *Period of Jahiliah* (Ignorance) and that they should now start living in the Light of Christianity or Islam, as their harassed brothers in the Fertile Crescent did. Since the paths of all these rituals led to One Brahm/Ishwar/Krishna, India was able to re-deliver polytheism from the womb of her own home-spun monotheist-monism, as rituals largely overshadowed the Faith itself, faster than the same process in the Abrahamic world. Krishna, the Designer God, was India's most long-lasting and mouldable clay toy that kept Indians ever-busy and never let them age mentally. The Hindu would marvel at the infinite capacity of Krishna to take shape and size according to situation, unlike the stiff and stern Abrahamic messiahs and their One Gods. As *Ashtavakra*, Krishna/Brahm could even be twisted at eight joints of His body, like the He-Man toys. The Hindus believed that Krishna will surely come to liberate you when the *paap ka ghada* (pitcher of sin) overflows. So, just forget all else. Keep deriving the material from the spiritual and vice-versa. The world is reversible; so wait for the situation to unfold itself, for the new 'Breaking News' to replace the old—like a TV news channel, trivialise the magnificent and magnify the trivial. Did not Krishna assure Arjuna that He would manifest Himself to re-establish Dharma? To the sceptic questioning this pious stuff, the Krishnaite would say that all the increasing evil and privation around you is, in fact, hastening His next coming (the pious Christian would say the same thing about the Second Coming of Jesus Christ!). As a matter of fact, it is He who, as the Creator, is decreeing whatever is happening. So forget about its finer nuances. All you can do is to stick to the ritual. All roads emanate from and lead to Krishna.

Evolution of god is like evolution of the state, in accordance with the Organic Theory. First of all you surrender all your powers to the fancies and fantasies you have yourself created so as to explain why the Universe moves the way it does; this pooling together of all human powers into That One makes the Latter mathematically greater than the sum-total of individual powers; the moment That One is Most Powerful, It starts moving, carries everybody in a particular, unknown direction as a willing slave of 'yours' that constitute 'You'. And That

You is Me, that is *Rta*, the Natural Law. This fatal, deterministic concept totally dwarfed men, their merits and capabilities, and enslaved their spirit to the extent that even in their personal sufferings and atomisation, they began to see a Divine Design: a beggar could now see merit in his 'pre designed' current purposeful profession. Your fate is a reflection of *Rta*, Brahm, Karma...with a Divine Purpose. This nearly killed private initiative for public good. India thus created a Frankenstein to ward off Satan. In this chemotherapy, India survived but lost her creative spirit for centuries together; but she denied pleasure to sadists and masochists. If at all a Hindu wanted a change, it was *he* who must change, not the circumstances; for he is a living being, capable of changing himself, unlike the circumstances which are abstract and incapable of changing by themselves, except due to their own force. The Buddha taught *Atmadeepo Bhava* (Be Your Own Light) and Gandhi said, 'Be the change you want to see in the world'. To scale the height of survival, India abstracted man to the minimum, brought down to the lowest rung from where he could not descend any lower. Now since *Rta* was the highest-placed, those on the upper rungs of society were better placed to 'see' It and know the truth about It, than the man down below on the ladder. The ruler of the day is, therefore, always right in India for he is in a better position and nearer to the Divine Purpose. So, even Nehru's defeat by China in 1962 did not really mean *India* had been defeated; for her, it was a subtle Chinese wake-up call to defeat Pakistan in 1965 and split it in 1971. India evolved a mindset of worshipping her arrogant rulers so much as to drive them to suffocation, as she did to Nehru in the 1960s or his daughter Indira in the 1970s; no other people mastered the art of strangulating their homegrown 'enemy' with a garland of flowers, turning it into a wreath; nowhere else is death so magnetic, musical and fragrant. No revolution is possible in a country having evolved such a robust protective mechanism through blind alleys and booby traps. India has, therefore, seen no real revolution that could really change the social fabric, on the gigantic, civilisational scales witnessed by Egypt, Persia, Babylon, Greece and Rome when they fell easily to the alien monotheistic creeds and lost much of their original national personality to Arab hegemony. Her converts largely remained what they were, converts. No wonder the Arabs continued to derisively dub the Indian and Pakistani Muslims as 'Hindu' or 'Hind' Muslims. India's Christians and Muslims are a peculiar lot: in their respective holy cities abroad, they are still identified as 'Hindus' but back home they continue to remain 'alien'. And although many of them consciously believe in their 'foreign' origins, their subconscious polytheistic roots drag them back to the soil. In *their* caste. In Abrahamic monotheism, God's Purpose was to free man from the clutches of an Absolute and Permanent Evil called Satan. In Indian polytheism, it was the other way round—all Hindu mythological villains or vamps would be *grateful* to their Deliverer for liberating them from the unwanted *yoni* of humanoid. All his sufferings were merely ephemeral like bubbles, an unreal manifestation of the Absolute Self, Maya. In this Absoluteness, there was no Problem of Absolute Evil in India because the Hindus believed in the non-existence of any Absolute Good either. Even gods and their reincarnations worshipped each other: Rama and Ravana would worship the same Shiva before going to war against each other. This unreal war is part of the Real Brahm. Since all is Brahm and I am part of It, how could I even conceive of any pain or pleasure. No Hindu, therefore, ever felt he suffered any moral dilemma; all Hindus suffered the mores of monotheism with equanimity, without even knowing it.

Now, there remained only one adversary that India faced within: the senses. To suppress and neutralise the six senses, the Indians evolved six systems or schools of philosophy, *Shaddarshan*, that kept professional chatterboxes busy splitting hairs and heirs for 3,000 years as real India, at a deeper socio-psychological level remained intact. To keep the ordinary people preoccupied, India developed countless *upayas* or rituals that kept them engaged in inanities and forget their own senses; her political parties now keep their workers similarly busy in similar inanities. The tortoise survived between the upper and lower shields of the shell made of the *Rta* and rituals. For monotheism it was the *God of Nature* that was important while in polytheism it was the *Nature of God* that took precedence. Monotheism discovered the cause of man's suffering *outside* his physical existence, ie. Satan, and used religion as a cure, while polytheism noticed that Satan was actually *inside* man himself and he needed to be quarantined against it. Prevention being better than cure and erring in haste worse than repenting at leisure, India learnt to fortify herself through fortitude and subtlety.

Ramanujacharya believed that one's Karma in the past lives compounded to entangle man in *avidya* (nescience) due to which the world was saturated with suffering and pain. Karma, being a huge loan recorded in a past ledger, cannot be waived off as a bad debt but *avidya*, the interest on this loan, can be paid for in small instalments to reduce the burden; once you have paid interest, your nescience is eliminated and you begin to see the same, rescheduled World Bank loan as blissful, even bountiful, as Pakistan does now. One begins to believe that he must change his perception, instead of hoping that someone else would do it for him. In other words, the seer taught that man should travel within himself to embalm his suffering soul and find solace, instead of depending upon or joining 'others', ie. converting to monotheism. That is, guard yourself against community religions by imploding within yourself. If monotheism believed its Faith is right, proclaim that you are personally wrong.

Belief in god hard-wires diverse people into one continuum. Monotheism provided connectivity to and basically appealed to the 'developing' minds which increasingly got complicated with the rise of the First Wave, primarily due to the slow change in food habits from carnivorous to vegetarianism, necessitating change in biochemical compositions, metabolic processes, hormonal re-balancing, mutations and genetic changes. It was one step up from what was the relic of man's past as an animal, a herd-mind. Polytheism appealed to those already ahead in evolution of the brain; it demonstrated the freedom of human spirit, although some people tended to shift from monotheism to polytheism and vice-versa, alternately, to rejuvenate, reinvent and revitalise; changes in environment and availability of food also dictated this choice.

Monotheism taught that the only human goal could be a one-way, one time unconditional merger with God; India made it recurrent, conditional and two-way for most of the people. Monotheism recognised transportation of man, virtually in flesh-and-blood, to join God at the end of the Mission; Hinduism separated wheat from chaff, man from Atma, and recognised wheat's capacity to be grown again and again; there was no monotheistic mission for India. The seers called this shapeless effigy Atma, soul, which, like *aqua regia*, dissolves all metallic human problems, and is indestructible: saying that this Atma eventually merges with Brahm or Paramatma meant that human problems can end only in death. Conversely, life is full of problems and one must accept this fact; the biggest problem is not man but God, the Almighty being a vast conglomeration of problems, the Primeval Motion. Chaos. Entropy. Practically, the Hindus propelled God to zenith, and jackbooted empirical man to nadir: this distanced him from Him so much that neither could really affect each other. Indians have saved themselves because they distanced God.

The fuel of the monotheistic engine was ***sin***, beginning with the Original Sin, and the Mission of God and His marksmen was to cleanse human beings of their sins. It was this mission that transported monotheism from one culture to another, like aerial pollination; monotheism succeeded primarily in societies at a lower rung of psychological evolution or ripened civilisations seeking rejuvenation through catalysts. But, given human tendency, most monotheists claimed to be sinless, and that infidels were sinners. In polytheism, however, the central theme was ***guilt*** and this was drilled deeper and deeper in the Indian psyche. India's guilt was a reaction to the Abrahamic sin: so, Indian villains were merely guilty, unlike Abrahamic Satan, the Indestructible and Inveterate Sinner. Guilt can be corrected, being an individual characteristic, but sin, a community trait, cannot be cleansed except by allowing it to accumulate until the Last Day; this sin is like a payment cycle on a credit card loan you would continue to pay even after you pay up *in toto*! No, not that the Hindus did not believe in sin; the three biggest sins for them were *straying* from (1) sexual sanctity (incest), (2) duty towards society (Dharma) and (3) human responsibility and continuity towards the chain of wombs (caste). The Hindus conditioned themselves to correct their guilt in a thousand ways; now since a guilt can be corrected, like sentence for a crime, there was nothing like blasphemy in Hinduism. No sin, no blasphemy: even gods were not beyond reproach! Hindus alone could punish and change their gods with seasons or at will; most other non-Hindus found their gods emerging as Voldemort, like Hitler, Mussolini or Stalin. One of the basic weaknesses of monotheism was that its God wore so lily-white clothes that the slightest spot would be visible; hence the concept of blasphemy. Contrary to an evolving selfish and monopolist God of monotheism, the eternal polytheist god was highly tolerant, wore colourful clothes and was not worried about—in fact He was even willing to repent—the man's curses to Him, since He, too, despite being the Prime Mover, was only a part of the Great Monist Machine called *Rta*: the only difference between a Hindu and his god was that the latter was a notch above on the ladder of evolution, and more evolved than his disciple. The Hindus had surpassed and outgrown even God until the Fertile Crescent forced them to retract a little in this psychological evolution; for them a god was no better than the politician-in-power at the time. And since the whole material world is moving simultaneously towards the same Goal, that is the merger of all Atmas with Brahm, everything is as holy as everything else, and working as part of the Great Design: for the pre-monotheism Hindu, therefore, a pebble was as divine as the Himalayas, faeces as important as food, the basic constituent of them both being the same. Whether you will it or not, you are inexorably drawn towards the Goal and get sucked into it eventually; you may, if you have higher ambitions or lower spirits, accelerate the process, cut the route short and merge with Him if you believe that is your liberation from the yoke of life. The monotheist God gives man a mission and retires him after he believes he has achieved it; monotheism sees man as the most evolved, perfect and the last, being—that is why all monotheists denounce Charles Darwin!—beyond which there is only God, the Divine One, Who blows a whistle if He doesn't want to see you win. Polytheism does not give you a mission and just asks you to keep moving, evolving along the way; the reason why some Hindu gods, for instance, have multiple arms or animal heads was that the faithful conceived them that way to distinguish them from lesser mortals: more evolved beings should have something other and more than what ordinary men and women have, an integration of physical animal and human characteristics, for instance. It deprives God of

His perceived infallible superiority and divinity and places Him only a few rungs above the human beings on the ladder of evolution: He is merely a little more evolved anthropomorphic form, in whose image man arrived, and is holding his hand, helping him climb by virtue of His being on a higher rung. He is like a venture capitalist or angel investor Who hand-holds a start-up like *Homo sapiens* to turn them into evolutionary entrepreneur; and like private equity, God must make good His Exit after reaching an investment horizon. All normal human activity is, therefore, aimed at the same Goal and when you see someone engaged in abnormal or special activity, like religiosity, it only means that the man is in a hurry and wishes to climb up—to the Cliff! And what is that Goal, up there on the ladder? Merger with the Brahm. What is Brahm? Pure Consciousness! How can I sense or achieve this? You cannot because it is beyond all senses.

It is your origins—nature, *guna*, caste, race—that determines your destination and compels and propels you into a peculiar manner. Your guna—*sattava, rajas or tamas*—is your duty for which you were born in the first place, your destination in Life, the justification for a division of labour based on your birth and inherited attributes. That is how Nature would propel a Buddha or Gandhi to do what they did.

This was the Krishnaite determinism, vis-à-vis the monotheistic certainty: Krishna transformed individual, self-imposed duty, Karma, into specified and cubicled work and each man and woman into little wheels predestined to rotate, even against their wishes, in the Great Machine: since you cannot fight this Machine, join in willingly and be a part of this Whole so as to enjoy being in the Being. Remain in the world as a lotus would in mud. This was India's feminine determinism, vis-à-vis the emerging masculine determinism of the Roman Catholic Church bracing for the Crusades, and the Islamic storm gathering at the Indus. India has survived with the fanatical tenacity and granite determination of a woman out to shield her children from advancing enemies; she waited for her turn until her enemies spent themselves. India bided her time till Christianity and Islam fought each other off *in this part of the world.*

And slowly pulled them both, globally, at a lower rung than ever before, the way *Mundakopanishad* taught:

'All those glad in ignorance, Think like a child: "Yeah, we have achieved our Goal!" Since doers of such deeds fail to understand Due to their passion, Therefore, when their world exhausts and collapses, Without achieving the Goal, They would sink down deep miserably Believing merit and sacrifice to be the greatest thing. Even now, they do not know any better (than they did earlier), For, they continue to be deluded. Having enjoyed on top of a perceived Heaven They felt until now they had won due to their good deeds, They re-introduce themselves to this world, *At a rung lower than ever before*. (MU: 1:1:7-10).'

Since zeroes cannot sum up into numbers, even the *Kathopnishad* had warned: How can one achieve the Permanent by resorting to purely temporary action? And the *Chhandogya Upanishad*, too, was aware of the flux the world will always be in due to the very temporary nature of motion and matter: As the world of those who acquire it by work would perish, so would, too, the work of those who acquire it by merit. For, matter-and-merit, motion-and-work are inseparable from each other

In monotheism, you are responsible for your own individual deeds and the fruits accrue to you alone; but in polytheism if you do not perform your enjoined social duty, you face the risk of your forefathers or progeny suffering for this omission on your part, in which case you must find cure in a *Narayan Nagbali* or *Kaalsarp Shanti* ritual. Monotheism offered a collective goal achievable through collective efforts while polytheism stressed on an individual goal (merger with Brahm) through individual, caste-enjoined, duty. Krishna, whose multiple attributes had fully evolved over 2,000 years, by the seventh century was now like an all-season overcoat. He consummated this polytheistic, individual goal in his *Karmayoga*, in actions aimed at actionlessness, while maintaining the social order within the caste-chaos. Until Krishna (when monotheism moving towards India was a largely peaceful, pre-monsoon drizzle), her culture evolved introvert response or socially-enjoined duty to resist the proselytising

Christianity; it did so by stressing on sacrifices (including study of the *Vedas* and *Upanishads*, alms-giving), austerity and psychologically binding man to his guru. However, some five centuries later, with the torrential Sandstorm of Islam lashing Indian culture like a full-scale monsoon, the response became extrovert with Krishna exhorting Arjuna to wage a 'righteous war' against self-righteous invaders, shed his kin's blood (as did the aliens) for *material and spiritual* well-being. Having achieved this end, you can go back to your origins—that was why the Pandavas eventually embraced sannyas even after winning in the *Mahabharata* War.

This was a ***new*** element in Indian thought as, until Adi Shankara's *Gita*, most scriptures would shun the material at the altar of the spiritual which, too, was merely a hoax. Krishna, like many Indians now, was *Jugadu* (Great Improviser); he re-assembled and recycled the available stuff on as vast a scale as was required to ward off the industrious Islam from assaulting the Indian mind. The *Qur'an,* meaning *Recital,* proclaimed birth of Knowledge in the nursery of Arabia; the *Gita*, *Divine Song*, made Karma more important and, despite proclaiming anthropo-monotheism (*Yada, Yada….*), Krishna did not stress on His being the *Last* Avatar, unlike Muhammed's proclamation of being the Last Prophet. Krishna did not make the Pandavas blue-blood of polytheism, nor did He create a One Book-One Church fixation. His aim was merely to bring the Indian psyche out of the barracks of the *Vedas* and *Upanishads* and deploy it to weather the Islamic thunderbolt: while the *Vedas* and *Upanishads* shielded India from the Testaments, the *Brahmasootra* and the *Gita* were her protective psychological caves vis-à-vis the *Qur'an.* In the monotheistic missions, the 'holy warrior' would target the 'infidel', acquire a killing spirit, and whenever this war-germ launched a new cycle, he would wage war against his own community, as the Christians saw during the Crusades and the Inquisition and the Muslim world sees now. Eventually a Jew, Albert Einstein, would provide monotheists their ultimate weapon for mass destruction in the atom bomb; it revived the 2,500-year-old unfinished, Biblical agenda of destroying Baghdad, heir of Babylon, and has logically dragged the Fertile Crescent to the scorched earth policy of Islamic State of Iraq and Syria (ISIS) and its even more ferocious successors-yet-to-arrive. Polytheism had no such unfinished agenda; it was more concerned with self-preservation from the onslaughts of monotheism on the prowl.

The sixth to eighth century period between King Harsha's and Adi Shankaracharya was challenging. While the Harsha era saw revivification of the Hindu 'religion' and, as a reaction thereof, reloading of Buddhism and Jainism as well to some extent in the North, the ancient Arab traders were no longer bringing just money for the spices they bought in the Malabar region, but also Islam, thanks to the generosity of some Hindu rulers. For the first time, India saw her pilgrims going ***out*** of Bharatvarsha, westward, as these neo-Muslims (and neo-Christians) went outside the subcontinent on *pilgrimage* to their new spiritual abode. This was like cultural diabetes in which a people would be unable to retain their sugar in body, although both Christianity and Islam also proved to be great catalysts, integrators-connectors and game-changers in India. Clearly, India experimenting with a new lifestyle had progressed, but also become diabetic! The Christian and Muslim pilgrimage abroad later encouraged the Hindus, too, to cross the oceans. This 'brain drain' slowly reversed in the 21st century as 'brain gain'. For instance, a section of the Indian Diaspora, forced by the license-permit Raj of the Nehruvian economy to migrate abroad, catalysed changes back home in the 1990s, paving the way for reforms; at the same time, the Diaspora acted as a pressure group and changed the attitude of their adopted countries towards India. Many among the Non-Resident Indians (NRIs) became an advance Indian 'army' in the countries of their current residence.

But this was not so then.

In the sixth century, India was plagued with political decentralisation and fissiparous, even deculturisation tendencies. Even before Muhammad could win Mecca, the world's first mosque outside Arabia, Cheraman Juma Masjid, was built in 629 in Thrissur district of Kerala. Barely four years after the Prophet's death (632), the Arabs launched their first small, exploratory expedition in India at Thane, near Mumbai, in 636, during Caliph Omar's era and the second from the land route in 644 in Western Sindh, via Makran, during

Caliph Usman's reign but without much success. For the next half a century, they were more busy plotting to kill the Prophet's grandsons and penetrating Africa and then Europe up to Spain, even as they struggled with their own Caliphal succession problems and saw their monotheistic Faith bifurcate into two, wondering they had One God, One Book and One Messenger but now two groups of the Faithful, Sunni and Shia. But they never forgot India. Clearly, India was waiting for the Islamic storm. And Mecca would not disappoint Mathura.

By 711, a Lankan king, freshly Islamised, was sending gifts to the Caliph but these were looted by dacoits in Sindh. Its weak King Dahir Sain of the Chhachh dynasty was unable to arrest these dacoits and compensate for the loot, as demanded by Muslims. This invited the Muslim attack, led by the 17-year-old Muhammad bin-Qasim. After his stunning victories at Deol, Nirun, Ravar and Multan, he was about to march on Kannauj, the Harsha capital, when political conspiracies claimed his life: his body was taken to Baghdad not in a coffin but in a cow-hide.

India had to protect her Cows: the *Upanishads*. Until now, the Upanishads were not holy cows but merely *Shrutis*, or Listened, something that would spark logical thinking process in the Hindu mind: *Sa Vidya Ya Vimuktaye*, or, the best education is one that liberates your mind. Thus far, the Hindu devout would endlessly debate the *Upanishads*; but debates were no solution to the crisis unleashed by axiomatic Abrahamic monotheism where debate, Reason, was seen as the third enemy of God, Satan and the infidel being the first two. The Hindu tradition of collecting facts to deduce faith—as in the worship of Five Elements—was no longer practical. Abrahamism was a mirage of the Crescent and a matching illusion was the call of the day. The proselytising, deterministic monotheistic creeds of Christianity and Islam, after the destruction of Zoroastrianism in Iran (which, being virtually non-proselytising, had so far been shielding India) had now posed an entirely new challenge and called for entirely new responses. To match the *Bible* and the *Qur'an*, both trans-Indus alien *Smritis*, India now needed an equally powerful *Smriti*, something the Hindus could remember, imbibe and follow without questioning or debate, which, at the same time, gave them inner strength against Abrahamism without affecting their native ethos of polytheism. Something that could keep them intoxicated, entranced, as long as the *Bible* and the *Qur'an* kept their followers spellbound.

In other words, there was an urgent need of a *designer* Book—did not, after all, the Biblical God *foresee* His Adversary destroying Him by writing a Book and Muhammed doing exactly that! Why should not India, too, write a similar Book? Adi Shankaracharya's *Bhagwad Gita* emerged on the scene as the Script culled from the Scriptures. The Adi Shankaracharya-reinvented Krishna was designed as the Milkman milching the ancient Cows for a modern dairy, as in Amul, through a cooperative of all Indian scripture. The *Gita* is a *Smriti*, worth memorising; for, if Shruti leads to logic, memory protects the seeds of change and circumstances offer challenge that make the seed sprout as opportunity. Change, after all, is the biggest challenge of Life and India's only constant. If the *Qur'an* made Muhammed unquestionable, the *Gita* made Madanmohan Krishna, unsurpassable. It was India's attempt to keep Islam at an arm's length. So, with such opportunist, alien enemies lurking around and weakling kinglets at home, what with the fossilising caste system and innumerable aliens from Central Asia also making India their home and flooding Hinduism with their own wares at the cost of Aryanism, desperation drove India to re-invent the *Gita* in the eighth century as a psychological fortress for Hinduism. A similar desperation, post-9/11, drove some of the South Asian Muslims to become 'liberal' and 'secular' in the 21st century, at least until the American pressure eased. Such was the mental math in the eighth century also. India's wisdom in restricted logic and her faith in unrestricted illiteracy shielded her from machinations of questionable 'friends' and unquestionable enemies. Educated Hinduism survived due to vast levels of illiteracy in the masses that were essentially compost for the evolution of India.

In order to make the Hindu Book unquestionably acceptable, it was incorporated into the Sixth Book of the *Mahabharata* in a backward integration, as a part of this already expanding *socio-political* Epic of War, to give it a spiritual flesh. The *Gita* was not incorporated into the moralistic *Ramayana* whose limited central theme, Kshatriya valour and piety versus Brahminical arrogance and decadence, ruled out such a possibility, especially when a Kshatriya Lord, Rama, was already its Hero. The *Ramayana* itself was created to fill the vast chasms caused by the casteless Buddhist and Jain sects, which themselves were the Hindu responses to the *Old Testament*—Valmiki, deriving his name from termites, was a tribal bandit who, reformed, penned the *Ramayana* to extol the Kshatriya virtues vis-à-vis the Brahminical guilt of Ravana, and while incorporating himself as a Hindu, the saint performed a forward integration of the natives into the Aryan fold; an *Uttar Ramayana* (Post-*Ramayana*!) was also evolved subsequently, this time by the Brahmins, as an attempt to deny the popular Rama some of his sheen, portray Him as an ordinary man questioning the virtues of His virtuous wife, seeing his own sons defeating his army, and drowning like an ordinary man in a rivulet in the backyard of his Ayodhya palace although the same Superman had conquered the ocean in the South. Even now, a section of the Brahmins views Rama as a Brahmin-killer, Ravana being a Brahmin. But, a majority of Brahmins also favoured Rama. With the last popular version of the Epic, the *Ramcharitmanas*, penned by a Brahmin, Goswami Tulsidas, a contemporary of Akbar, the North Indian Hindu society, which bore the Islamic assault to the maximum, came to be fully psychologically controlled by the Brahmins through the Muslim era.

But the *Ramayana* was essentially an epic of love, not war: even Ravana had abducted Sita not because of his hatred of Rama but because he loved his sister, Shoorpanakha, whose humiliation by Rama's brother, Laxman, the Lankan King could not stomach. But those were the times of social turbulence in which the Kshatriyas were ruling the roost, even in spiritual affairs. The Muhammedan centuries, however, necessitated not Kshatriya piety or valour but Brahminical learning and diplomacy. In the backdrop of an Abrahamic warfare, in which her next-door Aryan cousin, Iran, had surrendered to Islam, India needed to launch a low-intensity psychological offensive against her enemy. So far, India did not have even an all-encompassing, Omnipotent, Omniscient, Compassionate, Merciful God—the simple Rama, himself fighting to regain his lost wife was found worshipping Shiva to derive strength against Ravana, the way

India looked abroad for weapons to fight Pakistan. India needed a real Hero who could protect polytheism, a Hero who could perform truly heroic deeds, still remaining uninvolved and unscathed, beyond reproach or debate—a god who would *not fight himself* but manage a *political* war using spiritual weapons and holy warriors, as *did the Abrahamic God.* Something to match the Abrahamic Lord, *thy* God, and still not losing Indianness. Something that did not challenge, at a later date, the prevalent Aryanhood in the North and Dravidhood in the South nor changed the dual civilisational complexion of the subcontinent. Someone who appeared as warlordish as Yahveh but sang like the Prophet. Someone who performed all three roles of hero, comedian and villain Himself in the great epic. Someone who was God, Messenger and Prophet all rolled into one—all things to all for all times to come, *a la* Abrahamism.

In short, a *Designer God, the Ultimate Hero.*

This Hero came with Islam expanding to its last geographical posts in the Caliphal war, to Spain in the West and India in the East, both in the year 711. The *Shrimad Bhagwad Gita* (The Song of the Lord), or the *Gita* in short, was, apparently, 'synthesised' by Adi Shankaracharya to fulfil all these requirements of a designer hero; not that he actually 'created' it but, like an expert, enthusiastic cook, he prepared the recipe from the existing ingredients available in the Indian spiritual kitchen, which came down to him in a thousand years, like the government reports put together by faceless bureaucrats. Adi Shankaracharya, as had always been the Indian tradition, was a nameless Ved Vyas (Editor of the *Vedas*, ie. Scriptures), who would not lend his own name to what he edited, but only to the commentaries that he himself wrote. After thus apparently giving final shape to the *Gita*, in 703 Verses, he also wrote a commentary on the Book, this time under his name. *His* is the oldest commentary on the *Gita*, because the Book, in its present form, itself did not exist before him—he wrote the key to the puzzles, like modern maths teachers writing books as well as the keys to exercises. Did he have knowledge of Abrahamic monotheism before he wrote what he did? To some extent, because the logic he had mastered—that was why he could defeat the Varanasi Brahmins, led by Mandan Misra, immersed in inanities, superstition and obscurantism—made him conclude about the possible emerging scenario, about the theodesics emerging from the Cheraman mosque, and made him fortify the Idea that *was* India. This is how we discover a surreptitiously emerging nuclear power nation by watching its acquisition of centrifuges for nuclear enrichment, and take measures against such a 'rogue' country. Cultural responses being organic in nature, Adi Shankaracharya emerged as the best representative India could produce in his age. India treated most of her rulers with contempt and would rather turn to her gurus to solve existential puzzles. The *Gita* was like the government-sponsored National Anti-Poliomyelitis Campaign. He replaced metaphysics with theology and chatter-boxes with grave-looking saints-on-ramp parade who could, like the Jewish Judges, threaten the Hindus into submission: apart from the Four principal Seats of theo-thermal powerhouses, he also set up seven *Akhara*s or Holy Squads of God—somewhat like the Christian Hospitalers and Templers during the Crusades—whose order of pecking, camping and marching at the Kumbh Melas remains unchanged to this day: these squads, who sunk deep roots in rural India, were among the faceless forces in areas unpatrolled by and behind the ouster of the British, in 1857 and 1947.

When the first Hindu missionary, Shankar, the Adi Shankaracharya, (788-820), left Kerala for spiritual immunisation of Hinduism, ostensibly from an atheist, home-grown Buddhism but actually from alien Christianity and Islam, he apparently knew his objective: evolving a minefield full of booby-traps, a line of spiritual fortresses, a la Siegfried and Maginot in Europe, to protect the culturally-united pre-nation from an advancing monotheism, by using a monolithic hero who would not demand civilisational changes at a later date (ie. after finishing the task) as a recompense. In other words, someone who did the job without demanding a change in the Brahminical societal structure; that is, the Yadavs, by virtue of being the clan of Krishna, should not challenge Brahminical 'superiority', or disturb the Manuist society as a compensation for their Leader giving the *Gita* to the Hindus. Remember, the Hashimite 'superiority' among the Muslims had been established forever merely because Muhammed belonged to the Quraish tribe and the Hashim clan. Krishna allowed His Yadavs to destroy themselves in a fratricidal war after the *Mahabharata* War and the clan, ever since identified with internecine war against itself like the Afghan tribes, never rose to power except since the 1990s. In fact, the Yadavs acted first as an insulator between the *dwij* (twice-born, high-caste) Hindus and the *adwij*s (low-caste, non-Aryan Hinduised people) before turning against the latter in their quest for power. But the eighth century was different—and Adi Shankaracharya would have known that conversion to an alien faith was akin to deserting the Mother (synonymous with motherland) for many of the Hindus, although the Hindus' as a 'nation', in modern political sense, did not exist then. A 'Hindu' worshipping an alien god and going abroad for pilgrimage, could not be trusted, although a few of them, as traders, did travel abroad.

In north India, those crossing the seas were seen as *mlechchha*, impure, and must be shunned, or at least 'purified'; precisely for this reason, even Gandhi, when he went to England and South Africa in the late 19th century, was seen as an outcast by some in his clan. The traditional Hindu traders or the imperial arms of the South dealing with trans-oceanic trade or reign were, however, not included in this category; in any case, they did not go abroad for *pilgrimage*. Not that the Hindus did not have gods of water: Varun was the god of ocean and rains; Vishnu, CEO of the Hindu pantheon, had His Abode on the Kshirsagar, Ocean of Milk; Rama had crossed the Palk Strait to reach Lanka and the sage Agastya had 'swallowed' an entire ocean. And, of course, the southern kingdoms were busy creating a cultural 'Greater India' in South-East Asia. From 'Aryavarta' Who all were, therefore, crossing the oceans now who should be banned? Clearly, anyone crossing the seas for *spiritual* purposes was impure. In India of the times, particularly in the South, only the Hindus converting to Christianity or Islam fitted this category. And the Christian and Muslims, ruling here and there, knew that the word *mlechchha* was actually applicable to the converts in their ranks, but they could do scarcely anything to rub off this designation: they did not, perhaps, know that the word *mlechchha* virtually meant an untrustworthy, even 'traitor', to the Hindu Dharma, the way the word *Yavan* (Greek) meant an alien and, more recently, the word *Gora*, meant a Westerner. The North Indians did not have an ocean to think on these lines; but the Kerala saint had known about the Christians and the early Muslims crossing the Arabian Sea for pilgrimage. A ban on crossing the seas followed for the pious Hindus in general; they were now expected to take bath in the holy Indian rivers, collect water from one to mix it with others; keep the holy waters at home for rites from birth to death; collect water from the Gangotri in the Himalayas and take it to Rameshwaram in the South for ablution and rites; in order that the Dravids and the Aryans assimilated further, the 12 *jyotirlingas* were set up by the Shaivite followers of the saint across India; four main Shankaracharya Seats were also set up, three of them being at sea shores—which later swelled to 44.

Already, Christianity, in particular its Syrian Orthodox sect, was well established on the Kerala shores, and Islam, too, had entered there alongside westerly trade winds. Armed with this first-hand experience, the Malayali Brahmin energy burst upon the lazy North India which was still bracing itself to face the Islamic twister; the *Gita* was essentially a psychological disaster-management plan. Islam had spread to Spain and the Sindh Province, both in the year 711; by the time Adi Shankaracharya was born in the year 788, these two alien 'religions' were already eying India. And this time around, unlike in the past, this would not be a one-way absorption of immigrants *into* India; this invasion was like a gradual suction *of* India by the Middle East through the Indus straw. What Adi Shankaracharya, it seems, aimed at, therefore, was to create a thought-system that could withstand the monotheistic onslaught on Indian polytheism. He could as well have chosen Shiva as his Hero of the *Gita*; after all, he was a Shaivite. But Shiva was essentially a South Indian Hero; in the north, He was mainly a rural folk god whose temples dotted the countryside, a proto-god Rudra-relic from the pre-Aryan times. Moreover, a stern but simple, monogamous, unidimensional and pious Shiva was no match to the monotheistic foxes knocking at Indian doors. Only an urban and urbane, complicated, polygamous, diplomatic and practical Generalissimo like Krishna could have been the answer to the alien invaders. Like a South Indian filmmaker investing in Mumbai, Adi Shankaracharya, apparently, redesigned and repackaged Krishna Dwaipayana, the spiritual fount of the Central Asian Yadav immigrants settled in Central India (who were Hinduised, as a separate satellite clan and caste, but were not among the four Varnas) as his Hero of the *Gita*'s script. He culled and compiled the Book from the existing *Upanishads* and the Six Systems of Philosophy (*Shad Darshans*), besides the Bhagwat sect and different other sources to make Krishna a Central Asian Hero of a film based on Aryan script and Dravidian finance. Until then, people knew all that the Adi Shankaracharya wanted to say but, being polytheistic and liberal, would not put much faith in it; after all, the *Upanishads* etc. had dialogues but no heroes. By making Krishna a larger-than-life Hero, the Kerala genius packaged the script of the Book attractively, selected the best literary theatre, the *Mahabharata*, ensured that these ancient dialogues now found not only a Super Hero but also the people's Faith because the Song came directly, *this time*, from the Hero Himself. Thus was born India's own Supreme Lord, Sri Krishna, and the greatest Book, the *Gita*. There was no playback singing as in Abrahamism wherein the 'prophets' sang for and on behalf of the Lord; Krishna himself was a great flautist.

By the eighth century, the Aryans in the North and the Dravidians in the South had been past their respective Golden Ages and learnt to coexist in their domains, ending their civilisational competition at least at the level of polytheistic belief, if not as much at racial level of sharing food or inter-marriage. By making someone like Krishna his Hero, who was neither an Aryan nor a Dravidian in the strict sense of the terms, Adi Shankaracharya may have ensured that this civilisational balance between the Aryans and Dravids was not disturbed at a later date when the Gita and Krishna would finish their role of rolling back monotheism. Catalysts always come from outside to rejuvenate and control a halted process. Like Krishna, Muhammed, possibly of a Kurd descent, had also emerged as a *Messenger* to the fiercely tribal Arabs and as a Prophet to others

The *Mahabharata* is a curious narration of the struggle between Life and Death, for the existence of the Sperm and the Egg, to prevent

India's slip from the status of the Homo sapiens to a lower rung: the polygamous Krishna and the celibate Bheeshma fight-to-the-finish via mind-games and physical prowess, respectively, through their pawns, and the hermaphrodite hero, Arjuna, using the mind of Krishna and the shoulder of a eunuch Shikhandi, kills off the Grand Sire. Krishna is more of a Designer than Moral God evolved to meet the exigencies of the times; He does not exactly propound the *Sanatan Dharma* but the *Yug Dharma* or the *Aapad Dharma*, the 'what-to-do-in-an-emergency' plan, the rules for survival in times of a Crisis.

It was due to this peculiar psychological evolution that the Aryan Rama and the Dravidian Shiva became the moral High Gods in North and South India, respectively; Krishna turned out like a special purpose vehicle (SPV), a weapon to defend this social order. That was probably why the present Hindu orthodoxy did not launch any popular movement for the 'liberation' of the Krishna birth-shrine in Mathura (where the Lord was 'born' in a prison), as they did in the case of the restoration of the Somnath Temple of Shiva in the 1950s or Rama's shrine in Ayodhya in 1992. Even the Yadavs, supposedly the Krishnite clan, did not launch any movement to regain 'their' Lord's birthplace! If anything, the post-1990s Yadav leadership became 'defenders' of the very people (Muslims) against whom the *Gita* had apparently been conceived; but, by 'defending' the Muslims, they also kept open the channels for their reconversion to Hinduism! Not only this, the Yadavs slowly emerged as the neo-Brahmins, on the top of India's emerging *Third Civilisation*, who, thanks to the 'demographic dividend', are now collectively known as the 'Other Backward Classes (OBCs)'. Like the Germans and the Turks extracting the price as palace guards for protecting the Papacy and the Caliphate, the Yadavs also took advantage of their and the other non-*dwij* numbers in North India. That was, perhaps, why Krishna would rather have His Yadav clansmen destroy each other. The Yadavs are example of how India is sponging the remnants of Christianity, Islam and Communism simply by supporting them to the hilt. This Third Civilisation, unlike the Aryans and the Dravidians who largely remained confined to the North and South, is a nation-wide civilisation. The *Gita* is all things to all Hindus, but Krishna is nobody to anybody, except to the Vaishnavites, that too in the devotional 'Bhakti' form, not in His warrior gear any more.

The *Gita*, in its various avatars, was incorporated later into *Bhagwat Puran*, besides other scripture, including those of a hundred other sects with their own commentaries. Nowhere would Adi Shankaracharya mention the real enemy; he would merely sketch out and drop broad hints about the *concepts*, the *ideology* of Abrahamic cults his Book was written to fight against, to quarantine the Hindu mind against; so, unless the reader is well conversant with the evolution of religions in the Fertile Crescent and their continual, communal ideology, s/he would not be able to grasp the hidden meanings of the Verses in the *Gita* and, self-hypnotised, would merely meander in the wonderful 'philosophical maze' of this Book. No other nation had ever seen an evolving popular revolution and resistance movement shape up as 'religion'—had Akbar known it, he would not have, perhaps, celebrated *Janmashtami*, the birthday of Lord Krishna, to prove his 'secular' credentials, earning the mullahs' wrath in return. All the Kerala saint did was to give thumbnail sketches of the enemy phalanx, leaving the dots to be joined by those who could; he gave the Hindus the basics to absorb the perils of Abrahamism in their psyche and carry their societal defence mechanism to their collective mind. Defence was never so secretive, yet so widespread, so timeless.

Since Buddhism and Jainism were past their prime by the seventh century, unable to create a task force or a crack team for the looming Abrahamic crisis, Krishna was a logical and obvious evolution. He offers you competitive knowledge, *a la* Muhammed. But Islam came mounted on the horse of action, armed with the Sword in one hand and Word in another. How would India resist this flood of imported, aggressive, invading, globalising culture? How would she protect her domestic, cottage cultures? Of course by protective, progressive taxation, as a country would levy customs duty on dumped imports to protect her domestic industry. But who would dare take on the world in this hostile, cut-throat competitive world: the Lord Himself, as in *Yada, Yada*...(*The Gita. IV:7,8*). Krishna essentially instils in the Aryan devout the fear of recurring doomsdays, of apocalypses and His arrival to save him each time if he remains Faithful, a la Jesus and

Muhammed who, however, reserved for the Abrahamites one-time doomsday. The *New Testament*'s *Book of Revelation* triggered large-scale psychological upheavals among Christians at the turn of every millennium, Crusades against Muslims after 1000 AD, against the Jews after 1500 AD, against themselves after 2000 AD. In one go, Krishna also negates the Islamic belief in Muhammed being the Last Prophet of the world and assures the devout that He would continue to manifest Himself, time and again, until eternity. This gave India a recurring, renewable source of hope, unlike Islam in which the only and the last source of hope lay anchored in the far away past of the sixth century. But who were those Krishna was assuring so assiduously: Go to the *Gita*, IV:11-13. So, if you are unhappy in your adopted religion, it is because of your mode of worship and if you want to return, reconvert to *My* fold; the options are open for you. And you could return to the caste you originally belonged to, before you or your forefathers converted to the alien faiths, for all castes are My Own Creations and I created you the way you are because of the *guna* (predominant attribute, quality, or genetic specification) and Karma (work, action, level of knowledge, intelligence quotient) you were born with for the *first time* in this universe in whatever life-form. Thus, in just three above Verses, Krishna packs India's struggle against monotheism for 2,000 years: He leaves scope for conversion of the socially down-rung classes to Christianity and Islam, while still letting them adhere to the root Indian culture of polytheism, as an Aryan-Abrahamic hybrid, as a protective shield against rough weather, only to pull them back into the *Gita*-fold at a later date. Krishna also left enough space for a Jinnah, born as a non-practicing Indo-Islamic Khwazaite/Ismaeli and brought up in Victorian jurisprudence, to proclaim divorce of Islam from India, simply because he did not take even his own liberal Shia faith seriously while creating an inexorably fundamentalist Sunni 'state'; his sole aim was to cobble together a theocratic state, papering over the vast cultural chasms. The Lord left scope for a Gandhi, too, born non-practising into a Vaishnavite sect and brought up at the Bar in London, to organise the creation of a 'Ramrajya' (Domain of Lord Rama), a *nirguna* Hindu state, as we would see later.

The miracle of the *Gita* lay in the fact that it created a society in which the most religious and henotheistic people who believed in Krishna as the Supreme Lord, resisted monotheism and the most irreligious people—Jinnah, Gandhi—who were never known to be practising religious persons, would inexorably help create states of the semi-fundamentalist, pseudo-monotheistic variety. In the midst of all this slow, chaotic, snake-and-ladder-on-a-chess game—like Krishna calmly sermonising Arjuna with 700-odd verses right in the middle of a tense battlefield, bringing Order while standing at the centre of a Chaos as Time stood still—the Lord would declare that He was merely the author of this caste roller-coaster, not the doer, and was Changeless, *Achyut*. That is, like a magician keeping you spell-bound until the show lasted and then saying all that he produced out of his hat was merely Maya, and walks away. Indeed, the *Gita* was meant to last only as long as Christianity and Islam existed on the Indian subcontinent; to the masses with lower levels of psychological evolution, it was a marvellous book for all seasons. Faith kills logic; it would, therefore, mesmerise anyone who absorbed it the way the devout Christians or Muslims did with their Holy Books.

Contrary to the monotheistic stress on greed and procurement (ie. destroy if you cannot grab), Krishna, Himself the greatest reveller, laid emphasis on renunciation. While monotheism stressed interested action for the desired fruits, Krishna would have us believe (G:18.2) that sainthood, in the Krishnaite scheme of things, comprised a person working selflessly without expecting any award or reward in this or that world. But Arjuna does not know, until the first verse of the *Gita*'s eighth chapter, what exactly is a Karma, to which the Lord replies (G.VII:3), like the most ancient Jewish belief and tradition, that: The 'Imperishable is the Supreme Brahm. Its dwelling in each individual body is called *Adhyatma*; the offering in sacrifice which causes the genesis and support of beings, is called Karma'. The early Jews believed that through their 'burnt offerings' (the Aryans called it *yajna*) they could propitiate God to Create. In a *yajna*, therefore, the Hindus would sacrifice their material possessions so as to propitiate Him to procreate and create more: it was a little investment in the hope of a fabulous dividend. Fire, representing the

Aryan's Sun and being the 'purest' of all Elements, was considered the gateway to and fro god; sacrifices made into holy fire cyber-reached god and returned anew to the sacrificer. Thus, while the earliest principal *Upanishads* tried to wean the people away from the superstitious rituals aimed at the set goals, the *Gita* gave the movement a theoretical framework; but the later *Upanishads* and the *Gita*'s stress on one's caste-enjoined duties kept alive all the rituals that they once sought to bury.

Nature's irony is that it makes a fiery Sun's warmth melt a glacier into water at one place and heats water up in the oceans into clouds to rain back again as snow at another place. No scripture, not even the *Gita*, has succeeded in eliminating the basic and base instincts of the Eternal Tribal in India; even Adi Shankaracharya, who largely shaped the Hindu Mind since the advent of Islam, could not exactly decide whether the wise and the saints should engage themselves in rituals aimed at goals, in selfish action. India has fought with herself for 2,000 years on this issue: what may be individually selfless, could turn out to be communally selfish, ie. harmful to those outside. In this case, it would emerge that the duty you performed for the welfare of *your* people may have harmed other people, thus violating the symmetry of Brahm. Whatever you do or cause to do would violate Brahm and whatever you do not or cause to do not would *still* violate Brahm! Jainism taught India to totally abandon action; the *Gita* taught India to totally engage in action, *minus* fruits.

What is Karma? It is the Aryan Hindu's equivalent of the Jewish Covenant with God. The Jew would be born into the tribe of the circumcised; his prepuce would determine his ultimate identity, give him a 'passport' in this world and a 'visa' to the next; he would touch his testes in testimony as supreme belief in Creation—in medieval Europe, the Jews identified each other by swearing on their testes, hence the words *testimony, testament.* The Indian Aryan, on the other hand, would be born into a particular, virtually unchangeable caste, his ultimate identity; his birth in this particular caste had 'divine' sanction owing to his previous lives' statement of account; he would not shake a single hand with anybody but fold both the hands to demonstrate that he was not ready to surrender to or align with the aliens and would rather round upon himself like the benzene ring. Since the Jews were among the first refugees in an evolving geopolitical world of the First and Second Waves, migrated from one place to another time and again, their prime concern was *not* Jerusalem or Israel but preservation of their 12 tribes and Judaism. The prime concern of the Hindu Aryans, including the RSS, too, has *not* been India but the Hindu, their caste and habitat, Bharat, *swades.* In both the cases, a people displaced from their native cold or hot deserts, respectively, were harassed by their environmental and geopolitical circumstances and their peculiar dilemma, vis-à-vis other settled people having their own land and religion sprouting from culture, forced them to claim their *final* home from a vulnerable people; the late-coming Jews vociferously proclaimed the Cannanite land as their own, the Promised Land, even inventing scriptural support to protect it. Monotheism of the Jews was born out of this dilemma as was the Hindu's particular way of life, as a response to the Jews'. No wonder that similar circumstances and predicaments forced the Jews and Hindus into mutual admiration and friendship—during their Diaspora in 70 nations, the Jews could live peacefully only with the Hindus, the rank polytheists against whom, given half-a-chance, Judaism would have announced holy war! Circumstances forced the Jews and the Hindus to sit in the same boat despite theological split, to evolve unbreakable, diamond-hard religions, unlike other softer religions evolved by settled peoples, sure of their homeland.

Unlike others, the Hindus had evolved their 'religions' on two levels: intellectual level for the minority, the Gyankaandis, and popular level for the majority, the Karmakaandis. It was because of the fact that not all humans, due to their differential levels of psychological evolution, are as capable of absorbing nuances of beliefs and faiths. Even the same individual can demonstrate a lop-sided evolution; in the 21st century world, many scientists and technocrats fanatically believe in their inherited religions while apparently illiterate, tech-challenged people show amazingly liberal mind.

The manual called *Gita*, extolling survival, was meant for the minority Gyankaandi social leadership while the Epics, *Ramayana* and *Mahabharata*, were meant for consumption of the Karmakaandi majority—the former would subtly mould and control the latter by simply giving them switches to shut thinking process. The *Ramayana* was popular as a moralistic epic, but was also a documentary on the progress of Aryanism in the Indian subcontinent, the near-total replacement of the Harappan culture by an expanding Aryan one, the establishment of the new Aryan ethics and its adsorption by the pre-Aryan Dravidians, Nagas and others, in which process got weakened the classical Brahminism of the *Veda*s and *Upanishad*s, as demonstrated by the Kshatriya Rama killing the Brahmin Ravana. It also depicted the expansion of classical Brahminism, which had journeyed from the Caucasus via Afghanistan, from the Indian shores, up to Lanka in this case. This passage to India was the ultimate geographical limit of Aryanism in the subcontinent. It was due to this cultural connect that Sri Lanka invited the Indian Peace-Keeping Force (IPKF) in the 1990s to tame the native Liberation Tigers of Tamil Eelam (LTTE); but India also returned the way Rama, who got Vibhishan coronated, would not capture Lanka. India has never sought territorial expansion beyond the three seas and the Himalayas, not certainly by force; her *cultural* borders are largely confined, and have therefore survived, between the triangular landmass situated between the Himalayas, the Bay of Bengal, the Arabian Sea and the Indian Ocean.

In the *Ramayana*, the Lord does not proclaim any new principles—the Kshtriya Rama, who belonged to the Sun clan *Raghuvansh*, in fact, adheres to the old values and ethics—and, barring a couple of incidents (the killing of Baali, the banishment of his wife Sita), stresses on ideals of life and purity of means to achieve ends.He harbours no grudge even against the arch enemy, Ravana, whom he kills and *then* directs younger brother Laxman to learn the nuances of politics from the dying 'demon' king; for, traditionally, the Brahmins have been the political mind of India. After all, Rama, being the Indian response to the *Old Testament*, was modelled to meet the Biblical demands: the way Moses 'parted' the Red Sea, Rama, although he could, would not part the sea (the Palk Strait) to cross over into Lanka; the Lord would *request* the sea to do so, then prepare to dry it up but finally settle for a bridge on it. Somewhat like Jesus, Rama proclaimed an ideal, life as it should be, the mirage you would run after from cradle to grave. But Nature would not let you rest on your laurels even if you were a reincarnation like Rama. So, *because* He killed a Brahmin, Ravana, the Lord continues to be despised even now by a section of the Brahmins. Also, Rama had to suffer separation from wife and sons, following a curse from the Lankan Queen Mandodari after he killed Ravana and his son Meghnad. Rama, who had crossed the Palk Strait, died of *drowning* in the small rivulet, Sarayu, right behind his palace in Ayodhya! Similarly, Krishna lost all his *avatar* powers once the *Mahabharata* War concluded; the Lord who conducted the Great War to the Pandava victory, *died* of an ordinary tribal hunter's arrow. Clearly, the utilitarian Hindus do not spare even their SPV gods once their task is achieved.

The epic *Mahabharata* was something few North Indian Hindus would like to have in their houses; for, they believe, keeping a copy at home means inviting 'fratricidal war'. Instead, they would have the *Gita* and take oath on it in the courts. The epic was scripted like a real-life, unending drama in which the Song of the Lord was incorporated later like a unique selling proposition (USP), as some Indian producers add a song or two, sometimes even after releasing their Bollywood films. The biggest epic in the world, which expanded from just 6,000 verses of *Jai* (Victory) to more than a hundred thousand of what came to be known as the *Mahabharata* (Greater India) due to the massive psychological rivers flowing and glaciers merging in the Indian Mind, stressed the real life, the way Life is, in both noble and ignoble aspects; refrain from being parochial or emotional in matters of your mythology which is your collective response vis-à-vis the collective others. The moment you generalise Life, it turns special and vice-versa. Everywhere you encounter your enemies. From within, sex attempts to overtake your responsibilities and duties, like Shantanu falling victim to his desire to marry Satyavati, a mermaid: it was an accidental, retrogressive journey of Organic Life as a full mammal was marrying an amphibian half-fish, and, in the process, depriving his full-mammal son, Devvrata (Bheeshma) of his right to the throne, to progress of Life, to evolution. It was a mutation. The dutiful son, however, not only agrees to continue this human drama but, in fact, gives a fillip to it by releasing a long rope to and protecting the throne of his half-brothers and their siblings as the family's patriarch, as he had given word to his mermaid step-mother. As the drama unfolds further, colours of a rainbow life appear: the warriors wear distinctly coloured clothes—Bheeshma wears all white, Shakuni, the evil gambler, black—and the sons of Pandu, the Yellow King, take centre-stage. The Pandavas apparently depicted the yellow race, the originally atheist and morally-guided Central Asians (the Mongoloids, Shakas, Huns, Kushans and the Chinese were the most recent migrants to India who merged their respective gods in the Aryan pantheon and became Hindus by virtue of being new rulers of the day in this region or that and, with the energy of neophyte Rajputs, who later became defenders of polytheism; all these Central Asian ethnic groups, despite being enrolled under the overall Hindu architecture, protected their pre-Hindu traditions such as female infanticide, on-the-spot clannish decisions, etc). These Central Asians, later led by Genghis Khan, almost crushed Islam and half of Christianity but, *because of this familial affinity*, did not harm India, their closest and softest target. China would have perhaps died had she embraced monotheism, the way the accursed Yellow King, Pandu, died the moment he had sex with his second wife, Madri. Nature corrects this diversion of Life and puts it back on the rails of evolution in a slow, comprehensive, diabolical, manner. Such are the twists and turns of Life that even the elder Pandava, Yudhishthira, 'one who is calm even in a war', was forced to lie at least once,to his guru, the Brahmin Dronacharya, who trusted no one but his disciple and got, therefore, killed.

Since the *Mahabharata* came on the scene *after* the *Ramayana*, a Kshatriya Yudhishthira manipulating the killing of his Brahmin guru was of little significance. Bheem, fount of enormous energy, unleashed a gigantic force that annihilated his cousin and arch villain, Duryodhana, whose only weakness was his fig-leaf-covered genitalia and who was hiding in a reservoir. Arjuna, the third Pandava brother, the left-hand (Savyasachi) shooter hermaphrodite and recipient of the Song of the Lord's message, had an arch enemy in his own alter ego (eldest brother), Karna, 'born of the ear', ie. recital or constant pounding of ear making you mistakenly believe all your life something you are not. Karna was *not* son of a charioteer, but even after knowing his identity, he chose to fight against his brothers; he was the King of Anga (Assam), still longing for his 'lost' brothers, the wheel of whose righteous vehicle gets stuck up in the Earth and he gets emancipation only in death at the hands of Arjun, the way Pakistan was 'relieved' of Dhaka by India. The remaining two Pandava brothers, Nakul and Sahdev, are keepers of stables, for the sprint of Indian horses should match those of the enemies, who number a hundred brothers and a thousand allies. After the Great War, the victorious Pandavas would not reign in Delhi; instead, they would find liberation in the Himalayas.

The Pandavas, like Jesus, were believed to have been born of asexual, immaculate conception but waged a Muhammedan war. The *Mahabharata* was the saga and intense struggle, of how Life survives in the midst of a hostile ecosystem of Death, of how the tongue firmly kept in position outlasts the 32 teeth of opposition the Confucian way. The epic shows how the Aryans survived the apparent Abrahamism of the blind Emperor, Dhritarashtra (literally, 'one who believes *only* in a nation of his own offspring', *a la* Abraham, Father of Many Nations), a direct humanoid descendent of a retrogressively *converted* Shantanu and a 'progressive' and ambitious mermaid Satyavati, 'One who proclaims the *Truth*', ie. the lineage of monotheism (Christianity, and later Islam, both proclaiming Truth, with a capital T), the feminine Christianity, which had washed ashore like a mermaid when St Thomas was said to have landed in South India around 70 AD when the Romans were replacing the Jewish Temple in Jerusalem with that of Jupiter. Satyavati, also like the British coming through the East India Company washing ashore in the year 1600, later sought the Throne for her own progeny, and extracted the promise from her step-son, Bheeshma to protect the Throne till the end of Time. This was the last straw that broke the camel's back: Krishna had to come forward to teach Bheeshma a lesson and put the biological evolution back on rails after this short, retrogressive mutation; so did Gandhi in the 20th century by making phased retreat of Islam possible in 1947. In the epic, Krishna emerged as a blend of both Allah and Muhammed, God *and* Messenger. One can still come across some Brahmins in Central and Western India who piously believe that the Kauravas surviving the *Mahabharata* War escaped to become the Quraish of Arabia and returned to reclaim India as Muslims!

On the other hand, Christianity's attempts to convert India largely failed apparently because Satyavati, being a mermaid, conceived only sub-humans, despite her marriage with Shantanu: the Pandavas, being produced immaculately like Jesus, as well as the slain Kauravas, had to abdicate the throne despite winning the war—the way the British, despite their victory in the World War II, would be forced to quit India in 1947. Satyavati's ovum was that of a fish and could not have mutated overnight by a mammal sperm. It is the evolutionary stage of your ovum that determines your seed, the sperm being basically a stimulant and changer.

With Krishna, the downfall of classical Brahminism was accelerated-due-to-gravity as the intermediate castes of the fertile Yadav-led OBCs, who were essentially the cattle-breeders of Central Asia and Hinduised for being rulers in many of the little fiefs swarming across Western and North India post the Gupta-period, now emerged on the scene. They multiplied like contemporary Scandinavian, Germanic and Central Asian tribes flooding Europe and numerically overtaking the erstwhile ruling classes of Brahmins, Kshatriyas, Vaishyas and even the so-called Shudras, thus changing India's very demographic complexion. Krishna was a Yadav and, for the first time, the Brahmins were divested of their claims to all knowledge and Kshatriyas their claims to all armour. There was also another change: the early Aryan gods—including Brahma, Vishnu and Mahesh—did not belong to any caste but the Vishnu incarnations of Rama (Kshatriya) and Krishna (Yadav) did; with an 'Aryanised' Krishna, Nature apparently fielded the Central Asian atheistic mind face-to-face with the monotheist West Asian Abrahamic mind. Krishna's career in public life began with his rural struggle against urban monopolistic business represented by his maternal uncle, the demonised King Kansa of Mathura, who forced the villagers to pool all the milk they produced in the WTO-like royal kitty; milk, being produce of the holy cow, always remained the benchmark of Indian prosperity.

After killing Kansa and performing a hundred miracles before and after this incident, Krishna himself emerged as the supreme monopolist of the highest variety—demonstrating how a cruel Nature forces you to practice just the opposite of what you preach. As the 'Lord' Krishna eventually milches all the milk of the Cows (the *Upanishads*) into his own royal kitty (the *Gita*), although earlier he used to protest and smash the pots of milk his kin and villagers were taking to Kansa.

He delivers the Sermon on the Battlefield to Arjuna, vis-à-vis the Sermons on the Mount (at Mount Sinai by God to the Jews via Moses, on a hill by Jesus to his disciples and on Mount Hira by Allah to the Muslims via Jibril, Gabriel, via Muhammed), as if inviting, even forcing, the Archer to join a truly wordy duel on home turf. Having achieved the highest aim of making the *Gita* a howitzer gun to climb the two Mounts, Krishna, *the Lord* undergoes a retrogressive metamorphosis, watches the curtains falling on the whole human drama as Nature mops up the debris, the destruction of His own Yadav clan (who, however, survived even Krishna and His 'prediction'!), and died. Earlier, Rama, the superhuman, too, had died of drowning. India has been merciless to Her Gods as well!

Post-*Mahabharata*, even the mighty Arjuna, the strong arm of Krishna, Himself the strong arm of the Hindus against the alien foes, was unable to protect the Lord's 16,000-odd war widows taken by Him as 'wives' and was eventually defeated by ordinary tribal marksmen of Central India. The gambler-villain of *Mahabharata*, Shakuni, was the King of Gandhar, now in Afghanistan; many of the real enemies of India—from Mehmood Ghaznavi to Ahmed Shah Abdali to the Taliban, came from this Land of the Horses. Abdali's capital, Kandahar, smashed the Kargil pride of the 'Hindu' government in 1999 by forcing it to release three dreaded Islamic terrorists in return for 155 hostages of an airliner. No word or sword has ever been permanently strong; they all get rusted, even if they are made of chromium-laden stainless steel and come directly from God.

After waging the futile, fratricidal war, the Pandavas, now disgusted with the enormous blood-bath and ruling the haunting ghost capital of Hastinapur, abdicate the throne. Even Krishna and the *Gita* fail to console them (as the *Ishopanishad* taught them, perhaps, they were more distraught after the Lord's Sermon and the war *than ever before*!). They move to the Himalayan hills in search of the Real, which, clearly, the Song of the Lord did not represent or provide. Yudhishthira, the Dharmaraja (one who rules by the Law of Righteousness), is the eventual winner of the *Mahabharata*, not the warrior Arjuna through whom the Hindus received the Divine Message. India has always cloaked the Real from the Strong, the latter being merely the shield of the former. If Rama is the head of India, Krishna is the helmet to protect it. If Rama is an Aryan Kshatriya, Krishna came as an Aryanised Central Asian, the pre-Mongoloid, who defended *Bharatiyata* (India-esque) from monotheism by using the latter's own weapons.

In the 21st century, with the temporarily Arabised Indian Muslims now returning to their pre-Islamic Hindu roots, the Aryanised Yadavs, too, are being gradually elbowed out of mainstream classical Hinduism, by both the high and low priests of the social firmament. And with them the *Gita* itself; if anything, the appeal of *Gita* is weakening in its resolve as do the twice-born Aryans, and the Yadavs sought to control India's politics, in recent decades at the head of the Third Indian Civilisation comprising the rainbow of OBCs. Would the empowerment of the Yadavs *et al* further strengthen the hold of the *Gita*? Not really: the Yadavs flaunt Krishna as their own, but not seriously. They did not even launch any movement to liberate the Krishna Janmabhoomi Temple in Mathura, part of which was annexed by the Muslims and where an Idgah (Prayer Ground) now stands; secondly, a majority of the emerging Third Civilisation does not exactly believe in the basic Karma-centric teachings of the *Gita* (like sticking to your own caste, doing your own enjoined duty etc) and are continuously moving up the social ladder through empowerment. With the Dalits and 'lower castes', now outnumbering the Aryan *dwij*, the demographic dividend is favouring the pre-Aryan native population—and they could replace the hold of the *Gita* (The Book has already been much misused, as in the taking of oath in the courts). Even within the Third Civilisation, the Yadavs' role is getting minimised. Having performed their historical role of defending polytheism from monotheism, the Yadavs could eventually retire, like the Brahmins, from medieval Hinduism. This is somewhat the way Russia deStalinised itself by first purging the Georgian communist mafia of Josef Stalin—which had, in fact, defended the USSR from Hitler and Roosevelt!—in the Khrushchev era; this was followed by decline of the Communist Party's state, as a prerequisite to the folding up of the *Das Capital* and Marx also. Man is truly a Nature's creature: selfish and cruel, generous and emotional now and then, for he is a utilitarian and, in the end, a survivalist on the ladder of Evolution.

Krishna was the lone God in India to have been allowed flexible morals and mores—even now, wayward youths in North India often complain when caught by the police: *Krishna kare toh Leela; hum karen toh chhindrai!* (What Krishna did by annoying women was a divine drama, but what we do is eve-teasing!). All His actions, personal and social, were made part of His prophetic mission on earth, as was so assiduously believed by Christianity and Islam also in respect of Jesus and Muhammed. It is a common trait in all varieties of monotheism that all actions of the 'prophet' carry a missionary zeal, even a special purpose, to be followed by His disciples in words and deeds, without raising any questions about time, space or context of such actions. This led to the creation of vast schizophrenic societies, at war with each other, because they found their minds stuck in a time-warp and hearts in a space-bend. Indeed, Krishna was the only figure in Indian mythology to have been born with a clear messianic mission: *Whenever there is a decline of righteousness and rise of unrighteousness, O Bharata (Arjuna), then I send forth (incarnate) Myself* (*The Gita*, IV:7). He did not as much identify—except if we take the mythological Kauravas—the real enemy He was supposed to fight against. But He hinted that one's actions should be such as to protect his *race* from being polluted by others. Since the Kauravas and Pandavas belonged to the same race and family, clearly they could not be the real enemies in the *Gita*: they are only a smokescreen, dusted and brought forward from the original epic *Jai*, expanded and embellished in the *Mahabharata,* and used for the *Gita*'s real purpose to defend the race from the aliens *trying to convert India rather than be converted in India.*

India had, by the sixth century AD, been quite 'urbanised'. The polytheistic rural cult of Shiva was unable to meet the challenges thrown by the urban monotheism coming from across the Indus; the more India was urbanised, the more the simple Shiva cult was pushed towards the villages and the complicated, urbane and sophisticated Krishna cult emerged important in North India. With the *Om Jai Jagdeesh Harey*...the Shiva *aarti* penned by Shraddha Ram Phillauri in 1872, came the patently unHindu, Abrahamic, congregational monotheistic lines: *Vishay vikar mitao, paap haro deva*...(O' Lord, liberate us of our sexual desire and eliminate the evils of sex which are a sin!). Until Christianity claimed it as the Original Sin, the Hindus had a healthy approach towards it, as depicted in the temples of Khajuraho and Konark, and later popularised by Osho Rajneesh, that sex is only an external medium to attain Moksha (Liberation of the Soul). This was the influence Christianity still left on the Hindu mind. Similarly, the most long-lasting influence of Islam on the Hindus was the inclusion of the Moon as a 'cool star' in astrology, thus trying to change the very astral belief system of the Hindu mindset. The Hindus never regarded sex as a taboo until the arrival of Christianity; even polygamy, and in some areas polyandry, were socially acceptable and concubinage and prostitution were as important as civic drainage system. Christian influence made sex in India an obsession, until Rajneesh tried to free India of this virus. Jainism forbade sex, too; but here was a Jain saint who propagated free sex, virtually as an ideology but actually as a means to supersede it for higher aims, and became the biggest deChristianiser of the Hindu mind, one who dragged and propelled the surging Hindus on an aggressive superhighway, something they had never done before. Predictably, the Christians expelled him from America, 'the Land of a Free People'. Two others who freed India from her self-locked cage of poverty were a Gujarati, Dhirubhai Ambani, who demolished the Nehruvian socialist license-quota-permit Raj in the 1980s, and a Sikh migrant economist from Pakistani Punjab, Manmohan Singh, in the 1990s.

The spiritual space a declining Shiva cult had left in its wake was filled by the urban Krishna cult, rooted way back in the sixth century

BC in Krishna Dwaipayan, a rural deity of cattle-breeders; a thousand years later, in the sixth-seventh century AD, the Lord was reinvented and re-embellished by the *Gita* and the newcomer Yadavs, which served India well to fold back monotheistic carpets as they now had their own brand of homespun monotheism, and claimed to be the People of the Book. Thus, at a time when the Iberian Peninsula had picked sword to deIslamise itself, the Indian Peninsula re-invented and perfected a Word, the *Gita*, to roll back the alien ideology by waging a long-drawn-out psychological war against advancing monotheism. Since each city evolved its own brand of Krishna cult, and the *Gita* unified them all, the Cult and the Lord became multi-faceted; a thousand stories were woven in a hundred myths of Krishna as the Cult became, more and more, a federal and qualified monotheism like the 1950 Indian Constitution; eventually, the Krishna Cult, the crystallised form of Vaishnavism, ended up as the religion of the rich, and, as in Jainism, traders and businessmen flocked to it in large numbers because of the cult's carnival culture wherein every sensual pleasure was permitted if clothed in spiritualism, and its rituals became costlier with the passage of time.

Thus, the Hindus evolved a compensatory, conditional and strategic monotheism to stall the march of Abrahamism without much compromising with their inherent polytheism. The Krishna Cult allowed polygamy and many urban rich emulated the polygamous Lord, the way the Muslims emulated a polygamous Muhammed. Things had taken a curious turn in India: the simple forest-and-mountain-dwelling, monogamous Shiva of the Dravidian villages of South India had spread to villages of Aryan North India; the Krishna Cult of the Aryan towns found roots in the Dravidian hinterland in what became the assimilating focus of the two civilisations. Shiva prevented monotheism from intruding the Indian village while Krishna became the alimentary canal to digest monotheism. Together, Rama, Shiva and Krishna gradually became the head, body and sheath of the Hindu Turtle. With the Bhakti Movement in medieval Muslim era, the Krishna Cult got a further fillip as the religion of those rich Hindus *not converting* to Islam. During the British era began India's economic pauperisation as well as deAbrahamisation. Most of the pre-British invaders had looted urban India but they eventually settled down in the colony; the wealth largely remained in the country, even during the Muslim rule, and was recycled due to socio-political fluctuations. The British took away its wealth to England. With this flight of capital began pauperisation of urban India as well. The British piously believed, as did the Muslims before them, that they were converting India to their faith but, in doing so, they unwittingly caught polytheistic infection and weakened the world-wide-web of monotheism. Even the early Muslim invaders could not pauperise India much because they took away the looted wealth only on some camels and horses, unlike the British who did so on their ships. Also, since monotheism is essentially a trader's javelin, the poor could not sustain the rich Krishna Cult which began to take flight abroad in the form of different proselytising sects; the process intensified after India's Independence in 1947 and is still continuing.

In the sixth century India, mythology was pseudo-biology: the Theory of Incarnations included not only humankind and the animal and plant kingdoms but also gods and godlets as simple men wondered how Life would have evolved. Indeed, a biologically and progressively evolving Vishnu would incarnate Himself to eliminate devils of the day, as a *Matsya* (Fish, depicting that life originated in the marine water), *Koorma* (tortoise, amphibious, movement of life towards the drying land), *Varah* (mud-covered boar), *Narsimha* (half-lion, half-human), *Vaman* (half-grown man) *Parashuram* (fully-grown human with killer animal instincts still intact), *Rama* (fully humanised, but threatened with loss of self-control), *Krishna* (fully blossomed and humanised but threatened and powerless before the Eternal Tribal, ie. basic human nature), *Balram* (physically strong hulk), *The Buddha* (psychologically strong and emancipated sage) and the yet-to-come *Kalki* (combination of ultimate physical and mental strengths, the Superman).

As the eighth century unfolded, the booby traps of Malabar and Mathura awaited fresh arrivals from Mecca and Medina.

Guests

IN the pre-Muslim era, the *dwij* (twice-born) Aryans—the Brahmins and the Kshtriyas, later some Vaishyas, too—had opened Ashram-schools only for their own children; to some extent, they allowed semi-literacy to the Vaishyas and, barring exceptions, mostly denied it to their women as well as the so-called 'Shudras', enrolled by the pre-Buddha Aryans as their 'casteless' serfs, later incorporated as separate, lower castes in the Aryavarta. The early Aryan peers, still structuring their immigrant population's settlement plans, suspected their own women and the Shudras as being 'fickle-minded', ones who rarely went into larger issues like the *society's survival.* Survival of humans was different from that of animals in that the former's vital energies did not travel just one way between the mouth and genitalia; higher psychological development made humans think of *others*, too. Thus, in the Aryan worldview, most women and the Shudras, with their herd mentality, could be vulnerable to conversion to alien faiths through allurement. Not that those Indian Aryans were male chauvinists. They did respect intelligent and scholarly women—Gargi and Maitreyi, for instance, were greatly revered—and they made Saraswati the Goddess of Learning, and honoured learned men from the 'lower castes', like Valmiki, and later Ravidas, Kabir etc. But these were exceptions and also the limits of human nature, that reckless literacy to the undeserving people actually imperilled the society the way filthy riches degenerated the people. With the rigorous implementation of the Manu Code, literacy was further controlled after the first century AD. They treated 'knowledge' like we do with nuclear secrets which must not reach the undeserving 'rogue' people indiscriminately lest they misuse it; in modern times, educational institutions screen their intake through merit-based competitive entrance examinations because of the same reason. Apartheid has, in the larger context, always been obnoxious. But it has a silver lining, too: without enlightenment and democratic credentials being in place, indiscriminate 'equality' on this count produces rattle snakes like nuclear-armed Pakistan and North Korea.

These fears were borne of the vulnerable Shudra's easy conversion first to 'casteless' Jainism and Buddhism or hedonist heterodox sects and later to the imported alien cults like Christianity and Islam that threatened the Aryan worldview and lifestyle. The route to conversion had begun to take shape as early as the sixth century BC; although Jainism and Buddhism were seen as locally-produced godless competitors of the Brahminical Varna and later caste system—the way Communism would be a godless rival to the three Abrahamic ideologies, globally, from the 1850s to the 1980s—they inoculated the Aryans against future alien incursions and were eventually almost reabsorbed into the Hindu fold in the next 1,000 years. It was understandable because, howsoever benevolent the rulers might be, a country would always have some aggrieved souls, the catalysts, to churn the placid waters of the rulers' easy livelihood and luxury. Many amongst the Shudras and the Dravidians, the earlier settlers, still saw themselves as natives and the Aryans as 'outsiders', and, given a chance, were vulnerable to outside allurements on the basis of my enemy's-enemy-my friend dictum. It was not a question of 'patriotism' but the struggle for existence between the old and the new immigrants. Raja Jaichand and Mir Jafar represented this pack of 'traitors' in different settings and ages who wanted to settle local scores with alien reinforcements. With the advent of the British, a number of Hindu and Muslim rulers aligned with each other *and* the British in a free-for-all to settle personal scores that had nothing to do with their subjects who remained what they had always been: subjects. In the North, the Shudras were among the first to convert to indigenous rebel faiths like Buddhism and Jainism; in the South, the anti-Brahmin initiatives took the lead in conversion and later in political expressions, as in the Dravidian political parties. Sectional or wholesale population transfers from time to time and local rivalries led to change in demographies and international theo-couplings. This process continued all through Indian history and caused drifts in the Hindu civilisation. In a systolic and diastolic movement, in which one group of extra-fertile people demographically dominated the others, the Indus River inhabitants constituted the First Civilisation after the First Wave of agriculture peaked in the subcontinent. The Dravidians in the South and the Aryans in the North constituted the Second, a twin and composite, Civilisation; in the 21st century, we are witnessing emergence of the Third Civilisation, led by the non-Aryan, non-Dravidian Dalits, in the post-Mandal phase that began in the 1990s. This could be followed by the Fourth in which the Indian Muslims and Christians returning to the Dalit-led Hinduism could hold sway and share power with the Third.

The Aryans believed that education was a two-edged sword which could not be indiscriminately airdropped like food packets on the people stranded on the various islands of illiteracy, or they would kill each other in a stampede. They knew that different people evolved differently and remained at different levels of evolution like plants in a garden, had different worldviews, needs and limits of understanding, ambitions and emotions, ethics and morals, that, unlike cattle, they could not all be painted with the same brush or colour nor cut to the same size. The Aryans never believed in cultivating bonsai and gave freedom to all saplings to grow—until this freedom became a license against others, in which case an *avatar* would coerce-correct the wrongs. So, they were selective in imparting education. From today's criteria, one could denounce the Aryans as hegemonic; it was, and continues to be, the morality of each age and discrimination in one form or another has always existed the way racial discrimination has always existed. Heterogeneous' and democratic countries like India and America are forced to politically correct themselves from time to time by conceiving a B R Ambedkar or a Donald Trump, howsoever one may agree or disagree with them—'homogenous' countries like China do not have to go through this sham to hide their racism, as in Tibet. Despite the First Wave triggering complexities of human mind as a consequence of slow shift from flesh to food-grain, many in the masses in any country and culture remained automatons due to haphazard development of their brain, vulnerable to incitement and violence, though in a declining order; packing them with information not commensurate with their levels of enlightenment and mental development would only lead to lopsided development of the society, threatening it with the likes of 9/11 carried out by Arab youths trying to relive their forefathers' sixth century Islamist mindset in the 21st century modernity. The Aryans clearly distinguished between literacy, often inculcated at home, and education, offered in the disciplined environs of an ashram.

The Aryans were, therefore, selective in the spread of education and would not share their wisdom with the 'undeserving' people: the gurus kept even the kings under a tight leash and treated the princes at par with other students to make them level-headed. Only after teaching them to endure physical and mental labour would they begin to impart education. For 12 long years, the student would remain in the Ashram, the open school in Nature, and not allowed to meet even his parents; this inculcated in him a dispassionate responsibility towards the society, community service, and made him keep distance from emotional attachments or judgements. In other words, the Aryans' education believed in creating a batch of educated and conscientious societal rulers, rather than semi-educated 'professionals' manufactured in the assembly-line of a management or business school, or in an army academy. Lack of education would, at the most, make many people suffer the social mores and superstition. It would kill the person but save the society from invading and unwelcome 'knowledge' being thrust down the throat. This ultra-selective policy kept a large chunk of the society away from education—but that is how the India of 711 survived for 1947. Only after 1990 have the 'low-caste' Hindus and women really begun to find their voice in India, through the Mandal Commission recommendations and later the Women's Reservation Bill in Parliament, opposed by lawless lawmakers suffering from mental dysfunction.

Continuous suffering, generation to generation, had killed the spirit of these women and low-caste people, barring exceptions, as they were taught to enslave themselves in the world woven by the *Rta, Brahm*, *Karma*, *avidya*, *Maya* and rebirth...By keeping much of India illiterate, the Brahmins let the world outside crush itself under the weight of its own 'knowledge'. It is better to be illiterate and learn, wade slowly through a cesspool and let things fall in place theodesically, than undergo a crash course in monotheism, find oneself unable to cope, fast-track to obscurantism and mediocrity, and arrive at a Hitler to manage death through the asphyxiation called ignorance. In her *pranayam* and *shavasan*, India had learnt the art of breath-control and feigning death.

The armies use sandbags and junk on the forward front to duck behind and slowdown the enemy's intrusion. For the Aryans, the Indus River was this forward front and those settled between the Indus and the Ganges-Yamuna *Doab,* India's Mesopotamia, comprised the cultural war zone where this military strategy became necessary; it was *here* that the Aryans were the strongest and, as a corollary, those opposed to their worldview were the weakest and, therefore, vulnerable to the intruding belief systems. The maximum number of illiterates were also in this very zone and here the Hindus had to fight their fiercest battles for survival against Islam, in which the losers, eventually, retreated to become Pakistan and the winners Hindustan. All ruling establishments, since times immemorial, have used the masses as a fodder to realise the dreams of the classes. It is the masses that become compost to fuel the evolution of the classes. The Aryans were no exception. As an intricate, although largely unconscious, defence strategy against intruders' attempts or cultural desert ingress threatening to change the Aryan worldview and lifestyle, India, therefore, did not ignore the 'importance' of illiteracy and ignorance and used these the way Nature uses nitrogen in fixing a balance. It was not as much a question of reformist social engineering, political correctness, public welfare or affirmative action as whether who deserved what and whether it should be given in the large interest of the society's survival.

The Nature-loving Aryans followed Nitrogen Cycle that runs the Caravan of Life on our planet: the colourless, smell-less nitrogen is 'fixed' by Nature, in the beans of *Leguminosae* family of peas and beans, to maintain the Earth's fecundity through a cyclical journey; this protein-giving gas, like illiteracy, occupies three-fourths of the atmosphere. Each society has its own nitrogen cycle, illiteracy levels and Forrest Gumps and Mr Beans as 'role-models'—they are job guarantees to comedians and journalists. Plants cannot grow without shedding their today's foliage which, in turn, fertilises their tomorrows. Each nation retains its illiterates and nincompoops the way our bowels retain a certain minimum amount of faeces to maintain the balance of bodily fluids, in what may appear a cruel comparison. But it is a fact of our life, the metabolic reality of the society. The Aryans' ancient fears about the dangers of reckless literacy turned true post-1947 when India saw her most 'literate' States, with significant numbers of Christians and Muslims, increasingly embracing separatism, Communism, 'secularism' (a euphemism for Hindu-bashing) and social anarchy, as an alternative to the retreating Christianity and Islam, networking into a cartel and spawning denationalising forces. But these very states—Kerala and Bengal—also confused information with 'knowledge' and remained mired in age-less obscurantism and mediocrity, skipping the Second Wave, industrialisation, trying to force-land into the Third of information technology. Many of India's 'anarchists' came from these Communist-ruled States. Kerala witnessed the world's first elected Communist government in 1956 and continues to shelter the Muslim League, which led the Pakistan Movement, with a new signboard; Bengal, having chased out wisdom and prosperity, continues to get epileptic convulsions of still leading India. Thus, the Aryans thought, it was logical if education was made available only selectively; even the government's ongoing *Sarva Shiksha Abhiyan* (Campaign for

Education to All) aims at mere literacy, not education. If you inject health in undeserving prisoners of the past, chances are they would turn into hulks, break free and cause mayhem: 9/11 was perpetrated by such undeserving Arab youth, steeped deep in the sixth century Muslim Mindset, 'educated' in the West. Their fossilised faith has a disconnect with their modernist literacy; they used the future to beef up the past.

Christianity and Islam proclaimed 'knowledge' that had descended on humankind through Jesus and Muhammed and tried to lure India in their respective cult-based-faiths; as a subtle counter-attack, India, therefore, ensured that an ocean of ignorance and illiteracy made it difficult for this Abrahamic 'knowledge' to intrude her eternally fertile hinterland. The Brahminical selectivity ensured that large masses of Indians remained mired in superstitions, customs, rituals and illiteracy which kept the country free from any organised and long-term monotheistic bigotry; this policy became rigorous after the first century entry of Christianity and the resultant *Manu Smriti*. But the Indian virus of racial segregation continued to afflict Christianity as well as Islam and time and again split these faiths within and without. India let early brands of monotheism fight later brands, the way early settlers fought late-comers, the way the American 'settlers' oppose the 'immigrants' now. India alone offered a peaceful shelter to the non-proselytising Jews and Zoroastrians, although these two were the *real* fountainheads of monotheism and 'knowledge' as predecessors of alien proselytisers Christianity and Islam. From the Jews and Zoroastrians India learnt and charted her resistance to Christianity and Islam, the way the Afghan and French gunners taught the Hindus to defend themselves against the Turk sultans and the British chieftains in the 15th and 18th centuries, respectively. It was a Zoroastrian-Parsi General, Field Marshal Sam Hormusji Framji Jamshedji Manekshaw, who broke the myth of Islamic 'unity' in Pakistan by splitting that country and midwifing the birth of Bangladesh in 1971; not surprisingly, he became India's most loved General till date. If Indira Gandhi split Pakistan in 1971, her son Rajiv launched the second phase of retreat of Islam when he ignited the Hindu mind via Ayodhya in the 1980s. India treated religion and spirituality like hen-and-egg; and she never put all her eggs in one basket.

If your religion and the church is organised, chances are your society would convert wholesale. The absence of any organised church and her illiteracy, therefore, prevented much of India from moving in any particular direction in an organised manner, unlike neighbouring Persia which sank in Islam due to the surrender of its organised Zoroastrian church lock, stock and barrel, or earlier in Egypt and Rome where the defeat of a Caesar-cum-Pontifex Maximus would make the whole people surrender to the alien Christianity. In other words, India's chaos has shielded the country from the *Order* of God. Variety, pluralism, multiculturalism and polytheism, with the right of refusal to follow even a king or priest if they acted against the *Dharma*, prevented India from emulating the next door Iranian example. In the first four centuries, Islam tried to position and establish itself vis-à-vis Hinduism while the Slave Dynasties' Muslim rulers, whenever they had time from their chronically inherited tribal infighting, tried to encourage the Hindus' conversion to Muhammedanism.

Before we understand the complex socio-political-psychological processes in India as responses to the alien threat, it is essential to know what went into making this possible. A unified God hard-wires diverse people into a continuum; He is the quake that triggers the waves that multiply to become tsunamis few people know about. Such a God, monotheism, was born in the countries where desert was fast replacing agriculture, pushing the people towards greener pastures abroad. Monotheism, essentially, demonstrated a survival instinct in the face of climate change or mass extinction, even at the cost of retrogressive metamorphosis (the way some dinosaurs survived by shrinking their sizes into today's crocodiles or lizards), the revived relic of man's past as an animal, a herd-mentality. Polytheism demonstrated another survival instinct, to adopt to climate change, breaking free of the herd, survival of the fittest through natural selection, the emerging freedom of human spirit and victory of Darwinism, although some nations tended to shift from monotheism to polytheism and vice-versa, alternately, to rejuvenate themselves. Monotheism taught that the only goal for all humans could be a one-way, one time unconditional merger with God; India made it recurrent, conditional and two-way for most of the people. Monotheism recognised transportation of man, virtually in flesh-and-blood, to join God at the end of the Mission; Hinduism separated wheat from chaff, man from Atma (soul), and recognized wheat's capacity to be grown again and again; there was, therefore, no monotheistic mission for India.

The difference between the sixth-seventh century India and Arabia was similar as between King Harshavardhan and his contemporary, Muhammed: the former was a Hindu having a Sun-worshipping father, a Shiva-worshipping grandfather and Buddhist brother and sister and, at last, himself converted to Buddhism; the latter uprooted the traditional polytheism of the Sun-worshipping Kaa'ba and its priesthood, the Quraish, and planted lunotheist (Moon-worshipping) Islam in the Sanctuary. Muhammed, whose possibly Qurd-Quraish ancestors—his nephew and son-in-law Ali, the Fourth Caliph, mentioned this—had migrated from Syria to Mecca a thousand years before, was, apparently, the first surrogate theo-father in the world's known history as he gave the Arabs *their* religion. He was the greatest catalyst and aggregator, ever, among Homo sapiens.

Harsha, a Pushyabhooti King, began his reign in the year 606 in North India when Muhammed was still busy marrying off his step-daughters and was yet to emerge as a 'Prophet'. By the end of the Harsha era in 647, Islam had, through its monopolistic policy of hostile takeovers, diversification from the core business of Arabia, mergers-and-acquisitions, captured all citadels of polytheism as well as solar monotheism, crushed Judaism and even challenged Christianity in the Middle East—no wonder, this reckless expansion bequeathed differential work cultures, toxic assets, dangerous derivatives, subprime loans, weakened balance-sheets, adverse business cycles and eventual divestments as investors, mutual funds and private equity exited slowly over the next 1,400 years. But, post-Harsha, Islam's 'natural constituency' was that world of rank infidels, India, and that foremost Sun worshipper, Iberia. Before coming to India, the small holding company called Islam, with little equity and hazy bottom-lines but reckless valour, risk appetite and expansion, had become heavily indebted and leveraged due to the cost-ineffective acquisitions of top-heavy Sun-worshipping white elephants like Syria, Iraq, Egypt and, of course, Iran—and, later, its franchisees like Bangladesh and Indonesia virtually broke free from the main trunk to slowly revive their polytheist cottage industry.

With its protective gear and disaster management plan ready, India now waited for the alien invasion. Harsha was the last great *central* Indian Hindu monarch. By the end of his era in the seventh century AD, Hijri era was looming large on India as Islam had, by then, swept through Iran, wiped out the Aryan Zoroastrianism and was beginning to move eastward, towards the now Aryanised India, finally barging into the subcontinent with Muhammad bin-Qasim's conquest of Sindh in 711, the same year when the Muslims crossed Gibraltar to reach Spain in the West, and threatened to invade France as well. Already, Christianity had entered India from the South and now, with Islam threatening to trample the country in the North as well, the Hindus were, for the first time in their history, facing the *real*, pincer-like threat to their pluralism. Islam had already eliminated those two great, but bigoted and warring empires to India's west—Christian Byzantine Empire centred at Anatolia (from where the Dravidians and the Indus people, apparently, emerged after the discovery of agriculture, some 10,000 years ago) and Zoroastrian Sassanid Persia (the Indian Aryans' racial cousins and next door neighbours). The Muslims' next target could naturally be a heterogeneous India. The second Caliph, Omar, had, meanwhile, imposed his Islamic Code on the minorities, even on monotheistic Jews, in the nascent Crescent's empire and the Muslims had replaced many a shrine of other religions with their mosques. North India, having mastered the art of reading the monsoon winds, apparently sensed that these 'clouds' would not rain water and make the land green but erode the native soil, flood India with sand and desertify it.

All other immigrants in India had, hitherto, got assimilated within the umbrella-like Hinduism and settled down along with their gods. The arrival of Abrahamism was *different*: for the first time, the immigrant Christians and Muslims had not only settled down with their *alien* gods, unassimilated, but also converted Indians to *their* faith, who would, for the first time in history, go on pilgrimage *outside* India. Flight of this theo-capital was evidence of an emerging scenario that was fundamentally different from what had happened earlier. Clearly, India had to take precautions and corrective measures in view of these new realities and make tough laws vis-à-vis the newcomers, the way 9/11 forced America to frame stringent homeland security laws.

The Christians mainly came as missionaries, from the sea route, and their military assault, a spinoff of their Crusades in Eurasia, was still away until the 17th century. But Islam was the imminent danger to India. Unlike Islamists, the earlier invaders had not brought in or imposed their organised religion in India; on the contrary, they had Indianised themselves and adopted one of the innumerable existing native sects or invented one of their own, altogether new. Now, under the new dispensation, when the country was becoming more of a camp of pirates rather than a slum cluster of settlers unlike before, India realized that puny kings and great empires, religions and races would come and go. What really mattered was inoculation of a pluralistic society against the virus of a singularist community. The home-grown 'therapies' India had evolved so far during the last 1,000 years (700 BC to 700 AD) of the response to evolution of monotheism from heliotheism to lunotheism, could work only for the isolated individual not yet threatened by an organised community; the prevailing therapies had vaccinated and immunised him against a relatively less violent and semi-tribal solar monotheism, already hamstrung by selective breeding and the resultant low populations of non-proselytizing monotheists like the Jews and Zoroastrians—the small doses of these immigrant monotheists were like injections to evolve anti-bodies or an in-built inoculating defense system in the Indian context. This helped the Hindu to adapt to or forget the new social reality of lunar monotheism which he, being an isolated individual, was unable to alter. Post-711, in order to meet the new invading community's assault, the individual would have to dissolve himself *further* into society and create a pseudo-community.

Why? Christianity and Islam had broken away from selective inbreeding of the Semitic race and threw their net far and wide with inter-marriage and proselytisation that integrated, connected and aggregated diverse peoples in vast areas and expanded the challenge to the Aryan worldview multi-fold—it was like an erstwhile family-owned firm metamorphosing into a professionally-managed corporation which further expands into a multinational company threatening local businesses to either merge, get acquired or disappear. Islam was the fully-blossomed crystallisation of such a communal God, the final stage of theocrasia. As a reaction, India was forced to move to the other end of theo-spectrum: to a fully decrystallised society, to be created through implosion, giving way to cottage industry and subsistence economy with franchises from the *Gita*. Having seen the fall of ancient fossilized civilisations like Egypt, Syria and Iran, exhausted of their own greatness, to her west, India learnt her lessons and girded up her loins to pay a terrible cost no other civilisation had paid so far; those civilizations had simply surrendered before Christianity and Islam lock, stock and barrel. India struggled the hardest to perpetuate her polytheism, multiculturalism and pluralism at all costs, adopted and adapted—she even mutated and feigned death until the enemy left. No other sister civilisation could elbow out an intruding Islam the way India did because they had not evolved a strategy to fight out the Crescent through a long, psychological war that raged until the arrival of 1947. India, like an ostrich, buried her head into the Earth until the sandstorm lasted.

In Nature's food-chain, one man's food being another's poison, one culture's faith may turn out to be another's misfortune. So, proselytizing religions, which catalysed reluctant and fossilising cultures but were seen by the dominant classes as having 'poisoned' the indigenous cultures of their own or other lands, eventually evoked reaction and were slowly uprooted—Buddhism was nearly uprooted in India, Christianity in the Levant and North Africa, and Islam in Spain. Each culture evolves its own mechanism to control its beasts; evangelisation and proselytization were like drumming up and awakening the beast in men who find it as an escape route for the time being. But, like all good things, religion also comes to an 'end', and then begins its reincarnation as a destructive force. Islam was no different: founded by Muhammed *and only for the Arabs*, Islam, as apoptosis set in, began to transform into this destructive force once its capital, and the Caliphate, was shifted to Damascus in Syria, from where the Quraish forefathers had apparently migrated to Mecca.

Islam, which came as the life-giving water of Zamzam for the unsuspecting and simple Arab, became, for a time, a 'liberating' force for civilisationally advanced but theo-fatigued nations like Syria, Persia, Byzantium and Egypt; by the next 75 years when it reached its geographical limits, India in the east and the Iberian Peninsula in the west, Islam had quickly matured, even decayed into a destructive force, as it worked according to its *prakriti*: it did not humanise the civilisations it picked in Syria, Egypt or Iran; it not only whetted their own dehumanising tendencies, like Zoroastrian or Christian excesses in Iran or Turkey, *it also increased their threshold energy levels by unifying it for assault elsewhere.* In other words, the more Islam expanded, the more the Muslims became a force multiplier for further expansion, somewhat of a reckless bulldozer that levels the ancient ruins the way the Arabs are now doing in Mecca and Medina in what is a retreat journey! For a time, Islam did come as a whiff of fresh air, a great connector and networker of peoples across cultures and civilizations, a bridge between the East and the West, a disseminator of knowledge and one that *acquired great civilisations without really changing their native cultures, except in the mosque.* So, even after accepting Islam and 'Arabisation', Syrians largely remained Syrians, Egyptians Egyptians, Berbers Berbers. Also, Aryan Iranians remained Aryan Iranians, and, of course, Aryan Indians Aryan Indians. In a few decades after each such acquisition, Islam quickly degenerated to become an easy tool for all kinds of criminals, opportunists, upstarts and adventurers—the way Communism decayed into cacophony, the way democracy is now unfortunately degenerating into a mask for the West. Islam provided a mask to all sorts of barbarians who charged out straight from the cave to the mosque: in each century since Muhammed, Islam, while aggregating people on a vast scale, also stripped the masses of their capacity to think independently: it became a cheer-boy to the likes of Osama bin-Ladens, Mullah Muhammad Omars and Abu Bakr al-Baghdadis on their way from the caves to the mosques and rued when they were killed or returned to the caves. Mehmud, when he left Ghazni with his army of frenzied beasts, knew his mullahs would be satisfied with the Indian moolah. So, India decided to bide her time; her slow reaction against Abrahamism, which commenced in 1947, found its first *clear* target in Ayodhya in 1992.

This subterranean reservoir of blood has been in the making, not only in India but across those countries where Christianity and Islam entered as catalysts but wreaked havoc. This made life uneasy for our contemporary, unfortunate Muslims across the world; the Christians had already learnt the futility of the bloody Crusades and moved on as they no longer take their religion seriously. Peace activists are unable to fathom this red reservoir and should be forgiven as they do not realise how much did their own forefathers contribute to this vast pool due to alien orgies; they can only watch in pious horror when this hidden reservoir bursts out time and again in the shape of communal riots. In India, the Hindus never forgot Mehmood Ghazanavi's 11th century destruction, massacre and loot at the Somnath Temple; in each communal riot, they saw in the contemporary Muslim a descendent from Afghanistan and settled old scores, the last one being in 2002. Similarly, the Serbs saw the reflected image of the medieval Ottomans in their contemporary Muslims in the 1990s and readied themselves to be led by Slobodan Milosevik; America, too, marketing peace sermons for free along with price-tagged war merchandise until 9/11, suddenly discovered Frankensteins in Iraq and Afghanistan it had propped up against Iran and the Soviet Union, respectively.

In the beginning, however, Islam came as a catalyst. India was waiting to revive her stranded menstrual cycle, post the Gupta-Vardhan menopause, when the Indians had virtually forgotten the first principle of survival, warfare, amid prosperity-triggered easy life and peace. But Islam came to stay for longer innings—the guest would soon turn into a host! The Muhammedan conquest of India, particularly in the North, awakened and unified the Hindus. It was in this part of India that the Hindus fought their bitterest, pitched battles against the Muslims and evolved survival tactics. It was a tragedy because Islam was produced by a fine human being, Muhammed, but inherited by humans trapped in the beast's hide; it 'civilised' and united the Arabs but barbarised and uprooted other cultures, the poison being carried forward and forward by the zealous neophytes in a relay race. As Will Durant has observed, 'The Mohammedan Conquest of India is probably the bloodiest story in history. It is a discouraging tale, for its evident moral is that civilisation is a precarious thing, whose delicate complex of order and liberty, culture and peace may at any time be overthrown by barbarians invading from without or multiplying within.' India gradually threw out the barbarians from without until 1947 and is now dealing with those within whom she produced to defeat the former.

But Islam, or for that matter Christianity, could not be blamed. It was an idea whose Time had come in the India of the year 711, the way Christianity became an idea whose Time came in the India of 1764. These ideas became inexorable, inevitable as catalysts for *change* in India.

Not that India, politically weakened in the seventh century having forgotten Chanakya and thus afflicted with an acquired intellectual deficiency syndrome (AIDS), was not prepared to face this desert storm. On a practical level, Jainism and Buddhism had transformed India into a nation of peace-hawkers; monasteries encouraged any number of worthless Hindus turn into beggars in the garb of monks. India was swamped by impotent charlatans masquerading as 'holy men' and beggars flooding all centres of power. The last important Gupta emperor, Skandagupta, tried to arrest this slide by defeating the last batches of the Shaka invaders from Central Asia but an even bigger challenge was building up in Arabia which his otherwise worthy successor, King Harsha, could not stop. For 400 years from the sixth century, India's silence was the lull before the storm as it waited for the inevitable alien attack; and, at last, it arrived from Ghazni.

For about 300 years after the first Muslim invasion in 711, India prepared herself for a greater and deeper assault from across the Indus. The Turkish chieftain, Mehmud, who became Sultan of Ghazni in 997, left a bloody trail of death, destruction and decay in India in his wake, after destroying the Somnath Temple in 1024, the way Columbus and his post-Crusader gang would do in the Americas 500 years later.

Together, Mehmud and Columbus proved that civilisation is always a delicate and precarious thing which can be overthrown by barbarians who can also, at the same time, be inadvertent agents of change in the host country; and, the prematurely ageing American 'civilisation' is now being overthrown by similar 'barbarians' from across Mexico Samuel P Huntington was so concerned about. Mehmud's bloody legacy was carried forward by his successors who drove India more and more into shelter of the *Gita*, their emergency escape route; no wonder, a mastery of the *Gita* was considered the best Exit for a Hindu. The word *Prasthantrayi*, incorporating the *Gita* with the *Veda*s and the *Brahmasootra*s, itself meant the *triple exit route*. Muhammad Ghori's successors laid the foundation of the Delhi Sultanate and Medieval India in 1186 with Qutb-ud-Din Aibak as the first Sultan of the Slave Dynasty in an enslaved country—for the first time, a Delhi ruler was one whose religious loyalty lay *outside* India, ie. to Baghdad, Mecca and al-Medina. And, for the first time, the alien intruders, unlike their predecessors who had turned Hindus, Buddhists or Jains, had brought with them an imperial religion they tried to impose on India. India was no longer a Camp; it was a Colony.

But some Muslims slowly became the hard bark of the Indian banyan. The most prominent Sultan of this dynasty was Balban who, following Hindu India's cultural security theorem—*that the last come enemy should first bear the brunt of the next enemy!* If you came in the last and sat near the door, you'd open it to the newcomer, as it were—became India's response to the Mongol invasion. To some extent, even America has followed this theorem: in its War on Terror in Iraq and Afghanistan, the US armies have sometimes been led not by the Generals from European-American origins but by the Afro-American or Hispanic ones! In fact, if Islam drove away the dreaded Mongols in any nation, it was in India. No doubt Islam was now under the control of Islamised barbarians but Muhammed's religion had at least fed its early adherents well; the barbarian Mongols, being hungry, were an uncontrollable menace all over Asia and Europe. They even destroyed the notions of Islamic 'invincibility' and the Caliphate for ever, before some of them embraced Islam themselves. In fact, Islam's entire lifecycle was six centuries (632-1258), after which its Asiatic catalytic role ended and, in the absence of an external infidel enemy, it went into a self-destructive mode. The Mongols came as Islam's nemesis, launched its slow decline and fall and were responsible to bring it to its pathetic condition today. India had, therefore, been forced to use the contemporary lesser menace of Islam (Balban) against the greater one of Mongols. The only other important Slave Sultan was Allah-ud-Din Khilji who enunciated the principle of subsistence economy for the Hindus so that they did not rise in rebellion. '...the Hindus will never become submissive and obedient till they are reduced to poverty. I have, therefore, given orders that just sufficient shall be left to them from year to year of corn, milk and curds, but they shall not be allowed to accumulate hoards and property.' Later, the British, too, followed this policy, particularly when they forced the farmers to sow indigo in three-fourths of their land holdings, as in Champaran, Bihar—a place that gave rise to the Mahatma in Gandhi in 1917. And, Hindu India, since 1947, has been unconsciously following this same subsistence policy vis-a-vis Muslims!

But, as in Persia, the Indian 'Muslims' were infected with the Aryan principles of hereditary monarchy and primogeniture, which became the biggest weakness in achieving end of securing the whole of India for Islam. For, dynastic struggles sapped much of Islam's initial virility, leaving little time for evangelisation and proselytisation as the clerics remained busy justifying the rule of the day's Sultan, rather than increasing the number of the faithful for the Faith. The *Ahl-e-Hadith*, a fundamentalist Sunni organisation, diagnosed this weakness of Persianised Islam and set out to 'reIslamise' the Muslims all over the infidel world with the Jesuit zeal in the 20th and 21st centuries; in its dePersianising zeal, for instance, the South Asian organization even purged the popular Persian words and phrases beginning with the word *Khuda* and replaced it with Allah, as in *Khuda Hafiz* (Good Bye) or *Khuda Gawah* (By Allah). Sunnis now bid a goodbye to each other not by saying Khuda Hafiz but by *Allah Hafiz*.

As a result of these long-drawn-out Islamic attacks, barring some exceptions of assimilation and synthesis, 'composite culture', here and there, as the pauperising Hindus turned inside their soul and ferociously multiplied within, the Sultan remained 'Commander' of a lesser and lesser number of Faithful. Ironically, religious conversion was sometimes discouraged as it reduced the revenue from *Jazia* levied on all non-Muslims, the way prohibition policy is now unofficially discouraged in some states of India as less consumed liquor means lesser revenue for the State by way of taxes. Some of the Sultans, like Iltutmish, even got a robe of honour and recognition from the Caliph to buttress their Islamic credentials. Eventually, both Christian and Muslim missionaries failed to convert India's Hindus in large numbers to their respective fold and had to remain content with the multiplication of low-caste converts.

The Delhi Sultanate was, basically, a cartel of warlords of Turkish and Afghan origins who looted India to buy luxuries of India in India itself, unlike their successor European colonialists who were yet to arrive and would take the booty back home to make it 'venture capital' for the rise of their economies for the prosperity of their impoverished and uncouth people. The Mughals, descendents of Mongols, were, however, different. Having used the Turko-Afghan monotheists against the atheist Mongols, India now turned to tap the recently-converted pseudo-monotheist Mongols against the now-confirmed Islamists, as four centuries of Islam had seen at least ten generations of Muslims. The neo-Mongols a.k.a. the Mughals, were destined to regurgitate, assimilate and eject Islam. Zahir-ud-Din Muhammad Babur, a Sunni, founded the Mughal Dynasty in 1526; his Shia General Mir Baqi Tashkandi destroyed Lord Rama's Temple in Ayodhya in 1528, like Muhammed dethroning the Arab gods at the Kaa'ba as a pre-requisite for installation of Islam. They, erroneously, believed that only by destroying the Ayodhya Temple could Muhammedanism be planted firmly in India. Babur's namesake would help uproot Islam in the subcontinent—Nasirullah Babur, Interior Minister in the Benazir Bhutto government in the 1990s, was credited with midwifing the Taliban Movement, which 'invited' America to Kabul. Destruction of the Babri mosque in Ayodhya in 1992 was the first-ever collective act of Hindu zealots against Islam since 711.

The Hindus had rarely fought bloody religious wars amongst themselves and even allowed intra-sect poaching as normal human behaviour; they were happy worshipping each other's gods as guests.

They would not mind having even the prophets of West Asia for guests, provided they did not try to grab their host's house like the proverbial Arab camel. In this plurality of gods, Lord Rama had come to enjoy the status of the Chancellor, first among equals in the Aryavarta, the moral fibre of North India. The epic *Ramayana* has been an all-India respiratory system, blending and unifying the Northern Aryavarta and the Southern Dravidland in a unique twin-civilisational architecture, as its canvass spreading from Ayodhya to Lanka depicted the project of civilisational unity in the Indian subcontinent. Rama has, therefore, been the most important unificatory thread that bound much of India, unlike the greater epic, *Mahabharata*, whose centre of attrition was the North which mainly bore the brunt of Islam. *Ramayana* depicted fusion of the North and South India through victory over and reconciliation with Lanka, ie. the farther land across the sea, the geographical limit India set for itself after the maximum expansion of Aryanism. Lord Rama has been the ideal every Hindu was expected to follow as the son, father, husband, brother and as the ideal King who would renounce even his beloved wife to protect the realm from societal and royal controversies. Rama has been the soul of India, Krishna the body; the Kashmiri Brahmin-turned-founding-philosopher of Pakistan, Allama Iqbal, who rubs shoulders with Aurangzeb in a Lahore graveyard, called Rama *Imam-e-Hind.* The Kashmiris, as a racially conscious upper caste Hindus, mostly Brahmins, were the last to convert to Islam in the sub-continent and it was not surprising that one of them became the moving spirit for Islam's exit *out* of India in 1947—destiny had made him lie next to Aurangzeb 'Alamgir', 'Ruler of the World', the 'Derwish clad in the Imperial Purple'. A case of the weakest but wily Brahmin converting to Islam to defeat the 'ideal' Muslim ruler in India. If Jinnah and Iqbal formed the reigning couple that created Pakistan, Gandhi and Bankimchandra Chatterjee will become the guiding spirit for Islam's retreat.

The Gupta Emperor, Chandragupta Vikramaditya (375-415), had built a magnificent Temple at the Lord's mythological birthplace, Ayodhya (the City of No-War!) to house this Ideal of India. Muslim marauders like Mehmood Ghaznavi and Muhammad Ghori, who wanted to rush back to their trans-Indus caves with the Indian booty and beauties, did not have enough time to venture into this eastern Uttar Pradesh town to raid it. Their successor Slave Dynasties of Delhi Sultanate, too, were busy killing each other rather than the slaves they had made out of Indians. The responsibility to destroy the Rama Temple, therefore, fell on a vagabond refugee, Babur, who found his *el dorado* in India. Apparently, he knew he could create space for Allah only by displacing Rama—the guest must overthrow the host. Babur had come to know the 'importance' of the destruction of this Temple as the prerequisite to break the spiritual backbone of India, something his predecessors had failed to do; his lieutenant, Mir Baqi, destroyed the Temple and built a mosque, the Babri Masjid, on its ruins. Babur died in 1530, leaving his son Humayun, an opium addict, fugitive not from the Hindus but from the equally ambitious Afghan Muslim warlord Sher Shah Suri. The Hindus, adept at charming snakes, sheltered Humayun in Rajasthan and then Sind where his illustrious son, Akbar, was born in 1542. With some Persian help, Humayun returned to the Mughal throne and died where his mausoleum exists in Delhi, a posh area now hub of the communist and secularist establishment of India. Babur loved almonds and knew it takes some 12 years to get its first fruit. He cursed India for having none of it; but he did not know he had sown almonds in Ayodhya whose fruits will be continuously reaped by the unfortunate Muslims of India until the 21st century.

The Hindus of Aryavarta continued their struggle against the Muslim *mlechchha* for restoration of the Temple. Between Babur's death and Akbar's accession, around ten battles had been fought—the numbers may wary depending upon who is claiming what and why. During Akbar's reign, another 20 battles took place. Between 1528 and 1992, the Babri Masjid witnessed nearly 100 bloody battles between the Hindus and Muslims in which around 400,000 men were killed. Since the life of Hindus was worthless during Muslim and Christian regimes, these Hindu-only massacres were not often recorded in Muslim or Christian official records; the Hindus, multiplying furiously, also had little interest in chronicling these massacres. Rama was a civilisational figure and, therefore, the Ayodhya battle became a major flashpoint in the Clash of Civilisations at a time when Spain had already expelled Islam and was sending out exploratory armies of Columbus, Vasco de Gama etc to the infidel world. It was a big headache for Akbar who, as all ambitious men do, would embark upon making an opportunity out of a crisis. An illiterate brimming with wisdom, he perhaps knew how Ashoka had made an opportunity out of the Kalinga War; but he did not exactly know that the First Battle of Panipat (1526) his grandfather Babur had fought against the Rajput king Rana Sanga was the beginning of the *Mahabharata* to re-establish the *Ramayana!* Babur had inadvertently planted a Kurukshetra in Ayodhya, a Great War in the City of No-War.

In the process, the civilisational struggle commenced by Babur would reach a peak in his grandson Akbar, who would try to assimilate some Hinduism *into* Islam through rather 'peaceful' means, and slide back in the latter's great-grandson, Aurangzeb, who would, like the train's guard in the last coach, wave the green flag to a future Jinnah to take the train out of the subcontinent. It was Akbar who abridged Ashoka and Atal Behari Vajpayee. Islam, in this Mughal Emperor, arrived at its weakest link: the Sun myths. And Islam began its return journey in a slow halting procession. Jalal-ud-Din Muhammad Akbar (literally meaning 'the Glory of Religion of Muhammed, the Greatest') left little doubt that the glory of Islam in India was past. That the slow Indian counter-attack had begun.

For, Akbar began his political career (1556-1605) with the normal Muslim duty, as a 'Ghazi' (Holy Warrior, Slayer of the Infidel), after the killing of Delhi's Hindu king Hemchandra Vikramaditya (Hemu), already on his death-bed. In this pious act, the would-be 'Great' Mughal, who was, ironically, reared by infidel Hindus of Rajasthan and Sind when his fugitive father Humayun was running away from Sher Shah Suri, got the mullahs' nod to kill the Hindus, rule in peace and go to heaven when he dies. Hemu's corpse was cut to pieces until there remained a drop of blood in it. In 1568, he ordered a general massacre of some 30,000 Rajputs and innocent farmers at Chittor, Rajasthan, after the fort had fallen, four times 'improving' upon the earlier local record of Alauddin Khalji who could manage to kill only 8,000 Hindus. By his time, no Indian Sultan could expect reinforcements from West or Central Asia where Iran and Turkey were happy fighting their own intra-Brotherhood battles, and the Russians were pre-occupied with the trail left by Ivan the Terrible against the Mongols; a buffeted Akbar would, therefore, face grave difficulties both from within and without when the Shias hated him for ill-treating his Shia mentor Bairam Khan, the Sunnis for the fall of Tardi Beg and the Hindus despised him for Ayodhya, Hemu and other obvious reasons.

In the beginning, Akbar was a hate figure, despised but feared because of his ruthlessness combined with shrewd political management and improvisation that continuously fuelled his ambition; each success made his ambition more and more insatiable until, when he died, he found that he was alone and, like all over-ambitious men, hated. Many people, fidel and infidel, heaved a sigh of relief at his death. He had used both Muslims and Hindus as cogs in the fulfilment of his grand designs—to the extent that he ended up placing himself next only to Allah and Prophet Muhammed! Eventually he broke ranks from Islam as well and, like his middle name-sake, Muhammed, launched an altogether new faith with himself as its Pope, Caliph and Caesar all rolled in one. Had the rebellion of his son, Muhammad Salim alias Jehangir, not broken him, he would have probably ventured even further: declaring himself Allah and then, may be, even as Father of Allah! Unschooled future generations would gratefully remember him as *Mughal-e-Azam* (The Great Mughal). A better part of his reign was seen as the only Golden Era during the Muslim reign, with a hundred lore woven around him, and his minister, Birbal.

Akbar, like his Prophet, was illiterate, and as shrewd with great business-like and managerial instincts. He had a rare capacity to size up potential friends and foes and successfully use them against each other that makes an ambitious man's career a success—clear-sighted illiterates, who manage to acquire power from short-sighted debating literates, normally cultivate an uncanny habit to hire intelligent but powerless men for their advisors or, alternately, end up hating and eliminating such people. He knew the Muslim minority, to which he belonged, only too well and how they had behaved with his father, Humayun. Now, he would veer away to the other end and try to make bridges with the Hindu majority to protect himself from his own men. Like Ashoka, it was his ambition and far-sight, necessity and politics, rather than a change of heart, that guided Akbar's policies, on whom official historians and later the colonised Hindu mindset would thrust greatness. But, unlike his predecessors and successors in the Mughal Empire, Akbar alone could read the evolving Hindu Mind.

After Babur, three factors were shaping up the north Indian Hindu Mind and a possible general rebellion: (1) Demolition of the Lord Rama Temple of Ayodhya that prompted the writing of the *Sri Ramcharitmanas*, the 'new testament' of the *Ramayana.* It was penned by Akbar's contemporary poet Goswami Tulsidas, who reinvented the Ideal God and spread Him to the grassroots level in the people's own colloquial language, *Avadhi*, in the Doab heartland in North India where the Hindu-Muslim struggle was at its extreme, unlike Valmiki's *Ramayana* which was largely inaccessible because of its being in Sanskrit; Tulsidas has since been the Prince of Poetry in India, the greatest poet unsurpassed by anyone else and non-stop recital of his Book at thousands of places each year across North India is a common sight—it is he who shaped the Hindu Mind to implement the *Gita* plan of Adi Shankaracharya. The Book's several versions in colloquial languages were accomplishing the same task in their respective areas; (2) The emergence of Lord Krishna as the middle-class urban hero, the reincarnation of Vishnu and the next phase of Rama, who would deliver the Hindus from the aliens-from-across the sea. Krishna represented the traders amid competing influences of the Sufi and Bhakti Movements. The Sufis' 'unificatory' efforts were alarming due to their being under the overall Islamic umbrella, ie. Allah would eventually replace Hindu gods the way a 'peaceful' Muhammed did slowly at the Kaa'ba and later destroyed all the native Arab gods; the Sufis, unlike the violent mullahs, would 'unite' the Hindus and Muslims in a Track-II, Plan-B diplomacy, peacefully, 'under Allah' while the Bhakti saints were, essentially, the home-grown Hindu answer to this Sufi strategy, and (3) The emerging regrouping of the Rajputs, and then the Marathas, Jats and Sikhs, as a potent political force to strike back a decisive blow at the Muslims. Like any other wise king turning challenge into an opportunity, Akbar cut deals with some Hindus, married into a prominent Rajput family, but sired a fundamentalist Sunni Muslim son believing in brute 'justice'. Some of the earlier Muslim Sultans, too, had cut opportunistic deals with the locally-powerful Hindus but they were not as ambitious, far-sighted and spider-like as Akbar.

Tulsidas (1532-1623), ten years senior to Akbar, was born at a time when the entire *Doab* (the Ganga-Yamuna catchment areas) was seething with anger and agitation due to the demolition of the Rama Temple at Ayodhya and construction of a mosque in its place using the same temple material; the Hindus viewed it as the ultimate humiliation to their faith in their most ideal son of the soil whose teachings they would follow from womb to pyre. The Goswami was a Saryuparin Brahmin, who, ironically, were traditionally against worshipping Lord Rama, a Kshatriya, for having killed the Lankan King, Ravana, a Brahmin. But the poet's wife, Ratnavali, probably believed this little Brahminical unbelief in Rama was insignificant when compared to the civilisational struggle being waged by the Avadhi people at that time and felt her husband should better join this Hindu 'nationalist' movement and struggle against the Muslim marauders—after all, even Adi Shankaracharya had put his Shaivite belief on the backburner while reinventing the Vaishnavite *Gita*. 'Shame on you for loving me so much. Had you loved Lord Rama as much instead, you'd have been emancipated', the angry wife once famously snubbed Tulsidas, which changed his heart, made him travel to Ayodhya and write the Epic there. This metamorphosed him into the most potent force of Hindu unity and creator of the Hindi language, the like of which did not come until Gandhi. Tulsidas also penned the extremely popular 40 verses of *Hanuman Chalisa* to extol faith in the Lord's loyal disciple, the Monkey God: in this pocket-size booklet, the poet taught the Hindus to always remember Hanuman as the crisis manager who could contract or expand His Size when needed, One who could cross oceans and mountains simply by chanting Rama's name: 'When you recite Hanuman's name, the Devils and Monsters would be driven away... Lord Rama is the ultimate weapon with you, Whom you should always worship'. Hanuman represented the masses whose unity and power against the 'monstrous' forces Tulsidas extolled. And, Tulsidas was only the tip of the iceberg—more destructive Hindu storms were building up in the Punjab and the Deccan which would be reaped by Akbar's successors: Akbar became the Last Sigh of the Muslim Rule in India (1605); his successors increasing dragged Islam out of India.

The farsighted Akbar sensed early on that this accumulating anger could shape up into a rebellion and, if not attended to urgently, could eventually uproot the Mughal Empire itself. He, therefore, tried to befriend Tulsidas and bring him into the Mughal fold by offering him a place in his Court; the poet-saint, who grasped the Emperor's real intentions, rejected the offer, famously saying, '*Santan ko kahan Sikri so kaam*' (Saints have nothing to do with your Capital); nevertheless, in a bid to buy peace, Akbar met Tulsidas and sent his trusted Hindu lieutenants Birbal and Raja Todarmal to Ayodhya to build a makeshift temple on a *chabutara* (platform) just outside the mosque to placate the Hindus by acceding to their minimum demand. Had he so wanted, nothing could have prevented the 'Great' Mughal to solve the big problem once for all: but he did not, not because he could not but because he would not—if you solve a problem, you are merely a statesman; if you don't solve it, you can even become a politician! For, this one act, returning the 'disputed' land to the Hindus would have won this Sunni Emperor the implacable hostility of all Sunnis, while the Shias were already ranged against him: ironically, the Babri mosque was a Shia mosque and, therefore, the Sunni Akbar could have easily given it back to the Hindus. But he apparently had grandiose plans, *to emerge as a Caliph in the East*, now that the one in Spain had been done away with, and even that one in Turkey was too far away with the Shia Iran preventing Delhi to bridge with Istanbul. And, moreover, Akbar had not come to power to jeopardise the future of Islam in India; an 'illiterate scholar' as he was, as a politician he knew he needed the core support, the critical mass base, of Muslims for any imperial project and he could not totally antagonise his own community at any cost. Better, as any petty politician would do, play the two sides against one another. The Ayodhya issue, if 'settled', could antagonise either the Hindus or the Muslims; he could not have satisfied both. His middle-name was Muhammad and Akbar knew he could not afford to go down in history as a 'mosque-donor' to the infidels: similarly, our contemporary All-India Muslim Personal Law Board (AIMPLB), which would never be seen to be 'donating' the mosque to the infidel, rejected the Shankaracharya's proposal in 2003 because of this same reason. Moreover, Akbar had not come to the throne to destroy the Mughal Empire the way Winston Churchill had not become the Prime Minister in the 1940s to preside over liquidation of the British Empire!

The dominant Muslim Mind in India has, right from bin-Qasim in 711 to the AIMPLB, almost been the same; Akbar was no exception, at least in the beginning of his career. 'We have crushed the infidels by the sword, we will uphold Islam by the sword' has been the fanatics' pet slogan for ages—this imperialist dogma emerged almost as their Seventh Pillar of Islam, the Sixth being al-Jihad. Post-1947, the fundamentalist Muslim slogan was similar, '*Hans ke liya hai Pakistan; lad ke lenge Hindustan*' (We laughed our way to Pakistan; we will fight our way back into India to take it). Muslim, and later Christian, fanatics busy in the conversion business believed that beef-eating would permanently rupture the convert's old belief system and make it impossible his re-conversion. Next, the convert was brain-washed into believing that he had been 'reborn' in Islam/Christianity, *physically and in the same birth*, because of his residual 'good' deeds in the previous non-Hindu births, although he had strayed into the infidel and hostile territory for a while, from which he has just been rescued! He was then made to believe that now that he had arrived at his rightfully appointed place, he should help his co-religionists in pursuing the project further and help convert other 'straying' Hindus to the new Faith by all means; now, that the convert was part of the new Brotherhood he should treat India only as a guest house, his real home being Mecca/Rome, and do everything that could accrue benefit to the new Faith(s). With the increasing number of converts from the lower caste Hindus refusing to attack the upper caste infidels and temples, and the successful Sufi movements, the fundamentalist Muslims found this Islamic road via the Hindu's stomach much easier; with the weakening of the Muslim regimes, however, and the Sultan's own intra-Islamic problems, the full Islamisation project could not succeed in India.

The Delhi Sultanate, too, could not convert many Hindus due to its uncouth and ruthless policy of terror and slaughter and the in-house fratricide; the Sufis were more successful in this design through 'peaceful' means. They turned out more successful than the Sword of Islam because it worked at the lowest strata of the Hindu society many among whose 'untouchables' (including the vanquished Hindu soldiers forced into slavery as per norms of the era) were converted without much effort. Akbar, a disciple of the Sufi saint, Sheikh Salim Chishti (after whom he named his son), was achieving through words what his short-sighted predecessors of the Delhi Sultanate had failed to do through the Sword.

This was how a Hindu converting to Islam (and later Christianity also) was de-nationalised and uprooted by the missionaries. Only the operational details, not the Goal to fully Islamise/Christianise India, changed with the change of rulers. Akbar, too, was a part of this same project in the beginning but, for the misfortune of Islamists whose own fortunes had been put on the mat by the Mongols, he even had his own axes to grind. His successes intoxicated him and there began to lurk the idea that no Muslim had ever dared harbour: subconsciously, to challenge the authority of Prophet Muhammed! But not immediately. He would venture into this territory step-by-step; even otherwise, being a half-Mongol himself, Islam, for him, became more of a *policy* rather than a belief. Already, he was engaged on different fronts and did not want the divided Hindus and Muslims to open a united front against each other and, in the process, overthrow the Mughal Empire. The best possible alternative in these circumstances was to play them against each other in deft moves, to keep them busy through local anaesthesia, so that he could advance his ultra-ambitious project. Akbar, who, in the beginning of his temporal-imperial career, was a slave of his harem would eventually try to rub off this image by becoming spiritual Master of Islam and unsuccessfully launch himself as a new Prophet.

So, he decided to put the main existing problem of Ayodhya in a cold storage through the policy of checks and balances, as did the

Nehruvites and the Vajpayeeites more recently, simply by slipping the volcano under the Supreme Court and hiding themselves behind the cement bags of the Constitution. In order to mollify the angry Hindus, he married into the Rajput clan—Lord Rama was a Kshatriya, and the Rajputs were believed to be their descendents—and he met Tulsidas. Even Pakistani fanatic Maulana Fazl-ur-Rehman tried to fool the Hindu 'leaders' in July 2003 in India to placate them simply because his boys in terror-trade could not fight on two fronts: against India in Kashmir and against America elsewhere, post 9/11. In order to distract the Hindus' attention from Rama, Akbar embarked upon a 'Track-II' diplomacy also: he abolished the *jazia* (poll/pilgrim tax) slapped against the infidels of Mathura (1562), made the Krishna worship a state-sponsored programme, with the Emperor himself participating in the *Janmashtami* festivities. Both these steps—marriage and poll tax—were mainly cosmetic changes; he simply followed the Sufi policy and named his son Salim after Sheikh Salim Chisthti. Poll tax hardly earned any revenues now and was, therefore, safe to be axed. His marriage into a Krishna-worshipping Hindu family somewhat confused the Hindus. However, he took care to ensure that neither was the Ayodhya Temple restored to the Hindus nor did much of this issue come in the officially censored records—he would not undo his grandfather Babur's 'achievement' in Ayodhya and tried to ward off the problem by pushing it under the carpet through sops—just like the Indian governments did post-1992. Since Akbar was himself the Supreme Judge, he could not drag the matter to the court and take it as a cover!

It was due to the accumulating Hindu anger and possible revolt that he also shifted his capital from Delhi to Fatehpur Sikri, near Agra, so as to ensure that the presence of a big Muslim garrison in the Hindu heartland acted as a deterrent to the infidels and the Shias: from Agra, his army could now reach Allahabad and Avadh relatively faster, thanks to the Grand Trunk Road built by his predecessor, Sher Shah Suri. In a balancing act to all these 'pro-Hindu' policies, he figuratively banned cow-slaughter—in any case, this policy was created by Muslim fundamentalists as a Hindu-specific issue in India; the Arabs, or the *Qur'an,* did not even know cow! His son, Salim, as Jahangir, would turn out to be as ruthless a ruler as the Sunni Muslims expected him to be. But Akbar did not know that the Indian opium had made both his father Humayun and son Jahangir drug addicts! Akbar's greatness lay in that he was a better political manager, who could successfully manage contemporary contradictions, one who could size up men and situations in time and mould them into an overall scheme. He was the Sufi variant of the earlier Delhi Sultans, the latter's revised and enlarged, unabridged and embellished edition in which the mission of Muhammedans and the ambition of Jalal-ud-Din Muhammad Akbar had blended into what was later claimed to be his 'reconciliation' with the Hindus. His friendship with the Rajputs was only natural: for, the Rajputs, too, who had emerged as the militant representatives of the Hindus, had, after their arrival from Central Asia in the post-Harsha centuries and enrolment as Hindus, grown up alongside the Muslims and they understood each other better; similarly, the Tamils, Marathas, Punjabis and the Bengalis, who grew side-by-side in the British Raj, understood each other and the foreign power better. It was due to this inherent capacity to size each other up, even if unconsciously, that the British would be challenged most by these same-generation communities and a Rajput, Rajendra Singh, would head the RSS during the demolition of the Babri Mosque in 1992. This is how Nature arranges Pawns on its kaleidoscopic Chessboard across the world.

But the Ayodhya wound continued to fester like the mythological wound on the forehead of Ashwatthama, son of Dronacharya, the teacher of the Kauravas and Pandavas of the *Mahabharata*; when Ashwatthama tried to eliminate the Pandava progeny forever by using 'nuclear' weapons, an infuriated Krishna had surgically got removed the precious gem studded on the former's forehead with which he was born, leaving a festering wound on the forehead of the man who was condemned to live forever with it. That mythology still continues: many pious Hindus still believe that Ashwatthama would one day come to them seeking clarified butter to heal the festering wound. Ayodhya, therefore, lives in Ashwatthama. Some of the conscientious Muslims, too, knew that Ayodhya could turn out to be the inevitable exit door of Islam from India, if the rulers did not solve the problem.

That was why Mirza Muhammad Rafi 'Sauda' (1791-1852), the famous Urdu poet, said: *Tod kar butkhana masjid to bana di tuney O'Shaikh! Barahman ke bhi dil ki kuchh fiqr hai tumne ki; Kaaba agar dhaya to kya gham hai Shaikh, yeh koi dil nahin ki phir banaya na jayega.* (O Shaikh, you smashed a Temple and built a mosque on its ruins; did it ever occur to you how the Brahmin's broken heart could be mended? If the sacred Kaaba is brought down, it would not cause endless pain as it is not a broken heart that can never be mended.) But politicians are those who master the art of keeping a wound festering and Akbar had not come to power with the ambition to cure a cancer caused by his grandfather.

His name was Jalal-ud-Deen Muhammad. Jalal-ud-Deen literally meant the 'Light of Religion' (Islam). 'Akbar', meaning the 'Great', was the title he wore. So, his 'name' as *Akbar the Great,* so fondly recalled, had little meaning: The Great The Great! While Jalal-ud-Deen and Muhammad were both nearly forgotten, the facade remained.

Akbar, when burdened with the responsibility of managing a vast seething realm, slowly emerged as a tolerant, even if manipulative, Mughal, who, like Ashoka, was able to manage the emerging situations to fit into his overall imperial designs. In his own days, this 'secular' Emperor was tolerated because of his relatively better policies coupled with the threat of Muslim arms and absence of the adequate, pan-Indian Hindu muscle. His 'outsourcing' of security concerns to the contemporary affordable call-centres of local chieftains, called *Mansabdars,* always kept potential rebels in check as the otherwise local army could quickly transform into the imperial army at the Emperor's order and quell the rebellion, the way networking problems in computers are now solved from afar. He took extreme care not to appoint too many of bankrolled infidels as important or powerful Mansabdars; out of 137 Mansabdars of 1,000 horsemen and above, only 14 were Hindus but out of 12 provincial *Diwans* (Prime Ministers), as many as eight were Hindus—because the Hindu majority would not oppose being fleeced by the Hindu revenue official! Seventy per cent of Mansabdars were the *Muslims born outside India,* while the remaining 30 per cent were equally divided between Hindus and Indian-born Muslims. Why? Apparently, Akbar did not trust either the Hindus or those who converted to Islam, and made attempts to keep them at bay: many of his Diwans were Hindus who had the supplies but not the troops; and many of his 'subadars' were Muslims who had troops but not supplies—that was how he effectively checked the potential rebels. His successors did not adhere to this practice, promoted feudalism indiscriminately and eventually found themselves being gobbled up by the British. Like the British after him, he ensured that power and responsibility remained in inverse proportion, that rootless foreigners, who enjoyed power had no real support base and that the potentially powerful local chieftains did not become too big for their boots. He was, all in all, a consummate politician and brave soldier who knew the sources of power and the methods to keep them in control. So 'secular' were this romanticised Akbar's credentials and his policies of checks-and-balances and political management and so sweet-talking he appeared that he made a significant chunk of Hindus and their successors chronically culture-diabetic forever. But this was akin to the Hindus' Stockholm Syndrome: after their freedom being subjugated by Muslim fanatics for over seven centuries, Akbar allowed them to at least go to the loo; for this small mercy, the hapless Hindus of North India thought he was better in the Muslim pack and got beholden to him. Few Hindus could really see through Akbar's designs. A successful politician is one who can create an illusion of stability, security and prosperity—*Garibi Hatao* (Remove poverty), *India Shining*, *Achchhe Din*, for instance—and, in the anaesthesia thus generated, he emasculates a whole nation without the latter even realising it!

Not all Muslims were, of course, fundamentalists but most fundamentalists were Muslims—and they were in positions of power. Many of them wore the secular mask, the way many of the Hindus now wear one, cutting across political affiliations—you scratch them, just by asking if they would marry their son/daughter into a Muslim or Christian family and see them in their true colours. The Hindus *then* knew who was actually what, the way Muslims *now* know who is what—and this shaped the response of the ruled vis-a-vis the rulers. Many Hindus traditionally came to believe that although Islam could still be the best egalitarian religion, but the Muslim was the worst human being: they did not convert to Islam in large numbers because they would rather stay in a 'worse' religion rather than degenerate into the 'worst' human beings. The case of Christianity was different: the Hindus felt the missionaries were 'good' because they set up schools and hospitals but Jesus was a coward because, despite being the Son of God, he did not fight bravely and died on the Cross. For a Hindu, the Son of God *must be* a warrior who could defeat His Own Father, as Lord Rama's Sons Luv and Kush did; even Ravana's son, Meghnad, was braver than his father. For a Hindu, the ideal Son was one who could surpass His Father in all respects, even eclipse the latter, the way Ganesh and Kartikeya became more popular than their father Shiva in the North and South, respectively. Clearly, the Hindus mostly rejected both Christianity and Islam as inadequate, as they failed to satisfy the demands of their home-grown mythology and societal and moral behaviour. Abrahamism was culturally-incompatible with Hinduism the way foreign-made switches are incompatible in Indian electrical switchboards now. In return, both Christianity and Islam denounced Rama as a coward husband who could not protect his wife Sita from the evil Ravana, and Krishna as a slayer of his maternal uncle Kansa and the chief villain of the *Mahabharata* war, having plotted bloodshed in the Kuru clan.

Their common enmity against the Sunni Akbar had brought the Shias of Avadh and the struggling Hindus together. Interestingly, the Shias have mostly lived in peace and harmony with the Hindus; the 'communal' riots in the North and the West have often been between Shias and Sunnis, not Hindus and Muslims! —and this the Emperor wanted to avoid at all costs, lest they rise in a major rebellion—even the Sunni Muslims' current claim over the demolished 'Babri Mosque' of the Shias is part of strategy to drive a wedge between the Hindus and Shias of the erstwhile Avadh area as the Shias have, in the name of 'Islamic unity', been forced *not* to reinstate their controversial mosque to the infidel Hindus—the Shias are afraid that if they part with the mosque, the Sunnis would 'excommunicate' them from Islam as 'mosque donors'. Akbar could not win over the Shias who distrusted him because he had his own Shia mentor Bairam Khan overthrown and humiliated. The puritanical Shias, despite building this mosque from the ruins of the Temple, rarely used it as a place of worship because it had no minarets for *azaans* and its pillars and other structural detail still carried infidel insignia; the Shias also had support of Iran because of the latter's preoccupation against the Sunni Ottomans. For them, it was more of a monument of victory over the infidel Hindus, rather than a place of worship. But their common enmity having brought them together, the Shias now wanted to return the mosque to the Hindus as a gesture which the Sunnis, obviously, protested. The Sunnis pressurised Akbar not to yield to this Hindu demand and Shia readiness, and he did not. For, if the Emperor gave away a 'mosque' back to the Hindus and thus surrendered to the infidel, he would surely earn the wrath of his supportive Sunnis, *his core constituency*, who could declare him a Hypocrite, rendering him vulnerable to assassination as a religious duty of the Muslims for this blasphemy. And if he did not, the Hindu struggle would only gather momentum and possibly engulf his realm, at a time when Rajputana was posing a major challenge to him. In order not to offend Muslim sensibilities and pacify the Hindus, Akbar embarked upon the policy of political marriages and taking the Jaipur royals for his support, the then *coalition dharma*! He employed Rajputs to deal with Rajputs the same way the wily post-1947 Nehruvians evolved the policy of having token presence of Muslims and Christians, like decorative vases, to keep their communities smiling.

Having thus secured his position in the West, he turned towards the East. He always felt unsafe in Delhi from the Sunnis whom he distrusted now because of his matrimonial alliances with the Hindus *without converting them to Islam*. This was another reason why he moved his capital to Fatehpur Sikri, near Agra. Similarly, in 1573, when news of a revolt in Gujarat reached him, he marched from Fatehpur Sikri to shift his capital temporarily to Ahmedabad, securing Gujarat for the Mughals for 185 years; Aurangzeb, too, would nearly shift his capital to the Deccan with the same aim.

Akbar had 'secured' India from land routes; he did not, however, seem to have the foggiest idea that a more potent danger to the Mughal Empire was shaping up far away in Europe after expulsion of Islam from the Reconquista-infested Spain in 1498, the way Nehru did not believe that China was bracing for an attack on India in 1962. That this storm would come from the sea and that his son, Salim/Jahangir, would witness the beginning of the end. The British East India Company, like anaconda, washed ashore in India, in 1600—preceded by smaller fries from Portugal, the Netherlands and France. The Islamisation of both Spain and India, the geographical limits of Islam, had begun in the same year, 711; the deIslamisation, too, began in the same year, 1498, when Spain finally expelled Islam and the Portuguese arrived in India to midwife delivery of the 'unwanted' child—it is another thing that the Portuguese would leave their own scissors in the Indian womb which would be surgically operated out as late as 1960 in Goa.

Illiterate but successful adults often despise intellectuals and try to buy intellect and respect using the material means to offset the imbalance of their failure to burn the midnight oil as adolescents; uneducated and failed people, even if they are functionally literate, often force their progeny to fulfil their own unfulfilled ambitions and derive satisfaction in this 'our failure turned into our children's success'. Akbar had surrounded himself with intelligent 'gems' whom he used in carrying out different tasks but this did not satisfy his vaulting ambition. He knew Prophet Muhammed was 'illiterate'; couldn't Akbar, also illiterate and the most powerful Emperor of the vast Indian realm now, become a 'Prophet' in his own right? But Muhammed had declared himself the 'Last Prophet' and no true Muslim could, therefore, dare call himself, or Akbar, a Prophet. Akbar could at least become a Caliph, Commander of the Faithful, the *Amir-ul-Mominin*. But even this was not possible as he had only Turko-Mongol, not Quraish or Arab, blood in his lineage, nor did India under his rule enjoy proximity to Arabia unlike Turkey or Egypt where rival Caliphates could emerge because they had the power to control the holy places of Mecca and al-Medina, and influence Muslim politics. In fact, the Arabs often neglected the 'Hindu Muslims' and official Ummah never had any love lost with the Indian subcontinental Muslims whom they treated as lowly-born: barring equality in the mosque and pilgrimage, these Muslims were considered *mlechchha* even by the blue-blooded Arabs, the way the infidel Hindus did! The Arabs were aware that the first Muslim rulers of India were all Arab *slaves*. For the Ummah, India continued to remain a Muslim outhouse of the Brotherhood, founded by the *Slave Dynasties*; and the Ummah never trusted the Mughals whose Mongol forefathers had destroyed the Caliphate in the 13th century Baghdad. In other words, Akbar's vaulting ambitions were stopped in the tracks by his Turko-Mongol blood, distance from Arabia, and, above all, his utter dependence back home on the infidel Hindus for stability of his realm.

Clearly, even if Akbar declared himself a Caliph, few would recognise him as one. In fact, even the Turk Sultan-cum-Caliphs of the Ottoman Empire could never get official recognition by the Arabs (Mahatma Gandhi was, apparently, aware of this fact when he supported the zero-sum Khilafat Movement *in India* for restoration of the Caliphate *in far-away Turkey* in the 1920s, as we would see). The non-Hashimite Turks, not of the Arab and/or Quraish origin, and their 'Caliphate' always remained controversial until the Caliphate itself was scrapped by Mustafa Kemal in March 1924; it was another matter that the unrecognised Caliph would continue to issue recognition certificates to Muslim pretenders everywhere. For a proud Emperor like Akbar, such a 'certificate' was beneath his dignity anyway.

The Shia Iran was the unbridgeable gap between a largely infidel India and Sunni Arab nations like Arabia, Iraq etc. Akbar was, perhaps, in a dilemma. But he had an uncanny knack for balancing acts and finding a mid-course, and he had been successful so far. His policy of *Sulh-Kul*, Peace with All, had also brought in good dividends initially. Having revived in India the Persian imperial idea with a semi-divine Emperor controlling a vast imperial apparatus, Akbar believed he had secured India for the Mughals. But he had actually made the ground fertile for the British: his system essentially depended on the acumen of the Emperor, and since his successors were increasingly inept, and rank fanatics, they could not hold onto the emerging power of a united Hindu India, unlike in the Sultanate period when the Muslims had ruled so effectively because of disunity among the Hindus. Akbar, the Muslim, united India; Akbar, 'the Hindu', was its undisputed Monarch; so Akbar the Hindu eventually uprooted Akbar the Muslim! And Aurangzeb could not control the tide his great-grandfather had triggered. Akbar was the precarious mid-point on the Mughal Scale at the two ends of which hanged the pans called Babur and Aurangzeb: the Great Mughal tried to control the wolves unleashed by Babur but these were reaped in full force by Aurangzeb. Akbar tried to make Islam palatable in India and transform and settle the Mughal Dynasty essentially as 'Indian' in character at a time when China, too, was similarly trying to adjust to and live with the foreign Manchu Ching Dynasty that had replaced the native Mings. Akbar's imperial policies were aimed at proving this point and that India was one, indivisible entity whose 'natural' rulers were the Mughals. This notion was inherited by the successor British and the Nehruvian Congress rulers; culturally, India had always been one nation, though in terms of politics it oscillated between unity and diversity like glacier forming and melting with change of seasons. For India, unity has essentially been a cultural concept involving agreements on polytheism, pluralism and multiculturalism, a tolerance of a pyramidal social order and religious unanimity, rather than a political or economic expression which see cyclical ups and downs and are, at best, ephemeral due to rise and fall of nations depending upon technological quotients and trade cycles. Akbar tried to weld Islam with Hinduism into a temporary but rather impossible oil-water mix and ended up rearing an Aurangzeb and a Shivaji as implacable conjoined twins as theo-electrolysis progressed.

But, now, this balancing act between divergent forces, as in the Ashokan case, inexorably pulled Akbar's reign into the 'half-partridge, half-quail' mode, the way Nawaz Sharif once described Pakistan. In his lifetime, Akbar could seldom earn total or lasting faith and loyalty of either Hindus or Muslims. When the fires of his youth cooled down and he was bored and exhausted with his 5,000-strong harem, he revived in India what the Spanish Moors had lost in the Iberian Peninsula. Akbar, who knew that non-Arab Caliphs were seen as pretenders and Anti-Caliphs in the Muslim world, that he being a Turko-Mongol stood little chance of being accepted as one (within the Brotherhood, the Arabs believed themselves to be the only true and blue blood of Islam and the Persians as creator of 'Islamic culture'; the rest of the Brotherhood, they believed, was riff-raff and tolerated only because they were *not* infidel!). He was merely an Emperor of a largely infidel country like India far away from Mecca and Baghdad. He was a careful schemer and would not move in haste; he would not call himself a 'Caliph' straightaway but ensure everything else fell into place towards this grandiose project.

So, prodded on by sidekicks like Sheikh Mubarak, Akbar issued an Infallibility Decree (1579) at a time Europe was progressively readying itself to deny the same to the Pope in the next 300 years. By thus declaring himself first as *Mujtahid*, Supreme Arbiter in religious matters, he tried to emerge as the new, *de facto* Caliph in his own right with the additional title of Imam-i-Adil, Final Interpreter of Muslim Law, which he bestowed on himself, and indirectly placed himself next only to Allah and Muhammed. India's Muslim rulers before him used to obtain an affiliation certificate from the proper Caliph at Damascus, Baghdad or Istanbul but Akbar tried to annex this prerogative for himself and had it penned in a document. 'Obey Allah, and obey His Prophet, and those who have authority among you, and secondly, of the genuine tradition. Surely the man who is dearest to Allah on the day of judgment is the Imam-i-Adil; whosoever obeys the Amir obeys Thee; and whosoever rebels against him, rebels against Thee. And thirdly, of several other proofs based on reasoning or testimony; and we have agreed that the rank of Sultan-I-Adil is higher in the eyes of Allah than the rank of a Mujtahid. Further, we declare that the King of Islam, Amir-ul-Mominin, Shadow of Allah in the World, Abul-Fatah, Jalal-ud-din Muhammad Akbar, Padshah *Ghazi* (whose Kingdom let Allah perpetuate), is a most just, wisest and most Allah-fearing King... We do hereby agree that such a decree shall be binding on us and the whole nation.'

This Mongoloid attempt to convert Islam from being an Arabic, Desert Religion of Domination (*Deen-e-Ghalib*) into an Eastern Religion of God, to plant it firmly in the Orient by marrying it with the native culture, did not obviously go down well with the Sunni orthodoxy which suspected its claims and credentials; in West Asia too, similar Ottoman attempts followed—that eventually led Turkey to get embroiled with European politics, become a 'Sick Man of

Europe', abolish the Caliphate itself in 1924, thus leaving the headless Brotherhood in the lurch for the first time since the year 632.

Akbar, known to the Muslims as half-Hindu and to the Hindus as half-Muslim, fell between two stools; attempting to be all things to all and please everybody, he ended up pleasing none. Few, if any, took him seriously, not even the sidekicks who signed the document and pledged support. A Caliph could not be far from the injunctions of the *Qur'an* and the Hadiths, that is *expansion of the Dar-ul-Harb into Dar-ul-Islam*; and here was an alleged Caliph who wanted to earn the goodwill of the infidel! The very enemy he was supposed to eliminate! Although, in the Infallibility Decree, he had declared himself a 'Ghazi', Slayer of the Infidel, his 'Hindu-appeasing' policies had made him a laughing stock as devout Muslims ridiculed him; the Hindus, however, had nothing to do with all this fuss, a purely intra-Islamic affair, until Akbar decided to slide back to emulate the Slave Dynasties. Having thus ended up with egg in the face, the hyper-ambitious Emperor tried to rescue his sinking ship in a post-script: *Furthermore, we declare that should His Majesty think it fit to release a new order, we and the nation shall be bound by it as well; provided always that such an order be not only in accordance with some Verse of the Qur'an, but also of real benefit to the nation; and further, that any opposition on the part of his subjects to such an order passed by His Majesty shall involve damnation in the other world and loss of property and religious privileges in this.*' He thereby tried to divest the Muslim clergy of their right to persecute others for their opinions and orthodox theologians believed he had renounced Islam and become a 'Hindu Caliph'.

The 'infallible' Akbar soon discovered few were interested in his gargantuan designs; within two years, his caliphal claims came to a nought and fewer even remembered it. The Infallibility Decree fell like nine pins, like a much-hyped film flopping on the box office. But this did not detract the by-now intrepid and schizophrenic Akbar who had, like narcissists, become so addicted to his own early successes that each failure fuelled his ambition. His ambition was vaulting; he tried to match his own circumstances with those around Prophet Muhammed. Both of them were near-orphaned at an early age, both were 'illiterate', both of them faced insurmountable tasks before them at a tender age that had split their personalities. If Muhammed could launch Islam, why not Akbar? It was a case of Islam II: if Muhammad was 'Akbar' (the Great), why could not Akbar be 'Muhammed' (the Blessed One)? After the failure of the Infallibility Decree,Akbar was no longer interested in becoming a mere Caliph; even otherwise, after the Mongols overthrew them at Baghdad in the 13th century and the Spanish in 1492, the Caliphs were a mere shadow of their former glorious self; especially for an Akbar, who controlled a vast realm, the real competitor was no longer the Caliph but the Prophet himself! If an 'Arab' could become a Prophet and create an empire, why could not a Turko-Mongol, having already created an Empire, emerge as a Prophet in his own right in 1580!? Akbar, therefore, would indirectly try to dislodge Islam and Muhammed and enforce his own new faith and himself instead.

He now veered to the other end of this theo-psychological spectrum, setting up his own shop by floating a new purported faith in 1581, the *Deen-e-Elahi* (Religion of God!) or the *Tauhid-e-Elahi* (Unity of God). It was basically, in the typical Mongol style, revival of one of the oldest Central Asian Sun myths and an attempt to somehow impossibly blend it with Islam—which, interestingly, meant worship as well as condemnation of the Sun God simultaneously! —and a patently infidel Hinduism, to bring about a fresh brew billed to become India's 'national religion'. Its official 'philosopher' was his courtier and principal secretary Abul Fazal who was eventually got eliminated (1602) by Prince Salim for, among others, this crime. Akbar himself was, of course, its infallible Pope, the 39-year-old top pontiff of the new faith (Muhammed soft-launched Islam when he was 40) surrounded by aged lawmakers of the old, who admitted the novices into brotherhood on Sundays 'when the world-illuminating Sun is in its highest splendour'; the novice would surrender his turban, put his head at the Emperor's feet, to be raised up by His Majesty with his turban back on head. He then 'sacrificed', one by one, four things to the Emperor: property, life, honour and religion—so, there were these four categories of disciples. And, lo and behold, you have a new convert with a shast presented to him by the new Apostle. But Jalal-ud-Deen Akbar did not forget his middle name: Muhammad.

For, on the shast was engraved the symbolic motto 'Allah-o-Akbar' (God is Great!)—the new 'religion' was like an imperial club for Akbar's sidekicks and hangers-on to curry favour and, at the same time, remain what they were: Hindus or Muslims. Birbal was the only important Hindu to board this bandwagon. The Hindus had their own 'superhuman' kings in mythology and the Muslims believed in no such entity: the Deen-e-Elahi was, at best, seen as the eccentricity of an ambitious king given to self-exaltation and self-importance as a recompense for his own illiteracy, the way illiterate but successful people buy out scholarly recognitions the world over.

The Hindus tolerated him as there was no alternative; and, ironically, the Muslims tolerated him, likewise, for the same reason! It was the modern TINA factor at work in that medieval era: that, 'There Is No Alternative', a logjam that can be broken only by an *external disruptive intervention* as the Sikhs and Shivaji would do later. He established the cult of the monarch with himself as a semi-divine personage: it was a religious duty of all to obey him and a sacrilege to rebel; they were supposed to revere his aura and prostrate to him. Never was there any other Muslim king like him in a still largely infidel territory: he made the Mughals a necessary evil for the contemporary Hindus, the only Muslim dynasty they could somehow, minimally, relate to. Loyalty to the Mughal dynasty was one of the most important factors behind the 1857 First War of Independence, a hundred years after it had already lost its effective power; some of this mystique of 'divine power' was inherited by Queen Victoria when she was proclaimed the direct ruler of India in 1858—even Rabindra Nath Tagore was not free from this colonial hangover when he described the visiting King George V as *Bharat Bhagya Vidhata* (Maker of India's Destiny), in what became eventually the National Anthem since 1947; he had penned this ode when the King came to inaugurate the new capital of British-India in 1911 after its relocation from Calcutta to Delhi. The slave Hindus got so much accustomed to this yoke of *divine kingship of foreigners ruling India,* that, until Nehru, the Very Last Mughal, they could scarcely think of living without it; after 1947, the entire lot of hybrid, genetically modified Black Britons, that went severally by names like Nehruvians, secularists and communists, supported everything Anglo-Saxon *minus* the Crown. The Mughals' decline was pathetic, like the Congress Party's: Rahul Gandhi's reign does not even match that of Shah Alam II (1728-1806): *Sultanat-e-Shah Alam Az Dilli Ta Palam* (The Kingdom of Shah Alam extends from Dilli to Palam, the latter then a suburb).

But Akbar did give India back the idea of a *political and national* unity and an empire, lost long since King Harsha, in which the Hindus could have at least some say; in this sense, he was relatively more tolerant than other Muslim rulers even if for political reasons. It was, again, Akbar, who brought back the concept of imperial sanctity—his predecessors were forgotten soon after their last breath—and his paintings came to depict the halo, or nimbus, to the Emperor's head, which was copied by other Mughal emperors as well, like the Hindu paintings of gods, great personages and saints. At his best, Akbar was born Muslim, ruled over the Hindus, and died a heretic. He could not break any new grounds but tried to expand on the old; he did not solve any burning problem but succeeded in pushing them under the carpet. Ayodhya and Deen-e-Elahi were both examples of his monumental failures. But he was the tunnel through which the converted Hindus could return to Hinduism.

But, as Ashoka had through his *Dhamma* sapped India's virility for 500 years before the Guptas restored it to some extent, Akbar too, through his *Deen-e-Ilahi*, emasculated Indian mind for the next 500 years by spawning a whole swarm of synthetic 'secularists' who turned out to be severely afflicted by the Stockholm Syndrome. The patients suffering from this disease are like hostages who become romantically and emotionally attached to their captors: this Syndrome begins with shocking and sudden capture, terror and infantilisation where you cannot eat, talk, move or use even a toilet without the captor's permission; but, then, one of the captors turns generous and permits you to go to the loo... The 'gift' of life, this newfound 'generosity', conceding your minimum needs when you are imprisoned and under severe mental stress, results in primitive, primordial gratitude which, henceforth, is the foundation of all future feelings of love. You tend to forget the crime of the captor and, instead not only love him but even emerge as his protector and accomplice—in brief, the patient feels secure by *being patient* and even protecting the virus! He begins to feel safe with the disease, rather than find its cure, to try to have a mutual understanding in that kind of situation is not so strange, a peaceful co-existence between the patient and the disease. It is somewhat like survival of the 'unfittest' who struggles for existence by merely surrendering before the inevitable; it is not a reflection of throbbing life but postponing death, a sense of gratitude in which the victim and the captor continue their relationship even after the former's life is no longer at risk. So, in India, this mass Syndrome commenced with Babur inflicting a festering wound by demolishing the Ayodhya Temple and the secularist's romantic relationship with Islam, and later Christianity, began with Akbar providing that 'much-needed healing touch'; the latter became the generous captor who, while not releasing the hostage Hindus, would permit them to wash. For this generosity, the hostages would ever be grateful. No wonder, by the 21st century, post 9/11, the entire world has inherited the Stockholm Syndrome. Stockholm is where the Nobel Prizes are given. Only the Peace Prize is given at Oslo. Even President Barack Obama, who put a new label to America's own holy war, 'Just War', got one within days of his sending more American troops to Afghanistan!

The 'new' faith of Deen-e-Elahi was genetically different from the Islamic roots in being *Deen-e-Ghalib* (Faith of Domination). Except Akbar's hangers on, few had faith in it and, within two decades of official and royal patronage, it ended up reviving some of the Zoroastrian beliefs and the Sun myths and rites, promoted vegetarianism back among the Hindus at least and cremation, rather than burial, of the dead. All Hindus dead in North India were now taken in a funeral procession to their own pyres with the chanting of *Rama Naam Satya Hai* (Lord Rama, Thy Name is The Truth), until the singing of this chant became popular across the Hindi-speaking world. In other words, every Hindu cremated *thus* was seen as having died *for* the cause of Ayodhya! The Hindus could now go up in flames with head in the east, towards the Sunrise; conversely, all dead Muslims were buried with their head towards Mecca in whose defence they were thought to have breathed their last.

Like Ashoka's Dhamma, Akbar's Deen-e-Elahi was a nine-day wonder which, like the mirage, disappeared as soon as his sun set. Akbar married monotheism with pantheism: the practical deification of the monarch as *the* Vice-Regent of God on the Earth, the adoration of the Sun with veneration of fire and artificial lights and worship of Nature—the Aryan-Persian theory and practice of divine kingship, in which the younger males of a royal family normally remained unambitious and trusted in primogeniture, the right of the eldest son, in whom they saw the image of god to succeed father, was in vogue in India and Iran. The *Ramayana* was a saga revolving around this theme in which the Lord was denied this right, banished for 14 years and returned triumphant to Ayodhya in the end to restore *primogeniture* and Aryan Order. The Muslims of Arabia, when they won over Iran soon after the Prophet's death, found Islam infected from its earliest times with this Iranian practice; but since Islam was a Brotherhood of *equal* brothers, it did not have the concept of any *elder* brother—any Muslim, who could gather enough strength, thought it his right to kill all the males that could challenge his journey to the throne (in the *Mahabharata*, all the Kaurava brothers, too, were born almost simultaneously, artificially, but Duryodhana and Dushasana were the first two). So, the orthodox Muslims, who believed that it was their power of the sword that gave them the right to rule and the 'ideal' Muslim to cleanse the infidel land, did not like Akbar appropriating Aryan-Iranian culture of divine kingship, indirectly declaring himself a Descendent of God. Although many of the Mongols, after destroying the Abbasid Caliphate, had converted to Islam, they were still hated and suspected in the Brotherhood; the same was the case with the Turks who had usurped the Caliphate in the Ottoman regime. Here, in India, was a Turko-Mongol descendent, Akbar, who the Sunnis believed had reduced Islam into a caricature of itself. Clearly, like Julian the Apostate, when he died, few mourned: those who try to have no enemy, have no friends either. The Hindus now feared the arrival of an Aurangzeb, while the fundamentalist Muslims rejoiced at the death of this 'heretic' Emperor and boosted the morale of his successor Jahangir to atone for his father's 'sins': Salim alias Jahangir did not disappoint them as he midwifed Sikhism from the womb of Hinduism in the North, even as Ayodhya remained a volcano in the East; not to be left behind, Jahangir's grandson Aurangzeb, too, would midwife a Shivaji in the South; and, together, the Mughals ensured that the West came from the Waste.

Not surprisingly, Muslim orthodoxy reared its head against Akbar and, in 1580, believing that the Emperor had renounced Islam, his brother Muhammad Hakim became the figurehead of fundamentalist rebellion in Kabul, later crushed by the royal forces; already, the Brotherhood was under threat elsewhere and could not afford to remain complacent in a vast infidel territory like India, the Mughal Empire being the largest and the only relatively stable Islamic empire east of the Indus, especially for the Sunnis: Shia Iran divided the Sunnis into two contemporary halves, the Ottomans and the Mughals, and intra-Brotherhood politics required that Indian Islam did not go the Iranian way because, if successful, the Indo-Iranian Shia block would then have been more powerful than the Sunni Caliphate proper. Unless Sunni Islam reasserted itself in India, its days would be numbered and, while Sufism had links with the Shias in Iran, it came to rescue Sunnism in India: the Sufi 'peaceniks' became the reserve force of the Sunnis. 'Islam is in danger', announced Shaikh Ahmed Sirhindi (1564-1624), a contemporary of Akbar, Tulsidas and Jahangir—these four words were prophetic and have since shaped the Muslim Mind all over the world vis-a-vis the non-Muslims who spiked the third word—for them, it was, increasingly, *Islam is danger*. The Mongol menace had forced the Muslim orthodoxy into the ghettos of madrassas; the neo-Mongol, Akbar, now forced them to spread like a virus in the Muslim society. Sufism, which had begun as a half-way house between Islam and ancient mysticism *after total Islamisation* in West Asia, found its role fundamentally altered in India: here, it was not a half-way house between Islam and Hindu mysticism in a land where the infidel heavily outnumbered the Muslims, but would have to shoulder the onerous responsibility of *total Islamisation*! The Sufis had discovered that Muslim arms were of little use in this task as even the forcibly-converted continued to stick to their infidel culture and for any number of Muslim soldiers, it was impossible to convert a vast infidel country like India; emperors like Akbar, having their own ambitions and axes to grind, ended up only harming Islam and the fundamentalists, as elsewhere, did not comprehend the difficulties in ruling and running an infidel and immensely complicated land like India. And, of course, the Sufis, like Winston Churchill in the 1940s, did not want to preside over the liquidation of their own empire in India.

The only possible way to restart the halted project for everlasting and total Islamisation of India was to follow a carrot-and-stick policy. Already there were a dozen Sufi sects in India but the major ones were the Chishti, the biggest of them all, besides Suhrawardi, Naqshbandi, Qadiria, Nimatullahi and Shattari. Akbar was a disciple of Sheikh Salim-ud-Din Chishti, after whom he had named his son, Shekhu alias Salim, the would-be Jahangir. The founder of this sect in India, Khwaja Muin-ud-Din Chishti (1143-1223), had set up his theo-conversion business, the *Khanqah*, at Ajmer, to spread the message of Wahdat-ul-Wujud, a pantheic monism purportedly finding 'similarities' with the Vedas, something continued through TV evangelism by the likes of Zakir Naik with Arab funding. It aimed at converting the Hindus by persuading them to treat Islam as a 'continuation' of their Vedic monistic and monotheistic beliefs, *minus polytheism*. These Sufis differed with the Sunnis mainly due to their 'peaceful' means to convert the Hindus. Pakistani military dictator Pervez Musharraf, who sought to re-establish his post-Kargil War 'peaceful' credentials through a visit Ajmer in 2001, eventually backed off as he could not afford to antagonise the fire-spitting Sunnis back home in Pakistan!

The Naqshabandi Sufis were, basically, a shrine-worshipping fundamentalist clan and their name was derived from two words, *naqsh* (external appearance) and *bandi* (locking), that is, restricting the infidel belief in hand-made god to the construction of a god-less shrine as an external appearance, to facilitate the infidel's eventual absorption into the proper Islamic fold. Their next 'evolution' was the Deobandis, from 'deo' (gods) and 'bandis'—locking the infidel gods—

and anyone who was trapped in this Sufi maze eventually converted to the Sunni faith through this tactic on the road to Sunni Islam. For the record, the Deobandis provided the seed for germination of the Taliban and their ilk—through Ali Miyan, for example—although, under pressure, they could even hawk peace and harmony off and on, again as a tactic to buy time and gather strength. The Sufis provided the compost on which would mushroom the likes of Mushrraf, the Wahhabis, the Salafis, and, of course, Osama bin-Laden.

By the time of Akbar, however, the Chishtis had discovered that this strategy did not exactly produce the desired results despite 400 years of their being in business; on the contrary, it produced a disciple like Akbar who could *deIslamise* India! Sufism, therefore, must return to the Islamic moorings, barbarism and ruthlessness it had originally inherited from Zoroastrian Iran. So, Akbar's contemporary Chishti 'saint' Shaikh Ahmed Sirhindi (his title 'Sirhindi' meant one who vanquished Hind, ie. India) claimed to have been 'commissioned in a dream' by none else than Prophet Muhammed, who had, in turn, been once commissioned by Jibril (Gabriel), to Islamise the infidel; the Muslim 'intellectual' in Sirhindi tried to reconcile Sunni legalism with the religion of spirit, Sufism, in a bid to repel the tendency of syncretism with Hinduism. He declared that not only the Body of the Believers but also the Body of the Belief was important: when the Amir-ul-Mominin (Commander of the Faithful) in an infidel land like India failed to command the believers and temporal power protecting Islam collapsed, the Muslims could now fall back on the Sovereignty of Allah and the Congregation of the Faithful—the Islamic equivalent of the 'right to recall' in a modern democracy, the people's representative who failed to wage war against the infidel! While the Mughals evolved the concept of One India *under* the Mughals, Sirhindi gave birth to the germ for a *separate* Muslim state in the Indian subcontinent—Jinnah would merely be the surrogate mother for the frozen Sirhindi sperm to sire Pakistan. This Sufi 'saint' fathered all separatist and terrorist ideologies until Pakistan was created and Afghanistan destroyed by Mullah Umar and his Taliban gang. But, while trying to impregnate India with Islam, he ended up impregnating the Hindus against Islam and emerged as the biggest deIslamiser.

Protesting against Akbar's manipulative power policies, he shot off several letters to the Emperor' courtiers and Jahangir. Decorating himself with the exotic title of *Mujaddid-e-alf-e-Sani*, Renovator of the Second Millennium of Islam, he declared that Shariat could survive only under the 'Shadow of the Sword': 'The honour of Islam lay in utterly humiliating the infidel… they should remain constantly terrified and trembling', the recalcitrant peacenik Sufi said in his Letter number 163. Further, 'the cow sacrifice in India is the noblest of Islamic practices; for, the infidel could pay the jazia, but not agree to cow sacrifice', he declared in Letter number 81. He also was thrilled when the opium addict Jahangir resumed the 'commendable' policy of destroying temples and tortured Hindus, particularly the Sikh sect. It was the Sirhindi project and theology that spawned the Wahhabis in Arabia and later the Deobandis, the Aligarh Movement, the Ahl-e-Hadis, Pakistan, the Taliban, Osama bin-Laden, which all aimed at destruction of non-Islamic beliefs by using all means, ancient and modern, to impose Muhammed's medievalism across the world—but Arabia did not, apparently, know that in Sirhindi, it has imported the most dangerous antidote for Islam itself! Sirhindi was the Patriarch of Islamic terrorism and his admirers included Maulana Abul Kalam Azad, who was born in Mecca. 'But for these (Sirhindi's) letters, the Muslim nobles would not have continued to adhere to the Islamic cause and but for the efforts of Shaikh Ahmed, Akbar's heterodoxy would have superseded Islam in India', the Maulana once wrote. The poison tree of Sirhindi is now yielding fruit all over the Christian world as well.

So furious had Sirhindi become due to Akbar's attempts to push the Ayodhya issue under the carpet, befriend Tulsidas and promote Krishna worship instead—compare the stand-off between the then Prime Minister A B Vajpayee and the Vishwa Hindu Parishad (VHP) on the issue in the early 2000s! —that he declared that Rama and Krishna are 'insignificant creatures' begotten by their parents. 'Rama could not protect his wife whom Ravan took away by force. How can he help others? It is thousands of times shameful that some people should think of Rama and Krishna as rulers of all the worlds. To think that Rama and Rehman are the same is extremely foolish. The Creator and the creature can never be one... the Controller of the Cosmos was never called Rama and Krishna before the latter were born. What has happened after their birth that they have come to be equated with Allah, and the worship of Rama and Krishna is described as the worship of Allah? May Allah save us! Our Prophets who number 124,000 have encouraged the created ones to worship the Creator... the gods of the Hindus, on the other hand, have encouraged the people to worship them (the gods) instead.'

No wonder, although Sirhindi had named himself 'Sir-Hindi', one who would 'win India', ended up deIslamising India instead, through vivisection, by successfully plotting the incremental evolution of Pakistan and heralding a gradual deIslamisation of the subcontinent. India retained her cool, thanks to such nincompoops already anticipated by Adi Shankaracharya—when your boat is rocked in a choppy sea like this, refrain from swimming against the current lest you lose energy and drown; just lie down, on your back, till you regain your breath. Sirhindi lauded Jahangir for executing the Sikh Guru Arjun Dev, the 'chief of idolaters' and claimed, yet again, that Prophet Muhammed praised it in a dream that came to him (Sirhindi). Dream-inheritors! But he did not know that the capture of Samarkand by Babur coincided with King Ferdinand and Queen Isabella uprooting Islam in Spain in 1492 and soon after, Columbus discovering the New World of America (1498), nor that the Jihad he had launched against India was precisely what this infidel land wanted Islamists of all shades to do to come out in their true colours. For, he himself witnessed the slow beginning of the Hindu reaction: 'the Hindus are demolishing mosques, and erecting their own places of worship on the same sites. There was a mosque in the tank of Kurukshetra at Thanesar, as also the tomb of a Muslim saint. These have been demolished, and a huge Gurudwara has been constructed on the same sites. Besides, the infidel are holding many celebrations of infidelity.'

In the end, Sirhindi ended up where all those who father terror go: 'It is a thousand pities that the reigning King is a Mussalman, and we recluses find ourselves helpless. There was a time when Islam stood glorified due to the might and prestige of its kings, and the Ulama and the Sufis were honoured and held in high regard.'

Jahangir, Shahjahan and even Aurangzeb, like Akbar, often used the Sufis and other Muslim orthodox leaders like disposable sanitary napkins. Despite proving their Islamic credentials here and there, in varying degrees, the Emperors sometimes found themselves favouring the majority, the Hindus, if only to keep the lid on rebellion: while Akbar demonstrated his 'secular' bent of mind by trying to win over Tulsidas and donating land to the Sikh Guru Ramdas in the Punjab, even Aurangzeb sometimes did the same for administrative reasons. Akbar and Aurangzeb even favoured the family of Tulsidas by giving it some revenue collection authority at Chitrakoot, which were withdrawn by the 'secular' Congress Party in 1972 to celebrate the Silver Jubilee of India's Independence! The tenth descendents of the great poet still claim to preserve the hand-written *Ramcharitmanas* with them and wait for the reconstruction of the Ayodhya temple.

Akbar's ambivalence due to the very real problem of managing a vast infidel realm through political management and bribe—when he wanted to befriend the Hindu, it often meant that he would antagonise the Muslim—had forced him to go 'democratic', ie., majority Hindu-friendly in many cases. Citing some incidents, his Islamist detractors like Badayuni charged him with many a thing such as, after promulgation of the new faith, denouncing him that he issued many ordinances against Islam—that he forbade Islamic prayers, disallowed the call to prayer or *Azaan*, discouraged wearing of beard, stopped Muslim fasts, prohibited beef but allowed flesh of tiger or wild bear, ordered *Sijdah* (bowing before God) to be offered only to the Emperor, banned circumcision before age 12 and marriage of boys before 16 and girls before 14. He was also charged with disallowing pilgrimage to Mecca, discontinuing Muslim festivals, names containing that of the Prophet were disallowed, and wearing of silk dresses and ornaments made compulsory at the new faith's prayers; that mosques and prayer rooms were converted into horses' stables and given over to Hindu watchmen and that Akbar even ordered plunder of some mosques to get money, exiled Mullahs and Sheikhs and discouraged study of Arabic—most of these were mere allegations intended to charge up the devout Muslim, using unsubstantiated local and minor incidents; the Muslim bided his time, slowly turned screws on Akbar's petty successors until the Emperor's great grandson, Aurangzeb Alamgir turned these screws into nails in the coffin of the Mughal Empire. Nobody could diagnose the root cause of the disease the way the greatest Urdu poet Mirza Asadullah 'Ghalib' did about his own *Deen-e-Ghalib*, in the twilight of the Mughal 'Empire' in the 19th century: *Khuda ke vaastey parda na Kaa'bey se utha zahid, Kahin aisa na ho yahaan bhee yahi Qafir sanam nikley* (For God's sake, O'priest, don't lift the veil that hides the Kaa'ba, Lest you discover those beloved heathen gods there also)!

The Jesuits, European clones of Sirhindi, tried hard but failed to convert Akbar to Christianity; then these schemers began discrediting the Emperor, spread rumours against him, fomented trouble wherever they could, smelt conspiracy where none existed and created one instead, conspiracy being nickname of a successful Christian missionary. It was not their mistake, however: having kicked out the Spanish Caliphate and Islam from Europe, they fervently hoped that infidel India, too, was dying to be saved by the Christ. DeIslamisation was their sacrosanct mission and the more fundamentalists among them would continue to foment trouble here and there until a slow reaction and deChristianisation, too, set in what they identified as their pet territory, the geographical Gondwanaland part of India, the tribal belt spreading from South Gujarat in the West to South Bihar in the East: it was in these two extremities that the first violent expression of Hindu reaction against the Christian missionaries was noticed in the year 1999, when, anticipating the Second Coming of the Christ at the turn of the Millennium in 2000, they became hyperactive to harvest as many souls as they could to reserve a Berth Up There... and it is now the hub of Maoist-Naxalite bloodshed.

Jahangir (1605-27) was an able ruler but degenerate, given to alcohol, opium and barbarism; to win back the Sunni orthodoxy, he resumed the suspended but well-honed state policy of destruction of Hindu temples and suppression of infidels; and even wondered why the bubonic plague had broken out in his realm, claiming thousands of lives—he did not know the plague, afflicting Europe as well, had coincided with deIslamisation and that this drive, which began in Spain in 1492, was now washing ashore India. Nature was set to eliminate surplus populations. The Portuguese had already arrived in India during Akbar's time and had even snubbed the Great Mughal as well as other rulers in the South by their infamous uncouth and barbarian behaviour; seen as the scum of contemporary Europe, the Portuguese colonisers were the neo-Turks in India. A Kerala ruler had welcomed the Portuguese; in a return gesture, the self-invited guests, like their predecessor Muslims, claimed that India was theirs. By 1582, the Portuguese were well-entrenched all along the western coast and in the Arabian Sea because the Mughals did not have any navy. Akbar, too, who had just now failed to become a Virtual Caliph, was unaware that the Iberian Peninsula had overthrown the Spanish Caliphate and Muslim Rule in 1498 and the Portuguese had come to India with the same White Man's burden, and that the Portuguese were merely a trial balloon—the Dutch and French guests were on the way before the British finally replaced the Mughals. India, among the richest country in the 17th century world, had been socially sick for half-a-millennium and now needed a disruptive change to rejuvenate herself and turn into a breakout nation; she had also accumulated a lot of waste and compost we now know as surplus population and was ripe to receive a course of medicines and catalysts in quick succession. Prosperity, ease and comfort had socially ruined India, making it British-ready, the way it became Muslim-ready earlier.

While suppressing the Hindus, Jahangir had forgotten to suppress that 'other' infidel, the Christian. On the contrary, he permitted the East India Company, formed in 1600, to debut in India. He was unaware that he had effectively halted the process of complete Islamisation of India and that his Muslim successors would be swept away by the gathering British-Sikh-Maratha storm. It would be left to the British to segregate the grain from the chaff. And their guides were Captain W Hawkins and Sir Thomas Roe who had sensed that the Mughal Empire was now moth-eaten, ready to be captured when they obtained Jahangir's order to begin trade at Surat in 1615.

Akbar, due to his robust frame, had refused to die in haste despite Salim's prayers, but the latter, who once revolted against illustrious father, did not, at least, kill him. But Jahangir's son, Khurram alias Shahjahan, did not demonstrate any such pretensions. Islamists, essentially akin to military missionaries focused on goal and victory, generally recognised no human relationships; on the contrary, they despised such relations as a weakness and an obstacle. So, Khurram patiently waited for his father's death and, following his father's footsteps, revolted in frustration before surrendering to his drunkard father. In 1627, Jahangir died of alcoholism. Khurram killed all his competing brothers for the peace of his mind when he succeeded his father. He had massacred his brothers but forgotten to kill his own sons one of whom, Aurangzeb, dethroned and imprisoned him for nine years so that the Emperor could feel the Last Sigh of the Muslims in India in the form of the Taj Mahal before his own eyes. It speaks volumes for the Islamic mission in India that its best representative is not a mosque but a mausoleum! India became Islam's last major journey in the world. No wonder, the Taj Mahal is now the most threatened monument in India by human and external factors.

Aurangzeb—ironically but realistically described by Allama Iqbal as '*tarkashi maa raa khudangi aakhrin*' (the last arrow in the quiver of Muslim power in India!)—knew exactly how to bomb and deconstruct the great imperial edifice raised by his forefathers and restore Hinduism on its path of restoration. His activities united—and continue to unite—the Hindus like never before. For this 'pro-Hindu' monarch, it was not difficult. *The Hindus, as Gandhi would later realise, could only be united and whipped up into a frenzy by attacking them.* So Aurangzeb moved step-by-step: he expanded the Mughal premises but did not construct toilets for making the Hindus relieve themselves, nor provided after-sale services or maintenance. As a result, soon after his death, the Empire became a vast open toilet which the British inherited. Unlike his forefathers, he did not believe in building buildings; he was an expert in demolition through dynamiting. He, therefore, undertook a full-Islamisation project in India; only by launching this drive could he whip up the Hindus to revive their glory. A general of Babur had destroyed only the Rama Temple at Ayodhya; Aurangzeb reopened the project by targeting two more, Mathura and Varanasi, the holy towns of Lords Krishna and Shiva, respectively. He apparently felt that the Hindus could, over a period of time, forget that the Babri mosque was built on the ruins of a temple; lest they forget their humiliation, therefore, he ensured that the Temples at both Mathura and Varanasi be only half-destroyed; an Idgah was built at Mathura and a mosque at Varanasi (1669). He also took care to humiliate and provoke the Hindus, by additionally taxing them with jaziya, so much so that they soon came to be led by Shivaji in the South and Guru Gobind Singh in the north. In view of continued rebellion, Aurangzeb virtually shifted his capital from Delhi to the Deccan in 1681, spending the rest of his life in military camp, where the Muslim rule in India had actually originated; he did everything, indirectly, to uproot Islam from India and it was basically due to his 'untiring' efforts that Islam finally retreated in 1947 after centuries of evolution of Hindu consciousness. Sometimes, he also tried to curry favour with the Hindus if required for administrative exigencies in the realm. The austere Aurangzeb had earned his living by making skull-caps and copying *the Qur'an;* when he died, aged 89, he had virtually dethroned Islam in India and made his Holy Book widely hated, because more widely read and publicised now. The Hindus now, finally, knew that Islam was incompatible with India; Shah Waliullah, the spiritual founder of Pakistan, had ensured that Islam became a separatist force rather than an assimilative, catalytic movement it once was—still it took India two more centuries to regurgitate Islam and convert Waliullah's dream into a reality. Islamabad owes its existence to Aurangzeb and Waliullah, with Sirhindi's sperm; Jinnah and Gandhi would merely midwife the baby.

An updated edition of Sirhindi, Shah Waliullah (1703-1762) had emerged as the 'most revered' Islamic thinker among the 'Hindu Muslims' of South Asia and Afghanistan—his own sperm bank continues to help deIslamisers father test-tube babies like Islamic terror gangs. He found that Islam needed to be united before it destroyed the infidels. So he set out to unite the different Sufi-cum-Sunni sects first, reminding them that their original business is to finish off Hinduism and not each other. Like his *Ustad* (teacher), Sirhindi, he declared himself a *Qayam-al-Zaman*, a semi-divine personality given the responsibility to complete a mission by none other than Prophet

Muhammed, *not in a dream but in person*, to reform Islam. He travelled to the Hejaz, Arabia, to help spread the Wahhabi virus, created by his contemporary Abdul Wahhab (1703-1792) in a bid to effect mutations in all Muslim plants across Asia, a noble mission so fervently and feverishly taken up again, and again…more recently by Osama bin-Laden and his al-Qaeda, and latest by Abu Bakr al-Baghdadi in Iraq and Syria. Waliullah, whose father, Shah Abdur Rahim, was a 'Sufi scholar' who assisted in the compilation of *Fatwa-e-Alamgiri*, the voluminous code of Islamic Law under Aurangzeb, declared that Islam was *irreconcilable* with the infidel India and tried to unite the Hanafi, Maliki, Shafei and Hanbali schools of Islamic jurisprudence; he believed only in the *Qur'an,* not even in the Hadith, but tolerated the latter, selectively permitting it in obedience to the Prophet. In him, Islam had reached its next nemesis because the fundamentalists began to question even the Hadith! The Wahhabis, in their turn, would later virtually disown even Muhammed—and destroy his heritage in Arabia—saying the Message was more important than the Messenger whose job was over after downloading the Book! An abiding faith in the *Qur'an*, being a bundle of opposites, did not need any outside help to sicken the Muslim community. On a 'spiritual' plane, the alliance between these in-house groups sowed the seeds of Pakistan and its conjoined twin, worldwide Islamic terrorism, and its funding from Arabia. No wonder, the sources of 9/11 and other algebraic incidents were traced to Arabia and Pakistan.

Waliullah, a destructive man dubbed as a 'great Muslim thinker' of the 18th century, was a witness to the steady decline and fall of the Mughal Empire in the Indian subcontinent, unlike his predecessor Shaikh Ahmed Sirhindi who witnessed the rise of the 'Great Mughals'. Waliullah claimed lineage from the Quraish tribe of Prophet Muhammed and the Second Caliph, Umar. After a two-year stay in Arabia and interaction with the rising Wahhabis there, he returned to India in 1732 with a burning mission: to revive the Islamic glory and re-launch the conversion project with single-minded devotion to fully Islamise India because Islam was a 'separate' nation until the world became Dar-ul-Islam. Naturally, Mehmood Ghaznavi and Aurangzeb were his ideal heroes to be followed to re-establish Islamic hegemony in the subcontinent. He was particularly peeved at the rise of Hindu forces in different parts of India such as the Jats and Sikhs in the North and Marathas in the South, eating at the vitals of Islam. He rediscovered the Muslim-unifying slogan 'Islam is in danger', that became the political credo of many Muslims in the subcontinent; and he was not wrong! Even after separation from India in the form of Pakistan and Bangladesh, Islam continued to bleed itself like Ashwatthama's festering wound. Totally against integration of Islamic culture with that of the Hindus, he wanted to bring back the pristine Islamic glory of the Arab days, with the Shariat as their guiding spirit. The religio-political theory of Islam's revival and hegemony in India later became the most exotic dream the fundamentalist Muslims would harbour in India. Even within Islam, he did not want the Muslims to follow the third and fourth Caliphs, Usman and Ali; only the first two Rashidi Caliphs, Abu Bakr and Umar, both the Prophet's fathers-in-law, were worth emulation, not the other two who both were sons-in-law. Clearly, it was a backward journey of Islam, from the sons-in-law to the fathers-in-law of the Prophet.

Realising that the Mughals had become impotent, Waliullah invited Ahmed Shah Abdali (Durrani), the Amir of Afghanistan, to attack the infidel India and re-establish Islam. In 1761, he wrote to the invader: 'The Hindus alone being the only industrious and adaptable people, all control has now passed into their hands. They are rich and prosperous while the Muslims have nothing but poverty and misery. Currently, you are the only person with initiative and foresight, power and capability, to defeat the infidel enemy and free the Muslims from their clutches. God forbid, I am afraid if their domination continues, Muslims will even forget Islam and become undistinguishable from the non-Muslims.' Waliullah must have seen the Muslims and Hindus celebrating *Vasantotsava*, the Spring Festival, together, and happily engaged in the kite-flying competitions, the way the Lahorites do even today. This peeved the ultra-fundamentalist no end: 'We beseech you in the name of the Prophet to fight a jihad against the infidels of this region… the invasion of the Shi'a ruler of Iran, Nadir Shah, had only destroyed the Muslim power and left the Marathas and Jats secure and prosperous. With all this, the infidels have regained their strength and reduced the Muslim rulers of Delhi to mere puppets.' He also advised the Afghan warlord to prohibit the celebration of the infidel festival Holi and the Shi'a's Muharram: 'Draw your swords and not put them back in their sheaths again until Allah has separated the Muslims from the polytheists and the rebellious infidels and the sinners are made completely weak and helpless.' Even he did not realise that the same Afghans, exhausted of the killing machines of Taliban and Pakistan, would have to be brought back on their feet by the infidel India in the 21st century!

He also appealed to the Rohila warlord Najib-ud-Daulah and Nizam-ul-Mulk to do similarly. Abdali decisively defeated the Marathas in the Third Battle of Panipat (1761) but Waliullah died before he could rejoice. The later Mughals, propped up so far by the Maratha power, declined further and in this power vacuum entered the British, who had already established their supremacy after the Battle of Plassey (1757) in Bengal; all they had to do now was to systematically amputate the remains of the Mughal power in India. Islam continued to lose but Waliullah continued to gain: if Sirhindi was patriarch of terrorism, Waliullah became father of Islamic separatism and extremism in the subcontinent—together, they ensured that Islam took shelter in the Taliban caves. Ironically, amongst the pious Muslims, Waliullah is still known as an Islamic 'reformer' and modernist! An unending nostalgia. In Islam, the 'reformer' has often been the one who takes the Muslims back to the pristine Islamic glories of the sixth century. That is why Osama was the biggest Islamic 'reformer' of the early 21st century and he drew Muslim support on this very count; in India, all puritanists fall into the reformist category as 'Islamic scholars'. They all see Islam's future in the past.

Wahhabism had filled Waliullah with so much anti-Hindu hatred and blinded him politically so completely that, while inviting Abdali, he did not see the arrival of the British who had already destroyed the power of Nawab Siraj-ud-Daula of Bengal at Plassey; the boot was on the other leg now as the British found in the Nawab's deputy Mir Jafar, the Quisling of India, the same way the Muslim army of Muhammad Ghori had found a Jai Chand seven centuries ago. 'Traitors' are like toilet-cleaners used by Nature in any clogged society that needs to be cleansed and protected and it is they who, in fact, have accelerated the pace of change more than the patriots ever have—it is they who make possible the entry of disruptive change-makers. If Waliullah believed he was so intelligent that he was more of a Muslim than an Indian and, being an 'Arab', he could betray India for Islam, there would always be some Mir who would, simply by being a duffer, eclipse the Muslim rule in India. So, when Waliullah successfully removed the artificial respiration being provided by the Marathas to the Mughals, the latter were destined to seek euthanasia from the British. The single-most important factor behind the ensuing British Rule in India was Waliullah, the way the single-most important factor behind Muslim Rule in India was a weak Dahir Sain; Waliullah wanted to go down in history as a king among saints while Sain wanted to be a saint among kings!

Influenced by Waliullah's Islamic 'revivalist' movement, the Dar-ul-Uloom and its supporters like Muhammad Iqbal and Abul A'la Maududi, all believers of the Wahhabi school, participated in India's Freedom Movement in the mid-20th century—*not because* some of them loved the Hindus or India but because they hated the British and Christianity as 'intruders' who had upset the Islamic applecart. Once the British were thrown out, they fancied, the brave Muslims could easily defeat the coward Hindus and regain their glory. The Deobandis would continue to claim their 'patriotic' credentials, although their head master, Abul Hasan Nadvi alias Ali Miyan, became the spiritual founder of the Taliban 'students', one who had actually travelled to Pakistan to guide them in the mid-1990s. And, of course, Ali Miyan was also the respected voice of the 'secular' mafia in India!

The West, despite Christianity's own forked tongue, would scarcely understand this Byzantinian nitty-gritty of Islamists' duplicitous theory and practice nor that it is the Westernised Muslims, some among whom patronised the terror-network and provided 'intellectual' and 'secular' back office support using their 'democratic' rights, organise agitations and make strategic use of human rights etc by bribing the unsuspecting and award-awaiting non-Muslims. No one knows better but a devout Muslim in a non-Muslim majority nation how to exploit a person, an institution, a belief or a situation to promote a religious cause he so fervently believes in: full Islamisation of the world. The West, gloating after 'defeating' Islam in the Crusades, believed that the Muslims would forget Muhammed the way the Christians were increasingly forgetting Jesus and could, therefore, be 'processed' into modernity.

And it is a measure of the Muslim intellectuals' patience and forward planning that the Mujahidin-in-exile in Peshawar (1989) selected a Naqshabandi, Sibghatullah Mujadiddi, as the first President against the Soviet-supported Communist puppets; he was a descendent of Sirhindi and paved the way for the Taliban takeover in 1996. It was the 'philosophy' of Sirhind and Waliullah that the separatist Muslims—they were, in fact, escaping and retreating ones—adopted when Maulana Abul Muhammad Qasim Nanotavi founded their nursery called Dar-ul-Uloom ('Abode of Scholars') at Deoband in Saharanpur district of Uttar Pradesh (1879). In their doctrinal belief, and therefore source of Islamic anti-Indianism, anti-modernism, anti-Westernism, separatism and terrorism, the Naqshabandis, Wahhabis and the Deobandis fed each other. In 1761, the Third Battle of Panipat between the Muslims and the Hindus exhausted them both and made things easier for the British takeover. The Sirhindi-Waliullah duo ruled the roost. Deoband, which emerged as a major Islamic 'think tank' outside Arabia, was destined to welcome the founder of Taliban, Maulana Fazl-ur-Rehman of Jamiet-e-Ulema-e-Islam (Order of the Scholars of Islam) during the Vajpayee regime's twilight in July 2003.

For a time, the Hindus tried to digest Islam. The Sikh faith, propounded by Guru Nanak (1469-1538), tried to be a halfway-house between Hinduism and Islam: there was One God but the devotee could reach Him only through a Guru; it also borrowed fierce monotheism and the concept of Brotherhood from Islam. It was somewhat of an Indianised version of Abrahamic monotheism. Guru Nanak's successors, however, gradually became embroiled in local politics, with the Gurus trying to emerge as local chieftains in the Mughal Empire and oppose Muslim hegemony, which brought them in conflict with the Empire. Essentially a cult of the Punjab, ground zero of the fiercest struggle between Islam and the infidels, Sikhism gained respectability as a social reform movement with the Third Guru Amar Das (1552-74) banning the Hindu custom of *sati* and *purdah* system for women and gradually drifted away from mainstream Hinduism, despite remaining its sword-wielding arm. The Fourth Guru, Ram Das (1575-1581), who was granted 500 'bighas' of land by Akbar to buy peace in the Punjab, founded the city that later came to be known as Amritsar, the holiest place for the cult. The Fifth Guru, Arjan Dev (1581-1606), culled and compiled the Sikh Holy Book of the Adi Granth Sahib mainly from the Hindu and other contemporary sources; he was tortured to death by Jahangir for blessing the rebellious Prince Khusro. The Sixth Guru, Hargobind (1606-44) was the son of the Fifth who built the holiest Sikh shrine, Akal Takht, the Throne of the Immortal, in Amritsar, and began to turn Sikhism into a militant sect, assuming himself the title of *Sachcha Padshah* (the Real Emperor). He always dressed like a soldier and carried two swords—one, *meeri*, to defend the temporal order, the other, *peeri*, to protect the spiritual one. Jahangir confined him for a time at Gwalior while Shahjehan forced him to retire to the hills, with his grandson Har Rai (1644-61) succeeding him as the Seventh Guru, who made the mistake of rubbing Aurangzeb the wrong way by supporting the latter's rival but spineless brother, Prince Dara Shikoh. The Alamgir summoned the Guru who, instead, sent his son to explain certain 'un-Islamic' passages in the *Granth Sahib*. The son did it deftly by changing some words, incurred the wrath of his Father-Guru who disinherited him and appointed a five-year-old Har Kishan (1661-1664) as successor. The Eighth Guru died of small pox only three years later, paving the way for the Ninth Guru Tegh Bahadur (1664-75). He inherited the uninterrupted and implacable hostility of Aurangzeb, now even more pronounced, as the Guru supported and protected the Kashmiri Brahmins scared of the terrible methods applied by the Muslims for complete Islamisation of the Valley. Aurangzeb executed him when he refused to convert to Islam. The Tenth and the Last Guru was Gobind Singh (1975-1708), who decided that Islam was irreconcilable with India and must be defeated violently; out of the rarefied Sikh cult, he crystallised the *Khalsa Panth* (The Way of the

Pure) and completely transformed the new community as an aggressive anti-Muslim force: to meet the Muslims on *their* ground, he prohibited tobacco as the Muslims prohibited alcohol, added meat to the Sikh diet as the Muslims ate beef, eschewed idolatry and caste-system, made the recital of the Holy Book compulsory on solemn functions, evolved the idea of the *Akalis* (Eternal Warriors) on lines of the Muslim *Ghazi* (Holy Warriors) and glorious martyrdom in the battle against the 'infidel', that is Muslims. He turned the Sikh into armed resistance against the forces of Islam and transformed his followers into soldier-saints, himself moving over to the new capital, Anandpur Sahib, on the foothills of the Himalayas; his spirit continued in the Sikhs' resistance against the British as well. In successive campaigns, his four sons were done to death by the Muslims and the Guru himself was stabbed to death by a Pathan.

The Sikhs gained glory briefly during the reign of Maharaja Ranjit Singh; they prospered economically and militarily but the Punjab was too small a place for this ambitious and energetic, enterprising community. After weakening the Mughals, they busied themselves against the British, sought a separate homeland when the British promised Pakistan, denied, became restive when they found that the Nehruvian India was becoming a redrawn caricature of Mughal India on a home-made paper; they flooded defence services, prospered due to the Green Revolution, migrated from India in large numbers planting their little Punjabs in foreign soils, again demanded a separate homeland, Khalistan, picked up arms against the 'Hindu' Indian state they had originated to defend in the first place, now aided by their former foe, Pakistan. The separatist Sikhs' desire for a possible 'Khalistan' was due mainly to the dominating caste among the Sikhs being the Jats: they found that if the Muslim Jats could get away with 'Pakistan', and the Hindu Jats got Haryana, why couldn't the Sikh Jats get a State of their own?

India, which had slowly forced Islam to retreat by 1947 and had also slowly pushed out the Christian missionaries from the conversion business, found that it would now have to struggle against another, this time a home-made, organised religion, that of the Sikhs. Nehru wouldn't have done it, but his daughter Indira Gandhi did the unthinkable by sending the Army, for the first time in history, into their holiest shrine, the Golden Temple, at Amritsar in 1984, although she herself was gunned down six months later. Pakistan had found in the extremist Sikh preacher Jarnail Singh Bhindranwale a replica of the anti-Hindu ideology fostered by Shaikh Ahmed Sirhindi and Shah Waliullah, helped his terror gangs to inflict a thousand cuts on India and failed because a majority of Sikhs realised their home is the east of the Radcliff Line, not west of the Durand, and so they did not end up in the Afghan caves as did the Taliban. Indira destroyed two Theories: one, the Two-Nation Theory of Jinnah, that Islam was a 'separate nation' that led to the Partition of India and creation of Pakistan, and two, that India was a 'secular' state in which the state cannot violate or allow others to violate the alleged sanctity of a holy place: if Indira could rush the Army into the Golden Temple, her successors could never have prevented the demolition of the Babri Mosque. With Indira ended the Mughal-Nehruvian model of bridge-statecraft and on its ruins emerged the Hindu Reaction that had patiently risen like ferment since 711. Pakistan discovered that Bhindranwale had been reborn as Osama bin-Laden in a self-destruct mode! Because Pakistan, indeed many in the Muslim world, cannot survive without their regular dose of monsters to whom they could bow in submission.

In the South of the Vindhyas, parallel to the Sikh power in the North, rose the equally intrepid Marathas. They revived the Hindu restoration movement as an extension of the medieval Bhakti Movement, gained power, defeated the Mughals but lost against Islam, fought against the British; some of them tried to institutionalise continuance of power in the form of the RSS on lines of the Sikhs. The core of the RSS continued to be the Maharashtrian Brahmins dreaming of bringing back the glory of the 'Golden Age' of the Gupta Dynasty of the fourth century, just like the devout Sikhs would like to return to Maharaja Ranjit Singh's 19th century, or the Muslims to the sixth century, but they all found India far too complex for their simple faiths. India was *their* Truth. They believed it was simple, for truth is always simple; but the simplest things are often the most complex to understand. Sikhism never moved out of the Punjab nor the RSS took off her saffron glasses; the former named their dreamland as 'Khalistan' (Land of the Pure), the Marathas found that their state was named 'Maharashtra' (Great Nation), greater than India. Like their predecessors, they did not realise that India was like the dried cow-hide: you press it with your foot at one end, it rises on another! As it was found by Alexander the Great, who desisted from invading mainland India; as it was found by Akbar, who tried to stand on the cow-hide with multiple feet.

Within 17 years of Aurangzeb's death in 1707, the residual Mongol ragtag called the Mughal Empire, disintegrated and never revived; after the British interregnum, it revived briefly in another form, Nehruvianism. Nehru's supporters believed he was the last Englishman to rule in India; he was, in fact, the last Mughal. He converted the Congress Party into an election machine, just like Akbar had converted the Mughal administration into a long-term decentralised warfare machinery and centralised revenue collection machine, something continued by the British. But Indira understood India better than her 'historian' father, although she had inherited his weakness for greatness: he surrendered to China in 1962, she to Pakistan at Shimla ten years later. They both died of their own perceived greatness.

What was the South, where both Christianity and Islam had entered before they did in the North, but remained dormant, doing?

With the decline of the Delhi Sultanate in the 14th century, its attempts to establish an all-India empire had failed but it succeeded in stirring the South to go the Northern way in the evolution of the feudal system. The Bahmanis broke free from the Sultanate and ruled for two centuries in the northern Deccan at a time when the Vijayanagar kingdom came into existence as the repository of Hindu culture, religion and civilisation in the South, at a time when these were waging a grim and bloody battle against Islam in the North. The Krishna river divided the Bahmani and Vijayanagar kingdoms and struggle for control over the fertile Raichur *doab* between Krishna and its tributary Tungabhadra—still continuing in another way, on the Cauveri and Belgaum-type disputes in southern states in the 21st century—and over the diamond mines of Golkonda from 14th to 16th centuries eventually sealed the fate of the Bahamani and Vijayanagara kingdoms and their successor Bijapur, Ahmednagar, Golkonda, Bidar and Berar kingdoms. Political disintegration of the North had invited Islam; the same in the South invited Christianity. The Arabs already controlled trade in South India and South-East Asia; the Iberian adventurers and merchants, followed by the Roman Catholic and Protestant missionaries, particularly the Jesuits, fresh with religious fundamentalism against that 'infidel' Islam they eventually expelled from Spain and Portugal in 1492, discovered in the Muslim Arabs of South India the same face of their just-expelled enemy in Europe: the struggle between Islam and Christianity had now been shifted from the Iberian to the Indian Peninsula, the geographical limits of Islam. Tipu Sultan of Mysore was the Last Sigh of Islam in the 19th century South India as Akbar was in the North two centuries before. It was not just Vasco da Gama, the Portuguese, who reached the Indian coast in 1498; it was the anti-Islamic drive of Christianity that had arrived in India. The Pope, himself struggling against reformers, had 'gifted' the East to the Portuguese, and the West to the Spanish, to make converts and destroy Islam. The Crusades had failed to tame Islam in the Middle East but, ironically, succeeded in launching the Renaissance, Reformation and the Age of Reason in Europe against the Dark Age of the Popes; and with renewed vigour due to development of science and technology, merchant navies and overseas empires, revived the unofficial Crusades against the Jihadis all over the world—Christianity was losing the West but trying to compensate the loss in the rest of the world while Islam was losing the rest of the world and trying to control West Asia. India was just a part of this global pattern. Ironically, Christianity and Islam, true to form and like market forces, were not only fighting amongst themselves to grab more customers, even if through number portability, but each also against the local product, the infidel Hinduism.

At a time when the North suspected it had lost the Hindus to Islam forever, the South was showing the way. In the 14th century, the Bahamani army imprisoned the Warangal princes Bukka and Harihara and forcibly converted them to Islam in Delhi, before sending them back to the South to restore the Sultanate authority. There, in 1336, Harihara did the most amazing thing, by re-converting to Hinduism after being 'purified' of the *mlechchha* influence and set up the Hastinavati kingdom, centred at modern Hampi, which later became the bigger and brighter Vijayanagar Empire. Vidyaratna, a local priest, had, apparently, understood the hidden message of Adi Shankaracharya when he re-admitted the two brothers on the home page of Hinduism: he removed all restrictions against the brothers, declaring that, in fact, Harihara was the Vice-Regent of Virupaksha, the local Shaivite deity, who had been entrusted the task of bringing back the Hindus lost to Islam! Bukka and Harihara had done the hitherto impossible: it was the first time that Hindus converted to Islam had returned to the fold, something that would slowly gain momentum. Many more were now silently reconverting from Christianity and Islam to the Hindu fold, without admitting as much and their continuing caste-consciousness was their key to return. The Vijayanagar war against Hoysala in 1346 had made the former supreme power in the South: Harihara planned and built 'Vijayanagar' (the City of Victory) near Hampi and it became (1343) the capital after which the kingdom was later named.

The curious struggle for control of the Bahmani Kingdom between the local Muslim chieftains (*Deccanis*) and the 'outsiders' (*Pardesis*), who, too, were Muslim, led to haemorrhage of power and eventually led to its downfall in 1538; on its ruins were born five new kingdoms of Bijapur, Golkonda, Ahmednagar, Berar and Bidar which would eventually merge back to form the Nizamate of Hyderabad, the last Muslim fief forced to shut shop in India in 1948 through 'police action'. This was part of integration of 565 principalities by the powerful Deputy Prime Minister Sardar Vallabhbhai Patel who prevailed over the 'secular' Nehru, for removing this last remnant of the Mughal menace; in return, Nehru prevailed over Patel on the Kashmir issue—while Hyderabad was a Hindu-majority kingdom ruled by the Muslims, Kashmir was the Muslim majority kingdom ruled by the Hindus.

In 1564, four of the Deccan Muslim kingdoms had united to destroy the Vijayanagar kingdom. The descendents of the greatest Vijayanagar king, Krishnadeva Raya (1509-30), in whose reign the

South witnessed its Golden Era, turned out to be duds by the time the Mughals were spreading their wings from Delhi. But it was Krishnadeva himself, who had made the cardinal mistake of trusting the Muslim Bahmanis for a while: after defeating the enemy in 1509 at Raichur, he reinstated the Sultan out of humility, little realising that such human gestures carried no importance for Islamists, for, it was these very defeated ones who will unite and destroy Vijayanagar in 1564. Ironically, the Vijayanagar kingdom was founded by one who had reconverted from Islam to Hinduism; its end came because its greatest king reinstated the Sultan of Bahmani.

Krishnadeva's lasting contribution was the boost he gave to the Bhakti Movement, the ocean in which local devotional cults, like rivulets, eventually merged to call the Sufi bluff. Krishnadeva's popularity shifted the devotional cults' centre of gravity from the Tamil land to Mysore, to Maharashtra and beyond, until it spread all over, merging in it the streams of Kabir (1440-1518), Guru Nanak (1469-1538), Surdas (1483-1573) and, above all, Goswami Tulsi Das (1532-1624) and Chaitanya Mahaprabhu (1485-1534), the last two being the most important proponents of the Lords Rama and Krishna, respectively, besides a host of others—it was the low-profile Tulsi legacy that carried Rama in the 'Greater India' in South-East Asia and the Chaitanya movement that made Krishna being noticed in the West. If Akbar was the highest watermark of Islam in India, Tulsi Das was the highest form of resistance from spiritual India to oppose Muhammedanism, at the most fundamental level. Who could be the ideal ruler and why: Rama, who would renounce his family to save the society, or Muhammed, who would create a Brotherhood on the ruins of society? India chose *Rama*, whose literal meaning was Life. The Bhakti Movement was the Hindu response to the Sufis and prevented many of the gullible Hindus from falling into the traps laid by the Muslim missionaries masquerading as Sufi Peers and Faqirs: if God was one, as proclaimed by the Sufis, and all the ways led to Him, as the Bhakti Movement maintained, where was the need to convert to Islam!

The Portuguese had appropriately named their currency as *cruzado*, after the Crusades they were waging against Islam; later,

Brazil, too, named its currency *cruzeiro*, not letting Islam enter South America. The Portuguese had, early on, set out to fight against Islam wherever they could. Until Akbar, Islamic rulers and Sultans were but adventurists and upstarts, uncouth barbarians and devoid of any far-sight in managing affairs. But when Akbar tried to systematise the realm, Islam lost its 'moorings' and deIslamisation started! Not for nothing was Islam called 'Deen-e-Ghalib', Religion of Domination: if you cannot dominate others, especially non-Muslims, you cannot simply be a 'true' Muslim. At its most basic, Islamists demonstrated the animal instinct to rule a territory through force, not persuasion. That is why Islam and democracy have always been contradictory concepts. Even a devout Christian, A K Antony, as Chief Minister of Kerala running a coalition government with the support of Indian Union Muslim League, was constrained to admit in 2003 that the 'minorities' (read Muslims) wanted to reap all benefits through forcible gate-crashing; found 'politically incorrect', he, however, retracted it!

The same fate would await Christianity which was now entering the first phase of its glory in the South with the arrival of the Portuguese in 1498. These two new factors were now to fashion the future of both Christianity and Islam globally, although they thought they were shaping the future of India. The two aggressive, proselytising Semitic religions—both preaching 'peace'—had brought their Crusades and Jihad into the Indian territory: they had now come home to the roost. The Portuguese were the European-Christian variants of the Delhi Sultanate, as uncouth, hated and blood-thirsty, and they paved the way for the Dutch, French and, finally the British. In India, you have to sit on your own volcano in order to rule peacefully; the moment you begin to 'administer', you end up as a portrait in the hall of shame! India being a functional anarchy, it is governed the best—and least—when in chaos. That is why even democracy has flourished chaotically in this strange nation where human beings create, rule and destroy gods, not the other way round.

The Hindus had almost made India an object of ridicule and hate for these foreigners. In his memoirs, Babur, himself a Central Asian fugitive seeking asylum in India, wrote: 'This country of Hindustan has little pleasures. Its people are neither handsome nor friendly, nor mixing together, nor familiarising themselves with others. They have no genius, have no understanding of the mind, no humility of manner, no brotherhood, no creativity or inventing skills, no architecture, no horses, no flesh or fruits, not even ice and cold water, bread or baths, candles or torch.' Satan's fervent hope to be welcomed in Heaven! For one, he ruled in and around Delhi which had been made a ghost town time and again; secondly, he did not realise that India had *moulded herself the way* the likes of Baburs would find it; it was kept on hold by the Hindus who had asked their banks to stop payment from their account to the suspect fraudster, that this India was deliberately created and made foul-smelling to ward off the invader. The Mughals began their rule in India with Babur's hatred and ended it with Bahadur Shah Zafar's helplessness in finding even two yards of soil where he could be peacefully buried; with the latter's death in Burma (Myanmar) in 1857, the Mughal Empire, glittering externally but moth-eaten within, came to an ignominious end. The fanatic Muslims would succeed in 1947 in retrieving the Great Bath of Mohenjodaro from the Great Toilet of India.

Islam, however, remained an essentially urban phenomenon; the rural India has, always, been predominantly Hindu which slowly repelled the Abrahamic incursions—in the end, both Christianity and Islam have remained abortive forces in India. The Mughals, like their predecessors, spoke Turkish, with the Persian being their second, and eventually the first and official language. Ironically, the Ottoman Turks constantly quarrelled with the Safavids of Persia and tried to prevent the Persian culture from intrusion; the Mughals, on the other hand, despite their Mongol-Turkish blood, wholeheartedly accepted things Persian, which, despite being Shia, offered fine refinement. Iran tolerated the Mughals because they kept the recalcitrant Afghans in check; the Mughals did not attack the Persians because the latter held in check the Central Asian gangs who could have tried to replace the earlier gangs in India. This balance of power between India and Iran, vis-a-vis Pakistan and Afghanistan, has continued till today.

Ghosts

WHEN the British came in India, interesting developments were taking place—all those who viewed themselves as legatees of the Mughals wanted to join the British bandwagon, wherever they could, and they all thought the British were an alien interregnum after whose departure they would 'legitimately' rule India from Delhi. To begin with, the British were only traders who had neither an army nor a fort, nor any other base in India. In the North, the Sikhs fancied themselves as legitimate heirs of the eclipsing Mughals they had fought against from the very beginning. In the West, the Marathas had emerged with the same ambition. For some decades in the tottering post-Aurangzeb Mughal Empire, the Marathas had been the real power behind the Delhi throne: if the Germans/Turks, protectors of the Pope/Caliphate after the Hun/Mongol menace, could usurp the throne, why not the Marathas do likewise in India? They were peeved that Bombay became a 'wedding gift' of Charles II's Portuguese Queen Catherine, transferred to the East India Company. In the South, the Tamils felt that the North had, under Muslim influence, become far too 'corrupt'—its

Hindi-Urdu hybrid language 'Hindustani' they were so familiar with during Hyderabad's Nizamate being the 'worst' example of it!—and it was the duty of the South to extend the Rajendra Chola empire, this time, to Delhi instead of South-East Asia. In the East, Bengal thought enough was enough and it should now do a Pataliputra in Calcutta. It took them all a hundred years to realise that the British were here to stay, *themselves,* as the heir of the Mughals!

It was with this feeling of being 'cheated' that Madras, Bombay and Calcutta Presidencies, through which the British introduced Europe to India, became the hubs of veritable change and challenge to the foreign power, the *firangi*. And it was this latent and unfulfilled desire to rule Delhi, even if by proxy, as the successor of the Mughals (and the successive 'usurpers' British and the 'Indian National' Congress) that Madras (Jayalalithaa and N Chandrababu Naidu), Bombay (Sharad Pawar and Bal Thackeray) and Calcutta (Jyoti Basu and Mamata Bannerjee) tried to control a 'weakened' Delhi in the recent past. The East Pakistani Bengali desire to get even with Punjabi oppression, expressed in the victory of Sheikh Mujibur Rehman's Awami Party in 1970, triggered the creation of Bangladesh; a similar Sikh desire to 'control' Delhi drove them into an imaginary 'Khalistan' in the 1980s. Latent 'me-too' dreams, unfulfilled desires drive a people in each age, like the 'soul' of the dead going on the rampage, seeking emancipation; you can have some idea of the angst in this life by taking the subject through the 'past life regression therapy'. Despite India having been a nation of cultural unity, struggle for cultural and political hegemony between different constituents has always continued: it is due to this cultural hegemony, strong bias and mass support that, of all Indian non-Hindi languages, only the TV channels of Tamil, Bengali and Marathi languages have commercially flourished in the long run; proponents of these three languages and cultures have zealously guarded their turf and faith, although they sometimes played a second fiddle in the expression of their desire. Even in the Bollywood films, themes, music and songs specific to these cultures run in a cycle.

The Marathas, in particular, were notable because it was they who eventually became the fountainhead of Hindu nationalist movements. They were a hardy, able and rough-hewn mass that suddenly burst forth from the Western Ghats, spread over the Konkan, and across the Deccan towards Central India and finally to Delhi and Bengal. They were guided by a few intelligent Brahmins who, through their guerrilla language, Marathi, controlled a huge mass of low-caste people and shoved them into the furnace of guerrilla wars. Their endurance, enterprise, tenacity, frugal habits and bravery made them highly feared, and sometimes even hated, among the Hindus and Muslims, and later the British. They were poor, uninterested in raising magnificent monuments of the past, wedded fiercely to their 'traditions', and had a sense of belonging, dedicated to creating a future and history. Shivaji (1627-1680), their mascot and ideal, was the first effective militant Hindu reaction against Islam after the Sikhs chose to create an identity separate from the Hindus: the Maratha hero's attempts to defend the cow and the country, the Hindu religion and the nation, laid the foundation of an embryonic regional nation-state. Such has been his legacy that the post-Independence Maratha-dominated State around Bombay was christened Maharashtra (Great Nation). But the Marathas, whose sense of nationalism and self-importance was much more than they could handle, like the Prussians in Germany, invited ruin and devastation in the Third Battle of Panipat: casteism was their undoing. Fighting against the Mughals, they became imperialists themselves and ended up being entombed along with their enemies, the Mughals and the British. The rest of India did not accept their Lilliputian leadership and imperial designs; in the end, they became bitter and aggressive. They lacked the power and the resources, except as extortionists, to thrust themselves on the whole of India, had little interest in the new change agents like innovations in science, technology and industry, mostly preferred salaried jobs and saved more than they ate. For them, Maharashtra became bigger than Rashtra (Nation)! But they did give India and the Hindus the hope that they could meet Islam, and later Christianity, on their own turf, that, *without converting* to Abrahamism, the Hindus could become aggressive, violent, imperialist and defeat foreigners. It was Shivaji who gave India the idea that it was a 'Hindu nation' as he and his successors believed in the concept of '*Hindu Pad Padshahi*' (Hindu Imperium). The Marathas were expansion and shifting of the Rajput and the Sikh power against Islam; and the Shivaji dream of 'Hind Swaraj' (a self-ruled Hindu nation free from alien religions—Christianity and Islam) found full flowering in Gandhi, as we would see.

Post-Crusades Europe had come to India seeking Christians and cheaper spices, the former for Jesus, the latter for preserving beef and sausages on a large scale for use in winter. The European colonisers and missionaries sought to convert the infidels, including the Muslims, outside the Continent as a new global Crusade after 1500. Although the eight Crusades had failed to tame Islam in the Fertile Crescent, their fallout had been the Age of Reason and Renaissance that restricted the Pope's power and popularity in Europe. Losing spiritual market at home, the Papacy decided to continue the unofficial Crusades outside Europe; business and trade joined the spiritual bandwagon and the White Man's Burden was born. The core business of this conglomerate was the urgent demand for spices; newer money spinners like maize, sugar and cotton had fuelled the demand for slave labour, a one way outflow of populations from Asia and Africa to the West, which gradually infected Christendom with complacency and decay—to the extent that the Continent is now divided over the immigration issue with the British exiting the European Union.

With the fall of Rome and the rise of the Arab Muslims, trade had become a monopoly of the Muslims, until Columbus, who were purchasing cheap in South-East Asia and India and reaping whopping profit in the West. The spices were not a luxury but a necessity in Europe; these were needed to preserve meat through winter. Diseases like plague and wars, and decline in able-bodied population, had made it necessary for the people to keep stock of frozen and preserved cattle as food for adversity and invent machines to do manual work as millions of able-bodied men had died in the first five centuries of the Second Millennium due to the Crusades, wars and diseases. Bitter winter would kill the cattle due to lack of fodder; so the cattle had to be slaughtered in the autumn. To preserve it and to combat the taste of decay, spices were of utmost importance. On this lucrative trade, which yielded up to 5,000 per cent profit, the Venetians, Egyptians and the Arabs had virtual monopoly.

The spill-over of the crusading zeal against the Muslims and the commercial zeal against the Venetians etc were the motives that propelled Christopher Columbus to America (1492) and Vasco da Gama to Calicut, India (1498). Fortune-seekers continued to sail to the rich and prosperous India, the contemporary El Dorado, from the impoverished and bigoted 'Third World' of the 15th century, also known as Europe. One such sailor was the Portuguese, Pedros Alvares Cabral, who set off from Lisbon for India but landed in what came to be known as Brazil in 1500; still others 'discovered' a host of 'New Worlds' from the Americas to Australia subsequently—their only claim to fame was that the failures of the Crusades and the resultant success of an emerging scientific spirit had handed them new weapons which the 'Old World', still engaged in religious wars, did not possess; they too were the same old religious warriors with the same old mindset but with new weapons and new enemies. The Crusades and the Jihads had unleashed the animals hidden in human skin and the beast was on the loose outside the Papal Circus of Europe. Their failures in the Crusades against the Muslims had angered them no end and this frustration they carried to the new 'colonies' when they pounced on the hapless 'infidels'. Since the 'macho' Christian Crusaders could not defeat the intrepid Muslims, the former could now satisfy their animal lust for revenge on the infidels. The Portuguese were the worst example of this inherited mindset. Afonso de Albuquerque captured Goa on the subcontinent's western coast, off the Arabian Sea in 1510 from the Sultan of Bijapur and it became the capital of the Portuguese'eastern terror-cum-loot empire, the launch-pad of Europe in India. Thus, even before the arrival of Babur and Shivaji on the scene, the seeds of European imperialism had been sown on the Indian soil. The new Crusades to be launched in India, this time against the 'infidel' Hindus, were sought to be replacing the ongoing Jihads.

The uncouth and intolerant Portuguese, in whom Christianity had put its worst foot forward in India, quickly became unpopular and hated as they went about their killing spree, forcible conversion business and setting up factories to produce children in Indian women's wombs. At a time when Akbar was 'reconciling' with the Hindus, the

Portuguese set up the Inquisition (1560) in Goa where they allowed no Hindu temples and forced even the Syrian Christians of Malabar to 'reconvert' to the Roman Catholic faith! It was a Portuguese 'Sultanate' in India. They turned out be the neo Turko-Mongols, this time from Europe, coming from the Arabian Sea and the Indian Ocean, mounted on vessels instead of the horses. The Indians had little to choose between Christianity and Islam and had to guard against both. The hatred spawned by the warriors for Jerusalem, Rome and Mecca had winged its way to the East and the Far East where The Buddha had once issued the Edicts of love and tolerance. The Portuguese policy of seeking women, besides Christians and spices, led to mixed marriages; a population was reared which had Portuguese blood and Catholic culture and local, Konkani, ambience. They came to be known as 'Luso-Indians', after so many Louises amongst them, or simply as Goans or Goanese. Indian in blood, Roman Catholic in religion, a little western in outlook, a hybrid of Indo-Portuguese traditionsand an emerging bridge between India and Europe. Portugal tried to reclaim these lost children in 1960 and gave up. They were now increasingly happy being ruled by the Hindutva forces. In 2009, history came to full circle with one sect of Goanese Christians threatening to 're-convert to Hinduism' in their Second Millennium if the other sects, also of Christianity, did not accept its demands. Clearly, the Portuguese Christians are dissolving back into the Hindu ocean from which they had emerged.

When the Portuguese came, they found their match in Sheikh Ahmed Sirhindi and that the Muslims, like the Christians, viewed culture, religion, politics and business as part of the same seamless garment that had to be protected with ferocious energy against the infidel. Many Muslims, under the Mughals, had at least attempted to mingle with the things Hindu; the Portuguese remained aloof, alien, sterile and hated in the rest of India. The legacy of 16th century Portugal in particular and Europe in general, was the Goans and the educational institutions set up after their presiding deity, the Spanish Jesuit missionary 'Saint' Francis Xavier (1506-1552) who set up shop in Goa in 1542; many of the Xavierites, their minds infected with the same virus, became the home grown neo-colonialists in South

Asia even after the 1950s. They came to follow the Portuguese and entombed themselves successfully.

The first major European theo-cultural attack on India in the form of the Portuguese had failed much the same way the first Muslim assault in the form of Muhammad bin-Qasim had nearly failed in the beginning of Islamic imperialism—but they were only dry runs. The Hindus were tired of the 'disease' called the *mlechchha* Muslims and did not exactly relish the bitter 'cure' called Christianity; it needed a sugar-coated pill, even if more costlier. The British—who despised European 'Continentals', (even now their recipes are called Continental dishes)—believed they could provide this pill. They had set up their own shop called the Church of England (and that of Scotland etc.) separate from the Vatican and Protestantism, evolved a defence policy of ensuring that the British Navy was twice as powerful as all of the European navies put together, that they would not engage themselves in continental warfare and follow a foreign policy of 'splendid isolation'. They would not even call themselves 'Europeans', rather christening themselves as 'Men from the British Isles'; the same policy they now follow vis-a-vis the European Union and the European Parliament. India was, therefore, for the first time passing from the hands of continental colonialists of the Muslim and Christian varieties to the hands of the people from 'nowhere'! The amused Indians often mocked Europeans, including the British, as 'red-faced monkeys'. Although Christian missionaries still flourished during the British Rule in India, the Portuguese crusading zeal was no longer there. The British, who mostly had little stakes in the Crusades of Europe earlier, tolerated and even helped the missionaries but did not make religious conversion a state policy as some other Europeans did; instead, being businessmen, they loved to fleece and bleed the Indians slowly rather than converting them, just like the Muslims before them did. If you convert them, it would be difficult to fleece them in the long run, for they would demand Abrahamic egalitarianism and equality! A Christian/Muslim could not be, *theologically*, a slave to another Christian/Muslim! Imperialism called for evolving a system for long-term exploitation and nipping in the bud any future rebellion. Economic considerations had put religious goals on the back-burner and it was better to be a good businessman than be a bad missionary. A 'good' Christian or Muslim was not expected to fleece another from the same faith! So it was better to convert only as many as were required to run the local machinery. Eventually, their greed for Mammon would save India from God and Allah.

It was this India that the British inherited from the Mughals, a palace built on the marshes. Unlike the Mughals, they were more interested in controlling the Kitchen: they would cook in the Indian Kitchen what they wanted to carry to the restaurants of the emerging textile mills of Manchester and Lancashire. Unlike the vagabond Mughals in search of home and finally settling down in India, the British had no desire to make India their home. For them, it was merely a milk colony, to be used for mulching the Indian Cow; they did not, however, know they were carrying a Mad Cow back home! Both the fundamentalist Muslims and Christians continued to believe that they would one day fully convert India to their faith; the former settled down and found themselves being uprooted as encroachers and the latter came as encroachers and found themselves settling down—in their own Great Britain with the 'coloured' people, with the 1.6 million Muslims half of whom are Pakistanis, half of whom Kashmiris! The Great Mughals and their successor, Great Britain, found India 'small' enough to be trampled, ready to be devoured, ripe enough to be picked; once they tried to swallow it, however, India expanded in their throats. Like Hanuman.

The East India Company, founded on 31 December 1600, had its role slightly altered than the Portuguese and other 'continental' European colonialists. While the Iberians, brimming with their zeal to carry the White Man's Burden and continue their unofficial Crusade against Islam and the Hindus in India, aimed more at evangelisation than at epicureanisation, the British believed in the opposite. Gandhi understood very well that if India did not surrender to Christianity, it was because of its 'good fortune' of being ruled by Britain, a nation long since following the foreign policy of splendid isolation from Europe; had India been ruled by France or any other European country, it would have had a large Christian population. The Company had come here for business, not for evangelisation of a people who, the Stiff Upper Lip believed, were barbarians—and tamed barbarians could only be used as a labourer, not converted to your 'egalitarian' faith because, tomorrow, they would try to sit on the dining table opposite you. So, the early British kept the Indians at an arms length, even as the other Europeans would like to zealously harvest them to the Roman Catholic and/or Protestant faiths. The Church of England was the Church *only* for England and the English—it was not even for Wales and Scotland, not to talk of Northern Ireland. So, ironically, the English largely *shielded* India from Christianity; after 1947, a large number of Anglo-Indians', descendents of mixed blood of Indians and the English, migrated to the British Commonwealth countries because of this policy of aloofness vis-a-vis the infidel Hindu majority; it is another thing that many of these Anglo-Indians now find themselves neither English nor Indians, as the English believe they are Indians and the Indians believe they are English!

But why did the British come to India in the first place? India, except the extreme South, did not have much spices to offer, and was only the second best option. The first and the best option was South-East Asia where the Protestant Dutch would not allow the British to enter; in India, as the successors of the Portuguese, the Dutch had set up 'factories' (warehouses) at many places, including Agra, but, unlike their predecessor Iberians, they took little interest in local politics or culture and proselytisation. In Ceylon (Sri Lanka) they had bigger stakes. The British East India Company's total capital was only a tenth that of the Dutch and the Victorians were no match to the latter. Failure in South-East Asia due to the Dutch power forced the British to concentrate on India instead where the unpopularity of the Portuguese and unwillingness of the Dutch had left the field open to them. The Company soon became a maritime auxiliary, even unofficial Navy, of the Mughal Empire in the 17th century. In 1612, it set up headquarters at Surat on the western coast, looted several times by the Marathas and the Mughals, and shifted it to Bombay in 1674. The Company's fortunes went up and down as it got enmeshed with local Indian politics until its boastful Chairman Sir Josiah Child believed that the time was ripe for laying the foundation of a massive, safe and eternal English dominion in India. The Mughals, even if like a weak elephant, were weighty enough, defeated his forces in Chittagong; even Aurangzeb's officials kicked out the Company's merchants in Surat and Bengal. The chastened Company did not dare look into the Mughal eye until 1756. The only other important European rival to them was the French Company founded by Colbert in 1664, virtually a part of their state, whose rise and fall depended on local developments back home in France; but in 1720, Dumas and Dupleix founded a modicum of 'empire' at Pondicherry and Chandernagar, respectively, giving some sleepless nights to the British. It was, however, the Danes, settled at Tranquebar, who took missionary work more seriously than commerce in their Protestant zeal, particularly in South India. India had little to choose between the two evils called the Company and the Crown; but the North Europeans, including the British, turned out to be a little better and more civilised compared to the uncouth Portuguese and the French. The Mughals understood India relatively better and gave it back the imperial idea but never succeeded in really integrating the country; the British never really understood India, thought *they* united India for the first time after Ashoka and succeeded in creating modern infrastructure, if only in a bid to perpetuate their own superstructure back home.

Visibly, the Mughal Empire began to decline in 1712 when Aurangzeb's son Bahadur Shah I died after a brief rule of six years; the 'empire', however, dragged on through the hands of the kingmakers and puppets until the 1750s. Already, in the 1720s, the southern wing of the Empire had virtually broken away with the Nizam-ul-Mulk, Asaf Jah, setting up an almost parallel shop in Hyderabad. Unlike the Roman Empire, however, whose eastern wing, Byzantine, had completely broken away from the mother land and faith, the two wings of the Mughal Empire continued to coexist not like rivals but as partners; in fact, the Nizamate outlasted the Mughals and came to an inglorious end only in 1948. One by one, the limbs of the Empire continued to go paralytic and some parts even broke away. The Mughal 'emperors' increasingly became helpless against the rising tides of the Sikhs, the Jats, the Marathas on the Hindu side and a host of others—Avadh, Bengal, Kabul—on the other. The Rajputs were no longer partners of the Mughals who no longer received the constant supply of mercenaries and adventurers from the West and Central Asia to replenish their armour and army. The Muslims, who had defeated the Christians of Europe and had, in turn, been defeated by the Mongols, now found that they had become impotent. The boot was now to be on the other foot, the Hindus; only the socks were needed. These socks were provided by the British. But the Mughals, with the exception of Aurangzeb, had not been active religious converters as their mission and destiny. They were, at best, diluted and second-hand Muslims, descendants of the Mongols who had, in fact, destroyed the Abbasid Caliphate at Baghdad; they were also descendants of the Turks, who had, thereafter, captured this defeated Caliphate. Collectively, the Mughal *stake in Islam*, its future and its goals in infidel India was, therefore, as limited as the British stake in the spread of Christianity because the latter had little stake in the Crusades. To the Mughals, Islam was more of a vehicle rather than an article of *mass* faith; to the British, Christianity was more of an article of *personal* faith, rather than a principle of good business. Together, the Mughals and the British saved India from their own faiths. Reluctant Muslims, as the Mughals turned out to be, they had lost their sense of mission to rule India; reluctant Christians, as the British were, now had whale of a time to launch on a mission to rule India.

Not that there were no other claimants to the Mughal corpse. The Persians, led by the blood-thirsty Nadir Shah, dramatically appeared in Delhi in 1738 and proved that the Shias could also make the Sunnis run for their life, that Persia had exchanged new savagery of Islam in return for its culture and language to replenish its own Aryan barbarity; look how the nuclearised Iran, its baby Hizbollah in Lebanon and the Shias in occupied Iraq now cock a snook at the Arabs, the USA and Israel. The Sunni Mughals also found themselves at the mercy of the very same infidel, the Maratha Hindus, against whom they had been fighting for so long. The Marathas ruled the land under their direct control, called *Swarajya* (Homeland), and exacted *chauth* (one-fourth of revenue) and *sardeshmukhi* (one-tenth) from the 'Mughalai' land, both from Hindus and Muslims in a truly secular fashion, in what was also a new kind of Jazia in reverse; this unique extortion, now known as the mafiosi's 'protection fee' in Mumbai and elsewhere, has since continued in one form or another and the flow of such capital 'black money', from the rest of India would make Mumbai the nation's financial capital.

No wonder, the post-Shivaji Marathas in the 18th and 19th centuries ended up being as hated outside Maharashtra as the Mughals and later the Europeans for this exploitation. The Maratha rulers were an oligarchy of virtually independent eight provincial warlords, known as the *Ashta-pradhan Maratha Mandal* (Confederacy of Eight Maratha Chieftains), led by the Pune-based Peshwas. They succeeded in letting the Mughals cede to them the province of Malwa in 1738, thus effectively breaking the geographical unity of the Mughal Empire's two wings, the *predecessor* of the break-up of Pakistan in 1971. They fought on all sides: with the Mughals in the north (whom they came to control), with the Rajputs in the west (whom they could not), with the Nizam in the south (who bled them)...until they bled Orissa and Bengal. Eighteenth century India was like the India of the 8th century when rival kingdoms, almost evenly strong, sapped and exhausted each other in mock battles when the real warrior was knocking at the door.

In the early 18th century, the Afghans had overthrown the Persian monarchy and despite Nadir Shah crushing this revolt, the Afghans succeeded in carving out their short-lived empire out of the tottering Persian and Mughal Empires, thanks largely to the genius of their warlord Ahmad Shah Abdali. He had lost in Sirhind but was won over by the follower of Shaikh Ahmed Sirhindi, Shah Waliullah, who, like Quisling, invited the former to invade India in 1757. The impotent Mughals called in the energetic Marathas to help, who did repulse Abdali for a time but were decisively routed by him in the Third Battle of Panipat (1761). Allah did not, however, favour Abdali, whose own soldiers revolted for pay arrears and he had to beat a hasty retreat. There was now a power vacuum in India with both the Mughals and Marathas, bandaged from head to toe, finding their generals setting up separate shops in the carnival after the carnage. India was about to collapse and Europe was ready to take its domestic battles to this emerging colony.

With Frederick the Great of Prussia seizing Silesia in 1740, the War of Austrian Succession (1740-48) that followed found Britain and France on the opposite sides, as they would do again in the Seven Years' War (1756-63). In India, too, this Franco-British rivalry of Europe reflected in the political sides their Companies took in the politics and succession wars of the Nizamate that proved to be a turning point in this nation's history. A British clerk, Robert Clive (1725-1774), later the Baron of Plassey, had been made a soldier and administrator; he became a problem child in America and was transplanted to Madras. He turned out to be a genius in guerrilla warfare, forced the French to surrender at Arcot in 1751, using only 210 men, after a 51-day siege. All French attempts thereafter for a foothold remained half-hearted and they remained, till the very last, an also-ran in the marathon of European imperialism in India. The Indian rulers were now getting used to call in the Europeans to help and play them against each other; all European powers now had similar guns, muskets and cannons and superior firepower compared to the Indians, but the British were more focused, organised, disciplined and loyal to their Crown, ready to follow an imperial policy for commercial gains rather than religious reasons. They were always busy with business; they replaced the simple Hindi word *vyapar*, or trade, with the complicated 'business' that meant means fair and foul.

The biggest British contribution to India was that they made this lazy nation busy. She had learnt hypocrisy during the Muslim rule; now she learnt greed. For the first time, a bleeding India learnt to use sanitary napkins.

The 'British-India', to begin with, was an example of how to portray your nation's shady characters as 'patriots' abroad and discard them after they had played their role; he who could be your problem here could become a solution elsewhere. Robert Clive was one such example; first sent to America, kicked out from there, he became a success story in India. Britain retained the 'empire' he created in India, even made him a Baron, for establishing British Rule in India by victories over the French (1751) and the Nawab of Bengal (1757); on his return to Britain, their conscience suddenly pricked them and they accused him of 'abusing' power and making wealth, acquitted him, and when he committed suicide, forgot him for good. He had played his limited role and could now be disposed off like a disposable, clearing the British conscience. His legacy was carried forward by other notorious elements who included 'Christian' missionaries as well—even today European outcastes often emerge as Christian missionaries in the Third World. Since old habits die hard, many of them ended up as paedophiles, rapists and robbers at different places precisely because of this reason: that was why they were banished from their homelands in the first place. So, the British India, for 90 years from 1857, was ruled largely by a syndicate of imperialists, adventurers, fortune-seekers, industrialists, agriculturists, Christian missionaries and many of those who were misfits in their own countries. But, with the growing British Empire across the Seven Seas, these participants were too few in numbers to keep Great Britain going; their Indian collaborators, mostly feudal lords, were too stupid to understand the new machinery of the Industrial Revolution being used in empire building and colonisation for the purpose of seeking cheap labour, raw material and captive market for finished goods. The British, like Deng Hsiao Feng in the 1980s, knew that the cat's colour was unimportant, its ability to catch the mouse was; they needed black cats to catch mice in India as the white cats were few. At any given time, India never had more than 120,000 British and Europeans. Thomas Babbington Macaulay solved the problem of shortage of cats in India in the 1830s by introducing English-style education with the help of missionaries, so as to produce black cats that came to be known as the Indian Civil Service (ICS); its successor, Indian Administrative Service (IAS), which emerged as the *desi* kerosene to run a Westminster engine, eventually provided Black Cat commandoes to identify the Indian ruling class since the 1980s. Macaulay bequeathed these Cat-rearers to a nation where Mother India was astride a Lion!

The story of 'British-India' is, however, the saga of transformation from the original 'Delhi-Sultanate': both had hyphens to demonstrate that India was dominated by foreign aggressors but, while in the former it assumed a primacy of the British over India and became an all-India phenomenon, in the latter it was merely a Delhi-centric gang that masqueraded as an Indian regime. In both the cases, the hyphen was lost after the alien regimes felt that they had 'integrated' India with their parent country. The idea of India as a nation, of the Ashoka and Akbar vintage, got a new lease of life under the British. Seeing that the Muslim domination of a thousand years had been ended by the British, the Brahminical network began to function again. While the Mughal Empire, or whatever was left of it, was in the death throes at Delhi, its virtually independent Bengal unit, ruled by the self-appointed Nawab Ali Vardi Khan, since 1740, was heading a Muslim aristocracy in a large Hindu countryside. With warriors in short supply even in Delhi, his 'army' was woefully weak and he had to depend on still weaker Hindus. After his death in 1756, he was succeeded by his grandson Siraj-ud-Daula, 20, who had to face a Hindu uprising on one hand and the Franco-British Companies' rivalry on the other. The British Company, which had secured a Mughal *firman* (order) way back in 1717 for a free trade in Bengal, rubbed the young Nawab the wrong way forcing the latter to march on Calcutta, the British stronghold centred at Fort William made in 1696, but Clive rushed from Madras to save this citadel, restoring it after a few months in 1757. Clive found a willing Quisling in Siraj's general, Mir Jafar, who now succeeded as the British-chosen Nawab after the Battle of Plassey (1757); the 'guest' British plundered wealthy Bengal like a Mongol horde, eliminated challenges from the Dutch and the French, even obtained a Mughal title from Delhi, *Sabat Jung* ('Tried in Battle'). Clive then arm-twisted Mir Jafar to cough up 40 million sterling, and commenced financial bleeding of Bengal when the latter failed to pay up. With the arrival of these neo-Mongols, the Hindus of the bleeding Bengal were now being 'administered' by the clique of a Muslim usurper who had responsibility and his Christian protectors who had military power. The British mafia came to be called the Company *Bahadur* (The Valiant Company).

Having thus established British power without responsibility in Bengal, Clive returned to Britain to a hero's welcome in 1760, was sent back when his stooge Mir Jafar was toppled in 1765, and this time he extended the Company's Indian Dominion from Bengal-Bihar to Avadh, threatened even Delhi, and, in return, received the grant of revenue authority in Bengal and Bihar, becoming the Mughal's revenue collecting agency—its district-level revenue collecting officials were called District Collectors, as they are called even now. They mostly continued to be agents of their political godfathers for whom they collect both votes and wealth. The Company became virtual ruler of Bengal and Bihar, as the Nawab was the virtual imperial representative of Delhi. Clive, the White Plunderer, then tried to discipline his own plundering agents, invited a 'White Mutiny' by one of his brigadiers, returned to Britain after two years, this time got enmeshed in the machinations of the Company's in-house zealous politicians and, seven years later, proved that even high-profile robbers can commit suicide.

Bengal began to slide back; so the Company, threatened with bankruptcy due to mindless investments, now decided to fleece Bengal and Bihar, further, in a systematic manner: it sent Warren Hastings as Governor for 13 years, to cement the 'achievements' of Clive. Hastings hastily extended British power from Calcutta to Madras and Bombay as well and systematised exploitation so that the Company officials siphoned off wealth to the Company instead of lining their own pockets—with him began the notion that the Company could be dishonest, not its officials! True, even robbers and thieves should have morals and act honestly when it comes to distribution of booty. For this, the Company promoted him as Governor-General in 1773 with total control over Calcutta, Madras and Mumbai. For a time, he was cut off from Britain which was engaged in the American War of Independence (1775-78) but he dealt with the resurgent Marathas in Bombay and the reviving Muslim power in Madras provinces; for a time, the slave Hindus and their old masters, Muslims, united against the new masters, the British, in the South but, one by one, Hastings dealt with them and established the Company's power on firm footings in India. Under Hastings, India learnt to haste; she was grateful to the British missionaries for merely sucking her blood like leeches, unlike the Muslim marauders who killed her at will as well. Do not some people use leech to suck venom after a snake-bite?

Meanwhile, Her Majesty's Government, incensed over the Americas breaking away and the consequent loss of face in Europe, wanted to make good its losses elsewhere. India was the obvious choice, and the British could now boast that they had discovered the real India unlike Columbus who drifted to bogus India that came to be known as America. When the still bankrupt Company appointed Charles Cornwallis its Governor-General in India in 1786, the government, taking its lessons in America seriously, decided, for once, that the Company was accountable in England and responsible for the welfare of 'Indian subjects'. Since the British would always passionately do everything legally, including robbery, the government began by impeaching Hastings for having saved and secured 'British-India' through 'irresponsible tyranny'. It was like firing the chef and then relishing the dish so that you don't have to pay him and you have a clear conscience! British-India now came under His Majesty's parliamentary control, instead of the Company, the child being replaced by the parent.

Cornwallis, whose claim to infamy so far was that he was the British General who surrendered at Yorktown to end the American War of Independence, tried to restore his lost honour in India. A worthy successor to Clive. True to his British moorings, he called his predecessor Macpherson's government as a 'system of the dirtiest jobbings', divided his 'administration' into political and economic arms, thus laying the foundation of what later came to be known as the Indian Civil Service. He made the British government's say more important than a mere Company's trading and fleecing activity. 'Every native of India is corrupt' he declared—as if they should honestly and peacefully allow themselves to be plundered!—as he Europeanised the administrative and military services. But he did strike at the root of the people's continuing loyalty to the tottering Mughal Empire. Akbar's *Mansabdari* system had been caricatured into a *Zamindari* system by his successors; the hereditary zamindar, literally a landholder, had become a virtually independent land-owner and tax collector but the Company later roped them in as its own agents. They fleeced their own people marvellously even during the Great Famine of 1769-70, bringing the fabled and rich Bengal to a cycle of rural misery within a few years from which it never rose again.

Cornwallis, himself an English landlord, decided on what came to be known as the 'Permanent Settlement', making the zamindars government agents to keep the countryside quiet, collect tax and pay their annual fixed dues to the 'government' in return for security of their tenure; for his services, he was to retain one-tenth of revenue as his fee—this is also the business model of many start-ups providing services now. Having thus made the zamindari system 'merit-based' rather than hereditary, he created a new class of absentee landlords with no local connexions who bought estates as financial speculations. He stripped their police powers, strengthened the judiciary, took over criminal administration from Muslim hands, pruned the harsh *Shariah* Code, formed civil district courts at 23 places and separated their judicial and executive powers. In short, though he snatched the loincloth of the Indian, he dangled before him the pants he could purchase instead! The Bengali Hindu saw Muslim culture fading and being slowly replaced by the British one, a new and formidable class of middlemen arising in their midst as moneyed men, the old official patronage to religion and the arts waning in the urban areas whereas in the rural areas, life remained largely unchanged, submerging as it was now in the cesspool of poverty and illiteracy. In the midst of this subterranean anarchy, a significant number of low-caste Hindus and tribals of the North-East began to convert to Islam and Christianity. The high-caste Hindu saw them both as 'impure'; he had little to choose between the Persian-speaking feudal lords or the English-speaking 'Laat (Lord) Sahibs' as both were foreigners, cultivating their own cultures at the cost of the local one, unconcerned about public welfare. Old robbers had been replaced by a new gang, the latter systematising savagery for a long haul. In the Hindi-speaking areas, such rulers, together, came to be known through a dirty phrase: *Goo ka bhai Paad* (Faeces and Fart in Brotherhood, both as foul-smelling!).

Cornwallis thought the British were ruling India for its own good! That it was, for the first time, a law-and-order state, that the English landlords now ruling Bengal were better than their erstwhile Hindu or Muslim counterparts. Within 25 years after he left, most of India was under British control as his successor, Richard Colley Wellesley (1798-1805), a brother of the Duke of Wellington, a future foreign secretary and lord lieutenant of Ireland, proved. The fig-leaf of 'Company rule' was still there but, contrary to common belief, India unofficially came under the Crown in his time. Queen Victoria was now ruling India through the proxy of the Company whom she was increasingly using as a sacrificial lamb: anything good accrued to the Crown and all bad things were laid at the Company's doors—the policy of enjoying power and relegating the responsibility was followed not only by the British until 1947 but also by its Indian successor, the Congress Party. The British business in India was trade and the Company was its trading arm, the way the business of the Congress was to be in power and the civil servants were its arms. When Tipu Sultan of Mysore, otherwise the Aurangzeb of the South—aided by the French—challenged the British in 1799, the latter annexed half of his state, beginning the British territorial dominion in South India. Wellesley, true to his blue blood, then proceeded to arm-twist other states and tried to acquire their lands on one pretext or another, by hook or by crook, manipulations, bribe and fabrications. Thus Cape Comorin and Surat were 'absorbed' and so was half of Avadh; he appointed British Residents in vulnerable States which paid them their 'dues' in return for protection, and defeated the Marathas on behalf of the Nizam in 1803. He was recalled in 1805 in the midst of Britain facing the threat of Napoleonic invasion from France, that threw a spanner in the Company's expansion towards the Sutlej. For eight years, Britain marked its time while the French saw the rise and fall of Napoleon and his empire.

Taking advantage of this lull, there emerged a band of *Pindaris* (bandits) in Central India, recruited from the disbanded armies and uprooted villagers; it was their challenge that the British Crown began to take so seriously as to take India directly under the 'wings' of the emerging Empire. The rulers and the ruled, however, thought that the White rule was here to stay longer than anticipated, unlike the Muslim rule that suddenly snapped after eight centuries. The Company got a new Charter in 1803 and, after the final defeat of Napoleon two years later, its monopoly on the Indian trade was challenged by commercial interests in London who thought, correctly, that they had an equal right to rob India of its riches, that in that era of mixed economy, plunder could not be allowed to be an entirely state-owned enterprise in an overseas colony. But this should be preceded by the completion of British supremacy in India as a commercial imperative so that the victims could be dressed properly before being devoured. Thus was born the policy of the British forces being maintained at the Sutlej and policing the rest of India. For this purpose, a frontier war was waged with the Gurkhas (1815-16) who were then enrolled as permanent collaborators—the first batch of the new patients of the Stockholm Syndrome co-habiting with their Christian captors. All Maratha chieftains, whose glorious period was past, were brought to their heels by 1818.

By now, the British had established their hegemony in India up to the Sutlej banks: the Marathas, Rajputs, the Nizam and, last but not the least, the Mughals now became satellites of the British solar system. Lord Wellesley's 'nursery' created many officials who became cactus flowers of British expansionism in the subcontinent. Delhi, the political capital of India since the Chauhans last ruled it in the 11th century, was now a gaping hole in terms of political authority; this vacuum invited a spell of drizzle, followed by a thunder-shower and finally a deluge: even an adventurist like Charles Metcalfe, aged only 25, found himself to be the 'King' of Delhi for eight years from 1810. The Wellesley school kids, such as Mountstuart Elphinstone, wondered that they would continue to rule India till the end of Time simply by enrolling the patients of the Stockholm Syndrome; only a century and a quarter later, India forced them to eat crow in their own graves for they had forgotten that nothing changes like Change.

Increasingly, India's future was being decided outside India and the subcontinent was becoming part of the politics of Europe. Islam had helped India reach out to the Bosphorus; now Christianity helped India cross into Europe. The British catalyst, inadvertently, connected India globally like never before and integrated its evolution with other Homo sapiens, ending centuries of isolation from outside; this would provide greater survival benefits to the Indians in the 20th and 21st centuries. Earlier, under the Muslim Rule, India was part of the West and Central Asian politics. Policies of Ashoka and Akbar had churned India greatly—the former being gravy and the latter spices—but it had rendered socio-political India extremely supple, up for grabs by any marauder who could motivate and organise, bribe and manipulate, with a few thousand men under arms; Adi Shankaracharya had, perhaps, sensed that Ashoka and Harsha could morph into Akbars and he had tried to dyke the Indian psyche. But much of Europe lived in the caves at the time of Ashoka, and the British Isles marvelled at the Stonehenge when Harsha ruled; so the Kerala seer could not probably anticipate that the British would emerge in India as 'civilized' Mongols—but the potion he left for the Indians stood the test of Time.

After trading for 150 years (1600-1750) with India, the British took to arms and the Company, within eight decades, subjugated the whole subcontinent; it was yet another paradigm shift for the ancient civilisation of India when it came to be ruled by yet another alien culture, this time not even of Asian origin. For this feat, a lot of British thanked their own 'intrinsic superiority' and the 'exceptional qualities' of the Anglo-Saxon race, the way the Quraish once claimed superiority over the Arabs; to many Indians, too, the British appeared to be the Men from Mars. It was, however, a case of better leadership that the British found amongst themselves: they could organise, they could join heads with unity of purpose, and they could even join hands with those Europeans in India with whom they were fighting back home in Europe; the Indian 'rulers', on the other hand, were selfish, corrupt, undisciplined, caste and religion-ridden, rudderless, myopic, mostly men of fortune—in short, representatives of a decadent civilisation and culture. The Indian masses were, however, beginning to see through this maze of colonial politics and to its own shortcomings that had led them into this mess; despite all their flaws, the Muslims and the British came to India when she needed them the most to rejuvenate itself—and they were destined to eject themselves when their role in the great drama was up.

The pupils of the Sirhindi-Waliullah school, who still marvelled at the 'intrinsic superiority' of Islam (but anguished that the post-Aurangzeb Muslim rulers had been unable to keep it up), had, meanwhile, gradually come to occupy the Muslim Mind in India; while the Mughal Empire had shrunk to Delhi, the Muslim Mind, that they were *born* to rule an infidel India and would do so by the Sword, had begun to spread across the subcontinent, through the countless *madarsas* where this continues to be the dominant theme even now. They considered the British as 'usurpers' the same way the Hindus considered the Muslims as the previous batch of encroachers. Since the Hindus had to select between the two, they selected the *latest model* of the exploitative machinery! Some Muslim rulers, too, had tried to modernise their outlook: Mir Qasim, in 1763, trained an army on European lines, and Tipu would follow him later, as would the Scindias, too. So, it was the Indian armies that were being modernised and Europeanised *first of all* in an era when science and technology, secular and great levellers, had emerged as bigger instruments of imperialism, colonialism and expansionism, slowly replacing the role of religion in this respect. The Hindus were becoming aware of an even more important factor in the development of human societies and saw in the sciences a new, emerging religion, a liberating force. While the Hindus were, generally, beginning to come out of their primitive caves, the Muslims were creating ghettos in India. The Hindus were beginning to see the British as liberators much the same way the Persians and Egyptians had welcomed the energetic Arabs as liberators a thousand years ago. The colonial exploitation of India by the British was the price the Hindus had to pay to get rid of an overstaying Islam. Despite losing in America, the British had burst out on the world like the Arabs of the seventh century and found themselves uprooting the Islamic empires of the Mughals and then the Ottomans, one by one, and ***not*** planting the Christian ones in their stead. The job the British, in the end, entrusted themselves was to restore pre-Islamic, and even pre-Christian, credentials of the societies they ruled in India, Egypt and China, where they would unwittingly nurture the future monsters to devour Islam.

In other words, the British were the single most important factor for Return of the Infidel on the world scene.

Why did Nature choose the British to do what they did? Mostly unconsciously, sometimes even consciously, they had a burning sense of a mission. Many of them were exploiters, robbers and criminals in the colonies they ruled; some were even Christian missionaries; but it was the few, back home in England, who guided the destiny of the colonies by introducing new developments to the old societies that really mattered. Although the French Revolution had failed to unite Europe along Napoleonic lines and created the Metternich system instead, the Continent in the 18th century was now full of self-confidence, esteem and optimism. But, while the continental colonialists, such as the French, Belgians, Portuguese and the Spanish, had left a trail of blood in their respective colonies in order to make them look like their Masters through societal surgeries, the British in India did not do that. The very fact that they considered themselves 'superior' even over all Europeans put together, what to talk about those 'black, native Indian thieves', was why they did not assimilate with their slaves nor did they actively resort to supporting *medieval* practices like religious conversion. In fact, from the early 19th century, a combination of factors came into play: the imperialists were busy uprooting the Mughal Empire, the colonialists were busy fleecing and exploiting India of her raw material for the Industrial Revolution of Manchester and Lancashire, the Company was increasingly becoming a state enterprise with the Crown more and more interested in making the colony of India its permanent Jewel like *Koh-e-Noor* by 'enlightening' the Brown Sahibs to rule India on behalf of the British as the official Britain busied itself with acquiring and managing other colonies. Since the British monarch was also Head of the Church of England, she would not do anything that would disturb this imperial policy by inviting native revolt and, therefore, the British *refrained* from indulging in large-scale, officially-supported, religious conversion in India. They knew their Magna Carta, and that the attempts to kill a hen laying golden egg eventually end up in Cromwellian tragedies; they were fresh from the American humiliation and, although they had repeated Clive in India, they did not want to repeat their earlier mistakes they did in America. They had realised that they had come *for* business in India, nothing more and nothing less, and religious conversion was certainly not their business; some of them still dreamt of a 'manifest destiny' of Britain in India. On the contrary, if converted in large numbers, the neo-Christians could set up their own shop and demand equality! The British, therefore, maintained a safe distance from the dogma of the Church whose prime goal, even *raison d'etre*, was to harvest souls for the Christ; their job it was just to create a perpetual machinery for business that could work until the end of Time. They remembered very well that the Crusades ended up into a zero-sum game. They considered this whole business of missionary activity and drive for religious conversion as a relic of the 'despicable' practice of 'European' churches and, as in politics and diplomacy, followed the well-known policy of Splendid Isolation in this respect too. It was only after the humiliating defeat of the Ottoman Empire at the hands of Russia in the Crimean War in the 1850s and its eventual demise after the First World War, however, that the British began to take some serious interest in conversions: but again as part of their overall imperial policy, as the swelling number of adherents of churches other than the Church of England, or of the energetic neo-missionaries, the Communists, would have been detrimental to their Empire.

In this imperial task the British were lucky to use their local resources in forging their Empire in India, all for their own purpose, contrary to the native Indian rulers who divided amongst themselves the decreasing revenue and were, in the end, left with little resources for fighting wars on British levels. One by one, therefore, the British were able to make the Hindu and Muslim rulers toe their line until they reached Delhi themselves. The Muslims had subdued India because of the peculiar nature of Indian polity and the tensions produced by overlapping races and rival cultures in a multicultural, polytheistic subcontinent which provided few physical opportunities for the growth of integrated nationalism along European (or even the Middle Eastern) lines, that was now the modern mantra. Nevertheless, some groups, such as the Marathas and the Sikhs, grew into proto-nations, although without much intellectual capital; but they did not develop into empires, ossified into aristocracies and oligarchies and finally decayed and dispersed retaining a false glory, burden of history and superiority complex. India had never been a religious fundamentalist society as a whole, and would not mind having even a foreigner as a benevolent despot, submitting to a leader who would make good his claim to supremacy, provided he did not disturb the Hindu social order, traditions and beliefs. That was why they tolerated a non-

Hindu Akbar and even King George V as a *Chakravartin* but began to fall away from their successors when they stooped to disturb the Hindu psyche. Still the Mughal Empire lasted 230 years; the official British Empire, which began in 1858, lasted only 90 years. Why? The Mughals had made India sleep in hibernation; the British, on the other hand, whipped India up into activity and after flagging her off on a deIslamisation drive, retired in 1947. Among the Hindus, the only ruler who had the potential all through the Mughal-British period was the imperial and expansionist genius of Shivaji. Maharana Pratap, Ranjit Singh and Laxmi Bai fought the Muslims bravely but their vision was largely restricted to their own regimes, not all-India; but even Shivaji's twin policy of defending the *desh* (homeland) and the cow decayed during his successors' rule and eventually degenerated into the defence of Maharashtra, leaving the cow to die of eating the bio-undegradable polythene bags rather than end up in a slaughterhouse or the roads of modern India. The post-Shivaji Marathas could not become nationalists outside Maharashtra because they became imperialists in the rest of the subcontinent; and if other Hindu and/or Muslim rulers had to choose between them and the British, they often chose the superior force as per the Law of Nature.

The decay of the Marathas on the one hand and the Mughals on the other signified emergence of the British Rule in India. Although, superficially, the British came with their hackneyed commercial, colonial and imperialist aims like all powers of the day before or after them, their deIslamisation drive was only too apparent. They considered the Hindus merely superstitious, coward and backward and would like to whip them up from their dogmatic slumber if only to assist the Masters in fleecing the slaves, as Macaulay did, but they always suspected the Muslims to be their *real* enemy. They knew the Mughal Empire they were pulling down was tottering and that everybody, including themselves, was feasting at the dying body of this Baburite dynasty; they were always apprehensive of a possible strong reaction, or revolt, knew as they did about the continuing loyalty of all Muslims and many Hindus to the Mughals. The Macaulay project was meant mainly to raise from amongst the Hindus a *new caste* of pseudo-British so that they could assist the real British against the Muslims on a long-term basis. This became necessary because a vast India was much more than the few British could chew, particularly when they became increasingly involved in China, their current and best market from where their maximum profits came through trade in tea, opium etc. For the early 19th century British 'Company Raj', trade in India was increasingly becoming an unprofitable proposition as wars, bribes, cost of administration and policing and policy failures burnt a big hole in their pockets and dwindling profits were being absorbed by keeping the lid on in an era of Renaissance in Bengal and its after effects elsewhere. The commercial-minded British found India less and less attractive—but with those fancying their 'manifest destiny' syndrome, especially after losing America, being equally powerful, contradictions remained—but they had to maintain their hegemony in India for the preservation of China trade. On the other hand, private British business and free traders, jealous of the monopolist and government-supported Company, still viewed the Indian colony as a lucrative market if only the Crown followed a *laisez faire* policy and allowed other hands as well to trade in India; they egged the Crown on to continuing the British expansion in India as a withdrawal now would ruin their prospects and humiliate whatever remained of the post-American British pride and a *status quo* would leave them uncertain. So, the force of circumstances, policies of trade and imperialism, domestic and European concerns—and, above all, the Westminster pressures under which the Crown managed to stay on the monarch's uneasy head since Magna Carta and Cromwell—forced the British to favour and play the Hindus against the Muslims: their actions against the Indian Muslims were, however, muted as they were wary of their multiple interests in pan-Islamic lands. Additionally, there always lurked that intra-Abrahamic Brotherhood feelings of some of the British Christians *for* the Muslim Indians when it came to support the latter *against* the rank infidel Hindus with whom they both had refused to assimilate and were, in fact, comrades-in-arms in plundering. The British were angry with the Muslims also because the latter stayed put even after eight centuries and the former were not being given opportunity to milk India.

The British, who had frustrated the Napoleonic dream of a united Europe by 1815, however, fulfilled their dream of a united India just three years later through the Treaty of Amritsar (1818) with which they completed their hegemony in India from Bengal to Sutlej. *The most important fallout of this treaty was the plugging of Punjab from the porous mountainous passes from which hordes of adventurers and fortune-seekers had been coming to India since the very beginning. By thus effectively plugging the Punjab, the British made it impossible for anymore alien hordes to invade India from the North-West—the Making of India, its multiple societal layers, was now complete after 3,000 years of the Three Waves, as it awaited the Fourth.* India's recipe was now ready, its post-Indus, layered reorganisation complete and post-Harsha catalysis nearing end.

British-India had now begun to *contain* Islam in the subcontinent: the replenishment and reinforcement of Muslim warriors from Central and West Asia, that had kept the Muslim show going on in India, now became impossible; even in the early 1920s, during the Khilafat Movement, the Muslims could not invite Afghanistan to invade India. This removal of life support system was one of the major reasons why the Mughal Empire collapsed completely just four decades later, in 1858. The 'Indian' Muslims were rendered completely rudderless and leaderless and it was in this vacuum that the descendants of the likes of Shaikh Ahmed Sirhindi or Shah Waliullah, and their 'spiritual' followers like Sirs Syed Ahmed and Muhammed Iqbal, politicians like Muhammad Ali Jinnah and Nawaz Sharief, Generals like A A K Niazi, Zia ul-Haq and Pervez Musharraf and local chieftains like Z A Bhutto would descend in succession in the next two centuries. The 'fundamentalists' would try to bring the 'Indian' Muslims closest to the Arabic Islam, the 'modernists' would make them take to cyber-terrorism and crash hijacked planes to burn a civilisation down that did not regard the 'intrinsic superiority' of Islam. From now on, the aims of both the Islamic fundamentalists and the modernists would be well-defined, coordinated and organised: the former would unite the masses, the latter would *replenish* the power of Islam by using the means developed by the enemy. The fundamentalists absorbed the Qur'an, the modernists began to implement the Hadith, in a seamless full-circle. Not that all Christians or Muslims could be painted with the same brush; but the pro-Indians amongst them had the least voice before a recalcitrant and vocal majority amongst an overall numerical minority. How many Muslims in the 21st century India, for instance, would listen to an Arif Mohammad Khan? Some fundamentalists even asked Muslim Bollywood film stars to 'reIslamise' themselves as they had caught the Hindus' infidel infection. *Any conscientious Muslim trying to assimilate Islam with India was suspected and, clearly, unwelcome to the Muslim Mind.* Luckily, most Muslims, being illiterate, like their Hindu counterparts, continued to remain free of this communal virus and slowly merge back into the Indian Ocean.

The effect of this British supremacy in India was different for the Hindus and Muslims. While many among the Hindus, even if reluctantly, used things European to slowly eradicate their own social evils like *sati* and took to the sciences and modern education like a greenhorn, many of the Muslims could never overcome the loss of *their* Mughal Empire; they rued this loss which they believed was less due to the impotence of the Mughals and more due to the perfidy of the Hindus and the British who had 'united' against them. The Muslims were shocked to discover how fast some of the Hindus were recovering their lost civilisational ground and making up for the losses; having enslaved India for eight centuries, the dominant Muslim Mind could never tolerate this sudden collapse of the Mughal Empire and the resultant rise of the erstwhile slave Hindus, thanks to the British. But the Muslims had few options. Since the British plugged cross-border replenishment to Islam in India, the local Muslims had to *per force* show their 'loyalty' to the suspicious British so that the latter could make them partners at par with the Hindus; the idea was to learn modern science so that they could strengthen ancient Islam! Sir Syed Ahmed was the fruit of this school; no doubt some of the Hindus also believed that they could go back to the 'basics' through the modern route but a majority of Hindus had the capacity to ridicule them without being killed. For the 19th century Muslim in India, it was choice between the devil and the deep sea. Islam had established itself in India through the Slave Dynasty; now the Muslims found themselves being 'enslaved' by not one but two masters—and they were not as hostile to the British who was remote and 'superior' besides being a monotheist, but the sudden rise of the infidel Hindu, his very neighbour whom he used to lord it over until yesterday, became an eye-sore to him. It was this double whammy that made the Muslims in the subcontinent impatient with the Hindus: they would learn to be modern so that they could take on their ancient enemy, the Hindu. With this aim, Sir Syed Ahmed Khan established the Aligarh Movement and the Muslim University; with this aim, too, the fundamentalists established the mother-board of the Taliban, the *Dar-ul-Uloom* at Deoband in 1889.

Peeved at being dislodged and *dislocated* by the British, something the Mongols and the Turks had done earlier in the Cradle of Islam itself, the Muslim fanatics in India, eager to rediscover their roots *trans-Indus*, became extremely secretive; Islam was such a supreme truth that they could resort to any falsehood to uphold it! The British, despite their well-grounded suspicion, did not know the Muslim Mind in a largely infidel land where Islam had just lost to 'Christianity', undoing the hard work of 800 years. The India the British had inherited was a vast, exhausted and uninspired nation ruined economically by everyone who could participate in this scramble and mayhem. British officers like Metcalfe in the north, Elphinstone in the west and Malcolm at the centre did not know where to begin clearing this mess, a result of civilisational metabolism, the socio-economic disruption created by the internecine warfare of the Mughals with the Marathas and others, and the aftermath; this situation continued for several decades and India plunged deeper and deeper into the cesspool. One by one, the Rajputs, Marathas, Sikhs, the Jats, the Bundelas, all chronically feudal, were passing out in a parade as the new entrants—the Bengalis, the Tamils—were entering from the other end of the Aryavarta Ramp. Towards the end of the 18th century, across India, there was no link between the ruler and the ruled and everybody was free to fancy himself as the centre of the universe. This changed with the arrival of the British on the scene. After 1818, they restored a modicum of order in Bengal, Bihar and Orissa that constituted the hub of the erstwhile 'British-India' which had now extended up to the Sutlej in the north-west and Carnatic in the South.

Cornwallis had stamped out all 'unofficial' corruption, making the subjects grateful that banditry had at least now been institutionalised and systematised—post-1947, India witnessed it again, and post-1991, again and again—that fleecing was no longer a form of corruption but 'life tax' for letting you be alive, that robbery was no crime but religion. From the late 17th century many a people took to crime to make an easy buck; and they included unpaid and starving soldiers of different armies and even mercenary bands of alleged saints going by the names such as the *nagas*, *gusains*, *sannyasins* or *bairagis*; they controlled their domains like religious shrines with iron hands and evolved a system of fleecing the unsuspecting pilgrim. There were so many gangs of *dakoos* in the 19th century North India that the poor British, whose dictionary knew only one word 'robbery', other than banditry, until now, had to incorporate another, 'dacoity', the Anglicised replacement for the Hindi *dakaiti*. The dacoits were different from robbers and bandits in that they were often *caste-based*, would raid only the rich, followed a 'code' and certain 'principles', and many were even popular like Robin Hoods and christened themselves as *baagis* (rebels); the robbers on the other hand were secular in outlook and would, therefore, rob anybody nonchalantly and without any compunction whereas the bandits were the ordinary criminal gangs active on the highways, looting the caravans.

It was this vacuum due to the breakdown of the Mughal supremacy and the resultant feudal autonomies that was sought to be filled by the dreaded and pitiless *Pindaris* whose Hindu gangs religiously worked across North India for decades in the 19th century and whose descendants were the notorious dacoits of the Chambal ravines in the 20th century and the caste-based gangsters, Senas, politicians and the Naxalites-Maoists in the 21st. The Pindaris and the Thugs fancied themselves as representatives of the fierce goddesses Bhavani and Kali, incarnations of Durga, respectively. So rampant was this anarchy in 19th century India that even Islam had been somewhat 'Hinduised' along caste-lines, particularly in the countryside, due to breakdown of the 'egalitarian' Brotherhood into caste-based 'Muslims'. Several Muslims, who were merely local people 'converted' to Islam due to the force of circumstances, continued, or even revived, the use of part of their Hindu caste names to *shield* themselves from casteist Hindu gangsters who ruled the local area where the poor Muslim had to stay and survive. Fewer and fewer were now going to Mecca; most were slowly dissolving, like the iceberg melting back into the same Hindu ocean from which they had sprung up, and increasingly becoming indistinguishable from the Hindus thanks to the gradual adoption of Urdu (which had many Persian or Arabic words) and later its variant 'Hindustani' (having mostly Hindi words with a sprinkling of Urdu). Hinduism, as a silent killer, had now effectively begun to absorb Islam piecemeal, beginning with the villages, where the Hindus always remained a majority; Islam increasingly restricted itself to the urban areas.

Alarmed, the Muslim orthodoxy, which had already been increasingly finding itself driven to the wall, decided to hit back by opening religious seminaries at Bareilly and other places whose main job was to prevent the Indian Muslims (or Muslim Indians!) from melting back into the Hindu ocean. A school was set up at Bareilly which gradually forced the 'strayed' Muslims to discard their half-Hindu identities and names and adopt fully Islamic credentials; but, at the same time, the Bareilvi school, aiming to revive conversion of the Hindus to Islam, ensured that the Sufi traditions continued as a half-way rest house for the one-way traffic and, therefore, Islam was suitably 'Indianised' by adopting certain local traditions. This revived Sufi strategy, however, failed to stem the slide. So the orthodoxy did the best it could: just like others opening a university for those who fail in a school, its theologians branched out into the Dar-ul-Uloom at Deoband, at Saharanpur, hoping that Hindu pilgrims returning after taking bath in the Ganges at Hardwar could be made to take rest there! Subsequently, this university came to get brilliant pupils like Maulana Abul Kalam Azad and a host of 'secular' intellectuals and leaders who helped their *alma mater* float fundamentalist bodies like *Ahl-e-Hadis*, one of the fountainheads of Islamic militancy worldwide.

Not that the British were unaware of these machinations; they had taken to imperial policy after a thorough grind in European politics and knew their anti-Islamic roots lay in the legacy of Richard the

Lion Heart (1157-1199), the largely non-resident King of England, who had fought against Sultan Salahuddin alias Saladin to recover Jerusalem in the Crusades. For some time, the Company flip-flopped over whether to pursue business or religion aggressively. There was, in fact, a lively debate among the Company officials over religious issues of their Indian colony. Post-Napoleon, Europe was scene of intellectual ferment and the post-1818 British, having secured and controlled India, were still under the Tories, who were even now afraid of the Jacobins, Napoleon and the Revolution they had stirred, which gave a fillip to the Age of Reason and deChristianisation. In fact, the dead Napoleon was more feared now due to his increasing influence on European intellectuals who had begun to wonder about life after Christianity. Influential British leaders like Warren Hastings and H H Wilson favoured that the Company should not interfere in the Indian religious affairs and concentrate on security and trade, or else it could invite strong local reaction later. As a result, even the Christian missionaries had to be controlled and discouraged. Britain was not ready to lose a lucrative India *merely* for the sake of Christianity—as Rupert Murdoch was credited with having once said that truth could not be allowed to be an obstacle in the publication of a good story in his newspapers! The Company even discouraged those who were against Hindu practices like the *sati* and female infanticide. But the Evangelics, who equally abhorred Hindu idolatry and polytheism, Islamic monotheism, French Enlightenment and atheism and Jacobinism, found support among the 'secular' Tories. Here was a land where millions could be made to rush into the Christ, they argued, if only they could set up hospitals and schools in this land of temples. Like a woman knowing that the way to the heart of her beloved went through his stomach, the Evangelicals thought that the way for the Hindus to the Christ went through the Christian-run institutions that encouraged the infidel to question and hate their own traditions; what the Muslim fundamentalists wanted to do through terror, their Christian counterparts would do through 'service' and sustained Sufi-type campaign. They were supported by powerful Brits like Charles Grant and Wilberforce, the latter securing free entry into the subcontinent for the missionaries.

The third British group 'concerned' with India was that of the Utilitarians and the Radicals, who, together, shouldered the heavy 'White Man's Burden', that the West was inherently superior and the East chronically inferior, that it was the duty of the Occident to cure the ailing Orient. The Company enrolled James Mill, a Utilitarian, after he penned his famous *History of India* in 1817 along these lines. The fourth British group comprised Company officials like Metcalfe and Elphinstone who knew about the inherent and underground currents in India and cautioned that only a gradual change was advisable. They knew that the British had traded with India for 150 years before they came to acquire political control and any attempts to rush for a change would only trigger strong reaction. The Evangelicals and the Radicals were encouraged by the 'reformers' victory in 1830 and, for the first time since 1757, the West started sinking its teeth in India. Slowly.

There was, then, the fifth group of the Scottish. Although the United Kingdom came into being in 1707 with the 'union' of England, Scotland, Wales and (Northern) Ireland, there was little of 'Great Britain' in it. All these people continued to retain their regional identities for the next hundred years. The common 'British' identity emerged slowly only after Napoleon sought to create the common 'French' citizenry out of the Basque country and Brittany. While France was predominantly Catholic, the UK was primarily Protestant. Ironically, London's 'India mission' through the Company brought the English and the Scottish closer in making them acquire a British identity. The Scots were less than 10% of the British population but, by the end of the 18th century, they constituted over 60% of the Company's officials in India. In the British Empire, the Scots found a new, imperial identity: in London, they still found themselves being 'discriminated' against but in India they became Masters! The Scots thus helped create a modern common Indian identity and, in turn, carried the germ of separation back home when they returned in 1947, which waits to tear apart the Union Jack.

India now became more than a British Colony. It became the instrument of deIslamisation worldwide. From now on, in the favourite British cricket vocabulary, India would be like the 12th player who would ensure that one of the players fell sick in every match and he played in his place! The 'absentee' was to be the one who would always be present. That is, the Hindus would now play in place of the Muslim.

This change began with Lord William Bentinck, Governor-General (1828-35), who piloted India out of the morass, despite the hostility of Wellington's Tory government in the first two years. Bentinck realised that if Britain was all 'sexed up', India, too, was ready to receive the sperm and subsequent orgasm. The seven years of his reign were the most important in the history of India since the eighth century; these years provided the ignition key that restarted the Indian Juggernaut. Bentinck had earlier been recalled in 1807 while he was Governor of Madras but he bounced back, thanks to his father being a Whig Premier and the Company needing a strong official to run a complicated colony where others did not want to go. Contrary to common confusion that he was a 'reformer', the fact was he had no sympathy for things Indian. Understanding often leads to compromise, sympathy and non-action, he believed. He earned the Company's goodwill by balancing its account-books in India and that of the Indian upper classes by appointing judges from natives, ending the Cornwallis system of European monopoly in Indian judiciary. A confirmed westerniser, he was like a reformed Mughal putting back the revenue system on the rails on which depended India's prosperity in future. He enrolled half-westernised Hindu reformers like Raja Rammohun Roy and legally stamped out some of the Hindu superstitious practices like *sati*, the burning of widows on their husband's funeral pyres, religion-supported *thugee* and female infanticide and encouraged widow marriages.

But the most important thing he did was introduction of Western system of education in India. The 19th century was one bubbling with scientific spirit, secularisation of polity, economic imperialism; while the Hindus increasingly took to the Western education with the zeal of a neophyte, the Muslims, still intoxicated with the hangover of their fast-disappearing Mughal Empire, looked at Europe with suspicion—for them, Oxford and Cambridge spelled New Crusaders! In 1829,

Bentinck came to believe that the British language was the 'key to all improvements' and in 1834, that the 'general education is my panacea for the regeneration of India'. With support from James Mill at India House in London, who himself was a confirmed westerniser with a Utilitarian passion for dissemination of 'useful knowledge', and later from the radicals in Whig government, Bentinck then took the most important decision in the history of the still-in-place Muslim India: he changed the government language from a West Asian language (Turkish/Arabic/Persian/Urdu) to a Western European *English.* It is the language of your government that makes or mars your vision about the world around and the already westernising Hindus, cutting across their regional distinctions, soon felt the impact of switching over from the existing official Muslim language to English. In 1834, with the arrival of the powerful Thomas Babington Macaulay, the new Law Member, Bentinck did in a diverse British-India what Josef Stalin would do in a diverse Soviet-Russia a hundred years later: with the stroke of a pen, the language of the minority British would be forcefully imposed on a majority Indians. The British Resolution of 7 March 1835, declared that the 'great objects of the British Government ought to be the promotion of European literature and science...(by) imparting to the native population the knowledge of English literature and science through the medium of English language'.

In the colonial annals of Asia, this was a new development; the British were yet to fully control India as the Mughals were still, technically, 'ruling' the subcontinent. Before expelling Islamic rule from India, the British first expelled Islam's language of discourse; from then on, all Muslim languages slowly decayed and virtually disappeared from India, except in a microscopic minority. Even Urdu, the Indian offspring of the Arabic father and Persian mother, gradually emerged as the *Muslim* tongue, rather than as an Indian one and met the same fate; its poetry since the 19th century was more and more lamentation for the decline of a glorious past, its prose more and more 'revolutionary', that is attempting to retrieve this past; even Bollywood gradually reduced making Muslim-specific social films or penning Urdu songs with the rise of Muslim terrorism in the 1980s, the last such important film being made was Ismael Merchant's 1993 bilingual film, *Muhafiz/In Custody*, depicting the pathetic and slow demise of Urdu, the last language of the Mughal Empire.Still later, Muslim characters in Hindi films largely came to be depicted either in the stereotypical madarassa-type conservatives or as militants and criminals—depiction of the 'normal' or 'regular' Muslim became a thing of the past. The ordinary Muslim, fed only with the Mughlai dishes, continued to be overwhelmed with the sheer size of the vegetarian menu the new 'Rambharose Hindu Hotel' offered.

With the zeal of reformers, the successors of the Bentinck-Macaulay-Roy trio set up institutions imparting western knowledge in English language. English replaced Persian, the court language of the Mughals, as the official state language and the medium of the higher courts of law; even in the local courts, regional languages slowly elbowed out Persian. Muslim languages gradually got restricted mainly in the criminal procedure codes in the courts. English became India's vehicle of change as it indirectly promoted regional languages at the local level that led to their modern development, all at the cost of Islamic languages. Modern western science came to India in the form of western medicine, for which Calcutta Medical College became the first vehicle. More and more Hindus joined the bandwagon of western technology through engineering works like canals, bridges, roads and finally railways; eventually, the *administration* became more and more western in outlook and more and more Indian in staff. This was the second software developed by a hardware India, the first being the *Prasthantrayi*.

One of the major pillars of Islamic rule in India was its West Asian-type jurisprudence; despite occasional and short-lived 'secular' outlook, the Muslim courts in India were heavily what they were, pro-Muslim, serving the interests of the minority rulers of Islamic persuasion in an infidel-majority nation they ruled. This control of judiciary and all that went with it kept the Hindus in check in the name of 'law' even as the Muslims enjoyed benefits and trappings of being the 'ruling' class, at least in the urban areas where the influence of Islam was the strongest. It was also one of the mantras of the Hindu 'loyalty' towards the Islamic rulers. Unless a new ruler transforms this *way of thinking* and moulds the public opinion in his favour, his rule cannot last long. As the Law Member, Macaulay understood this intricacy of public administration: if the British were to really replace the Mughals and rule India for a long time, the whole nature of Indian jurisprudence must be changed. So, he commenced codification of Indian public law from the main basis of Cornwallis's system of revising the Mughal-Islamic criminal law, which was completed in 1861. It was in this department that the British first handed over power to the Hindus. They worked according to the English legal procedures, attained high positions and interacted with western ideas. *For the first time, the Hindus came to believe that they enjoyed equal and as many rights as the Muslims.*

The post-Bentinck Governors-Generals were afflicted with the colonial mindset; they believed that the British would continue to rule India until eternity. Influential officials amongst the British-India regime, together with Christian missionaries of various hues, found India neck-deep in paganism and superstition and decided to harvest it to the Christ. 19th century Britain was getting more and more embroiled with European politics in that era of colonial and imperial expansion, the Scramble for Africa, the moves towards Down Under (Australia) and China. The Ottoman Empire was, like its Mughal counterpart, readying itself to sleep into the grave. For the Church, it was an era of jubilation: with the weapons of science and technology, it had launched the unofficial Ninth Crusade against Islam! But a pagan land like India, which they believed must be retrieved from the hands of Islam, and which they fancied could be 'Christianised' easily, must first be understood for its strengths and weaknesses.Since 1813, these missionaries had succeeded in pressuring the Company to grant them entry. With this aim, European countries, particularly Britain, set up schools, colleges and hospitals across India and a number of missionaries like Max Muller 'studied' Indian (say Hindu) classics and translated them into European languages. Few of them were interested in Islamic-Indian studies because they knew the Muslims were a hard nut to crack while the Hindus could be a soft target if encircled methodically. Overall, learning from its earlier failure of the Crusades, Europe was now encircling the Fertile Crescent from all sides: Britain in India, Russia in Central Asia, France and Belgium in Africa; it was foolish trying to create a joint Christian command to take on Islam as despite the aim being one, the haphazard armies were defeated by the united Muslim resistance in the eight earlier Crusades. The Crusaders believed that now was the time to revive the Crusades, this time the aim being one but the participants were free to evolve their policies in their specific colonies. The policy would culminate in the defeat of the Ottoman Empire in the Crimean War (1854-56) at the hands of Russia, barely two years before even the Mughal Empire was uprooted. But, at the end of the First Afghan War, Edward Law (First Earl of Ellenborough) gave the Hindus a dream (September 6, 1842) and the belief that the victorious English Army had brought back to India from Ghazni those gates of the Somnath Temple which were looted away by Mehmood Ghaznavi in the 11th century. 'Our victorious army bears the gates of the Temple of Somnath in triumph from Afghanistan and the despoiled tomb of Sultan Mehmood looks upon the ruins of Ghazni. The Hindus' insult of 800 years is at last avenged', Law declared. A Christian securing back the infidel's looted property from the Muslims! Although the Hindus were not amused as the gates were not found to be genuine, the Muslims felt immensely humiliated—but it did sow in the Hindu mind a dream to undo the various humiliations heaped by the Muslims—later even by the British/Christians—and this was done the very next year after the Independence by Sardar Patel who vowed to reconstruct the Somnath Temple in 1948. Truth always being stranger than fiction, Lord Ellenborough was ridiculed, like all those seeing through the mirror, but it was he who, for the first time, *clearly* summed up, although subconsciously, why the British had come to India and where India was headed to.

The 'First War of Independence' in 1857 was part of this evolution. Overall it was, as it turned out eventually, despite jingoistic battle-cries, politically correct sabre-rattling. 'Secular' historiography and the Congress greed to force the Hindus and Muslims into the same sandwich for perpetuating its regime, made this the Hindus' battle for independence from the Muslim rule, rather than an 'Indian' war of independence from the British. The Muslims were led by, who else, the Wahhabis, well-entrenched by now in the Islamic orthodoxy, as they continue to remain in 2017, and their aim was to restore a *Mughal* Empire, not a Hindu/Indian one. Clearly, the revolt collapsed because (1) the Hindus were still divided and reluctant, unsure as to who was worse, the Muslims or the British; (2) the Muslims were now as powerless vis-a-vis the British as the Hindus were at the time of Muhammad Ghori's invasion—it was a battle between a revivifying and an eclipsing culture and everybody knew who would win in the end and (3) because the British successfully used the railway, telegraph and the army to move speedily against the 'rebels' who were still busy giving a medieval sparkle to their rusted guns even as the *firangi* bombarded their hideouts. In the event, the Hindus, the Muslims and the British used each other against each other in this musical chair race and the one who had the whistle to blow, won. In fact, the British were still not fully entrenched in India which was not yet a 'British Dominion' and it continued to be, technically, ruled by the mummy of the crumbling Mughal Empire, which had been entombed early in the 19th century. Therefore, if at all there was to be an element of 'independence' to it, it could only be the half-hearted attempt of the Hindus to get rid of Islamic rule—in fact, many of the Hindus had become so much used to the Islamic yoke that they would feel the discomfort of ridding it even in the 21st century, trying to somehow assimilate sand and snow in a sundae! The British were, therefore, not much off the mark calling the 1857 uprising a *Gadar* (Revolt) in the Muslim armies of Delhi and Lucknow and some other places for the re-establishment of the Mughal Empire with the specific aim of defeating the British. The Hindus who joined it were mainly the subjects of feudal lords and vested interests who wanted to perpetuate the Mughal regime for their own ends, the British believed.

The Hindu angle of this episode was an entirely different case, although the Muslim and Hindu aims did join against the British for some time. Indian Muslims, unlike many of their brethren elsewhere, have always reacted strongly to any Muslim-specific problems *anywhere in the world*, be it Turkey or the Palestine, by going *against the infidel Hindus*, the local receptacle to cool down their erectile function! Being a minority in an infidel majority *Dar-ul-Harb*, they always cried the loudest to register their presence and take whatever benefits an emerging situation provided in the larger 'Islamic Cause'. The Muslim Indian clergy were peeved at the stunning defeat of the Ottoman Empire at the hands of Russia only recently (1856) and wanted to take revenge against the Europeans wherever they could, the way they sought to take revenge, post 9/11, against American interests everywhere, including India. So, the 1857 episode in India was basically an extension of international Muslim grievances against the former Crusaders. The British-Mughal-India's 'mutiny' was part of this mindset of the *Ummah* (Muslim Brotherhood). In fact, defeat of the Caliphate and the Ottoman Empire that protected it was an issue extremely more sensitive to the Indian Muslim than to the West Asian Muslims themselves; the Muslim Indians, left alone on the Blue Lagoon of the still unconverted, alien, infidel Hindu ocean, felt insecure and would like to re-attach themselves to the Fertile Crescent at any cost—it was this mindset that created the Khilafat Movement *in India*, in the early 1920s, aiming to re-establish the Caliphate *in Turkey*, whose own people led by Kemal Ataturk had overthrown the Muslim Papacy. Being a minority even after some nine centuries, the Muslim Indians tried to prove themselves to be more Muslim than even the Arabs who were themselves struggling against the Caliphate and the Ottoman Empire! The Caliphate always remained the most sensitive spot in the orthodox Muslim Mind, so much so that even a Nehruvian Indian politician-academic like Rafiq Zakaria remained the lifelong Chairman of the All-India Khilafat Committee, formed in 1919 by the Ali Brothers, until he died in 2005. Interestingly, Nehru was an agnostic and admirer of Mustafa Kemal while Zakaria himself had been a former aide of the 'Islamic' State of Pakistan's founder M A Jinnah (a non-practising Shia-Khoja Muslim). Sadly, Muslims had to wear so many masks in so many countries because they felt their mosques were threatened!

These mosques were threatened even in 1857. The more India was welded with the expanding British Empire, the more she became part of European politics and 'British interests' to be protected not only from the Ottoman-Mughal mindset but also from Russia, denied warm-water and all-weather ports in Europe, was now expanding from St Petersburg towards South Asia and towards Vladivostok in the East, thus becoming the largest country in the world. The British, who loved to do business at the crossroads of both Heaven and Hell for maximum profits, as always, were sailing in two boats simultaneously: in the case of the Ottoman Empire, they supported the case of Turkey, the Caliphate and the Muslims, the integrity of their Empire whose parts were Mecca and Medina and, as per Palmerston's policy, would like regeneration of the Turk virility 'to cure the Sick Man of Europe' *even if this meant the Ottomans crushing the rising tide of Christian nationhood in the Balkans*! Because, the British, having now been sufficiently advanced in their own deChristianisation drive in their country, their business being business, their politics part of this business meant no Christ, saint or the Pope really affected the British imperialist project. For supporting Turkey, the British had extracted their own pound of flesh by seeking concessions and managed to put a valuable share of Turkish spoils into her own pockets. In the case of the Mughal Empire, however, the same British were wary of the Muslims, because here they were directly involved in the affairs of their colony, technically still a Mughal Empire. It was as if the British wanted their Turk concubine to look more beautiful than their Indian wife!

The Mughals, therefore, rightly suspected the careful British moves on the Indian chess-board; even otherwise, like minorities everywhere else, the Muslims' sixth sense of politics in an infidel land like India was always more advanced than the generally complacent Hindu's. Although many of the urban Hindus had followed the British-triggered 'modernisation' (it was merely Westernisation/ Europeanisation), with the zeal of a neophyte, they were rather reluctant to get rid of the old diapers, their familiar comfort zone. The slave could still not imagine life without the foreign yoke and the Hindus' modernisation merely meant that they wanted the youthful and energetic British to replace the tired and ageing Mughals as their new masters. There was little sense of 'Hindu' nationalism until 1857, not even Muslim nationalism—they were all parochial in nature due to their *caste-and-desh* enjoined heritage. The Hindus were still energetic slaves of the old masters, the Mughals; the Muslims, on the other hand, wanted to restore their Mughal pride by temporarily joining hands with those they saw as their permanent slaves, the Hindus, and avenge the loss of the Ummah in the Ottoman Empire by exacting the price in India. Overall, in the mid-19th century, the Hindus would like to modernise but not shake off the Mughal or British yoke while the Muslims wanted *not* to modernise or emulate the British and still retain control over India.

But one mistake of a certain Dalhousie, an admirer of Warren Hastings, forced the British to change their hitherto policy of enjoying power and pelf without any actual responsibility whatsoever. The British always suspected the Mughals who they thought would, someday, try to overthrow the Company Rule. The British, who had supported the Muslim Turk in the European part of the Ottoman Empire *against the Christian Serbs*, were so far supporting the Marathas, the 'Indian Serbs', vis-a-vis the Mughals; the Marathas, defeated by the Muslims a century ago in Panipat-III, through the Scindias, had a balanced equation with the newcomer British trading Company who, they fancied, would leave India after some time and the Marathas would be back to business, that is, against the medieval Mughals! The Marathas hoped to remove the Mughals. A century's complicated politics had evolved in such a manner in 19th century India that there was hardly any distinction between friends and foes and slaves and masters as they constantly changed equations and positions in the contemporary kaleidoscopic scene; even the Mughals, who had weakened themselves by playing puppets to power brokers and puppeteers and inviting the Nadir Shahs and the Abdalis against the Marathas and others, had eventually reduced themselves to seek support from the same Marathas! India was a veritable flux, a concrete mixer.

The national urge of the British to fully annex India—the imperialists wanted the Crown to remove the Company; the Crown, Head of the Church of England as well, was being influenced and egged on by the Christian missionaries in the same direction; but the colonialists, the Company that is, wanted to continue the then arrangement of keeping India just what she was, a colony, for collecting raw material and selling the finished product in this vast market—was fully flowered in the 35-year-old Lord Dalhousie. He had entered

British Parliament at the tender age of 25, knew how to play to the gallery and go down in history as the 'builder of the British empire'. So, when he was sent to India as Governor-General (1848-56), he adopted a *policy* of outright annexation of state after state with the use of naked power, winning accolades back home in Britain—he was an unelected but 'democratic' forerunner of Hitler. The cardinal mistake he, however, committed in this zeal was to unite the reluctant Hindus with the seething and waiting Mughals by doing something even Bentinck and Roy had not thought of in the name of reform. When Dalhousie denied the Hindu royal houses the tradition and the right of the adopted children rising to the throne, he touched a raw nerve. The traditional Hindus had always been extremely sensitive to the *Gotra* system: a Gotra is a family tree that emanated from the founding father of a clan in the Vedic Age; from these seers of antiquity, the Brahmins believed, had arisen different Hindu families and this arrangement was unalterable at any cost; even in the 21st century, the most 'modern' Hindu could be found eating the beef but not marrying in the same Gotra; marriage in the same Gotra is still seen as akin to incest and punishable by society in parts of northern and western India, as also in Pakistan; natives of these areas settled abroad, too, follow it.

Marriage between members of the same Gotra, even if they are thousands of miles apart and separated from generations, was considered incest—only now some Hindus have come to agree to their children's marriage in the same Gotra if the two families are separated by seven generations, by when, they believe, the genetic impact of incest is no more. The Gotra was inviolable except in two circumstances: marriage in case of girls and adoption in case of boys. Normally, a girl's Gotra would *change* upon her marriage into another Gotra, a boy's upon adoption: at the time of marriage or adoption, even during funeral rites, the priest would ask the candidate/successor of the dead to utter his/her Gotra aloud and declare its continuance/change. Thus, the Gotra system lay at the very foundation of the Brahmin-led Hindu society. Religions came and declined, nations evolved and degenerated, masters changed and empires were reduced to dust but this basic structure of Hindu society continued unabated, something that kept the nation together even if the Hindus did not lord it over themselves due to changing fortunes and masters. In the Muslim Brotherhood, caste or origins did not, technically, matter and cousins got married in what the Hindus abhorred as incest. In the Hindu society, caste and origins mattered above everything else: it was this networking of the society, keeping it insulated from harmful wires where necessary for long-term survival, that had kept the Hindus alive in their struggle for existence. The Gotras respected each other, although each believed that Kalki, the Last Incarnation of Lord Vishnu, would be born in it *provided* it retained the fundamental Gotra system.

Dalhousie's so-called 'Doctrine of Lapse' and the act of denying the right to throne to the siblings *adopted* by royal families, therefore, touched the Hindus at their rawest nerve—what if, the Hindus thought, the British also disallowed caste-based marriages as the Portuguese had already reared a 'casteless' Goan people and the number of casteless Anglo-Indians, too, was rising to provide butlers to the British, teachers to the convent schools and nurses to the missionaries' hospitals; the Dalhousie attempt must, therefore, be nipped in the bud. At several places they joined forces against the British who, however, still had the powerful Scindias on their side in the vicinity of Delhi and crushed the short-lived rebellion. Dalhousie thus kick-started the Hindu 'nation' that was refusing to wake up even after the most stunning defeats such as the Third Battle of Panipat. He was a reckless man and it is such reckless men, not the careful and slow reformer, who have the capacity to change the course of history in a sudden move—his intervention proved disruptive in the placid Hindu society, now emerging as the breakout nationhood. Otherwise a politically far-sighted man, he started the general movement of troops from Bengal towards the West to meet the growing challenge of Russia as well as to keep the Mughals at Delhi in check, and shifted the Army Headquarters to the Himalayas, at Shimla, enlisted the brave Gurkhas into the Army, urged his superiors to send more 'white' troops as, knowing the weaknesses of his projects, he *rightly* suspected the loyalty of native recruits. To make sure the British penetrated India further, as and when needed, he promoted the Posts and Telegraphs, the Railways and Public Works Departments to make troops movement faster. At the instance of Sir Charles Wood's Dispatch of 1854, he laid the foundation of the first Indian Universities in Bombay, Calcutta and Madras Presidencies, which came into being in 1857, and a number of schools imparting education in Anglo-vernacular languages sprang up.

Leaving India in 1856 ripe for rebellion, Dalhousie, broken in health but high in spirit, had nearly lost his voice. In completing Hastings' work, he had drained himself of life-blood. The Company crushed the first-ever Hindu-Muslim revolt in which the interests of the two communities had matched against the British, even though temporarily. In fact, Dalhousie would not have committed the mistake of attacking the Gotra system had he derived right lessons from the earlier mutinies (Vellore-1806, Burma-1824, the 38th Native Infantry-1852) when the caste feelings of the Hindus and the religious sensibilities of Muslims triggered revolts. The 1857 mutiny was different only in that it was relatively widespread with a hazy hope of overthrowing the British even as the Hindus and Muslims soon started working at cross-purposes—the 'differences' as to why they actually participated in the Revolt, soon resurfaced as they both lost and ended up replacing the Company with the Crown. Sir Syed Ahmed represented the *true* Muslim Mind: that the Muslims lost the Mughal Empire because of their weakness vis-a-vis the Hindus; if the Muslims wanted to restore the Mughal Empire they must be superior first to the Hindus and then to the British—and for this purpose, the Muslims should follow the British and European ways. In other words, the Muslims should defeat the Hindus first and then take on the British and the former Crusaders—he was a hybrid Muslim trying to 'reattach' the fragmented Indian Muslims with the Ummah.

After the defeat of the Ottoman Empire at the hands of the Russians in 1856 and that of the Mughals the very next year, the Muslim Mind in the entire Ummah largely got disoriented and became defeatist. Their pride of Islamic 'invincibility' had earlier been broken by the Mongols but the Brotherhood consoled that many victors had adopted the 'victorious' religion. But the new case of the twin-defeat of the twin-empires of the Sunni Muslims(although considered and despised by the Arabs as second-hand Muhammedans), at the hands of European Christians, who had earlier lost in their Crusades, was unpalatable to the Muslim Mind. Nothing could be as humiliating for the Muslims, who had ruled India for 800 years, as the defeat at the hands of Christians in an infidel, Hindu land. Always politically savvy, the Muslim Indians now had few options. They were no longer the 'master race', the Hindus were demanding and commanding and retrieving more and more space in all fields of life thanks to their slow but sure westernisation. But there was one difference in the Muslim and British rule: the Muslims broke the Hindu temples but could not and did not prevent them from worship whereas the British refrained from breaking temples but began to kill the Hindu desire to go to the temples.

Several factors were at work in India of the mid-19th century. Between 1757 and 1857, the British had completed their dominion in India through a carrot and stick policy, divide and rule, persuasion, bribe, fraud and naked imperial show of strength, as all imperialists have been doing throughout human history. Since the defeat of Napoleon, Russia had emerged as the strongest power in Europe, encroaching upon both the Ottoman and the Persian Empires, thus directly threatening British interests in Afghanistan and India. On the one hand, therefore, while Bentinck was busy in the twin-task of capturing and cleansing India, Palmerston was trying to check Russian advance in the Near East, Middle East and the Mediterranean; in the East, Lord Dufferin completed the task by annexing Burma in 1886 to protect the Dominion against the French in Indo-China. The British traders, eyeing markets even in Tibet and Burma besides India, formed a formidable Company-free pressure group for increased British activity in India while the Evangelicals, having become emboldened with the suppression of sati and thugee, succeeded in forcing the 'Christian' island of a government in an infidel ocean to withdraw official patronage of certain Hindu temples and festivals. America, the former British colony, was engaged in post-Independence war between the White neo-feudals and the Black old slaves. Those of the imperial British stock, who saw in India the Red Indians Reloaded, formed the third important pressure group arguing that only by force and 'superiority' could they continue to control the subcontinent; this group still rued the British failures that led to the loss of America and did not want to lose India this time, come what may. And Dalhousie subscribed to this view. Yet another group of the British, influenced by the optimistic rationalism of the French philosophers, believed in the 'intrinsic superiority' of the European-Christian civilisation, burdened with the noble mission of civilising the 'static' civilisations in the rest of the world. This wound inflicted on the European psyche by Napoleon was still festering in the American dream of 'democratising' the world in the *American* way in the 21st century.

But the most important changes in classical Europe were wrought by science and Marxism. Scientific advancement gave the European Christians chance to avenge their defeats in the Crusades and they expanded into Asia and Africa; Marxism, as the latest revolutionary member of the Abrahamic ideological Family, *minus God*, was the product of those who were unable to adapt to the changes wrought by the steam engine, the telegraph and the railway, having already adopted the printing press to print the Bible. Marx did not believe any society could witness the class struggle unless its transition from an agricultural-feudal to industrial society was complete; that was why he did not view the short-lived 1857 revolt against the British in India as a class struggle or even as the 'First War of Independence' as the Indian revisionist Marxists would later claim!

The overall strategy of this science-and-economy-triggered European expansion in Asia and Africa was the product of the Christian subconscious effort to encircle Islam in what would in due course turn out to be the long-drawn-out Ninth Crusade. The Christians, having stripped the papacy of most of its clothes, no longer exactly needed the Pope to trigger this Crusade, much the same way the Muslims of the 21st century do not need the Caliph to launch them on a Jihad. Their respective matrices of ideologies, now on auto-pilot, had made each of the 'true believer' a potential Caliph/Pope, or a Marx or Hitler, as the case may be. The Europeans were fighting their wars everywhere against each other but joined hands against their common medieval enemy, Islam, whenever they crossed swords with it. That was what they did in India too. The British, who had taken active interest in 'reforming' the majority Hindus, were, however, shaken from their stupor by the 1857 uprising. Until now, they were suspecting only the Muslims whose Mughal Empire they had brought to an end. Now, with the Hindus rising, was the time to Divide and Rule.

The British Raj had, until now, seen two phases: Warren Hastings' start of the British rule was an attempt to impose neutral rule over a traditional society divided along the minority Mughals' pro-Muslim policy and the majority Hindus, most of whom had no notion of self-respect or even an iota of thought as to why a few Muslims or a fewer British could rule them—many amongst the Hindus had chosen to be the 'permanent' slaves and it was up to their Masters to fight it out amongst themselves as to who would rule India. Nobody in the world had the power or the wherewithal to shake the whole of the Hindu masses which was nose-deep in the cesspool created by divisions in the society; many of the Muslims, too, were neck-deep in the same morass. By 1818, an exhausted India was ready to accept *yet another* foreign catalyst, provided it left the socio-religious fabric of both the declining Mughals as well as the declined Hindus untouched. Bentinck changed all this, and the Hastings' policy of neutrality; he actively rescued the Hindus from their nose-deep to neck-deep status but the Muslims correspondingly descended deeper into abyss. Hesitant in the beginning, the Hindus then went whole hog with the British innovations, shaking off their cowardice and lethargy cultivated over the ages as a survival tactic amidst Muslim barbarism; some Hindus accepted the British logic that only by modernising themselves could they shake off the yokes. Not that all the Hindus absorbed these British innovations; in fact, many, being still conservative, suspected government countenance with the Christian missionaries in running down the Hindu religious sentiments, seen as an attempt to Christianise India; like the Muslims, conservative Hindus also thought the telegraph was 'evil'.

The mid-19th century British-India was the setting for the resentment of the dispossessed and multiple fears of the orthodox Hindus and Muslims for their own reasons—and they included Indian soldiers of the 'British Indian Army'—something more potent than what the British thought should have been the gratitude of the beneficiaries or the fervent hopes of the small, 'emancipated' new westernised class. Dalhousie's 'Doctrine of Lapse', empowered him to take over the states of Hindu princes without direct heirs, thus triggering a new Hindu thought even the Muslims had not done so far: 'Today you are challenging our right and tradition to adopt, tomorrow you could force us to marry in *another* caste or the *same* Gotra! Forcing us to indulge in incest'.This was the Hindu orthodox argument against the neo-*mlechchhas*, the British. And, therefore, for some of the Hindus, the Muslims, the old *mlechchhas*, were relatively 'better', and Bahadur Shah 'Zafar' deserved to be reinstalled as the Mughal Emperor. The slave-and-seige mentality of the majority of Hindus, including the Marathas who were now a burnt out candle as were the Sikhs, was such that it did not even occur to them to replace both the Mughals and the British once for all; they would wait for a nominal Muslim, M A Jinnah, to force them to reluctantly eject Islam from India! The Hindus proved to be the most immovable people in the world. Bentinck's silent flogs had woken up only a few. Dalhousie opened the gates but few horses bolted and they too returned soon, finding the short-lived freedom of thought and action more suffocating than the enchanting slavery and the familiar foul smell of the stable that guaranteed security of idiocy and mediocrity. Only a few Hindus were, therefore, opening their eye; and most Muslims chose not to rise at all.

For the British, however, this would simply not do. They were the latest soldiers of fortune on the globe and the decline of France, integrating Germany and expanding Russia were giving great impetus to imperial Britain. Until now they had a lobby only amongst the Hindus; post-1857, they decided to create one amongst the dispossessed Muslims as well who were deeply suspicious of British actions after uprooting of the Mughal Empire. The British discovered amongst the Indian Muslims a British Knight: Sir Syed Ahmed Khan of Delhi (1817-98) believed that the Muslims should follow Sheikh Ahmed Sirhindi and Shah Waliullah's 'theology' of re-establishing Muslim hegemony over the infidel Hindus and, in doing so, utilise the modern British and European education and science. In other words, he professed use of modern means to achieve medieval ends;

in still other words, he became one of the spiritual forefather of the 21st century's Muslim terrorists who realised the importance of Western learning in re-imposing Islam on the societies where its hold had weakened. Muslims 'intellectuals' would, henceforth, filter out Christian elements of Westernism, and simply replace it with Islam in what would later come to be known as 'Western Islam'. Fancying himself as the Raja Ram Mohun Roy of the Muslims, the Syed, who belonged to a Mughal official family but found himself serving the British judicial service, earned the goodwill of the British by remaining loyal to them in the 1857 Revolt. He believed that the Christians and Muslims, who shared the common Judaic heritage as well as goals to convert the infidel Hindus, should unite for a common cause. He joined the Viceroy's Legislative Council in 1878 and remained the unquestioned leader of Muslim Indians until death. His whole 'philosophy' revolved around the premise that Islam was born to rule and should adopt each and every means to achieve this end; that the young Muslims should absorb western education, language, science and technology *for the benefit of Islam*. To achieve this, he founded in 1875 what came to be later known as Aligarh Muslim University, the third fountainhead of Islamic separatism in South Asia after the Deoband and the Barelvi seminaries. The Syed was the best friend of Islam: he firmly believed that democracy was nonsense and Islam could survive only if it established its dictatorship over the infidel Hindus of India. So, while he supported the things British, he opposed British democracy *in India*: democracy meant rule of the majority, the majority was the Hindus, and, therefore, democracy meant rule of the infidel Hindus over the Muslims! No wonder, he was the spiritual father of Pakistan and all such 'freedom' movements.

The Hindus were, however, fortunate to have a Muslim like the Syed lead the Indian Muslims and effectively turn many of them into *Muslim Indians*! In fact, the 'dynamic' Islam was tired of the lethargic Hindus and preparing to leave India lock-stock-and-barrel; the Syed, M A Jinnah and Sir Allama Iqbal were merely flag-bearers of this beating-the-retreat. The only thing the Hindus had to do was just to huddle together like walruses on the coast and soak in as much sun as they could before they jumped back into their chaotic ocean.

Towards this end, there could have been no better service provider than Dalhousie, the convinced westerniser who began to give India a modern face in the 1850s, won over the middle and lower classes but, at the same time, angered the royalties with his Doctrine of Lapse. In particular, the way he rubbed the Brahmin component of the British-Indian Army the wrong way, put paid to all his achievements; the Brahmins, first among the Hindus to go the British way, had come to fancy themselves as indispensable to the British Army within India but, due to religious reasons and eating habits, hated to be deployed outside India. The 1857 Revolt proper had been, as an immediate cause, triggered by the greased cartridges for the newly-introduced Enfield rifles, smeared with the fat of cow and the swine, holy for the Hindus and unclean for the Muslims, respectively; this blatant British roughshod convinced both the communities that the British were plotting to destroy their old cultures. The dethroned Mughal Emperor, Bahadur Shah 'Zafar', who believed the Hindus were fighting to reinstall him, contented himself with the couplet: *Na Iran ne kiya na Shah Russne, Angrez ko Tabah kiya Kartoos (cartouche) ne.* (Neither did Iran nor Russia destroy the British; it was the cartridge that damaged the British.)

The early unofficial British policy of keeping the missionaries away had also undergone change and they were now employing more and more missionaries to penetrate deeper areas to make inroads for the imperial administration—convents, schools and hospitals, set up basically for the British, were now increasingly thrown open for the Hindus as well; the Muslims would mostly go to the madrasas. With the advent of steam engine and telegraph, the movement and activities of the Christian fundamentalists and arrogant missionaries, supported by a section of the British and Europeans, had got a fillip; even some district collectors held meetings with these elements in their offices. Having got entry in 1813, these rogue elements in the garb of saints and fathers, had further enraged the Hindus with the Converts' Inheritance Act of 1850, allowing a convert to inherit property from his infidel family. Rubbing the Indians the wrong way, Rev M A Sherring claimed that 'The whole land has been shaken by the mission to its innermost centre. The Hindu trembles for his religion, the Mohammedan for his'.

Dalhousie acknowledged the conversion of Maharaja Duleep Singh and the daughter of the Raja of Coorg; the Ten Commandments in Urdu and Hindi, inscribed on four pillars, appeared in Fatehpur town at the order of the Commissioner. The Christian missionaries were a medieval, indoctrinated and intoxicated gang like the 21st century Taliban, intolerant, dogmatic, fired by Victorian zeal and ready to harvest India to the Church of England before the Roman Catholics and the Protestants did. Like militants, they infested not only the churches but schools, hospitals, prisons and even markets, force-marketing their ware, threatening, cajoling and using every trick in their bag to convert India, so succinctly narrated by Gandhi in his autobiography. If the Wahhabis wanted to drag India to the seventh century, the Christian missionaries wanted to drag India further back, to the first century! India was not merely seen to become a British jewel, but also to be a Christian jewel, the largest potential Christian nation in the world. Between 1813 and 1857, many of the British gradually became active peddlers of Christianity. As Jomo Kenyatta would rightly say later, Africa had the land and the Christian missionaries the Bible when the latter came; finally, the Africans had the Bible and the Christians the land when the latter left. Similarly, now, the British missionaries aimed at thrusting the Bible into all Indian hands and annexing the remaining land for this great service. The well-known Delhi Proclamation of May 1857 aimed at forcibly converting the infidel elements of the Army to Christianity with, as Nana Sahib said in July 1857, the British 'calculating' that 7,000 or 8,000 Europeans would be sufficient to convert all the Indians, then numbering around 300 millions, to Christianity! On 25 August 1857, Bahadur Shah 'Zafar' called upon all Indians to join 'jihad' against Christianity which stood condemned by the Islamic Sunna and Hindu Shastras! Maulavi Liyaqat Ali of Allahabad openly declared jihad against the British and invited the Muslims to massacre all the Christians; Birjees Kudur Wali of Oudh made a similar call to the Muslims, and so did Mirza Feroz Shahzada…the Ninth Crusade, launched unofficially by Napoleon Bonaparte had arrived in India. The scramble of Europeans in the Ottoman Empire post-Crimean War had convinced India that the Mughal Empire was now an incurable 'Sick Man of South Asia'.

But all this turmoil was in North India; the South was virtually peaceful. The Revolt was, therefore, sporadic and localised, like free-floating trial balloons here and there. The Sikhs, enjoying the bliss of irrelevance after the demise of the Mughal Empire, remained calm even though Sir John Lawrence, otherwise an unpopular man, sent out practically all the Punjabi troops to quell rebellion elsewhere. British stooges like Sir Dinkar Rao and Salar Jung ensured that the Revolt did not cross the River Narmada and the Vindhyas. The Revolt was more of a minor civil war in which everybody, who was even if a nobody, was free to go out on the street to settle scores with whoever he would like to; it lacked focus, united purpose and leadership. But, overall, as its results showed, it was a chaotic overthrow of the Muslim Rule in India, the medieval era well-entrenched at Delhi since the 11th century, which heralded the dawn of a New India. The Muslims had settled down in India over the Hindu chaos; the British now settled down in India over the Hindu-Muslim chaos. Islam, which created Muslims out of the Hindus, now found itself infected with the incurable Hindu disease of atomisation into castes before being absorbed piece-by-piece. It was the end of the road for Islam which could never go beyond Indian borders; if re-energised, it could now only return towards Arabia. In India, both Christianity and Islam had come home to roost. Thus commenced the Return of the Infidel.

The chaotic North India had played its role of uprooting the Mughal Empire; now was the turn of the Bombay, Madras and Calcutta Presidencies to make the next move

The Revolt, which began at Meerut on 10 May 1857, came to an end at Gwalior on 20 June 1858. The biggest reason for its failure was the peace and support of Punjab to the British: having got rid of the Mughals, the Sikhs had lost their virility and the very *raison d'etre* of their origin and existence. They would rise again thrice, briefly, in the 20th century and some even cooperate with Pakistan, but only to make a protective shield for India against the advancing Soviet Union and start melting back into the Hindu masses thereafter. If anything, the Revolt's failure was the success of the Hindus in many ways: first of all, they got rid of the moth-eaten Mughal Empire, even if they replaced their old Masters by bringing in the Crown, the Taj being replaced by the Raj. Secondly, they got their first-ever and united net-practice in 'modern' warfare; thirdly, back-to-back crushing defeat of both the Ottomans in the Crimean War and the Mughals in the Revolt in less than a decade convinced them that Islam was no longer invincible, nor the New White Masters. The British, who barely won back India, could never sleep in peace thereafter; the Muslims, who lost India forever, could never sleep in peace either. Only the Hindus could. For, to them, both the Mughals and the British, wedded as they were to their respective decadent monarchies—the Hindu monarchs were, any way, fossils by now—came from the same Abrahamic stock. By 'helping' the Muslims, the Hindus had indirectly assisted the British in uprooting the Mughals; now was the time to assist the British to uproot Islam in India. It was only a question of time; opportunities were knocking at different doors. And the British imperial 'heyday', that began in 1858, gave them ample opportunity to slowly do away with what even Britons would not dare do even in the 21st century Britain: get rid of the monarchy.

The British came down heavily on the Muslims who were more violently anti-British during the Revolt. The Nawabs of Jhajjar, Farrukhnagar, Farrukhabad and Vallabhgarh were hanged in Delhi and so were two dozen other Muslim princes on 18 November 1857; the dethroned last Mughal Emperor, Bahadur Shah 'Zafar' was exiled to Burma where he died unsung; the Muslims' properties were seized at many places. The Hindus, too, had participated in the Revolt but this 'discriminatory' and selective communal approach of the British infuriated the Muslims now more against the Hindus than against the British. Sir Syed Ahmed, who had once-upon-a-time famously described the two communities as the two eyes of India, would freshly discover that the storm had left more tears in one eye than the other. The Muslims, who hitherto enjoyed all positions of power, pelf, prestige, were now worse off than Hindus. Jealous, many of them continued to drift away from the Hindus; but swallowed pride and, as a recompense, their tendency to snake their way inside the royal palaces and influential places, cultivated and honed over eight centuries, soon made them sing paeans for the British, the New Sultans who, unlike the Hindus, were at least *not* infidels—given a choice, a Muslim would always choose a Christian or even a Jew—and vice-versa—over a Hindu or other infidels, because of their ideological affinity of belonging to the same Abrahamic *Gotra*! There were no prizes for knowing why the Muslims were now hobnobbing with the British the way there is no prize for the two-way Pakistan-US-Israel bonhomie during the 'War on Terrorism' and their own internal contradictions and intra-Abrahamic battles.

The ultimate battle was, after all, between the Abrahamites and the rest of the *infidel* world. The Hindus, therefore, had nothing to choose between the two sets of *mlechchhas*. The post-Mughal Empire Muslim Indians thought the best way for a former landlord to survive after losing his property was to serve the one who now owned this property, like the promoter of a small company joining the Board of Directors of a bigger company that acquires the smaller one.

The British, wary of the upheaval and having just proclaimed the Raj in India, would not, however, be ready to be fooled so easily and early; they had enough time to do so! The Wahhabis, whose policies kept shifting in India as an extension of the politics of the Middle East vis-a-vis the European powers, having found the British 'better' than the Russians in the Ottoman muddle—despite the overthrow of the Mughals!—now keyed up their Muslim robots to cooperate with the new Raj that replaced the Taj. Henceforth, the 'Indian' Muslim Mind would largely become a puppet of the Wahhabis; even during the Mughal rule, the Muslim Indian was not as well-networked with the Middle East as he would now be. The fundamentalist Muslim Indians would not only become an extension of Arabia in India but also an inseparable part of the loop and circuit and sleeping cells of international conspiracies; from time to time, the Wahhabis would successfully electrify the Muslim Indians and later leave them to die of electrocution.

The Wahhabis, being a highly indoctrinated and intoxicated, ultra-puritanical sect of Islam, which had come to occupy the centre-stage now, were working to a plan to weed out the later accretions to

Islam and reinstall the purest form of their Faith so that the ancient glory of Muhammedanism could be restored all over the world. They detested modernism and westernism but were careful to use its fruits to advance their own agenda. All else was to be sacrificed for this noble cause. So, from Syed Ahmed Barelvi, who founded the Wahhabi movement in India, they would inevitably move towards Syed Ahmed 'Aligarhi', also known as Sir Syed Ahmed. Discovering that the Sir was only a reincarnation of (Sheikh Ahmed) Sirhindi, they ignored all the British retaliation against the Muslims, or that there were only 92 Muslims against 711 Hindus among 2,141 persons employed by the British Bengal government even in 1871. They made Verse 36 of the Qur'an, exhorting the Muslims to martyrdom, very popular. All they aimed was to ensure somehow not to let the Muslims slip down further *than* the Hindus; some of the Muslims would be the first among the slaves of the British.

The Hindus were not amused at this metamorphosis of a third rate master into a first rate slave after the new master came on the scene. They had reasons. From the Land of the Rising Sun they could now learn more lessons than from the Land of the Noon, Arabia. It was a forward march for them and they knew, unlike the Muslims, that nobody could move forward while looking backward.

In Japan, a fierce westernisation drive had begun in the 1860s and within 50 years, that tiny nation became powerful enough to defeat a major European power, Russia (1905). The progress of Japan startled the Hindus: if such a small 'infidel' nation could do it, why could not they? The Hindus, too, who until now reluctantly followed the West and detested *firangi* government and Christian missionaries, suddenly took to English education in a big way on their own. In a generation, they were able to take over the Indian National Congress, formed by a *firangi* in 1885. The British themselves triggered this social electrolysis post-1857 by replacing the strong Brahmin component of their Indian Army with the induction of the Sikhs, Gurkhas, Jaats and Rajputs, along caste-lines, and later Pathans and Punjabis—thereby, they unwittingly pushed the shrewd Brahmins, who no longer trusted the British after the Gotra and greased cartridge episodes, into the legal and political arena. This coming together of the different strands of the

Hindu masses under the British auspices in the Army, administration and educational institutions—the Muslims mostly kept aloof—brought in them a sense of oneness. The British Governor-General was now also the Viceroy and concerned to retain India as a Jewel in the Crown at all costs; in the light of the abolition of slavery in America and the assassination of President Abraham Lincoln, no Viceroy would now be foolhardy enough to rub the Indians the wrong way. Post-1857, the British handled India with care, though not necessary with love, always suspicious, scheming, plotting and putting the Hindus and Muslims against each other. In the first 100 years (1757-1857), they were full of energy and drive under the Company Rule, controlling only patches in India; in the next 90 years, until 1947, they controlled a lot of the subcontinent but remained unsure of when they would be uprooted completely. The forces they had unleashed would soon begin to overwhelm them.

During the Dalhousie regime, Britain had created a Legislative Council in 1853 having *British* representatives from the three Presidencies of Madras, Calcutta and Mumbai; post-1857, Indian aristocrats were added to this remodelled elite Council. From this hitherto insignificant remodelling, the Indian participation in government at the top began. Another British attempt to cool the ruffled Indian feathers was to buy off and reward their loyal Rajput, Maratha, Sikh and the Nizam princes who had helped check the 1857 Revolt; these States were now 'integrated' with the ever-expanding British-India, members of the New Order having a personal relationship with the Crown, like local franchisees of a multinational corporation in an era of mergers and acquisitions. Lord Lytton even proposed an Indian peerage for them. The promulgation of the Indian Penal Code (1861) was a strong unificatory strand in a multicultural, heterogeneous land like India. But the British cautiously refrained from hurting caste or religious sentiments of Indians; there was no longer to be something like the Widows Remarriage Act or allowing the converts to inherit property. The Indian Railway, commenced in 1853, went apace furiously until it was virtually complete by 1900, giving India the best system in Asia; thereafter, most expansion was within. The British thought they were cautiously and zealously dressing the Indian chicken, that the Raj would continue until eternity. Behind all these modernising moves was the idea that while the pre-1857 Raj depended on British-Indian Army having a strong component of Brahmins, the post-1857 Raj came to depend upon the BritishIndian Army having a strong non-Brahmin component *plus* a modicum of *Indian* participation to run this great exploitative machine, just like multinational cola companies employing local salesmen to hawk their stuff.

This heyday of the British Raj continued from Lord Canning's proclamation of the end of the revolt in 1857 to the Partition of Bengal in 1905; they and their Indian collaborators continued to believe in the inherent British superiority, that Great Britain was the best thing ever to have happened to Little India. Or so the Raj believed, and Gandhi mockingly 'convinced' London. It did not know what was there in those minds the British had ignited: the English-speaking 'Yes Boss'-type clerks, chatter-box professionals like lawyers and teachers, subordinate officials. The slowly enlightened middle classes created by Britain were no longer ready to remain mere franchisee of the British shell: it was here that the fissure between the Old Britain and New India began to appear. The post-1857 British-Indian history saw the first Period of Reconciliation (1858-1880), the second Period of Neo-Imperialism (1881-1905) and the third Period of Retreat (1905-1947). The British, having once again become complacent, did not know where the foxes of India would drive them before killing: Lord Mayo, Governor-General and Viceroy, in whose regime was laid the Red Sea cable and the British began to take interest in the Suez Canal and Egypt, was assassinated in 1872 by a fanatical Pathan of Afghanistan in the faraway Andaman Islands!

The British thought they were happily skiing using the alternate Hindu and Muslim sticks; they did not realise they were sliding down and an avalanche was catching up behind them.

All their land reforms and the Permanent Settlement had come to naught with the recurrence of famines and cholera across India in the last three decades of the 19th century. Nothing moved India, they thought, and so nothing would move Britain either, they believed. They did not realise what the Tatas were doing; they did not know what the 1,000-odd members of the Indian Civil Service, the maids-for-all-jobs, were up to; they did not know what the Arya Samaj was doing; they did not know what their very own Sir Syed Ahmed Khan was doing. No, they actually knew all this, but were so convinced of their own power at the end of the 19th century that they, like the USA until 9/11, decided to let the show go on, on and on: they could be woken up from their dogmatic slumber only by an explosion called Hitler the way the Americans could be woken up only by an Osama bin-Laden. Until then, they believed, everybody who complained was an idiot. The omnipotent and omniscient British were largely blissfully unaware that they had sown the seeds of Hindu Renaissance and retreat of Islam in the East. In them, India found a *non-Muslim, non-Roman Catholic, non-Protestant, fast deChristianising* colonial nation: only a Britain could have deIslamised the Indian subcontinent. The Criminal Procedure Code (1873) further strengthened India's march forward. The racial profile of superiority—intoxicated Europeans, however, came up in sharp contrast when they refused to be tried by Indian sessions judges in the Ilbert Bill controversy (1883) during the Ripon era. The Indians saw through all the bogus claims of the West in this controversy. This further widened the fissures between the Hindus and the British—the Muslims were happy at this growing gulf between the British and the Hindus. Having lost 'Hindustan' to the British, their keen political sense of survival in an infidel country was inexorably driving them into a yet-unheard-of 'Pakistan'.

After defeating Napoleon, Russia was advancing in Asia throughout the 19th century in search of warm waters and all-weather ports. The British feared a Russian advance towards India and it led to the First Afghan War in 1839; by 1841, the hardy Afghans had put Russia in its place. This was the ancient Indian policy to prevent invasion from the North-West by all means, even by vivisection of a part of India to form a buffer zone. Post-Ashokan India saw the rise of Afghanistan as a buffer between India and Central Asia/Iran; post-1757 period saw the rise of Punjab against further Persian or Afghan attacks; post-1850 era witnessed the rise of Pakistan; post-1970 India witnessed the rise of the movement for 'Khalistan'—in all this Darwinian-cultural warfare, India continued to shrink and create yet another protective layer against the North-West to plug the Passes used by the invaders of all shades, including Muslims, and the layers would slowly disappear, one by one, after the danger receded.

Knowing that the Afghans were the best defendants of their own independence—the USSR learnt it the hard way, the USA is learning it the harder way now—the British employed the policy of 'masterly inactivity' thereafter, the way the Americans are now following, despite occasional convulsions of activity. When Russia, the European orphan in search of its parents and dissatisfied with its Asian asylum, got entangled in the Balkan Crisis in 1875-78 due to machinations of that German old fox, Bismarck, the two British gentlemen, Salisbury and Disraeli, used Afghans again against the Polar Bear to keep the latter away from Europe. Their stool pigeon, Lord Lytton, was only too happy to oblige them and declared a march into Turkistan, plunging himself head-on into the Second Afghan War (1878-80). For the British and Muslims, little came of the Afghan wars except that Russia, denied south-ward movement, continued to expand east and north. Once again, the British realised that the Afghans were easier to defeat but difficult to be subdued, the way America would discover in the 21st century Iraq and Afghanistan.

In these Afghan wars many Muslims from India had participated in the British-Indian Army; it was these wars that forced the British, who were until now suspecting the fidelity of Muslims disrobed of their Mughal Empire and supporting the Hindus, to reverse their policy; even otherwise, given a choice, they would prefer the Muslims over the Hindus due to *theological affinity*. From now on, they began supporting the Indian Muslims even though in Europe they were still opposing the Ottoman Muslims. But the British scarcely knew that the Hindus were already on an auto-pilot post-1857; the British merely thought they had put the Muslims on auto-pilot by supporting Sir Syed Ahmed Khan. From 1875 onwards, the role of the British continued to shrink more and more and the ground beneath them eroded faster and faster. After impregnating India with steam engine, railway and telegraph, they were destined to be gobbled up like the male termite being swallowed by the queen after sex.

For, the waves of New India were rising from Gujarat, which never forgot Mehmood Ghazanavi and never forgave the Muslims: otherwise a peaceful place, a Gujarati Hindu would become savage whenever he saw the Muslim's image in a mirror reflecting the Ghazanavi. The Somnath Temple's ruins in the now Muslim-ruled Junagarh state were a constant reminder to the Indian Hindu of Islam being an occupation force, just like the Jews wailing at the Wall of their Solomon Temple in Jerusalem, destroyed similarly by the Romans. The epic struggles to retrieve these two Temples by these communities, respectively, saw the simultaneous resurgence of the Hindus and the Jews and the re-establishment of their rule in 1947 and 1949.

Although a number of localised movements, some with political shades, had cropped up on the ashes of the Bhakti Movement in the 19th century India, none of these—Brahmo Samaj, Prarthana Samaj, the Theosophical Society, Ramkrishna Mission, the Dev Samaj—had the weapon the Arya Samaj, founded in 1875, used. Its founder, Swami Dayanand Saraswati (1824-1883), a Gujarati Brahmin, knew how the Brahmins had failed to unite society against the Ghazanavi invasion due to the caste system. When Mehmood reached the Somnath Temple, instead of defending their God of Thunder and Destruction with swords, the Brahmin priests merely tried to invoke Him, crying 'Over Our Bodies'—and Mehmood Ghazanavi simply marched over their bodies. In the 1940s, Gandhi would similarly cry, 'Pakistan? Over My Body!' and Jinnah would simply walk over the Mahatma's body. Dayanand knew that Islam drew its inherent strength from the 'immutable' *Qur'an*; if the Hindus were ever to regain this same strength, they must also bind themselves to their *Veda*s, rather than gods-made-of-human-hands. This was as revolutionary an idea as Adi Shankaracharya's: the Kerala saint came with the arrival of Islam while the Gujarat saint arrived when Islam was just beginning to retreat from India. Both the saints knew the weaknesses of Hinduism and the strengths of Islam; both ended up trying to make Hinduism a 'religion of the Book' with shades of Islam, like monotheism and iconoclasm, a call to shun the later accretions and outgrowths and return to the pristine past.

Like Adi Shankaracharya setting up the four principal Hindu seats, the followers of Dayanand, too, set up a chain of what came to be known as the Dayanand Anglo-Vedic (DAV)—later also known the Dayanand Aryan-Vedic—colleges, schools and *gurukuls*.

He discouraged idol worship and his schools produced a number of patriots. The British suspected these institutions to be Hindu 'madarsas' and the Muslims as the Hindu 'Salvation Army'—the hotbeds of political activism and Hindu Renaissance against both the British and the Muslims. The Arya Samaj did a lot of social reform work in the fields of untouchability, women's education, weakening the caste system, widow remarriages, discouraging the child marriage; it made the Hindus militant and aggressive, teaching them why they had lost their virility and how could they regain it. What alarmed the Muslims most was, however, its active promotion of *re-converting* Muslims willing to return to the Hindu fold by 'purifying' them. The 'Shuddhi Movement' constantly reminded the Indian Muslims how they had been 'polluted' by Islam, how, despite ruling over the Hindus for nine centuries, they continued to be *mlechchha* (impure), lower than even the Untouchables. This touched the Muslim raw nerve and hurt him the most who saw in Dayanand's 'Go Back to the Vedas' appeal a parallel to the Sirhindi-Waliullah duo's 'Go Back to the *Qur'an*'—a move to manufacture Hindu 'terrorists' and steal from Islam its 'legitimate' grazing ground, the lower castes among the Hindus. What was more, Dayanand published a critique of all religions, denouncing even Islam, in his famous book, *Satyarth Prakash* (The Light of Truth). The reformer, having played his role of igniting the Hindu mind, even traced the future of science in the past of the Vedas. As happens with all illiberal 'reformers', in order to fight their rivals, they tend to use the same weapons and end up in the same pit, Dayanand, too, like Muhammed unto the *Qur'an*, believed that the Vedas as interpreted by *him* contain all the truth. But he demonstrated to the Hindus how they could lift themselves from the mud of their own creation and have faith in their future. His social reforms and removing evil practices to cleanse the Hindu society were preceded by those of Ram Mohun Roy and emulated by Gandhi and Ambedkar.

No wonder he was killed by a Muslim woman by secretly making him drink powdered glass in milk in Rajasthan. Another Muslim killed another Swami, Shraddhanand, in the 1920s. The Hindus, who cared to understand the *fundamentals* of Islam, or for that matter Judaism and Christianity, would continue to be killed the same way—for they knew the source of all Holy Terror lay in those very Holy Books.

The Muslim leadership, stripped of their imperial clothes (who never liked the Hindus except as slaves and India as an unfinished mission possible of Islam), was now in the leaguc of the likes of Sir Syed Ahmed—the 'modern' face—and the faceless Wahhabis; the Syed, like the Wahhabis, declared that the Qur'an was the only authorised Book of Islam and all other books were useless. He would see everything else, including science and Christianity, only through the prism of Islam and how he could fleece modern knowledge to advance his own faith. Anything that did not conform to the *Qura'n* was evil, declared the 'reformer'. 'A civilised life is impossible until freedom of thought is established', he claimed, and urged the people to adopt a 'critical' approach. He was all things to all, gave a call against 'obscurantism' and appealed to the students to be 'tolerant and liberal'; like most Muslim 'reformers', he, too, wore many a mask to defend the mosque. He was the modern Sword of Islam. But this Sword was double-edged: while planting separatism and secessionism in the Muslim Mind, he effectively stopped the spread of Islam, made Islam more and more ghettoised and transformed it from a religion of palaces to the religion of slums.

In fact, the Wahhabis had won over many among conscientious and progressive, modern-looking Muslims; even in the 21st century, they would appeal to Muslim film stars not to marry with the Hindus *without converting* them and 'reIslamise' themselves to re-establish their Muslim credentials. The fanatics indoctrinated these impressionable Muslim minds that the great, halcyon days of Islam could return and they could re-dominate India by redoubling their efforts and using modern education and sciences in the service of Islam and its unfinished mission of fully converting India. There was a parallel to this amongst the Christian missionaries who, too, egged on the British rulers similarly and spread out with their 'educational' institutions and 'hospitals' to woo the Hindus, Mother Teresa included. The Arya Samaj and other Hindu reformist groups understood this strategy and set up their own parallel institutions to keep the Hindu flock within. Thus, modernism was increasingly becoming a shield of the orthodoxy in all the three religions—unlike in the West, where sciences had stripped the people of their spirituality. In India, the emerging sciences became the rescue boats of the sinking ships of religions.

Nothing demonstrates it better than Sir Syed Ahmed. Being a Mughal official, he knew how to keep the Master—old or new—in good humour while shooing away his non-Muslim neighbours, the Hindus. Always ready to salute the rising sun, he had been, as a 'British' official, through the 1857 Revolt and even helped the new, youthful Master, to eliminate the old. With grateful help from the British, he set up the Muhammedan Anglo-Oriental College at Aligarh in 1875, the same year as the founding of the Arya Samaj, which grew up into the nursery of 'Islamism' in 1920 as the Aligarh Muslim University—and continued to foment trouble in India thereafter until the Hindu leaders decided to ignore its gargantuan claims. The whole gamut of the Syed's thinking was that the Muslims, who ruled India until 1857, had been left behind the Hindus in respect of Western learning, and consequently the Hindus practically monopolised the higher offices of the state; if the Muslims were to regain their earlier status and importance, and *eventually rule India again*, they must undergo modern education and *compete with the Hindus rather than the British*. Thus the aims of the Wahhabis and the Syed were no different, re-control of India; they only differed in strategy, in the beginning, and then joined hands with their clear-cut zones of influence: the 'modernists' who were to be the 'new face' of Islam and the faith's bridge to the West as well as Indian 'secularists', were supposed to be serving and servicing the 'traditionalists' back home. This nexus gave rise to the widespread Hindu belief in Central India that the more literate a Muslim, the more fundamentalist plotter he could be. If India remained largely 'secular' even after the Independence, it was because, ironically, most Muslims, who stayed back after the Partition, were illiterate! The educated Hindus tended to shun their temples; the literate Muslims would force their government offices to grant permission to leave for *namaz* in the midst of office duty hours, else charge it with 'discrimination'. There was never another community which believed that the more modern you are, the more ancient you should become!

This legacy of the Syed, absorbed so zealously by so many 'modern' Muslims across the world, culminated into the rise of terror masterminds, now led and updated by ISIS, a logical development of the networked Matrix called Islam. After the Wahhabi 'revolution' in Arabia in the 18th century—in Islam alone a 'revolution' takes you backward, not forward!—the continuous decline of the Ottoman and Mughal Empires necessitated an urgent thinking on how to regulate the flow of oxygen in a Faith that allowed no bypass surgery despite clogged blood vessels threatening death. Now, even as Christianity sought fresh souls in the Orient to offset the losses in the Occident, Islam's main concern was to retain the already converted flock, rather than seeking new converts. Islam was as much concerned with poaching by Christianity—dozens of Christian missionary outfits actually attempted this even at the turn of the Second Millennium and their websites boasted to convert the Muslims!—as by the new challenges of the rising Jews and the Hindus, the 'infidels' believed to have been suppressed and subdued 'forever' a thousand years ago. This was *not* the thinking of the illiterate millions of Muslims; this was the monopoly of the literate few among them. The literate Muslims often thought of dominating others; the literate Christian often thought of converting the infidel and colonising; the literate Diaspora Jew often prepared for a return to Israel; the literate Hindu would often shed copious tears without doing anything himself and hoping others to do what *he* thought was right. In India, the holy warriors of Islam took inspiration from the Hindu festival of Holi in which women wearing a man's mask at the back of their head could dance their way through the heart of both the sexes!

Syed Ahmed Khan did not need to be egged on by the fundamentalists in the service of Islam and did what they wanted him to do as the flag-bearer of Islam after the departure of the Mughals: he ended up charting the birth of a future Pakistan as a mushroom on the moth-eaten grave of the Mughal Empire. As soon as the Indian National Congress came into being in 1885, he discovered in it a 'civil war without arms' and the very next year he set up an 'Educational Congress' as a rival organisation claiming—what else but—that the Muslims would not benefit by the discussion of political matters, and education was the only means of ensuring their progress. Ridiculed for this patently communal step, the Syed then swung to the other extreme. He now set up, not one but two Associations to oppose the Congress: one was the United Indian *Patriotic* Association (1888), having both Hindu and Muslim members who *supported* the British, and the second, exclusively, the Muhammedan Anglo-Oriental *Defence* Association, confining its membership to the Muslims *and* Englishmen! How patriotic! It was for such nationalists that Albert Einstein once said: 'Nationalism is an infantile disease. It is the measles of mankind.' Syed Ahmed Khan gave a new meaning to 'patriotism': since the Muslims had lost their Empire, they must do everything to ensure that the Hindus did not regain theirs. Like any fundamentalist Muslim, he had a forked tongue and always double-spoke. While he supported 'democracy', he abhorred it in India because he believed the Muslims, constituting one-fourth of the population, could never hope for justice vis-a-vis the three-fourths Hindus; democracy *for Muslims* was welcome only in so far as they could retain their dictatorship! He became a role-model for all those who wanted to see the mummy of the Islamic past returning to life in a Western attire. No other Muslim ever poisoned the innocent and poor Indian Muslim's mind as much as he did, and he proved his loyalty to the British who had knighted him precisely for this servitude. The Syed was ably assisted by the principal of his Aligarh college, Theodore Beck, from 1883 to 1899, and others like Archibald and Morrison, for their common belief that it was better to bring new masters from abroad rather than be lorded over by a liberated slave; but even these scaffoldings could not prevent the decrepit fortress of Islam from crumbling further. Islam's twilight was fast approaching in India.

Despite such efforts to control the steadily rising Hindu Wave, these attempts were bound to fail as the things were no longer even in the British hands. In any case, they, like any other imperialist power, had little love lost for the Muslims, their predecessors, in a now love-now hate relationship; they were mostly using them as tools against the Hindus. The Syed school was aware of this, but they saw a dim opportunity even in this servitude. The Hindus had to contend with two Masters, with the old one sulking and serving the new one. A unified Germany and Italy had compounded problems for the British in Europe as these new powers were demanding colonies wherever possible; this had led to the Scramble for Africa. With new threats in Africa, the Suez Canal, the proposed Berlin-Baghdad railway line, the Opium Wars in China, the Boer War in South Africa, the British had their plate full of woes and their forces were spreading thinner and thinner; the British Empire was set to be defeated and dismantled everywhere in the beginning of the 20th century, the way the American Empire is crumbling everywhere in the beginning of the 21st. The Bismarckian politics was far more dangerous for the British than the Czarist or the Napoleonic before that. Imagine the current politics: the USA is far more 'engaged' now than it was in the Soviet era! The way the USA rejected and then sought the UN fig-leaf in Iraq proved the limits of a super power. No Hercules has ever been immortal.

The blue-water navy of the British was increasingly thinning out towards the end of the 19th century and, in India, as the USA now, they increasingly wanted to franchise and outsource their rule to someone who could proxy for them. Genetically, they were not warriors but merely cunning businessmen, full of bravado but essentially insecure, cowards of the first order, boastful not because of the man behind the machine but because of the machine ahead of the man, paranoid at the prospect of body-bags returning home instead of loads of gold, something the Americans inherited from them. The more the Hindu consciousness was awakened, the more the British hired the Muslims to do the dirty work for them, not because they loved the Muslims but because they were scared of the rising Hindus—their 1830s policy of enrolling the Hindus to run the emerging British Empire on the ruins of the collapsing Mughal Empire had only triggered a Hindu *renaissance*. Like other imperialists, they believed in the policy of hitting two birds with one stone: hiring the arrogant enemy to suppress the docile subject. This gave the Muslims the separate vote, Pakistan, and subsequently the veto power during the Congress-secular regimes to the Indian Muslims after the Independence; this somehow, to some extent, satisfied their ego vis-a-vis the Hindus. The fanatic Muslims wanted to restore their 'honour', which they got with Pakistan and Taliban; the Hindus wanted their national-cultural pride restored, which they got in 1965 and 1971! So, the British policy of keeping both of them happy and dividing them simultaneously, succeeded cent percent.

For the first time after the 11th century, 19th century India was seriously considering an alternate, non-Islamic way of life; the Marathas, the Sikhs, the Rohillas, the Bhakti saints, the micro-kings and macro-emperors, the swords and the big guns, all had passed out from the bloody pageant, having displayed their assets, covered and uncovered, as their wardrobes malfunctioned every now and then as India marvelled at the variety of Life in the Great Carnival. The year 1857 was a watershed development when both Christianity and Islam convulsed with a paralytic stroke; their limbs would now move involuntarily. Even the British, who had risen to real power in 1858, began to realise by 1898 that they were, in fact, sitting on their own volcano, that they wore a Crown of Thorns. India was in ferment as never before and discovered that Christianity was no better than Islam; this was to become the basis of Indian nationalism and transformation at the grassroots level. The fact that Christianity had been virtually defeated in the West, not yet as a religion but as a way of life, that the Pope was no longer, after all, the Invincible Commander and the Vatican had shrunk to just 44 hectare even in Italy, that America had just seen a bloody Civil War between the Blacks and Whites, both Christians, over the issue of slavery, that Bismarck was waging a relentless war against the Church in his German *Kultur Kamph.* Islam, too, was, being the branch of the same Old Tree of Abrahamism, in the throes of similar crises, and had now made the Indian task all the more easier. Here were the 'egalitarian religions' that had been losing at home while dreaming to conquer the world. India decided to conquer the home first; the foreigner, the 'impure', could be dealt with later. The West was slowly exploding against an invader Christianity; India was slowly exploding against an invader Islam. The world would slowly explode against all invading ideologies. Each culture would exorcise the ghost of a non-compliant 'guest' civilisation.

It was not exactly xenophobia but a pride in the tradition that was to be taken care of after the invading catalyst had played out its assigned role—no guest would now be allowed to overstay and claim benefits. At a deeper level, the role of *male* catalysts like Christianity and Islam in impregnating the *female* sperm-seeking societies, and prodding them to conceive Change for the next stage of socio-biological evolution, was to be over; they had to separate after sex and then leave space for the next batch of catalysts. There were intense debates as to what kind of Hindu traditions should be revived by those who championed revivalism as the panacea to restore the ancient glory. Mahadev Govind Ranade wondered: 'What are we supposed to revive? Those old habits of our forefathers when the upper castes were devouring the despicable non-vegetarian food and liquor? Or revive the 12 ways of begetting a son or eight of marriage, that included abduction? Shall we revive sexual orgies and indiscriminate sex even with animals? Or the animal sacrifice every year, or even human sacrifice to please the gods? Or the killing of the widows and children?'

As this debate raged in the Hindu mind, more enlightened minds were busy enlightening other minds. They still numbered only a few but the Hindu ethos largely allowed them to get away with liberal ideas and fresh thoughts that dissociated them from the strings of the past, unlike in Islam or Christianity. Having toppled the Islamic regime in Delhi, now was time to consolidate the Hindu moorings and, at the same time, unite and modernise these; no doubt Islamists would create every conceivable obstacle, as Syed Ahmed Khan had amply demonstrated, but that would only accelerate exit of Muhammedanism. The Hindus picked up threads from where they had lost. They discovered that the very cause of their slavery, first to Islam and then to Christianity, was two fold: internal divisions and 'evils' of the Hindu society and their tolerance of the invader. This realisation, together with the 1857 fiasco, dawned, as in the case of the aftermath of the Third Battle of Panipat, first in the Maratha mind that had, as the last Hindu regional force, sought to displace the Muslims. But the Marathas, like the Prussians in unified Germany, did not know how notorious they had become due to their domineering attitude across India; they were forcing the rest of India to choose between the

Maratha Raj and the Muslim reign and this very fact had brought in the British Raj, as the proverbial monkey taking advantage of the two fighting cats. But the Marathas could be the launching pad––the very first missionaries of Indian Independence, beginning 1857, were, of course, mostly Marathas—but players in a cultural Olympiad had to come from across India. Even abroad.

The Maratha consciousness, in the wake of the failure of their *Ashta Pradhan Maratha Mandal*, a loose confederation of eight states ruled by almost free-wheeling Maratha generals who once treated Pune's Peshwa almost as a Hindu 'Caliph', gave way to Indian nationalism; but the Marathas continued attempts to restore hegemony across India and both the Communist/Socialist movements and the RSS were products of this mindset. The Indian attempt to pit the 'newcomer' Christianity against the old, entrenched Islam had, at best, produced only mixed results: living with Islam, India had adjusted with the Muhammedan idea of egalitarian equality of all human beings at least in religious matters; living with Christianity, India now accepted the Christian idea of equality of all human beings at least in secular matters. If the 'godless' British could be successful against the 'god-filled' Muslims, why could not the 'god-like' Hindus; if you cannot remove them physically, then join them politically and use their own ideas against them. So, the Hindus dusted their own ancient emphasis on reason, adopted the Christian's emphasis on human rights...these thought-processes of the 19th century had culminated in the Hindus joining the Indian National Congress in 1885. That old tree had begun to wear new foliage after a long, hot summer.

The Hindu Renaissance, that began with Ram Mohun Roy, now branched off into two streams: secular and religious. There was no parallel Muslim renaissance in India although the Muslims in West Asia were witnessing nationalistic, culture-specific feelings against the Ottoman Empire drawing inspiration from European colonialists and new, culture-specific nations were emerging on the ashes of the Ottomans. In India, the Muslims, afflicted with the minority syndrome, sought to acquire a veto-power against the majority Hindus and, further afflicted with the triple cocktail poison of Aligarhi-Deobandi-Barelvi separatism, would support *only* that 'democracy' in which they could effectively exercise this *Islamic* veto against the Hindu infidels. The Syed had successfully funnelled the Indian subcontinental Muslim society into this fatal Mindset and put them on an auto-drive that would take them away into their cherished but truncated dreamland called Islamabad and then into the Taliban caves.

Even those supporting the Hindu Renaissance had three streams to follow: in the Roy school influenced by European rationalism were those who, taking inspiration from the Anglo-Indian Derozio, wanted to restructure the whole Hinduism and rid it of its archaic past and superstitions. The second school regarded adoption of Christianity as a natural corollary of a general acceptance of the West, as suggested by the Scottish Presbyterian Alexander Duff, and produced literary figures like Michael Madhusudan Dutt and other high-caste Hindu converts to Christianity who briefly provided leadership to the Hindus; the third stream was that of Hindu traditionalists who, like the Muslim Wahhabis, wanted to use the Western toolbox to repair their vintage bullock-cart and make it run in Formula One.

The Arya Samaj, from 1875 onwards, became the fountainhead of all Hindu revivalist movements in the North, a thought process which would, through gradual aggression, lead to eventual exit of Islam in 1947; it was not as if India would exactly expel Islam but would, instead, create conditions increasingly suffocating for Islam, forcing it to withdraw. Islam, being a desert faith, is *genetically incompatible* and *unadoptable* in other environs, the way a rose cannot survive in a desert. Therefore, Islam cannot survive for long in any democracy that allows co-existence of divergent human minds. With India now getting democracy-ready, Islam's exit was a natural evolution. The educated Hindu middle class, carrier of this democracy, felt a vacuum due to their disbelief in ancient superstitions that passed off as religion and customs; this vacuum was now filled by political nationalism at the end of the 19th century just like the seed of an evolving cultural nationalism at the end of the 20th century resulted in the BJP coming to power. Mother India, which had failed to rise in the Marathas, now woke up in Bengal with Bankim Chandra Chattopadhyaya announcing that India was a matriarchate, *Vande Mataram*; it went without saying what the fundamentalist aliens were like, vis-a-vis this Mother. That was why this Song has since been abhorred by the adherent of alien faiths as an abuse.

Like mules, many lethargic Hindus had cultivated the habit of being shaken into action when flogged *only* by a rank non-Hindu alien—be they Muhammad Ghori or Allan Octavian Hume. A retired British official, Hume flogged India to gather in the Indian National Congress (INC). At the end of the 19th century, it had nearly 100 active members; it is always the dynamic minority that changes the shape of nations. At the end of the 20th century, the Congress had millions of static and seasonal mosquito-type non-members as witness to its demise because from a movement, the Congress had degenerated into a Party and finally decayed into a sect worshipping a demi-god—its off-and-on electoral successes notwithstanding. The Bengali-dominated INC was set up in the Maratha land, at Bombay, with W C Bonnerji as its President. But Hume was not an enemy of the Raj he had served so long: he had disclosed that the Congress was merely a safety valve to let off the rising Hindu steam to avert a repeat of 1857; the British already controlled the troughs of Islam, thanks to the Syed Ahmed knighthood. Overlooking the 'noble' aim of Hume, the Marathas and the Bengalis, under the leadership of the Parsis, gradually made the Congress a mobile post office and a suggestion box where the Indians could post their grievances to and against the British. The Parsis, having been the last immigrants in India chased away from Persia by the Arab Muslims, predictably, became the first protective shield of the Hindus against the British.

Tortoises may win the race in the end but the rabbits always win the claps. The Congress moderates of the Gopal Krishna Gokhale school soon found themselves being clapped away by the Bal Gangadhar Tilak school that offered a faster courier service. A strong Brahminical element had, in fact, snaked its way into the Congress, as it would, later, in the Communist and the RSS movements as well. After the inaugural, the Maharashtra Brahmins, including the Chitpawans, had captured the Congress leadership; the emerging Maratha role was like a combination of the Serbs' against the Ottomans and the Prussians in unified Germany. The Marathas considered the British merely as an 'alien interregnum' between the Mughals and their dream of a Hindu Raj and had found expression to this after the 1857 fiasco in the form of the INC. Reviving the Shivaji cult, therefore, Tilak was able to arouse patriotic feelings, particularly after the government failures in controlling thc Bombay Plague of 1897, and gradually wrested leadership from the Gokhleite moderate school. Tilak's efforts to bring about a Hindu awakening through the idiom of cultural festivals was like electrolysis in a rarefied solution. Only a strong electric current was needed to make it boil and crystallise things that were waiting to happen for centuries.

The Napoleon-like George Nathaniel Curzon, who was the Viceroy (1899-1905) and who would, as Foreign Secretary (1919-22), set up the British protectorate over Persia against the emerging Soviet Union, wanted to immortalise himself like Wellesley and Dalhousie in the annals of the Jewel's history—so that he could become the British Prime Minister! He ended up as the swan-song of British imperialism in India. For, while he remodelled the whole frontier policy, administering the British Forward Policy to fully administer the territory up to the Durand Line, drawn between India and Afghanistan in 1893 and sending the Younghusband Mission to Lhasa in 1904 to strike deal against Russian designs, he did one worse elsewhere. To influence the British back home, he organised the Delhi Darbar in 1903 to mark the accession of Edward VII; to win over the British in India, he tried to control the middle class education, ending up antagonising the latter and giving them an opportunity to launch the first Indian mass movement in 1905 when he partitioned Bengal along communal lines. He demonstrated to the Hindus that the Muslims *could be winnowed out.* Bengal was an overgrown British Presidency of nearly 78 million people comprising the east and west Bengals, Bihar and Orissa—of these, the East Bengal would become East Pakistan in 1947 and Bangladesh in 1971. Curzon created a new province, East Bengal and Assam, with 31 million *mostly Muslim* population, having its capital at Dhaka, and reducing the mainly Hindu Bengalis to a minority even in West Bengal wherein Bihar and Orissa were the mainstay. This was the ultimate humiliation to the proud Bengali who had so far been fancying himself as the legatee of the British whenever they leave India; the Bengali gentry, which inherited the British superiority complex and saw the rest of India, just like the Marathas or the Tamils did, as mere riff-raff, discovered that their claims were as hollow and untenable in 1905 as the Marathas' were in 1764; soon, the Bengalis would be stripped of Calcutta as the Capital of India just like the Marathas lost Bombay to the rest of India. Regional chauvinism was found to be as baneful as other evil Hindu social customs and practices. If Mother India was washing Islam out, she was also washing her own coloured children.

Curzon's stupidity, triggered by his wisdom, surcharged and revivified a moribund Congress which would, henceforth, promote Hinduism in the garb of nationalism; likewise, it encouraged Muslim separatism in the garb of 'equality'. Curzon returned to Britain in 1906 and discovered that he could not be the Premier, thanks to the Liberal landslide that would reunite the now-volatile Bengals; the new Viceroy, Minto, aided by the new Secretary of State, John Morley, undid the partition of Bengal, only to push the ignited Muslim separatist process further leading to the Partition of India, 1947.

Although the British, according to historians, had hanged some 27,000 Muslims in Delhi alone in 1857-58 to crush the Revolt, they were always apprehensive of the possible Muslim backlash. Lord Lytton warned Salisbury on 23 June 1877, that there 'is no getting over the fact that the British empire of India is a Muhammedan Power; and that it entirely depends upon the policy of Her Majesty's Government, whether the sentiments of our Muhammedan subjects is to be an immense security or an immense danger to us.' It was under this policy that the British patronised the Muslim fundamentalists on the one hand and the Hindu liberals on the other, thus while effectively crushing any rise of Islamic liberalism, triggering, at the same time, a Hindu fundamentalism. Principal Archibald of Aligarh facilitated a meeting between Minto and the Agha Khan that led to the formation of the Muslim League on 1 October 1906, with Salimullah Khan, the Nawab of Dhaka, owed as he did to the British Rs14 lakh, to emerge as the new Mir Jafar by becoming the President of the new party. As a reaction, there began the crystallisation of the Akhil Bharatiya Hindu Mahasabha in 1907 as the daughter of Arya Samaj.

The basic flaw of Islam, despite its great role as a catalyst across Asia and Europe, was that while it could become a carrier of modernity, it would *itself* not adopt it—for instance, the Muslim terrorists 'popularised' AK-47 and AK-56 the world over but none of the Islamic country would manufacture it; even Pakistan's 'Islamic Bomb' has been theft-based. Like those hoteliers who would not eat in their own hotel, Islam and change were antithetical. The Abbasids, who gave back the Greko-Roman heritage to Europe that, post-Crusades, triggered the Ages of Renaissance, Reformation and Reason leading to the ouster of Papal hegemony from secular life, would not adopt the same progressiveness *within* Islam. The British came to India like these Abbasids and reopened Indian eyes to her 'glorious', pre-Islamic past but could not control the forces this policy unleashed and found themselves uprooted in a few decades. The more Islam became inflexible vis-a-vis its host Hindus, the easier the task of ejecting Islam became.

With the formation of the Muslim League and the Hindu Mahasabha, therefore, the fate of Islam in South Asia was decided—it only indicated that Islam had failed to uproot, convert and absorb the Hindus fully, that even the coward Hindus had rejected Islamic superiority. There was no looking back now. Even the perceived 'superiority' of Europe, of Britain, and, above all, of Christianity, stood shattered forever with Japan defeating Russia in 1904. Shinto-Buddhist Japan had defeated Christian Russia; now was the time for Hindu-Buddhist India to defeat both Islam and Christianity.

Several factors went into making the exit of Islam from India possible as the Hindus continued to win back the space once occupied by the Muslims, as the Spanish had done before in the 15th century Iberian Peninsula. Had Islam not been in the throes of crises everywhere, it would never have retreated from India. But the Hindus, who always believed in the circularity of Time and the phases of good and bad, fortune and misfortune, of business cycles, knew that like all 'good' things, even the Islamic rule, would come to an end eventually. This same ingrained trait largely shielded India from the global economic meltdown in 2008-10—because, in a diversity-infested India, not all the people go the same way—even their elections only produce first-past-the-post winners, that do not exactly mean a 'preference'.

India's, particularly Adi Shankaracharya's, long wait of 11 centuries was now coming to an end. Why did India wait so long in ejecting Islam if it was antithetical to the natural evolution of Homo sapiens? Why did the victim wait to strike until the assaulter grew old and infirm? Why was India so patient?

All thought-systems and ideologies that seek to dominate human minds are products of an astral belief system of their promoters, their beliefs in the different aspects of Nature, the elements, the sky and the Earth, the flora and fauna—and the role they play in human life. Christianity had begun to weaken in the West not so much because of Protestantism but due to the combined, and indirect, efforts of isolated individuals like Galileo, Copernicus and Newton, who, together, changed the very notion of the Universe and the forces that controlled it. They altered the primordial belief in Christianity-bred egocentricity, back to the native European heliocentricity. In the beginning of the 20th century, this thought process was accelerated globally with Einstein, Max Planck, Michelson-Morley, Neils Bohr and others, in bits-and-pieces, striking at the very roots of belief system spawned by the Moon-cultist Christianity and Islam and restoring the Sun-cultists after a gap of nearly 3,000 years. This change in thinking was slow but sure, basically in the common people's uncommon minds, not in the uncommon fundamentalists' common minds—and this was what unhinged the well-entrenched Christianity from its very roots; the number of believers in Galileo continued to grow and that in the Christ decline correspondingly. That was how deChristianisation began. Other Abrahamic ideologies like Communism, Fascism and Nazism, came to their desired ends quickly simply because they emphasised mainly on the politico-economic aspects of human life, unlike religions which sought to change everything, including astral belief system of a people.

The biggest challenge *to* Islam came after Karl Marx. His emphasis was mainly on politico-economic development of human beings—he even declared that economic conditions determined culture and religion—but a few aspects of Marxism unhinged all existing thought systems from their very roots. Nietzsche believed that God was dead. But He never died; the very idea of God is due to the common belief in the existence of someone Perfect out there Who constantly reminds us of our imperfections, and we all strive to become Perfect like Him. But to say that this Great Perfect One runs the life of imperfects like us, and selects those He would like to at the End of the Day, the Little Perfect Ones, is in itself a 'blasphemy'. Had God created man, He would create them all alike in His Image and there would have been no inferior or superior religions or men or the struggle between these Children of God; that is, God did not create man in His Image, it was the other way round: *man created God in his image*. God was therefore not an entity but an idea which reminds men of their imperfections, that he should strive to become That One and must become his own destiny.

Such revolutionary ideas slowly eroded the soil from under Christianity's feet of clay. Swami Vivekanand (1863-1902) made the Hindus draw a line longer than those drawn by Christianity and Islam; he knew the limitations of Abrahamic ideologies, based as these were on an individual 'prophet', all One Man Shows. Clearly, these couple of religions could not be culture-compliant for long in a comity of nations numbering a couple of hundred and would come apart as soon as they stopped being nourished by their roots. In the modern context, this could be understood in the same way as restrictive and monopolistic trade practices: each country would try protect its domestic market from alien invasion—and missionary religions were like dumping of a nation/empire's surplus technology by MNCs in another by hook or crook—Christianity was dumped on other cultures when it became outmoded after the Renaissance in its bases of Europe while Islam was dumped elsewhere mainly by force. Nothing remained to be proved after the failure of the Crusades and the un-success of Jihads as to the perceived 'superiority' of a religion. The first CEO of an MNC in India was Robert Clive.

The simultaneous decline of Islamic power in Turkey and India was not a coincidence but a foregone conclusion. While, out of the disintegrating Ottoman Empire, the gradual and inexorable rise of the basically Sun-worshipping societies of Turkey, Transjordan, Syria, Egypt and other constituent nationalities into nations freeing themselves was the clearest sign of the Moon-worshipping Islam's losing appeal as a cementing and absorbing force, the rise of India out of the morass called British-India, like the lost Atlantis re-emerging in the Atlantic Ocean, was a parallel process. While Islam, centred around the idea of Allah and the personality of Muhammed, tried to project itself as largely intact, the men who peddled this idea found themselves increasingly out of sync in the torrent of change and were forced to carve out their little enclosures where they could shelter their beloved God and the Prophet from their enemy, that is Change. This Change came in phases: militancy of different shades prepared the soil for the next generation, *of separatists*; they were followed by *retreaters*. Globally, terrorists of all hues, who would eliminate surplus populations believing in the Old World, came *as disruptive change-makers*, as Malthusian Terminators!

The formation of Muslim League was a desperate attempt of the retreating faith to find a shelter in India, like an encroacher trying to hold-on to his kiosk when the municipal removal gang arrives. Even if the British were not there as 'facilitators', Islam's fate in India would, at best, have been slower but not different; the British only accelerated Islam's exit. Why? Because the abiding interest of India's increasing middle class was in the emerging disciplines of science and law, which, both, ironically, were the prime movers of all anti-Mosaic Law movements in the West, and, by extension, would have been anti-Islam in India as well. Most Congress leaders, and even those who were out of the Mother Party, were lawyers who interpreted in the secular courts the meaning of religions; it was not for nothing that even in an Independent India, the most 'popular' discipline continued to be the law for many decades. The rise of scientific temper, similarly, affected the thought-process of educated Hindu Indians. They accepted the secular law and sciences immediately like *prasad* after a *pooja*, unlike most of the literate Muslims who chewed for some time these modern secular disciplines like '*paan*' (beetle leaf), vomited it completely and grinned their coloured teeth to 'prove' that they had 'modernised'!

Narendra Nath Datta, a Kayastha, when he became Swami Vivekanand, knew. He was full of Darwinian ideas of struggle for existence and survival of the fittest, Herbert Spencer's emphasis on *laissez-faire* and application of Darwinism to the entire spectrum of human knowledge, as expounded in his ten-volume *System of Synthetic Philosophy* he began to pen in 1862. An atheist to the core himself, to begin with, Vivekanand took off from where the earlier Brahmo Samaj had stopped. He set up the Ramkrishna Mission which, in turn, opened modern education centres and overturned the very Hindu notion that religion meant asceticism and meditation. The Swami asked the Hindus to practise their religion not through obscurantism but by devoting themselves absolutely to the welfare of men. 'Vedanta, you said? Leave that to the next life, leave meditation to the next life. Put your body, here, at the service of others. Now. The noblest truth is that God is present in all human beings. If you serve the human beings, you serve God. You cannot see God but you can see these humans. They are His multiple forms. There is no other God up there to seek. He who serves humans serves God.'

For the first time, Hinduism had been brought down from its ideal and lofty pedestal to the concrete reality on the ground. In Chicago to speak in the Parliament of Religions, he found himself penniless in 1893; there, he spoke eloquently on the 'unity' of all religions, indirectly disrobing Christianity and Islam of their perceived *uniqueness* and exclusivity and making 'heathen' Hinduism stand on the same pedestal, made atheism a 'noble religion'. The infidel-in-saffron was, in turn, honoured by some of the theo-fatigued Believers. 'There is no other God than the souls of living beings', he told the Hindus, 'and we want a religion that makes man. Give up these sickening mysticisms and be strong...Make all other vain gods disappear from your minds for the next 50 years. Have only one God awake, *our own race*, which sees His Hands, His Feet, His Ears everywhere. He is omnipotent, omniscient. The first worship must be of those who we see around ourselves, men and animals, and the first gods we want to worship are our own countrymen.'

The post-1875 India was once again in ferment, in a parallel process to the reconstruction of Europe after dismantling of the Metternich Matrix. It reached a crescendo in Bankim Chandra's stirring patriotic song, *Vande Mataram*. This was the trigger to the fundamentalist Muslims, who controlled their society, and their 'secular' slaves amongst the non-Muslims. They despised it first in Bengal, then in India, because this theme song of all freedom fighters asked them to worship Mother India. How could they? Their holy land was far away in Mecca; for them, India had always been a camp: a base camp, an army camp and, finally, alas, a relief camp—they never treated India as their home unless they owned this motel; this 'trait' of Muslim fundamentalists, who had a complete hold on the Muslim Mind, created untold miseries for the common, poor, innocent Muslims who eked out a living like the common, poor, innocent Hindu. Islam was a major denationalising force in India, even bigger than Christianity and the Muslims felt 'liberated' from the Hindu-yoke when Bengal was partitioned in 1905; instead, they were prepared to be slaves of the British who had usurped the Mughal Empire; even the Hindu preferred the British at least as a 're-civilising' force.

The Song did bestir the freedom fighters across India but did not shake them further into decisive action. It was mainly because of the intellectual-cultural arrogance of many in the emerging Indian leadership from the three British-Indian Presidencies of Madras, Calcutta and Bombay, each of which fancied itself as the torch-bearer of 'modern' India, the legatee of the British, and, of course, the rest of India as just *hoi polloi* they would like to *lead*—even post-1947, this intellectual ghettoisation and superiority complex continued and the 'Indo-Britons', Delhi-bound, did so as if they were the in-house, neo-colonialists. Congress leaders of these three Presidencies were, therefore, unable to make themselves an all-India voice; at best, they were local vortices—you would be sucked in by them only if you went closer. Due to continuous, serial assaults by the aliens, the North refused to be allured by other sides, undressed briefly to make them spend themselves and woke up when Gandhi gently tried to make it sleep in peace rather than be tortured in war.

The early Congress leaders, led by those who believed they would *persuade* the British to leave India and were fascinated by the very idea of being the Raj inheritors, did not have the foggiest idea of the Abrahamic Mindset that had enslaved India for a thousand years. Only, the face of the day's encroacher changed when the Muslim rule changed from the Slave dynasty to the Mughal dynasty or the Dutch/Portuguese/French were replaced by the British. Therefore, at best, these 'intellectuals' of the Congress variety were like the assistants who cleaned the vegetables and dressed chickens like other Black Butlers did until the Master Chef came. Their biggest problem was that they fancied themselves as 'intellectuals' and 'liberals', galaxies away from the hard-rock-bottom of practical politics; they were doomed because they deemed. They did not know that the Muslims, stripped of their Mughal rule in 1857, were not going to sit idly if and when the British left India; the Marathas, the Bengalis and the Tamils fancied themselves as the rightful heir to the British—they did not weld themselves fully into India, and largely remained the unassembled parts of the next vehicle. Like the British, they wanted to rule India without caring for its majority's sensitivities; their linguistic chauvinism and hatred of Hindi and North India, that constituted majority of the Hindus, continued throughout the 20th century, and even in the 21st...that was why no Maratha, Bengali or Tamil could ever become the all-India leader, even after Independence—to the ordinary North Indian, all the people east of Bihar were 'Bengalis', being part of the British India's Calcutta Presidency; similarly, all the people south of the Vindhyas were 'Madrasis', being part of the Madras Presidency. Most of the 'Leaders' from these two Presidencies, despite supporting democracy, never cared to learn the language of the majority of Indians (Hindi) and ended up passé even before the *real* End Game actually commenced. Leaders from the third Presidency, Mumbai, although proponents of Hinduism and even learning some Hindi, did not matter much eventually: they carried the heavy burden of the failure of the Third Battle of Panipat (1764), unpopularity of the Marathas outside Marathwada increased when they turned hegemonist and looted various areas during and as the Mughal Empire weakened—and, post-Independence, the assassination of Gandhi.

Back then, in the early 20th century, however, Only One Man Understood This Great Game and the approaching End Game… and, therefore, overtook, raced past all other Indians to successfully arrive at The End Game. And, above all, unlike other contemporary leaders, he did not carry the burden of his 'intellectual prowess', history, or ambitions. He learnt and promoted Hindi, wore the minimum of clothing, ate a morsel or two…he looked like a mouse far below in dimensions of a Gokhaleite reformer, but was an elephant who thought and worked far beyond Tilak's symbolic *Ganeshotsava.*

Gandhi was *the* Enigma whose Arrival was unstoppable.

The Game Changer

'WELCOME, and dissolve yourself in our people, like sugar into milk', thus famously said a king in Gujarat when a group of Parsis (Zoroastrians), fleeing Iran from Arab invaders soon after the Prophet's death, sought refuge near the port town of Surat. Earlier, many immigrants from different places had got assimilated in separate Varnas and castes under the umbrella Hinduism.

This assimilative pattern continued until Islam's arrival in the eighth century, and a resuscitated Christianity's in the 18th century. By then, India had, due to continuous influx of immigrants, become socially dysfunctional and top-heavy. In the beginning, the two Semitic faiths came as a whiff of fresh air and catalysts to rejuvenate the sluggish society. But, as game-changers from the Fertile Crescent, they changed the rules in which the newcomers, for the first time, had not only brought in their own *aggressive* faiths but actively sought *converts* in India, unlike their predecessors. The Semitic sugar refused to dissolve into, and began to dictate terms to, the Aryan milk! Clearly, a guest cannot set up own kitchen in the guesthouse.

In the resultant society that emerged, the age-old Hindu belief system, although still hard as rock, eroded slowly until the implosion of Gandhi. The Hindu Bharat, particularly in the Cow/Hindi Belt (North India), emerged as a largely socially decayed biomass even though its threshold to implode—and then explode, as after the 1990s—continued to increase. Eventually, the British came as the fresh game-changers, set up a neo-Sultanate and a neo-Mughal Empire, resuscitated the Hindus, and left by 1947.

Since India never had a nationally-organised church to stall this implosion within Hinduism, *avidya* continued to sink further and further down in her psyche: if India survived as a predominantly Hindu nation during the last 2,000 years, it was because she *stuck to illiteracy* as little knowledge is a dangerous thing. Christianity and Islam eventually failed, also, because the India they found waiting for them was largely illiterate, even if prosperous until the 18th century: they got tired of blowing a flute before a ruminating buffalo, the way the Communists failed to usher in a Red Revolution for the same reason. A highly decentralised, even chaotic, society defeated the centralised faiths and ideologies. This was not an organised response from a enslaved Hindu country to a master Muslim or Christian coloniser but an emerging societal response in a polytheistic, multicultural society adhering to variation, enforced by a belief system spawned by a cake-like society architectured over some five millennia: it outnumbered the enemy by multiplying, hid its claws, Shivaji-like, and waited for Afzal Khan to enter into striking distance; once swallowed, it will expand like Hanuman in Sursa's mouth.

The slow process of deIslamisation of India had started when Islam suffered a mortal attack from the Mongols at Baghdad in the 13th century, followed by emergence of a Shia Persia as a wall between Delhi and Baghdad; the Sultanate, basically, influenced the *Doaba*. Islam actually impacted the rest of India only under the Mughals. This creative destruction continued apace between Muhammad bin-Qasim and Muhammad Ali Jinnah.

The Arya Samaj tried to organise the Hindus along the irreconcilable *Christian missionary* lines but waned precisely because it tried to pull the steam engine and telegraph revolutions using the sacred *Yagnopavit* thread; even the Ramkrishna Mission met a similar fate for the same reason.

It was a complicated checkmate, the end-game, understood and played by Gandhi *alone*. A non-practising Hindu, he *led* the Khilafat Movement whereas a non-practising Muslim, Jinnah led its next stage, the Pakistan Movement.

Islam's exodus from India took place in four stages: (1) Rupture of Islam between India and West Asia after the post-Mongol destruction of the Caliphate at Baghdad beginning in 1258, and the ensuing First Battle of Panipat, leading to the foundation of Mughal dynasty (1526); (2) While the atheist Mongols destroyed Islamic 'invincibility' in West Asia, they diluted Islam in India after the Second Battle of Panipat (1556) as 'assimilative' Mughals increasingly followed only a third-hand, largely Caliph-free Islam, unlike the Arab-influenced Delhi Sultanate; (3)The subsequent indigenisation and Indianisation (de-Arabisation/de-Persianisation) of Islam, beginning with Akbar, with a hybrid Urdu slowly replacing Arabic and Persian languages, then *English* gradually replacing them all, and beginning of the first-ever major armed Hindu reaction culminating in the Third Battle of Panipat (1761) and (4) Retreat of Islam in the next nine decades of the staggered Fourth Battle of Panipat, or 'Partition' (1857-1947). It was, therefore, the atheist Mongols who actually saved a polytheist India from a monotheist Islam until imperialist Christianity hurriedly retreated, taking Pakistan in tow.

It was the Mongols, again, who aroused India from her dogmatic slumber after 1947 and paved the way for her second yawn. Most of the modern Chinese are actually descendants of the Mongols who kick-started India in 1962, and prepared her to dump fossilised ideas like Panchsheel, peace, nonviolence and non-alignment in the world of *realpolitik*. This war enabled India to modernise her armed forces and launch her first-ever consolidated attack on Islam(abad) in 1,200 years (1965) and split Pakistan (1971). The birth of Bangladesh (1971), or for that matter many a nation on the ruins of Ottoman and Mughal Empires, proved that neither Islam nor any other religion can be the basis for a separate nation in an alien soil, that Ummah (Muslim

Brotherhood) has been destroyed by the resurgence of suppressed cultures—the supposed 'revival' of Islamism now is an attempt to reunite the Muslims against the 'common enemy', the infidels that, incidentally, includes the West, the Jews and the Hindus—besides, of course, the 'lesser Muslims' like the Shias, the Ahmedias etc. The monotheist Muslims do not, *so far*, include the atheist Chinese in this kill-list! The political alliance of Pakistan and China can ensure that no outside power prevents China's entry into Mecca *via* Gwadar!

Unlike other fossilised First Civilisations (Sumer, Babylonia, Assyria, Egypt, Persia etc), which virtually sank into the quicksand of Islam, eighth century India was merely exhausted; she accepted Islam only as a cola, a catalyst, the way China and Japan would also do subsequently in respect of Islam and Christianity. In a jelly-like Indian society, Islam could not, therefore, strike as deep roots as it did in the Fertile Crescent. So, when Islam turned demanding and sought to change rules of the game, India began to plot exit of the overstaying guest.

Nature had now readied the Chess Board: the Grand Master was awaited. Gandhi was this Game Changer, the one who would break India out of her psychological seige.

Each idea flowers only when its time arrives, that is the soil is ready to germinate the seed. They yearn for a host to make a home, for a people to impregnate, and then as active carriers; in these hosts, the guests mutate and evolve, before mating and multiplying, leaving them for another set of hosts for another lifecycle. *The* idea often lies dormant before it suddenly wakes up to complete a 'germ cycle' when the host gets bouts of the disease. Sometimes we see the feverish idea ebbing after false starts—it is, in fact, gathering energy and would be the force multiplier for a bigger show in the offing.

Ridding India of the *alien* ways of life was a long dormant idea. The *Gita* had warned as much: *Better is one's own Dharma, (though) imperfect, than the Dharma of another well-performed. Better is death in one's own Dharma: the Dharma of another is fraught with fear.*

(III, 34-35). No other part of India had borne the full fury of Islamic sandstorm the way the great temples at Somnath, Mathura and Ayodhya did. Due to the demographic and political 'imbalance' however, the Hindus of Mathura and Ayodhya could not take decisive action against the Muslims for a thousand years—until the 1990s.

Not so in Gujarat, which appeared to bc the chosen place for *this* decisive action. After 1857, Gujarat was, for the first time in a thousand years, paying the Islamists in their own coin. It had suffered the full flowering of Islam in the personas of Mehmud of Ghazni destroying the Somnath Temple in 1024, followed by the devastation caused by, in varying degrees, Allah-ud-din Khilji (1297), Muzaffar Shah (1375), Mehmud Begda (1451) and finally by Aurangzeb (1701). In the early 20th century, therefore, the seething Gujarat was a ready host for this *idea*—the 2002 communal riots in this state were indicative of how the Hindus' frozen anger continues to melt in Gujarat. Gandhi was the Carrier-in-Chief of this idea, the *new Idea of Islam and Christianity-Free India*. His Time had Arrived. This Idea consummated, crystallised and personified in him, like a glacier emerging from the Indian Ocean. The Gujaratis were to be the 'chosen' community to incubate this Idea and expand it to sub-continental and later global levels. The Idea and the Gujaratis had found each other as guest and hosts in the 20th century, the way lunotheism and the Jews had found each other in the sixth century BC, or Islam and the Arabs found each other in the sixth century AD.

Luckily, Gandhi had no literary pretensions, intellectual arrogance, chalk-and-board fundamentalism or scholastic snobbery unlike some of the upstart, narcissist dreamers from the three contemporary British-Indian Presidencies of Madras, Bombay and Calcutta who fancied themselves in messiah-type roles and as rightful inheritors of the Raj if and when it managed to decamp with whatever was left of the Indian rags. On the contrary, Gandhi would often present himself as a vulnerable simple man—that was how he came to scan through the countless silent majorities believing in simplified solutions to survive in a complicated biological chess-game. He silently played a highly complex mind-game with the British and the Muslims, but, at the same time, outwardly, he offered an uncomplicated solution one could buy. And, unlike most other literate Indians, boisterous and sulking alternately—like milk boiling up or down in a moment—he had two other rare qualities: subtlety and patience. The impact of his words, which many mistook he spoke or wrote casually, would be felt long afterwards.

He was born into the Modh Vaishya caste: these people often defied common business wisdom and produced supplies *before* creating demand! The two most famous Modh Vaishyas of the 20th century, Mohandas Karamchand Gandhi and Dhirajlal Hirachand Ambani did exactly that: while the former helped *create* a demand for Pakistan, the latter created demand for polyester, *only after* they had ensured supplies.

A practical survivalist people, Gujaratis seldom had any traditions of flowering of great intellectuals; having struggled against Islam, particularly in Central Gujarat, many among them had, somewhat like medieval Venetian merchants of the Crusades era, come to believe more in costs and prices than in 'values' and emerged as successful traders. They would *buy* literacy rather than earn it; some parents would even guard their promising children from falling 'prey' to the unwelcome infection of intellectuals. This tendency made them incapable of helping intellect evolve or doing anything that flowers wisdom; they only managed to emerge as prosperous but mediocre people. They largely shunned the armed or paramilitary forces, sports, sciences and the arts—anything which requires patience, scholarship and longer gestation periods. They developed strong common sense, *minus* civic sense, and have rarely been good manufacturers as they lacked sanctity for quality by genuinely respecting talent. That was why science and technology, even information technology, remain a pipedream for Gujarat, which mostly shunned learning languages, including the English language. The only notable scientist Gujarat ever produced, Vikram Sarabhai, father of India's space programme and a great visionary and institution builder, was an exception; but even he came from a business family! The daily mood of the Gujaratis would fluctuate alongside the Bombay Stock Exchange's sensitive index (Sensex), which they largely control. But they could at once be generous and miserly—they would fleece one another to the last penny, but donate millions to sects and cults and splurge wantonly as tourists and pilgrims. But, like many Indians, they trained their children only for the next minor battle, not the Great War of Life. Most Indians won small battles but lost big wars.

Such traders, given to bullish or bearish trends, tended to follow cults blindly as they provide them an escape route from their many inherent insecurities and the hidden guilt of having fleeced others. Religion itself being big business and money-laundering racket, businessmen's cults and sects flourished in and infested Gujarat; they bought quick-fix 'spiritualism' rather than inculcating or experiencing it personally. They used 'religions' like towels to cover their stark cerebral nudity and loved their many gods the way they loved their many cuisines. Gods have, for them, been like seasonal fruits: each season has had a different god. Overall, the Gujaratis have generally been a crazy, practical, jovial, fun-and-festival-loving people in things religious and commercial, social and political—they immediately accepted the profitable and at once rejected the 'harmful', without any compunction.

Gandhi was no exception. Few of his 'theories' had any logic or intellectual depth, such as the First Wave cottage industry he supported while being guest of big industrialists and in the midst of the Second Wave colonial wars for global markets and industries, vis-à-vis the emerging Third Wave 'temples of industry' and modern knowledge his disciple, Jawaharlal Nehru, advocated. The 'Gandhian' theories were mostly shallow and old, recycled stuff which would not stand intellectual inquiry anywhere. What stood him apart was, however, that he was honest about borrowing this very stuff and admitted as much on the back cover of his 'autobiography': 'I have nothing new to teach the world. Truth and non-violence are as old as the hills'.

It was his genius that he used these same Stone Age rocks as missiles against the medieval Abrahamic ideologies in a New World. Since he had nothing new to offer intellectually, Gandhi had no ego problems common amongst those burdened with academia; he could present himself as the humblest man, and easily slip like a fish from one position to another leaving others in 'intellectual' tatters.

In Indian business circles, they say a Gujarati is one who buys from a Marwari and sells to a Sindhi, making profit! Only an infidel Gujarati trader could have, for instance, *sold* a Khilafat movement *to the Indian Muslims*, for restoration of the Caliphate in *far away Turkey*, only to withdraw when it had served its limited purpose; he was like a successful salesman marketing a refrigerator in Antarctica.

He could not but have been a Gujarati!

Gandhi was, perhaps, the first Hindu *Mujahid* (a guerrilla fighter), even a *Fidayi* (one who sacrifices his life for God). He was the strangest 'Order' churned out by a chaotic India over the last 2,000 years, the Hindu Uncertainty to counter the Abrahamic certainties. With him began India's Second Age of Enlightenment.

When Sir Richard Attenborough met Jawaharlal Nehru in 1959 while planning his biopic *Gandhi*, the Indian Prime Minister asked the celebrated filmmaker not to glorify the Man as a saint. 'Richard, whatever you do, don't turn him into a saint. He (Gandhi) was much too human and complex to be a saint.' But this is exactly what the Nehru-led Indian National Congress (INC) did thereafter. Let us not, therefore, fall for the Congress attempts to glorify Gandhi, nor the cries of the Rightist Opposition to vilify, or adopt, the great man. The Congress and its successors found in him a holy cow, resting in peace at Raj Ghat in New Delhi, behind which the corrupt political machine could operate safely for decades. The Congress created a false propaganda and xenophobic voices to continue the Nehru Dynasty which succeeded in brainwashing gullible large Indian masses into believing in a carefully crafted Gandhian mythology that would strip them from thinking their own way. Gandhi was far beyond the mental horizons of Indian politicians of various hues.

What follows here is a tapestry of strands from various streams, swinging back and forth, weaving designs, connecting contemporary roaming wavelengths in a global mobile telephony and seamless voice-overs from world history, particularly that of the West and West Asia between the two World Wars. Gandhi was not a linear personality; there could, therefore, be no straight story emerging from him. We can understand this Nature's unique son better and soak ourselves in the Gandhian Sun only by running *his* India's history along side that of the world, particularly of a sulking China, a chest-thumping Japan, a declining Europe, an eclipsing Britain, an emerging America. Many of us would find contradictions galore taxing our mind; but without them, we would not, perhaps, be able to fathom his immensely great persona.

It is easy to become a copy-and-paste intellectual but takes a real genius to play a simpleton. He was the rare genius India was waiting for, for a thousand years; he represented, collectively, the Indians' aspirations and innovations, foibles and limitations, confirmations and contradictions—with his being a Gujarati and his *bania* caste getting activated when he 'struck' deals with others. Millions glorified him without understanding his mission; many demonised him when he paid them in their own coin. Few actually understood him without glorifying but were drowned in the cacophony of this irresistibly rising Sun. Some even turned sheep and virtually followed him blindly to the bottom ash of his funeral pyre; still others turned into Gandhian fundamentalists and living non-violent fossils of today.

He was an unstoppable Sun India was waiting to see rise and rise for long. He knew that those who claimed to know the most, knew the people the least. Like a modem in today's Internet, he would spot and modulate social desire and action into social communication and then demodulate it into political communication and action; for him, his 'experiments' were all directed to achieve the goal he had set himself when, as a boy, he took to non-vegetarianism to make himself muscular enough to kick the British out of India—the level of his motivation, his silent self-indoctrination, even radicalisation, was such that he could go to any extent, even pretend as a peacenik, in this psychological warfare. As slippery as a fish and as enigmatic as Krishna, Gandhi was the fox India needed to deAbrahamise herself; he was the greatest thing to have happened to India after the penning of the *Gita* in the eighth century, from which he frequently quoted. While the contemporary Congress leaders in India furiously burnt their typewriters petitioning the British in politically correct English, he learnt the art of foxing the Raj through bad handwriting—in South Africa, he had already sized up the British to their bare bones and knew that, these Cromwell-fearing rulers were ultimately vulnerable to argument, a reason why in the 21st century, they helplessly see Islam and other religions forcing out whatever is left of Anglicanism.

In South Africa, Gandhi first came as a Brown Briton, *against* the native Africans; he spent a fortune emulating the British in dress and behaviour as a lawyer. Then, when the White Britons famously kicked him out of the train, he began to understand the rulers' snobbery, and quickly turned into a messiah of both the Africans and the Indians there. When he returned to India he underwent a complete transformation by paring down clothing to just a loin-cloth like millions of Indians; he spoke the simple language they could comprehend, he raised the issues they could support; he lived the life they were always living; he ate what they did; his hand-writing was as bad as any third grader at school; he openly declared that he was a third-class student all his life, like most others, and he travelled third-class; unlike other 'leaders', he enjoyed self-deprecation and humbled himself to the bottom level from where nobody could humiliate or depose him any more. He easily foxed those who roared like lions, but himself mixed like sugar-to-milk with the millions of sheepish Indians. His critics would burn him alive, but his admirers would die for him; he evoked strong emotions and ambitions. India had never produced anyone as multifaceted as Gandhi to take on the professors of Abrahamism. He alternated between good and evil and, like an expert driver, changed gears to negotiate the way ahead smoothly.

And, above all, despite having an amazing capacity to argue and tie up the enemy in verbal knots, he was never proud to have been educated as a lawyer. 'Practice as a lawyer was and remained for me a subordinate occupation', he wrote in *My Experiments with Truth*. Little wonder that he did not apparently believe in the alleged sanctity of man-made law, any law, and was, therefore, able to use, circumvent or challenge it, find loopholes and exit routes in it when he actually began the Battle of the Indian Mind as a mass psychiatrist out to cure his people of their multiple inherited ailments. He could challenge the British laws with as much ease as he did in case of the *Manusmriti*. His source of strength lay in his amazing capacity to read the human mind and size up individuals and issues, and his real university was

Nature, not those brick-and-mortar graveyards of the mind. He was among those rare Hindus who never go to a temple, never worship at home, but are still viewed as saints and formidable social reformers and revolutionaries. Gandhi bloomed like a lotus in the Hindu reservoir whose water had remained calm and stinking for a millennium.

That the Hindus should unshackle themselves from the outdated notions of Abrahamic superiority or their own inferiority and, at the same time, shake off the chains they had tied themselves into, was his unmistakable message. Like Adi Shankaracharya in the *Gita*, Gandhi, too, left enough hints for those who could really understand, in *My Experiments with Truth*, published in 1927 when he was barely 58 and had two more tempestuous decades to go; he closed the book with the events of 1920s when his most important works were ***yet*** to begin! He did not even update and revise the book. Few could have such an extraordinary control over their own mind, pen and the tongue and the will to resist the temptation to become immortal. Why did he leave it half-finished, merely by saying that his post-1927 life was an 'open book', a public knowledge, that need not be written about? Perhaps because the forces he helped shape and unleash in the early 1920s, he probably knew, were inexorably leading to the creation of what would become Pakistan, the most important event of his life, and of India in the last 1,000 years. How could he reveal the truth behind his many silences to abort it midway by writing about his foot-soldiers, the aim being winning the War and not court-martialling the soldier that could distract others. Already, both Christianity and Islam abhorred this reawakening of the sleeping giant of Hindu India; that they now apprehended an India slipping out of their hands was obvious but Nature had arranged human pawns and nations in such places and kept moving them so deftly, globally, that nothing could be done to prevent the inexorable arrival of the enigmatic 1947; Gandhi was the man of this hour, this millennium. The Soul of India, the sum total of India's cultural response to Abrahamism since Jesus.

He was viewed by many a British as a comic cipher, or, at best, as a cunning politician; from him emerged infinity. All Indian history would now be either pre-Gandhi or post-Gandhi as he stood at every corner across India, even abroad, surveying the Grand March of History, the way Jesus and Muhammed did in respect of the societies they left behind—Gandhi was the delayed Hindu response to the Son of God and the Last Prophet. He was the logical and national culmination of the Hindus' unifying and 'connecting' movements such as the Brahmo Samaj and Arya Samaj at local levels and much more than all these put together; it was in him that an incredible India fully flowered. He was the product of India between Muhammad Ghori and Mountbatten, *the* representative personalities of those 1,000 years. Without studying Gandhi, we would never know India nor how she rid herself of alien chains, the 'religions' that sought to unhinge her polytheistic culture; without knowing the Mahatma, we would not know how India chased away her ancient ghosts and evolved while still drawing sustenance from retreating Christianity and Islam. Gandhi and the Ganges went together; unlike Nehru's dynasty, the Mahatma's descendants mostly remained low-key, as if consumed by the Holy River.

He alone understood survival tactics of fanatic Christians and Muslims in alien lands: whatever their in-house battles against each other, all shades of European Christians had united in the Scramble and loot of Africa and China in the 19th and 20th centuries. Similarly, the Christian Britons had joined hands with the Muslims in setting up the Aligarh Movement, dividing Bengal in 1905 and creating the Muslim League in 1906—giving rise to the Muslim hope that they would regain their Mughal Empire, lost in 1857, if and when the British left, particularly due to the First World War. Clearly, putting aside their market-share dialectics, the Abrahamic Sector of world politics—Judaism, Christianity and Islam—had the potential to unite against the re-emergence of non-Abrahamic competitors like China, Japan or India, whom they perceived as their common *infidel* enemy. When it came to common enemy like the Hindus or Chinese, even the Crusaders and the Jihadis could join hands; but they could scarcely do anything. That was how Abrahamism survived all odds. Gandhi had a first-hand experience of this the way we now know why a 'democratic' Christian America supports a 'dictatorial' Muslim Pakistan vis-à-vis India, or China. A realistic China understands this global politics; India pretends not to.

Gandhi was a rare raw genius who did.

Although not as brilliant as he was, he had the support from a pageant of leaders that India produced in his era in different fields. Gandhi arrived on the Indian scene in 1915 but more important than him, at that time, was Rabindranath Tagore. After Vivekanand squaring off with invading religions in the 1890s, Tagore had squared off with the invading Western and Middle Eastern literature, with the 1913 Nobel Prize. He was thus the first Asian, Black, Non-European-Non-American, Non-Christian, Non-Muslim, Non-Jewish, Colonial, and, above all, Infidel, to be in the 'august' company of those stiff jaws. Tagore unshackled Hindu Word from the Abrahamic Word, just as Gandhi would decouple the Hindu Mind from the 'Abrahamic Mind'. The defeatist mindsets bequeathed by the Christian and Muslim colonisers to infidel Afro-Asian cultures were waning and their strengths in the global anti-colonial movements rising. With Tagore and Gandhi, Chandrashekhar Venkat Raman completed the trinity with his 1930 Nobel Prize in Physics: 'Monochromatic light, having a single wave-length, scatters when it passes through a transparent substance', was the essence of the Raman Effect. Imagine Christianity and Islam as the monotheistic lights, having a single Prophetic wave-length, scattering in a transparent India! Each of the two Nobel Prizes re-ignited a million Hindu minds; although the Nobel Prizes were not exactly the mark of nobility, India had to use this foreign vaccine against foreign virus. Jagadish Chandra Bose, on the other hand, had scientifically proved the ancient Indian eco-sensitive wisdom that even plants had similar sensations, life and responses as animals; and Satyendra Nath Bose would eventually co-father, posthumously, the Higgs-Boson Particle, or 'God's Particle' in the 21st century. The Hindu mind was undergoing a slow, sure and total transformation when that new Chanakya, Gandhi, arrived to play a no-holds-barred gamble. Until him, politics merely meant the Hindu *response* to the Muslim or Christian initiatives; Gandhi took the political *initiative*, like Chanakya, foxed both the British and the Muslims, and before they realised what he was up to, their Game was up.

The much-trumpeted British policy of divide-and-rule, of sowing seeds of hatred between the Hindus and Muslims, was, at best, a peripheral issue as all imperial and colonial powers would indulge in this time-tested policy anywhere in the world; of course, the British were less brutish and less barbarian and, unlike other European colonial powers, they did every dirty work 'legally'. This made the task of the Hindus relatively easier—Gandhi would not, perhaps, have succeeded against his contemporary Hitler or Stalin had they been the colonial power in India—they were biped monsters trapped in human skin. He knew the British were, perhaps, the laziest imperialists in history—that was why they 'invented' an idlers' game like cricket to kill time, a game they could play endlessly for days together, at leisure and without bothering about actual victory or defeat; a lazy, chaotic India, teeming with millions of nincompoops, was a perfect match for this zero-sum game, host as this Hindu 'nation' already was to the 430-odd inanities called 'rituals'. A grateful compost component of India would lap cricket up with the zeal of a neophyte until politicians and actors realised its business potential and pimped for it full blast in the 21st century. The British would leave India in 1947 as if returning after a cricket match!

Without a British preference for an 'amiable' Gandhi over the more 'extremist' Tilak school and the armed revolutionaries, London would not have succeeded in getting its exit ticket from Delhi. Gandhi, therefore, made himself acceptable to the British as much as to the Hindus and, for a time, the Muslims; because this was the only way he could eventually isolate the fanatic Muslims. The Hindus trusted him because they felt he was strong; the Muslim fundamentalists, at least till he squeezed them like lemon, believed in him because they thought he was the softest stupid *they* could squeeze at will; many Britons 'trusted' him because they believed his 'non-violent' ways were a guarantee for prolonging their stay in India. By thus making himself indispensable, he was able to dispense with both the British and the Muslim separatists.

Here was a man who, as a *political* successor to Vivekanand, Tagore and Raman, was emerging like a Sun after the shadows of night began receding. Although the Partition of Bengal had ended, it apparently charged up some among the Hindus about the much larger issue that raged in the Hindu minds for the next 100 years: for instance, the ordinary Hindu, conscious of Muslim terrorism in 2017, would ask himself 'If 150 million Muslims *in* India, vis-a-vis 900 million Hindus, could be the way they are, what would have happened had India remained undivided, with 450 million Muslims, in such a "united" subcontinent!' Gandhi had no love lost for the Christians or Muslim fanatics either but since he could not just wish them away, he had to play hard ball with them. He had seen enough of them back in Gujarat and then in England and South Africa. He studiously refrained from saying anything against the Muslims, however. In his autobiography and elsewhere, time and again, he merely referred to how he '**swallowed the poison**' or '**pocketed the insult**' on difficult occasions which demonstrated his extremely intense struggle to control himself, keep his cool and move in his chosen direction come what may. He was a consummate, practical politician, not really the saint his cronies believed, who did so aiming to achieve larger goals: he was a Chanakya attired as a Mahatma, the fulfilment of Adi Shankaracharya's Krishnaite Sermon in the *Gita*. For him, liberation of India from the Abrahamic yoke was his religious calling. Gandhi was a revolution India was waiting to happen; it was in his Matrix that Modern India took shape.

Many of his critics mocked him as a charlatan—they actually saw their own mirror image in him! Most of his devotees viewed him to be a Great Soul. Few, however, thought his life as an inevitable evolution of the Indian psyche, the consummation of the *Body Indique*, who could have been born and succeeded only in Brand India; as a man, he was extremely common but as a phenomenon he was extraordinary. His mental mathematics and thought processes, like those of Einstein, were extraordinarily complicated and his moves so subtle as to appear innocent long after he had ended the game; like Einstein, he would use the back-of-envelopes for his 'equations'. With a single-mindedness, he worked against alien civilisations, religions and communities, political philosophies and social patterns, economic upheavals and cultural dynamics on a global chess-board with as much aplomb as Bismarck played with five European nations to unify Germany. Gandhi was born in the year Bismarck was preparing for the decisive Franco-Prussian War (1869) that would make Germany one nation after hundreds of years of disunity, and pave the way for the Third Reich forcing the Diaspora Jews out of Europe in a diabolical human metabolism; he died in the year Israel was reborn (1948).

Born on 2 October 1869, at Porbandar, 130 km from Somnath Temple in Gujarat, he felt that, in the end, he was going to sacrifice his life for India. 'But I should certainly like to narrate my experiments in the spiritual field which are *known only to myself*, and from which I have derived such power as I possess for working in the political field... *What I want to achieve*,—what I have been striving and pining to achieve these 30 years,—is self-realisation, to see God face to face, to achieve Moksha (salvation). I live and move and have my being in pursuit of this goal. All that I do by way of speaking and writing, and all my ventures in the political field, are directed to this same end...I am prepared to sacrifice the things dearest to me in pursuit of this quest. *Even if the sacrifice demanded be my very life, I may be prepared to give it.*' Was it a death-wish for a cause? Unlike other leaders, he shoved himself into the fire so that India could rise like a Phoenix; not for nothing had he christened his Ashram near Durban, South Africa, after this mythological bird. As the first Hindu 'Mujahid', highly-motivated, self-indoctrinated, extremely patient and secretive about his plans, he outwardly appeared calm like an ocean but inside he harboured many a hidden volcano and earthquake that triggered giant tidal waves few knew about. In South Africa and Great Britain, his westernisation and Briton-like attire protected him; in India, he used his loin-cloth like the soldier's sandbag to duck behind after throwing grenades at the enemy. He knew many a people could be influenced by external paraphernalia and attires. So, as a lawyer, he ducked behind his British attire in South Africa; in India, where holy men were seen beyond reproach, he turned a 'Mahatma'. And he used *ahimsa* much the same way Arjuna had used the eunuch Shikhandi to protect himself from the attacks of Bheeshma Pitamah, in the epic *Mahabharata* War, before slaying the Patriarch. A consummate politician-diplomat, he had the rarest of the rare capacity to force his friends and foes alike toe *his* line merely by threatening to harm *himself* and they buckled each time because, weak-kneed, they did not want to harm a 'Mahatma' who protected his warehouses brimming with stuff largely seen in hard politics and the rough-and-tumble of practical human life at micro-level as unusable and termite-eaten—truth, non-violence, peace, love etc. His numerous fasts hardly had any effect on his own health because, like Jain saints, he had learnt to live without stomach—on the contrary, each fast made his resolve steelier and his will-power only stronger, the way each failure as well as success makes the contemporary Muslim terrorist more fanatic. No other man in the Occident or the Orient more effectively used these utopian weapons of ethics to attain practical ends in politics; like Hitler and other dictators, he evoked strong emotions among the people—he himself had strong likes and dislikes and had fierce 'friends' (or, better, disciples of his strange political cult) and 'foes' (idiots who thought they were using him while, in fact, he was using them). That he was not what he portrayed himself to be was apparent when, while selling democracy and basic education etc, he remained a dictator on the domestic front, imposed his iron will on his wife and sons.

He had learnt the difficult art of remaining silent and transformed this weakness into his biggest strength; he would observe *Mondays* as silent days for a purpose, as we would see. Under the heading 'Shyness My Shield' in his *Experiments*, he said: 'This shyness I retained throughout my stay in England. Even when I paid a social call, the presence of half a dozen or more people would strike me dumb....My hesitancy in speech, which was once an annoyance, is now a pleasure. Its greatest benefit has been that it has taught me the economy of words. I have naturally formed the habit of restraining my thoughts. *And I can now give myself the certificate that a thoughtless word hardly ever escapes my tongue or pen. I do not recollect ever having had to regret anything in my speech or writing*. I have thus been spared many a mishap and waste of time.' (Italics mine).

Remember these words: they will help us fathom Gandhi.

No wonder, millions admired and hated, read, wrote and spoke about or against him but very few really understood Gandhi. What he said was less important than what he left unsaid but casually dropped broad hints about. He cultivated these 'saintly' and diplomatic qualities to make others open up before him while he closed in on them. For him, freedom of India was a spiritual bliss and quest.

The young Mohandas, the last of the offspring of Karamchand—one daughter and three sons—was most influenced by two Hindu mythological characters. He wanted to be as truthful as King Harish Chandra and as dedicated a son as Sravan Kumar; he was a dedicated son but his 'truthfulness', later, remained, at best, strategic. Like his contemporary Hitler emulating the German mythological character Wotan all his life and dying like his hero, Gandhi, too, found solace in Harish Chandra and Sravan Kumar, his psychology of sacrificing his family for his beliefs, and get killed in the process, shaped by these two characters in his formative years. At school, he was an ordinary student with an atrocious hand-writing ('bad handwriting...a sign of an imperfect education'), which remained so infamous and easily identifiable that his 'treacherous' draft of a letter to the Afghan Amir during the First World War became instantly known to many people. His Sanskrit teacher persuaded him to learn the ancient language: 'Every Hindu boy and girl should possess sound Sanskrit learning.'

Married at 13 with Kastur, he worshipped his father like god and served him like a dedicated nurse. His indulgence in sex with his pregnant wife at the time of such a revered father's death psychologically affected him for some time, particularly after his newly-born first baby, too, died within four days. It was this extreme sense of loss of near and dear ones in quick succession that played a vital role in driving Muhammed to prophethood in the seventh century. The sense of this double-loss devastated Mohandas as well, as he cited in his *Experiments*. This only added to his missionary zeal as a panacea or recompense to the losses he suffered. His apparent split personality grew with age, particularly in South Africa, and fully blossomed when he returned to India in 1915 as the ultimate mixture of opposites. Like the hero Neo in the Hollywood film *The Matrix*, he could easily weave in one breath war as well as peace in a seamless whole and still retain the mantle of the Apostle of Peace—exactly like Moses, Jesus and Muhammed. Gandhism was, therefore, destined to be the warriors' peace!

Although he advocated truth and non-violence, but, being a practical Gujarati, he also knew that many others, particularly in the ruling class, would hardly subscribe to these themes which would not normally attract the non-Hindus with proclivities to violence. Therefore, while dealing with them, he carefully used these themes like the two-piece shield of the tortoise in which he would instantly turn cautious and duck when in the slightest trouble; silence was his third weapon. His experiences in formative years were very important to shape his future personality: 'I saw that *a man of truth must also be a man of care*.' A Christian class-mate in high school made this Hindu Vaishya boy secretly turn to non-vegetarianism for a time to become a 'strong' man physically. Why did the adolescent Gandhi want to become physically so strong? Marvelling at the power of the British, the young impressionable mind felt that 'if the whole country took to meat-eating, the English could be overcome...I wished to be strong and daring and wanted my countrymen also to be such, so that we might defeat the English and make India free.' *Clearly, the boy was shaping himself up to take on the British even at an early age and would do everything*, including eating meat, that is crossing over one of the most important Hindu Vaishya threshold of vegetarianism, to achieve this end; thereafter, when he hit the streets, only his strategy differed, not the aims and objectives, and he shaped himself up first as a lawyer, social activist and finally as a 'Mahatma' to achieve his aim—he would even declare himself a loyal subject, a 'British citizen' whenever necessary! Ironically, he had also taken to meat-eating with a view to 'reform' his friend and later learnt it the hard way that a bad company could ruin him. The episode demonstrated the level of his *self-motivation* and *radicalisation* with a certain aim.

A vegetarian Vaishya boy who could secretly turn to even eating meat and thus outgrow the Hindu religious borders by resorting to such patently irreligious step just to fulfil his ambition of expelling the British would, when matured in an ocean of politics, have no qualms in masterminding the expulsion of Islam and Christianity that had 'enslaved' India for a thousand years. He was brought up in the best possible Christian way for a traditional Hindu family: schooled at Alfred School, Rajkot, and educated at the Bar in London; therefore he understood Christianity better than Islam.

Only, he would criticise Christianity openly because the British were relatively more tolerant; later, he would plot against Islam but secretly because many of the Muslims were intolerant. He attacked Christianity, while praising Jesus; it was like attacking the shopkeeper for higher price while praising the product it sold! Like praising Bill Gates but attacking Microsoft for 'monopoly', even while using the Windows! Clearly, Gandhi's praise of Jesus was strategic, to win support in the West; he knew the British were, in any case, deChristianising—Bertrand Russell would even declare, in 1927, *Why I Am Not A Christian*—and attacks on Christianity meant little to these businessmen who thought even Jesus was a tradable commodity, as they did in Africa by trading the Bible for the land and mines. In the case of Islam, however, his strategy was different: he supported Indian Muslims to the hilt—while tactically ignoring their fanatic fringe's barbaric instincts such as in the Moplah massacre case of the early 1920s—with the aim of 'leveraging' this 'minorityism' for triggering a never-before Hindu reaction elsewhere and consolidation and eventual backlash that led to the amputation of 1947. The first defining moment was his father's death and the guilt associated with it; the second bout was when he crossed the borders of Hindu Vaishnavite beliefs in Gujarat by eating meat: he now knew how missionaries of Christianity—and Islam—had mostly expanded in India and converted the Hindus, through force, fraud, and allurement.

And, at an early age, with these episodes in his early life embedded deep in his mind, he had come to view Christianity in its true colours: 'Only Christianity was *at the time* an exception. I developed a sort of *dislike* for it. And for a reason. In those days, Christian missionaries used to stand in a corner near the high school and hold forth, pouring abuse on Hindus and their gods. I could not endure this...I heard of a well-known Hindu having been converted to Christianity. It was the talk of the town that, when he was baptised, he had to *eat beef* and drink liquor, that he also had to change his clothes, and that thenceforth he began to go about in European costumes, including a hat. These things got on my nerves. Surely, thought I, a religion that *compelled* one to eat beef, drink liquor, and change one's own clothes did not deserve the name. I also heard that the new convert had already begun *abusing* the religion of his ancestors, their customs and their country. All these things created in me a dislike for Christianity.'

The mature Gandhi had to deal with this *very* Christianity on its own turf, and its sisterly Islam, which had honed these 'skills' over the last 2,000 years; no wonder, the Mahatma discovered that the cesspool he wanted to clean up was much larger in size, much deeper than he thought, much awfully smelling, and he had to tread his way extremely slowly through these labyrinthine underground drainage system. If only to survive, he would have to become a modern fox in this jungle full of medieval foxes.

The boy had begun to understand how Christianity sought to uproot humans from their native culture and traditions and make them go on pilgrimage to Rome and Jerusalem as their new spiritual abodes; his experience of Christianity denationalising those it converted in India were to magnify later and equip him with an understanding of the finer nuances of British and European, denominational Christian, and finally world politics and the Islamic abracadabra which others failed to spot due to the multiple blindfolds they wore or total ignorance about alien religions, their aims and their tactics.

At school, he abhorred mathematics until he read *Euclid's 13th Proposition*: 'If a straight line stands on a straight line, then it makes either two right angles or angles whose sum equals to two right angles.' Later, he apparently applied it to his struggle *for* India. The horizontal, straight-lined India had the Christians and Muslims as the two sides of the same line standing on it and whatever angle it stood on, the sum total would remain equal to two right angles! The angularity was unacceptable to him—all struggles between Christianity and Islam *in India* were going to lead to only two right angles, 180-degress, one of them winning now and losing then. In any case, the ultimate losers would, of course, be the Hindus. That is, any regime headed by these two religions in India was unacceptable. Once Gandhi understood this Proposition at school, 'the utter simplicity of the subject was suddenly revealed to me. A subject which only required a pure and simple use of one's reasoning powers could not be difficult. Ever since that time geometry has been both easy and interesting to me.' And geopolitics afterwards. For a time, when he regretted having taken to smoking and stealing, too, he plotted even to commit suicide but gave up the idea. 'And since then, whenever I have heard of someone threatening to commit suicide, it has had little or no effect on me.' In fact, he would drive such people, and communities, to *harakiri*, and he did so meticulously in the case of fanatic Muslims. A dichotomy of mind in which one having a death-wish at one stage would manage to survive himself but drag others to it later on! But, at the same time, he was able to force the British to release him prematurely whenever he undertook fast in jail; he used his famous fasts to slow down the enemies, both within the Congress and without.

Being a Vaishnavite Hindu, he was almost a Jain in following the principle of *ahimsa* (non-violence), the corner-stone of Gandhiana. Few, however, understood the finer nuances of the dynamics of non-violence that he followed and mistook him to be flogging the long-dead horse of the *ahimsa*. The concept of non-violence, over the ages, had itself undergone a sea-change and evolved by the time of Gandhi. Only the uneducated believe that non-violence must be *absolute and unconditional*. Now, for many of the Jains themselves, as the venerable Jain saint the late Acharya Mahapragya told this author in 2003, violence is seen to be *conditional, relativistic* and of three categories: (1) Occupational, as in the case of a butcher, which cannot be avoided unless he is given another livelihood; (2) Defensive, in which the soldier's violence is a categorical imperative like vaccination because, without using this violence, he would not be able to defend the peaceful nation from invasion of violence from across the borders and (3) Intentional violence, to harm others deliberately. Gandhi tried to introduce reforms to reduce the first category of violence through the removal of untouchability, actively promoted the second category either as a nurse (as in the Boer War in South Africa), as a recruiter of soldiers (in the First World War) and as a manipulator to get concessions from the British (in the Second World War) and, thirdly, as one asking the Indian soldiers to throw out the Pakistani intruders in Kashmir in 1947. His non-violence was a dynamic and virile concept, not a static and sterile one, which meant the right to defend oneself was inalienable. He deftly extended this concept as part of his overall political strategy and allowed the fanatic Muslims to expose themselves as violent people; this strategy sparked reaction amongst the Hindus so that exit of Islam and creation of Pakistan could be justified.

The socio-religious extremism of *Manusmriti*—that actually shielded the *core* of Hinduism from alien assaults until the *Gita* came—also, however, put him off, indeed making him almost a non-practising Hindu, although he himself may have failed to see the logic behind the Manusmriti's pyramidal social engineering as a means to defend Hinduism. But he had high regard for the *Ramayana* of Tulsidas and his dream of India was to create a Ram Rajya (The Reign of Ram), an ideal, utopian nation. He left it unsaid that this Ram Rajya could not be established unless the arch-foe of the Lord, Ravana, the evil genius Demon King, was vanquished but, by actively propagating Rama, he influenced the people to identify who the contemporary Ravana (s) were!

When he matriculated in 1887, his middle class family sent him to England for further education, infuriating the orthodox Modh Vaishya community enough to excommunicate him for being the first one from the caste to cross the ocean and live among the *mlechchhas* ('unclean' people, with whom a caste Hindu would not eat or marry). He was expelled from the caste and he would later work to expel the caste system itself! As a lawyer, he learnt that 'One golden rule is to accept the interpretation honestly put on the pledge by the party administering it. Another is to accept the interpretation of the *weaker party*, where there are two interpretations possible.' No wonder he followed the latter when he would support the *minority* British liberals and anticolonialists in the 1890s, the *minority* 'Moderates' of the Gokhale School in the Congress in the 1910s, the *minority* Khadi-spinning, peace-grazing Congressmen during nationwide armed resistance in the 1920s and 1930s, the *minority* Nehruvians against the majority Bose supporters in 1938, the *minority* anti-Pakistan Muslims in the 1940s, and, finally, the *minority* choice Nehru over the majority choice Patel for the premiership in 1947—with his ultimate threat to go to Pakistan to support the remaining 'minority' Hindus after 1947! He was a rare agitator who knew that by actively supporting the minority, the *desired* majority could be created at the other end of the spectrum. It was Archimedes' principle of using a small lever to lift a great weight; in Newtonian physics, this came to be known as 'action at a distance'; in investment banking parlance, post-2008 global meltdown, it became known as derivatives, 'toxic assets' or 'leveraging', using a small investment to build a huge asset, even if as an albatross around your neck! He may have drawn this inspiration from the *Mahabharata*'s Barbarik, grandson of Bheem, who had the power to support the weaker side, alternately, until both were decimated! Gandhi, therefore, 'supported' both Christianity as well as Islam.

Why? He was not a self-seeking politician who would try to create a majority so that *he* could come to power; he was a statesman and diplomat who, like a prophet-on-the-mission, wanted to create a majority for *his* people and their future generations, not himself. Making the Hindus trust him because of his loin-cloth, he was able to support the minorities to the hilt. He knew that directly supporting a minority on emotional issues creates a far wider but indirect majority support towards your ultimate end; see how the minority 'secular' Hindus, simply by opposing the Hindu 'fundamentalists', empowered the majority Hindutva in India since the 1990s! No wonder, Gandhi could see through the minority Christianity and Islam in India so fully and create the Hindu majority simply by nursing the pregnant minorities. Politics is, after all, like billiards in which you aim at a ball by hitting it by another...and Gandhi played these on a Chess Board, where he could stop the rolling ball at will and in the square he chose. And, he knew what Archimedes had said: 'Give me a lever and a place to stand and I will move the earth.' Therefore, he occupied the minimum space on the political firmament and, manipulating boastful leaders, achieved the maximum results.

Why did Gandhi do so? He, like many, was aware that he could not defeat the contemporary British weaponry; the moribund Hindu society, even after surviving Abrahamism, lagged a dozen generations behind Christianity and Islam. The Mahatma's task was to upload the artificial satellite onto a bullock cart to take it to its launching station—the way parts of the first satellite project of Indian space programme were actually transported on bicycles and bullock carts in the 1960s in Kerala. Therefore, Gandhi had to become a warrior of the mind rather than warrior of the muscle. He would play Christianity and Islam against each other in a highly subtle manner and defeat them at their own, old game—they had a common goal, were united in their scramble for India, just like the rival European nations and different Christian denominations were united in the scramble for contemporary sub-Saharan Africa where he had a first-hand experience and cut political teeth, or in the contemporary China, Japan and South-East Asia where the same colonial, Abrahamic brotherhood of European exploiters was at display. Christianity and Islam may have been mortal enemies for a thousand years and a half, but their ultimate goal in India, indeed in the whole infidel world, was the same: competitive conversion of the Hindus and others. So, Gandhi chose to be a unique customer who would make the rival shopkeepers fight it out amongst themselves! Many amongst the Hindu converts to these religions had been denationalised who damaged the very idea of a pluralist India and, in order to revive it, he had to negotiate through the treacherous Abrahamic maze. 'A convert's enthusiasm for his new religion is greater than that of a person who is born in it', he wrote because he knew the post-1857 activities of Christian missionaries and the post-Deoband Muslim parallel that were eating at the very vitals of India, its polytheism, its multiculturalism—that a convert to these religions could not be trustworthy because his absolute article of faith, his frame of reference, was *not* in India, unlike the Hindus'; and he could not be blamed because he would only do what his religion expected him to do, his soul-calling. Gandhi wrote about what he felt of Christianity because some of the conscientious and liberal Christians, already deChristianised at different stages, could read, reflect and agree with him; he did not write as much about Islam because of the fanatic and illiberal character its fundamentalists had come to acquire; they needed to be handled carefully before surgically removing the enlarging tumour.

The British, indeed all European colonisers, had fattened themselves through breed, creed and greed. He knew the British inside-out, that they were, at best, guests in the Indian motel who would one day check-out; but the Muslim fanatics had become encroachers, claiming India as their ancestral property. Indeed, the most famous slogan of fanatic Muslims in Pakistan has been: *Hans ke liya hai Pakistan, Ladke lenge Hindustan* (We laughed our way to Pakistan, we would fight our way into Hindustan). Many among the Muslims, who generally enjoyed the status of the 'ruling class' and cornered power and pelf until 1857, were peeved at the loss of the Mughal Empire because of this very reason; that the post-1857 British slowly cultivated the Muslims first as partners, then as collaborators and finally as Partitioners was understood only by a few—and they included Gandhi. 'Jinnah, My Brother', he would gently try to make the *Muslim* leader see the 'sense', presenting himself as more and more vulnerable, making the fellow Gujarati-Sindhi more and more recalcitrant and adamant at getting Pakistan. For, Gandhi may have felt he could persuade Jinnah, and whet his appetite, to demand Pakistan ***only*** by patiently and persistently 'rejecting' the demand: 'over my body', the chief Brahmin priest at Somnath Temple was said to have cried before Mehmood Ghaznavi and the marauder had simply walked over his body, and the corpses of hundreds of others. Gandhi understood the typical fanatic Muslim character in an infidel land: if you are humble, he would think you are a fool he could fleece; you hammer him, he would instantly become 'secular' and 'democratic', and regroup, Taliban-like, if and when you look away—the post-1947 Indian administrators and police have known this peculiar Muslim streak and enrolled the community's most violent faces on the 'peace committee' formed after communal riots in the towns and cities as a temporary measure. Gandhi knew that only by being humble could he whet the Muslim appetite and he used this cultivated art to the fullest. Abrahamism was a glass-house and Gandhi had to dismantle it without breaking it! He, therefore, improvised at each step and played the emerging circumstances so subtly that the British were forced to return to Britain and Muslims had to declare themselves as a 'separate nation' and decamp with Pakistan. He did it all by merely supporting the *minority-of-the-day*. Never was a lawyer so unsuccessful in professional life and just the opposite globally! To generate Hindu anger, he supported the Muslims to the hilt—even promising Jinnah the Prime Ministership after Independence but the wily Muslim leader, *finally*, saw through the Mahatma's game-plan knowing well he could not last even a single day in this hot seat and would end up with egg in the face; but even he did what the Mahatma expected him to do, demand Pakistan with renewed vigour! Gandhi was in a win-win position and Jinnah in Catch-22; like a cuckoo, Gandhi had the crow nurse his eggs.

While in England, Gandhi read Sir Edwin Arnold's translation of the *Gita*, 'the best book on metaphysics and spirituality'. In Manchester, a priest wanted him to read the *Bible*. 'I began reading it but I could not possibly read through the *Old Testament*. I read the *Book of Genesis*, and the chapters that followed invariably sent me to sleep. But just for the sake of being able to say that I had read it, I plodded through the other books with much difficulty and without the least interest or understanding. I disliked reading the *Book of Numbers*.' But he liked the Buddhist 'Sermon on the Mount' and Arnold's book on Buddhism. In Thomas Carlyle's *Heroes and Hero-Worship*, 'I read the chapter on the Hero and learnt of the Prophet's greatness and bravery and austere living. Beyond this acquaintance with religion, I could not go at the moment.' From atheism, however, he was back to theism, but not the kind of monotheism of the Abrahamic brand. At 20, his last year in England (1890), he witnessed the contrast of Christianity in Paris. 'I had read a lot about the fashions and frivolity of Paris. These were in evidence in every street but the Churches stood noticeably apart from these scenes.'

Returning to India in June 1891, he was influenced by Leo Tolstoy's *Paradise in Your Heart* and John Ruskin's *Unto This Last*. He tried to establish himself as a lawyer but failed for what he said was his adherence to principles of ethics, truthfulness and honesty, which are sometimes seen as weaknesses in that profession; a successful lawyer was supposed to be the one who shuns all this 'nonsense'. But, his education as a lawyer made him value facts. He was extremely careful about facts and consciously cultivated the art of impressive letter-drafting. After his initial experiments in Rajkot and Mumbai to eke out a living, he was hired by a fellow Gujarati Muslim businessman in South Africa, where he went in April 1893 for a year but would return two decades later. Africa became the incubator of this emerging political start up entrepreneur looking for 'angel investors'.

Stay in South Africa became his test driving, a trial balloon, for what Gandhi was to achieve back in India; his travels between India and South Africa gave him an opportunity to study the chessboard divided into 64 black and white squares, how these pieces moved only on their respective colour and took those in the rival camp. This gave him a clarity of thought: novices believe they have 64 squares, but the wise men knew they had only 32; and even in these, the maximum, eight, were mere pawns who could only move in one direction—forward—although they could kill sideways as a collateral advantage-cum-damage; the Rooks, the Bishops and the Knights, and even the Queen, were all there to shelter and protect the King. So, the whole system, in each walk of life, was the army of the King who, when in the centre of this chessboard, was the most potent and mobile piece; only when cornered, could you check and checkmate the King. But, even the King was a mere pawn of his religion. Gandhi's biggest asset was his critical and comparative study of religions, particularly Christianity and Islam—the revival of India that he inaugurated was, therefore, to be religion-centric, and, in an era of Indian brand of minority-servicing, majority-bashing 'secularism' financed, sponsored and supported by the ruling class, he actively evolved the 'spiritual' angle of politics. He knew that the misfortune that visited India was the after-effect of these alien religious armies: his father had been the *Diwan* (Prime Minister) of three royal houses successively in Gujarat and he knew a mere change of government did not mean the change of the people's fortune. One exploitative system replaced another. India could no longer progress unless these very systems were uprooted. Comprehensively. This could not be done by any worldly leader; in India, this could be achieved only by a 'saint', and he shaped himself up as one. So much so that the Christian missionaries continued their efforts to convert him knowing not he would, in fact, overthrow the British; so much so that the fanatic Muslims, despite seeing through his game, did not know that more than a weakling Pakistan along the Indus, they were creating a much stronger 'Hindustan' in India along the Ganges; so much so that the Hindus, ever-confused, fanatically believed in what he said without understanding what he achieved. He wore loin-cloth because it was his ultimate fortress; even those, like Nehru and Patel, who understood some of his politics, could do nothing but help him as the numbers were with this man seen as a cipher by the arrogant British like Churchill and Muslims like Jinnah. Churchill would even talk of 'eliminating' the Mahatma! Because Gandhi was paying Church-ill in his own coin!

His first host in South Africa, Abdullah Sheth '...was by nature suspicious... He was proud of Islam and loved to discourse on Islamic philosophy. Though he did not know Arabic, his acquaintance with the Holy Koran and Islamic literature in general was fairly good. Illustrations he had in plenty, always ready at hand. Contact with him gave me a fair amount of the *practical knowledge* of Islam.' This name, Abdullah, would annoy Gandhi no end until his last years. Having already experienced Christianity, he was now experiencing Islam; but something of more immediate importance churned his mind. European racism and apartheid in South Africa gave him an opportunity to tackle first things first and emerge as leader of the Indian 'coolie' community, and even the Blacks, in a country as notorious for Western and Christian social leprosy as for its gold and diamond mines. Initially, Gandhi unsuccessfully tried to distance himself from the Blacks and get closer to the Whites by emulating the latter in attire. After being famously thrown out of a train due to the colour of his skin, however, he dissected all kinds of discriminations everywhere—even if he had not been thrown out of the train, he would have perhaps plotted to throw the British out of India as he had started preparation for it much before going abroad. 'The hardship to which I was subjected was superficial—only a symptom of the deep disease of colour prejudice. I should try, if possible, to root out the disease and suffer hardships in the process.' If it was the apartheid of colour in South Africa, it was the apartheid of religion back in his native India where the Christians looked down upon the Hindus and Muslims, the Muslims hated the Hindus, the Hindus hated each other and, when tired, even hated the lower castes which, in turn, hated the tribal. In Pretoria, a fundamentalist priest, A W Baker, also tried to convert him, again: 'He upholds the excellence of Christianity from various points of view and contends that it is impossible to find peace, unless one accepts Jesus as the only son of God and the Saviour of mankind.' Some other Christians tried to lure him into their faith while denouncing Hinduism: 'If this be the Christianity acknowledged by all Christians, I cannot accept it. I do not seek redemption from the consequences of my sin. I seek to be redeemed from sin itself, or rather from the very thought of sin. *Until I have attained that end, I shall be content to be restless.*' Later, the still-hopeful Christian missionaries in India tried to persuade him to become yet another St Francis Xavier but he did not want to restrict himself to the tiny Portuguese colony of Goa! And, like Christianity, Islam, too, was, by extension, not useful, both being members of the same Abrahamic Family.

Abdullah Sheth, like some other Muslims, particularly the Memons, thought that their faith was one thing and business altogether another and different thing. True to the old Abrahamic stress on faith being more important than conduct, it was logical for them to find no relationship between the two. His legal activities funnelled Gandhi into socio-political field as well, particularly in Transvaal and Orange Free State and he was irresistibly drawn into public life, thanks to the time he had at hand due to his financial failure in legal profession. Only a 'k' separates money from monkey: money turns us into an evolved monkey; money-freed, we can plan higher, humanly aims, as it were! The Christian missionaries wanted this emerging socially-active youth to be brought into their fold and took him to a religious congregation. 'Mr Baker was getting anxious about my future…the Protestant Christians organise such gatherings every few years for religious enlightenment or, in other words, self-purification. One may call this religious restoration or revival. Mr Baker had hoped that it… would inevitably lead me to embrace Christianity…It was impossible for me to believe that I could go to heaven or attain salvation only by becoming a Christian. When I frankly said so to some of the good Christian friends, they were shocked. But there was no help for it… My difficulties lay deeper. It was more than I could believe that Jesus was the only incarnate Son of God, and that only he who believed in him would have everlasting life. If God could have sons, all of us were His sons. If Jesus was like God, or God Himself, then all men were like God and could be God. My reason was not ready to believe literally that Jesus by his death and by his blood redeemed the sins of the world…According to Christianity only human beings had souls, and not other living beings, for whom death meant complete extinction; while I held a contrary belief.'

How could a man who did not agree that Jesus was the *only* Son of God, could ever believe that Muhammed was His *last* Messenger? Clearly, Gandhi, as he himself admitted, would carefully weigh his every word before saying or writing; he wrote about Christianity because the Christians were a small minority in India; he refrained from writing about Islam because the Muslim fanatics were intolerant and violent, leading a large minority that needed to be handled with kid-gloves even if one wanted to throw it out of the window. In his *Experiments* penned mostly in the Yarwada jail (1925), soon after he helped trigger the Muslim volcano in India via the Khilafat Movement and the resultant Moplah Massacre in the early 1920s, making them expose themselves fully, he cautiously avoided mentioning Muslim activities. A year before, 1924, Hitler too had penned his own *Mein Kampf* while in the Landsberg jail where he had been lodged after the infamous Beer Hall Putsch. Hitler did not criticise Christianity until he came to power, but denounced the Jews; Gandhi criticised Christianity, but did not denounce the Muslims. They both were against Christianity as a common enemy to their respective 'Aryan' nations; additionally, and more importantly, Hitler was against Judaism and Gandhi against Islam which they both worked against to eliminate from their respective countries. Their strategies, however, differed radically, although revival of Israel and creation of Pakistan involved bloodbath of 5-6 million people each. Gandhi criticised the Christians openly but did little against them; he remained silent in case of the fanatic Muslims and even 'supported' them to the hilt, while working for their overthrow.

He declared, 'I could accept Jesus as a martyr, an embodiment of sacrifice, and a divine teacher but not as the most perfect man ever born. His death on the Cross was a great example to the world, but that there was anything like a mysterious or miraculous virtue in it my heart could not accept. The pious lives of Christians did not give me anything that the lives of men of other faiths had failed to give. I had seen in other lives just the same reformation that I had heard of among Christians. *Philosophically there was nothing extraordinary in Christian principles. From the point of view of sacrifice, it seemed to me that the Hindus greatly surpassed the Christians.It was impossible for me to regard Christianity as a perfect religion or the greatest of all religions...* Thus if I could not accept Christianity either as a perfect, or as the greatest religion, neither was I then convinced of Hinduism being such. Hindu defects were pressingly visible to me. If untouchability could be a part of Hinduism, it could but be a rotten part or an excrescence. I could not understand the *raison d'etre* of a multitude of sects and castes. What was the meaning of saying that the Vedas were the inspired Word of God? If they were inspired, why not also the Bible and the Koran?' An enlightened and practical Hindu, after impregnating ancient India with modernity and change, like a male honey bee to the queen, his role was up in 1947; only, a man so opposed to so many Hindu sects and castes, would bequeath to India his own cult, Gandhism, and caste, the Congress.

But what about Islam? Gandhi simply glossed it over. He would not die at the hands of a Muslim at least until his life's actual 'work' was over; did not, after all, a fanatic Muslim Pathan, Sher Ali, assassinate Lord Mayo in 1872? Or, later, Swami Shraddhanand, a prominent Hindu leader once close to Gandhi in the 1920s, who was murdered by a Muslim? Apparently, he aimed at slowly elbowing Islam *out* of India, unlike what the 15th century Spain did violently during *Reconquista* (re-conquest of Christians who overthrew the Andalusia Caliphate), or like his contemporary Japan which, after being suddenly woken up by Christianity, had turned against the alien faith, defeated Russia in 1905, and turned anti-West. The Jewish, Christian and Muslim fanatics denounced as 'infidels' all those who did not subscribe to their respective Abrahamic religions; most of these infidels were in Asia which largely remained unconverted for centuries; and these same infidels were now returning on the world theatre at the cost of the Christians and Muslims. One by one. The more he read about Christianity and Islam and interacted with Christians and Muslims, the more reformist Hindu he became. '(Edward Maittland) sent me his book *The Perfect Way*...the book was repudiation of the current Christian belief. He also sent me another book, *TheNew Interpretation of the Bible*. I liked both. They seemed to support Hinduism.' He repeatedly said that his faith lay in Hinduism, criticised Christianity wherever he could, and indefatigably worked to eject Islam as we would see shortly.

Why?

What did Christianity—or Islam, for that matter—do with those it converted? Gandhi felt that conversion mostly meant denationalisation of the native; at least some of those converted to these religions could not be loyal to India and its traditions. When he asked his client Abdullah Sheth whether South Africans of Indian origins could help him, the latter demurred. '"But", said I, "there are so many young Indians born and educated here. Do not they help you?" "They!", exclaimed Abdullah Sheth in despair. "They never care to come to us, and to tell you the truth, we care less to recognise them. *Being Christians, they are under the thumb of the white clergy men, who in their turn are subject to the Government.*" This opened my eyes. I felt that this class should be claimed as our own. Was this the meaning of Christianity? *Did they cease to be Indians because they had become Christians*?' The same was true of fanatics of Islam which, like Christianity, tended to rob the converted people of their inherited traditions and culture and plant them instead in the West or West Asia—they became extensions of Rome or Mecca in India. If some in the two per cent Christians in contemporary, undivided, India could be like this—and they were the ruling class under the British—what about the 22 per cent Muslims—who were trying to *reclaim* India and re-emerge as the ruling class again after the 1857 fiasco robbing them of this status. Gandhi was like a prism reflecting a rainbow: each ray of light, when it passed through him, scattered into its seven constituent true colours, VIBGYOR, and he could know the frequency and wavelength of each of these colours. He was the Newton of Indian society, despite his weaknesses, some natural and others cultivated. South Africa made him see through Christians and Muslims.

Like Frederic Engels nursing a Karl Marx in the mid-19th century, dreaming to launch the Communist revolution in Europe, some Indians in South Africa nursed Gandhi in the 1890s to hone his skills that he would put to perfect use in India. So, in order to register himself as a practising lawyer there, he swallowed his pride like poison in the many confrontations he had with the White-Christian authorities. South Africa, the Cape of Good Hope, was the training ground, the launch pad, for this ambitious youth before he returned to the land of Cape Comorin to fight bigger battles.

He knew how and when to remain silent, not how and when to speak, the common disease afflicting politicians and other sundry chatterboxes; and being a statesman, rather than a salesman, he did not reveal himself fully except on odd occasions: in 1915, when he returned to India from South Africa, he may have spotted his would-be rival instantly and dubbed this fellow Gujarati, Muhammad Ali Jinnah, as a 'Muslim' leader, thus making the latter *conscious about his religion*, inaugurating his continuous drift away from the Congress; in 1947. The 'Apostle of Peace' wanted the Indian Army to repulse the Pakistani incursion in Kashmir with full force for, 'that's what an Army is expected to do'. Even while adhering to his 'principles' of selective and practical non-violence and truth, he knew the Army was indispensable; for him, even his principles, like his own family, were his laboratory and, like a trained political scientist in public life, he knew the limits of his principles which he had used as armoured vehicles and travelled so far in. For, truth, non-violence, love, peace etc were quite lofty ideals, to be kept on the loft where they returned after being used, like a suitcase. To Gandhi, these sometimes did provide a moral fibre, the best things for human perfection in an ideal life. But, then, he was fighting a psychological *Mahabharata* War even while promoting a Ram Rajya in a world teeming with demons. The Bombay Stock Exchange was established in 1875 as Asia's first bourse, and the Gujaratis were settling around it in large numbers. He hailed from the traditionally-intrepid Gujarati business community and knew the net worth and market capitalisation of such bearish equities as truth and non-violence, lacking fundamentals, on the bullish stock exchange of *realpolitik*. He, therefore, kept up the show, resorted to insider-trading and artificially jacked up stock prices, invited foreign direct investment (FDI) into his product marketed mainly between the two World Wars, often effectively using non-violence and truth as private equity and promissory note. In the beginning, these were not exactly articles of faith to him in a world being reshaped by Nature through the basic survival of the fittest, but as conveniences to achieve the ultimate goal. These were the scaffoldings, to be removed when the edifice was ready—towards the end, however, he became obsessed with his own concoctions the way a tea-taster often gets addicted to tea. He knew the 'Gandhians' only too well but he used them. A man active in practical politics and seeking success could not absolutely love non-violence etc for, after all, politics is the ancient art of rubbing the people against each other, like marbles, to generate fire.

The Abrahamites had ruled India for a thousand years; Gandhi was the first Hindu who strode across the whole spectrum of Hindu life—religious, political, social, economic; like other dictators, he never had any long-time real friends or associates nor did he cultivate one. One could only be either his crony 'Gandhian' or his enemy; he used the former like his pawns and puppets and defeated and ignored the latter. In 1927, he declared Chakravarty Rajagopalachari as his 'could be successor' but changed his 'will and testament' in 1942, as it was now Jawaharlal Nehru who fitted the slot! Why? Because in the 1920s he apparently needed support in the Madras Presidency, especially after the Moplah Massacre of the Hindus; but in 1942, he may have foreseen the Partition coming and so a Kashmiri Hindu bathed in a 'composite' culture (Nehru) was the natural heir, particularly when Pakistan became the dreamland of many Muslims of the Hindi heartland. All those who preceded or followed him were men of their moment, partial persons with partial successes because of partial understanding of the complexity of human nature and their response to alien cultures. Why and how did Gandhi understand what he did: because nobody was as ideally placed in those circumstances. Here was an extraordinary man emerging from the 'non-violent' Hindu traditions who knew the limits of violence too, that what the British abhorred most was the Cromwellisation and re-barbarisation of *their* own society—and, therefore, would at best be businessmen rather than Muslim-like 'victors' in India. Knowing the limits of the British brutality, it was easy for him to mould India on his Potter's Wheel. Here was a man who came from the land of Somnath; here was a man whom Sheth Abdullah Haji, who had invited him to South Africa, tried to nearly convert to Islam, as did his Christian 'friends'. 'As Christian friends were endeavouring to convert me, even so were Musalman friends. Abdullah Sheth had kept on inducing me to study Islam, and of course he had always something to say regarding its beauty.' And the more Gandhi studied Christianity and Islam, the more he assured himself that there was nothing better than Hinduism! 'On a dispassionate view of the question I am convinced that no other religion has the subtle and profound thought of Hinduism, its vision of the soul, or its charity.' He never forgot the *Gita*: *Better is one's own Dharma, (though) imperfect, than the Dharma of another well-performed. Better is death in one's own Dharma: the Dharma of another is fraught with fear.* (III:35). Those who do not understand this Krishna calling would never understand Mohandas Gandhi. He opposed tooth-and-nail the Christian and Islamic fundamentalist attempts to convert others. 'Why can't we all be Sons of God', he would ask the Christians. He knew his band of 'Gandhians' were mostly naive people, bereft of any understanding of Nature and Things, ready to shove themselves into the rising Elements of the Time; did not, after all, Marx know that the 'Marxists' were, likewise, a bunch of stone-heads, ever ready to wage holy wars against 'infidels'?

But what about the others who had already converted, back home in India? In South Africa, he was a number among ciphers; in India, he would be a cipher amongst those who claimed to be numbers. Gandhi knew his first targets in India would *not* be the British but the well-meaning, well-fed contemporary Congress 'leaders', many being merely pleaders and dealers—unless this *first line* of British defence, the shock-absorbers, was removed, one could not make the real enemy visible and vulnerable. In India, he used the British as the white ball he would appear to be striking against but actually hitting it onto the other balls as on a billiards board.

Here he found his mission. But he was also aware of British perfidy, the Muslim barbarity and the obnoxious accretions in Hinduism that he wanted to clean up. He had to negotiate his way through the Byzantine minefields of Islamic, Christian and pseudo-Hindu origins. The self-esteem of most of the Hindus, due to their enslavement for a millennium, was so low that they would not recognise any indigenous product or innovation nationally and with pride; only a 'foreign-recognised and returned' Indian was fit enough to harangue them. Gandhi had seen how Naoroji and others were marvelled at in the Congress; so he honed his skills in South Africa, mainly through socio-political work in a British colony infested with racists and apartheid, the scum of Europe reigning as cream in America and Africa, later in Australia, New Zealand etc as well. Few ever understood the importance of the 'lowly' and patient social work as a prerequisite for dizzying political success.

That he was destined to lead the Indian National Congress was clear even in 1894 when, on 22 May, Gandhi, aged only 25, founded the Natal Indian Congress in South Africa, in Abdullah Sheth's house, *because* the British had come to abhor it in India; at that time, he was not perhaps aware that Allen Octavian Hume had assembled the Congress merely as a safety valve to let off anti-British steam to avoid recurrence of 1857. Gandhi bided his time, experimented with the British in South Africa before sizing them up in India. He knew the Indians, like the Indians in South Africa, were mostly illiterates he was going to deal with. 'And they were mostly illiterate, the men no less than the women. The fight in South Africa was for such, and it was fought by illiterate soldiers; it was for the poor and the poor took their full share in it.' He also realised the importance of fighting his battle in India through the rough-hewn across-the-board Hindustani dialect as the common link, rather than any of the regional languages that tended to be exclusivist. His conscious use of the Hindustani was a major reason behind his success; his rivals from the three Presidencies were, at best, parochial Congress leaders who shunned Hindi and cried either in English or in their own languages to which they fanatically adhered. Clearly, unlike Gandhi, they could seldom connect to most of the Indians; they could never strike a chord with the majority heartland of India, the Hindi Belt, where the decisive battles, leading to Pakistan, were actually shaping up.

Returning to India, Gandhi made all the right, inaugural, politically-correct and British-friendly noises: 'Hardly ever have I known anybody to cherish such loyalty as I did to the British Constitution, can see now that my love of truth was at the root of this loyalty…In those days I believed that British rule was on the whole beneficial to the ruled….Preparations were going on for the celebration of Queen Victoria's Diamond Jubilee when I reached India.' By that time, he had perfected those bizarre 'experiments' in diets, health and commune-like life and attained name and fame back home in India; his alleged experiments on *brahmacharya* (celibacy), too, generated quite a curiosity in the sex-starved minds. His 'celibacy'—two decades of marriage, a lot of sex by his own admission and five children later when his fires of youth had already begun to cool down—was like fasting after a sumptuous meal.

But Gandhi was adept at such sabre-rattling mind games and knew about their electrifying effect on the unsuspecting, illiterate and poor Hindus even as he dismissed the elites who laughed at him. He was emerging as all-things-to-all and nothing-to-nobodies. The married, ageing celibate devoted two chapters in his autobiography to celibacy and tried to cure the Hindus' erectile dysfunction; they did not notice the inconsistency that celibacy was supposedly the period in the life of a Hindu/Brahmin adolescent boy between leaving the house for education after ceremonially wearing the sacred thread and returning home for marriage; *here* was a man who claimed celibacy while approaching his 40s and after siring five children! But the Indians glossed over such minutae for the larger battle the Man was fighting for them. Gandhi created a huge constituency in India by giving at least something to so many of the customers: he influenced some through his 'experiments', others through his 'non-violence', still others through 'patriotism', etc. Being member of a traders' community, he knew the simple dictum: no customer should return empty-handed; if you want to long last in business, gather the maximum number of customers by charging the minimum price for the longest time. The Wal-Mart way.

He knew how the Christians defended their religion and zealously used new converts to cover their old Bible. In South Africa, he would doze off in a Church, as some other Christians also would; but a Christian boy, under Gandhi's influence, chose to become vegetarian. This was not liked by the boy's mother who used to invite Gandhi every Sunday; she also disliked Gandhi narrating stories about the mercy of Gautam the Buddha, and, finally, severed her relationship with him.

He did not send his four sons to school. Revolting, his eldest son, Haridas, would even convert to Islam for some time later in life to teach his father a lesson. 'Never did it occur to me that I did not fulfil my duties towards them nor do I regret for this. On the contrary, the sorry state of my eldest son seems to be the echo of my own immature past.' Even then, in fact even until he breathed his last, he never spoke openly against Islam which he would so deftly push out of India. Many a sapling would fail to grow under him because he was drawing *their* share of nourishment. Greatness is like a tree that grows at the expense of its immediate environment which becomes barren due to excessive flow of nourishment to make the tree tall; nothing grows under a banyan tree, he knew, and was ready to pay the price to become one. While his friends and contemporaries found him to be quite eccentric, particularly in the 1930s and 1940s, they had to remain with him because he, like magnet, had the crowds on his side. In particular, celibacy became a controversial issue but when he returned to India, it added to his stature; at a time when the supposedly celibate saints were turning debauch, here was a married man who had adopted celibacy while still remaining in family and society. Celibacy, for him, was an extension of his attempts to control the senses, like speech; it also demonstrated the highest level of motivation to do what he ultimately did in India from where there was no looking back, even if some viewed him as an eccentric or even mad. He knew the *importance of celibacy in the Hindu Mind*; and also reversed the order in which celibacy was practised. He was accused of being a hypocrite in this respect; Nehru was also linked to several women.

But Gandhi was able to incorporate even his private 'sexual' life in his overall ambitious planning, as no one had done before him. The bizarre 'experiments' he performed with his family and others would have been denounced elsewhere and in other leaders; he made these very same things admirable in India, particularly among the masses. It was this genius to turn his private brain-waves into social storms that made Gandhi stand apart from others. He had seen not only the true faces of *practical* Christianity and Islam but also the decadence of Hinduism in different parts of India: he witnessed the pointless animal sacrifice at temples in a Calcutta that boasted of being the 'intellectual capital' of India even after the political Capital's shift to Delhi and the educated people's indifference, even support, to this practice. In Varanasi, he witnessed the cesspool Hinduism had been reduced into. There, he also went to the famous Kashi-Vishwanath Temple of Lord Shiva, half-rebuilt after Aurangzeb had destroyed it and constructed the Jana-Vapi Mosque in its place in the 17th century: 'When I reached the Temple, I was greeted at the entrance by a stinking mass of rotten flowers…I went near the Jana-Vapi. *I searched here for God but failed to find Him.* I was not, therefore, in a particularly good mood. The surroundings of Jana-Vapi too I found to be dirty.' This Mosque is one of the three principal mosques now being claimed for 'liberation' by the Hindutva forces, the other two being the Krishnajanmasthan-Idgah at Mathura and the Ramjanmabhoomi where the remains of the Babri Mosque were dismantled by the Hindus in 1992. Soon, he also visited Veraval, the town of Somnath Temple in Gujarat, where plague had broken out. He did not mention these mosques for obvious reasons but his journey from Varanasi to Somnath, where flagship Hindu temples were destroyed by Aurangzeb and Mehmud of Ghazni, respectively, spoke volumes about his self-motivation.

Now was the time for playing the chess in the land of its origin. He had learnt it from the captain of a ship on his way from India to Natal. 'He was fond of playing chess, but as he was quite a novice, he wanted one still more of a beginner for his partner, and so he invited me. I had heard a lot about the game but had never tried my hand at it. Players used to say that this was a game in which there was plenty of scope for the exercise of one's intelligence. The Captain offered to give me lessons, and he found me a good pupil as I had *unlimited patience. Every time I was the loser, and that made him all the more eager to teach me. I liked the game, but never carried my liking beyond the boat or my knowledge beyond the moves of the pieces.*' He was now entering India with the 'reluctance' of a grandmaster to play chess because he knew the movement of all the human pawns. He began to find holes in this Whole: 'I likewise taught the National Anthem to the children of my family...Later on the text began to jar on me. *As my conception of ahimsa went on maturing, I became more vigilant about my thought and speech.*' The lines in the British Anthem: *Scatter her enemies, And make them fall; Confound their politics, Frustrate their knavish tricks*, was the snook he could cock at the British now and hurt them with their own Anthem: Bobbies, you are not the bloody peaceniks you claim to be, as it were! The British, the Anthem meant, were no less barbarians than the Muslims—the British Anthem sounded straight from the *Book of Revelation* or the *Qur'an*. 'I, therefore, deplored the civilisation of which the Natal Whites were the fruit, and which they represented and championed...I had in my speech described the Western civilisation as being, unlike the Eastern, predominantly based on force.'

At 37, he vowed to become a celibate; this set him apart from others in the Indian community in South Africa and he began to fashion himself for a bigger role, a Mahatma-in-the-making at a time when the whole world colonised by Europe was in ferment as a resurgent Japan had defeated Russia, ending the jinx of the 'invincibility' of the Christian world vis-a-vis the 'barbarian' Afro-Asians. In fact, it was the Land of Rising Sun that had launched the Eastern drive to kick out the Europeans from their colonies in 1904, although it had to pay the price four decades later with the destruction of Hiroshima and Nagasaki for its own conversion from liberator to oppressor. Flaunting his 'British citizenship', Gandhi had willingly participated as a nurse, along with 1,100 other Indian volunteers, to mend the British soldiers' wounds in the Boer War in the late 1890s for which he was later decorated with the title *Kaisar-e-Hind* (Lion of India); the British did not know they were siring a lion which would kill them without wounding! He even gave a new definition to 'loyalty' while he was in South Africa, although, when a child, he wanted to throw out the British: 'Suffice it to say that my loyalty to the British rule drove me to participation with the British in that war. I felt that, if I demanded rights as a British citizen, it was also my duty, as such, to participate in the defence of the British Empire. I held then that India could achieve her complete emancipation only within and through the British Empire.' He used his 'loyalty' as a tool, an anaesthesia to perform surgery on the British, although the latter were not much amused. Now was the time to perform surgery on the elitist Congress leaders.

When he finally returned to India in 1915, Gandhi was 46, mature enough to be wise, young enough to be a good leader; most of the pirated Indian editions of Britons that populated the Congress leadership then were often like hot-metal composed letters in a contemporary printing press, recycled each day. Full-time money-makers who *also* cared for their nation three days each year when the Congress met in session; they included British sycophants and spies who travelled business class and helped their Masters run colonial business. Gandhi saw through this leadership. When he approached the 'uncrowned king of Bombay', Sir Pherozeshah Mehta, he saw two more Knights in the same saloon of the train, Sir Dinshaw Wacha and Sir Chimanlal Setalvad. 'They were discussing politics. As soon as Sir Pherozeshah saw me, he said, "Gandhi, it seems nothing can be done for you. Of course we will pass the resolution you want. But what rights have we in our own country? I believe that, so long as we have no power in our own land, you cannot fare better in the Colonies."' Gandhi had to cross hurdles like ***these*** leaders who meant a lot, understood little and did nothing concrete. 'I was taken aback.

Mr Setalvad seemed to concur in the view; Mr Wacha cast a pathetic look at me. I tried to plead with Sir Pherozeshah, but it was out of the question for me to prevail upon the uncrowned king of Bombay.' Clearly, unlike in South Africa, where he played the political chess only against the British, here, in India, he had to make the Blacks and the Whites play against each other. The first line of British defence in India was, ironically, in the Congress itself, founded as it had been by a Briton, AO Hume. Gandhi, therefore, decided to be an activist-umpire who would reframe rules of the game, shift goalposts and force the two teams to play against each other as *he* would want them to.

Gandhi, who dressed like the British in South Africa, now decided to dress like the *hoi polloi* in India: he also decided to work his way up right from the bottom, rather than parachute straight onto the podium; he worked as a clerk and a waiter, even as a scavenger, in the Congress conferences so that the grass-roots workers came to know him directly. Three decades before Jinnah's call for 'Direct Action', that led to the creation of Pakistan, Gandhi's 'direct action' against the established Congress 'leadershop' had begun to catapult him to the dizziest heights that would force India shed lethargy. He used the three-day Congress jamboree each year to further push himself against the Muslims and the British. The contemporary Congress was a caricature of the Marathas' 'Indian' army in the Third Battle of Panipat (1761) with each regional group and castes blowing their own trumpets separately; everybody wanted *the others* to fight in the battle. If the Chinese were down in the dumps with opium the British exported for them from India, the Indians were down with the sheer sense of producing the herb. The Hindu leaders and pleaders, who led this society, were like dinosaurs, eating and defecating a lot, ruling at will, killing for game and snoring when tired of boredom. They were the last link in the Muslim-Christian chain that bound India, and the first one, therefore, to be rusted and thrown away—it was they who, as the first line of infidel defence of Abrahamism in India in the 20th century, were the first to be removed from the scene, just like the 21st century Hindutva forces targeting the 'secularists' defending 'minorityism' as the first line of defence. It was this great churning at the bottom that had thrown up this slug at the surface—Congress

Liberals at the end of the 19th century, 'secularists' at the end of the 20th—that would be removed. The 'last' battle of Hindutva is yet to be fought, and it would *not* be led by the Sangh Pariwar! India has been a cultural refinery in which the slug, asphalt, is created at the top, not at the bottom: 'In a few days, I came to know the working of the Congress. I met most of the leaders, I observed the movements of stalwarts like Gokhale and Surendranath. *I also noticed the huge waste of time there.* I observed too, with sorrow even then, the prominent place that the *English language* occupied in our affairs. There was little regard for economy of energy. More than one did the work of one, and many an important thing was no one's business at all.'

This deadwood, within the Congress and without, had to be removed. He clearly saw how these overrated, highly-regarded, pea-sized Congress brains had summarily 'passed' his proposals and forgotten them 'unanimously'. 'The procedure was far from pleasing to me. No one had troubled to understand the resolution, everyone was in a hurry and, because Gokhale had seen the resolution, it was not thought necessary for the rest to see it or understand it!' Why should then he, Gandhi, the most experienced man in the heap of rubble called Congress, carry the dead weight of these dinosaurs hanging around India's neck like albatross? Better he bury them, for if he carried this burden his own back would bend. Until now, Gandhi was a mere participant in the Congress movement; now he decided to wait for the opportunity to lead it from the front. He spent a month with Gokhale: 'As a result, some of those whom I had regarded as stalwart fighters began to look quite puny.' At Gokhale's suggestion, he travelled across India, third class, to gain a first-hand experience of the battlefield he was to conquer; other leaders travelled first class and, therefore, had a third class experience of the ground realities. And they all died unsung.

Like a possessed man, burning with ambition and sense of a mission, self-indoctrinated and motivated, wherein all doubts were to be chased away, he waited for his opportunity to strike as the First World War, beginning in July 1914 raged in full force, with the British fully focused on Europe rather than the East. By this time, the Capital of British-India had already been shifted *back* from Calcutta to Delhi

(1911), Muslim separatism was growing in leaps and bounds under the Muslim League and the issue of separate electorate had all charged up the Muslim Mind, the Indian National Congress had emerged more and more as the voice of the 'majority' Hindus, although the Muslims, feeling cornered in Europe due to the Balkan Wars eating away the Ottoman Empire and during the First World War, were trying to work out a *temporary* truce with the rising Hindus—just like Pakistan trying to wage peace upon India in the wake of the 9/11 when the American pressure increased. Islamists would never fight on two fronts simultaneously; so if it was war against the monotheist Christianity or even Judaism for the same space, they would temporarily befriend the infidel and polytheist Hindus and even the atheist Chinese—given a choice, however, Islamists would prefer Christianity and/or Judaism, even Zoroastrianism, over polytheism and atheism—its ultimate enemies. Believers in the three Abrahamic religions were, after all, *Ansar-al-Tawhid* (Partners in Monotheism).

The British fancied themselves as democratic and benevolent and hated to be dubbed as despots. Gandhi knew this congenital British weakness and he patiently waited to exploit it and prove that the foreign power was despotic, something the Crown abhorred no end. Once that done, the political initiative would be in his hands: in order to buttress their 'benevolence', the British would continue to alternate between liberalism and despotism, more and more, giving Gandhi more and more opportunity to ascend, concede more and more space in the contemporary print media and society; in other words, he would *provoke the British to use force* and thus fall in his trap! Gandhi carefully avoided being extremist because this would be playing into the hands of the enemy: after all, he, too, would grab leadership from Tilak merely by being a 'moderate'. A basic principle of practical politics is to portray yourself as weak and vulnerable until the sympathetic people begin to support and make you strong; foxes do not last long in politics, rabbits do, but tortoises become immortal. He knew about the British diplomacy in Europe, the Policy of Splendid Isolation and to join the weak *against* the strong to maintain balance-of-power, whenever needed. And he exploited this second weakness of the British to the hilt. Gandhi had learnt the art of supporting the weak in order to emerge strong. He outgrew Adi Shankaracharya's Krishna and Arjuna and added Barbarik to his persona, strategy and tactics.

The 1905 Partition of Bengal probably gave food for thought to Gandhi. In fact, the beginning of the 20th century was heralding momentous changes in different spheres of human thought and outmoded thought systems that had outlived their utility were now being buried across civilisations. Revolutionary changes in one sphere of life were triggering similar changes in others; the very way discerning people looked at the shape of things had begun to change. There was a certain clerk in the Swiss Patent Office, Albert Einstein, who did not believe in the constancy of the Newtonian system in natural philosophy; so, when the Michelson-Morley Experiment (1887) failed to make sense between the existing 'theory' and practical results, the Jewish youth hit upon the idea of relativity: light has a dual nature of wave-particle, travels at a universally constant speed and bends due to gravity. There was a David, Japan, that had just defeated the Goliath, Russia (1904). A number of such global events were triggering a million minor mutinies in human thought. Gandhi had a fertile imagination: *could the Partition of Bengal, a trial balloon, lead to the Partition of India*!

A treacherous, even blasphemous, anti-national idea in an era of patriotism being the badge of youth. But Gandhi had cultivated a style of looking at things from the 'other end' of the telescope. What, to others, appeared to be too far, it was, for him, so near; he was an expert political driver who knew that the objects seen in the rear-view side mirror were closer than they appeared. The Calcutta-centred Bengal Province had 78 million souls; Lord Curzon divided it by creating a new one of East Bengal and Assam of 31 millions, mostly Muslims, for 'administrative' purposes. In the truncated Bengal of 47 millions, the Bengali Hindus found themselves in a minority due to the presence of Bihari and Oriya Hindus amongst them, whom they would avoid as uncultured riff-raff, as they sometimes do even now—the same way the West Pakistan would later find East Bengal! Having honed their cultivated gift of the gab, many amongst the cultural hegemonist Bengali Hindus raised a lot of hue and cry, boycotted British goods, cried their hearts out in *butler's English* (a heavily accented salad English with Indian words sprinkled liberally) across India, enrolled the support of Gokhale and Tilak, and gave birth to armed militancy. India would never be the same again. And with this last sigh, Bengal would slowly cease to be the intellectual heart of India, with the Marxists performing the last rites a century later in a dialectical opportunism. The Hindi-speaking middle class gradually flooded the Congress and revivified it; nationalism and patriotism—of the Hindus—overshadowed Bengali xenophobia, Maratha chauvinism and Tamil parochialism which many of their early leaders exhibited. Many intellectuals from Calcutta, Bombay and Madras Presidencies—a hybrid of the 'Hindu Church' variety—had one common trait in fancying themselves as born rulers and looking down upon other Indians as barbarians, the *rightful* heir to the British if and when the aliens left India: Jyoti Basu's description of the Vajpayee government as 'barbarian', Bal Thackeray's contempt for the North Indians and the Dravid parties' anti-Hindi/anti-Brahmin politics were all relics of this self-supremacist, pseudo-British mindset in which alien colonialists were perceived to be replaced by domestic ones. Post-1947, thanks to Gandhi and Patel, India survived this mindset and emerged united—shunning *dependence* on the three former Presidencies for political survival. These India's own 'Boston Brahmins' could not, however, translate themselves into a mass-based national-level political platform where one would have to tolerate a viewpoint other than one's own. No wonder Bengal and Madras would come to be ruled by their *representative* leaders, Mamata Bannerjee and Jayalalithaa!

Gandhi had witnessed these personality traits of 'presidential intellectuals' at first hand and he never allowed leaders from these three British Presidencies to take control of the Congress or India; he had eliminated the Gokhale-Tilak leadership and when Bose challenged him in 1938, he made the great Bengali-Oriya leader clash with the Telugu leader, B Pattabhi Sitaramayya, thus virtually splitting the Congress (barring a Narasimha Rao interregnum, even the Nehruvian Congress reserved most leadership in the Hindi Belt and ensured that no Bengali, Maratha or Tamil leader ever become the Prime Minister!). In Bengal, it was the intellectual and cultural hegemony and arrogance of the Hindus, particularly the Kayasthas, that had forced a large number of people into Islam and Christianity that changed the demography of the East; in the West and South, it was the Brahminical tyranny that did the same.

The 1905 events had other effects. The Congress found itself split into the Pro-Changers' group headed by Tilak and No-Changers of the Gokhale variety and the Bengal Partition was undone. But Muslim leadership in India, unhappy at having lost the Mughal Empire in 1857 and then East Bengal, *the first Muslim-majority island in an infidel ocean*, now found it necessary to exhibit their 'separateness' from the Hindus in every sphere of life—even without Gandhi and Jinnah, they were headed in the same direction: Pakistan. The Muslim League, founded in 1906, was unable to make them an all-India force because of two reasons: one, the Muslims were spread only thinly across the most-populated North India, except in pockets, and two, they lacked active, unconditional and prolonged British support vis-a-vis the Hindu-dominated Congress; the crumbling Ottoman Empire in Europe and West Asia, thanks to the Urdu press it financed in the Indian subcontinent, was a major concern for them, although most of them did not even know where Turkey was! The Muslims needed a 'modem' between them and the British on the one hand and the Hindus on the other. There was no Muslim leader available to do this all-important job; the bearded *mullahs, maulanas and maulavis*, who led the Muslim 'intellectual' community, were no match for the English-speaking and boisterous Hindu leadership: the Hindus looked to the West, but that was Europe and America; the Muslims, too, looked West but to the outgoing Ottomans and the incoming Saudi-Wahaabi fundamentalist Arabs. All the Muslims could do, therefore, was to *import* a Hindu leader, at least on a temporary basis, to propagate the Muslim cause! Such was the pathetic state of the post-Mughal Muslims, who had 'led' the whole of India for a thousand years, that they no longer had a single leader who could lead them even for a decade: the long-marching India had brought them to this ironic stage that they were forced to import leaders from amongst the *infidel* Hindus: Gandhi and Nehru to Mulayam Singh

Yadav-Laloo Prasad Yadav to N Chandrababu Naidu to Atal Behari Vajpayee and Lal Krishna Advani and, of course, the 'headless chicken' called Communists; they all, willy-nilly, temporarily, supported different Muslim causes at different times due to different reasons. No, no, Jinnah was *not* really the 'Muslims' Leader'; he was merely the transporter of what Gandhi produced; that was why the Qaid-e-Azam, who was actually a *Hypocrite* by strict Islamic standards, was dumped by the Muslims themselves as soon as Pakistan was transported out of India.

The shrewd 'Mahatma', having his ear to the ground, realised that even by keeping alive the Ottomans on a post-Crimean life support system, Europe could not contain Russian ambitions in the Balkans simply because the time of Russia had come, despite the 1904 defeat at the hands of Japan. Similarly, the British would not be able to contain the emerging, resurgent Hindus even by supporting the Muslims. All he had to do was to prod the Muslims to demand more and more while stressing that the *Hindustanis* (read the Hindus) were getting less and less! To support the Muslims to the hilt was, for now, the Mahatma's seed-capital, the equity, to raise and leverage a huge derivative loan from global consortium to make the Hindu India rise. Post World War I, he was, therefore, waiting for venture capitalists and angel investors in his political start-up, assured to attract Series A and more funding.

Gandhi's job was, apparently, tailor-made: take the aborted Bengal Partition to the logical conclusion of India's Partition through well-calibrated steps as the first requisite of the departure of Islam. He had studied Christianity in South Africa; now he studied Islam in India. He was aware how the fanatic Muslims were trying to revive their bygone Mughal Empire in India at a time the Ottomans were struggling to retain their sick empire in Europe where a host of Christian nations were separating from Muslim hegemony through the contemporary Balkan Wars in the early 1910s. If the Christians could dissociate themselves from the Muslim Ottomans in the West, why would not the Hindus dissociate themselves from the Muslims in India in the changing world order? The way 9/11 created a worldwide reaction against Muslims, the falling apart of the Ottomans as the last Muslim Empire in the world was similarly viewed as the herald of a 'Muslim-free' world, particularly in Europe. Gandhi would bring this anti-Muslim, essentially European, drive to India to spark a Hindu reaction, consolidation and unity. But, for this purpose, he must *unite* the Muslims first, to convert them from Indian Muslims to Muslim Indians, as it were! Like the immensely patient Muslim fanatics, he, too, had immense patience and waited for the opportunity to lead the Muslims so that *he* could take them up on their chosen garden path. The fall of the Ottomans was his first opportunity, the 'rise' of Afghanistan was second and the ambition of the Nizamate of Hyderabad the third—he deftly utilised all these opportunities in the next three decades to whet the fanatic Muslim appetite to cure Hindu indigestion.

Turkey, already reeling under the after-effects of the Balkan Wars of 1912-13, joined the First World War on 29 October 1914, by attacking the Russian ports on the Black Sea. When Gandhi decided to support the British, his friend, Henry Polak, telegraphed him questioning 'the consistency of my action with my profession of *ahimsa*'. Gandhi wrote back why, despite being a worshipper of ahimsa, he had to take part in the War, 'a spiritual dilemma'. 'Even today, I see no flaw in that line of argument, nor am I sorry for my action, holding, as I then did, views favourable to the British connection.' He may have had a bad handwriting but he had mastered the art of writing political material. Having studied the *peaceful warriors* of Christianity and Islam, he proclaimed to be professing non-violence uncompromisingly, but revealed his mind in a rare moment. During the 'Recruiting Campaign' in the First World War, when he asked the people to gather arms and 'assist' the British, they declined saying, 'You are a votary of Ahimsa, how can you ask us to take up arms?' Gandhi ignored these doubting Thomases, published a leaflet and told the Commissioner protesting against the British decision to disarm the people: 'Among the many misdeeds of the British rule in India, history will look upon the Act of depriving a whole nation of arms as the blackest. If we want the Arms Act to be repealed, if we want to learn the use of arms, here is a golden opportunity. If the middle classes render voluntary help to Government in the hour of its trial, distrust will disappear, and the ban on possessing arms will be withdrawn.' Why did the Mahatma want the people to own arms and learn to use these? Clearly, he was aiming high and looking far into the future.

And he revealed it in a subsequent letter to the Viceroy, giving enough hints of his political strategy and boasting as if he had already overshadowed other Congress leaders in 1916, as if he had become spokesman even for the Muslim League: 'I recognise that in the hour of its danger we must give…ungrudging and unequivocal support to the Empire of which we aspire in the near future to be partners in the same sense as the Dominion overseas…people are entitled to believe that the imminent reforms alluded to in your speech will embody the main general principles of the Congress-League Scheme, and I am sure that it is this faith which has enabled many members of the Conference to tender to the Government their full-hearted cooperation. If I could make my countrymen retrace their steps, I would make them withdraw all the Congress resolutions and not whisper "Home Rule" or "Responsible Government" during the pendency of the War.' Then he narrated why it was not possible for the Indians to give up their demands, he cajoled and threatened the British in the same breath before unfolding his aims: 'In Champaran by resisting an age-long tyranny I have shown the ultimate sovereignty of British justice. In Kheda, a population that was cursing the Government now feels that it, and not the Government, has the power when it is prepared to suffer for the truth it represents… Thus Champaran and Kheda affairs are my direct, definite and special contribution to the War. Ask me to suspend my activities and you ask me to suspend my life…Lastly, I would like to ask you His Majesty's Ministers to give definite assurance about Mohammedan States. I am sure you know that every Mohammedan is deeply interested in them. As a Hindu, I cannot be indifferent to their cause. Their sorrows are our sorrows. *In the most scrupulous regard for the rights of those States and for the Muslim sentiment as to their places of worship, and your just and timely treatment of India's claim to Home Rule lies the safety of the Empire.* I write this, because I love the English nation, and I wish to evoke in every Indian the loyalty of Englishmen.' He had shown that he was the emerging leader after Champaran and Kheda agitations….and that he was *creating a Muslim demand* for a product he was going to launch: the Muslims' 'places of worship' were Mecca and Medina which were now threatened due to the First War in which the British were forced to fight their old ally, the Ottomans; the 'those states' were Arabia, Syria etc where nationalist movements were striking at the root of the tottering Ottoman Empire, which Gandhi did not identify *then* for obvious reasons. Contemporary *world history* makes it easier to understand Gandhi and his deft moves, *in India*.

While he was touring Central India promoting Hindi language, he got the venture capitalists he was waiting for. Some prominent Muslim leaders, including Hakim Ajmal Khan and Asif Ali, requested him to lead their proposed *pro*-Khilafat Agitation, seeking restoration of the Caliphate and the Ottoman Empire that protected it *in Turkey*. Never had Muslims requested an infidel to help restore their Caliphate! In the absence of their Caliph, the Sunni Muslims felt like global orphans; time and again they tried to restore it, the latest experiment being in 2014 when the Islamic State in Iraq and Syria (ISIS) was born with the same aims.

During the War, Muslim soldiers of the British Indian Army were angry with their British bosses who piloted these soldiers to attack Mecca and Media, then part of the Ottoman Empire, which also housed the Caliph (Khalafa); in other words, the British ordered Indian Muslim soldiers of their Army to attack *their own* Holy Mosques; in still other words, the infidel Christian British plotted the Mominin Muslims' attack on their own Brothers...After winning the War, the British conveniently forgot to implement their promise that they would withdraw the victorious Army from the Holy Places. To rub salt in these Muslim soldiers' Ottoman wounds, the British *celebrated* in India their victory against the Ottomans, knowing well that most Indians, Hindus in particular, were perennially festival-friendly; all successful Indian leaders, from Jawaharlal Nehru to Narendra Modi, therefore, mastered the art of keeping them in a perpetual festival mode, something that turned large masses into psychologically dysfunctional and mentally castrated people. But the Muslims were different, and never ignored their ultimate objectives.

In the midst of the War, Gandhi folded up his shop in South Africa and returned to India via England. Soon, he went to the Kumbh Mela, 1915, in Hardwar, where he would have the opportunity to see millions of Hindus of all shades. At railway stations on the way, he found vendors selling 'different' waters. 'The pangs of thirst, caused by even such a journey as this, could not persuade orthodox Hindus to take water if it was "Musalmani". They waited until they could get the "Hindu" water. These very Hindus, let it be noted, do not so much as hesitate or inquire when during illness the doctor administers them wine of prescribed beef tea, or a Musalman or Christian compounder gives them water.' He regretted the hypocrisy of many of the Hindus, said the day of the fair was a 'red-letter day for me'. 'I have never thought of frequenting places of pilgrimage in search of piety. But the 17 lakh of men that were reported to be there could not all be hypocrites or mere sight-seers. I had no doubt that countless people amongst them had gone there to earn merit and for self-purification. It is difficult, if not impossible, to say to what extent this kind of faith uplifts the soul.' He wanted to electrify these very masses so that they could shed their inertia and alien viral sickness.

He saw through the strengths as well as weaknesses of the Hindus. On 25 May 1915, soon after returning from Hardwar, he set up his Satyagraha Ashram at Kochrab, Ahmedabad, the capital of Gujarat and the Muslim stronghold in western India where he began to weave the different strands of Hindus into a vast carpet, starting reform movements and launching political agitations. When he went to Bihar for the Champaran agitation, he met Maulana Mazhar-ul-Haq, President of Muslim League, who had once been a student in the Mahatma's London college days. Continuing political networking, he decided to reverse his South Africa policy of financing an agitation. In South Africa, it was the Indians who financed his stay there; but, in Champaran, a 'Mahatma' was not supposed to collect money from the people. Champaran, 'the land of King Janaka' (father-in-law of Lord Rama), particularly attracted him; 'I still remember the Ramnavmi Prasad among them.' 'I had made up my mind not to accept anything from the Champaran ryots. It was bound to be misinterpreted.' He had begun to shape his political strategy, alongside the all-embracing social reforms.

It was, however, the Hindu-Muslim relations that he paid his maximum attention to. It was already in the air that the upcoming annual meeting of the Congress at Lucknow in 1916 was a platform to bring together the two factions of the Congress as well as the Muslim League, for the first time after 1907. Most Congress leaders did not realise that the Muslim fundamentalists were demonstrating this new-found 'affinity' to the infidel Hindus *because* they (Muslim) were losing their Ottoman Empire in Europe and Asia. Tilak was an orthodox man, father of Hindu cultural nationalism; but he was equally tolerant towards the Muslims, his main enemy being the British. Gandhi saw through the Hindu idiocy and Muslim tactics. The Lucknow Pact brought the two communities together for the time being, not as a union of hearts but merely as a political exigency as Muslim League needed the Hindu support against the British involvement against Turkey in the War; the League maintained the separate status of the Muslims by continuing the Communal Electorate system. The two Home Rule Leagues were virtually non-starters. The year 1916 proved that the Hindus and the Muslims could be mixed only as water and oil! It also proved that despite being pro-changer, Tilak was old and static, that Gandhi, despite being a 'disciple' of the no-changer Gokhale, was young (47) and dynamic. Tilak would construct half-the-platform and leave the remaining half for the Muslims to construct; Gandhi, the Gujarati takeover expert, would let the Muslims construct the whole platform and then occupy the centre-stage himself. 'I was seeking the friendship of good Musalmans, and was eager to *understand the Musalman mind through contact with their purest and most patriotic epresentatives.* I therefore never needed any pressure to go with them, wherever they took me, in order to get into intimate touch with them. *I had realised early enough in South Africa that there was no genuine friendship between the Hindus and the Musalmans.* I never missed a single opportunity to remove obstacles in the way of unity. It was not in my nature to placate anyone by adulation, or at the cost of self-respect. But my South African experiences had convinced me that it would be on the question of Hindu-Muslim unity that my ahimsa would be put to its severest test, and that the question presented the widest field for my experiments in ahimsa. The conviction is still there.'

A self-proclaimed peacenik who could weave arguments to support the War was now weaving arguments to forge unity between the Hindus and Muslims despite knowing well that there was 'no genuine friendship' between the two. The same Mahatma would write four years later when the Non-Cooperation Movement was a 'rising tide', that 'I had long discussions on the subject with the late Maulana Abdul Bari and the other Ulema, especially with regard to the extent to which a Musalman could observe the rule of non-violence. In the end, they all agreed that Islam did not forbid its followers from following non-violence as a ***policy***, and further, that, while they were pledged to that policy, *they were not bound faithfully to carry it out*.' Clearly, the Muslims were ready to follow non-violence only as a policy, not as a conviction, the way Gandhi was following ahimsa just as a policy, not as a conviction. The ever-cautious 'Apostle of Peace' left more evidence for those who could read between-the-lines that non-violence was merely a political exigency, his well-thought-out strategy, as far as the 'aliens' were concerned. Lala Lajpat Rai was to preside over the September 1920 All-India Congress Committee's special session on the Khilafat issue in Calcutta. 'At the request of Maulana Shaukat Ali, I prepared a draft of the non-cooperation resolution in the train. Up to this time, I had more or less avoided the use of the word non-violent in my drafts. I invariably made use of this word in my speeches… In the original draft, the word 'non-violent' had been left out by me. I handed over the draft to Maulana Shaukat Ali who was travelling in the same compartment, *without noticing the omission*. During the night I discovered the error. In the morning I sent Mahadev with the message that the omission should be made good before the draft was sent to the press. But I have an impression that the draft was printed before the insertion could be made.'

Gandhi, who could as well have inserted the word 'non-violent' the next morning when the Maulana would wake up in the 'same compartment', apparently chose to wait until the Muslim leader left and the resolution went to print; Gandhi 'forgetting' his god, ahimsa, was like Muhammed omitting to mention *Bismillah*… in the opening lines of *Surah IX* of the *Qur'an!* The word 'non-violence' was not something our astute lawyer-turned-Mahatma, who had mastered the art of drafting and who self-admittedly wrote and spoke very carefully, could have forgotten, unless it was a deliberate tactic to launch a national-level struggle whose exact nature, violent or non-violent, was yet to be decided—and he himself admitted that, so far, he had used the word 'non-violence' only in his speeches, not in the drafts of resolutions! It is important to note that Gandhi, ever meticulous with his facts and having a strong will-power to speak only what *he* wanted to reveal, had this to say of himself: '*My other aptitude which the Congress could utilise was as a draftsman. The Congress leaders had found that I had a faculty for condensed expression, which I had acquired by long practice.*'

How would this playing of words like violence and non-violence impact his emerging leadership? Wait! This is how he would now control the Movement, without giving any assurance to anybody about its exact nature, and, as he eventually did, withdraw it at the most opportune time of *his* choosing.

So, the AICC resolved to launch a Non-Cooperation Movement whose violence-component on the Khilafat issue was left *vague* in writing. The silent Mahatma had begun to weave his web against the ebullient Ali Brothers and their ilk and slowly encircle and corner them before they realised what he was up to.

Gandhi had begun to mould the Congress as well for his purpose. When he returned to India in 1915, it was Tilak's Congress all over, Gokhale being overshadowed. Tilak spoke, wrote and did a lot but planned little; on the contrary, even when he promoted India's cultural festivals as the cement of Hindu national unity, he also tried to soften the Muslim stand by supporting their 'separate electorate' demand. On the face of it, it appeared that Tilak was trying to reunite the Muslims and the Hindus by supporting the former's separatist demands; it was like an attempt to re-attach a severed arm with the body. Gandhi was aware that the Lucknow Pact (1916) between the Congress and the Muslim League on the one hand and the Tilak and Gokhale factions on the other would be short-lived, what with its stress on bringing together the two communities as 'separate' entities which believed in give-and-take—give more to the minority Muslims and take less for the majority Hindus, that is. Gandhi, therefore, instantly looked through the sieve-like Pact and waited for his opportunity. Gokhale was no more; even the Lokmanya passed away in 1920. By now, Gandhi had already become an important leader having participated in the agitations related to the Rowlatt Act, Champaran, the Ahmedabad Mill Strike and the Jallianwala Bagh Massacre. People looked with awe at this half-clad saint who, in his frail body, hid an iron will: when necessary, he could be flexible like a snake, slippery like a fish, leaping like a frog, strong like elephant and killer like a cheetah.

So, when the sun of the Ottoman Empire was setting, Gandhi did the most amazing thing: the man who was working *against* the relatively secular and alive British Empire *in India*, began to work *for* the revival of the fundamentalist and virtually dead Ottoman Empire thousands of miles away, *in Turkey*. Imagine the Hindu Right prodding Indian Communists to agitate for the revival of the Soviet Empire! Even the Ottomans—and why, even the Prophet—would have been amused at this rank infidel trying to revivify a Muslim Empire and the Caliphate! A self-proclaimed liberal and religious Hindu leader vociferously supporting re-installation of a Muslim Caliph, not in India but in far-away Turkey—at a time when the Muslims of the Fertile Crescent, above all the Young Turks, were themselves furiously attacking the last crumbling Islamic Empire. They wanted to follow a modern and democratic Europe but not Gandhi! And, by extension—because the Muslims were a global Brotherhood, the *Ummah*—did Gandhi want the Indian Muslims to remain backward by supporting such a retrogressive and reactionary 'movement'? At a time when a dozen Muslim nationalities, including Arabia, were trying to get rid of the moth-eaten Ottomans, our Gandhi was virtually forcing the Indian Muslims to rush inside a crumbling fortress!

Why?

Because the far-sighted Gandhi, apparently, knew he was playing a zero-sum game as far as the Muslims were concerned. He realised that neither the Caliphate nor the Ottomans were going to survive for long—in the 1940s, he also knew that Jinnah, who was suspected to be suffering from debilitating diseases (later diagnosed as cancer and terminal tuberculosis), would not survive for long even if he became the Prime Minister of India after the Independence! It was a time of cartographic reshaping of Europe and the world, at a time when even the Continent, particularly Britain, had begun to be eclipsed by the USA, with Woodrow Wilson being the new rising Sun on the horizon, when the Tsarist Russia had been replaced by the Soviets and Germany had lost the Hohenzollerns' Second Reich. By supporting the bailout of a bankrupt company like the Ottoman Caliphate, Gandhi would like the fanatic Muslims to invest in it, thus pauperising them of whatever trust and goodwill they were still left with. He was supporting the dead Caliphate far away because he was targeting the live Muslims of India, right here. Gravity is nothing but Newtonian action-at-a-distance, and in a contemporary relativistic Einsteinian reshaping of classical physics, gravity of matter could even force-bend the straight ray of light. It was an era of growing uncertainties in science, and dying permanances in spirituality; space and time were now a continuum, space-time, a particle could simultaneously be a wave and vice-versa; a saint could, likewise, be a politician and vice-versa; Gandhi could be both violent and non-violent.

Until the 1910s, only three men understood relativity of natural forces— Einstein, Henry Poincare and Bertrand Russell. But, here, Gandhi alone understood the relativistic dynamics of religious and socio-political forces unleashed by the First World War with a potential to reshape the world. There were Hindu nationalists like Vinayak Savarkar who could not look beyond Indian borders, had lofty dreams of a 'united' Hindu India, warning Gandhi about the inherent dangers in his 'policy'. There were, also, fundamentalist Deobandis—Maulana Abul Kalam Azad also came from the same seminary—who, while remaining in the Congress, feared that Gandhi would eclipse the Muslim hegemony forever and, therefore, they 'opposed' the Khilafat Movement in the garb of patriotism. Gandhi would see through them all, suffered them silently, and continued to move like the long-range turtle, come what may.

He would have none of these myopic Hindu and Muslim leaders and their lofty 'ideals'. The Russian Communists had just ousted the dominant Greko-Russian Orthodox Church after fall of the Tsar.

Whether India could do likewise with Islam? For him, it was a now or never opportunity to shape post-Turkey events in India to encourage and *unite* the Muslims, heat them up with theo-adrenaline to such a high temperature that, when frustrated at being unable to do anything abroad, they would turn their violence against the Hindus and spend themselves here—the way terrorists now strike at will within Pakistan in a 'spiritual' catharsis. If the Slav Christians had thrown away the Ottoman yoke in Europe, if the Arabs were chopping away at the hated Ottomans in West Asia, if the Turks themselves were heaving a sigh of relief at the loss of their own Empire and eventually the Caliphate, Gandhi would not miss any opportunity to repeat the same in India: get rid of the medieval alien baggage. But, here, he had a problem: the Christian Britain as the Key and the Muslim relics of the Mughal Empire as the Lock, clamped on a warehouse of the vast Hindu majority. He, therefore, had to play the Muslims and the British against each other in such a subtle manner that when the British left with stock and barrel, they took along the Muslims, key and lock. And he may have known that, within Islam, the regenerative and creative powers were left only in the heretic sects, like the Khoja Shias, to which Jinnah belonged, or the Ahmedias who would produce the only Nobel Prize winner Muslim scientist, Abdus Salam; the Sunnis and the official Shias had mostly sunk into their ancient mire, bereft of any regenerative powers or renaissance: all Islamic 'revolutions' were, therefore, destined to be reactionary and retrogressive leading to a throwback to the past. The seventh century was fast catching up in Islam of the 20th century.

For him, Jinnah was such a promising leader who could be cornered enough to demand eventual separation of the Muslims in India at a time when everybody else was dissociating from the Ottomans in West Asia. The Islamisers had come uninvited in India and now was the time when they retreated to what would become Islamabad, the *Abode of Islam*. Gandhi had already identified Jinnah as the point-man for this; only, Jinnah needed to take the path *Gandhi* had chosen for him.

Their caste backgrounds, the ultimate 'intranets' of social life in India only the sub-continental people could understand, were compelling the rising nation towards this logical end. Only those who understand the nitty-gritty of the Indian subcontinent's caste system would fathom why and how Gandhi and Jinnah did what they did, or why and how Pakistan and Bangladesh may eventually be reabsorbed in India—*minus* Islam. Reading their actions without knowledge of the world history, particularly of the 19th and 20th century, would not yield a complete picture.

Gandhi belonged to the Modh *vania* (traders') caste whereas the nominally Muslim Jinnah, despite his forefathers' conversion to Islam in the early 19th century, continued to share his Lohana-Thakkar caste's headstrong and obstinate habits. Both the rival castes were seen as great innovators, achievers and business-minded. The Modhs originated at the famous Sun Temple town of Modhera near the ancient capital of Patan in North Gujarat and scattered after the invading Muslims did a Ghazanavi in the 16th century to Patan and shifted the capital to what is now known as Ahmedabad (Karnavati). The Gandhis, who originally sold fragrances and scents (hence the word 'Gandhi', meaning those who sold fragrance) first shifted to Kutch and then to Saurashtra (Kathiawar), in the coastal Gujarat town of Porbandar—remember, Prophet Muhammed was also fond of fragrances. Their rivals saw the practical Modhs as scheming, cunning and vengeful. The Modhs, who thought big and planned silently, were an upwardly mobile caste and few realised what they were up to until they suddenly surfaced like scuba-divers.

Curiously, after the 1990s, the upward caste mobility through migration, inter-marriage or economic upliftment reversed and many castes and sub-castes, even fair-complexioned, tall and socially powerful intermediate castes like Jats, vociferously demanded the status of 'backwardness' in the hierarchical system to derive political benefits dictated by numbers. The Gujarati Ghanchi sub-caste of the Modhs, that crushed seeds to extract oil, sold grocery or milk, was declared an 'Other Backward Caste' (OBC) in 1994—Prime Minister Narendra Modi hails from this sub-caste.

The Lohana-Thakkars, on the other hand, were typical Saurashtrian, headstrong people who tenaciously continued their business in the most adverse of circumstances. Often aggressive, they inherited their caste traits even after conversion to Islam. The Thakkars-turned-Khoja Muslims set up their business in coastal Gujarat, centred at Porbandar, controlling both crime and business syndicates and, therefore, acquiring both notoriety for their killing spirit and fortune for their offspring. The Gandhi-Jinnah rivalry, that led to Pakistan, was rooted in the medieval Modh-Thakkar rivalry and the Mahatma's first impressions of Islam came from the Thakkar Muslims' behaviour in coastal Gujarat that produced a lasting image in his mind about Jinnah's caste and religion. More than Islam—Jinnah had hardly ever been a practising Muslim, like Gandhi a non-practising Hindu—it was the 'Mahatma' that became *the reason* for the 'Quaid-e-Azam' to slice off Pakistan. For Jinnah, *the* Thakkar, Pakistan was not any national or even a spiritual quest but a slap to Gandhi, *the* Modh. Only, Jinnah being a 'Muslim' led to the creation of a 'Muslim state' of Pakistan. The Thakkar Khoja Muslims continued to wear both their Hindu and Muslim identities: in alternate generations, they had Hindu and Muslim names. Even Jinnah's only daughter was named Dina, a typical Hindu-Parsi name, not one of a Muslim girl. And, barring Jinnah and his sister Fatima, other members of the family remained nominal 'Muslim' and chose to settle down in India. Clearly, Jinnah was as much an aberration in his family as Gandhi was in his. And, of course, the Gandhis traditionally belonged to the *Pranami Sampraday*, a Vaishnavite sub-sect which, like iconoclast Muslims, worshipped no human images of Lord Krishna but only His attributes. Who else could have better understood Islam and Jinnah but Gandhi?

The battle for this oneupmanship between the wily Modh Gandhi and the headstrong Thakkar Jinnah slowly matured into the ultimate battle between Hinduism and Islam in the decades leading to 1947. Typical to his Modh nature, Gandhi worked secretly whereas, again typical of his Thakkar caste background, having once decided, the boastful Jinnah did not waver from 'Direct Action' that created Pakistan. Gandhi fully understood Jinnah up to his bones and knew what he would do under which circumstances; he, therefore, sized up the brilliant and ambitious Muslim lawyer, worked against Jinnah right from day one after landing in Mumbai in 1915 on return from South Africa when he, knowing that Jinnah was a Thakkar, singled him out and, as a clear taunt, described the latter as a mere 'Muslim' leader. Ironically, in that *Gurjar Sabha* meeting, Jinnah spoke in *English*—praising Gandhi and Kasturba for their work in South Africa—while Gandhi spoke in *Gujarati*, remarking that he 'was pleased to find a *Mohammedan* member of the Gurjar Sabha as the chairman of this function'. Also, 'I had acquainted myself with the programme *beforehand.* Mr Jinnah was present, *being a Gujarati*, I forget whether as president or as the principal speaker. He made a short and sweet little speech in English…Then my turn came, I expressed my thanks in Gujarati, explaining my partiality for Gujarati and Hindustani and entering *my humble protest against the use of English in a Gujarati gathering.*' Gandhi described Jinnah first as a 'Muslim', then tried to rob him of even his being a Gujarati! Jinnah took this slight to heart, just as Gandhi would have liked, and the Thakkar headstrong, having been slighted again and again—once even beaten up by the Khilafatists!—eventually decided to teach the Modh a lesson once and for all, again as Gandhi may have wanted! Ironically, Jinnah, accused of being father of Islamisation of the sub-continental politics, wanted Pakistan to be a 'secular' state while Gandhi, whose successors claimed to be 'secular' in outlook, wanted to create a Ram Rajya! None of them, however, succeeded.

Apart from shaping this inner caste dynamics of Gujarat, that helped create Pakistan, Gandhi had identified the four aces, the Kings, he had up his sleeve in his emerging project to eject Islam. He invested heavily into the rival Muslim community by supporting the crumbling causes dear to their feverish heart—the Caliph in Turkey, the Amir in Afghanistan, the Nizamate in Hyderabad—realising that each of these would, in the end, be a zero-sum game—the fourth was the British Crown. Being a Modh, Gandhi would not make worthless investments for merely worthy 'ideals'—he was like any other Gujarati trader, except that he made socio-political transformation the commodity he traded and emerged as a socio-political entrepreneur. Having cut his teeth in the apartheid politics of South Africa and honed his skills as a silent operator, his knowledge of international politics and instincts and improvisations were legendary—no other contemporary Indian leader, Jinnah included, had such a vast sweep of knowledge on almost everything under the sun; no wonder, few, if any, actually understood the deft Gandhian moves; he would gently sow the seeds quite early and wait patiently for their germination. In the post-World War I scenario, he, therefore, knew exactly what he was doing and going to achieve through his 'truth-non-violence-the supreme religion' brand of politics that moved millions of illiterate Indians no end but not exactly the ruthless businessmen that the matching British were. Cloaked behind his saintly 'spirituality'—more enlightened spiritual leaders like Maharshi Aurobindo Ghosh ridiculed the Gandhi cult for his bizarre 'secular religion' perhaps without knowing that these were merely his tools in a long-drawn-out plot—was a sharp mind where violence and non-violence, truth and falsehood, were as seamless as his loin-cloth. The Modhs were known to create wealth out of nothing through sheer dint of mind and hard labour and Gandhi knew well that no leader could take on the far-more powerful British by resorting to conventional politics and armament—either Congress-type petitioning or through the likes of the militant Gadar Party. He would rather have the Congress ride the Muslim camel and cross the fiery desert, a policy its successor Nehruvite Congress Party continued since. He, therefore, evolved the politics of engagement and agitational path, looking for issues to launch strikes that created disturbances and made him the leader; whenever he was arrested, he wrote prolifically, improved his health, fasted to force the British to release him each time before his sentence ran out and came back from jail stronger. Due to his sabre-rattling tactics and being all things to all, he flummoxed the British and the Hindus alike who alternated in pushing him up and up on the ladder.

But not Muslims, not particularly Jinnah.

Gandhi was aware of the Muslims' contradictions and dilemma: on the one hand, the fundamentalist Muslims were struggling in Europe and Asia to re-install the uprooted Caliphate and the Ottomans as much as they were dreaming to re-install the Mughal Empire in India if and when the British left; on the other hand, the Muslim elitists and intelligentsia were heralding nationalistic freedom movements in Arabia, Egypt, Syria, Iraq and even Turkey to free themselves of the ramshackle Ottoman yoke and the Caliphate. While he was part of, and then would lead, the forward-looking Indian nationalist freedom movement, Gandhi *also* decided to support the backward-looking, reactionary and retrogressive Muslim clergy of India who wanted the Ottoman and Mughals back! Theoretically, since he was leading an anti-colonial, progressive, nationalist movement in India, he *must* have supported the Young Turks and other Arab/Muslim progressives and nationalists against the Ottomans. But he would not! By supporting Muslim fundamentalists and Hindu liberals in India, simultaneously, he rode a mule and a horse at the same time in what Aurobindo described as using 'unintentionally sophistic logic'. Why did he do so? First of all, he knew that even if he supported the elitist Muslim Leaguers' nationalists, their leadership would eventually slip into the hands of their mullahs who, from as long as Islamists could remember, were seen as the only 'repository' of knowledge, particularly in a still-infidel country like India; and these mullahs could relaunch Ghazanavism of the Somnath and Modhera varieties—he was proved right again and again, the latest being the Muslim leadership slipping into the hands of the 'intellectual' mullahs since the Shah Bano and Babri Mosque episodes of the 1980s...until a medical professional doctor, Dr Zakir Naik, suspected as 'Dr Terror', led the pack of preachers.

No minority can claim to have a veto. Gandhi knew the Muslims were *not* a minority and they ruled India for 800 years; they still had a veto, they used it at will simply by resorting to violence, what with nearly half the population of the subcontinent having been converted to Islam. For the time being, it was better that they remained in the tent and pissed outside, rather than standing outside and pissing in, as it were: that is, they should be encouraged to look outside India, pick up issues of Islam rather than participating in Indian affairs. Gandhi knew that even Sir Syed Ahmed Khan, the 'most enlightened of Muslims' who once described the Hindus and Muslims as the two eyes of the same India, had eventually decided to wear a monocle! The very reality of the Muslims living in an infidel India meant that they would re-launch what they had lost in 1857 in case the British left. The Mahatma was aware of the well-known activities of the likes of the Wahhabis, Deobandis and the Maulavi Jamaluddins who were criss-crossing India for decades inciting the Muslims to work for the revival of the Mughal Empire; his successors turned a Nelson's eye to the attempts made by Ahl-e-Hadis, Dawat-ul-Islam and others, to radicalise some of the Muslims, motivating them into terrorism in the 21st century.

This he would not let happen; the celibate Gandhi decided to sleep with the enemy. He knew that many amongst the contemporary Thakkars of Gujarat became successful because they set up shops in problem-areas where no sane businessman would like to go; for this, the Thakkars often used muscle and money power. But, being a Modh, he knew that merely opening a shop was meaningless unless one had customers. The Hindu customers would not come to a problem-area and would, instead, set up shop in their own area. So, he set up a kiosk in the Muslim areas, so that the angry Hindus could be encouraged to set up their own. He was aware that the three issues that could unite the scattered Indian Sunni Muslims were the questions of Turkey, Afghanistan and Hyderabad, the issues that could make them hyphenated 'Muslim-Indians' with extra-territorial loyalties: Turkey, because it was home to the 'Caliph', Afghanistan because it was the only important Sunni Muslim power next door to India and Hyderabad because it was the largest Indian princely state inhabited mostly by the Hindus but ruled by the Muslims. The Indian Muslims had invested heavily in these three issues as, everywhere in the contemporary world, Muslims were being cornered as they are now in the post 9/11 world, forcing them to unite.

At the turn of the 20th century, the Muslims in the Indian subcontinent were divided into 70-odd sects and communities plagued with fissiparous and anti-Islamic activities; the rise of 'heretic' sects like the Ahmedias that questioned Muhammed being the 'Last Prophet', had further weakened them. They were all claimants of what they thought was their 'heritage', heirs to the bygone fortune; it was to put an end to so many claimants that Gandhi decided to gamble and buy the three sick units. By uniting the Muslims, he would unite the lethargic Hindus as a *reaction*.

Yes, the Ottomans, 'Sick Man of Europe', had lost their erstwhile possessions in Eastern Europe after the First World War even as their Islamic colonies like Egypt, Syria, Arabia and Iraq were in ferment, each having a national movement for independence from the Turkish yoke. In the rising tide of anti-colonialism and nationalism, sooner or later, they were going to achieve independence and Turkey, with Mustafa Kemal Pasha 'Ataturk' as its strongman, would no longer be the seat of the Caliphate because the newly-independent republican nations would not recognise the Sultan who had annexed the Caliphate; and it was not the Sheikhs and Sultans but the British, the French and the Russians who, in order to control the Fertile Crescent's newly-struck petroleum, would actually control West Asia. Oil, not Islam, was to be the new driving force for neo-colonisation of this region. There were a hundred paradoxes and contradictions in the midst of which Gandhi had to play deftly.

But that was still a few years in the future, although Gandhi had begun to feel the signals with his ear to the ground and eyes across the oceans. The Arabic word *khalafa* or *khalifa* meant *temporal successor* to the Prophet. Many unlettered Indian Muslims could not distinguish between *khalafat/khalifat* and *khilafat* (opposition)! So, when the Khalafat (Khilafat) Movement (1919-24) started with the aim of restoring the Caliph-cum-Sultan in the Ottoman Empire, uprooted by the First World War and its consequences, they thought they were opposing the British (who were supporting the Caliph!). In this confusion, Gandhi realised that the Caliphate itself was controversial amongst the Muslims themselves; the Caliph was not only pro-British but also under protection of the British even though he had temporarily sided with Germany in the First World War, that the Young Turks were trying to overthrow the Caliph, that the Ottoman Empire was breaking up everywhere in what the Indian Muslims mistook was the Christianity-versus-Islam Clash of Civilisation but was, in fact, due to nationalistic movements, amid global Islamic Retreat, within this last Sunni stronghold. The whole world knew, except the Ottoman-funded Urdu press and the Muslim leadership in India which decided *not* to know, that the acquisition of the Caliphate by the Ottoman Sultans itself was a disputed matter. They had claimed that the office had been 'transferred' to the victorious Ottoman Sultan Selim I by the defeated al-Mutawakkil, a descendent of the Abbasids of Baghdad, in 1517. Interestingly, al-Mutawakkil himself was living in exile in Egypt as a pensioner of the Mamluke ruler Baybars and was, therefore, a man without legitimacy, authority or the crown to do so—he was merely an Abbasid, a symbol. To their credit, the Ottomans never made a claim to acquire the Caliphate except for occasional political reasons; instead, they preferred the humbler title of 'Ghazi', the Holy Warrior. Formally and officially, the title of Caliph was not used by the Ottomans until 1774, again for political reasons. When, during negotiations with the victorious Russians of the Treaty of Kucuk Kaynarca, the Russians described their Empress, Catherine the Great, as the 'Head of the entire Christian Orthodox Church', the negotiator of the Sultan, too, described the latter as the 'Caliph of all Muslims'. That was how Europe came to know that the Ottomans were 'Caliphs' too! But, having been adept at sleeping with the 'Donation of Rome' hoax for so many centuries, the Christians accepted the Muslim hoax as well. It was the British who, reeling under the 1857 kick in India, enrolled their ally Ottoman Sultan Abdul Aziz (1861-76) as the official Caliph in what was their attempt to heal the Indian Muslim's Mughal wound in the Turkish bath; even earlier, the British had bought the Ottoman support against Tipu Sultan of Mysore.

The Abbasid Caliphate, for all practical purposes, had been uprooted by the Mongols in 1258 and all those who claimed it later were, at best, pseudo-Caliphs. When Gandhi joined the Khilafat Movement in 1920, the Caliphate had multiplied like mushrooms; at one stage there were as many as 82 'Caliphs' spread over every nook and corner of the Muslim world as each minor Muslim factotum wore this title! In the Indian subcontinent itself, chiefs of hundreds of Hindu and Muslim *akharas* (gymnasia) were known as 'khalifas', as they continue to do so even now. So, the issue of the Ottoman Caliphate's so-called 'future' was no issue at all. And Gandhi knew it.

The clever Gandhi also knew he was investing in a drowning company; still he did it. Why? Not because he was a bad investor or had any sympathies with the gullible fanatic Muslims of India when he supported them on the issue of reviving the Khilafat (Caliphate).

The Indian Sunni Muslim opinion was framed by the Barelvi and the Deoband seminaries. The Barelvis, supported by the majority, the more superstitious, relatively tolerant and indigenised Muslims of India, refused to accept the legitimacy of the Ottoman claim because they were not Quraish; the minority, fundamentalist and puritanical Deoband school, Dar-ul-Ulum, on the other hand, supported the Ottoman claim to the Caliphate. And Gandhi, having perfected the art of supporting the minority everywhere through his gift of the gab, roped in the Deobandis, despite knowing well that the Indian Muslims were rather tolerant and their opinion was generally with the Barelvis. In the fresh Gandhian approach, his principal interlocutor was Maulana Abul Kalam Azad. The Deobandis, like their Wahhabi counterparts in Arabia, were emerging as a strange and heretic school that would, slowly, disown even Prophet Muhammed as an intercessor/modem and set up a direct, satellite communication with Allah. Azad, a highly learned Muslim scholar and leader, belonged to this school that viewed the relatively tolerant Barelvi practices with suspicion. The Deobandis felt that India's full Islamisation was still incomplete, to achieve which end the Muslim Indians needed international help. It was with this view that Azad supported the spurious Caliphate issue and claimed that the Caliph was, in fact, *Khalifa at-Allah* (Allah's Caliph), meaning that the Ottoman Caliph was next only to and successor of Allah—Muhammed being nowhere now! Islamic scholars like al-Mawardi protested against this concoction saying one could be a successor only to such a person who has died or disappeared. Had Allah died or disappeared, so that the Caliph could succeed Him, they asked!

But Azad, adept at arousing the illiterate Muslims through extravagant claims, much like Gandhi's practice of addressing illiterate Hindus with equally ridiculous promises—for instance, the 1920 promise of '*Swaraj*-in-one-year' etc.—had found each other, both manipulating each other to further their own aims. Intelligent successors of Gandhi continued with this policy of instant gratification for instant results: for instance, post-ideology, post-media political entrepreneurs like Arvind Kejriwal, in 2013, promised to pass laws for a *Janlokpal* and *Swaraj*, within weeks, if they came to power! Unlike Azad, M A Jinnah was a more straightforward, modern and secular man; but he was an anathema to Gandhi who preferred cronies as cogs in his emerging Great Machine and where he had openings only for mechanics, not engineers. Ironically, the pro-British Syed Ahmed Khan, long dead now, did not regard the Ottomans as the Universal Caliphs but only as administrative head of the Muslim Brotherhood who controlled the holy places of Mecca and Medina. But there was no place for such theological niceties and logic in the *realpolitik* of Gandhi whose tenacity of purpose dictated that he rope in the likes of Azad who could parrot his voice even if temporarily. The Mahatma did not mind the anti-British and nationalistic Non-Cooperation Movement sleeping in the same bed as the essentially pro-British and extra-territorial Khilafat Movement. Maulana Abul Kalam Mohiyuddin Ahmed Azad, born in Mecca in 1888, overlooked even the fact that he was supporting an essentially anti-Arab Khilafat Movement because the Arabs were happy at the ouster of the Ottomans and were struggling to gain their nationalistic independence under the leadership of even a British military-man T E Lawrence (the 'Lawrence of Arabia'), happy even at being jackbooted by the home-grown ultra-Islamic Wahaabis rather than the foreign yoke of the relatively secular Turks. Gandhi, and his supporters, had long honed the hobby of running with the hare and hunting with the hound as long as it amused the audience in the political circus.

For, Gandhi knew that the plural of the word *madrasa* was *madaris*: the former meant an Islamic seminary but the latter *also* meant street-side jugglers, the snake-charmers, the rope-tricksters, the monkey-choreographers. He used Azad until he served his cause. Some of his opponents may have seen through his political game and horrified with the possible consequences; he ignored them. This was *precisely* what he wanted: to unite the Muslims so that they looked *out* of India, rather than *in* India, while he played his game against the British simultaneously. Apparently he knew that small-minded men constituting big masses could be moved only by big, emotional issues for small political ends. In this mind-boggling, complicated game, he used the Khilafat Movement as a force-multiplier, even a multiple rocket launcher, to para-drop a dozen political Maulanas onto the Muslim masses in the subcontinent.

It was a dangerous game. Gandhi only hastened the demise of the Caliphate! The Movement was destined to fizzle out but its lasting legacy was the legitimacy it gave to the Muslim clergy who replaced their community's 'nationalist' elite of the Muslim League and eventually formed the Jamiat-e-Ulama-e-Hind and its successors after Partition; if Syed Ahmed had politicised the Muslim elite, Gandhi politicised the Islamic clergy. Why did Gandhi want the Muslim elite to be replaced by the clergy in politics? Because, the Muslim elite raised on the Syed Ahmed legacy since 1857, had slowly come to terms with the post-Mughal scenario and were even integrating with their Hindu counterparts; Tilak's Lucknow Pact (1916) had enhanced this bonhomie, despite separate electorate, and Jinnah was a fine example of this development. It appears that, post-Tilak, Gandhi would not want Islam to be indigenised and Indianised like this; he may have been thinking not of a mere separate electorate but probably dreamt of a separate nation for the Muslims! Raised on the staple diet of puritanical Hinduism of the Vaishnavite variety, wherein even *evil* vegetables like onions and garlic were not allowed in the Hindu kitchen, he would rather Islam make an exit from India. In his childhood, he had experimented with meat and turned a staunch vegetarian as a reaction—now he was experimenting with the Muslims and Christians and arousing Hindu nationalism in the same vein. In this stratagem, he supported the Maulanas so that they could replace the Muslim 'intellectuals', who were basically descendants of landlords, in the political game. And his game-plan was not confined to India alone; the reactionary, counter-productive Khilafat Movement helped trigger anti-Caliph movements in the erstwhile Ottoman Empire and led to independence of several nationalities. On the Khilafat issue, India was the only important country, *an infidel one at that*, where the Muslims were supporting the Caliph's cause; all other Muslim nations were *against* the restoration of the Ottomans and were creating their own nations on the ashes of this last Muslim Empire. He achieved this feat by doing a simple thing: never before in Indian Muslim history had the clergy ever been accorded such an exalted place in political life, not even by Aurangzeb. *Gandhi demonstrated what the Muslim clergy would do if they ever entered politics*. His successors continued this policy.

Gandhi also knew that the literal meaning of the word 'caliph' was 'successor'; it did not connote any office nor gave any spiritual claims to anybody. The word came in use after Abu Bakr became the first 'caliph' or 'successor' to the Prophet after the latter's death in 632. Being a caliph did not mean anything except that the man was the administrative and temporal head of the Muslims, Muhammed having left no spiritual successor at all; he was the Last Prophet, the last spiritual resort for all Muslims. The nominal spiritual head of the Muslims was supposed to be the Imam but his duty was largely confined to leading the prayers in the mosque. But the Umayyed counter-Islamic revolution had led the Sultans to annex both the caliphate and imamates and the Abbasids continued the tradition; despite this, several Muslim rulers continued to wear the title as the Muslims had, over the ages, come to mistakenly believe that the Caliph was their temporal and spiritual head and successor of the Prophet. In fact, while Abu Bakr styled himself as the Caliph, his three successors—Umar, Usman and Ali—were content with only being *Amir-ul-Mominin* (Commander of the Faithful). These four were called the *Rashidi Caliphs* (The Rightly-Guided Caliphs), implying that other self-styled Caliphs may have been wrongly-guided! Gandhi also realised that the Christians and Muslims were not just engaged in a civilisational clash; in fact, what the contemporary world was witnessing was ethnic nationalistic anti-colonial and anti-imperialistic movements all over the world wherein the old monarchical order was yielding place to democratic and republican aspirations. He succeeded in not only drawing the attention of Indian Muslims out of India but also painted the British as anti-Muslim by supporting the Khilafatist claim that the Ottoman Sultan was a 'Universal Caliph'. Gandhian politics not only hastened the demise of the Caliphate but also left the Indian—and the world's—Muslims in the lurch, without a Caliph, for the first time in Islamic history. Not only this, the Indian Muslims became suspects in the eye of the Arabs and other Muslims for supporting the hated Ottomans! Never did they recover from the Arabs pasting on them the stigma of being 'Hindu Muslims'; they remained isolated from the rest of the Ummah until the post-1973 petro-dollars acted as their bridge with the Wahaabis—and, thereafter, the Indian Muslims did everything to amuse the Arabs.

Few people in India, particularly non-Muslims, then knew about the Hyderabad connection to the Caliphate and Sultanate in the Ottomans' Turkey. Fatah Jang Nawab Asaf Jah VII, or Nawab Mir Usman Ali Khan, born as Osman Ali Khan Bahadur (1886-1967), the seventh and last Nizam of the Hyderabad State and founder of Osmania University (1918), was said to be nursing the ambition of becoming the Caliph himself! He had seven wives and 42 concubines from whom he had fathered some 40 children. His eldest son Azam Jah was married to Durru Shehryar, a daughter of Abdul Mejid II, the last Ottoman Caliph and cousin and heir of the last Ottoman Sultan; his second son, Moazzam Jah was married to Princes Niloufer, a princess of the Ottoman Empire. When the going became tough in Turkey, the Hyderabad ruler fiddled with the idea of acquiring the Caliphate for his descendants, of course with the British help. But the British could do little when Mustafa Kemal Pasha 'Ataturk' abolished the Caliphate-cum-Sultanate itself. It was then that the Nizam looked into India to inherit the Mughal mantle and then supported the Pakistan movement; he had his men trained in the Moplah incidents in the early 1920s and later raised a Razakar force of his own in a bid to declare independence from India in 1947, but failed, again. Unlike many other leaders, the Mahatma knew of this Hyderabad connection to the Caliphate when he supported the 'Khilafat' agitation.Gandhi was also aware how the Ottomans stumbled into the First World War *against* their old ally, the British. Nature so willed that the Germans and the Turks, who had destroyed the Holy Roman Empire and the Abbasid Caliphate, respectively, and all that went with these, joined hands. The British, who were fighting the War in a temporary partnership with Russia, did not want their old ally Ottomans to be part of the first major European war as the Tsar opposed the Ottomans for the latter's support to the Slav independence movements in the Balkans. Bismarckian Germany, which had constructed the famous Berlin-Baghdad railway line a few years ago, however, made the possible spoils of the post-War period an irresistible prospect for the Ottomans who jumped into the fray from the other side now, in October 1914, by declaring war against Russia in an attempt to recover from the Crimean War's shame of the 1850s. The War proved to be the death-knell for the Sick Man of Europe, although the British continued to protect the Caliph until he was finally overthrown by the Turks themselves in 1924.

None would have laughed more in silence but Gandhi when he found the Indian Khilafatists supporting the Caliph and the latter's arch-enemy, Mustafa Kemal Pasha, the 'Ghazi', in the same breath; interestingly, the Kemalists were denounced by the monotheist Caliph as atheists! The Mahatma realised the value of this confused lot, the chaos in which he loved to play his mind-game as his adversary proved more and more incapable of perceiving the nature and significance of that conflict between the monarchical rule of the Caliph and the democratic aspirations of the Republican Nationalists, the Young Turks, as well as other nationalists in different Muslim nationalities in the Ottoman lands. When Mustafa overthrew the Caliphate in 1924 and declared Turkey a secular state, the Khilafatists were left totally bewildered, unable to comprehend what befell them; nor did they know why Mustafa had, in his famous six-day-speech described the Caliph as 'treacherous' and that the Muslims no longer needed a Caliph. It was Mustafa who forced the British to abandon the Caliph, the same British who had abandoned the Pope centuries ago. But the Kemalists and Khilafatists, despite the demise of the Caliphate, were of the view that Arab nationalists—from Muhammed Ali of Egypt to the Lawrence of Arabia—be suppressed and denied their right of self-determination, that they be continued to be kept under the Turkish thumb. This further annoyed the Arab nationalists; the Indian Muslims, and later Pakistanis too, were made to pay for this anti-Arabism when the Arabs paid only lip-service to their problems. Post-1918, the Ottoman lands were under Anglo-French control and the Arab nationalists were trying to get rid of this new yoke much the same way they are now protesting the US occupation of Baghdad and other Muslim lands in West Asia.

The Mahatma, having his ear to the ground, was aware of the facts about all these fast-changing global scenarios; the Maulanas he was playing around with knew only what the Ottoman-sponsored Urdu press fed them with in India, and what suited them to run their political shop. Politicians all over the world always keep their warehouses full of idiots that comprise their prized inventory. So, Gandhi began to weave his web around the Muslim clergy which invited him to participate in a joint meeting with the Congress in Delhi in November 1919. The invitation letter said the issue of cow protection was *also* on the agenda along with the Khilafat issue. Cow was as much holy to the Hindus as the swine were unholy to the Muslims; cow protection being a sensitive and emotional matter for the Hindus, any meeting that discussed this as a means of forging communal harmony between the Hindus and Muslims should have been welcomed by any normal Indian politician; it was, therefore, welcomed by the Tilak supporters who thought it would be yet another feather in their cap if they could persuade the Muslims to stop eating beef as a *quid pro quo* to the Hindu support to their Khilafat issue; after the Lucknow Pact of 1916, this would have been yet another step in better relations between the two communities and the important question of cow protection—one of the prime reasons of conflict between the two communities—would, perhaps, have been settled once for all. It has remained unsettled even in 2017!

But Gandhi, by now an expert in political somersault and oratorial sabre-rattling, would have none of this; for him, cow seemed less important than his aims. If, in his childhood, he ate meat to throw out the British, he could now swallow this issue to eject the Muslims! Within the Congress, whose supreme leader he wanted to be, his target was now Tilak, the only towering leader left to be dealt with after the demise of Gokhale. The Mahatma would not join his 'guru' Gokhale's Servant of India Society; he wanted to capture his enemy Tilak's Congress! But one must have an issue to ride; Gandhi now had the cow, but in a different way. 'Before the conference I contended that, if the Khilafat question had a just and legitimate basis...the Hindus were bound to stand by the Musalmans in their demand of the Khilafat for the redress of the Khilafat wrong. It would ill become them to bring in the cow question in this connection, or to use the occasion to make terms with the Musalmans, just as it would ill become the Musalmans to offer to stop cow slaughter as a price for the Hindus' support on the Khilafat issue.' Interestingly, many Muslims, led by Maulana Abdul Bari, favoured a deal with the Hindus on the issue but Gandhi virtually sabotaged it! The astute businessman as he was in his dealings with the British and even with other Congress leaders, Gandhi suddenly turned around: 'But, in spite of my warning, Maulana Abdul Bari Saheb said: "No matter whether the Hindus help us or not, the Musalmans ought, as the countrymen of the Hindus, out of regard for the latter's susceptibilities, to give up cow slaughter." And at one time it almost looked as if they would really put an end to it.' Gandhi realised that the deal would be yet another victory to the Tilakites and he, Gandhi-the-Mahatma-in-the-making, would be left out in the cold; and, moreover, his aim of capturing the Congress leadership and then using it effectively to oust the Muslim extremists would remain unfulfilled.

Why did Gandhi want the Muslim fanatics to be shown the door?

'But it would be another matter and quite graceful, and reflect great credit on them, if the Musalmans *of their own free will stopped cow slaughter out of regard for the religious sentiments of the Hindus, and from a sense of duty towards them as neighbours and children of the same soil.* To take up such an independent attitude was, I contended, their duty, and would enhance the dignity of their conduct. But if the Musalmans considered it as their neighbourly duty to stop cow slaughter, they should do so regardless of whether the Hindus helped them in the Khilafat or not. "That being so", I argued, "the two questions should be discussed independently of each other, and the deliberations of the conference should be confined to the question of the Khilafat only." My arguments appealed to those present and, as a result, the question of cow protection was not discussed at this conference.'

By thus effectively sabotaging the sensitive cow issue, Gandhi would kill four birds with one stone: one, dislodging Tilak (who, however, died soon thereafter) from the top leadership of the Congress; two, capturing the Congress leadership *and* political initiative; three, appealing to the Muslims to decide on it 'of their own free will' and 'from a sense of duty towards them as neighbours and children of the same soil'—he thus put the Muslim goodwill and patriotism to test!; four, he buried forever any chance of Hindu-Muslim unity on the basis of *quid pro quo* on religious issues. Gandhi realised that the Muslim fanatics would get nothing out of the Khilafat issue and their violent and restless nature would eventually force them to vent their ire on the Hindus. He had now only to wait for the fanatic Muslims' barbarism to flower in full force. These Muslims did not disappoint him; they would massacre thousands of Hindus in the Malabar region and the communal riots elsewhere spread in India like an angry bull on heat, sexually aroused but finding no cow to funnel heat into would go rampaging in a China shop.

Not only cow, even the burning issue of Punjab, after the Jallianwala Bagh Massacre (April 1919), was of no use to Gandhi: 'there was a suggestion from some quarters that the Punjab question should be tacked on to that of the Khilafat wrong. I opposed the proposal. The Punjab question, I said, was a *local* affair and could not therefore weigh with us in our decision to participate or not in the peace celebrations. If we mixed up the local question with the Khilafat question, which arose directly out of peace terms, we should be guilty of a serious indiscretion. My argument easily carried conviction.' So, for the Great Soul, Amritsar was local, to be kept out of India, and Ankara (Istanbul), Turkey, was to be brought in! He would not discuss the Jallianwala Bagh Massacre because it was a local issue of Punjab; he would discuss the Turk issue because it related to the *foreign* Muslims! And their supporters, the Muslim Indians.

Clearly, Gandhi wanted the focus to remain *exclusively* on the Khilafat issue, overlooking the Hindu issue of cow protection and the 'local' issue of Punjab which had aroused strong reaction even in England where General Dyer was later tried for his barbarism. The Mahatma knew that most participants in a meeting, *any meeting*, are like unthinking robots, worth only their raised hands, controlled by their Masters. This meeting was no different or else the participants would have easily nailed him: in one breath, he was supporting the Muslims in the latter's protest against the British 'atrocity' on the Khilafat issue, he was not supporting the Hindu demand on the cow issue and he was, simultaneously, overlooking the British atrocity on the Hindus and Sikhs in Punjab. Not that other contemporaries of

Gandhi were so stupid as to not see through the Gandhian game, but they had no guts to become parallel 'Mahatmas' themselves, or duck into the fortress of loin-cloth, and helplessly witnessed the wily pied-piper marching past with the gullible, mesmerised crowd the way they would follow cult leaders across the world. Gandhi knew that Indian saints were seen as beyond all human laws, conventions and traditions; they could not apparently be tried or sentenced by normal courts.

After thus pushing the focus of the meeting effectively on the Khilafat issue, throwing the on-agenda cow protection item to the dustbin, Gandhi now created a dramatic spectacle even the Last Prophet would not have forgotten: the sacrifice of a *qafir* (infidel) for the re-establishment of the Caliphate!

Gandhi began slowly: he aimed at *mobilisation* of Muslims, as a prerequisite for the eventual mobilisation of the *Hindus as a counter-reaction*. Maulana Hasrat Mohani had proposed the boycott of British goods to force the government on the Khilafat issue; the Muslims had realised the importance of this patently 'Hindu' method which had played an important role in undoing the Partition of Bengal. The way Gandhi had slighted Jinnah in Mumbai, he now belittled the Maulana in Delhi: 'As the Maulana was delivering his speech, it seemed to me that *it was vain for him to talk about effective resistance to a Government with which he was cooperating in more than one thing*, if resort to arms was impossible or undesirable. The only true resistance to the Government, it therefore seemed to me, was to cease to cooperate with it. Thus I arrived at the word non-cooperation.'

And then, suddenly, the Mahatma declared, even before the assorted leaders and the maulanas could get a glimpse of what he would say next: 'The Mussalmans have *adopted* a very important resolution. If the peace terms are unfavourable to *them*,—which may God forbid,—*they* will stop all cooperation with Government. It is an inalienable right of the people to withhold cooperation. *We are not bound to retain Government titles and honours* or to continue in Government service. If the Government should betray us in a great cause like the Khilafat, we could not do otherwise than non-cooperate. We are therefore entitled to non-cooperate with Government in case of a betrayal.' He thus declared, *on behalf of the astonished Muslims*, that *they* had adopted a resolution to non-cooperate with the British government, even before they could know they had! The Maulana had merely suggested boycott of the British goods. And then Gandhi gave them yet another shock, benumbing those present into admiration and exhilaration, by announcing to surrender the titles like *Sergeant-Major* and the *Kaisar-e-Hind* conferred on him by the British for his services in South Africa, which, in any case, were worthless now. The ensuing cacophony drowned all the doubts and the illogicality of the Mahatma's shenanigans. It had the desired dramatic effect on the participants and Gandhi became the first-ever infidel leader of the Muslims in their 14 century history, though temporarily, and, more importantly, the eternal Number One leader of a recharged Congress. Even Tagore had renounced his Knighthood against the Jallianwala Bagh Massacre—but he was merely a Nobel Laureate in Literature! And Tagore had not done so theatrically in a meeting of the Hindu-Sikhs.

Gandhi was aware of the importance of his political drama: the Sergeant-Major-turned-Mahatma was emerging in India at a time a certain Lilliputian corporal was mending his wounds in a German hospital to emerge as Fuehrer Adolf Hitler. Both were products of the First World War; both nursed deep-seated antipathy against the Fertile Crescent's religions as a culmination of hundreds of years of conflict—Hitler against Judaism and Christianity, Gandhi against Christianity and Islam; both were honing their oratorial skills to mesmerise millions to deal with their perceived religious enemies; both wrote their autobiographies in the 1920s, while in prison, after they tasted their first blood—Gandhi's Non-Cooperation-cum-Khilafat Movement leading to the Moplahs killing of some 5,000 Hindus in Kerala and Hitler's Beer Hall Putsch; both attracted women by their declared 'celibacy'; both shunned their families in the pursuit of their political and messianic goals; both were vegetarian, did not smoke or drink liquor; both would die unnatural deaths when the war they had declared against their perceived enemies would recoil on them.

The Mahatma had now effectively 'entered' the Congress. The first two things he did was to collect half-a-million rupees for the

Jallianwala Bagh memorial and ten million rupees for the Tilak Fund—the first because his 'initiation' in the Congress had taken place in Amritsar where he wanted to impress the Hindus and Sikhs, and the second because he needed money for the Khilafat Movement, for which only the Hindus would contribute and that, too, in Tilak's name (the Muslims would not contribute to *their own* religious Khilafat cause as long as the infidel Hindus were associated with it, as much as they would not like to go to Hajj in Mecca with infidel's subsidy!). Gandhi could swim in such inherent contradictions with the ease of a fish in a turbulent ocean. Reminiscing about these early days in the Congress he was now moulding to do his bidding, he said: 'They used to invite me to their informal gatherings where, as I found, resolutions for the Subjects Committees were conceived. At these gatherings only those persons were invited who enjoyed the special confidence of the leaders and whose services were needed by them. Interlopers also sometimes found their way to these meetings…'

But neither the Khilafat nor the cow protection issues were *his* babies; Khilafat was patently a Muslim issue and the cow protection that of the Hindu Mahasabha and the Arya Samaj. A newly-established leader must have his own mule to ride to the cliff. This Gandhi found in *swadeshi*, or preference to indigenous products over the foreign ones, and *swaraj* or home-rule; the concept of swadeshi was, in fact, evolved during the agitation against the Partition of Bengal in the first decade and that of *swaraj* by Tilak in the second decade of the 20th century. Gandhi, who had *opposed* the boycott of British goods for the Khilafat cause, ***now*** thought it fit to be used for his Non-Cooperation Movement; the Mahatma, who had, until now, *opposed* the Tilakite Home Rule League, admired the British democracy and declared himself a British citizen, ***now*** adopted Tilak's call and 'promised' that India would get *swaraj* (home-rule) in a year! Only a Gujarati businessman would have understood his tactics: a Gujarati businessman, as they say in Gandhi's home state, was one who bought from a Marwari, sold to a Sindhi and made profit. The Mahatma would ridicule your product, encourage you to dispose it off to him for cheap, praise it sky-high and sell it to another, thus making profit! And you could not complain because he had a bigger shop. That 'Gandhi' metamorphosed from a product to just a brand-name was proved by the Congress Party which continued to market the pseudo-Gandhis even after 1948; this brand-loyalty determined market capitalisation of the political company having weak fundamentals and investments.

In that era many Congressmen, particularly the ever-confused Hindus, believed that Gandhi had adopted the Khilafat issue because it was of immediate concern to the Muslims, as also his foil to the British attempts to communally divide the Indians' Freedom Struggle, that he promoted the Ali Brothers and 'sold his heart' to them, that he even anointed one of them, Mohammed Ali, as the Congress President—in other words, he 'appeased' the Muslims to stitch them to the Hindus. Very few contemporaries, however, could have fathomed his politics—most have not even now, in 2017—as they continued to graze at the Gandhian grass with the zeal of newly-born calves. Once they realised how a single puritanical Hindu had defeated the gang of puritanical Muslims at their own age-old game, and had merely used them instead of they using him, the bitter Ali Brothers retreated. But credit must go to him: Gandhi never rubbed even a defeated rival the wrong way. He would just leave him to nurse his wounds and move on: 'We must not be upset that they are no longer with us. On the contrary, we should be thankful that they travelled with us this far,' he counselled his supporters who complained how the Ali Brothers were being dismissive and contemptuous of him. In any case, the Ali Brothers were not his real rivals…Ali was their last name. His real rival would be someone who sandwiched Ali as his middle-name: Muhammad Ali Jinnah.

In the backdrop of this political situation, the All India Khilafat Congress, which met in Delhi in November 1919, decided to launch the Khilafat Movement *under* Gandhi's leadership; the Mahatma, adept at making politically correct noises with a perfect sense of timing, declared the agitation as 'an opportunity of uniting Hindus and Mohammedans as would not arise in a hundred years.' Early in 1920, he publicly declared that the Khilafat question was much more important than the constitutional reforms and the Punjab issue and that *he would lead* the Non-Cooperation Movement in India if the terms of peace with Turkey did not satisfy the Indian Muslims. Gandhi would have known that the demands to annul the Rowlatt Act or make amends for the atrocities in the Punjab would not be accepted by the British, for, that would give boost to the separatist Irish movement in their own backyard; but the Mahatma went ahead with his plans to raise political temperature in India. In June 1920, an all-party conference decided in Allahabad to boycott educational institutions and law courts; on 31 August 1920, the Khilafat Committee launched its movement. Lokmanya Tilak having passed away on August one, Gandhi was now the uncrowned king of the Congress, with Chitta Ranjan Das and Motilal Nehru being his new Sancho Panzas.

At the annual session of the Congress held in Nagpur in December 1920, Gandhi declared that 'the British *people* will have to beware that if they do not want to do justice, it will be bounden duty of every Indian to destroy the Empire.' Now, the Gandhian target was not only the British Indian government but also the British people! The Nagpur meeting was of crucial importance for Gandhi: 'The question of the goal of the Congress formed a subject for keen discussion. In the constitution that I had presented, the goal of the Congress was the attainment of *Swaraj* within the British Empire if possible and without if necessary. A party of the Congress wanted to limit the goal to Swaraj within the British Empire only. Its viewpoint was put forth by Pandit Malviyaji and Mr Jinnah. But they were not able to get many votes.' The meeting passed resolutions about routine issues like Hindu-Muslim unity, the removal of untouchability and promotion of Khadi as an alternate means of livelihood, especially for the untouchables…'and since then the Hindu members of the Congress have taken upon themselves the responsibility of ridding Hinduism of the curse of untouchability, and the Congress has established a living bond of relationship with the 'skeletons' of India through Khadi. The adoption of non-cooperation for the sake of Khilafat was itself a great practical attempt made by the Congress to bring about Hindu-Muslim unity.' He foresaw the attempts to divide the Hindu community and took up the issue of untouchables through social reforms.

After writing about this conference, Gandhi declared Farewell to the readers of his autobiography. Why did he abruptly close the book, while his work had just begun in the Congress? 'The history of the

Congress, since the great changes in it that I have described above, is still in the making. And my *principal experiments* during the past seven years have all been made through the Congress. A reference to my principal *experiments with the leaders would therefore be unavoidable, if I set about describing my experiments further*. And this I may not do, at any rate for the present, if only from a sense of propriety. Lastly, my conclusions from my current experiments can hardly as yet be regarded as decisive. It therefore seems to me to be my plain duty to close this narrative here. In fact my pen instinctively refuses to proceed further.' He was aware that the Hindus would not like him to say unpalatable things about those leaders who had passed away, nor would the Muslims like him to reveal the truth about the selfish Maulanas who exploited the Muslims for non-causes. He confined himself to his 'experiments' with Hindu and Muslim leaders and their issues, until 1920, and exploited them for what he, missionary-like, believed was *his* truth and *his* non-violence, the way *he* saw Satya and Ahimsa: 'It is not without a wrench that I have to take leave of the reader. I set a high value on *my* experiments....To describe truth, *as it has appeared to me*, and in the exact manner in which I have arrived at it, has been my ceaseless effort.'

Outwardly Gandhi was calm like an ocean; inside, he was struggling with his gargantuan storms. He was a non-practising Hindu, away from ritualism and the only solace he could draw from was in his 'achievements' without the aid of a God of others who believed in Him this way or that. Like the angry Hindu sage Vishwamitra, Gandhi had constructed his own make-believe world, with himself as its Creator-Prophet, and came out of this shell only to ensure that others believed in the truth of what he believed. Like other similarly possessed missionaries, his 'experiments' were the only relief from these excruciating psychological pains: 'The exercise has given me ineffable mental peace, because it has been my fond hope that it might bring faith in Truth and Ahimsa to waverer.' Protesting against Christianity and Islam had perhaps made him think like those two founder-prophets, *the way they saw the truth*, the way they would bend others to it. If you want to fight a prophet, become one yourself!

'My uniform experience has convinced me that there is no God than Truth...the only means for the realization of Truth is Ahimsa'. Unlike monopolistic and absolutist Abrahamic prophets who would not let any other competitor emerge, he was a multi-cultured, multi-layered Hindu for whom destination, rather than the vehicle, was important: 'And, even though my efforts in this behalf may prove fruitless, let the readers know that the vehicle, not the great principle, is at fault. After all, however sincere my strivings after Ahimsa may have been, they have still been imperfect and inadequate...But this much I can say with assurance, as a result of all my experiments, that a perfect vision of Truth can only follow a complete realisation of Ahimsa.'

If he were a saint, what drew him to politics: 'To see the universal and all-pervading Spirit of Truth face to face one must be able to love the meanest of creation as oneself. And a man who aspires after that cannot afford to keep out of any field of life. That is why my devotion to Truth has drawn me into the field of politics; and I can say without the slightest hesitation, and yet in all humility, that ***those who say that religion has nothing to do with politics do not know what religion means.*'** Unlike other careerist politicians sweeping fundamental societal questions under the carpet to hide the cesspool beneath it, he thus brought to the centre-stage the question of Hindus and Muslims, their belief systems and deftly rubbed them against one-another, like Jesus playing his disciples, particularly Judas Iskariot, against his Jewish enemies or Muhammed juggling the wavering Ansars, the 'Hypocrites', in Medina to establish his leadership once for all. Despite his greatness, Gandhi had to stoop to the level of Christian and Muslim fundamentalists to shield India from the Abrahamic shenanigans continuing unabated since the last 20 centuries and defang them in 1947. His greatness lay in finding the needle successfully in a haystack the Gandhians continued to be lost into thereafter.

He chose to close the book suddenly, perhaps, because, while writing this in 1926-27, he would not want to say how his support to the *patently* anti-Hindu Khilafat Movement—because, theologically, the Caliph was responsible for elimination of non-Muslims and Islamisation of all infidel lands like India; the Hindu support to reinstate the Caliphate was like the calf trying to revive the big cat!—

had achieved his unsaid objective of dividing the Hindus and Muslims, rather than uniting them as he claimed outwardly. And how would he now further widen the gap between the two rival communities. He was the only autobiographer who would end his work mid-way because he did not want to declare his successes prematurely.

And, ironically, the Ali Brothers, who vociferously led the Khilafat Movement in India, played the key role in hastening the demise of the Caliphate in Turkey: they distributed pamphlets to fellow Muslims there, urging them to restore the Caliphate's honour, at a time when the Turkish Muslims were ambivalent about the institution's future; even Mustafa Kemal dare not abolish it before 1924. The 'foreign intervention' of the Ali Brothers, from a *British India*, alarmed the nationalist Turks, already anti-British, to abolish the Caliphate quickly!

Gandhi had learnt really well from Euclid's 13th Proposition.

But Mohandas Gandhi was much more than his Autobiography; and left many hints about the Mahatma and his mission outside this book. His other writings, too, revealed his tactics few people could understand *at that time* because they blindly glorified him believing he was not only thinking for India but was also somewhat of a Hercules shouldering the Earth for them. Faith kills logic and the capacity to think and analyse independently, and the unquestioning disciples could never become really educated people—the Gandhians proved it again and again. They chose to be in awe of him but never shocked by him; like all cult leaders, the Mahatma continued to benumb their senses because none among them could outgrow his genius and intercontinental mind—his admirers and critics were simply unequipped psychologically even to fathom him. Why? Because they had a limited vision about the *Things of Nature*, unlike their Master who grasped the *Nature of Things*, the way from Goat to God.

Gandhi, who returned from South Africa to India in 1915, had, within five years, become the undisputed political leader of India, leaving those miles behind who had toiled for decades through that petitioners' club, the Congress. These leaders—G S Khaparde, Bipin Chandra Pal, Annie Besant, and, above all, M A Jinnah—did not like the Gandhian tactics, the new, active street-smart agitational turn the national freedom movement had taken under him, the transformation of static electricity into a dynamic one using the First World War as a dynamo. They strictly believed in traditional methods of agitation and political work confined within the four walls of the law, a slow evolution of political consciousness and the slow demise of the British Empire, a Dominion Status for India until these ends were achieved, thanks to the perceived *benevolence* of the British. The main proponents of this idea were the leaders who had now begun to see the interests of the Hindus and the Muslims as their lifetime rewards; they were Pandit Madan Mohan Malviya of the Hindu Mahasabha and the debonair, three-piece-suited M A Jinnah, the latter being the source behind the Lucknow Pact of 1916 but increasingly sidelined by that fellow Gujarati in one-and-a-half piece loincloth. These community leaders preferred the Dominion Status rather than Swaraj because they suspected that any sudden departure of the 'powerful' British would make India a chaotic state ruled by the Hindus/Muslims—their fears were proved correct in 1947 when the Partition left some five million people dead. Gandhi knew better, as all successful politicians do, because he cast his net far and wide, looked beyond India to spot the British weaknesses and Muslim vulnerabilities, *abroad*—and he was not scared of chaos and anarchy as he knew, the Darwinian way, that Life evolves only through turbulence and churning. One by one, these protesting leaders left the Congress and, except Jinnah, disappeared almost without a trace even as Gandhi and his associates set up parallel educational institutions across the country in a bid to undo Macaulayism.

Post-1857, the Muslims had evolved into mainly three streams: *Muslim Indians*, led by the clergy, who would, given the opportunity, revive the dead Mughal Empire and become the feudal ruling class once again; *Indian Muslims*, the patriotic minority Muslim elite who, having been processed through European traditions, knew the futility of reviving their bygone Empire in the contemporary era of nationalism, especially in the face of the fast evolving Hindus, and would, therefore, like to share the reign with them—they were led by Jinnah—but eventually they mostly turned into latter-day clones of Jinnah; and, the vast majority of *India's Muslims*, who, like their Hindu counterparts, could be used as cannon fodder by the two earlier categories.

Gandhi's politics led to the near-merging of all three streams, and made the Muslims appear as a solid block; from his study of Islam, he knew that Muhammedism provided the perfect Matrix for creation of this block and he trusted the Muslim clergy to turn their community into fuel if only he could win their trust, even if temporarily. For this purpose, he deftly used the three issues—Khilafat, the Afghan 'invasion' and Hyderabad—to unite them to make him emerge as the soul of the 'Hindu Congress', as the perceptive Jinnah called it. Strangely, most Hindu leaders who went round Gandhi like his satellites were of the progressive bent of mind but the Muslim leaders supporting him were retrogressive; in the case of Jinnah, it was just the reverse and the Muslim clergy almost shunned him initially as an infidel (indeed, many Deobandi fundamentalists, frustrated at the re-emergence of a vast Hindu India flanked by two miniature Pakistans on the corpse of the Mughal-British India and thus undoing the achievements of Islam in a millennium, denounced the Qaid-e-Azam as *Qafir e-Azam*, the Great Infidel, in the 1940s).

Delineation of these streams had begun to appear more clearly, although its outlines were marked by Sir Syed Ahmed himself in the 1880s, with the creation of the Muslim League. On 1 October 1906, a group of Muslim leaders, led by The Agha Khan, presented a Memorandum to the Viceroy seeking *special privileges* to the Muslim Indians, such as reservation in the Army and separate electorate; these demands were readily accepted and prepared the soil lying fallow after 1857 for the four-phased germination of Pakistan in the next four decades. Of course, the British, who had played a double-game with backdoor support to the formation of the Indian National Congress in 1885, played their imperial game again: Aligarh's Muslim Anglo-Oriental College Principal William A J Archibald was the brain behind this Memorandum, drafted with able assistance from Harcourt Butler, the Viceroy's private secretary. This led to the formation of the Muslim League on 30 December 1906.

By the time Gandhi returned to India, Jinnah had already emerged as the 'best Ambassador for the Hindu-Muslim unity' and as a possible successor to Gokhale, particularly after the 1916 Lucknow Pact that 'united' the two factions of the Congress with each other and with the League. The only way Gandhi could establish himself vis-a-vis such a formidable and brilliant lawyer as Jinnah was to somehow appear *different* from the fellow Gujarati Muslim. Jinnah was moving step-by-step, within the framework of the law, as a backroom boy away from street politics which he abhorred; predictably, Gandhi chose to hit the street, using as seed capital the political dividends he had brought back from South Africa. They did not miss any opportunity to run each other down—but always maintained the facade of bonhomie in the public. Ironically, despite their outward appearances, Gandhi evolved as a global Hindu leader, and Jinnah as a local Muslim leader. There was a difference between their perceptions of the British, the issues, the people: while the elitist Jinnah was a full-time lawyer, part-time politician, had the illusion of the 'supreme' power of the British who could only be *persuaded* to deliver the goods, Gandhi, full-time politician and part-time lawyer, knew the British hollowness better in terms of world politics, that the Empire was facing similar anti-colonial movements across the seven oceans and was yielding one concession after another, that the Crown could be *forced* to bend provided you have the force multiplier to make it kneel, and, if necessary, crawl.

This force multiplier could be brought into existence by emotional, religious issues that affected the people the deepest. To the Hindus, the Mahatma would offer Ram Rajya and Swaraj; to the Muslims, Mr Gandhi would offer the Dar-ul-Islam of the Caliph! Nobody realised that the wily Gujarati businessman was selling the same property, India, to two rival buyers because the Ram Rajya *for the Hindus and in India* was antithetical to the Dar-ul-Islam for the Muslims globally. But, he revived the ancient, mythological dream of the Hindus to re-establish the ideal reign of Lord Ram that necessitated the killing of Ravana, the Demon King, leaving unsaid who the latter was but created a situation in which poor Jinnah was forced to fit the bill. Gandhi continuously worked to weave his sticky and thin web, laid a trap and waited for the enemy to fall within his striking distance. At the beginning of the First World War in 1914, when he, like Jinnah, was in England, Gandhi was enrolling recruits to the British Army *against*, among others, the Ottomans/Caliph; after the end of the War, the same Gandhi would enrol the Muslims in *support* of the Ottomans! In 1917, when both Gandhi and Jinnah met the Viceroy, Lord Chelmsford, to discuss the issue of sending Indian troops to Europe to fight against the Germans in the First World War, the former supported and the latter opposed!! Emerging from the meeting, the media-savvy Mahatma said he had spoken to the Viceroy in *Hindi* language—this, and not Jinnah's opposition to the troop-sending, hit the headlines the next day!!!

It is necessary to understand the tactics of the master strategist Gandhi's so-called Khilafat efforts, which he, as the astute Master of global politics, alone knew. A majority of Muslims, including the ebulliant Muslim Indians and the silent Indian Muslims, cutting across all their differences, were almost unanimously behind the Ottoman Sultans who doubled as the Caliphs—it was another thing that even the Arabs treated the Turks as barbarians and were happy at the end of the Ottoman rule as a good riddance. Gandhi suspected that some of even Gokhale's 'secular' disciples, including H C E Zacharias, were pro-Caliph and against infidels like the Hindus—barring Gandhi, none of the Hindu leaders cutting across their political parties, uneducated as they were in things Islamic, understood their contradictions or short-sightedness; the Ottomans' inevitable end due to rising Muslim nationalist movements in West Asia or the fanatic Islamists' secret strategies and tactics to keep the Hindus in good humour for the time being.

Gandhi, targeting as much the Christians as the Muslims, saw in the Khilafat issue the golden opportunity to corner the British by temporarily enrolling the Muslim support to the Hindu cause of *Swaraj* as well. Interestingly, while supporting the Non-Cooperation Movement envisaging *Swaraj*, the Muslims did not realise that the very word 'Swaraj' was coined by the great Hindu king Chhatrapati Shivaji, who humbled Islam's 'ideal' ruler, Aurangzeb, and that Swaraj or self-rule, then, meant *freedom fromMuslim rule*! Swaraj, now, did not merely mean a freedom from the British; it also meant revival of the

Hindu Empire and end of the Muslims. And Gandhi was enrolling Muslim support in this agitation! For, the more the Muslims united, the more their aspirations would grow and more they would trigger the *desired* Hindu reaction: in other words, if one aimed to unite the diverse Hindus, *he must*, first of all, unite the Muslims. Besides the Khilafat issue, the Muslim fanatics were also electrified about their Plan-B: an Afghan 'invasion' of 'British India' if the British failed to reinstall the Caliph, so as to complete India's stalled Islamisation.

Before Gandhi handed over what came to be known as the 'blank cheque' to the Muslims, he was aware that the Muslim soldiers of the British Indian Army, recruited mainly from Afghanistan, North-West Frontier Province (NWFP) and the Punjab, had brought the news back home as to how the Muslims in the Middle East felt relieved at getting rid of the Ottomans and this was the prime reason why Afghanistan would not 'attack' India despite the Muslims' desire. Clearly, he knew that the 'blank cheque' he issued to the Muslims was bound to bounce as the bank account had no money. Even anti-Gandhi Congress leaders were appealing to the Muslims not to fall into the trap of the Non-Cooperation Movement whose declared goal was Swaraj.

But, hats off to Gandhi's political genius that, despite some of his enemies having the idea of what he was up to, he played with fire like an expert and was able to persuade the Muslims in the early 1920s to set their foot on a slippery path which would take them straight down into the Islamabad of 2017 aligning with rank atheist, China!; no other leader, an infidel one at that, would have led them down their perceived Eden Garden.

In his *Young India* of 6 June 1920, Gandhi wrote: 'Mrs Besant and Dr Sapru strongly dissuaded the Mahomedans present from the policy of non-cooperation. The other Hindu speakers made non-committal speeches. Whilst the other Hindu speakers approved of the principle of non-cooperation in theory, they saw many practical difficulties and they feared also complications arising from Mahomedans, welcoming an Afghan invasion of India. The Mahomedan speakers gave the fullest and frankest assurances that they would fight to a man any invader who wanted to conquer India, *but they were equally frank in asserting that any invasion from without undertaken with a view to uphold the prestige of Islam and to vindicate justice would have their full sympathy if not their actual support.*' That is, if the Afghans invaded India to 'uphold the prestige of Islam', the Muslims of India would sympathise with the invaders, against the infidels, that is the Hindus (and the British, for that matter). Gandhi's efforts to prove that even modern education and westernisation would not really change most Muslims had begun to bear fruit. 'It is easy enough to understand and justify Hindu caution. *It is difficult to resist the Mahomedan position.*' Why was it difficult to resist the Muslim position? Because this was precisely what official/political Islam, increasingly under the spell of Wahhabism, expected them to do—to either convert or eliminate the infidels! 'In my opinion, the best way to prevent India from becoming the battle-ground between the forces of Islam and those of the English, is *for the Hindus to make non-cooperation a success* and I have little doubt that if the Mahomedans remain true to their declared intention and are able to exercise self-restraint and make sacrifices, *the Hindus will play the game* and join the campaign of non-cooperation.' Gandhi left no one in doubt that his Non-Cooperation Movement and its declared goal of Swaraj was purely a *Hindu* phenomenon; likewise, the parallel Khilafat Movement he was using so deftly for his purpose, was purely a Muslim agitation—like a true businessman, he was selling rival brands from the same outlet...pick and choose. Many of his contemporaries did not understand his game-plan; even Jinnah had only a hazy idea of what Gandhi was up to—the future Qaid-e-Azam, Great Leader, cautioned everybody of the dangers of this 'Gandhian' policy which would, he was afraid, not only lead to Hindu-Muslim conflicts but also give an opportunity to the British to crush the Indians, particularly the Muslims, the way they had post-1857.

Jinnah thought Gandhi would throw back the Muslims to the same abyss; but even he did not realise that Gandhi was apparently working not merely against the Muslims *in* India but to despatch Islam *out of* India! 'I feel equally certain that the Hindus will not assist Mahomedans in promoting or bringing about an armed conflict between the British government *and their allies*, and Afghanistan.' That is, the Hindus should keep off the Muslims if the British *and their allies* (the Hindus?) faced Afghanistan! On 20 June 1920, he wrote in the same periodical 'I consider it (the Non-Cooperation Movement) to be perfectly consistent with my loyalty to the British connection. But I would not go with the Mussalmans in any campaign of violence I could not help them in promoting, for instance, an invasion of India through Afghanistan or otherwise for the purpose of forcing better peace terms. *It is I hold the duty of every Hindu to resist any inroad on India, even for the purpose specified.*' On the one hand, he was being accused of drafting a letter on behalf of India's Muslims to the Afghanistan Amir inviting him to attack India—Maulana Muhammed Ali, who sent this telegram ('Don't sign the treaty. Situation in India hopeful.') to Afghan Amir Amanullah Khan, had shown to veteran Hindu Mahasabha leader Swami Shraddhanand its draft written in Gandhi's infamous and easily recognisable hand-writing—and, at the same time, he was cautioning the Hindus! The Amir was 'Ghazi', slayer of the infidel; since the British, being Christians, were *Ahl-e-Qitab* (People of the Book), they could not be infidels. Only the Hindus were the infidels who were to be, the Muslim leaders believed, used as cannon fodder; indeed, Muhammed Ali had clarified in a Madras speech that the infidel Hindus *will have to* cooperate with the Muslims if the Afghans invaded India to 'liberate it'. Clearly, Gandhi's purpose was to somehow incite the Muslim Mind so that, when frustrated, they pounce on the Hindus.

His political moves were becoming clearer: of the two enemies, the British and the Muslims, he would befriend one at a time and use them against each other. When a Muslim fanatic murdered Swami Shraddhanand in December 1926, Gandhi, in one of his rare, uncontrolled, outbursts, reacted sharply: '(The) Mussalmans have an ordeal to pass through. There can be no doubt that they are too free with the knife and the pistol. *The sword is the emblem of Islam.* But Islam was born in an environment where the sword was, and still remains, the supreme law. The message of Jesus has been proved ineffective because the environment was unready to receive it. So with the message of the Prophet. The sword is yet too much in evidence among the Mussalmans. It must be sheathed if Islam is to be what it means—peace.' But even he did not, perhaps, realise that Islam **never** meant peace—it always meant, literally, ***surrender***:

unconditional surrender of the Muslims to Allah and Muhammed and unconditional surrender of all non-Muslims to the Muslims. When Islam moved out of Arabia, it got acculturated and softened up somewhat in contact with other highly-developed but sick companies, the twilight civilisations and cultures it acquired, (Syria, Persia, Egypt and the Mesopotamia); however, as deIslamisation progressed post-Abbasids, particularly after Russia defeated the Ottomans at Crimea and Britain snatched India from the Mughals, both in the 1850s, the retreating Islam, led by the Wahhabis, slowly reclaimed its original moorings of death and destruction when it found that its Word as well as the Sword were being rendered increasingly irrelevant by science, technology and democracy. Gandhi, who lived in the midst of this great churning process, had come to understand this Islamic dilemma of irrelevance versus irreverence and his reaction, as above, effectively showed what he really thought of the Muslims' tactics and strategy and why and how he crafted the ejection of Islam from India.

The whole theme of Non-Cooperation-cum-Khilafat Movement was hilarious. Gandhi was leading one 'Movement' and participating in another, parallel, simultaneously. Non-Cooperation was against the British and non-violent; Khilafat was violent in India, later, and pro-British (because the deposed Caliph continued to be pro-British! But the British could not reinstall him due to the rise of Kemalist movement in Turkey itself and nationalist movements across the Arab-Muslim world against the Ottomans). The Khilafatists, too, not to be left behind, were both pro- and anti-British and pro- and anti-Hindu all at one and the same time. Take your pick—both the sides were consistently inconsistent. As per what he said on 20 June 1920, in *Young India*, cited above, he was trying to pin the blame for any possible violence on the Muslims and preparing the Hindus to resist any Afghan invasion for which he was himself one of the alleged conspirators! At the same time, his 'loyalty to the British connection' remained intact; this, when he had surrendered the titles the British conferred on him; this, when he was leading the Swaraj and Swadeshi drives against the British....but Gandhi was a rarest of the rare breed who could have his cake and eat it too, run with the hare and hunt with the hound simultaneously, one who would encourage the thief to break-in and, also alert the policeman to catch him. Apparently, he felt that his contradictory positions were being read closely by his enemies who could use these in future against him; he, would, therefore, cover the tracks himself. On 15 June, 1921, he wrote: 'It is not enough for a non-cooperator not to mean violence; it is necessary that his speech must not be capable of a contrary interpretation by reasonable men!'

Age-old slogans of 'Islam in danger' and the like had stirred the Muslims of the sub-continent which was still full of infidels and although the Afghan Amir was unwilling to attack British-India to protect Islam, his restless tribes found an opportunity to loot India by flooding in. The British-Indian Army tried to prevent this flood and more than 5,000 soldiers were killed between 1 January 1919 and 30 April 1921. On 4 May 1921, Gandhi wrote: 'I warn the reader against believing in the bogey of an Afghan invasion. A weak, disarmed, helpless, credulous India does not know how this government has kept her under hypnotic spell.' However, less than a month ago (13 April 1921), the same man was writing thus: '*It is no use isolating me from the rest.* As Maulana Mohammad Ali often puts it, war is bad but there are worse things than war. The Ali Brothers are honestly and industriously endeavouring to secure a peaceful settlement. But should their effort prove vain either for want of response from the government or the people as lovers of their faith they will not hesitate to precipitate in war if they could. *As for my own attitude, whilst my faith would not permit me to invite or encourage a war of violence, I do contemplate with equanimity a state of war in preference to the present state of effeminate peace imposed by force of arms. And it is for this reason that I am taking part in this movement of non-violent non-cooperation even at the risk of anarchy being the ultimate result.*' Never was a lawyer-turned-politician more eloquent about creating a situation that could lead to anarchy!

Not that the British, or others with their heads equidistant between the shoulders, did not know about the Mahatma's political somersaults and that the celibate was sleeping with several sworn enemies at the same time, in the same bed; perhaps the only people in the dark were the die-hard, blind-folded, Gandhians finding solace behind his loin-cloth which they thought was the ultimate shelter for the Hindu soul harassed for a thousand years. Home Member Sir

William Vincent, who had the 'intelligence' as well as intelligence to analyse and understand the ground situation, told the Legislative Assembly on 23 March 1921, that 'the two prominent Muslims identifying themselves with Mr Gandhi (ie. the Ali Brothers)' were conceiving the 'idea of a Mussalman Empire in this country…with the aid of foreign enemies.' Some intellectuals, such as Sir Sankaran Nair, exclaimed at the Mahatma's foolhardiness in 1922: 'But for the fact that he (Mr Gandhi) is well-known to be a saint and Mahatma, I would have had no hesitation in saying that his observations about meeting the Afghans show him to be either a fool or a knave.'

Although Gandhi had drafted his 'secret' letter to the Afghan Amir and the Ali Brothers and others tried to dissuade the Amir from entering into negotiations with the British, its patently anti-national content became controversial, maligning the name of the Mahatma. Gandhi, always careful with words spoken and written—he drafted his 'anti-Indian' letter in his own hand-writing to make sure that the Muslims whipped themselves up against the British with ***this*** extent of 'Hindu support'—never lost any of his well-honed skills in his classic reply at the Allahabad District Conference of 10 May 1921: 'I cannot understand why the Ali Brothers are going to be arrested as the rumour goes, and why I am to remain free. They have done nothing which I would not do. If they had sent a message to the Amir, I also would send one to inform the Amir, that if he came to India, no Indian, so long as I can help it, would help the government to drive him back. If a man is true to his religion no Afghan or any power on earth can make him transgress his religious precepts.' But the controversy dogged Gandhi all his life; when the people began to question Jinnah's patriotism, the Mahatma's patriotism, too, came under cloud. Finally, he washed his hands off all this by writing on 10 February 1940, in *Harijan*: 'So far as the charge of my intriguing with the Amir is concerned I can say that there is no truth whatsoever in it. Further, I know that the Brothers stoutly denied the charge when it was brought to their notice. And I believed them implicitly. I do not remember having drafted any telegram on behalf of Maulana Mohammad Ali to the then Amir. The alleged telegram is harmless in itself and does not warrant the deduction drawn from it. The late

Swamiji never referred the matter to me for confirmation. *It is wrong to say anything against dead men unless one has positive proof and stating it is relevant.'* So, on the one hand he totally disowned having drafted the telegram, on the other he even declared it to be 'harmless', which did not warrant the deduction everybody was drawing from it; it could warrant the attention only Gandhi could draw from it, that it was a harmless telegram that had not been penned by the Mahatma! Why did Gandhi take two decades to officially deny he drafted the telegram? Because all three men concerned—the Ali Brothers and Swami Shraddhanand—were dead by 1940! And, Mr G was now directly fighting his last battle against Mr J, who was far more potent a force than the Ali Brothers or the Swami, one who could *now*, in the midst of the Pakistan Movement, use the controversial letter to question the Mahatma's own patriotic credentials!

Interestingly, at a time when Britain was fighting a grim battle against the Germans in the World War II, suffering heavy losses in 1940, and was at the same time getting crippled in India due to extremist movement, Gandhi justified why he would not invite the Afghans: 'For one thing, it would be contrary to my creed of non-violence. For another, I have too great a respect for English bravery and arms to think that an invasion of India can be successful without a strong combination of different powers. In any case, I have no desire to substitute British Rule with any other foreign rule. I want unadulterated Home Rule, however inferior in quality it may be...*Let me further remind the readers that I do not believe in secret methods.*' He was reluctant on possible reincorporation of Sind into the Bombay Province—in 1940, it meant that Gandhi may have felt that Muslim-majority Sind could soon be part of an emerging Pakistan!—when he said: 'As for Sind my advice stands. Reincorporation of Sind in the Bombay Province may or may not be a good proposition on other grounds, but certainly it is not for the purpose of greater protection of life and property. Every Indian, be he Hindu or any other, must learn the art of protecting himself. It is the condition of real democracy. The state has a duty. But no state can protect those who will not share with it the duty of protecting themselves.' He was now beginning to refer to every Indian as 'Hindu or any other', but no longer Muslim! And they must learn the art of protecting themselves (against Muslims?), ostensibly with the help of the British, since the state has a duty. No wonder a number of leaders accused Gandhi of changing the creed of the Congress; from advocating the interests of 'all Indians' in 1885, Gandhi's Congress had, by 1920, come to speak for the 'rule of the people, by the people, for the people' (that is, rule of the majority, Hindus!). By constantly speaking about the Ram Rajya, the recitation of the *Gita* and similar other Hindu symbolism, Gandhi had converted the very *raison d'etre* of the Congress from secularism to Hinduism: the Mahatma prepared the ground on which would germinate both the RSS and Jinnah.

The Gandhi-Alis' invitation to the Afghan Amir to invade India against the British was different from the invitations sent in the 10th and 16th centuries by King Jaichand and Ibrahim Lodi to Muhammad Ghori and Babur, respectively. Gandhi was aware of the Islamists' real intentions in doing so, but he still gambled because he knew the lethargic Hindus could not be whipped back into their battle gear without a *fear of the Muslims*—the way Islamist terror unites them now!—by scaring them of being once again attacked by the Muslim invaders, especially by the Afghans, and reviving memories of the Three Battles of Panipat; the last such battle had been fought against Ahmed Shah Abdali in 1764 which crippled the Mughal Empire as well the Marathas and led to the establishment of the British Raj. Gandhi would not want a Fourth Battle of Panipat between the Hindus and Muslims and he knew it would not come about either, what with the British at the helms in Delhi. He merely used the Ali Brothers as firewood, as agent provocateurs for this purpose. When his crony C F Andrews questioned him about an article he penned on this subject, his reply was remarkably cryptic. On 5 May 1921, he wrote in his *Young India*: 'Is not my article on the Afghan bogey an invitation to the Afghans to invade the Indian border and thus do I not become a direct party to violence? Thus asks Mr Andrews. My article was written *for Indians and for the Government*. I do not believe the Afghans to be so foolish as to invade India on the strength of my article…' Clearly, by 'Indians', he meant the Hindus, as he had already made the Non-Cooperation Movement a Hindu movement; simultaneously, he also *cautioned* the British 'Government' about what the Muslims could do! But wasn't the Mahatma accused of being anti-Indian (or, anti-Hindu in this context)? 'But I see that it (the article) is capable of bearing the interpretation put upon it by Mr Andrews. I therefore hasten to inform all whom it may concern that not only do I not want to invite the Afghans or anybody else to come to our assistance but I am anxious for them not to come to our assistance.' But what if the Afghans invaded, after all? 'I am quite confident of India's ability to settle with the Government without extraneous help', he wrote, and then the customary, default Mahatma-brand popped up, 'Moreover, I am interested in demonstrating the perfect possibility of attaining our end only by non-violent means.' He thus effectively left the Khilafat and Afghan issues high and dry once they had served their limited purpose of inciting the Muslims. Through the Non-Cooperation Movement, he not only wanted to charge up the political scenario but was also trying to energise the Indian soldiers of the British Army: 'What however I would do is totally different from what I can do. I am sorry to have to confess that the movement has not yet acquired such hold on the soldier class as to embolden them to refuse assistance to the Government in time of need. When the soldier class has realised that they live for the nation, and that it is a travesty of a soldier's calling when he undertakes to kill to order, the battle of India's worldly freedom is won without more.' After inviting the Afghans to set India on fire, it was time he also kept the fire-tenders ready: '...I, therefore, so far as my creed of non-violence is concerned, can contemplate an Afghan invasion with perfect equanimity and equally so far as India's safety is concerned. The Afghans have no quarrel with India. They are a god-fearing people. I warn non-coöperators against judging the Afghans by a few savage specimens we see in Bombay or Calcutta. It is a superstition to suppose that they will overrun India if the British post at the frontier was withdrawn. Let us remember that there is nothing to prevent them from overrunning India today, if they wished to.'

After investing his zero seed capital in a shell company called Khilafat Movement, and having managed an unprecedented 0:100 equity-debt funding from a consortium of contemporary imperial banks—that would also lead to the Initial Public Offer (IPO) in 1947—now was the time to make a quick exit from the start-up itself. This made the Movement bubble into a massive non-producing asset (NPA) but the consortium did not know how to recover its investment as the first promoters, the Ali Brothers, had retired and the second promoter, a saint, did not even have to file for bankruptcy; Jinnah, who eventually bought the bleeding firm was not even sure of its fundamentals! What was, however, NPA for the consortium, would be a huge realty for the second promoter to raise the future Pakistan.

How?

When nothing came of the Khilafat Movement and Gandhi's Swaraj promised in a year failed to arrive, the Muslims debated the next course of action. Many, including Maulana Abul Kalam Azad, believed that India was no longer Dar-ul-Aman, but a Dar-ul-Harb and that the only theological exit available to the Muslims was either to leave India for a Dar-ul-Islam or wage *jihad* (holy war) against the 'infidels' that included the slave Hindus and the masters British; Azad, who was to become the Congress President two decades later, had said that 'Against the non-Muslim Government, Islam prescribes only sword, protracted battle and the cutting of throats.' This, when his 'leader', the Mahatma, was promising Swaraj to the majority (the Hindus) within a year! Clearly, even Azad knew that Swaraj would trigger Islamic jihad against any possible Hindu Swaraj because the Muslims could not, theologically, remain subject to the infidel rule. But the Mahatma was not only a great snake-charmer, he also loved to gift his enemies the reptiles attractively packaged. Some 18,000 Muslim families left India for Afghanistan, to settle down in that next door Dar-ul-Islam, in 1920-21, in what was to be the first *reverse-flow of Islam* since the arrival of Muhammad bin-Qasim in 711; it was the beginning of transfer of population in the would-be 'Pakistan'. But not all Muslims, vast majorities of whom were innocent converts, illiterate and poor, still steeped deep into the Hindu caste system and traditions, could leave India.

The only course left for the frenzied Muslim militants was to turn against the Hindus to relieve themselves of their erectile function.

What if they could not revive the Caliphate in Turkey? Had not they been the only Muslims in the world to have agitated for this revival of the Ottoman Caliphs? Therefore, if not in West Asia, they could at least revive the Caliphate in South Asia! Therefore, on 1 August 1921, the first death anniversary of Tilak and expiry of the Mahatma's Swaraj-in-one-year bluff, the 'Khilafat Raj' was established by the Mappilahs or Moppla (Moplah) Muslims in the Malabar region of Kerala, ostensibly as a 'proletariat' revolution against the local Hindu *jenmis* (feudal lords)—the Marxists still glorify this Hindu-only massacre as a 'freedom movement', underlining that Communism is merely the Allah-free, Marx-attached variety of Islam, member of the same Abrahamic Family. The Muslim 'revolutionaries' exclusive targets were the proletariat poor Hindus; between 5,000 to 10,000 of them were massacred in cold blood as the first qualification for the devout Muslims to enter *Jannat* while leaving behind the hell of rape and rapine. In the next 20 days, the Muslim jihad spread all over Kerala, the Khilafat flags were hoisted on police stations and government offices for over two months. The *Mappila Lahala* 'rebellion' was actually a culmination of similar mini-massacres in the 19th and early 20th centuries when Islam began to flower again in Kerala. A number of 'secular' reports probing the massacres came, mostly white-washing the Hindus' bloodshed; Annie Besant estimated that the Muslims killed or drove away some 100,000 Hindus and forcibly converted many 'infidels'. The venerable lady observed that 'Malabar has taught us what Islamic rule still means, and we do not want to see another specimen of the Khilafat Raj in India'.For six months from August 1921, the 5,200-sq km-area of the Malabar region remained prototype of future Pakistan.

Gandhi had *thus*, through his stratagem, succeeded in exposing the Wahhabi-type, default Islamic barbarism to its full-flowering; all he needed to do was to inflate the Muslim ego more and more to have them work for political Islam's flowering season. Soon, the sporadic communal riots became an all-India phenomenon as Gandhi continued to preach peace and love of the goat. Only a hapless goat could whet the killing spirit and 'bravery' of the fanatic Muslims; he was aware that the fanatic Muslims could surrender only to a more barbaric and superior force and would never, *therefore*, take up arms against the British. This was a terrible psychological warfare in which the relative loser of today would be the absolute victor tomorrow in the age of Sigmund Freud and Albert Einstein. *Gandhi would just demonstrate to the Hindus what the Muslims would do if and when the British left and the Mughal Empire was resurrected*; he apparently trapped the Muslims to make sure Islam blossomed in its true colours: '*shameful inhumanity* proceeding in Malabar', was his cryptic comment on Islam, as his colleague, Maulana Hasrat Mohani, predictably, justified the massacre as a 'military necessity driven by the Muslims' self-defence'.

The 5,000 Hindu corpses in Kerala in 1921 were the seed whose crop would yield 50,000,000 transmigrated and massacred souls India will harvest in 1947. Islam had entered India from Kerala; its return journey, too, began in the same coordinates.

In fact, with the decline of the Mughal Empire, the Islamists were on the back foot in India from the beginning of the 19th century, the way they were sliding back in the West due to the decline of the Ottomans in the 19th-20th; they were concerned with the future of their faith in an infidel India which they, unlike other civilisations they invaded, had failed to fully Islamise in their 1,000-year-long rule. The utter defeat of the Ottomans at the hands of the Tsarist Russia in the Crimean War in the 1850s had further made them believe that they must pool their resources globally to protect Islam from infidels and bring back the glory of Muhammedanism of the seventh century which modernism had eroded. In India, with the Wahhabis' support, they had declared a *jihad* against the Hindus as early as in 1824—thereafter, only their tactics and strategy differed while the goal remained unchanged; and, when the British abolished the post of *Qazis* (Islamic district magistrates) in 1864, the Muslim fundamentalists were all the more concerned about the future of Islam. It was this concern that made them launch a two-pronged strategy: the Aligarh Movement of Syed Ahmed, who visited Mecca in 1822 and returned radicalised with the aim of turning Muslim youth into circumcised 'Britons' and the Deoband Movement and the Ahl-e-Hadis, the spiritual foundation of the Taliban and the al-Qaeda, which both commenced in the 1860s in league with the Wahhabis as frontline organisations aiming to complete Islamisation of India, left incomplete due to the demise of the Mughal Empire midway. They both had similar aims with seamless strategies: while the Syed would aim at 'educating' Muslim administrators and judges along British lines, the Deobandis would turn the unsuspecting poor youth into madrasa-trained Islamists—many among the former would eventually metamorphose as sleeper cells and cyber terrorists, the latter as foot-soldiers, bomb-blasters and *fidayeen* (suicide bombers). 'Peace' masked these underground efforts the same way the Black Curtain covered the Kaa'ba in Mecca. Many a devout Muslim rued the loss of the Mughal Empire, their perceived property and alleged family silver, and tried to help the fanatics in their attempts to restore it; this, more than any alleged 'injustice', has been the basis of the 'sleeper cells' scattered across the Indian sub-continent as the substratum and Matrix of Islamic terrorism in the 21st century. How tenacious this re-Islamisation aspiration of Islamists has been was proved with import of thousands of Qur'ans by Ahl-e-Hadis into Gujarat in April 2009.

Like the barren Khilafat issue, the Afghan bogie, too, was also a sterile post-menopause situation as the Ali Brothers, taken for a ride by a loin-cloth man because they wore too many clothes, realised to their dismay and dejection. With the Young Turks eliminating the Caliphate itself, a host of new Muslim nations mushrooming on the corpse of the Ottoman Empire, the new order fast emerging with the defeat of the reactionary White Army and firm establishment of the atheist Communist rule by the revolutionary Red Army in Russia, it was inevitable. In India, while most other leaders kept their eyes and ears firmly shut about this changing global scenario, Gandhi alone was keeping an eagle's eye on these developments and the debilitating diseases of the British but, unlike other professional chatterboxes, he kept mum; he alone x-rayed this fluctuating stock market correctly when he dared to make investments. Frustrated, the Ali Brothers gained nothing out of the Mahatma's 'generous' help in the zero-sum game. Finally, in his Congress Presidential Address at Cocanada, Maulana Mohammad Ali was forced to say, 'I have heard that my Madras speech of 1921 had not found much favour even in Afghanistan.'

This was the virtual death-knell for Pan-Islamism in India. Even the next door neighbour, Afghanistan, was not ready to help infidel India's Sunni Muslims to 'protect Islam'! In a few deft strokes, Gandhi had undone the decades of patient work of the likes of Maulavi Jamaluddin who fanned Pan-Islamism in India. He still remembered and smiled when he recalled what Hakim Ajmal Khan, the 'simultaneous' President of the Congress as well as the Khilafat Conference, had said at Ahmedabad. In his presidential address, the 'Hakim' (Doctor), in Gandhi's presence, had blurted out publicly: 'India on the one side and the Asia Minor on the other are but two extreme links in a chain of *future Islamic Federation*, which are gradually but surely joining together all intermediate States in one great system.' Interestingly, to rub salt into the Muslim Indian's wound, the British concluded the Anglo-Afghan Treaty on the day the Bardoli agitation was to commence.

The Khilafat and the Afghan issues were inter-related. Many Muslims were made to believe that after the 'departure' of the British, the Mughal Empire would be reinstated, that the Afghan Amir would be the 'new Caliph', that the Hindus' help against the British in this 'Islamic cause' was merely a tactical, temporary ploy for the good of Islam. Colonel J C Wedgwood noted in his book, *The Future of the Indo-British Commonwealth*, 'That the Amir should become Khalifa is the wish of every raging Muslim in India. He is on their borders, almost in hand, a permanent threat to British India. Every conqueror save one (ie. the British) has come down from the Afghan passes. India as a whole does not want what the Muslims want. The leaders of Indian thought and politics desire democracy and fear ruler, whether Ranjeet Singh from the Punjab or an Amir from Kabul. The temporal power of a religion seems to them as wrong as it does to us. *As education spreads India may convert the Muslim or the Muslim may convert India. It is quite certain that after what has passed the British cannot convert the Indian Muslim from his rage, either by force or fraud or kindness, that conversion be left to time and India.*' Few understood the 'Muslim Question' in India better.

Many thought that Gandhi's 'invitation' to Afghanistan to invade India was actually a tactic intended to force the British to compromise with the Congress or that it was yet another, but foolhardy, attempt to forge unity between the Hindus and Muslims by giving the latter a 'blank cheque' without seeking anything in return. A body of literature and newspapers during the Khilafat-Non-Cooperation Movement period deplored Gandhi and his cronies for their anti-Hindu and pro-Muslim policies: none asked why the Mahatma was driving even the Muslim elites, such as Jinnah, into the arms of the Khilafatists and other Muslim fundamentalists—by 'supporting' an Islamic cause, he was first uniting all shades of Muslim opinions into a 'political action', whip up their frenzy at the frustration of failure and then suddenly withdraw leaving them to feed on the embers they produced. None but Gandhi had seen the real face of political Islam, or for that matter Christianity, as global imperial and colonial forces, their hide-and-seek and cloak-and-dagger tactics, divide-and-rule regime, running through generations after generations to achieve the Goals set by their respective Founders.

Apart from the Khilafat and Afghanistan issues, he also played with the Hyderabad issue with the same motive and deftness. Two decades after exploiting the two issues to whip up a pro-Congress hysteria amongst the Hindus and pro-Caliph fever amongst the Muslims, and when the Congress had been agitating for *Poorna Swaraj* and the Muslim League for Pakistan, he was writing this in *Harijan* of 10 October 1940, of course after a long exposition of 'Gospel According to Gandhi': '...If independence is taken by force of arms, then the strongest power will hold sway over all India. And this may be Hyderabad for aught I know. All the big and the petty States will be free willy-nilly from the British yoke. They will each fight for their existence and succumb to the strongest who will be the Emperor of India. This presupposes unarmed millions lying prostrate at the feet of the combination of armed States. Many other things are, however, conceivable. The Indian part of the British Army will probably have consciousness of strength and an independent existence. There may be Muslim arms, Sikh arms, Gurkha arms, Rajput arms and what not. They may fight amongst themselves, or, having allied themselves to some nationalist party, may present a united front to the princes. There may also be the descent upon India of the warring tribes from the Frontier to share the spoils or the sovereignty itself.' Clearly, he was warning of the dangers that the Muslim League's policies could lead to, that the Nizam could emerge as the 'Emperor' of India, a Muslim Raj could arise and as a result, India could be dismembered due to invasions and fissiparous, civil war-like tendencies.

And what should the Congress do in this grim scenario? 'The Congress, *if it still has anything of its non-violence left in it*, will die in the attempt to establish universal peace in India.' He knew the Congress' popularity was being eroded by the extremely popular armed revolutionaries like Sardar Bhagat Singh and his associates and the Congress would be forced to adopt a more activist role rather than harp on its ancient peace-and-harmony 'policies'. He then advocated for a strong centre—unlike the Muslim League whose policy was to have a weak, federated centre as a pre-requisite for a separate Pakistan, as the next best option if the neo-Mughal Empire remained a pipedream—and how the things could be pushed to weed out the Islamists: 'It is not impossible that all the warring elements will find it profitable in more ways than one voluntarily to surrender themselves to the moral authority of a central power. This means universal suffrage exercised by a disciplined and politically intelligent electorate. It also means a decent and permanent burial to communal and other discord.' The 'universal suffrage' here was for the Hindus as the Muslims already had a Separate Electorate and separate seats in the Central and Provincial Legislatures, mostly won by the Leaguers—that is, Gandhi's proposed democracy was basically meant for the Hindus!

He also warned of the possible anarchy, the threat of the 'cent percent domestic' rule of the Nizamate as the new, revivified Mughal Empire, but only as an interregnum to the Hindu reign: 'But this may not happen. The existing state of things does not warrant an optimistic outlook...But supposing the worst happens and there is anarchy in the land, if there is God upon earth as He is in heaven, then you may depend upon it that I shall not live to make any choice. I shall die in the anarchic flame whilst I am vainly attempting to still it with my tiny, shaky hands. *But if you ask me in advance whether I would face anarchy in preference to foreign orderly rule, either British or any other, I would unhesitatingly plump for anarchy, say, the rule of the Nizam supported by the Chiefs become feudatory to him or supported by the border Muslim tribes.*' So, he would rather prefer *anarchy*, say, *the rule of the Nizam…supported by the border Muslim tribes*!

Did he really want to die in this anarchy, or would he prefer to live as a slave under the Nizamate? As an adolescent, he had tried to commit suicide by consuming the poisonous *datura* seeds when lack of 'independence' to smoke frustrated him and a relative: 'But our courage failed us. Supposing we were not instantly killed? And what was the good of killing ourselves? Why not rather put up with the lack of independence? But we swallowed two or three seeds nevertheless. We dared not take more. Both of us fought shy of death, and decided… to dismiss the thought of suicide. I realised that it was not as easy to commit suicide as to contemplate it. And since then, whenver I have heard of someone threatening to commit suicide, it has had little or no effect on me.'

Clearly, in 1940, he did not contemplate his own death in the anarchy he helped create; after having encouraged the Muslims for two decades, he was now merely arousing the Hindus, this time, by hinting that he may die if they did not heed his advice. Through a convoluted and labyrinthine 'logic' he now revealed his actual plan. The Nizam rule, the neo-Mughal Empire, 'In my estimation will be cent per cent domestic. *It will be home rule though far, far from self-rule or swaraj. But you must let me repeat that, while I can write thus academically, if the reality faces me, my choice will be death or the rule of the people by the people for the people.*' That is, even the Nizamate will not be swaraj, and he would prefer the majority (read Hindu) rule, 'the rule of the people by the people'. He had, in fact, clearly hinted that even if the Muslims succeeded in wresting the Mughal Empire back in the garb of the Nizamate, the struggle to establish democracy will continue, at any cost, including that of his own death; often, when he gave contradictory statements such as supporting the Nizam as the 'Emperor of India' and also the 'rule of the people by the people for the people' in the same breath, his actual view, the *operative part* as any lawyer knows in a judgement being the last piece in a tome, was the one which formed the latter part of the writing. Like any successful judge, he seemed to write the judgement, the last part, first of all, and then 'develop' the whole argument backwards! He seldom forgot to add his favourite customary, default, pop-up words like non-violence, peace, truth and 'academic interests' in such sentences; these were his escape routes although the moralists and Gandhians fattened themselves by grazing on this very stuff.

Not that Gandhi was, by nature, immoral or unethical, violent or brutal or he supported these tendencies as any unscrupulous politician would do: amoral and dispassionate like Chanakya, his entire vision of India was the promotion of 'Ram Rajya' as his childhood ideal, moral universe. But, he had to put such tendencies to effective use, because, at the same time, he was aware of the enemies of this utopian Ram Rajya: if there were to be a Ram, there would invariably be a Ravan, to be killed with the help of a turncoat enemy brother, Vibhishan; if there were to be a Baali, the Lord would have to kill him from behind a tree to help the enemy's twin brother, Sugriva. *Only by killing the demon could you create a godly world.* That was why he was using all at his command to deAbrahamise India, through stratagems and stonewalling and tactics and smokescreens and booby-traps and landmines... Even after being a moralist, after all, Rama had to kill Baali from hiding, an immoral thing for a Kshatriya; and Krishna had to use numerous tactics to eliminate the evil Kauravas. Gandhi was, despite his numerous contradictions, a Rama, Krishna and Chanakya all rolled into one. He was all too human. There was little godly about Gandhi, as his selfish, glorifying followers made him out to be; he was the great Hindu patriot who wanted his country to be free of all slavery, at any cost.

For this, Gandhi even donned a 'saintly' exterior, making many believe he was a saint out to liberate his country and the people from foreign yoke. His opponents often criticised him in hushed tones, and some openly as well; but, using a unique blend of logic, threats and blackmail like any astute politician, he silenced them into either submission or dispatched them into oblivion. And he was wholly successful—because it was *he alone* who called the shots and had the capacity to hypnotise the masses, the way Hitler would say, 'I alone did it'. Being a Gujarati, he knew that one could destroy the enemy non-violently by simply persuading him to invest in woolly companies! Didn't he, after all, write thus on 23 March 1940, in his mouthpiece *Harijan*: 'It is the Muslims who will impose their will by force singly or with British assistance on an unresisting India. If I can carry the Congress with me I would not put the Muslims to the trouble of using force. I would be ruled by them for it would still be Indian rule.' But why was he 'supporting' the Muslims out of the way? On October 21, 1939, he had already replied in the *Harijan*: 'The question therefore resolves itself into not who is numerically superior but who is stronger. Surely there is only one answer.' Seen from the Indian context, it would merely mean that the minority Muslims were stronger than the majority Hindus and that Gandhi was, therefore, supporting the former; but, internationally, the Muslims were a much larger majority than the Indian Hindus, and the Pan-Islamist Muslims, all-around Gandhi like the Ali Brothers, openly boasted of this. Who was it then the Mahatma was actually supporting? Obviously, compared to the Muslim Ummah, the Hindus were a minority!

That Gandhi was following a well-thought out plan of exposing both Islamists and the British, and warning the Hindus to strengthen themselves had begun to emerge in 1924 itself. At a time when the Muslims had massacred many Hindus in Malabar and other places out of frustration over the utter collapse of the Khilafat issue and Mustafa Kemal Pasha having overthrown the Caliphate, Gandhi wrote in his *Young India* on 18 September 1924: 'I hate duelling, but it has a romantic side to it. I am engaged in bringing that side of it to the fore. I would love to engage in a duel with the Big Brother. When we are both satisfied that there is no chance of unity without bloodshed and that even we too cannot agree to live in peace, I must then invite the Big Brother to a duel with me. I know that he can twist me round his thick fingers and dash me to pieces. *That day Hinduism will be free. Or if he lets me kill him in spite of the strength of a giant, Islam in India will be free. He will have atoned for all the bullying by the average Musalman.*' Obviously, he was anticipating a strong Hindu reaction to his well-rehearsed 'policies'. 'The way to get rid of the Hindu cowardice is for the educated portion to fight the goondas. We may use sticks and other *clean weapons*. My Ahimsa will allow use of them...That would remove the Hindu cowardice in a moment.' Thus spake the Prophet of Peace! The very next year, 1925, Keshav Baliram Hedgewar took his advice seriously and founded the Rashtriya Swayamsevak Sangh (RSS), whose volunteers, wielding sticks and other *clean weapons*, permitted by the Gandhian non-violence, set out to make the Mahatma's dream become a reality! Indeed, the stick was the common bond between the Mahatma and the RSS. For him, the Congress was a tool to achieve these objectives, just like Jinnah would be using the Muslim League to achieve his own ends. But the extremely careful Mahatma would not advice use of other 'unclean weapons': he knew the Muslims and the British would outdo the Hindus in such weaponry and all his labour would go waste. Gandhi had a unique way of accusing and reprimanding others. Cool-headed and cold blooded, even humorous, he would, for instance, accuse Maulana Shaukat Ali of betrayal thus, in 1924: 'My dear Shaukat, I cannot bear the people accusing you and your brother of having broken your promises to me. I cannot bear the thought of such an accusation. I must die for it.' Ready to undergo fast, observe silence or threats to die were the tools the Mahatma deployed to emotionally make others submit: he knew the immense value of benumbing his disciples as well as foes by injecting moral dilemma as an anaesthetic and making them watch him escape, helplessly, with *their* clothes. He did not care for those who glorified him; they were his fodder. He ignored those who criticised him; they brought in more support for him.

Gandhi's Mall did not return any customer empty-handed. During his fast of 1924, his assistant Mahadeo Desai asked him what was he doing his penance for. 'My error?' the Mahatma replied, 'Why, I may be charged with having committed a breach of faith with the Hindus. I asked them to lay their lives and property at the disposal of the Mussalmans for the protection of their holy places. Even today I am asking them to practise Ahimsa to settle quarrels by dying but not killing. And what do I find to be the result? How many temples have been desecrated! How many sisters came to me with complaint? As I was saying yesterday to Hakimji, Hindu women are in mortal terror of Mussalman goondas. In many places they fear to go out alone. I had a letter from….How can I bear the way in which his little children were molested. How can I now ask the Hindus to put up with everything patiently? I gave them the assurance that the friendship of Mussalmans was bound to bear good fruit. I asked them to befriend them regardless of the result. It is not in my power to make good that assurance. Who listens to me? And yet I must ask the Hindus even today to die and not to kill. I can only do so by laying down my life.' Obviously, the Mahatma had succeeded in whipping up the Hindu anger and driving them against the Muslims to the logical end. Why did he do so? It was necessary because, as he wrote in *Harijan* of 21 October, 1939: 'Hinduism is an elastic, indefinable term and the Hindus are not a homogenous whole like the Muslims and Christians.' A pseudo-Abrahamisation of this Hinduism was the Gandhian strategy to create the exit route for Islam and Christianity from India; he succeeded in eliminating the elasticity of Hinduism and made the Hindus more homogenous than ever before, at least with reference to Islam and Christianity.

The Ali Brothers, who realised long afterwards that the Mahatma had taken them for a ride and to the precipice on the Khilafat issue and that the resultant communal riots had made the Muslims a hated community, were bitter no end. During the Calcutta Special Session of 1926, Maulana Shaukat Ali told his supporters: 'Mahatma Gandhi is a shrewd *bania*. You do not understand his real object. By putting you under discipline, he is preparing you for guerrilla warfare. He is not such an out-and-out non-violenceist as you all suppose.' By 1928, finding that the Muslim League was nearly defunct due to the Mahatma's policies, the same Maulana bitterly said publicly that the worst Muslim was better than the best Hindu, even if the latter were a Mahatma! For the first time, the two *imported* Cults had discovered their match in a *native* Infidel.

There was no dearth of those, even amongst the Hindus, who demonised or called Gandhi a pervert; there were, in fact, many who even called him a sex maniac, pointing to his bizarre experiments of '*brahmacharya*' and sleeping with many women. But such nincompoops, as also those who glorified him no end, would not disturb him: disregarding such bouquets and brick-bats, it was his genius that he continuously rearranged the pawns on the Great Indian Chessboard making it impossible for Islam to remain embedded in India. With a self-exposed thorax and a seamless loincloth, his unmatched fortress no one could penetrate, he could easily defeat moralists, doubters, and a whole bunch of chest-beaters of different hues. In a rare self-appraisal, he said: 'I refuse to be considered so simple as to be readily taken in by my companions.' (*Young India*, 13 April 1921.) While changing the creed of the Congress and incorporating Swaraj as its goal, he had left the definition of the word 'Swaraj' amorphous—merely to its literal meaning, 'self-rule'—without explaining that this was the word coined by Shivaji for the re-establishment of the Hindu Raj in the 17th century after attempting to destroy the Mughal Empire. If the Muslims were trying to revive their dead Mughal Empire, Gandhi, too, was also resuscitating and reinventing the emerging Hindu consciousness that disappeared prematurely due to the arrival of the British in the 18th century. And it was no secret; many leaders, including Jinnah, were aware of it. Even Bipin Chandra Pal, close friend of Tilak (who gave the slogan, 'Swaraj is my birth-right and I will have it'), had some idea of this Gandhian strategy when, on 4 September 1925, he wrote in *Comrade*, the periodical edited by Maulana Muhammed Ali: 'The Congress started in 1920 with a new creed and constitution framed by Mr Gandhi. In this constitution, Swaraj was declared to be the goal of our national endeavours. *But the Mahatma would not define Swaraj. He would not allow anyone else to do so.* Mr Mohammad Ali gave me the reason of it in the course of a conversation I had with him on the subject at Mr Byomkesh Chakravarty's place in the heyday of the Non-Cooperation campaign. *I then learned that Swaraj was left without any definition because the moment we tried to do so, the unity in the Congress would break up.*' Clearly, both the Mahatma and the Ali Brothers, the Non-Cooperation Movement and the Khilafat Agitation, were into a temporary marriage of convenience aimed at 'uniting' the Hindus and Muslims into instruments of power to be used by the Congress and Muslim League under the garb of their so-called 'national' movements. The Alis failed because Gandhi was set to win.

But Gandhi's contemporaries in the Congress were either his yes men or his enemies; few ever tried to understand him why he was doing what he did and fewer still took the hints, nor spotted the straws in the wind, and supported him in his designs. No wonder, he was, like the Grand Master, playing the game against a whole lot of Hindus, Muslims and the British, who all fancied themselves as 'chess players'. Even Pal, the erstwhile member of the 'Pro-Changer' Group within the Congress, together with Tilak and Lala Lajpat Rai, was unable to comprehend Gandhi: 'At Nagpur, I moved an amendment to Mr Gandhi's draft, adding the adjective 'democratic' to the word 'Swaraj' and rendering it into English as 'full responsible' government. But Gandhi opposed it and it was necessarily lost. My amendment was opposed by a prominent non-cooperator (Gandhi) who openly declared that he saw no reason why we should not welcome autocracy like that of Ranjeet Singh, if it would replace the present foreign domination.' Gandhi was using symbolism again, but deliberately avoiding the word 'Hindu Raj': he was advocating Shivaji's Swaraj and Ranjeet Singh's Khalsa Raj, both of which grew upon the ruins of the Mughal Empire in the South and North India of the 17th and 18th century respectively; at *Nagpur*, he could not have called Shivaji's Swaraj 'autocratic' but he called Ranjeet Singh's reign as 'autocracy', just for the sake of effect on that monarch's victims (the Muslims), because Amritsar, the seat of the Sikhs, was far away! And some understood him, as Pal noted: 'That speech, which was more or less openly applauded, was a clear indication of the political philosophy of those who declared that they were out to destroy the Satanic British Empire; but this opposition to define our objective and clarify our vision of the ideal which we were pursuing, concealed also deliberate design.' Even the Ali Brothers later realised that Gandhi was befooling them, as, indeed, he knew that they, too, were exploiting him for the Khilafat cause: 'I cannot believe that such astute politicians as the Ali Brothers did not realise the confusion of thinking, which characterised the whole Non-Cooperation campaign; but they were only interested in helping the destruction of the present government leaving the future to take care of itself.' The Ali Brothers believed that once the Caliphate was re-established, or at least the Muslims, in a temporary alliance with the 'stupid' Hindus, energised sufficiently to kick out the British, the Mughal Empire could be revived and India's halted Islamisation could be re-started, even completed; for this aim, they, too, played the ball with Gandhi. 'I voted against your amendment', Muhammed Ali told Pal, 'because I did not believe in tautology. I am convinced that Swaraj cannot be anything else than democratic.'

At the height of the Khilafat Movement, Gandhi was convinced what the frustrated Muslims would do when they discovered they got nothing out of it: they will precipitate war, not against the British, but against the Hindus, as they did in Malabar and elsewhere, a situation that would, given the seed of the Separate Electorate, would theodesically culminate into the fruit of Pakistan, the Separate Nation. On 13 April 1921, to repeat it, he wrote in *Young India*: 'The (Ali) Brothers are honestly and industriously endeavouring to secure a peaceful settlement. But should their efforts prove vain, either for want of response from the Government or the people, as lovers of their faith, *they will not hesitate to precipitate war if they could.* As for my own attitude, whilst my faith would not permit me to invite or encourage a war of violence, *I do contemplate with equanimity a state of war in preference to the present state of effeminate peace* imposed by force of arms. And it is for this reason that I am taking part in this movement of non-violent non-cooperation even at the risk of anarchy being the ultimate result.' This sort of Gandhian peace left many a leader red-faced. Pandit Madan Mohan Malviya then arranged a meeting of the Mahatma with Lord Reading the same month in which the latter was able to extract an apology from Gandhi as from the Ali Brothers as well—the British were able to tame political foxes, but only temporarily.

The Moplah massacre in the Malabar region of Kerala was just a beginning of the 're-flowering' season of Islam in India. Gandhi would let the Muslims continue to kill the Hindus at will—hold your breath, he would later say India may have to swim across the 'sea of blood'—but he was not ready to cross swords with the British simultaneously. Having learnt enough from the Christians' and Muslims' tactics of one-enemy-at-a-time, he would not fight two at the same time. Even after the angry Non-Cooperators killed 22 policemen at Chauri-Chaura village in Deoria district in eastern Uttar Pradesh on 4-5 February 1922, he continued to support the Movement; he even wrote to the Viceroy, on 7 February 1922, justifying the violence as 'undoubted dangers'. However, much to his chagrin, the situation took a sudden turn *outside* India that would have freed the British to crush the Movement with an iron hand; this would have left the Mahatma high and dry, without any moral authority, and nipped his game-plan in the bud. But Gandhi, too, was a political genius. Keeping his eyes fixed outside India and ears to the ground, he learnt that the British-Afghan Treaty of 22 November 1921, had come into force with King George signing it on 6 February 1922. This only meant that the Non-Cooperation Movement was now going to be crushed like the British did in the 1857 uprising. This was the time to suddenly call off the Movement itself to deny the British the opportunity to do so. So, even after having justified the Chauri-Chaura killings as 'undoubted dangers' on 7 February, Gandhi took a U-turn *within four days* and, on 11-12 February 1922, withdrew the Movement, citing the Deoria killings as the reason, even as his Deobandi mullah associates, such as Maulana Sobhani, principal advisor to the Mahatma at that time, continued to pour venom, inciting the Muslims not against the British but against the Hindus! Always clean-shaven himself, Gandhi gave these fanatic clergymen every opportunity to grow their beards and long ropes to hang themselves. Barring exceptions, a majority of Muslims across the Indian subcontinent were now infected with the Islamisation virus, to revive the Mughal Empire by throwing out the British with the temporary Hindu help and then crushing the Hindus as well. But Gandhi understood this ancient Islamic tactic of making a herd of goats kill a lion before themselves moving in to kill the goats—in the 1920s, even Communists had adopted it in the Soviet Union where the contemporary minority Bolsheviks were crushing the majority Mensheviks and capitalists with the help of bourgeoisie and preparing themselves to deal with the bourgeoisie as well and was paying the Muslims in their own coin. He ignored the mullahs now that he had squeezed them fully to serve his purpose; like a farmer, having sown the seeds, he now waited for the onset of monsoon when these seeds would germinate and spread a green carpet.

Imprisoned on 10 March 1922, for six years, Gandhi effortlessly donned the mantle of a martyr. Meanwhile, Mustafa Kemal led a Turkish uprising in November 1922, toppled the Sultan-cum-Caliph, secularised Turkey's polity by melting the Islamic flab, nationalised education, granted women extensive rights, eliminated Islam from the Constitution, introduced legal codes based on European models, developed agriculture and industries—*all anathema* to the Islamic orthodoxy the world over. Then he dealt a mortal blow to Islam: he *deArabised* Islam in Turkey, had the Holy Book written in Turkish, made compulsory the recitation of the *Qur'an* only in Turkish language. He completed this task by 9/11 of 1924 when Turkish Parliament sealed the fate of Islam in that country. Turkey became the first Asian nation to be somewhat deIslamised. Islam never forgot this date, 9/11; Islam would not forget this date, 9/11: for, on this very date in 1948 the founder of Pakistan, Muhammed Ali Jinnah, too, passed away leaving his 'separate nation', what its own Prime Minister Nawaz Sharief would call, a 'half quail, half partridge'. And no prizes to guess why al-Qaeda chose 9/11 to attack America.

With this stunning pace of deIslamisation in the land of their own last Caliph, the Khilafatists of India, too, virtually disappeared from the political scene in India. But the Caliphate did not disappear from the Muslim Mind; in fact, the Wahhabis gave it a fillip when they formed the al-Qaeda at Peshawar, Pakistan, in the 1980s, or in 2014, when the al-Baghdadi-led Islamic State declared a 'Caliphate' in the Mesopotamia. Back then in the 1920s, however, it was a dream turned into a nightmare for some. They had been made to believe that they would re-establish the Caliphate in Turkey as a pre-requisite to India's being made the Dar-ul-Islam, the biggest Muslim country in the world, with the resuscitation of the Mughal Empire. Now, even that ultimate Dar-ul-Islam in Islamic politics, Turkey, had turned into Dar-ul-Harb! Across the mediocre political spectrum of Indian Hindu politics, only the Mahatma understood this nitty-gritty of Islam's struggle to survive internationally. He knew no purpose would be served, post-1924, if the Congress continued to agitate on the streets against the British; already, he was aware of the ticking bomb called Weimar Constitution of Germany and its deadly impact in Europe, which became clear with Hitler's aborted-for-the-time being Beer Hall Putsch in 1925. The best strategy, for now, was to wait and watch. He, and the Congress, therefore, devoted themselves to constructive and social work. He himself utilised this time in writing the *Experiments*, dreaming of the Ram Rajya. In fact, the only two motion films he ever watched were *Raja Harishchandra*, after his childhood ideal, and *Ram Rajya*, his young-age ideal.

Like the Mahatma, even the title of his autobiography was enigmatic: it is through experiments that one arrives at truth. One cannot 'experiment' with the truth, which is the end of inquiry. The Mahatma's ubiquitous 'experiments with truth' were, therefore, his quest for truth. In different fields, the truth he propounded was different: in Hindu society, he sought amelioration of the lot of the Untouchables, in industry he promoted cottage industries and khadi etc. But, when he found that he could not do much in a British and Muslim-dominated politics, he set out to expel the two 'aliens' as he already was, from childhood, prepared even to lay down his life in this quest. He knew that the British conscience could be aroused merely by dubbing them as tyrants but the Muslims were not afraid of any such appellations. The only possible way to deal with the Muslims was to appease them, give them preferential treatment, ignore their boasts and somehow persuade them to rush to the precipice, making them feel they owned the entire (Kashmir) Valley before them, and make them jump into it—this was what the Congress and, indeed, other political parties in India silently followed since 1947. It was a typical, time-tested, *bania* tradition in Gujarat honed by businessmen and traders: they would lick you until you tasted sweet and then drop you like bubble gum. Gandhi was no exception. He knew that the Muslims supported the Hindus on the Swaraj and Swadeshi issues in as much as it meant shunning of all European aid, material and propaganda but favoured help from even China and Peru, even seeking the Afghan invasion, when it came to redress the 'wrong' to Turkey or dealing with the Hindus. From 1915 to 1925, he tried to keep the attention of the Muslims away from India and that of the British inside it; now, he would make the Muslims look inside India and the British outside.

For this purpose, he needed to groom a Muslim leader who could articulate the Muslim demands not in terms of the medieval Caliphate aims but in terms of modern 'values'. Unlike the uncouth cactus-like maulanas he had gathered for the Khilafat Movement, whom he discarded once they ceased to be useful, Gandhi found a leader of his 'liking' in Jinnah, whom he could promote merely by demoting. The most brilliant and successful lawyer in the Indian subcontinent, articulate, obstinate, well-cultured, a Grey Briton in tastes, Jinnah was the farthest man from Islam—like the farthest planet Pluto orbiting the Sun *elliptically*, in 248 years—and, therefore, the one who would fulfil the Gandhian dream of deIslamisation of India. The Mahatma was one soul who could attempt to do the impossible and mostly achieve it. The only thing needed to mutate Jinnah from being the son of India into the Father of Pakistan—the latter's sister, Fatima, was called *Madar-e-Watan* (Mother of the Motherland) in Pakistan—was to attack and exploit his weak spots which the Mahatma now set out to do. Jinnah soon became an instrument of Gandhian political machination, although the former thought he was using the latter, the same mistake committed by the boastful Ali Brothers who could no longer even shed tears on a turkey that became Turkey.

The Pied Piper

EARLY on, an ever-alert Gandhi had spotted Jinnah's three major exploitable 'weaknesses': his belonging to a micro-minority Shia sub-sect of Ismailia and near-total ignorance of Islam and its practices; his obstinate belief in slow progress, step-by-step, by the letter of the law and three, his overconfidence that he would one day lead *India* as its supreme leader. In the end, his stubbornness and dislike of Gandhi led him to lead only a corner of India, which became Pakistan. Gandhi was aware that Jinnah was basically an armchair but brilliant lawyer who dreaded street-fights, political movements and life in jail. The Mahatma, who had once claimed he would make patriots out of the Ali Brothers and other sundry Muslim clergy, would eventually make an 'Islamist' Jinnah out of a secular lawyer who would have inherited the mantle of Dadabhoy Naoroji, Sir Perozshah Mehta and Gopal Krishna Gokhale in 1915 but was cooling his heels after being virtually forced, like others, to quit the Congress in 1920.

The Jinnahs' Hindu Lohana-Thakkar family hailed from village Moti Paneli in Rajkot district of the erstwhile princely state of Gondal in the Kathiavad region of Gujarat. Eldest among seven children, Jinnah's entire personal life, even his parents' and other family members', was a series of tragedies; his six other siblings were brothers Ahmed Ali, Bunde Ali and Rehmat Ali, and sisters Maryam, Fatima and Shireen. Their mother tongue was Gujarati but they also came to speak Kutchi, Sindhi and English. Afflicted with an identity crisis, the *discovery* of Pakistan could not change him: for him, it was more of a consolation prize, a panacea, a catharsis, even a slap to Gandhi, than fulfilment of an ambition or the good of Muslims at heart. Despite his Hindu roots and known 'heretic' background even in Islam, many in the newly-carved out nation fondly called him *Baba-e-Qaum*, Patriarch of the Nation, almost equating him with Abraham. Like his dream project of Pakistan, he was himself 'half quail, half partridge', a personality split to the core that could neither become fully Islamic nor could discard the Hindu credentials—so much so that, in 2008, the lawyers of Dina Wadia, his 88-year-old daughter, would claim Mumbai's 'Jinnah House' property on the basis of Hindu inheritance law, not Muslim law! Indeed, Jinnah, Father of Pakistan, had, in his will, divided his assets in accordance with the Hindu Law, not Islamic Law!

He was everything his bitterest rival, the Mahatma, *was not*; together, they complimented each other and constituted the climax of the great saga of the rise and fall of Islam in India in a seamless whole. Gandhi's apparent 'vulnerability'—his tolerance of all faiths and his tactical 'appeasement' of the Muslims, even if for political reasons in this case—demonstrated why the naive Hindus were continuously defeated by the wily Muslims, and then the British; Jinnah's obstinacy showed how and why the Hindus, who had absorbed so many people and faiths, were forced to expel Islam, as also Christianity, out of India. Gandhi and Jinnah would have been ciphers without each other: they scaled the wall on each other's shoulders, alternately. Gandhi had a way of letting Jinnah say what the Mahatma actually wanted him to: for instance, in January 1940, Gandhi described Jinnah as a 'patriot', forcing the latter to deny the 'accusation' thus: 'Let me say again that India is not a nation, nor a country. It is a subcontinent composed of nationalities—Hindus and Muslims being the two major nations.'

In a dozen such instances, the Mahatma merely provoked Jinnah to say something the former wanted the latter to utter, prompting the 'Muslim' leader, like a pied-piper, to push himself and his hot-headed community out of India, the way Moses had lured the Jews out of Egypt 12 centuries before Jesus.

How did Gandhi virtually manipulate Jinnah into 'demanding' Pakistan? How was the Mappila/Mopplah's massacre of the Hindus in the Malabar area of Kerala enlarged into the plot of an even greater genocide of 1947, guided from Jinnah's bungalow at Malabar Hills of Bombay? And how was the failed Partition of Bengal in 1906, pushed, logically, into the successful Partition of India in 1947?

In order to understand this saga, one must understand nitty-gritty of the 'intranet' of Indian caste system, the fulcrum around which has revolved this banyan-like society for 3,000 years, and its 'internet' connectivity with those outside their caste. For three generations, the Jinnah family was struggling to find their Islamic identity after being excommunicated, post their conversion to Muhammedanism, from their Hindu caste, Lohana-Thakkar of the Saurashtra region. This caste was believed to have had a Raghuvanshi descent, from the family tree of Lord Rama, and some thought they were Bhatia Rajputs. Like some other drifted Hindus who had, due to the force of circumstances, found themselves on the Islamic island, many of the Thakkars, too, continued to use both their Islamic and Hindu names and maintain traditions in alternate generations to retain their roots in both the old and the 'new' worlds. Jinnah's grandfather was a faithful Hindu, Premjibhai Meghji Thakkar. In the early 19th century, Premji was forced to convert to Islam's Shiaite Khoja sub-sect after his excommunication by strictly vegetarian Hindu orthodoxy due to his fishing business, considered 'dirty' and identified with the *mlechchha* (impure, non-Hindus) people. Adamji Khoja, similarly converted two generations ago, was his business partner who had encouraged him to embrace the new faith to teach his detractors a lesson. But, Premjibhai soon had to rethink over the long-term implications of his action on his family. Even his wife and other family members opposed this conversion, and they tried to get him re-converted. But the priests refused to re-induct him into the Hindu fold, forcing Premjibhai to stay a nominal 'Muslim'. His son, Poonjabhai, born in 1850, was underweight and so nicknamed *Jhiniabhai*, due to his wiry physical constitution. He had married Mithibai, who, in 1876, gave birth to the man who would be Father of Pakistan. They all remained nominal Muslims throughout life.

Interestingly, Premjibhai had not converted to either the mainstream Sunni or the Shia beliefs, Islam's two main branches, because there was no religious or spiritual reason for this conversion. He had 'converted' to the heretic Khoja-Ismailia sub-sect for two reasons: one, he knew this conversion would help him spread his business far and wide as the rich followers of The Aga Khan, head of the sub-cult, were ready to assist him financially, and two, this would also teach a lesson to his fellow Hindu caste people who were jealous of his success in business but had succeeded in having him excommunicated for 'violating' his Gujarati Vaishnavite credentials of pure vegetarianism. For a long time after his 'religious' conversion to Islam, Premjibhai continued to worship the family deity Srinathji, an incarnation of Lord Krishna, and the Thakorji, besides the Tulsi tree in the courtyard of his house, as millions of other Hindus did; outside the house, he, however, would go to the mosque like other nominal Muslims who had converted from Hinduism to Islamic sub-sects of the Memons, Bohras and Khojas or Khwajas. Premjibhai had joined the Khojas' sect, thanks to Adamji Khoja, his friend, philosopher and guide, who had brought him into the fish trade and then into The Aga Khan's fold.

Premjibhai had three sons—Gangji, Natthu and Poonja alias Jhinia—who found it difficult to marry in their Thakkar caste because of the conversion of their father. They had to marry in similarly converted families and decided to move out of the conservative village where they could neither hide their trade nor their family from others because of the small population of a couple of hundred people where everyone knew everyone else down to their generations. Jhinia settled down in Karachi to look after the booming trade in this port city, developed by the British after their Gujarati port of Lakhpat, in Kutch district, was destroyed by a devastating earthquake in the 1819; Karachi became an important trading centre after the completion of Suez Canal in 1869. Jhinia's wiry physical constitution was inherited by his illustrious son as well. With assistance from Adamji, his fortunes smiled on him. Like his father accepting the fate of remaining a nominal Muslim, Jhinia had to remain a nominal Muslim. And like many in Gujarat, his family had also adopted the grandfather's name, Premji, as a surname so as to hide their caste, a practice that continues; so, Jinnah's father's full name was Jhinia alias Jhina Poonjabhai Premjibhai Thakkar.

The word 'Jinnah', which the Father of Pakistan derived for himself from his father's name, had nothing to do with a matching Arabic word, meaning 'wing' as of a bird or army, as the Pakistanis tried to give him an Islamic 'ancestry' in Sindh; many of wiry Gujaratis are identified as 'Jhinias' even now. True to the traditions in the freshly converted families, who wanted to hide their exact religion and caste from others, Jhinia named his eldest boy 'Mamad', instead of Muhammed. Jinnah's full, original name was Mamadbhai Jhiniabhai Thakkar: in short, M J Thakkar.

The boy, indifferent to studies, loathing arithmetic and logic all his life—unlike Gandhi who was strong in these—avoided studies at home. Fond of argumentation, winning brownie points and settling scores, even as a child he was seen as a future lawyer. His father, concerned at the son's 'waywardness', consulted Adamji who advised Jhinabhai to make Mamad join business. Accordingly, Jhina asked his sister Manbai to take Mamad to Bombay in 1887. But the boy returned after six months. He had no interest in the Islamic seminary, or *madrasa*—for a time, he studied at the Sindh Madrasat-ul-Islam at Karachi—and, therefore, was admitted at Christian Missionary Society High School on Lawrence Road, Karachi. At that time, his future rival, M K Gandhi, was also studying in a Christian school, Alfred High School, in Rajkot; both of them, brought up in Christian educational traditions, will fight Christianity in their own ways, besides each other's faiths. He was dissatisfied with his date of birth (20 October 1875) and changed it later to 25 December 1876, to share it with Jesus Christ! His devoted sister, Fatima (born: 31 July 1893) died on 9 July 1967. All his life, Mamadbhai remained underweight and wiry, like his father; at birth, he weighed a few pounds less than normal while at death, his mortal remains weighed only 70 pounds.

At school also, he was an average student like Gandhi; for a time, he also studied at Gokaldas Tej Primary School, Bombay. When he failed in his matriculation examination, his concerned father again consulted Adamji who advised Jhinabhai to send him abroad; but he finally managed to pass matriculation from the University of Bombay. He was then sent to London in 1890 to assist Jhiniabhai's partners Douglas Graham Shipping and Trading Company. There, Mamad came in contact with his godfather, Sir Frederick Leigh Croft, the company's general manager, who influenced the young boy in British etiquettes and other 'good things' of life. Sir Frederick was attracted towards the young boy, a nominal Muslim, argumentative and having a capacity to make one's head turn in disbelief. It was he who, in 1892, arranged for Mamadbhai to join home office as an apprentice. But Mamad's mother protested at this virtual separation from her 16-year-old son and, as a precondition, decided to have him married to her niece, the 14-year-old Ami, a Khoja girl in Moti Paneli village; her name *Ami*, a common Gujarati Hindu name, meant 'raw mango'. As the first deal struck with his own mother, Mamad quietly married his cousin Ami, went to London and never met her again—he never had any compunctions to justify the means so long as these took him to his goal, so typical in his business caste; she died young, unseen and unsung. The British, businessmen of the world, would later discover what would happen to an outsider caught in the cross-fire between two Gujarati businessmen separated by the Gulf of Kutch.

In January 1893, Mamad decided to go to England for three years. Like many other Indians making it to England and returning as Black Britons, he found that, like his date of birth, even his name was dissatisfactory. His name, Mamadbhai Jhiniabhai Thakkar, was against the current fashion; moreover, his name was such as would not clarify his exact identity. So, he first tried to find an identity as a 'Muslim', by changing his name into 'Muhammad Ali Jhiniabhai of Karachi' but found it, too, was difficult. He then tried another name, Muhammad Z Thakkar by changing Jhinia into Zina. Finally, he decided to name himself as 'Muhammad Ali Jinnah', or simply

M A Jinnah, dropping his Hindu Thakkar identity altogether. His transformation now seemed complete: he was no longer a fence-sitter on the Hindu-Muslim religious divide—he was now to be a Muslim, named after the Last Prophet and the first Sunni (Muhammed) and the first Shia (Ali), and shared his date of birth with the Only Son of God, Jesus Christ! This transformation was indicative of his vaulting, messianic ambition, the desire to lead India, to carve out a niche for himself, to become a historical figure: he did lead a truncated India, carved out a nation from an India that had forced his grand-father to convert to Islam, but also became a historical figure for *halting the progress of Islam* in the sub-continent. Jinnah's Pakistan was as much his revenge on Hindus and India for forcing him and his family into Islam, as what he thought was a personal slap to his bitter rival Gandhi; after the Mahatma's assassination, he virtually lost interest in Pakistan itself and died within nine months. Using a typewriter and a clerk, he would say, he carved Pakistan out of India. Alas! None from his family, except Fatima, went with him to the new nation, not even his only daughter Dina (a typical Gujarati name for a Hindu girl) who chose to settle down with her Parsi husband Neville Wadia in Bombay and London. Clearly, even his family did not share what Jinnah claimed was the desire of the Muslims of India; he had cut himself off from all his family roots, except Fatima, the way he split Pakistan from India.

In London, he lived life king size, completely anglicised, having 200-odd hand-tailored suits in his wardrobe, becoming a model of fashion thanks to the father's money. He had no interest in anything concerning India or even Islam; his 'Muslim' name merely gave him an identity. He even ate pork, according to his once-close associate Muhammed Carrim Chagla (who later became Chief Justice of Bombay High Court), never went to the mosque nor read the *Qur'an*, nor even participate in his Khoja sect's functions or festivals; he smoked heavily, and loved his wine. In short, his outward way of life made him a misfit in any religious outfit, least of all in Islam or in carving out a nation for his 'religious' community. He could even bluff his way to make his point. Half-a-century later, while addressing Karachi's Bar, he claimed having joined Lincoln's Inn because, on its main entrance, the Prophet's name was inscribed *on a painting* as a great law-giver.

The Prophet's paintings were forbidden in Islam; but, to impress the lawyers, he got away with this bluff! His near-total ignorance of Islam was proved again in 1947 when, as Governor-General of Pakistan, he invited Lord Mountbatten to lunch without knowing that it was the holy Ramzan month of fast for all Muslims; after this was pointed out by associates, Jinnah hastily revised his invitation as 'dinner' the same day. Even Gandhi and Mountbatten knew more about Islam than did the Father of Pakistan!

After his stint at Lincoln's Inn, he joined Dadabhoy Naoroji, the Grand Old Man of Indian politics in London, and cut his teeth in the nitty-gritty of imperial politics as his assistant for some time under the wings of this Indian Gladstone. Jinnah was now a politician, a Liberal nationalist, joining the Indian National Congress soon after he returned to India in 1896, and remained a Congressman until 1913. Extremely ambitious—physical misfits sometimes find solace in psychological acrobatics as a recompense for their own shortcomings—he had become a successful lawyer as a pre-requisite for becoming a successful politician in contemporary India. He was no longer a 'Sindhi upstart ingrate', as his godfather Sir Frederick had found him. In London, he even had a fling with theatre and, for a time, dreamt of acting as a career; he, however, soon gave it up, perhaps sensing that, even as a lawyer or politician, he would be an actor after all, with a life-long career at that. He used histrionics to telling effect in his later days as a proponent of Pakistan; his opponents mistook him with acting when he was most serious! But, back then, when he wrote his father about his interest in theatre, the latter warned his once-wayward son not commit the mistake: 'Don't be a traitor to the family', the father scolded him, not knowing that most Hindus would love to hate him forever as a traitor.

Jinnah came to Bombay in August 1896 in a metropolis infested with Black Death, the bubonic plague from China. Here, he was all alone at home; he had severed all his ties with Karachi, as he would cut all his ties with India later. During the plague months, he had developed a strange habit of washing his hands as many times as was possible in a day; this idiosyncrasy remained with him all his life along with his extreme habits in cleanliness. Working under acting Advocate-

General John Molesworth MacPherson, Jinnah had established his credentials as a lawyer by 1900. His father, Jhinabhai, whose fortunes had meanwhile declined, decided to settle down in Bombay with his wealthy son, but 'Mr M A Jinnah, Esquire' was no longer interested in his erstwhile family members, except Fatima in later years. To him, his simple, half-Hindu father and other siblings appeared uncouth and unworthy of being associated with him. Realising that the rising sun of Bombay was no longer his rising son, poor Jhinabhai rented a small house in the Khoja district of Khajak; unable to make the two ends meet, Jhinabhai, in the twilight of his life, had to move, in 1904, to the Ratnagiri coast of Bombay Presidency to eke out a living for his remaining family; his wealthy and worthy son had finally betrayed the family.

Jinnah, who had so far shunned his birth date, his family and his entire background in his quest for upward mobility, now decided to shun even his religion, which had, anyway, played no role whatsoever in his life so far—he had cultivated a use-and-throw habit to cast anything away that became a hindrance in the fulfilment of his highest ambition: to lead the country like an all-powerful man. Since his 'Sevener' Khoja community had to work under the leadership of The Aga Khan, he decided to join the rival sub-sect of the 'Twelver' Khojas, or *Isna' Ashari*, who acknowledged no leader and had less stringent hierarchy. Not that he would not hobnob with The Aga Khan in his later political career. But, in the first decade of the 20th century, he chose the 'Twelver' because of one important reason: Justice Badruddin Tyabji (1844-1906), the first Muslim judge of Bombay High Court and third president of the Indian National Congress, was an Isna' Ashari—Jinnah thought by 'converting' to the Twelver sub-sect of this mentor, he could further move up the ladder under the wings of Tyabji. Clearly, the way he changed his clothes, Jinnah was ready to change his religion as well if that brought him closer to his goal; it was this mindset that when he discovered that he could not become Father of India, he decided to Father a portion of it as Pakistan; he would have, perhaps, reconverted to Hinduism had the Mahatma made him the Prime Minister of undivided India specifically on this condition!

But his joining the Twelver sub-sect proved a great deIslamising step for India. For, the Khojas' beliefs slowly made Jinnah what he turned out to be. In Shia belief, each generation of the Fourth Caliph, Ali, to the Twelfth, was said to be headed by a divine incarnation or the Imam; the Twelfth Imam was to be the Last One, the Redeemer—some even believed that Ayatollah Ruhollah Khomeini fitted the bill in the 1980s. The Sixth Imam, Jafar al-Sadiq, had appointed his son, Ismael, as the Seventh but soon replaced him with another son, Musa, in the year 760. The supporters of Ismail were called the Ismailia, headed by The Agha Khan, and those who dismissed this claim continued to wait for the Twelfth. Perhaps finding the slot open for him, and suitable for his learning and personality, Jinnah joined the Twelvers; the Muslims, particularly the Sunnis, who became great supporters of Jinnah in the 1940s, ignored the fact that the anti-Sunni Ismailis had destroyed the Caliph's army completely in the year 900, plundered Mecca, slew 40,000 Sunnis in the holy city and made away with the Black Stone; and that in the next century, they spawned a new, notoriously drugged and murderous sub-sect, the Hashishuns, or the Assassins, the forerunners of opium-peddling Sunni Taliban!

This change of god(s), as in other cases, split Jinnah's psychology: as a half-Hindu, he would shun Islam but as a half-Muslim, he would press for Pakistan.

In December 1904, Jinnah attended, for the first time, the 20th Annual Session of the Congress in Bombay. Its reception committee Chairman Sir Pheroz Shah Mehta chose Gokhale and the newcomer Jinnah, 'the Muslim Gokhale', to be sent to London the next year to lobby with the freshly-elected Liberal government on Indian issues. But the British, irrespective of their domestic politics and party affiliations, were confirmed imperialists outside their shores; they divided Bengal in 1905, a move that Jinnah considered shrewd, and which ignited the Muslim Mind enough to form the Muslim League the next year, under the guidance of The Agha Khan. For the first time, in their 1 October 1906, meeting with the new Viceroy, Lord Minto, at Simla, 35 prominent Muslims used the words 'national interests' of the Muslims which they said needed to be protected vis-a-vis the Hindu majority; they demanded, and got, *Separate Electorate* and seats in various places for the Muslims. They were decorating the horse on which would mount their groom, Jinnah, after some initial hesitation. But, Jinnah, who recently quit The Agha Khan's Ismaeli fold, had nothing to do, for now, with the Muslim League outfit created in Dacca (Dhaka) on 30 December 1906; on the contrary, Jinnah was the only well-known Muslim to have opposed the separate electorate as 'dividing the nation against itself'.

He, along with 44 other 'like-minded' Muslims—in official Islamic Brotherhood, unlike-minded Muslims do not exist: one is either a Muslim, or a Hypocrite/infidel, vulnerable to physical elimination—joined the 1906 annual session of the Congress in Calcutta. It was presided over by Naoroji, with Jinnah as his secretary. The 33-year-old Jinnah and the 40-year-old Gokhale were the eyes and ears of the ailing, 81-year-old Naoroji. Jinnah soon emerged as the 'Ambassador of Hindu-Muslim Unity'. He became Congress spokesman for the newly-adopted goal of *Swaraj* (self-government), realising that the only hope of succeeding his liberal mentors and friends like Naoroji, Mehta and Gokhale as *the* leader of the Congress could be by virtue of his secular national appeal and not through his triple-minority status, ie., a Muslim, a Shia and a Khoja—he was a minority within a minority within a minority; in fact, in the Indian context, he had a quadruple minority status as he was a Muslim, a Shia, a Khoja born into Seveners and converted into Twelvers. Thus, he was, to begin with, the unlikeliest candidate to give a call for Pakistan as the Sunni-majority homeland for the 'Muslim nation'. Within a decade after returning from London, he had emerged as the heir apparent for the Bombay Congress triumvirate of Naoroji, Mehta and Gokhale. However, the Congress was facing teething troubles with the Pro-Changer group of Bal Gangadhar Tilak, Bipin Chandra Pal and Lala Lajpat Rai promoting the cause of Swaraj as a *totally independent* India, not Swaraj with a British *Dominion* status for the country. This caused the Congress split in Surat in 1907, which continued for nine years. In 1908, Tilak was arrested for 'treason'; Jinnah, as his counsel, tried to secure his release. Even in 1916, Jinnah represented Tilak in another case and, this time, won.

By 1909, Muslim League politics had gathered momentum and even Minto had a spat with Morley over the 'excessive representation granted to Mahomedans'. Jinnah himself was undergoing a slow transformation: the Separate Electorate formula, which he rejected in the beginning, was now raising his personal consciousness of having a 'Muslim' identity. It just remained for Gandhi to fan the spark and exploit it. In 1910, he was elected, besides five others fellow Muslims, as a 'Muslim member from Bombay' on the Viceroy's 60-member Central Legislative Assembly at Calcutta (Kolkata), the then political capital of British India. He soon clashed with Viceroy Minto over the question of indentured Indian labours to South Africa whose case had been taken up by a certain lawyer, Mohandas Karamchand Gandhi, in Transvaal and who was leading a *Satyagrah* (*Insistence on Truth*, ie. non-violent resistance) on behalf of these workers. The wiry Jinnah, adept at tongue-lashing his opponents with his razor-sharp mind, soon won over the next Viceroy, Sir Charles Hardinge, who undid the Bengal Partition in 1911. Jinnah's first legislative victory was also his first legislative measure, in March 1911, with regard to the Waqf (tax-exempt Muslim endowments). He soon won over an influential clientele amongst the Muslim elite—the Nawab of Bhopal, the Raja of Mahmudabad, the Nizam of Hyderabad—who all had some dispute or the other over the waqf lands, with the British, or in their own families. This clientele would become the bricks and mortars of his 'Pakistan' project in the years to come.

With the annulment of the Bengal Partition and relocation of the British Indian capital from Calcutta to Delhi in 1911, politics underwent a sea-change in the country. While, on the one hand, the Muslim League lost one of its pet causes and turned its ire against the British, joining hands with the rival 'Hindu' Congress, the Indian National Congress itself saw the focus and its leadership shifting from the predominantly *Bengali* leadership to the rest of India, particularly to leaders from the Northern and Western India. Jinnah attended annual meetings of the Congress as well as the League in Bankipur in December 1912. Although he had not joined the Muslim League, it praised him sky high for piloting the Waqf Validating Act; League Secretary Syed Wazir Hasan and Maulana Mohammad Ali, the Pan-

Islamic champion and editor of *Comrade*, invited him to join the Muslim League. He promised to join in 1913, travelled to England along with Gokhale, visited Karachi after 17 years and attended the Congress there. From there, he went to Agra for the League meet in December 1913. He was now emerging as a national figure like no one else: besides having his feet in both the Congress and the League, he was also privy to the government in London and Calcutta as member of the Imperial Legislative Council. He was now trying to evolve what would be known as the Lucknow Pact: at Agra, he proposed to the League to postpone its reaffirmation of faith in their quest for communal representation at least for one year and come closer to the Congress.

By now, he had planned a political future for himself as an 'Ambassador of Hindu-Muslim unity' and, but for Gandhi, who was yet to emerge on the scene, would have been the Congress' supreme leader; had there not been Gandhi around, India would have never had her Nehru dynasty either. Ever since the demise of the Mughal Empire in 1850s, the Muslim opinion had been divided into two main streams in British India: the elites of the Aligarh School had come to believe that they could re-establish a modern Muslim empire in India with the possible cooperation of the Hindus against the British and, in such a dispensation, they would be the *benevolent* rulers sharing power with the Hindus.The second school, of the reactionary Pan-Islamists of Deoband, would have none of this—they wanted to complete the halted project of full Islamisation of India and reinstatement of the dead Mughal Empire after expulsion of the British. Thus, both the streams wanted to re-establish the Muslim *supremacy* in India vis-a-vis the Hindus: Jinnah belonged to the Aligarh school and his support to the Muslim League's 'communal electorate' and later proportional representation was part of this particular ideology. Gandhi, having mastered the Qur'an, understood this Muslim Mind very clearly and continued to corner both Jinnah and the Muslim League—with the initial support of the Deoband Pan-Islamists!—until they migrated to Pakistan, to the two corners of India.

But Jinnah's initial appeal to the Muslim League to give up separate electorate did not cut any ice with the League stalwarts—it was their lifeblood, the *raison d'etre*, the policy for which the League itself was set up; had they given it up, the League would have merged in the Congress! On the contrary, it was this very issue that, after being nearly shunted out of the Congress due to Gandhi's 'machinations', Jinnah would expand into a demand for Pakistan: from separate electorate to a separate homeland for the Muslims was but a small, logical step.

In April 1914, Jinnah sailed to London along with some other Congress leaders, at a time his would-be rival, Gandhi, had also reached there due to diversion of ship as the First World War began. The 'peace-lover' Gandhi was urging the Indians to volunteer for military service and 'think imperially', inviting them to join the Field Ambulance Training Corps he had floated. Jinnah joined the gala reception for Gandhi in London; there, the would-be Mahatma would size up flowering potential of the ambitious up-and-coming 'Muslim' seen as the 'Ambassador of Hindu-Muslim unity', the heir apparent to the Bombay triumvirate of the Congress, may be the future ruler of India if and when the British left. Lord Crewe had already described Jinnah as the 'best talker of the pack'.

When he returned to India in January 1915, Jinnah did not realise what Gandhi was up to. The *Gurjar Sabha* (Gujarat Society), of which Jinnah was the President (and, therefore, Gandhi knew he was a Thakkar-Khoja convert, whose family once belonged to Kathiawad, Saurashtra), organised a garden party in the honour of fellow Gujarati (Gandhi), who had earned name and fame throughout the colonial world for his series of agitations against imperial powers. With Jinnah in the chair, Gandhi responded to the welcome: 'I am glad to find a *Muhammedan* not only belonging to my own region in the Gujarat's Sabha, but also chairing it.' There was nothing wrong, factually; but it was a deep insult to a man of Jinnah's taste, the Black Briton who had come so far after shedding so much of his past baggage and embracing so much of modernity and who was even urging the League to shed its Muslim identity. It was Gandhi's way of letting everyone know that Jinnah was, after all, a *mere* Muslim. From this inaugural tiff emerged their historic rivalry and they mutually found in each other their natural enemy, a fatal embrace. Nemesis.

With both of his mentors, Gokhale and Mehta, passing away in 1915, and the ailing, aged Naoroji away in London, Jinnah alone remained the top leader of the Moderate faction of the Congress in Bombay. Tilak, released from the Mandalay jail in Burma in June 1914, was very popular but ailing; he entrusted some responsibility to Jinnah who was working furiously not only to bring the two factions of the Congress but also the Muslim League together. In December 1915, both the Congress and the League held their annual sessions in nearby tents in Bombay, facilitating members to attend any or both at will. In the 31 December session of the League, with Bengali Barrister Mazhar ul-Haq in the chair, angry Muslim clergy, led by Maulana Hasrat Mohani, took the English-speaking Jinnah to task in chaste Urdu and Pashtu for his 'anti-Islamic' activities, as thousands shouted at him. Jinnah urged Haque to adjourn the stormy meeting. The very next day, as President of the Bombay Muslim Students' Union, he reconvened the League meeting. The 1 January 1916 meeting paved the way for the famous Lucknow Pact the same year. But Gandhi had, looking from the sidelines of the adjacent tent of the Congress, meanwhile, come to know who were most opposed to Jinnah: the bearded, Urdu-speaking mullahs. He would cultivate these very clergy very soon, whom, initially, Jinnah ignored.

His 'secular' credentials and progressive views echoed in the attempts he made to forge unity between the two major communities, although the Lucknow Pact, arrived at after Jinnah appealed to the Hindus to sacrifice more, turned out to be deftly tilted *in favour of Muslims*—he had joined the Muslim League in 1913 and remained in it until 1920, alternately remaining active or inactive later as well. Gandhi sensed this pro-Muslim tilt in the Pact that would widen the Hindu-Muslim gulf in the near future, once the ongoing First World War was over. For, **disproportionate** to their *actual population* and viewed as a 'veto', the Muslims got guaranteed seats in each of the provincial legislative councils: 33 per cent each in Bombay and at the Centre, 50 per cent in the Punjab, 40 per cent in Bengal, 30 per cent in the United Provinces (UP), 25 per cent in Orissa and Bihar and 15 per cent in the Central Provinces (CP) and Madras Presidency. Thus, the 'Ambassador of Hindu-Muslim unity' had very cleverly begun to provide a veto to the Muslim community: Jinnah was doing everything legally and peacefully that the Pan-Islamist mullahs wanted to do by sword! The lawyer was creating a core-constituency of Muslims on which to build his future, 'secular' career as the Leader of a largely Hindu India—in other words, a modern Akbar, with an updated *Mansabdari* system. On 30 December 1916, speaking from the League platform in Lucknow, its President, Jinnah, promised additional safeguards to the Muslims, leaving no loopholes in the 'contract' he drafted with the Hindus: 'The decisions that you take...will go forth with all the force and weight that can legitimately be claimed by the chosen leaders and representatives of 70 million Indian Musalmans. On the nature of those decisions will depend, in a large measure, the fate of India's future, of India's unity, and of our common ideals and aspirations for constitutional freedom.'

Unlike most idiots populating the existing political leadership, Gandhi, himself a master of reading the fine-print-between-the-lines, fully understood what this Lucknow Pact of the so-called Hindu-Muslim 'unity' *actually* meant: Jinnah was bringing in from the backdoor and legal way what the Hindus feared the violent mullahs would snatch from them at sword-point. Jinnah seemed to be using his legal talent to gift-pack a cobra to the Hindus. The Lucknow Pact, therefore, remained merely a ceasefire between the two rival communities although it was initially billed as a 'great step' in forging national unity. In 1917, Jinnah raised in the Central Legislative Council the issue of the Ali Brothers' imprisonment (since 1915), forcing the British to reply that they had been interned for their sympathy with the King's foes, that is, Caliph Abdul Hamid of Ottoman Turkey. But, Jinnah could not become darling of the Muslim clergy as they did not pardon him as yet. It was the Mahatma who jumped at the prospects of aligning with Jinnah's enemies, the Muslim clergy, led now by the Ali Brothers, and used them to the hilt as springboard to parachute himself on to the national centre-stage.

So absorbed was Jinnah in giving shape to his ambitious plans for himself that he had almost forgotten he had once even been married. He had not seen his cousin-wife Ami for 28 years. But now he felt it was time to have a wife and raise family. After a romance with the 18-year-old Ratanbai or 'Ruttie', the granddaughter of the wealthiest Bombay Parsi Sir Dinshaw Manockjee Petit, the 42-year-old Jinnah got married on 19 April 1918, much against the wishes of her family. Ruttie was now nominally converted to Islam as 'Marium' or Mary. Even before his honeymoon was over, he had to participate in the Delhi War Conference the same month, which Gandhi, too, attended. The Mahatma opposed non-inclusion of the Ali Brothers in the conference and then seconded the resolution on recruiting Indians for the British Army, abandoning his non-violence etc.; his loyalist role at this conference completely upstaged the 'anti-British' Jinnah, whose heart was more with his new wife than with age-old diseases like war and peace. Although Tilak and Annie Besant supported him as their Home Rule League colleague, the British had taken cue from Gandhi. Bombay Governor Wellington, too, in his own war conference of 10 June 1918, passed unsavoury remarks against the Leaguers, meaning Jinnah, who was present. The Jinnahs and the Wellingtons, thereafter, had many a spat. This lowered the prestige of Jinnah and the British now began to think of him as an arrogant, obstinate, self-righteous upstart vis-a-vis a manageable and malleable Gandhi. At a time Gandhi was recruiting Indian soldiers in his native Gujarat for the British Army, they observed, Jinnah was honeymooning! But Jinnah proved them wrong very soon. In July 1918, he turned out as a moderate, brilliant and flexible constitutional expert on the proposed Montague-Chelmsford Reforms. Edwin Montague, a Jew, was the first secretary of state for India to have visited this country; the impact of the Balfour Declaration and Israel were still away in the womb of the future and a Jew could still praise the would-be Father of a Muslim Nation; he praised Jinnah as '...armed to the teeth with dialectics, and insistent upon the whole of his scheme...and it is, of course, an outrage that such a man should have no chance of running the affairs of his own country'. But that was in 1917; by next year, Gandhi had begun to upstage Jinnah.

Ironically, Jinnah himself had set the stage to paint himself in a corner. The obstinate leader, now on the wrong side of his 40s, further compounded his woes when he organised a massive public demonstration against the Wellingtons whose term had ended with the War in November 1918. It was a small issue: the Bombay Parsis had merely planned a send-off party to the retiring Governor. Finding this as the last opportunity to settle their personal scores with the Wellingtons, the Jinnahs went out of their way and virtually gate-crashed in the party. This was the first time that Jinnah had taken such an openly anti-British stand and also the first when he was roughed up, bruised and forced out of the Town Hall. Overnight, he became a public hero of sorts. But his debonair image was shattered forever; however, this one-act play did not bring any lasting glory to the former actor and he could never become the street-fighter like the Gandhians. Like his former Ismaeli chief, The Aga Khan, the new leader was now a specimen of a personality cult; his burning ambition to emerge as *the* Leader of India had begun to vault when he described his settling personal score with Wellington as a 'Red Letter Day' as he spoke at a public meeting to celebrate this 'triumph' at Apollo Street in Bombay. To commemorate the event, his supporters collected Rs 65,000 and built what became known as the 'People's Jinnah Memorial Hall' (or, after 1947, the P J Hall), ironically in the compound of Bombay's Indian National Congress building. If Jinnah could have a memorial to his 'historic triumph' at the age of just 42, could Gandhi have remained far behind in writing his autobiography two decades before his death? In their acts, the two rivals tried to defy death even before they had begun to actually live for the causes that would make them world famous.

Having won their temporary peace in an essentially Europe's so-called First World War, Britain now set out to win the ongoing 'war' in India by adopting repressive measures, instead of ushering in democracy it had promised to gain support during the War. Justice Sir Sidney Rowlatt, chairman of the British government's Sedition Committee, found it justifiable to go back on the British word and decided that the Black Act was the most suitable for the blacks of India. So, in March 1919, the Rowlatt Act was passed, prompting Jinnah to resign from the Legislative Council as a protest. As Britain was busy collecting trophies of the War and raising Hitler in the Weimar incubator, Muslim League President A K Fazlul Haque complained of the Christian nations' 'land-grabbing' in the Islamic countries. With the Khilafatists, as also Maulana Azad, behind bars, the League despatched Jinnah to London at the head of a delegation to protect the Muslim interests. There, on the intervening night of 14 and 15 August 1919, was born Jinnah's only daughter, Dina—precisely 28 years later, same day and hour, will be born Pakistan, his second child! His third child, Bangladesh, was born 23 years after his death. For now, however, Britain only gave short-shrift to Jinnah as the deceased Ottoman Empire was being sliced out between Britain and France at Versailles. Wellington, still smarting under the humiliation Jinnah had heaped on him in Bombay, now saw to it that the Muslim leader returned empty-handed; the former Bombay Governor poisoned the ear of everyone who mattered in London against the now-former member of the Council.

Back home, Jinnah's first major failure was music to Gandhi's ears. He organised agitations against the Rowlatt Act. On 6 April 1919 a nation-wide strike and on 13 April the Jallianwala Bagh Massacre followed. Gandhi, his sixth sense intact, reckoned that the British, gloating over the War trophies, would commit mistakes; he let them kick their own ass. The road to freedom would start from Amritsar where General R E Dyer killed 400 and wounded 1,200 unarmed people. Jinnah tried to save his leadership now slipping out of his hand like quicksand. This he could do only by appearing to be 'different' from Gandhi; his Thakkar-pride would not let him *follow* the Modh Mahatma. So, he tried to continue his hitherto unsuccessful line of slow, moderate, legal, constitutional and legislative changes. His problem was that he was still wearing the old, worn-out gown he had inherited from the Bombay triumvirate and thought he was the successor of Gokhale; however, Gokhale himself had not seen Jinnah in the same light—the Maharashtrian Brahmin leader had seen his successor in the Modh Gujarati *bania*, not the Thakkar Muslim. Jinnah was brave but obstinate; Gandhi was 'coward' but knew exit routes. Together, they were sketching and shaping an emerging Pakistan.

Using carrots-and-sticks alternatively, the once-bitten-twice-shy British now tried to rub off their tyrannical colour. In December

1919, the Montague Reforms were passed to buy peace in India and to enjoy power-without-responsibility at the Centre while giving away responsibility-without-power to the 'bloody black thieves' in the provinces—the British monarchy had now given birth to a diarchy in an India where the existing princely states made it a triarchy! Meanwhile, both the Muslim League and the Congress held their annual meetings in Amritsar. Jinnah, the old thespian, now elected as President of the League for 1920, declared in the presence of the new-kids-on-the-block, the Ali Brothers, that 'there was no Government but the Government of Allah'. He appealed to the gathering to consider whether the Gandhian agitational programme, with the support of the Khilafat Conference, could be supported. He had realised that his star was declining and that of Gandhi rising; the latter was the new action-hero superstar on India's political horizon, eclipsing the old one who looked tired and outdated, his typecast movements and histrionics too predictable to be attractive. Gandhi, flavour of the new season, was now the mass leader in his many avatars and Jinnah still the mediocre, middle class, 'Muslim' hero, always in a three-piece suit, smoking like chimney, always speaking English. The Mahatma, with the Ali Brothers and Motilal Nehru in his tent, easily walked over Jinnah and his supporters C R Das and B C Pal at the Calcutta Congress.

How did Gandhi do it? Simple. The Gujarati trader knew the British steps had enraged Indian business community and he exploited it to jack up his own leadership. His businessmen supporters, such as Bombay's leading man Mian Mohammad Chotani, brought in train-loads of Khilafatist Muslims to Calcutta to support Gandhi's leadership. Tilak, a Brahmin, who would not work under the leadership of a *bania*, or support a Muslim cause like the Caliphate, passed away in August 1920. With all other leaders of the Old School of the Congress finding themselves prisoners of their armchairs or bed, Gandhi sprinted to the leadership of the Congress. He changed, what his detractors accused him of, the very 'creed' of the Congress: until now, the Indian National Congress had a secular outlook, though it had compacted the Lucknow Pact with the League; now, it was actively supporting even 'religious' causes. And no wonder which way the Congress would turn inevitably, slowly, inexorably, comprehensively and eventually: it would be to the majority's Hinduism. It was destined to, because democracy is the rule of the majority and the forces of history would ensure that Gandhi, *any* Gandhi, would find himself/herself presiding over from the crest of the wave. If the Old School could compromise with the League, why shouldn't Gandhi have compromised with the Khilafatists? The 'creed' of the Congress was, therefore, changed in 1916 itself; Gandhi, who understood this better than anyone else, blossomed fully when the opportunity came. How confused the Old School and their British acolytes were could be gauged from the fact that even Montague suspected the polytheist Gandhi and the monotheist Khilafatists to be in 'league' with the atheist Bolsheviks of Russia!

With the Ali Brothers in his tent, now was the time for Gandhi to ensure that Jinnah was stripped of his Congress badge altogether. From Calcutta, both of them went to Bombay to attend the Swaraj Sabha (Home Rule League) meeting in October 1920. The Mahatma, who presided over the meeting, proposed 'total independence for India according to its people's wishes' which, Jinnah, predictably, opposed with his hackneyed 'self-government under the British Commonwealth' line. Like any class leader, Jinnah did not know *what the people would support*; like any armchair politician and 'intellectual'—including the ready-to-vomit sound-byte 'experts' of our TV news age—he believed that the best thing *for the people* was the one in which *he* believed! He, therefore, declared that he would not accept what Gandhi proposed. This was the opportunity the Mahatma was waiting for. 'Anyone', he announced, 'who could not accept the majority's decision is free to resign from the Sabha'. Jinnah's problem was that he thought for India like the British imperialists did, and what was to be *given* to its people; Gandhi's advantage was that he knew what the Indians *wanted to take* from the British. Jinnah would realise it only later, and to a great cost, that the masses could be moved *only* by emotional issues, not saner voices: this realisation he would use to telling effect when he would declare 'Direct Action' in 1946, hinting that the Muslims massacre the Hindus, en masse, to terrorise and force the latter to agree to Partition. A politician unable to blackmail and exploit the masses using emotional issues would simply morph into a statesman!

But, for now, Jinnah was heading to a twilight zone. His pride was wounded and he had to confess that he no longer had 'any voice or power'. At the geographical centre of India, Nagpur, where Gandhi was on 28 December 1920, he declared India's goal as the 'attainment of Swaraj by the people of India by all legitimate and peaceful means'. Jinnah, once again, objected to it saying he was against removing the British unless the people were adequately prepared for independence. Typically, Gandhi too supported that the British connection was a necessity 'so long as it benefitted the Indians': 'I know before we are done with this great battle on which we have embarked...we have to go probably, possibly, through a *sea of blood*, but let it not be said of us... that we are guilty of shedding blood, but let it be said by generations yet to be born that we suffered, that we shed not somebody's blood but our own; and so I have no hesitation in saying that I do not want to show much sympathy for those who had their heads broken or who were said to be even in the danger of losing their lives. What does it matter?'

Jinnah saw through the sugar-coated bitter pill his rival was slipping down the Congress throat: Gandhi, ever careful with his words, was mentally preparing the people to face the 'sea of blood', presumably to be shed by the British/Muslims, and also warning the would-be victims not to resort to violence. Like a Hindu Noah, he was readying his people to jump onto his boat. When Jinnah tried to reason with him, the 'Muslim' leader was shouted down. The Lucknow Pact lay in tatters: in Calcutta, the Khilafatists had opposed Jinnah while in Nagpur the Hindus did the same. So humiliating was his experience that he, even though he was elected its President only three months ago, refused to participate in the Nagpur session of the League, charged up as his own organisation was with the Gandhi-Khilafat battery.

In the 1920s' India, it was an age of competitive Islam—as since the 1990s, it was of competitive Hinduism—in which a wily Gandhi had out-manouvered Jinnah and other 'moderate' Muslim leaders. The Muslim community in the Indian subcontinent felt threatened with a post First World War British 'anti-Muslim' backlash, as in the wake of the Ottoman Empire's dismemberment, the way it was post-9/11 and the US destabilising the Islamic apple carts, one by one. In a minority throughout their 1,400 years presence in an infidel land like India, the Muslims could not have fought on two fronts simultaneously, against the other *Ahl-e-Kitab* (People of the Book, ie. the Jews and Christians) of the UK/USA and with the *Qafirs* of *Hindustan*. So, the Ali Brothers, like Pervez Musharraf and others of his ilk, bought temporary 'peace' with the Hindus. Gandhi knew then, like India knew later, that the Muslim fundamentalists could be trusted to turn anti-Hindu again as soon as the British/American loosened their grip on Turkey/Pakistan and allowed the latter to go hammer and tongs against India. But Gandhi played along with the Ali Brothers, the way India played with Pakistan, for the stakes were higher: in the 1920-47 period, Gandhi supported the Muslims because he apparently wanted their fanatic fringe to destabilise India and create Pakistan while in the post-9/11 era, the stage was being set for deIslamisation of Islamabad, as well as Dhaka, as the next phase of 1947 and 1971.

Why was Gandhi doing so? Extremely careful with his words, he sometimes found them slip: 'The Sword is no emblem of Islam. *But Islam was born in an environment where the Sword was, and still remains, the supreme law... The Sword is yet too much in evidence among the Mussalmans.* It must be sheathed if Islam is to be what it means—peace.' (*Young India*, 30 December, 1926). Clearly, he knew Islam much, much better than most world leaders put together. That was why he played the Chess with Islamists with an unprecedented finesse no one had done before, and after, in order to ensure its exit from India. Jinnah, on the other hand, despite his manipulating the 1916 Lucknow Pact to benefit the Muslims, had lost touch with the reality, at least for now. He did not even realise that his strategy of the 1916 Pact was destined to be the first step for him to father Pakistan three decades later.

Shattered to the core due to Gandhi eclipsing him politically, the post-1921 Jinnah was much occupied as a lawyer and—unlike Gandhi who became a full-time politician and health-hygiene-brahmacharya freak now—aged much faster. He strongly felt the double loss of his most passionate subjects of interest as he could neither become an actor nor a successful politician. Even now, however, he had no personal rancour against Gandhi; he still respected 'Mr Gandhi', but never believed or called him the 'Mahatma'. Having learnt from the 1857 fiasco of losing the Mughal Empire and the Ottoman Empire as well so recently, no important Muslim leader would launch any major agitation against the British; he was, therefore, opposed mainly to Gandhi's agitational methods that had changed the creed of the Congress. Even after retreating in his shell, Jinnah agreed to address his guru, Gokhale's Servant of India Society, Nagpur, on 19 February 1921, and attend the Ahmedabad Congress in December that year. The year saw the Hindu-Muslim accord on the Khilafat issue shattered, leading to the outbreak of communal riots, the Moplah Massacre and the migration of nearly 20,000 Muslim families to their nearest *Dar-ul-Islam*, Afghanistan.

From concept to conception: Mother India was now pregnant with 'Pakistan'.

In January 1922, as a violent India drifted on the shoulders of the 'non-violent' Mahatma, Jinnah called an All-Parties Conference in Bombay, trying to create an alternative path to the Gandhian highway project. Nearly 300 leaders, Gandhi included, came to the meeting headed by Sir Sankaran Nair of Madras, the former Congress President who had studied the Moplah Massacre from close quarters. The Non-Cooperation and Khilafat Movements had, by now, charged up India and Gandhi was waiting for an exit route. This was provided when the British-Afghan Treaty came into force freeing the Raj to act against Swaraj activists; the agitators killed 22 policemen at Chauri-Chaura in Deoria district of United Provinces in February 1922, prompting the Mahatma to halt the twin Movements. The Gandhian Satyagraha collapsed as Jinnah had predicted and the Mahatma, too, had envisaged: the Muslims and the Hindus returned to their medieval cat-and-mouse game with renewed vigour and hatred. Gandhi, the Celibate, knew that 'sudden withdrawal' was the most ancient human tactic to make a woman cry for more: he would now wait for the Khilafatists collapse of their own wait and the British commit another round of mistakes. Jinnah, on the other hand, tried to rope in M R Jayakar and Motilal Nehru to float a new liberal and moderate party in 1922 but they spurned the offer, leaving the 'Ambassador of Hindu-Muslim unity' high and dry and cut off from his Hindu friends within the Congress. In November 1923, he was re-elected to the Central Legislative Assembly, now called National Assembly, again as a 'Muslim' member from Bombay, and thus regained the seat he had resigned from in the wake of the Rowlatt Act's passage.

In the Assembly, he organised a powerful block of 23 'Independents' in 1924 at a time Mustafa Kemal Pasha of Turkey was consigning the Caliphate to the dustbin of Islamic history. He collaborated with the 42-member-strong C R Das-M L Nehru-led Swaraj Party and worked hard in the evolution of parliamentary, Westminster-model government in India, becoming the most important member of the Assembly, while Gandhi cooled his heels in a prison, planning to write his autobiography. The Muslim League, in doldrums, now called Jinnah back to preside over a special session in May 1924 in which he stressed the need for a Dominion Status for India in the British Commonwealth as the Gandhian Satyagraha and the Khilafat Movement had failed to achieve anything. Jinnah, who had joined the League in 1913 and returned to it a decade later, proclaimed that Swaraj was an 'almost interchangeable' term with Hindu-Muslim unity! The League resolved to work for *its* goal of Swaraj: a federal union of fully autonomous provinces, delegating some of the concerns to the Centre, guarantee of full religious liberty and 'separate electorate' for the Muslims. In other words, a weak Centre and the strong States in a loose federation a la the latter day Mughal Empire in which the minority Muslims would always have veto power against the majority Hindus!

But Gandhi, too, was not sitting idle. He knew how revolutions uproot monarchy, upstage mediocrity and flower the real national potential, even if temporarily: that the aftermath of the First World War would trigger a popular, republican revolution in Turkey as well. Russia was now well under a Bolshevik rule; Hitler was organising the Beer Hall Putsch and threatening to pull Germany out of the League of Nations and bury the Weimar Constitution; Spain was hurtling towards a Civil War; the Fascists were gaining strength in Italy; France, as usual, was hoping to create yet another, nth Republic... China was in turmoil, the Indo-China was in ferment. He knew the British would accord topmost priority to save *their* Crown rather than its Jewel. If the Jewel were to be left to fend for itself, the Muslims would not be part of a democracy in India, that is, the Hindu Raj. The fanatic Muslims, frustrated at the unceremonious collapse of their Caliphate, had gone berserk and were organising massacre of the Hindus across the subcontinent; the Hindu Mahasabha and the Arya Samaj, in retaliation, were organising their own 're-conversion' (*Shuddhi*, 'purification') programmes to wean back those lily-hearted people who had embraced Islam/Christianity. At each opportunity they got, the two communities were increasingly going at each other's throats, preparing grounds for a 'Pakistan' no other leader foresaw in that age of slow-motion-photography.

But this Hindu-Muslim tension was yet to fully charge up the most crucial and populous part of the subcontinent: the vast, Hindi-speaking, 'cow belt' of North India—the ground zero and sub-continental Mesopotamia of the Infidel which would script the saga of Islam and Christianity's return journey. Neither Gandhi nor Jinnah really knew the pulse of this region that had actually faced the full fury of Islamic terror since the coming of Muhammad bin-Qasim to Sindh in 711, the heart of India that had lost its self-esteem to the maximum extent. It was in this area that the future of India, and the beginning of Pakistan, depended, simply because it housed the maximum density of Muslims in the subcontinent and had catalysed the Hindu civilisation like never before to rejuvenate it over the last 1,000 years. In 1927, Gandhi declared Chakravarti Rajagopalachary (CR) of Madras as his temporal successor but would later revise his 'will' and make Jawaharlal Nehru the first 'Hindu Caliph'. Why? Because only a North Indian leader could charge up the Hindi belt. While Jinnah scarcely knew any Hindi and had little command over Urdu, Gandhi's knowledge of 'Hindustani' was better and he had floated several pro-Hindi outfits across India.

It was, again, a hilarious situation in the Congress politics. The Mahatma had called off the Non-Cooperation Movement but his

Satyagraha continued! He continued to boycott all councils and British connections even as his confidante Motilal Nehru, who headed the Swaraj faction within the Congress, remained in the Assembly and cooperated with Jinnah. The senior Nehru was a successful lawyer like Jinnah but, unlike the latter, needed support to climb political pillars; his son, Jawaharlal, was an unsuccessful lawyer and a failed 'historian' but shared some of the Mahatma's histrionics. The father-son duo, social climbers from Kashmir who had made it good in *Allahabad* (The Abode of Allah), were the ideal foster-sons of Macaulay. Gandhi was preparing to pit the half-Hindu Nehrus from Allahabad against the 'half-Muslim' Jinnah of Karachi. Motilal was indecisive about his own political career but wanted his son to climb up the ladder called Gandhi; Jawaharlal, the new kid on the block, on the other hand, was ambitious to 'lead' India, just like Jinnah, and had begun to throw around his weight as an 'intellectual' of sorts; short-tempered, a lover of 'good things' of life but generous, romantic and a gifted orator, even a visionary who cultivated international connections, Jawaharlal became popular next only to Gandhi—what he lacked was the Mahatma's political vision.

Gandhi could now either become the Congress President himself or have his trusted man head it. He could anoint his acolyte Motilal as the top Congress leader whom he could use against Jinnah. In August 1924, the Mahatma made this known to the senior Nehru, putting him in a dilemma: if Gandhi became the Congress President himself, it would eclipse him (Nehru) and as per the Mahatma's continuing boycott of the Assembly and other Councils, Motilal would have to resign from it and end his alliance with Jinnah. In what Jawaharlal called a tug-of-war between his father and Gandhi, the latter won. Putting aside his claims of disinterest, Gandhi presided over the 1925 Congress meeting 'only as a businessman presiding at business meetings'. Between 1921 and 1925, while the Muslims vent their frustration at the Hindus wherever they could, an important development had taken place: the 1921 census had proclaimed both Bengal and the Punjab as Muslim majority provinces with India's 'minority' community being more than 50 per cent in these eastern and western regions. With this, as Gandhi knew, the Muslim League's demand for increased representation of the community and revision of the Lucknow Pact became more and more vociferous. Jinnah, his consciousness about being a Muslim increasing, and the League, which drifted apart from the Congress over the Pact, found themselves in the same boat. Gandhi, his Non-Cooperation and Khilafat tactics exposed, found that he was no longer able to use the Muslims as 'friends'.

Meanwhile, the retiring Lord Reading tried to rope in Jinnah with the offer of Knighthood which the Great Leader spurned; even his wife threatened to divorce him if he became an honourable Sir Muhammed Ali Jinnah! The League shifted its office from Dhaka to Delhi in February 1927 making it easier for Jinnah to frequent it from Mumbai. This brought him closer to the League again with its secretary Sayyed Shams ul-Hasan trying to patch up Jinnah's increasing differences with his wife. Gandhi, on the other hand, was waiting like an eagle for his next opportunity to strike at the British and the League—in the interregnum, he worked as a social worker. With the Communist Russia increasingly active in China, India and other countries of interest to the British, it was only a matter of time before revolutionary extremists, a Gadar Party Version 2.0, would gather momentum; Europe, too, was slipping in the undemocratic mire of Fascism, Nazism and similar extremist 'ideologies' and monarchist Britain would soon find itself in a 'democratic' camp to save its colonies, making the Second World War inevitable. Post-First World War, Britain was no longer following the foreign policy of Splendid Isolation in Europe but was actively trying to have a decisive edge in the 'Continental' as well as world policies. The Westminster was pitted against Weimar. Even in Britain, the Tories were becoming unpopular; Ramsay MacDonald's main Opposition of Labour Party would eventually come to power in 1929. In order to keep its hold on the Crown's Jewel, India, the imperialist Tories constituted, in 1927, an all-white Commission under Sir John Simon to work out something on the decade-old promises of a Dominion Status for India, or what the Indians called 'Swaraj'. The entire public opinion in India was anti-Simon, forcing the British to invite the Indians to draft a forthcoming Act agreeable to both the Hindus and Muslims. The Indians accepted the challenge and called the All-Parties Conference at

Delhi in January 1928, and another two months later, a third again in May that year; but no agreement could be reached on the issue of the rights of the 'minorities', mainly Muslims. Finally, a committee under Motilal Nehru was formed to frame a 'Constitution'. Jinnah opposed the panel's all-white constitution none of whose seven members, including Simon, knew anything about India. Gandhi, on the other hand, realised that the opportunity he was waiting for had come.

Jinnah tried another go as his favourite theme of Hindu-Muslim 'unity', a euphemism for Muslim *veto* vis-a-vis the Hindus simply because the westernised Muslims could no longer hope to revive their dead Mughal Empire. Considering separate electorate to be the main hurdle in improving Hindu-Muslim relations, he came out with a Six-Point Formula, known as the Delhi-Muslim Proposals, which, if the Hindus accepted as the Muslim's safeguards, the latter would give up its demand of separate electorate. Consequently, these Proposals were formally approved at a conference of Muslims in Delhi in 1927—these were first accepted and then rejected by the Congress. Why? Because the cure seemed worse than the disease. The Proposals began with the separation of a (Muslim-majority) province of Sindh from Bombay Presidency and introduction of 'reforms' in the North-West Frontier Province and in Baluchistan—first steps that would form the basis of a future 'Pakistan' (ie. separate electorate being replaced by a separate homeland!). Furthermore, the Hindu minorities in the Muslim-majority areas were to get the same concession as the Muslims in the Hindu-majority areas; all right, *but* the Muslim representation in the Central Legislature would not be less than one-third! As if these were not enough, Jinnah wanted to ensure that the 'minority' Muslims enjoyed a veto in any future democratic, majority rule: he wanted a constitutional guarantee that, on communal matters, no bill or resolution could be considered or passed without three-fourths of members agreeing to it! He wanted to create a new democracy in which decisions were to be taken not by a simple, not by a two-thirds, but by a three-fourths majority! In this psychological warfare with the Hindus, Jinnah, who had never really embraced Islam, was laying the foundation of Islamabad. Gandhi's fears with regard to the Hindus converted to Christianity, as he found in South Africa, were coming true even in the case of Muslims like Jinnah: once converted, Abrahamism tended to denationalise them and *theodesically* forced them to take the path of separatism, even treason; Christian or Muslim belief system would eventually equip them with a particular mindset to work secretively to exploit and/or overthrow the infidel rule if they could not convert them.

It was this very menace Gandhi was silently fighting against because he knew that 'People of the Book', the fanatic Christians and Muslims (in the Indian context), could not live peacefully *with others* in an infidel land; it was not a question of Muslims alone—Independent India discovered the same problem with Christian-majority areas in the North-Eastern States and fervent attempts being made by rabid Christian missionaries to convert the tribals and others wherever they could to change the demographic composition, misusing the Constitutional safeguards like right-to-religion, under the shelter of 'human rights'; the evangelists believed in buying out souls for the Christ, the millennialists went berserk with the 'Second Coming' of Jesus as the year 2000 approached and tried to convert the Hindus, *en masse*, in tribal areas, leading to Christian-Hindu spats in States like Gujarat and Orissa.

The Muslim League was divided on whether to support the Simon Commission; Jinnah, re-elected permanent president for another three years, thought that his time had come. Speaking at the League's annual meeting at Calcutta on 30 December 1927, he extended an olive branch to the Congress and Hindu Mahasabha. The bonhomie between the Hindus and Muslims seemed to be re-emerging, the moribund Non-Cooperation Movement suddenly got its life back, communal riots stopped for the time being. For once, Gandhi and Jinnah found themselves in the same boat. For once, even Gandhi 'congratulated' Jinnah on the success of the boycott of the Simon Commission in February 1928; the British, taken aback at this unexpected turn of events and of having stoked the latent fire against themselves, decided to divide the two communities so as to perpetuate their rule. A hyper-active Jinnah, trying to wrest the leadership from Gandhi at this god-sent opportunity, attended the

All-Parties' Conference called by Congress President M A Ansari in Delhi the same month, aimed at suggesting alternative constitutional path. Gandhi, having little faith in such British-style niceties, remained in Ahmedabad, spinning yarn at his Ashram. He knew the Thakkar-Jinnah would not budge from his 'Muslim' position. Hindu leaders like Lala Lajpat Rai and Madan Mohan Malviya wanted to do away with the very idea of separate electorate for the two communities while Jinnah wanted its continuation as a cost of unity between the communities. He even produced proposals, which would later mature into a 14-point formula (to match Woodrow Wilson's 14-Points!) which, if accepted, would have given Muslims control in five provincial governments. But the Hindu Mahasabha mounted pressure on the Congress against it. Dismayed over its rejection, Jinnah returned home, only to find his wife had left for Europe in his absence. He, too, followed her to London.

Here was an opportunity for the Congress, whose President M A Ansari chaired a meeting in Bombay of All-Party Conference; it set up its own 'Commission', headed by Motilal Nehru, to draft a nationalist constitution. Gandhi ensured that Motilal became the Congress President that year, 1928. And with this, the Mahatma bounced back onto the centre-stage.

How?

The Jinnah proposals and the Nehru Report ensured that. The Report negated the Lucknow Pact without any compensation being offered to the Muslims; moreover, at Gandhi's instance, it proposed to make *Hindi* the official language, something Jinnah abhorred to the extreme, given his own poor knowledge of not only that language but also Urdu (he was always most comfortable in English; he did not like to converse even in his native Gujarati or Sindhi either!). For Jinnah, this was a bolt from the blue. After anointing a leader like Motilal from the *Hindi* belt as Congress President and setting up a large number of Hindi-promoting cells across India, Gandhi was now promising to make Hindi the national language. Knowing well the importance of a language in nation-building and integrating a people—as Stalin did by making the Russian the national language of the Soviet Union, or Mustafa Kemal did by replacing Arabic by Turkish—Jinnah sensed the gravity of what Gandhi was up to: it was a road that began at Hindi, went through Hindustan, and culminated at *the* Hindu. Predictably, he dubbed the Nehru Report as a 'Hindu' document. As a reaction to this growing Hindu-isation of the Congress, he decided to become an out-and-out Muslim leader, as Gandhi had guessed *he will* way back in 1915. It took 13 years for Jinnah to become one: in November 1928, while in Sindh defending the Peer of Pagaro in a case, Jinnah, for the first time in his life, participated in a function like a Sindhi Muslim, wearing typical native costume.

Back home, even the League was divided over the Nehru Report; except Jinnah, no important leader was for outright rejection of the Report which was considered fairly democratic for a Dominion of India under the British Raj; many Muslims realised that if one minority got special rights, others, too, would demand the same and make democracy dysfunctional. In short, it was a struggle on whether the Muslims should be 'compensated' for the loss of *their* Mughal Empire in India and who should pay for it. The British were unlikely to pay for it; so, naturally, the Hindus, who, as a majority, would come to rule, must pay as inheritors. This same question haunted Independent India and the government had to resort to the policy of Privy Purses for the former rulers after integration of *their* domains into the Republic; Indira Gandhi scrapped this scheme. The British had pensioned off the last and deposed Mughal Emperor Bahadur Shah 'Zafar', who died in Burma; but his ghost had come to haunt India.

Jinnah, no less quarrelsome with his Leagues colleagues either, had his way and parted ways with the Congress. Forever. He began to prevail upon the League like Gandhi did in the Congress. The Jinnah League now firmed up its demand for a weak centre 'controlling' strong provinces, separate Muslim electorate and special 'weightage' to them in provincial, central government as well as in all departments of social, political and economic life. Jinnah argued that, being a 'minority', the Muslims were in no position to offer anything to the majority Hindus; the Hindus should, on the contrary, be 'generous' enough to offer everything possible to the Muslims. This, which he termed as a 'contract', was necessary for national unity—the Jinnah argument was repeated *ad nauseum* by the Muslims and their parroting, short-sighted Hindu secularists of Independent India until 2014 when Narendra Modi came to power firmly denying any appeasement to the Muslims. The majority Hindus viewed this 'contract' as an instrument of blackmail used by the Muslims, a veto against the majority and democratic community, without giving anything in return to the nation. This was a one-way surrender of the forward, majority community to the largely backward minority merely because it had ruled India for a thousand years, because it could enforce its will, make or mar political fortunes of a political party in a number of poll constituencies through its ghetto voting directed mainly by Friday sermons from the mosque. The Hindus dubbed it as a policy of 'appeasement' of the Muslims; the Congress, a pendulum between the Hindus and Muslims, described it as a price for national unity—the Rajiv Gandhi Government, in the 1980s, meekly changed a law after a Supreme Court ruling granted alimony to a Muslim divorcee woman, Shah Bano, when the fanatic Muslims threatened another flowering season of Islam; only in the year 2003, a Congress Chief Minister, A K Antony of Kerala, could muster courage to expose the Muslim veto when he said the ganged-up community was forcing the democratically-elected government to change its decisions; but the Congress forced Antony to retract his statement! Not to be left behind, even the Hindu rightist BJP tried to change the party creed in 2005 when its top leader, L K Advani, sang paeans to Jinnah and recalled the latter's 'secular' credentials during a visit to his native Sindh in Pakistan; another BJP leader, Jaswant Singh, forayed on the Jinnah route briefly and embraced irrelevance. Clearly, Muslims have been the favourite pastime of idle Hindu leaders in India the way we nostalgically listen to old songs!

Gandhi, therefore, knew how such pseudo-Hindus, many of them, could be trusted to become turn-coats, particularly when afflicted with seasonal secular virus. That was why, for his tactics, he trusted a half-Muslim like Jinnah more than he trusted the half-Hindus within the Congress. Jinnah was pregnant with what would become 'Pakistan' but he would not declare it as yet, even if he knew about his paternity blues. Like a skilful lawyer, he was going step-by-step at a time Gandhi was preparing to leap-frog. Jinnah attended the

All-Parties Muslims Conference presided over by The Agha Khan in Delhi in January 1929. The Agha Khan, happy at Jinnah's 'return' and his own 'importance' disproportionate to his known sources of support, did not mind the Leader's change of creed from his Khoja antecedents and rejecting His Holiness's leadership: two 'heretic' Shia Muslims (The Agha Khan and Jinnah) were now going to decide the future of the largely Sunni, Wahhabi-infected Muslims of South Asia! Within a decade, the Muslims had collectively slipped from espousing the cause of the Caliphate to defending The Agha Khan whose ancestors had done so much against the Caliphs, the Holy Places and even Prophet Muhammed! The successor to the first Agha Khan, who had fled from Persia due to persecution by the Shias, had now found shelter among the Sunnis of the League! Islam was never so helpless in its entire history. Minorities within Islam were now deciding the future of Islam the world over: and, ironically, they were also the driving force in the ongoing deIslamisation drive across the world by making Islam an object of global hatred it had never been.

With his estranged, 29-year-old wife's death in February 1929, the 53-year-old Jinnah was now free to pursue full-time his political career in the direction he wanted; even otherwise, he had little attachment to his small family, the only exceptions being sister Fatima and, for some time, the only daughter Dina; the two women never saw eye-to-eye. Jinnah now produced his famous 14-Point Proposals, ironically, supported by his biggest in-house enemy Maulana Muhammed Ali, who was totally disenchanted with Gandhi. But, within three months, the League was back in doldrums and the Conference of The Agha Khan all but ceased to exist. Jinnah was too strict a lawyer to be palatable to these mercurial political foxes. The Mahatma, on the other hand, true to his salt of the 1919 call for 'Swaraj in one year', now electrified India with his new call of a 'national Satyagraha' if Parliament failed to implement the Nehru Report 'within 1929'. In the Calcutta Congress, where Gandhi moved this resolution, Subhas Chandra Bose, the Mahatma's own new *bete noire* within the Congress, demanded 'Complete Independence' immediately and protested against the 'slave mentality'. Finding each door being closed in his face, Jinnah sought help from his old friend Ramsay MacDonald, the new Prime Minister of Great Britain, who assured him that the government would soon declare India a Dominion. A happy Jinnah, although politically on a slippery wicket, found himself assisting the Viceroy, Lord Irwin, in preparing for what came to be known as the Round Table Conferences to discuss the Dominion Status. Jawaharlal Nehru, the new Congress President, was being egged on by his ambitious father and the wily Mahatma; they had stone-walled all Jinnah efforts to recognise that there existed something called the 'Muslim problem'. The Congress, they declared, represented the 'whole' of India and all of its communities—the representative body of the British colony that would negotiate with the Crown for a Dominion Status like that of Canada and Australia. If Jawaharlal succeeded in this plot, he would emerge as the Prime Minister of India! Or, so Jinnah and Jawaharlal fancied.

Not Gandhi, however. He knew the British saboteurs and chameleons only too well from his personal experience in South Africa and thereafter. Spider-like, the British would hang on to India with the last and the thinnest thread. The Mahatma, therefore, decided to change the creed of the Congress once again; if in 1919-20, the creed was changed from peaceful and constitutional path to the agitational path, the new creed was to virtually declare a war on the British. At its Lahore session in 1930, the Congress declared *Poorna Swaraj* (Complete Independence) as its goal, with Sunday, 26 January 1930, as the Poorna Swaraj Day. Jawaharlal unfurled the National Flag on the banks of the river Ravi, and the Congress was back on the roads for the first time after the Chauri Chaura incident. Jinnah, all alone in his Malabar Hill bungalow of Bombay, with no Muslim League left to give him company, knew he was wasting his time in India, which was once-again in the grip of a Khilafat-II fever: a decade ago, the Indian National Congress was agitating to restore the Muslim Caliphate, in Turkey; now, in Khilafat-II, it was going to launch a drive to oust the Christian British. The energies released by the Khilafat-I drive force multiplied and fuelled Khilafat-II and would eventually lead to the Khilafat-III and Partition in 1947. The Mahatma alone knew how to transfer hydro-energy towards gravity, from higher to lower levels, to create hydroelectricity.

In these muddy waters of Indian politics, Jinnah and Gandhi were emerging as two islands. Jinnah's 14-Points were aimed at making Indian democracy moth-eaten; if the Muslims could not win back India through arms, as they did in the past, they would cripple it constitutionally. More than fears of a minority, it was a case of a psychologically possessed and programmed community to re-boot India to complete Islamisation, or, at the very least, slice out the parts where Islamisation had been completed—the way the Hindu and other minorities have been eliminated in Pakistan, and then in Kashmir, since 1947, is an example. In his 28 March 1929, 14-Points programme, Jinnah not only wanted a weak centre and strong, autonomous provinces (what a functional democracy!), but also one-third Muslim members in each Cabinet at the Centre and in the provinces (even where the meagre Muslim population did not command it!). Clearly, his aim now was to make it impossible for the Indians to have democracy; his successors would pay the price for this folly in Pakistan. Jinnah was merely the Tip of this tumour, dormant since 711, which began to swell post-1857; Gandhi, the Surgeon General, merely pierced this Tip to make the pus ooze out. The frenzied Muslims never realised that Jinnah was the worst thing to have happened to Islam, not only in the Indian subcontinent but globally—he, alone, was the Pied Piper who launched Islam's retreat from across the world.

How prophetic Gandhi proved to be became clear in 1930. After Aligarh, Prayag or Allahabad, the oldest centre of education in British India, had emerged as the centre of North Indian politics. In anointing the Kashmiri Nehrus, the Mahatma had taken a far-reaching decision to integrate the North around at this confluence of the three holy rivers of the Hindus. From *Allahabad* to *Islamabad* would be a short route—just 17-years-long. It was in Allahabad where a Kashmiri poet, Dr Allama Iqbal alias Sir Muhammad Iqbal, another converted Hindu, was giving shape to the future 'Pakistan' as its philosopher and guide. He called a meeting of Muslim leaders at Allahabad in 1930, declaring the community as a 'nation', that there could be no peace unless this fact was recognised by one and all. The embryo of

Pakistan had now bumped up with limbs. The way a crackpot British, H S Chamberlain, provided the 'intellectual' basis for Nazism, Iqbal became the messiah of the separatists; with his feverish mind, the 'philosopher' once composed eloquent verses extolling the virtues of India, only to replace words in the same to extol the Muslims later! He wavered between Hinduism and Islam, like other Kashmiris getting lost in the maze of Shaivite dualism; even the Nehrus were a hybrid of Hinduism and Islam. Gandhi, and then Jinnah, were using these hybrid varieties, Nehru and Iqbal, to achieve their respective, but similar, aims. Iqbal's poetry became clarion calls for both the Congress and the Muslim League to gather their respective flocks! The 1930 India was charged up again, this time the womb bulging out.

No miscarriages or abortions now. Mother India was getting ready to deliver....

So far, Jinnah's main problem was that he was a brilliant general without an army of dependable, trained soldiers; the 'leaders' of the Muslim League, barring a few mullahs and fundamentalists, were mostly fickle-minded and self-seeking opportunists, like their counterparts in the Congress, the bandwagon-jumpers, the fence-sitters raising hands wherever their Leader wanted. Even Jinnah despised most of these leaders who had no vision whatsoever and whose only weapon was rhetoric; Jinnah himself was no less a demagogue but he also had matching brains. It was his dogged determination to emerge as the supreme leader of the nation and his pique against Gandhi that drove his frail and ailing body. But he had neither energy nor resolve nor interest in launching an agitation to prove his point. All he wanted was from *above*, from the British, on the basis of his own brilliance; on the other hand, Gandhi believed in generating biogas, mass support at the grassroots, from *below*, for his agitation and forcing the government to accept his demands. When the British government failed to respond positively, Jinnah would sulk for the opportunity lost and Gandhi would wait for the next opportunity.

Extremist Hindus had failed to make their point. Gandhi knew the basic problem of imperialism was not the arms but the psychology of dominating others and it could be defeated only by waging a psychological war against the enemy. The Indians needed to be deprogrammed of their fears while the British must be stripped of their white supremacist ideas. The British were only too happy to crush the extremists, trade unions and the Communists with an iron hand but even they realised the gravity of the Salt Satyagraha of the Mahatma who, on 12 March 1930, launched his second Civil Disobedience Movement with his 78 associates and marched 200 miles from Ahmedabad to the Dandi coast of the Arabian Sea in South Gujarat. It was largely symbolic but Gandhi made the Indians realise that the British could be challenged on their own turf, that they were *not* invincible. In one stroke, as he successfully defied the British laws, he freed the Indians of their siege mentality: for 1,000 years, the Hindus feared the Muslim barbarians and their arms and, then, the British 'laws' had programmed their minds to resign themselves to fate. Gandhi's very *raison d'etre* was to first liberate them from the British clutches and then to deIslamise India. He knew the immature imperialist British, if and when they left India, would partition it as a parting kick, the way they had done in Ireland: their culture still stranded in childhood, mature democracy still trapped in monarchy, they believed in breaking a toy if they couldn't snatch it from another kid. So, addressing his massive audience at Dandi, he said, 'The British rule in India has brought about moral, material, cultural, and spiritual ruination of this great country. I regard this rule as a curse. I am out to destroy this system of Government…Sedition has become my religion. Ours is a non-violent battle. We are not to kill anybody but it is our dharma to see that the curse of this Government is blotted out.' This, from someone who had declared himself a loyal 'British citizen' just about a decade ago!

Jinnah had nothing to do with such agitations; in fact, he despised agitations and even his closest aides found this opposition so 'unIslamic'—the Muslims were, after all, agitating against the British and the French in West Asia, but not in India! But that did not prevent him from using his gift of the gab to as telling an effect as an agitation. Like a spirited lawyer, he knew how to bluff his way to success. On 12 November 1930, he told the First Round Table Conference in

London: 'I am glad that they (the Prime Ministers and representatives of the Commonwealth) are here to *witness the birth of a new Dominion of India* which would be ready to march along with them within the British Commonwealth of Nations.' This, at a time, when the very idea was being merely discussed. Sir Malcolm Hailey, former Governor of the Punjab and the United Provinces, remarked that Jinnah remained secretive, elusive and was, therefore, not trustworthy. '..Jinnah, of course, was always the perfect little bounder and as slippery as the eels which his forefathers purveyed in Bombay market.' The brilliant Thakkar was living up to his caste reputation even after conversion to Islam by his grandfather a hundred years ago. Thus, while he was bluffing the Conference, he was warming up the British to consider his demands and, at the same time, threatening that '70 million' Muslims would join Gandhi's Civil Disobedience Movement if their demands were not conceded. Refusing to listen to these trademark Jinnah noises, the British, unimpressed by the finely-stitched three-piece Savile Row suits he copied from them, replied to him in kind: on the expiry of Lord Irwin's term as Viceroy in April 1931, the government appointed none other than Lord Wellington, the Great Leader's topmost enemy, as the new Viceroy (1931-36). Jinnah, who was now almost demanding a homeland for the Muslims of India, was himself forced to flee to and live in England while Wellington remained in India! For, Wellington had not forgotten the humiliation the Jinnahs had heaped on him in 1918. During his absence from India, where the Muslim League was in one of those many doldrums, it was Iqbal, whose Brahmin family had converted to Islam 300 years ago, who would hold the Muslim fort until his death in 1938—it was left to this former Kashmiri Pandit to whistle out Islam and perform the last rites of the Muhammad bin-Qasim legacy. He was now openly articulating, as he did at the Muslim League Conference on 29 December 1930, at Allahabad, the 'two-nation theory' of irreconcilable Hindu-Muslim differences, that the principle of European democracy could not be applied to India until its communal problem remained unrecognised. 'The Muslim demand for the *creation of Muslim India within India* is, therefore, perfectly justified', he told his audience, and criticised Ramsay MacDonald for refusing to see that the problem of India was 'international'. Like Gandhi and Jinnah, Iqbal, too, understood the real nature of the big problem: the doctors were waiting for the cancerous tumour to mature so that they could perform surgery! But the Muslim fundamentalists, who knew that a new mullah cried for prayers the loudest, did not realise that these relatively recent Hindu converts were, in fact, creating a Hindu majority Bharat by slowly edging Islam out of Hindustan!

After considerable loss of face, the British were forced to negotiate with Gandhi who had, in one stroke, left Jinnah far behind, once again. The Mahatma had prepared for eight years and launched his agitations for the remaining two years of the decade. He had won half of India in 1920; he had won the whole in 1930. Realising that their follies could make them end up with egg in the face, the British government summoned in London in 1930 the First Round Table Conference of Indian leaders to discuss the Simon Commission Report—without the Congress participating in it, unless the government released its leaders from jail. After going round and round, the government was forced to ink the Irwin-Gandhi Pact, paving the way for the Mahatma's participation in the Second Round Table Conference.

Jawaharlal wanted to accompany Gandhi, but the latter refused to take his acolyte along. The Mahatma would have benefitted had he taken the Nehru junior whose Fabian and other connections in England were legendary. But Gandhi insisted on going alone as the *sole* Congress representative; apparently, he did not want to share the London publicity with anybody else and, more importantly, he knew his very presence would infuriate Jinnah no end and the latter would vociferously describe 'Mr Gandhi' as the representative of the Hindus. Gandhi would like Jinnah to communalise the Conference; but Jinnah, who was staying in London, largely kept off the Second Conference! With a warm send-off to Gandhi, Wellington had told MacDonald that the Mahatma was, in fact, a 'little devil—always working for an advantage. In all his actions, one could see the "bania" predominating over the saint!' Not surprising because Gujarat was, traditionally, infested with businessmen doubling up as saints and vice-versa!

As the last speaker, in his midnight speech of 1 December 1931, Gandhi declared that the Congress represented the whole of India, 'all other parties at this meeting represent sectional interests' (meaning that Jinnah, too, enjoyed only a minority support even amongst the Muslims, as Hindu leader M R Jaykar had said), and then surfaced the real Mahatma: '...*Believe me, the* (Muslim) *problem exists here* (Jinnah and his supporters?), *and I repeat...that without the problem of minorities being solved there is no Swaraj for India, there is no freedom for India.*' For the first time, he indirectly hinted that the Muslims were a problem, even if in the incarnation of Jinnah who 'exists here' (in London), and that this needed to be solved for attainment of Swaraj. Who created this problem, anyway? Gandhi would not blame the Muslims; instead, he blamed the British, whose Raj was the culmination of conflagration called the Third Battle of Panipat (1761), for the 'wars' between the Hindus (including the Sikhs) and Muslims.

Jinnah was a living example of the pathetic state of his Faith: the current flowering season of Islam the world over, was like bamboo's flowering season in which new flowers spell death for the parent tree as multiplying rodents gnaw at the roots. With whatever sobering effect Ruttie had on her husband no longer there, Jinnah was lonelier and lonelier, the sole comforts that soothed his mind being tobacco and the Muslim issues—the more he thought about the Muslims, the more he chain-smoked (up to 60 cigarettes a day). He had his sister Fatima hold the home-front; Begum Liaqat Ali Khan would call her a 'wicked-witch' who hated her niece, Dina, Jinnah's only offspring, now 13. While Fatima was driving Dina out of the Islamic fold—Jinnah's daughter would marry a Parsi, thus re-converting to her mother's faith—Jinnah's British friends were driving the Great Leader out of India. For, at the end of the Second Conference, in August 1932, the British government announced the 'Communal Award', placating the Muslims with 51 per cent seats in the Punjab legislature and nearly 50 per cent in Bengal and, after the Third Conference ending in December 1932, announcing that the Muslims would get one-third of all seats at the All-India Federal Centre. The Communal Award did not restrict itself to the Muslim 'minority'—interestingly, Jinnah always insisted that the Muslims were *not* a minority but a *Qaum* (nation) and that he himself was a 'minority within a minority'. Finding it increasingly difficult to hang on to a resurgent India, the

British wanted to smash the toy they could not hold on to. So they gave the right of separate electorate not only to the Muslims but also to all the other minority communities in India—in a hundred years, they would relish the same cuisine in Scotland, Wales and Ireland. Aiming to dismember India—with Christian missionaries copying their Patriarch Abraham's fathering of many nations, so that small morsels of beef could be gobbled up when swallowing the whole cow became difficult—the British gave 'special interest Europeans' of Bengal the balance of power, retaining separate electorates; in all Hindu majority areas, the Muslims were given representation in excess of total population proportions. This was what Jinnah aptly called the emergence of 'Muslim India'. Gandhi, unlike Oxford-Cambridge-returned-nincompoops, was the only learned man who was aware of this British strategy.

Strengthening the Muslim claims far beyond their population and expectations, the British now went further to deconstruct the Hindu society—their latest aim was to unite the Muslims of India and divide the Hindus, reversing the 1857 'imperial policy'. Having honed the practices of dubious democracy since the *Magna Carta* (The Great Charter),1215, the self-appointed guardians of all that was good in the contemporary expanding universe of Sir Arthur Stanley Eddington's astronomy, now declared even Hindu 'untouchables' as a minority, giving them a number of special seats in areas where their voters were concentrated. Turning 'democracy' on its head, the British had discovered a new definition: democracy is a government of a minority people, for a minority people, by a minority people! Ironically, the same British would not declare separate electorate and seats for the Roman Catholics, Protestants and others in their own 'United Kingdom'.

By thus trying to hang onto India, the British only whetted the Muslims' appetite, taking up from where the Mahatma had left. Gandhi knew that, when it comes to facing the Infidels, at the end of the day, ALL *People of the Book*—the Jews, Christians, Muslims, or their modern God-free variants like the Nazis, Fascists, Marxists or Maoists—would gang up, being birds of the same Feather. For, they all believed Abraham to be their Forefather, who they thought had fathered many nations. The Muslims claimed they numbered

56 per cent of the total population of the Punjab but were given only 86 out of 175 seats in their Assembly, thus reducing them into a 'minority', and charged the British with favouring the Sikhs. The Muslim League, at its November 1933 annual session declared that 'though the decision falls far short of the Muslim demands, *the Muslims have accepted it in the best interest of the country, reserving to themselves the right to press for the acceptance of all their demands*'.

It was becoming increasingly clear that Partition would be a parting kick of the British to an India they had mistakenly 'united'. While the Mahatma would welcome 'solution' of the minority problem as a prerequisite for Swaraj, he did not want self-rule at the cost of dismemberment of the Hindu society. He was a *dwij* (twice-born) Hindu although he did not wear the sacred thread; for the first time after Emperor Ashoka in the third century BC, a Vaishya (businessman/trader) was leading the Brahmins and others to their destiny in India—only a Vaishya would engage in *deals*, not the caste-arrogant Brahmins or power-arrogant Kshatriyas. Gandhi, the *bania*, therefore, struck a deal with the revered leader of the depressed Hindu castes, B R Ambedkar, in what came to be known as the Poona Pact. In 1915, Jinnah's Lucknow Pact had extracted concessions from the Hindus for the Muslims that whetted the latter's appetite and would have increased conversion to Islam; in 1933, Gandhi's Poona Pact gave concessions to the lower castes and nearly closed the door for religious conversions! If Poona was the last important Hindu post under the Peshwas in the 18th century, Lucknow was the last Muslim post under the Nawabs in the 19th century. The reversal of fortunes, for those who could sense, was, therefore, unmistakably clear. The Gandhi-Ambedkar Pact ensured special privileges to the depressed castes and retained them into the Hindu-fold; these privileges continued and increased in Independent India, forcing those who had embraced Christianity or Islam to reconsider their conversion to the alien faiths. Religious conversion to Abrahamic religions was no longer necessary in India.

Why?

The assaults of Christianity and Islam on India and other multi-cultural and polytheistic societies of Asia were the products of the empires based in Europe and West Asia. But, after the First World War, the centre of gravity of *European* politics had shifted across the Atlantic to the USA, with Woodrow Wilson and the League of Nations taking increasing interest in world affairs, the former winning and the latter failing eventually. Secondly, with the demise of the Ottoman Empire and the rise of ethnic 'Muslim' nations on its ashes as the different communities once-upon-a-time forced into Islam began to revive as culturally-conscious masses and reassert themselves in a Caliph-free West Asia for the first time after the death of the Prophet in 632, the focus of Muslim fundamentalists was, for the time being, on self-preservation rather than evangelisation of the infidels. Never had Islam faced such a hostile weather, not even after the Mongols destroyed Baghdad in the 13th century as at least the Caliphate had 'survived' then. And this attack was more from within than from without—Islam, like an aged star, was imploding. Vast populations of Muslims were no longer ready to suffer the yoke of their mullahs and demanded democracy—except in Saudi Arabia where the Wahhabis emerged in an attempt to stop this flood. In India, too, finding it increasingly difficult to convert any more Hindus, the Muslim fanatics wanted to break-away from the infidel well in time with whatever they could decamp with, or they would be helpless witness to the melting masses of Muslim islands disappearing into the rapidly expanding Hindu oceans—it was like investors dissociating from a drowning company. If the newly-emerging West Asian Muslim nations were increasingly apprehensive of the progressive re-emergence of Israel in their own womb (the Balfour Declaration of 1917 had encouraged Zionists to go on a land buying spree in the Palestine that would eventually become 'Israel' in 1948), the Muslims in the Indian subcontinent were scared of a resurgent Hindu society led by the Mahatma. While the West Asian Muslims had lost the Caliphate but gained nations, their counterparts in India had not only lost the Caliph but were not getting even a nation after the demise of the Mughal Empire; on the contrary, they were threatened with the possibility of dwindling numbers vis-a-vis the Hindus.

It was this churning in the great melting pot called India that gave Chaudhary Rahmat Ali the idea to create 'Pakistan'. In 1933, the 35-year-old Punjabi 'student' at Cambridge produced a pamphlet, prophetically titled *Now or Never: Are We to Live or Perish for Ever*, and demonstrating the pathetic dilemma of Islam's survival in an infidel country that had refused to convert fully for 1,000 years and that was now, on the contrary, threatening to swallow Muslims themselves. With three other 'students', he founded the Pakistan National Movement. Taking their cue from Zionists who were similarly active, these overgrown Muslim 'students', egged on by their British 'teachers' (including Sir Michael O'Dwyer, who ruled the Punjab during the Jallianwala Bagh Massacre, the nearest namesake of General Dyer!) and financed by the Muslim 'intellectuals' and 'charities', such as Ahl-e-Hadis, from which the stench of terror emanated, produced a road-map for what they recognised as the 'solution of the great Hindu-Muslim problem': having failed to fully convert the Dar-ul-Harb, the Muslims should try to protect whatever little they had of Dar-ul-Islam in India! They publicised the name PAKSTAN, the proposed 'nation' of the Muslims living in the five northern units of India—Punjab, Afghan Province (or, the North-West Frontier Province—the very name of the nation presupposed that Afghanistan was 'part' of it. No prizes for guessing why Pakistan nursed the Taliban!), Kashmir, Sindh (and Baluchistan); to this strange combination of PAKS, they added the Persian word *stan* (as in Sanskrit/Hindi word *sthan*) meaning living place, the same as the contemporary Nazis' *libensraum*, to make it PAKSTAN. Still, when pronounced, the newly-coined word did not sound a complete one—PAK had no phonetic or linking vowel to link it with STAN, and, therefore, seemed artificial. Which of the five vowels should, then, be added: PakAstan? PakEstan? PakIstan? PakOstan? Or, PakUstan? The first two and the last two further compounded the problem as the name of their nation sounded rather comic. The Chaudhary and Company had, therefore, to settle for PakIstan—they did not know that 'I'ndia would always be a wedge between PAK and STAN, between Western and Eastern wings of a future Pakistan, between Pakistan and Bangladesh, between Islamabad and Dhaka, between the temples of Rawalpindi and Dhakeshwari. Between the Muslims themselves, and it would metamorphose the Two-Nations Theory into the True-Nations Theory in 1971, that ethnicity, culture and language *were,* not Islam, the true basis for nationhood, that a deCaliphated Islam would no longer remain a Brotherhood in the absence of the Brotherhood's Commander-in-Chief (*Amir-ul-Mominin*). Interestingly, there is no 'P' in Arabic; so the Arabs pronounced Pakistan as 'Bakistan'! In the late 1970s, the then Indian Prime Minister, Morarji Desai, clearly diagnosed Pakistan's existential dilemma when he said that Bangladesh was not liberated from Pakistan in 1971; it was the other way round! Pakistan would continue to 'liberate' itself from itself!!

The 57-year-old Jinnah, who refused to meet Chaudhary Rahmat Ali and discuss the 'nation' he was to Father later, at the instance of Liaqat Ali Khan (later, Pakistan's first Prime Minister) returned to India in December 1934 to head and revivify the moribund League, once again; Jinnah did not know the Chaudhary had already named the child the Great Leader was carrying in his frail womb.

Three months ago, in September 1934, Gandhi had announced his 'retirement' from Congress and devoted himself to the causes of the abolition of untouchability and village reforms as part of his brand of socialism called *Sarvodaya*, 'upliftment of all'. Why did the 65-year-young Mahatma, still busy with his brahmacharya-experiments, seek 'premature' retirement in the pink of his health, even though the seeds he had sown had yet to bear fruit? Probably, because he had now begun to entrust his Hindu farm to somebody other than the Congress, through what was known as *bataidari* (share-cropping, in which the landlord takes a portion of produce from one who tills his farm). Even as Jinnah began to pump life back into the League, on 25 December 1934, Gandhi visited an RSS camp set up next to his Sevagram Ashram at Wardha to encourage the Hindu nationalist volunteers in their nation-building lessons; he unfurled the saffron flag of the RSS there along with Appaji Joshi, his friend. Next day, he invited RSS chief Keshav Baliram Hedgewar, who was a Congressman until 1920, to his Ashram. The Mahatma may have sensed the future of the RSS, and that it was to this organisation that the Congress would pass the baton to, off and on. Meanwhile, in 1936, Jawaharlal returned to India after his wife died in Germany, and took over Presidency of the Congress from Rajendra Prasad. From Germany, Jawaharlal had brought home some of the Nazi infection—no, not against the Jews but against the Muslims—and this found expression in his anti-Jinnah stance; he did not speak against the Muslims as such as this was the constituency of the Hindu Mahasabha! On the other hand, Jinnah, having perfected the art of what came to be known his 'pendulum negotiations', was going forth from one end (the Congress) to another (the British), and even swinging occasionally to the Mahasabha and others, to wrest the maximum concessions for the Muslims and to make *his* community hold the veto—he had thus degenerated from once being the most promising politician to the now most untrustworthy one. By a strange coincidence, both 'Pakistan' and 'Israel' were taking shape simultaneously in the 'Aryan' wombs of India and Germany in the 1930s—Europe, that had massacred the Jews over the ages, was now despatching them back to the Palestine (in the Christian world, America was the only country that had not persecuted the Jews; in the East, India was the only country where the Jews remained safe); similarly, India was now beginning to eject Pakistan.

Luckily for Jinnah, his *bete noire* Wellington was replaced by Lord Linlithgow as Viceroy in April 1936 but the newcomer's impartiality in honestly implementing the Government of India Act, 1935, the new Constitution, pained him no end. He swung back to the Congress to bargain more for the League and contest elections. Luckily, again, his foremost rival in the League, Sir Fazl-I-Husain of the Punjab, died and Jinnah found himself in the arms of Allama Iqbal. It was the age of the Third Reich with the Nazis proclaiming that what Emperor Friedrich the Great envisioned, the Diplomat Bismarck prepared, in the First and Second Reichs, and the Soldier, Adolf Hitler, was achieving; in India, the Muslim fundamentalists, similarly, believed that what Iqbal envisioned, the Chaudhary planned, was being politically implemented by Jinnah.

Jinnah's efforts to woo the Congress, however, did not cut much ice due mainly to his own untrustworthiness and the 'economic policies'. The League, a rag tag bunch of Muslim landed gentry and feudal lord leftovers of the deceased Mughal Empire, firmly opposed expropriation of private property. Nehru and Bose, on the other hand, favoured socialism, although of their own varieties. India was, therefore, destined to hit the path of mixed economy and Pakistan that of 'minced' economy. Jinnah was fortunate that a large majority of the Muslims was backward, illiterate and poor who were kept busy and made to survive on regular, rationed doses of Islam; if they complained of constipation, they were administered purgative, both being Islam. That is why most Muslim countries live comfortably in dictatorships and periodically turn 'democratic' the way other people turn to their toilets to relieve themselves.

Controversial remarks by an ambitious Jawaharlal, who was known for such gaffes, had made Jinnah's task rather easy, however: 'May I suggest to Mr Jinnah that I come in greater touch with the Muslim masses than most of the members of the Muslim League.' It was not the Kashmiri Iqbal nor the Cambridge-based Punjabi, the Chaudhary, still a 'student' who brought the drawing room barrister Jinnah on the street, to seek support of the Muslims for *their* League and become a mass-based politician, to the drawing board called Pakistan; it was the Kashmiri Jawaharlal who completed Gandhi's task of forcing a still somewhat unwilling Jinnah fully into the Muslim fold by constantly challenging and prodding him to prove his worth. Jinnah discovered that the age-old slogan of fanatics, 'Islam is in danger', electrified the Muslims both in the urban and rural areas to take up arms against the Hindus; he calibrated his policies more and more to assure the Muslims that Islam was 'safe' in his hands. Never was Islam safer in the hands of a heretic! Of course Gandhi had laid the foundation but it was Nehru who unwittingly 'ensured' that Jinnah formed Pakistan, the way Hitler pushed the Jews to create 'Israel'.

Political flip-flops of the 1930s saw some of the Muslim Leaguers being weaned away by Maulana Abul Kalam Azad to the Congress fold as power equations became a salivating temporary attraction rather than the 'Islamic cause'. An exasperated Jinnah, unwilling to seek Nehru's help, turned to his old foe, Gandhi, at his Wardha Ashram. The cryptic Mahatma, Chanakya-like even in his 'retirement', replied: 'I wish I could do something but I am totally helpless. My faith in Hindu-Muslim unity is as bright as it always was; but I see no light out of the impenetrable darkness and, in such distress, I cry out to

God for light.' A helpless Jinnah, who was now paying for his own follies, blackmail and 'pendulum negotiations', smoked and coughed his way through a meeting of Muslim leaders at Lucknow, called to decide upon the steps to be taken to hold this off-and-on erosion in the Muslim rank and file. In the same Lucknow, where he had forged the Hindu-Muslim unity Pact two decades ago, the same Jinnah witnessed the first scuffle between the Muslim League and Congress workers. First of all, Jinnah brought around Sir Sikander Hayat Khan's Unionist Party of Punjab into the League's fold and unfurled a green flag with a giant 'P' over the League's Kaisar Bagh near Mahmoodabad. This signalled the maturity of the embryo called 'Pakistan' that would be born in 1947 after a Caesarian section.

Jinnah was now determined to pay Gandhi and Nehru in their own coins. To symbolise the dramatic change after Lucknow session of the League, he even changed his attire, the way Gandhi had already done in 1915, for public appearance. For the first time in public, Jinnah became the true *Qaid-i-Azam* by donning a black Punjabi *sherwani* (long coat), shedding the Savile Row suit in which he had reached the town, and a black Persian lamb cap loaned by Nawab Muhammed Ismael Khan, that later came to be known as the 'Jinnah cap', the Muslim equivalent of the 'Gandhi cap'. The transformation was now complete. The man once hailed by Gokhale as the Ambassador of Hindu-Muslim unity addressed some 5,000 Muslims, assuring that the 'Eighty million Musalmans in India have nothing to fear'. He set out to make the League a mass-based party and by the Lahore meeting, where the Pakistan resolution would be adopted in 1940, its membership sky-rocketed from a few thousand to more than half-a-million, thrilled as the Muslims became at the prospect of having their own tiny kiosk at the corner of a great Mall-under-construction, India, which they once fancied they owned. In order to distinguish itself in every respect from the Congress, the League declared the Congress anthem *Vande Mataram* as anti-Islamic, for it hailed a Motherland, India, whereas the Muslims believed in a Fatherland, Arabia. A devout Jewish/Christian Indian, for the same reason, would also not like this song, for their Fatherland was in Jerusalem/Vatican. Only, they did not number as many as the Muslims in India so as to raise their voice against it. It was a matter of inherited faith and mindset of the devout People of the Book who now found themselves abandoned on an infidel island.

The League also announced to make Urdu, rather than Hindi or Hindustani, the 'universal' language of India. Addressing the League's student wing meeting in Calcutta in December 1937, Jinnah told the audience that, at Lucknow, he had only rung an 'alarm bell' and exhorted the Muslim youth to become the muscle of the League. January 1938 saw him in that nursery of the future 'modernist' extremists and the modem between Islam and technology, Aligarh Muslim University, where he excited the students by declaring that the Muslims were 'slave' in India for 150 years, that having made them free from the British, the League was now endeavouring to make them free from the Congress, the 'successor of the British Government. It is a Hindu Government.'

In March 1938, the 41-year-old Subhas Bose replaced Jawaharlal as Congress President. As the League jumped by leaps and bounds in membership and popularity, Jawaharlal tried to mend fences and reconcile with Jinnah who, however, wanted to strike a deal with Nehru's godfather, the Mahatma. Gandhi, as he had been earlier 'guided' by the two Maulanas, the Ali Brothers, said, now he was being 'guided' by Maulana Abul Kalam Azad; Jinnah got the message and backed off. Clearly, Gandhi did not want Jinnah to be recognised as the sole leader of the Muslims, *at this stage*. On the other hand, Jinnah was as anxious to ensure that the Muslims did not melt away into the Congress and the Hindus as he was to make sure that the League alone represented the Muslims. Gandhi, himself a health freak and nurse, had sensed Jinnah's illness, his over-smoking and constant coughing and fever, as the marks of an incurable tuberculosis or cancer, and that the obstinate Muslim leader was racing against time. Waiting for an opportunity to strike next, the Mahatma had watched Europe kneeling before Hitler; apparently, with evil clouds gathering over the European skyline, he was also waiting for the Second World War to break out that would, once again, force the British to seek the Congress support. Even the League was keeping Jinnah's illness under wraps as he was its only true leader, first and last. By this time, the League had expanded its base in seven of the 11 British Indian provinces. Jinnah, adept at rhetoric, was threatening the Congress, here and there, to 'respect and fear' the Muslims, ie. the League, and collected complaints of the Muslims' 'grievances' in the Congress-ruled provinces, to be discussed in its session. Gandhi saw in it the opportunity to meet Jinnah first-hand, ostensibly to discuss the 'grievances' but, in fact, to see for himself the ailing old rival. Predictably, Jinnah agreed to meet the Mahatma at his own house in Mumbai, minus Azad. Gandhi saw Jinnah from the closest quarters, constantly smoking and coughing, complaining of congestion in the chest and frequenting fever, and almost diagnosed that the Great Leader was inching toward death, that his old foe would precipitate things soon so as to fulfil his lifelong ambition to 'lead' before he breathed his last. During his three-and-a-half hour meeting of April 1938, it was Jinnah who mostly spoke; Gandhi merely took 'notes'.

What were the Muslims' 'grievances', anyway?

The Congress-run provincial governments that came to power in July 1937 and ran through the next 27 months, turned out to be pro-Hindu. Even before the formation of these governments, the Congress started a Muslim Mass Contact Movement, with the aim to convince Muslims that there were only two political forces in India: the British and the Congress. The aim was to totally neglect the importance of the Muslim League. As soon as the Congress came to power, it made Hindi the national language and *Devanagari* the official script; the Congress flag, the Tricolour, was given the status of the 'national flag'; cow slaughter was banned; educational institutions were directed to display the Gandhi photo and *Vande Mataram* was pronounced the 'national anthem'; under its Wardha Taleemi Scheme, the Congress introduced the 'India-as-one-people' theme song, much to the chagrin of Muslim separatists; in the Central Provinces and Berar, the *Vidya Mandir* scheme was introduced with schools displaying photos of Saraswati, the goddess of learning, and singing hymns to her. Clearly, all these steps were like straws in the wind as to what would happen if the Congress came to power at the Centre as well. The Muslims claimed that the local Congress leaders were now openly threatening the minority community to take revenge for the atrocities the Muslim rule had perpetrated on the Hindus since the attack of Muhammad bin-Qasim on Sindh in 711.

To investigate the Muslims' 'grievances', the Muslim League formulated the 'Pirpur Report' under the chairmanship of Raja Syed Muhammed Mehdi of Pirpur. Some other similar reports were from the Congress-run provinces, such as A K Fazl ul-Haq's; the Congress also continued this periodical window-dressing, such as the Sachar Report under the Manmohan Singh government in the first decade of the 21st century. Even some of the British officials corroborated the resurgence of the Hindus. For instance, the Marquees of Lothian, in April 1938, termed the Congress regime as a 'rising tide of Hindu rule'; Sir William Barton, in his article of June 1939 in 'National Review', described it as the 'rising tide of political Hinduism'. And whose policies was the Congress following when it came to power? Gandhi's 'nationalist' policies were a death-knell for the Muslim identity. The Abrahamic cults lose their distinct identity the moment they are stripped of their perceived superiority and *equated* with other faiths. This was precisely what Gandhi did; he simply exposed Christianity and/or Islam and put them on the same pedestal with Hinduism, equating the global Goliaths which remained Davids in India, with indigenous David, Hinduism, that threatened to emerge as a global Goliath.

While the Congress was doing all this, Jinnah, fearing that the League would be completely cornered by the Congress in the 'cow belt' and other provinces it ruled, inched closer to the British. More determined to break away, on 8 October 1938, he told a Muslim League audience in Karachi that 'If the Musalmans are going to be defeated in *their national goal* and aspirations it will only be by the betrayal of the Musalmans among us as it has happened in the past'. This was his first public reference to a 'national goal' of the Muslims. With a view to expand his party's base in Sindh, he tried to rope in Khan Bahadur Allah Bux, the United Party premier of Sindh, but Sardar Patel robbed Jinnah of this opportunity with the Muslim leader's own province (Sindh) slipping out of his hand. The League fanatics murdered Bux in May 1943; his assassin was never caught.

This was the first blood drawn for the 'cause' of Pakistan.

On 10 December 1938, Jinnah was officially declared as *Qaid-e-Azam*, or the Great Leader, by Maulana Mazharuddin Ahmed, editor of Delhi's Muslim daily, *al-Aman*, in recognition of his contributions to the community; there was already another 'Great Leader', the *Fuehrer*, Adolf Hitler, in contemporary Nazi Germany. Basking in its reflected glory, Jinnah told his annual League audience in Patna that the Congress had 'killed' every hope of Hindi-Muslim settlement in a 'fascist' fashion: 'We, the Muslims of India have made up our mind to secure our full rights…the Congress is nothing but a Hindu body…I challenge anybody to deny that the Congress is not mainly a Hindu body. I ask, does the Congress represent the Muslims?' After this diatribe, came the crux: 'Who is the genius behind it? Mr Gandhi. I have no hesitation in saying that it is Mr Gandhi who is destroying the ideal with which the Congress was started. ***He is the one man responsible for turning the Congress into an instrument for the revival of Hinduism. His idea is to revive the Hindu religion and establish Hindu Raj in this country, and he is utilising the Congress to further this object***…Today, the Hindu mentality, the Hindu outlook, is being carefully nurtured and Muslims are being forced to accept these new conditions and to submit to the orders of the Congress leaders.' Only a Thakkar would have thus radiographed and understood the machinations of a Modh so completely. But Jinnah would not say that he, too, had similarly captured the League, changed its creed from the possible re-establishment of the Mughal Empire across India to the approaching establishment of Muslim rule in a corner of the country, and using this platform to further his own agenda against Gandhi while appearing to be working for the 'Muslim cause'. Never were two foes so friendly after, perhaps, Richard the LionHeart and Salahuddin (Saladin) during the Crusades!

Jinnah alone perhaps had some idea of what Gandhi was actually doing and why; in turn, Gandhi, too, understood what and why, Jinnah was aiming at. They, being fellow Gujaratis, 'helped' each other achieve their respective goals. They being Saurashtrians, would always be adequately courteous to each other, refraining from abusing even when sharpening their knives to cut each other's throats. Only those who understood the nitty-gritty and intricacies of India's caste system, which enables one caste to virtually X-Ray another, would generally know why and how. Jinnah also went hammer and tongs at other Congress leaders—Nehru, Patel, Bose, Prasad—of these, the first would not let Pakistan take the whole Kashmir, the second would end the Nizamate in South India, the third would expand the concept of the Indian National Congress to Indian National Army and the fourth would inaugurate, in the early 1950s, the Somnath Temple in Gujarat heralding Hindu renaissance, destroyed by Mehmud of Ghazni in the 11th century.

Jinnah changed the creed of the League again. The brilliant lawyer who had hitherto stuck to his Constitutional guns to further his aims, now realised that most of the Muslims did not understand such niceties of the law and soon got fed up with the slow pace of change. Traditionally, having fast-forwarded themselves on the evolutionary ladder due to sudden mutations and, therefore, bereft of slow genetic variation, they understood one language better: the Sword. Taking into account the exaggerated reports of the 'Hindu atrocities' on the Muslims in the Congress-ruled states, Jinnah had a 'revolutionary... departure from the past' resolution passed unanimously the next day. Fanatic Muslims had always been thrilled with the prospects of loot and kill anywhere, sanctified as *ghanimat* by Islam. An once catalytic and promising Islam had, after all, decayed into an imperial ideology that prepared the have-nots to resort to the shortest cut to 'progress' by simply robbing the haves. Hitler's 'Final Solution', elimination of the Jews simply by killing them *en masse*, was in the air; Jinnah fancied something similar in India. There was, however, a small catch here: Jinnah was *not* the Chancellor of India, the Hindus were *not* a minority, and the Muslims were *not*, the British were, the rulers. So, the League authorised itself to resort to 'Direct Action' to 'redress' the grievances and to 'protect the elementary rights of the Musalmans' of Bihar, the Central Provinces and the United Provinces, the three Hindu-majority, Congress-ruled provinces that had reported 'atrocities' against the Muslims. In turn, the League authorised Jinnah to give a call for Direct Action. The Hindu-past of Jinnah had virtually evaporated, the

Muslim present was lurking now on his mind: if the Ismaelis could once destroy even the Caliphate, kill 40,000 Muslims in Mecca and loot even the Black Stone, why could not *this* Ismaeli, Jinnah, do something similar in India, which was anyway full of infidels, whose only right was to get killed?

Direct Action was, simply put, a call given by the Muslims to the Muslims to kill the Hindus wherever they could. But why should the Muslims kill the Hindus in the first place in India where they had lived together for centuries, although as Masters and slaves at many places? It was not a simple question of India witnessing what Spain did five centuries ago; it was not merely a *Reconquista* in the East, the Hindus regaining their territory by pushing back the Muslim boundaries. The questions related to the very basics of biological evolution: the Muslims had refused to evolve and were, therefore, going out of the evolutionary loop everywhere as they continued to do in the 21st century, at an accelerating pace. The post-Ottoman world had become increasingly un-monotheistic and uncertain. The world was watching the death of permanence; it was an age of uncertainty that upstaged all certainties, such as those of Judaism, Christianity and Islam on one hand and Fascism, Nazism and Communism on the other—all offspring of the domineering Abrahamic Mindset which was increasingly turning inconsistent, incongruent and incompliant with modernity, democracy and science—they were the global civilisation's metabolic faeces, ready to be egested everywhere. The very age-old mindsets were changing and giving way to new 'certainties': the sciences had moved from mechanics to quantum mechanics, the Newtonian physics had been replaced by the Einsteinian, the stock markets had favoured John Maynard Keynes' Theory of Liquidity Preference, sex became a Freudian determinant of human behaviour, monarchy fossilised, the certainties of Moses, Jesus and Muhammed had been replaced by the young Werner Heisenberg's Theory of Uncertainty, that fetched him a Nobel Prize...the uncertainties of one area triggered the uncertainties in another. All over the world, all types of certainties were on the back-foot and, as a reaction and a last gasp, these fossilising certainties crystallised themselves in Nazism in Germany, Stalinism in Russia, Fascism in Germany, Churchilism in

Britain, Zionism in Israel and Jinnaism in India in the two decades between the two World Wars.

In this reshaping of the world, 'new' ethnic nations emerged on the corpses of the old empires. This remapping, like child-birth, was accompanied by some blood-letting, and Jinnah was no exception. There were two exceptions, however: while most countries coming in and going out of this evolutionary loop were either Christian (Israel included) or Muslim, India and China were the only major infidel countries, the former a central issue, the latter a marginal, at that time. Even the Christian and Muslim nations emerging in the wake of the World Wars, one by one, were not the ancient 'Brotherhood' types; they were, on the contrary, active deAbrahamising agents what with the different constituent ethnicities fighting with each other after they attained independence as a Christian or Muslim nation, down to Serbia, Croatia, Bosnia, Chechnya etc in the 1990s and thereafter. So, Christianity or Islam were no longer the glue that eternally bound these ethnicities together into Brotherhood(s) but only a temporary means to achieve freedom from the day's master. The Muslim League's emergence and Partition were, essentially, the beginning of deIslamisation of the Indian subcontinent; the Jinnah Theory of Two Nations, that depended on Islam as a binding force among diverse ethnicities, came apart in just 25 years, in 1971.

The irony, the dilemma, and how the Muslim fanatics were trying to unite against the rising global tide against Islam was demonstrated by another resolution in this same League meeting of Patna. On the third day, it passed its Palestine resolution, warning the British government 'forthwith...to stop the influx of Jews into Palestine', that the problem of Palestine is the problem of the Muslims of the whole world; and if the British government 'fails to do justice to the Arabs...Indian Muslims...will be prepared to make any sacrifice...to save the Arabs from British exploitation and Jewish usurpation'. The Indian Muslims conveniently forgot that it was they who had opposed Arab nationalists fighting for freedom against the Ottoman Empire just a decade ago. They also forgot that while they, as a 'minority', were urging the British to give them special privileges in India, they were opposing the same British giving similar privileges to the Jews, a minority in Europe; they even forgot that while they demanded a separate Pakistan for Muslims, being carved out of India, they were opposing a separate Israel being carved out of the Palestine for the Jews! In Palestine, they argued that it was the Muslims, not the Jews, who were the permanent residents; in India, their argument was that it was the Muslims, not the Hindus, who were the 'permanent' residents of the areas that would become Pakistan; in Palestine, they described the Jews as 'outsiders'; alas, they could not describe the Hindus as outsiders in India! The only thing the Muslims could not prove by any stretch of imagination was that they came to India *before* the Hindus. In fact, the Jews and the Hindus, when they began to reassert themselves, had become a pain in the neck for most of the Muslims. While discussing the resolution, Abdul Sattar Khairi dubbed 'both the British and the Hindus were Jews to Muslims', that is, their enemies. 'In India, Mr Gandhi was the leader of the Hindu Jews'. But, in this surcharged atmosphere, when one Muslim was outdoing another in rhetoric, even Jinnah, himself a rhetorician *par excellence*, was appalled when a delegate, Abdul Khaliq, denounced the British and the Hindus as the Jews of the West and the East, 'both sons of Shylock'. Thus, in 1938, India was inexorably, inevitably, irresistibly hurtling, heading towards Pakistan—no power on Earth could have reversed this natural process of deIslamisation. Islam was trying to reassert itself without reinventing itself, flaunting its continuing 'supremacy' vis-a-vis the Hindu infidel, at a time when India itself was preparing to push Islam back across the Five Rivers. Gandhi or no Gandhi, Jinnah or no Jinnah, India was destined to vomit Pakistan and would have discovered alternate leaders if the Mahatma or the Qaid-e-Azam were not around—they were merely the natural outgrowths on Mother India, products of their life and times and circumstances within and without, the Idea whose Time had come. In that tumultuous year, when the Second World War was looming on the horizon, Gandhi, who, despite his 'retirement' from the Congress, controlled its levers, saw to it that Bose was replaced by Prasad as party president in 1939. The reason was the same old one: the egotist typical Bengalis, despite being great patriots, artists and scientists, despised other 'uncouth' Indians as riff-raff and sub-cultured, fancied themselves as being superior than others, were highly opinionated and self-important, given more to rhetoric rather than reason and, above all, believed themselves to be the rightful heir apparent, even inheritors, of the British if and when the latter quit India. The flamboyant Bengali youths had joined the Congress in large numbers after Bose became its President and were 'spoiling' the silent chess-board the Mahatma had laid out so meticulously for Jinnah and the League in the Great Game that called for patience, not patients. Bose, a fierce, fearless nationalist, found himself a victim of his own followers' uncalled for over-enthusiasm and rabble-rousing; the Bengalis despised silent diplomacy and believed in their own 'direct action', having been the latest victim of the Abrahamic bug-bite—that was why Communism sunk roots in Bengal and Mamata Bannerji became a Jyoti Basu-II—from Christianity/Islam, Communism was just a short-cut, as in Kerala also. So, Bose resigned in 1939 and floated his own party, the Forward Block, which continues to remain backward and blocked even today for the reasons cited here. The great Bose launched an epic struggle against the British in the Second World War and came to be lauded as 'Netaji' (The Leader) across a grateful nation. With these developments, Gandhi was back in his political business, unofficially and unannounced. When The Agha Khan visited the Mahatma in January 1939, the latter asked Nehru to get in touch with Jinnah about the 'atrocities' perpetrated by the Hindus on the Muslims. Jinnah replied with several such 'reports' compiled by Fazl ul-Haq. The 'Apostle of Peace' was waiting for the Second World War.

In May 1939, Jinnah fell seriously ill and signed his last will and testament; he left, from his vast estate, a living of Rs100 a month to his three sisters, brother Ahmed and for his daughter (he did not name her) Rs200,000, while making Fatima overall in-charge. On 3 September 1939, when Lord Linlithgow broadcast the news of Hitler's invasion of Poland two days ago, Jinnah knew his moment had arrived with this beginning of the new World War: the wedding horse was ready and so was he to mount. The very next day, he urged the Viceroy to dismiss the Congress-ruled provincial governments to ensure Muslim support for the War, and that the only solution to the Hindu-Muslim problem lay in Partition. On the other hand, Gandhi, true to his salt, promised his 'personal' support to the British, saying he would do so with an 'English heart' but he could not commit Congress—the same Mahatma would try to force them to 'Quit India' three years from now, this time with an 'Indian' heart! Meanwhile, the Congress intensified its Hindu policies in the provinces it controlled, thus further infuriating the League; the Arya Samaj, many of whose leaders doubled up as Congressmen, was re-engaged in re-converting the Muslims back to the Hindu fold through their 'purification' drive; this created tension between the two communities.

Politicians, like monkeys, have similar simian habits across the world; the British parties had their own axe to grind. Winston Churchill did not want to preside over the dismemberment of the Empire by giving undue importance to the Indian National Congress; on the other hand, Labour leader Sir Stafford Cripps egged Nehru on to ensure that Congress remained united like a 'rock' and that it did not accept anything from the government unless it was of conclusive nature. So, Nehru declared a slave India could not help Britain and Gandhi, who, within a month cast away his English heart he was wearing on his sleeve, declared that the Congress will be no party in either the British policy of divide-and-rule or its war against Germany. The Congress demonstrated its sudden Gandhian gear-shift by resigning from its provincial governments. This brought Jinnah closer to the British; this put the Congress away from the Empire. In November, Gandhi urged Jinnah, through his *Harijan*, that now with the Congress no longer in power in eight provinces, the League could make its choice and hoped that the League would not 'want to vivisect India', thus indirectly *reminding* Jinnah about his ultimate objective, just in case he had forgotten! He also asked Jinnah to hold talks with Nehru. Jinnah talking to Nehru was like Hitler talking to Churchill, though, unlike a mercurial and romantic Jawaharlal, the cold-blooded Muslim leader never decided on impulse. Even now, he did not want to come out openly for Pakistan. First of all, he wanted to marshal his forces and organise the Muslims for 'political' action. Since March 1939, he was discussing with his associates the various options for the Muslims' political future; Sir Sikander Hayat Khan had proposed an alternative 'Outline of a scheme of Indian Federation' with as many as seven Muslim 'zones', the eastern and western ones in this arc through North India being what would eventually be Bangladesh and Pakistan. Jinnah knew the five zones between the eastern and western zones were the areas of *real* conflict between the Hindu and Muslim populations, the latter being a clear minority; it was from here that the Muslims would eventually migrate to Pakistan as *Muhajirs* (Immigrants) and keep turning against India, as more Muslim than the Muslims, like Pervez Musharraf. Jinnah knew that neither the British nor the Congress would dismember India like this and, at the most, he would get the eastern and western zones only, as the 'moth-eaten' nation of Muslims in which there would be no tunnel through the five zones 'identified' by the current Sikander (Alexander) to win India. Still, Jinnah wanted this imaginary tunnel to pressurise the British and the Congress.

So, he declared Friday, 22 December 1939, as the 'Day of Deliverance and thanksgiving as a mark of relief that the Congress regime has at last ceased to function'. The Congress, which had by now shaken off the Gandhian strategy of holding fire and the policy of claws of steel hidden in a velvet glove, openly went against Jinnah, dubbing him as the 'Dictator of Malabar Hills'. The League leaders in the eastern and western regions, who had found the Congress a convenient tool for political power, were disappointed as they saw all the possibility of power and pelf drifting away for the time being with this open war against the Congress. Therefore, they decided to break away from Jinnah. Unfazed, Jinnah, whose aim was to unite the Muslim minority amid the Hindu majority areas, and not vice-versa—by now he understood the full implication of the Gandhian policy of creating a majority out of a minority!—and he knew that the pressure built up in the Hindu-majority areas would ensure creation of Pakistan in the eastern and western zones. He was now pressuring the Muslims in Hindu-majority areas by exploiting their fear of being absorbed in the infidel sponge. In this strategy, he also got the support of Periyar E V Ramaswami Naicker, the 'Dravidistan' Justice Party chief in South India, who was opposed to the North Indian 'Aryan' Congress Party of the Hindi-Hindu-Hindustan mould—though this did not mean he would support the Muslims! Naicker found himself in the same boat as Jinnah, who, like Noah, was gathering all those concerned due to the Congress (Hindu) flood; for a time, they included even BR Ambedkar, leader of the Independent Labour Party who, despite his Poona Pact with Gandhi, was in the opposite camp to extract further concessions for the depressed classes. It was an era in which few had their fingers only in their own pie as most leaders were running in and out of the revolving doors with whatever they could lay their hands on in the scramble and confusion of the War kitchen. Even the Muslims were divided: the para-military Muslim Khaksars had made even the League leaders' life miserable the way they were hostile to the Hindus and Sikhs in the Punjab; despite Jinnah trying to win them over, they could never be placated and even tried to assassinate him time and again.

In this great melting and churning pot, nothing remained stationary. Except one thing: the top layer that had started cooling off as Pakistan, which, in fact, was also the bottom-line of the whole process. In the 22 March 1940, meeting of the League at Lahore in the presence of 70,000 Muslims and guarded by sword-wielding bodyguards of his trusted Bombay Muslim League—for, Jinnah did not trust even those Muslims of the east and west whom he was going to gift their homeland in the name of Islam!—the Great Leader, now frail with pleurisy, tuberculosis and suspected cancer and mostly enveloped in the tobacco smoke he belched out like chimney while constantly coughing and clearing his throat, spoke a few words in Urdu before quickly switching over to his favourite English. Amidst the drawn swords of his bodyguard, the occasional shouts of the Khaksars and cheers from others, he spoke for two hours in what was the greatest performance of the once failed but now successful thespian before his largest audience ever. Like a resurrected Mughal Emperor, he harangued his patient audience, denounced his rival Azad whom Gandhi had now drafted as Congress President as a foil to his 'brother' Jinnah and who was instrumental in calling all non-League Muslim leaders to a conference next month in Delhi. Such steps, Gandhi knew, would further charge up Jinnah and League, and that was what he exactly wanted; he knew that, by now, Muslim public opinion had come to favour Partition. The time was coming when the British would not be able to hold on to India and decamp, leaving India and Pakistan in their wake; but he did not want a moth-eaten India as Jinnah did not want, at least publicly, a moth-eaten Pakistan. All those Muslim leaders who favoured Partition and Pakistan had joined the Lahore meeting. There were still some, mostly from the Deoband School, who disliked Partition *not* because they loved the Hindus or Hindustan but because they loved the emerging 'India' and its 'secular' and 'democratic' character so that they could exploit it to further their pending aim of full Islamisation of the world's biggest infidel land—had they also supported Pakistan, India would have emerged a Hindu dictatorship, detrimental to the interests of Pakistan itself! So they decided to stay back in Hindustan, virtually as Pakistan's extension. Gandhi knew these leaders were, therefore, for Hindu-Muslim 'unity' etc. But he still cultivated and used them like blower to make the embers red-hot at the other end of the oven. Many of these Muslim leaders were no more than the ornamental cactuses in the Congress living room, bereft of any support in their own community—they mostly remained so even in Independent India.

Jinnah also knew the worth of these *Gandhian* Muslims who exploited the accident of their birth in a 'minority' community and he ignored them with the contempt they deserved. At Lahore, that day, he announced: 'The Musalmans are not a minority. They are a separate nation by any definition.' He may not have realised that he was actually undoing the Islamisation mission started by the victory of Muhammad bin-Qasim in 711; in fact, he was not only halting Islam's further progress but presiding over its return journey and liquidation, globally. It was not a Hindu-Muslim problem alone; it was an international, civilisational war. '*The problem in India is not of an inter-communal but manifestly of an international character, and it must be treated as such.* So long as this basic and fundamental truth is not realised, any constitution that may be built will result in disaster and will prove destructive and harmful not only to the Musalmans, but also to the British and the Hindus… The only course open to us all is to allow the major nations separate homelands, by dividing India into "autonomous national States.' Few understood the fact hidden behind eloquence of this Jinnah speech—even America needed a 9/11 to understand the words italicised above. But, the USA, having many an axe to grind, may yet pay heavily for each such axe.

Jinnah did not yet mention the word 'Pakistan' in this speech nor in the forthcoming resolution that later went by the name 'Pakistan Resolution'. There was no turning back now, neither for him nor for the League. Gokhale's disciple and the Ambassador of the Hindu-Muslim unity in 1915 had, by 1940, totally metamorphosed into the Ambassador of the *separate* existence of the Hindus and Muslims, one who, being half-Hindu, had dutifully and successfully undone the work of Islam in India since bin-Qasim. And most of the Muslims did not even realise this; on the contrary, they applauded Jinnah. In the Congress, he was of assimilative character; in the League, he became a separatist. His forefathers had to sacrifice merely their Hindu fold; he had to sacrifice his faith, his belief-system, his family, his nation, his reputation. And he did it. He alone could have done it. For, he emulated the Bahamanis of South India where a few Brahmins converted to Islam to protect fellow Hindus from Muslim onslaughts: perhaps he realised that he could protect India from Islam only by becoming a 'Muslim' and leading the flock out, the way Moses, the Egyptian priest, had similarly led *his* Jewish flock out of Egypt to save his land from 'diseases'. Circumstances had shaped Jinnah, Gandhi, and India's mission and put them all on the same Road. With the same destination. India would always be grateful to Jinnah, the Pied Piper.

Jinnah's greatest contribution, therefore, was not the creation of a Muslim Pakistan but the making of a Hindu Bharat, shielding India from any further enforced Islamisation. Imagine the Arabs' petro-dollars pouring into an unPartitioned India, since the 1970s, well after the British had left, and the activities of Islamist Wahhabi front organisations like Tablighi Jammat, Ahl-e-Hadis and Dawat ul-Islam in an undivided India having 1,000 million Hindus vis-à-vis 500 million Muslim population, and one can guess what impact it would have on the world. In that case, an undivided India would have become the largest Muslim nation in the world, with a rock-solid block of *no-changing* 500 million Muslims. This would have been detrimental to the very biological evolution of the world and survival of Homo sapiens. Jinnah halted that process; that was why he was more of the saviour of India than the creator of Pakistan; perhaps even he did not realise this. Sadly, he was also the most misunderstood leader, both by the Muslims and the Hindus.

But omission of the word 'Pakistan' in what passed off, then, as the 'Pakistan Resolution' created a confusion in that crucial year, 1940. So much so that Sir Sikander, already an 'enemy' of the 'Pakistani' Muslims, until his death, thought the Resolution was merely a bargaining point to extract concessions from the Hindus in a post-British federated India. But neither Jinnah, nor Gandhi, nor even the British thought so; they all knew that Pakistan was a *serious* business: the first two of them had, by now, come to understand Islam very well as detached, un-devoted, observers while the last one had vast experience of manipulating Muslims in the Empire. On 1 April 1940, satisfied that his efforts since 1915 had finally begun to bear fruit now, when asked if he would start agitation against the British or the League, the Mahatma replied: 'I admit that the step taken by the League at Lahore creates a baffling situation. But I do not regard it so baffling as to make disobedience an impossibility… *The Muslims must have the same right of self-determination that the rest of India has. We are at present a joint family. Any member may claim a division.*' Other Congress leaders, mere patriots, some xenophobes included, reacted more sharply, with Nehru calling the Resolution as 'fantastic'. Ironically, the same League meeting carried through a second resolution as well, denying the right of self-determination to the Jews in the Palestine! It expressed 'grave concern' at the British Empire's 'inordinate delay…in coming to a settlement with the Arabs in the Palestine'. Jinnah felt especially relieved after having seen these contradictory resolutions through: 'I have thoroughly enjoyed my stay in Lahore because of the result; otherwise I was worked to death.' The Congress had, meanwhile, painted Jinnah as the villain of the piece; Gandhi, on the other hand, found in Hitler a not-so-bad a man, after all! The Mahatma knew that both the Fuehrer and the Qaid-e-Azam were reshaping the world-map from where Mustafa Kemal Pasha had left—it may not have been designed so but its *result* would become the unwritten international policy of containment of Islam.

Three weeks before the German air-attack on London, Gandhi wrote to Lord Linlithgow a strange letter on 26 May 1940, offering to go to Germany or anywhere required to plead for peace: 'I do not believe Herr Hitler to be as bad as he is portrayed. He might even have been a friendly power as he may still be.' This when the German plans for extermination of the Jews were already in the air. The Viceroy, therefore, did not allow Gandhi to fish in troubled waters outside India. Jinnah's League, on the other hand, passed a pro-British resolution, against the Nazi Germany: even the League was sailing in two boats—on the one hand, it was happy at the genocide of the Jews due to the Nazi policies and opposed the creation of 'Israel' in the Palestine as a result thereof; it was, on the other hand, also supporting the British for opposing Hitler and supporting the Jews! A week after the Germans attacked London, Jinnah met with Linlithgow at Shimla on 27 June to tell him that the Lahore Resolution demonstrated the 'universal faith of Muslim India'. Gandhi, on the other hand, tried to do a Jesus in Britain by appealing the Empire to let Hitler and Mussolini take whatever they wanted even as the Mahatma was preparing to give a call in India to kick out the British! The British, who had never got so many kicks in their ass from so many in such a short time, did not know who to turn to in India as those two Gujarati foxes, Jinnah and Gandhi, alternately kicked and caressed their imperial buttocks.

At a time when Linlithgow was trying to sew up Indian political support for British war efforts, Jinnah threw in his spanner: he wrote to the Viceroy that the Congress Party's enrolment and the extent of its say should be approved by the League. The Viceroy saw through the game and felt that Jinnah wanted to eliminate Nehru's candidature and probably, eventually, become the Prime Minister! On the other hand, Gandhi braced himself to launch yet another agitation as Jinnah was denouncing everyone around—the Viceroy, the 'Hindu Congress', the 'Muslim Congressmen' etc. Everything seems to have gone haywire for everyone and each politician and party found itself entrapped in its own web. The Second World War was raging and freedom movements throughout the world colonised by Europe had come a cropper as the world riveted its attention on the inevitability of blood-shed as continents and people reshaped their nations and destinies by eliminating surplus or use-by-date populations. The biggest shock of the 1940s was destruction of self-importance and invincibility of Britain: the Master, that ruled the waves, suddenly found himself begging the slaves for support.

It was in such vulnerable situations that Nature reorganises the Elements. In February 1941, Shah Nawaz Khan drafted a secret plan for Jinnah on 'What is Pakistan?' detailing his plan on how to move about to demand the various areas where the Muslims were in a commanding majority, a weak majority and a minor minority. Had this fantastic plan been implemented, there would have been a Hindustan in the midst of Pakistan, not the other way round! But Jinnah, and the League, indeed Islam itself, had been surviving on such fantastic diets for long. If Jinnah had passed the Pakistan Resolution in the former Sikh Capital of Lahore, he now chose Madras to announce the clear demand of Pakistan! On 12 April 1941, while recuperating from a nervous breakdown, with the 'Dravidistan' *Periyar* (the Great Sage) by his side and under the shadow of drawn swords of his trusted bodyguards from Bombay, he declared: 'We have defined in the clearest terms that our goal, about which Muslim India has been groping in the dark, is Pakistan.' Then he charged his natural enemy, Gandhi, with his favourite question: 'I should like to ask any man with a grain of sense, Do you really think that Gandhi, the supreme leader, commander and general of the Congress, has started this Satyagraha merely for the purpose of getting liberty of speech? Don't you really feel that this is nothing but a weapon of coercion and blackmailing the British, who are in a tight corner, to surrender and concede the Congress demands?' Now was the turn of the British to 'please stop your policy of appeasement towards those bent upon frustrating your war efforts and doing their best to oppose the prosecution of the War and defence of India at this critical moment...You are not loyal to those standing by you; you desire to placate those having the greatest nuisance value in the political and economic fields...If the British Government want the whole-hearted cooperation of Muslim India, they must place their cards on the table.'

The British were not impressed with this request-cum-appeal-cum-threat nor did they think Jinnah, the Lincoln's Inn alumni, had imbibed anything from Abraham Lincoln. They tried to cut Jinnah to size in the League itself by inviting all anti-Jinnah League leaders—Sir Sikander Hayat Khan, Fazl ul-Haq, Sir Muhammed Saadullah, the Premiers of the Punjab, Bengal and Assam—to the newly constituted National Defence Council. Jinnah struck back by taming or expelling these armchair politicians with egos inflated beyond their crania. Meanwhile, Japan's attack on Pearl Harbour brought possibility of the War visiting the shores of India from the East. The British now realised the importance of the phrase, 'uneasy lies the head that wears the Crown' in a new context as both Jinnah and Gandhi braced themselves to race ahead of each other and the British. On 26 December 1941, Jinnah told the All-India Muslim Students Federation at Nagpur that the 'League's goal would lead you to the promised land where we shall establish our Pakistan. People may say what they like and talk as they like. Of course, he who laughs last, laughs best'. The British took this laughter seriously and decided to charge Sir Stafford Cripps to bring the political leaders together.

Jinnah, having sensed his own precarious health, the fact that he was host to several debilitating diseases, and the fear of an approaching death, was now talking in matching terms even in his political speeches. He told a League meeting in Calcutta on 13 February 1942, that 'Our blood had become cold, out flesh incapable of working, and the Muslim nation was, for all practical purposes, dead. Today, we find our blood circulation improving, our flesh getting stronger, our mind more clarified'. At Serajganj he said, 'We are going through a life and death struggle...we must stand on our own legs and rely on our own strengths if we are to achieve anything in this world'. Clearly, it was not Chaudhary Rahmat Ali but Jinnah who had become one with 'Pakistan', with all its contradictions, diseases, confusions. The unbottled *jinn* of Jinnah, who was still alive, had begun to drive Islam out of India; with Pakistan inching towards staggered self-destruction in the 21st century, the genie would repeatedly come haunting the Hindu Right in India, too.

Even the British were hoist with their own petard. Bewildered at the fast pace of changes overtaking their five-day-cricketing, easy-going imperialist habits, they were astonished to see 60,000 well-armed soldiers of their British Indian garrison simply surrendering to Japan in Singapore on 15 February 1942, without firing a shot! Clearly, the Crown could no longer trust the colony. Everywhere, Indian soldiers—both Hindu and Muslims—were defying their British superiors and such 'mutinies' sent chills down the Whitehall spine. For the first time after 1857, Indian soldiers of the British Indian Army were no longer trustworthy and the only way out for the British was to get out of India—at the best of times, the Raj never had more than 120,000 Europeans, including the British, stationed in the Indian subcontinent having a population of 400 million, most of whom were now ready to throw out the White yoke. The British did not want to face another bloody 1857 in their largest colony, particularly when they hoped to get little help from the Isle itself, still suffering from the bouts of the War. They had no option but to leave. Better leave honourably, or they would have to be ready to be kicked out the way the Americans did unto them in the late 18th century. The British could no longer trust either the Congress or the League, as much as these two distrusted each other and the British.

Sir Stafford Cripps, brought into Britain's War Cabinet as Leader of the House of Commons and Lord Privy Seal, met Gandhi on 27 March. The Mahatma proposed an offer which Jinnah knew would, if accepted, have finished off the Great Leader in one brilliant stroke: the *British* should make Jinnah the Prime Minister of India and the Great Leader should *then* try to get the Congress support—in which case, of course, Jinnah would have to come with a begging bowl to Gandhi! It was just like the short-lived 'secular' governments led by Prime Minister(s) Charan Singh/VP Singh/H D Deve Gowda/ Inder Kumar Gujral/Chandra Shekhar being supported from outside and toppled at convenience from inside by the Congress in the 1970s-1990s period. Jinnah, who knew how close Cripps was to Nehru and Krishna Menon, saw through this non-violent Gandhian game being played by the Hindus' leadership that had pushed the Muslims, post-Khilafat, in a corner. Cripps, aspiring to replace Churchill if his Indian experiment paid off, even drew up a Cabinet ministers' list, with Maulana Azad as Home Minister, in the proposed 'National Government'. Jawaharlal, never ever accused of far sight, subtlety or political acumen, and Azad, who hated Jinnah for being a show-piece Muslim in the Holy League—although Azad himself was, in Jinnah's views, merely a 'show-boy' Muslim in the Hindu Congress—could be trusted to reject the proposal. Even Gandhi knew this but he made this proposal known to everybody; at least some of the mud would stick on Jinnah. Not ready to appear anti-Jinnah, anti-League or anti-Muslim, the Congress rejected the proposal on 10 April 1942, on the pretext of being denied 'full powers' in the proposed National Government which, Azad said, would be a mere extension of the Viceroy's Executive Council; the British did not want to part with the technical and defence matters. A relieved Jinnah told the Press the very next day that unless all the parties agreed to Partition and Pakistan, whose details could be settled after the War, the National Government could not be formed.

A dejected Cripps decided to return to England as US President Franklin D Roosevelt criticised the British for their unwillingness to recognise the rights of the Indians to self-determination and self-government; if this right could not be granted, how could the Congress grant the right to self-determination and self-government to the Muslims! Hence the deadlock. The situation had come to such a pass that the departure of the British only meant the arrival of Pakistan. Never was the League, therefore, as much pleased with the Congress rejecting to be led by Jinnah; reacting to the Congress rejection, the League Working Committee resolution noted with 'gratification that the possibility of Pakistan is recognised…The Musalmans cannot be satisfied by such a Declaration on a vital question affecting their future destiny'.

Few had the cerebral capacity to absorb Gandhi's one-step-backward and two-steps-forward policy. Some even saw the failure of the 'Jinnah-as-Premier' experiment as a failure of the Mahatma. Among them was Gandhi's son's father-in-law, Chakravarti Rajagopalachari (CR) who now sought to lead the Congress to cooperate with both the British and the Muslims and directly challenge Gandhi and Nehru. The All-India Congress dismissed such lofty claims, forcing Rajaji to resign from the Congress in April 1942 at a time when Gandhi was planning his biggest anti-British *Experiment*, ever. Spinning yarn at Wardha, Gandhi had his resolution passed on 1 May 1942, at the Congress meet at Allahabad, saying, among other things, that India had no quarrels with Japan and that 'She is warring against the British Empire...If India were freed, her first step would probably be to negotiate with Japan...The Congress is, therefore, of the opinion that the British should withdraw from India.'

It was the Mahatma's flowering season. Again.

He knew his views should now be made known to America, the new kid on the imperial block; the British were bored with Gandhi but the United States could still find him exciting. Particularly if the aloof Americans could be made to believe that India was doing unto the British precisely what they had themselves done unto the Crown in 1776. Having been dragged into the War by an unwitting Japan which attacked Pearl Harbour, America was now leader of the 'free' world with Britain hanging on to its coat-tails; in fact, much to the chagrin of Premier Winston Churchill, US President Roosevelt had dispatched his former Assistant Secretary of War Colonel Louis Johnson as his 'personal' representative to study and help in finding a political solution to the Indians' demands. So, Gandhi thought, the Americans should be made psychologically ready to see the British departure *from* India. How to ready them? The best way was to arouse in them indignation, to touch their raw nerve, to make the contemporary largest democracy realise that America was no better than Nazi Germany, Fascist Italy or the brutal Britons—not to compare with Japan! If you could needle the British merely by saying they were brute and uncivilised, the biggest criticism of contemporary America was that it was 'undemocratic'—in the 21st century, they no longer take the barb seriously, for they know that they have become one while dealing with non-Christians and non-Whites! So, when two American journalists interviewed Gandhi in May 1942, he told them: 'I have not asked the British to hand over India to the *Congress or to the Hindus*. Let them entrust India to God or in modern parlance to anarchy. Then all the parties will fight one another like dogs, or will, when real responsibility faces them, come to a reasonable agreement, I shall expect non-violence to arise out of that chaos.' He did not even mention the words Muslims or the League; he was now, although indirectly, advocating handing over of the power to the Congress or to the Hindus! This was a subtle shift in his policy, or was it really? Earlier, he had advocated Hindu-Muslim unity as a prerequisite for Swaraj; now he was seeking Swaraj as a precondition for 'unity'. He was no longer using even words like 'Hindu-Muslim unity': 'There could be no unity until India has achieved independence.' Unity between whom? The Mahatma, ever so careful about choosing his words, said: '*Time is a merciless enemy.* I have been asking myself why every whole-hearted attempt made by all, including myself, to reach unity has failed, and failed so completely that *I have entirely fallen from grace and am described by some Muslim papers as the greatest enemy of Islam in India.* It is a phenomenon I can only account for by the fact that the *third power, even without deliberately wishing it, will not allow real unity to take place.* Therefore I have come to the resultant conclusion that the two communities will come together almost immediately after the British power comes to a final end in India.' He left the words 'third power' undefined—clearly, it was not Britain, but the USA! He had this innate ability to see through the Americana as an upgraded, updated, revised and enlarged edition of the now dog-eared Britannica.

Jinnah smoked at the mouth; Gandhi through his mind. So the Qaid-e-Azam did not perhaps fully realise how the Mahatma was pushing Pakistan out of India and making him, the Great Leader, believe that it was, indeed, *he* (Jinnah) who was doing so. 'I am glad', Jinnah reacted on expected lines, 'that at last Mr Gandhi has openly declared that unity and Hindu-Muslim settlement can only come after the achievement of India's independence and has, thereby, thrown off the cloak that he had worn for the last 22 years'. Only a Thakkar convert to Islam could see through a Modh, who refused to convert, so perfectly! Or did he really understand Gandhi so perfectly? Even now?

In early August 1942, Gandhi gave his most-famous call asking the British to 'Quit India': 'We shall get our freedom by fighting. It cannot fall from the skies. They will have to give us freedom when we have made sufficient sacrifices and proved our strength.' After the default Gandhian pop-ups of truth, non-violence and love for the British, et al, in place, he said it was the 'biggest fight' in his life and expected a 'change' in Jinnah's mind. Why did the ever-cautious Mahatma give this crucial call? The British Army, already hounded out by Japan from Burma, was so demoralised that it was ready to quit India as well any time; Sardar Patel told Gandhi that the Quit India movement could charge up the people in an unprecedented manner and it could be successful within a week. But the stiff-upper-lipped British, unaccustomed to give up without being booted out by the likes of the Boston Tea Party, decided to arrest the Mahatma for this 'open rebellion'. Jinnah's in-house enemy in the League, Sir Sikander, disclosed to the British that the Mahatma and the Qaid-i-Azam could join hands against the Crown, with Gandhi promising Pakistan! The Mahatma, thinking on similar lines, renewed his earlier offer of Premiership to Jinnah on 8 August saying the Congress was ready to play second fiddle to, and even join any Government headed by the League if the latter fully cooperated with it in attaining 'immediate independence'. Why did Gandhi make this offer again? In the surcharged atmosphere across India, particularly in the North, if at all Jinnah and the League came to power at the Centre, there would emerge a hundred Chauri Chauras, or anarchy against the re-appearance of the Muslim rule, that would consume both Jinnah and the League—along with their cherished hope of Pakistan!

Predictably, Jinnah reacted sharply, charging Gandhi with 'fooling' the Muslims. Gandhi gave a call for 'Quit India' on 8 August, asking the people to 'do or die'. The British arrested the Mahatma and 'imprisoned' him in Jinnah associate Agha Khan's Palace at Pune! Next day, Jinnah regretted that the Congress had 'finally declared war and launched a most dangerous mass movement in spite of numerous warnings' and, a week later, the League deplored the Congress for this open rebellion meant to 'establish Congress Hindu domination in India'. Interestingly, many in the Muslim League believed the Quit India movement was actually aimed at the Muslims! Its resolution, passed after four days' deliberations at the Jinnah House, claimed that the Quit India movement was an attempt being made by the Congress to 'force the Musalmans to submit and surrender to the

Congress terms and dictation'. Truth had finally begun to emerge in the Caesarian opening.

And with this, violence was the natural corollary. The British tried to conceal the movement and the violence it triggered from the 'outside world' as Linlithgow complained to Churchill about American 'intervention' in Indian affairs. Meanwhile, sensing the imminent demise of the British power in India, all shades of princes and feudal lords, both Hindus and Muslims, became apprehensive of their own future; since the Congress was openly anti-imperialist and anti-feudal, they financed the League like never before—the League leadership itself was mostly feudalistic. On the other hand, the British were finding their hands full on all fronts: with 500,000 Indian troops abroad and the industrial boom in parts of India preventing British imports, the Crown already owed 400 million pounds, which doubled by mid-1943, to India: retaining the slave had become an expensive affair now! The problem was complicated with Churchill, who was more like an elected British version of the mainland European dictators he was fighting against, not heeding to Cripps who had to resign on 22 November; indeed, like Churchill, Hitler and Mussolini had also come to power through election. For India, there was nothing to choose between the decomposing triumvirate.

The situation worsened in 1943 with the Japanese invasion looming large on Calcutta and the century's worst famine in India, prompting the Mahatma to threaten a fast-unto-death. The British developed cold feet. Gandhi renewed his offer to make Jinnah the Premier which the League rejected as a 'tenancy-at-will as a favour'. The League was rightly wary of such Congress-laid traps, much the same way the non-Congress parties were wary of the 'Gandhians' who pulled down the various 'secular' governments in New Delhi and denied premiership to leaders like Jyoti Basu, Mulayam Singh Yadav, Purno A Sangma etc. who all consequently hardened their anti-Congress stand, favouring instead the rightist BJP in the 1990s! As news about Gandhi's 'deteriorating' health due to the fast spread, the Quit India Movement became more and more strident across the country until he broke his fast on 3 March, losing the weight he would now throw around.

In April, the League's annual session began in New Delhi with the map and slogan that 'Freedom of India lies in Pakistan!' The 'P' word became a fashion statement amongst the thrilled Muslims of India much the same way the 'K' word (Kashmir) became in Pakistan in the coming decades. Jinnah accused Gandhi of trying to convert the entire India into a Hindu Ashram but offered to meet his *bete noire* if the latter conceded the demand for Pakistan beforehand. Unlike Gandhi, he still over-estimated the British 'power' which, he believed, would drag the War on for many more years; this had forced him to remain on the right side of the British for the time being. During the New Delhi session of the League, he told the British to 'guarantee the Musalmans the right of self-determination' without further delay, and addressed the Muslims thus: 'I say to the 100 million Muslims...the way I see them now is that the phoenix-like rise and regeneration of Muslim India from the very ashes of its ruination...is a miracle.... Now it is time to take up the construction programme to build up this nation so that it can march on the path of our goal of Pakistan... The goal is hither, you just have to stand united, persevere and march forward.' Never had a heretic Muslim so allured the Sunnis; never had a twig-thin pied-piper mesmerised-magnetised and taken away so many with him to their own ruination.

The War continued unabated outside India. Inside, the foetus of Pakistan was continuously shaping up. On 26 July 1943, Rafiq Sabir Mazangavi, a Khaksar-cum-League activist from Lahore tried to assassinate Jinnah at his house in Bombay. The reason he gave was that the League was doing nothing for the Muslims except talking. Jinnah's miraculous escape from the jaws of death—his jaw had been badly cut in the knife attack—prompted the Muslims to view it as a divine grace; they celebrated a 'Day of Thanksgiving to God for sparing the most precious life of the sub-continent'. As both Gandhi and Jinnah now waited for some really divine intervention in their favour, Lord Wavell estimated in September 1943 that both 'Gandhi and Jinnah are dictators. Gandhi because he has shaped himself up as a saint; Jinnah because his party has no other leader to match him in ability'. The Viceroy was not sure about the boundaries of 'Pakistan'—even Jinnah was not!—but knew it was a serious plan. But, like Gandhi, even Jinnah was now running out of patience as nothing seemed to move any further. As famine deaths mounted in the Muslim League-ruled Bengal of Khwaza Nazimuddin, and the anti-British wave swept the eastern province, Jinnah condemned the British: 'Supposing in England a few hundred people had died every week of starvation, would the Churchill Government be able to stand for 24 hours? And here we are calmly and coolly told about not indulging in recrimination. It is our misfortune that we are living under a system of Government which is irremovable and irresponsible and, I would add, thoroughly incompetent to handle any big issue.'

This was Jinnah at his worst anti-British outburst in a quarter of a century since the Rowlett Acts row. The Great Leader had carefully refrained from donating anything to the starving Bengal and had compensated this shortcoming by denouncing the British. The Sick Man of India, on the eve of his 67th birthday, coughed his way through the 31st annual session of the League at Karachi amidst thunderous shouts of 'Long live, conqueror of the Congress' even as he was shadowed everywhere by his 2,000-strong private army of trusted Bombay bodyguards with swords drawn throughout; but he was also shadowed by his own diseases like tuberculosis and pleurisy with suspected lung cancer, too, arriving. Unimpressed, Lord Wavell said of Jinnah: 'He does not really represent solid steady Moslem opinion (in fact, Jinnah himself is hardly a Muslim) but he can sway opinion, and no one seems to have the character to oppose him.'

Gandhi's wife Kasturba died in February 1944, forcing the British to release the ailing Mahatma who, however, recovered miraculously. Even as Sir Sikander's son Shaukat accused Jinnah of 'importing' into the Punjab a number of maulanas from North India to rake up communal trouble, the Great Leader braced for a new meeting with the Mahatma on old lines. Gandhi, who never missed a chance to needle Jinnah, wrote a letter on 17 July 1944, *in Gujarati language*: 'Brother Jinnah, *There was a day when I could induce you to speak in the mother tongue. Today I take courage to write to you in the same language... We will meet whenever you choose*. Don't regard me as the enemy of

Islam or of the Muslims of this country. I am the friend and servant of not only yourself but of the whole world. *Do not disappoint me.*' The operative parts of this letter, the trigger words, were the words typical of the Mahatma reminding Jinnah of their first joint public meeting of Gurjar Sabha in Bombay in 1915 in which Gandhi had virtually berated Jinnah as a mere 'Muslim' leader and ridiculed him for speaking in English as he himself spoke in Gujarati; now, 29 years later, in the midst of yet another World War, the same Gandhi was speaking to the same Jinnah in the same language! How could Jinnah *disappoint* him?

On 30 July 1944, Jinnah told the League at Lahore that 'Insha'Allah, Pakistan is coming'. The Gandhi-Jinnah, rather *the* Jinnah-Gandhi, talks began on 9 September at the Great Leader's Malabar Hill house. Jinnah told Gandhi that he wants 'Pakistan now, not after Independence' and that the two of them should first agree to it before going to the government. The Muslims insisted on *talaq* from the Hindus. Before going to the *qazi*! A divorce is caused by the partner's dissatisfaction with the spouse and the Muslims had indirectly conceded that they were unable to convert the whole of Hindustan and now wanted to separate the parts they had succeeded in converting to Islam. 'The Muslims want Pakistan. The League represents the Muslims and it wants separation.' The impatient Jinnah wanted a premature child through caesarian surgery; and Gandhi was unwilling to deliver it; so the 'talks' continued for another round. An exasperated Jinnah, knowing well the futility of this drama, wrote, and again wrote, to his 'Dear Mr Gandhi' that he was still waiting for a reply and that: 'Please, therefore, let me have your reply as soon as possible with regards to the various points mentioned in my letter.' Gandhi wrote back on 14 September for the first time almost using the word Pakistan. 'With your assistance, I am applying my mind very seriously to the famous Lahore Resolution of the Muslim League', that is, the demand for Pakistan.

Gandhi would be no Gandhi if he would let go of any opportunity to make pawns out of words: 'The Resolution itself makes no reference to the two-nation theory which was in any event wholly unreal. **I find no parallel in the history for a body of converts and**

their descendants claiming to be a nation apart from the parent stock. If India was one nation before the advent of Islam, it must remain one in spite of the change of faith of a very large number of her children.' And Jinnah would be no Jinnah if he let slip any opportunity to hit out at Gandhi: 'It is my duty to explain the Lahore resolution to you today and persuade you to accept it. *I have successfully converted non-Muslim Indians in no small number and also a large body of foreigners, and if I can convert you, exercising as you do tremendous influence over Hindu India, it will be no small assistance to me.*' Here, Jinnah was referring mainly to Ambedkar with whom Gandhi had entered the Poona Pact a decade ago and who now believed in the inevitability of Pakistan.

Of the two geniuses, Gandhi was greater because he would not claim credit for what he did; Jinnah, on the other hand, would forget that he was merely product of and influenced by the circumstances in the world and claim, like Hitler, 'I alone did it'. So when Jinnah 'explained' to Gandhi what the Lahore Resolution was all about, the latter wrote him back: '*The more I think about the two-nation theory the more alarming it appears to be. Once the principle is admitted there would be no limit to claims for cutting up India into numerous divisions which would spell India's ruin.*' After making Jinnah drive thus far, Gandhi was complaining about the distance covered! No longer was he refusing to recognise Jinnah, the Muslim League or Pakistan.

Meanwhile, Chaudhary Rahmat Ali, still financed by monarchist and fundamentalist charities, was busy like bee dividing India further; not satisfied with Pakistan as the Muslim 'nation' of South Asia, he worked overtime—he was to India the inverse of what the British-German national H S Chamberlain was to Nazi Germany. He described the infidel country as *al-Dinia Milli* ('Religious Nations') and was now advocating as many as ten 'Muslim nations' apart from Pakistan. He penned a new pamphlet, 'The Millat and her Ten Nations' from his headquarters at Cambridge on 10 June 1944. India was to be divided into the so-called *Usmanistan, Farooquistan, Haideristan, Maplistan, Muinistan*....and counting more. For this ultra-Muslim Chaudhary, wherever there was a single Muslim in an ocean of infidels there should be a separate nation for that Muhammedan! Because, theologically, the

Muslim was ***not*** supposed to live in an infidel land at all; if forced to, he must get his own nation and it was his paramount duty to either convert the infidels or destroy them. It was no matter of joke: after the demise of the Caliphate, the Chaudhary had revived the Prophet's directives to Muslims in an infidel land; and all non-Muslim nations across the world would continue to face this music in the 20th and 21st centuries because of this.

Gandhi played music for Jinnah's failing ears, saying that even Pakistan could, tomorrow, be a victim of its own theory. As expected, Jinnah rejected the Gandhian 'principles' and stuck to his own theory. Like estranged soul-mates, they exchanged a few more letters, came together for 'talks' and arrived at no decision until Gandhi's last letter to Jinnah: 'You keep on saying that I should accept certain theses, while I have been contending that the best way for us, who differ in our approach to the problem, is to give body to the demand as it stands in the (Lahore) Resolution and work it out to our mutual satisfaction.' But Jinnah would not fall in this simple trap: it only meant the League entering into a possible agreement with the Congress. Had Jinnah agreed with Gandhi, Pakistan would be a gift of the Hindus! This he did not want, and that too from the Hindu Congress and the Modh Gandhi. He wanted Pakistan on *his* own terms. And *from* the British! In order to achieve this, he must cut Gandhi to his (Jinnah's) diminutive size so that he and the Mahatma could go to the British as 'sole' representatives of the Muslims and Hindus, respectively, with the former demanding Pakistan. Gandhi, who had declined to be converted to Islam by his Muslim benefactor Sheth Haji Abdullah in the 1890s, now refused to be converted by Jinnah to the demand for Pakistan as well: the Mahatma did not want either to gift away or give away Pakistan to Jinnah—he would rather the Muslims ***drag away*** this 'trophy', walking in an ocean of blood just like Mahmood Ghazanavi had returned after loot and massacre from Somnath a thousand years ago. It was the Indian version of the 15th century Spanish *Reconquista*, with a difference: while in Spain, the Christians shed the Muslim blood and pushed them out of the Iberian Peninsula and re-converted many, in India the Hindus were forcing the Muslims to shed *Hindu* blood so as to re-establish the brutal nature of Islam as an enduring political ideology, much the same way as Nazism, Fascism and Communism were the contemporary fruits of the Abrahamic Tree.

After 'breakdown' of the talks, Gandhi returned to Wardha to tell the press that, '*My experience of the previous three weeks confirms me in the view that the presence of a third power hinders the solution. A mind enslaved cannot act as if it were free*'. Next day, he told *Bombay Chronicle* that, '...*Mr Jinnah is sincere, but I think he is suffering from hallucination when he imagines that an unnatural division of India could bring either happiness or prosperity to the people concerned*'. He was inciting and putting both the British and Jinnah in the auto-drive mode now, to begin taking steps against himself, the Congress, the Hindus.

How?

Until October 1944, the Viceroy did not believe in the two-nation theory. In fact, so deChristianised and technology-softened had the Europeans and the Americans become that they would refuse to see or recognise the deep-rooted historical problems of Asia and Africa—even 9/11 could not much wake them up from their dogmatic slumber. Their ostrich-like habit of burying head in the sand in the midst of a storm and stubbornly refusing to see what *they* did not want to see made them believe that even others would do so similarly; for instance, they might have forgotten the atrocities they had committed against the Muslims and other Afro-Asians, coloured or colonial people throughout history but axiomatically believed that the victims would also not remember these either. Socialism and communism had further stripped them of their ancient spiritual moorings and their science and democracy had not exactly replenished them with wholesome mental processes that guide and shape the destinies of vast populations. They all split and simplified the problems of their colonies the way *they* chose to, into 'political', 'social' or 'economic' ones, the way the West 'recognised' the causes of Muslims' 'backwardness' in the 21st century while enforcing democracy from the above, not recognising that the bases of these problems were these regions' history and religions that had shaped up these societies and that were only now beginning to be deChristianized or deIslamised in what would be their own slow, bloody, painful and long-drawn-out *Renaissance*.

Instead of recognising it as a civilisational and cultural drift of continental proportions, Lord Wavell, too, saw in the Pakistan Movement only a religious pressure tactic of the Muslims to draw political concessions in governance of British India—Jinnah and Gandhi, on the other hand, were deadly serious in deciding the future of Islam and Muslims in the Indian sub-continent even as many a League and Congress leaders still believed that Pakistan was a mere hot-air balloon, a fantasy, a bargaining counter, a political wishful thinking, than a potential reality. Only the Mahatma and the Qaid-e-Azam, perhaps, knew that they were leading a civilisational shift, even a drift, in the sub-continent involving *Homotectonus*, the ideologically-driven and connected human species that moved like the Earth's tectonic plates and silently generated tsunamis.

Early in 1945, both the titans were bed-ridden, giving an opportunity to the younger but confused lot to give their fantasies a try. Bhulabhai Desai and Nawabzada Liaqat Ali Khan 'settled' for an Interim Government at the Centre with the Congress and the League taking 40 per cent of Cabinet seats each and leaving 20 per cent to the Sikhs and the Untouchables, and claiming that Gandhi and Jinnah had 'approved' this so-called formula. Predictably, Jinnah rejected the move and Gandhi, waiting for his *bete noire* to strike first, kept mum. The British believed that both Gandhi and Jinnah were losing control over their respective fiefdoms, Congress and the League; the Crown did not realise that they were not mere political leaders who could be swept aside by their age or diseases—they were formidable crests of the waves their respective societies had generated over a thousand years and would continue to churn their societies long after they were physically dead. As Jinnah told his faithful in his Pakistan Day message of 23 March, 'I have my fingers on the pulse of Muslim India...and I feel confident that ten crores of Musalmans will stand as one man at any critical moment and will not hesitate to make every sacrifice, if we are to be thwarted, ignored or by-passed by those in power...Pakistan is within our grasp...Insha-Allah, we shall win'.

With Hitler committing suicide in April 1945, the War ended in Europe—although, in Asia, it will continue until August that year. To his chagrin, Churchill apparently discovered that that there remained no dictator of his stature in Europe to continue his pow-vow with and he resigned in disgust—like most other Western Europeans, he saw the surviving Stalin as an 'Asian' dictator! Badly mauled in the War, the British were reduced to their own caricatures, left with no strength or the will to carry the burden of their Empire: the White Man had himself become burdensome and would not like to pull the Indian chestnuts out of civilisational fires. The British would soon have to dismount from their high horse, and pass on the baton. They would appoint Mountbatton to make the Crown disMount and relieve itself of the Baton.

Wavell was to prepare the ground for Mountbatton. Returning to Delhi on 7 June 1945, Wavell ordered release of all Congressmen from jails and called a conference of 'Indian leaders' who told him to make an immediate declaration of 'complete dominion status' for India. Both Gandhi and Jinnah objected to the inclusion of 'caste Hindus' and 'non-League Muslims', respectively, to represent their 'communities' in this Conference, forcing the Viceroy to call the Congress and the League to a conference in Shimla on 25 June. Gandhi was represented by Azad, Jinnah represented himself: it was a struggle between the inclusivist nature of Hinduism and the exclusivist nature of Islam—and the latter won as the former desired. Wavell, however, found Jinnah nervous but still determined and sticking to technicalities. On 11 July, Wavell called both Jinnah and Gandhi and informed the latter of the breakdown of talks once again. The Mahatma knew, took the 'news' 'calmly, but said that ***His Majesty's Government would have to decide sooner or later to accept the Hindu or the Muslim point of view, since they were irreconcilable***'. Three days later, Jinnah announced that 'Pakistan and United India are diametrically opposed to each other, that…the Muslims are determined to have Pakistan'.

Failure at Shimla forced Wavell to call a Governors' meeting in New Delhi, warning them of the possible civil war, particularly in the Punjab, which could snowball to other areas. On the other hand, Jinnah was unable to control his rage; he knew his time was fast running out and he must be able to create Pakistan while still alive. He became more and more Gandhi-centric, obsessed with the

Mahatma as much as with his own diseases, even as his *bete noire* retained his 'magnanimous' cool at finding the seeds he had sown long ago finally germinating. Soon after Shimla, Jinnah poured venom at Gandhi out of frustration in a statement at Bombay: 'When it suits him, he represents nobody, he can talk in individual capacity; he is not even a four-anna member of the Congress; he undertakes fast to decide the political issue; he reduces himself to zero and consults his inner voice; yet when it suits him, he is the supreme leader of the Congress! He thinks he represents the whole of India. Mr Gandhi is an enigma…how can we come to a settlement with him?' In his by now well-known default diatribe, he then accused the Congress of 'coercing, threatening, ignoring, humiliating, discouraging, bullying and hammering down' the League.

With Hiroshima and Nagasaki going up in tragic nuclear flames in August 1945, the War came to an end in the East as well. The former British colony of America now politically eclipsed the Empire completely. Unlike other major imperial powers of the past, Britain had aged too fast and would be losing all her major possessions within a few years; for the first time, a former Master would beg from erstwhile Slaves, but not without flaunting those stuffed heads of big cats on his wall. Above all, the first slave to secede, America, would not only write obituary of the Empire but also replace it. But, while the American Independence had been mostly a Tea Party, India's Independence will be a savage, blood-washed barbecue.

Some British sensed it, but they were unable to convince those marble-headed jackasses who happened to be their bosses due to the accident of their births or connections. The failure of Shimla Conference and release of the Quit India activists was to be followed by elections to the Central and provincial bodies. In particular, Governor Glancy of the Punjab was scared of the gathering storm in that province so notorious for its massive carnages over the ages. He did not want elections that would communally polarise the volatile province already fertile with the likes of the dreaded Khaksars whom even Jinnah feared. 'If Pakistan became an imminent reality', Glancy warned, 'we would be heading straight for bloodshed on a wide scale;

non-Muslims, especially Sikhs, are not bluffing, they will not submit peacefully to a Government that is labelled "Muhammedan Raj"'. Why did he fear that Jinnah's Raj would, in fact, be a Muhammedan one? Glancy was aware of the peculiar character of Islam: modernity would not easily liberate the Muslim mind from the yoke of his medieval religion; on the contrary, the literate Muslim would use his modernity to strengthen his medievalism, like a stem-cell being grafted on a frozen mummy to revive it. Many of the League leaders, including Jinnah, were highly educated and, *therefore*, highly orthodox and reactionary having no compunction in bloodshed on a vast scale: they were English-speaking rebooted and programmed barbarians, far more brutal, organised and complicated than the simple Arabs whose simple cult they had embraced.

It was, therefore, no surprise that Glancy found Jinnah's stock rising and that he, who belonged to the anti-Sunni Ismaeli sect, was being hailed as the true 'champion of Islam'. 'I must confess that I am gravely perturbed about the situation, because there is a very serious danger of the elections being fought, so far as Muslims are concerned, on an entirely false issue...The uninformed Muslim will be told that the question he is called on to answer at the polls is—Are you a true believer or an infidel and a traitor?' This would be exactly the same line future Pakistani politicians will take to annex power. And like a tumour that sucks the infected blood, 'Pakistan' was more attractive to the Muslim minority who did not want to 'suffocate' in a Hindu majority around which they had failed to curdify, areas of the real Hindu-Islam interplay such as the United Provinces and Bihar; these Muslims, afflicted with the Mughal nostalgia, would rush into their 'homeland' in a few months and remain there as *Muhajirs*, permanently, like Altaf Hussain and Pervez Musharraf, hostage to and vociferous 'defenders' of Islam because that was their only weapon to survive there.

Lord Wavell also noted that the Sikhs were going to fight for their own 'Holy Land', the Punjab, instead of succumbing to a permanent Muslim rule there; he said the support for the idea of 'Pakistan' was much more stronger in Hindi-speaking areas rather than in those provinces that were supposed anyway to become a new Muslim 'homeland'. Nothing could be more heartening to the ailing Jinnah who was criss-crossing India and trying to lure the ailing Muslim souls to the proposed spiritual hospital called Pakistan. Cripps now asked the Viceroy to meet Gandhi who appeared 'ready and willing to influence Indian public opinion towards moderation'. By November 1945, the British countdown had begun with the whole nation charged up with the trial of Indian National Army (INA) heroes, brought in from Singapore, whose charismatic leader Subhas Chandra Bose had 'died' mysteriously in Formosa (Taiwan) a few weeks ago. Jinnah's first task was, however, to win elections in the 'Pakistan provinces' to consolidate his hold and increase bargaining power. Neither he nor Gandhi had now been left with many arguments: Pakistan's moon was rising on the horizon irresistibly and they were, like devout Hindu wives on the *Karwa Chauth* evening, rushing to their rooftops to witness the celestial spectacle and break their slow-paced fast.

Apparently, Jinnah had never forgotten how Gandhi had 'manipulated' his exit from the Congress on the Khilafat issue: in fact, the Qaid's political career thereafter was based on the premise that if a Hindu could make political capital out of a *Muslim* issue, why not he (Jinnah), although a nominal Muslim, do the same. On 24 November 1945, at a public meeting in Peshawar, he ridiculed the Congress asking him about the sacrifices he had made for India: '... Who made the sacrifices in 1920-21? Mr Gandhi ascends the throne of leadership on our skulls.' He thought he was paying Gandhi in the same coin as a recompense to the worst trauma of his life, the deepest wound on his psyche, when he had to quit the Congress because of the Mahatma's 'machinations'. Jinnah had shaped up this personal political battle against Gandhi into a civilisational war between Islam and India out of the millennium-old forest of cultural warfare. Gandhi, on the other hand, having nursed Mother India so far, was now only waiting for the Pakistan-birth and preparing for post-natal precautions.

Bengal Governor Richard Casey, who met Gandhi in Calcutta, reported that while the League was 'suffering from Hinduphobia', the Mahatma seemed to run out of options when he said that Jinnah had 'constantly raised his price', shifted goalposts, until he reached Pakistan. Anything less would not satisfy the Great Leader, Gandhi said, who he believed was a 'very ambitious man and that he had visions of linking up the Moslems of India with the Moslems in the Middle East and elsewhere and that he did not believe that he could be ridden off his dreams'. Amid the continuing drought and famine, bloodshed, election campaign, interspersed with communal riots, the reports that the Army may not really obey the British orders in India, the INA 'mutineers' emerging as public heroes, the number of European soldiers, already fatigued, rapidly going down, the alarmed Crown, finding that the Viceroy had become a pigmy in the face of the gargantuan problem called India, decided to send a Cabinet Mission. On 3 April 1946, Gandhi appeared before Wavell and told him that he sympathised with Jinnah and Muslims but, to him, Pakistan was a 'sin' he would not commit. For a moment, the Mahatma even appeared a 'patriot' in the classical sense, before he began, what he did best, to weave the web: 'The substance of Pakistan as he understood it was independence of culture and a legitimate ambition'. That is, the independence of the Muslim culture—from the Hindu culture, of course—and the legitimate ambition of Jinnah—to lead *his* country. Gandhi had an uncanny genius to create word-screen to keep his real intention hidden as he targeted the enemy: 'The two-nation theory is far more dangerous. The Muslim population is a population of converts...all descendants of Indian-born people'. That was the same as his argument before Sheth Abdullah in South Africa in the 1890s, only the converts there were Christians! Then he moved to prove Jinnah wrong: 'Jinnah is sincere but his logic is utterly at fault especially as a kind of mania possesses him. He himself was called a maniac and he therefore honoured Jinnah for his mania', is what Viceroy Wavell reported on what Gandhi told him about Jinnah. That is, Gandhi, the maniac, honoured Jinnah, the maniac! After this self-deprecation in one breath and Jinnah-bashing in another (if you hit yourself before hitting the enemy, you have the luxury of being non-violent!), 'He asked Jinnah whether his own son (Harilal Gandhi) who had gone over to the Muslim religion changed his nationality by doing so?'

And after this foreplay came to the fore the 'magnanimous' Mahatma, yet again: 'Let Mr Jinnah form the first Government and choose its personnel from elected representatives in the country.

The Viceroy would appoint them formally but, in fact, Mr Jinnah would choose. *If he does not do so then the offer to form a Government should be made to Congress*...The Interim Government must be absolutely national. Mr Jinnah could choose who he liked for his Government. *They would be subject to the vote of the Assembly from which they were drawn.*' Since, in any case, Jinnah will never form a government ***in*** India, Gandhi knew it was the Congress that was going to be invited to form the Interim Government; even if, by any chance, Jinnah did fall into the Congress trap, his ministers will be subject to the vote of the Assembly, that is, Hindu-majority! The 'Great Leader' would come abegging to the Mahatma to keep his government afloat. These intricacies were beyond the grasp of many of the 'secular' British who, being believers of high living and simple thinking, had no idea of the complicated Indian thought processes. But some Britons still had an inkling of what Gandhi meant. Lord Pethick-Lawrence 'reminded' Gandhi that since the Muslim League had not won a majority of Assembly seats, most of Jinnah's ministers will have to be Hindus! From parties other than the League! Gandhi smiled and said he understood the 'difficulties of the situation'!

Predictably, Jinnah would not fall into the old, Khadi-woven trap Gandhi had set up again for him in a new situation; the 'Great Leader' would rather be the Sultan of a small island than be the *Samrat* (Emperor) of an infidel sub-continent his enemy was offering: a veritable beehive gift-packaged! When he met the Mission, the humiliation his own grandfather had suffered from the caste Hindus way back in the 19th century Gujarat was, apparently, uppermost on his mind. Arguing that India had never been united except under the Muslim and the British rule, Jinnah came to the core of the Muslim problem in the country: 'A Hindu will wash his hands after shaking hands with a Muslim...No Hindu will let me (Mr Jinnah) have a room in his building. Hindu society and philosophy are the most exclusive in the world...How are you to put 100 million Muslims together with 250 millions whose way of life is so different.' When Cripps told him that a Bengali Hindu was more similar to a Bengali Muslim rather than a Punjabi Hindu, Jinnah said the 'fundamentals' were common to all Muslims: all the Muslims, he said, believed in

One God, in the equality of men and in human Brotherhood. 'The Hindus believe in none of these principles.' The Mission offered Jinnah to provide a defence cover for Pakistan but he demanded a completely sovereign Pakistan, saying that once the principle of the new nation was accepted, its areas could be discussed. He wanted six provinces as also Calcutta whose 600,000 Hindus, mostly depressed classes, he hoped would go to Pakistan—and convert to Islam!

Even as Jinnah debated Pakistan with Britain—no lawyer trained at the Bar in London had, perhaps, ever discussed dismemberment of the British Empire with His Majesty's Government itself!—the newly-elected Muslim representatives to the provincial and central assemblies took a pledge in New Delhi in April 1946, 'in the name of Allah, the Most Beneficent, the Most Merciful', to dedicate themselves to achieve and safeguard Pakistan. On 5 May, Jinnah, who had complained to the British about Hindu puritanism, refused to shake hands himself with Maulana Azad when they met Wavell in Shimla. As Nehru, Jinnah, Patel and others engaged in wordy duels, Pethick-Lawrence came up with a three-tier formula—a powerful All-India Union Government and Legislature, provincial governments and the Groups of Provinces (ie. Pakistan)—which Gandhi rejected arguing that *90 million Muslims would enjoy 'parity' over 200 million Hindus, an idea worse than Pakistan*.

For the first time, Gandhi had shown his aces. No longer was he talking in terms of giving concessions to the Muslims to keep them in India. Now he openly said he did not want the minority Muslims to be equated with the majority Hindus. He thus pushed Pakistan one more step out of India.

Never used to such hard-bargaining, the exasperated British found themselves at the end of their tether—in any case, India was a mere colony annexed by the British through intrigue and bloodshed for the simple reason of sophisticated robbery; they had no emotional, spiritual or religious, or even political, attachment to the land to indulge in prolonged, hard bargaining and had no stakes whatsoever in this so-called Jewel of their Crown. Pethick-Lawrence asked Jinnah to give him in *writing* the precise demands. On 11 May, both Jinnah and Azad submitted their demands in writing: two Muslims arguing over the 'ownership' of Hindustan! Five days later, the Cabinet

Mission rejected the demand for Pakistan saying it would not solve the communal minority problem but only raise many more. It proposed a modified three-year system for India. In a statement, the Mission warned India of a 'grave danger of violence, chaos and even civil war. The result and duration of such a disturbance cannot be foreseen; but it is certain that it would be a terrible disaster for many millions of men, women and children', and appealed to the '400 million Indians' to cooperate in implementation of the proposals.

Gandhi ignored the warning and welcomed the arriving British departure. The British had taken the call for 'Quit India' quite seriously. The Mahatma remarked that 'Whatever the wrong done to India by the British rule, if the statement of the Mission was genuine, as I believe it was, it was in discharge of an obligation they had declared the British owed to India, namely, to get off India's back. *It contained the seed to convert this land of sorrow into one without sorrow and suffering*'. Thus, he clearly saw the British taking along Pakistan in their wake and thus rid India of its sorrow and suffering. Why? Because Gandhi knew that the British would never depart without dividing India—irrespective of their historic in-house animosity, a devout Christian, howsoever mild or liberated, would tend to favour a Jew or a Muslim, and vice-versa, over a Chinese, Japanese or a Hindu because of their common ancestry in the Abrahamic Family—but it would still be a good riddance for the Hindus as the step 'contained the seed to convert this land of sorrow into one without sorrow and suffering'. Jinnah reacted sharply over the Mission's statement but sought time to 'consult (his) working committee'—all working committees in all political parties in Independent India as well have often been rubber-stamps of their Presidents, who pack these panels with their toadies—as the hot-headed Khaksars were readying for a Jihad against the Hindus of Punjab that would have spoiled the Jinnah recipe he had so arduously prepared. The Mahatma and the Great Leader waited for each other to make the next move; Gandhi, meanwhile, engaged in scuttling the British move to keep its armies in the 'Groups of Provinces'—a euphemism for the gang of feudal lords who were mortally afraid of losing their fiefdoms.On the other hand, on 24 May, Jinnah told Major Woodrow Wyatt that the need of the hour was a 'surgical operation'. That the British should remain as the uniting forces at the Centre for at least 15 years and deal with defence and foreign policy matters for 'Hindustan and Pakistan'. Unlike the Congress, which insisted on the total withdrawal of the British, he wanted the Crown to remain in India until Pakistan found its feet. By June 1946, he, therefore, came round to let his League become part of the Interim Government. This would make him a 'reasonable' leader; and he was sure that Nehru, a popular leader with gift of the gab but cursed with lack of political subtlety, administrative or diplomatic capability, would mess up the things to prove that no Throne has place for two Kings, perhaps even before the Interim Government came to power. Expectedly, Nehru did not disappoint Jinnah.

Gandhi warned Field Marshal Wavell that he 'will never succeed in riding two horses at the same time. Choose the names submitted either by the Congress or the League. For God's sake, do not make an incompatible mixture and in trying to do so produce a fearful explosion…I hope I have made my meaning clear'. By now, Wavell had seen through the Mahatma's game and described him as an 'exceedingly shrewd, obstinate, domineering, double-tongued, single-minded politician; and there is little true saintliness in him'. Realising the futility of its attempts, the British government in London now braced secretly to evacuate Europeans from India should the two-nation country explode in the increasingly widening political vacuum. It was like the year 711 when Muhammad bin-Qasim had found India attractive because of a similarly widening political vacuum in which Islam could step in; now, Mamad Ali bin-Jhinabhai Thakkar had created a reverse vacuum to enable Hinduism to step in again and make Islam exit.

After failure of the Shimla Conference in that summer of 1946, even Jinnah had lost faith in the British; he had lost faith in the Congress in 1920 itself. Nothing seemed to work for this brilliant lawyer who had once touched the zenith in his profession but nadir in the dirtiest game of politics now. He apprehended that, with his health continuously failing, he would not be able to see 'Pakistan' in his lifetime if the Muslims did not use their ultimate weapon, the Sword, that had brought and established them in Hindustan. Like any other consummate, professional politician, he had no compunction in using any means if that brought in the desired end. His Thakkar-brand obstinacy had brought him so far and created a huge Muslim constituency for him in the sub-continent; his Ismaeli genes now catalysed him to unsheathe his sword to draw blood. Late in July 1946, he told a League council meeting in Bombay: 'If there is not sufficient power, create it. All efforts of the Muslim League at fair play, justice, even supplications and prayers have had no response of any kind from the Congress. The Cabinet Mission have played into the hands of the Congress...We worked with clean hands. The League is the only party that has emerged from these negotiations with honour and clean hands.'

Jinnah had forgotten everything of his own past. He now remembered only one thing: Pakistan. After many false starts so far, Gandhi's first turning of the ignition key in 1915 had finally started the Jinnah engine. From his experience in South Africa, the Mahatma had known that conversion of the infidel to any of the Abrahamic religions, in effect, potentially uprooted and orphaned the convert. If a man like Jinnah, at best a heretic Muslim, could denationalise himself to this extent, imagine the effect on others. How far had his Faith brought him from his roots became clear when, reacting angrily to Pethick-Lawrence's comment in the House of Lords that he (Jinnah) could not have a monopoly to nominate Muslims in the Interim Government, the Great Leader lost his balance: 'I am not a trader. I am not asking for concessions for oil, nor am I higgling and haggling like a *bania*.' He did not realise that he had patiently negotiated his way up like an obstinate bania that had brought him so far and was now rejecting his roots, his forefathers' profession, like a Sunni orthodox.

On 29 July 1946, the League resolved that, '...it has become abundantly clear that the Muslims of India would not rest contented with anything less than the immediate establishment of an Independent and fully sovereign state of Pakistan...the time has come for the Muslim nation to resort to **Direct Action** to achieve Pakistan to assert their just rights, to vindicate their honour and to get rid of the present British slavery and the contemplated future Caste-Hindu domination'.

And Jinnah declared: 'We have taken a most historic decision. Never before in the whole life-history of the Muslim League did we do anything except by constitutional methods and constitutional talks. We are today forced into this position by a move in which both the Congress and Britain have participated...Today we have said good-bye to constitutions and constitutional methods. Throughout the painful negotiations, the two parties with whom we bargained held a pistol at us; one with power and machine-guns behind it, and the other with non-cooperation and the threat to launch mass civil disobedience. This situation must be met. We also have a pistol.'

This demonstrated three basic weaknesses of political Islam, indeed of classical Judaism and Christianity as well, although to a lesser extent: that it never believed in democracy and modernity and preferred violent means to achieve ends and short-cut evolutionary processes; that it has always, like its predecessor Judaism and Christianity, believed that those not following its dictates were *persecuting* it and that there could be no side of truth other than the one shown by the Founder of the Faith concerned. And this also demonstrated the utter frustration of Islam when forced to retreat by a hostile people unwilling to accept its perceived 'superiority'. In Jinnah's case, however, this frustration was of a peculiar nature: the Great Leader had made the defeated Muslims believe that, in departing from 'Hindustan', they had, in fact, been *victorious*! Unlike the retreating Moors of Spain in the 1490s, the retreating Muslims of India in the 1940s were not sighing but beating their chest in a wholesome, exhilarating defeat! It was truly Jinnah's miracle that he created a counter-mirage of 'freedom' for the Muslims who did not want to unshackle themselves from the mirage of Islam. But even the Hindus were not exactly above board: the Congress in 1965 and the BJP in 1999 similarly beat their chests after the Indian Army drove out the intruding Pakistanis from Kashmir as if kicking out an encroacher enemy from your own house called for celebration!

Wavell, who now understood Gandhi so well, did not know that Jinnah, despite his protestations, meant business. The Great Leader, as most Muslim leaders do, chose a *Friday*, 16 August 1946, as the ***Direct Action Day***, about which the League had 'authorised' him long ago. If, in their 'Final Solution', the Nazis wanted to weed out the minority Jews of Europe, in the Indian sub-continent, the League, representing a minority, wanted to root out the majority Hindus, or at least terrorise them into submission. Jinnah discovered an able Himmler in Bengal, Hussain Shahid Suhrawardy, who derived his surname from a 'peaceful' Sufi sect, to organise carnage of the infidel Hindus meticulously in his capacity as the volcanic province's Chief Minister. As Islam unshackled itself from the culture and civilisation of India, he declared to his armed mob: 'The Direct Action Day would prove to be the first step towards the Muslim struggle for emancipation.' Emancipation of the Muslims who were supposedly 'enslaved' by the Hindus! He then assured them that he had made 'all arrangements' with the police and military not to interfere in the holocaust he was plotting against the Hindus. Even the British, who had chosen to forget the 'mutineers' they had massacred en masse in the 1850s, were shocked at this unbridled savagery in which the Matrix called Islam had fully flowered now, first of all in Bengal where Muhammedanism had reached the last in India: the first smell of this Rafflesia had come from the nearly 20,000 bodies that lay strewn in the City of Death. Asked to react about the Great Calcutta Killing, Jinnah justified it like the Ismaeli leader killing 40,000 Sunni Muslims in Mecca a thousand years ago: 'If Congress regimes are going to suppress and persecute the Musalmans, it will be very difficult to control disturbances…In my opinion, there is no alternative except the outright establishment of Pakistan.' The Bengali Muslims would, however, be meted out the same treatment by the Punjabi Muslims in 1970, leading to vivisection of Pakistan and emergence of Bangladesh—and history is yet to come to full circle for them both. Wait, for the Jinnah seed has not yet reached its natural course of fruition.

Apart from Calcutta, Islam's flowering season hit other areas as well. The Interim Government headed by Nehru took office on 2 September 1946, and those Muslims who joined the bandwagon were targeted by their fellow fanatics. Next day, the Mahatma declared at his prayer meeting at Birla House, New Delhi, that the 'door to Poorna Swaraj (Total Independence) has, at last, been opened'. The elephantine British, having evolved into mice in their retrogressive metamorphosis in just seven years of the Second World War, realised they no longer ruled the Waves and decided to evacuate nearly

200,000 Europeans, half of them British soldiers, from India which they saw as a drowning Titanic. Wavell was neither a wave nor well, but flat; he was disliked by the 'ruling' Congress which demanded that he be removed for being 'supportive' of the League and for failing to convene the Constituent Assembly without which the Interim Government would remain what it was, interim. Wavell was forced to call in Gandhi, Jinnah and Nehru to meet him individually and found the Congress leaders did not want Jinnah and the League at all in the government or in the Constituent Assembly. In particular, the Viceroy reported to London, Gandhi wanted the Congress Party's 'domination'. 'The more I see of that old man', Wavell said, 'the more I regard him as an unscrupulous old hypocrite'. But the Viceroy somehow persuaded Jinnah, in October, to soften up and agree to let the League join the Nehru government. But the Great Leader was Great as a Leader: if Gandhi could use Azad, a Muslim, as a pawn, Jinnah, too, could nominate a Scheduled Caste Hindu member as one of his five 'Muslim' members in the government! If Gandhi could flaunt 'nationalist' Muslims like Azad, Jinnah could as well flaunt the Scheduled Castes as uncompromising with the Caste-Hindus! So, J N Mandal was included in the 'Muslim' League team, headed by Liaqat Ali Khan, to play against the Congress—in the continuing drama, another Mandal (Bindeshwari Prasad Mandal) would, through his famous report, decimate the age-old stranglehold of the high caste Hindus on Indian politics in the 1990s and bust the well-entrenched political gangsters through social engineering. The new 'coalition' of the Congress-League, like an impossible mixture of water and oil, was formed on 15 October, each directing its cadre not to take things lying down against the other. Liaqat Ali continued, as in a speech in Karachi on 20 October, to press for 'winning the goal of Pakistan'. The 'new' government of old, tired foxes assumed office on 26 October, as Wavell prodded Jinnah to stick to his strategy and gather support and strength for the Final Goal through the Interim Solution.

As the newly-elected Central Legislative Assembly met in New Delhi on 29 October, Nehru and Liaqat, pawns of Gandhi and Jinnah, respectively, sat side-by-side without recognising each other's presence while the Great Leader declared in mid-November that his League colleagues were in the Nehru ministry as watchdogs of the Muslim interests and soon thereafter announced that the League would not participate in the Constituent Assembly meeting called in to frame a Constitution for 'Hindustan'. Stumbling from one stalemate to another, British Prime Minister Clement Attlee decided to no longer waste his love of Labour and that delivery of an overgrown foetus, Pakistan, was the only solution; it could no longer be delayed. He called Jinnah to London. The Great Leader, keeping his approaching death a closely-guarded secret, embarked on his last journey to London in the Viceroy's plane at Karachi airport amidst chants of 'Pakistan Zindabad'(Long Live Pakistan) to give birth to a nation he believed was 'new', on the opposite banks of the River Sindhu or Indus that gave its name to Hindustan or India. It would, as 'Islam as a separate nation', be short-lived; its East Bengal wing, that became Bangladesh in 1971, was never any natural part of the separate 'nation'; the Rawalpindi-based military-theocratic mafia that always ruled 'Pakistan' never treated Dhaka as a brother but as a burdensome, despicable brother-in-law that came with the reverse-dowry and no one in 'Pakistan' really shed a tear at this Second Partition on the eve of the silver jubilee of the First. So much for the claim that monotheistic Islam acted as a cement to disparate ethnic people; on the contrary, the fissiparous, polytheistic Hinduism would be more tenacious in binding its adherents.

But, back in 1946, Jinnah, now the Sick Man of Asia, looked stronger at the end of the Second World War unlike the Caliph-cum-Sultan Mehmed Reshad, the Sick Man of Europe, at the end of the First War which eclipsed Islam in Europe: by retreating from India in the 1940s, Islamists sought to exhibit their exploits just like they had done in Spain in the 1490s. The British were 'happy' that their Empire was dissolving; and the Muslim Indians, too, being siblings of Christians, were happy at the prospects of Pakistan, not realising that Islam was, in fact, retreating. So no argument moved Jinnah in London as the Constituent Assembly met in New Delhi for the first time under the Chairmanship of Rajendra Prasad on 9 December 1946, with the League boycotting it completely; in a reversal of the tide of history, Prasad, as the first President of India, would soon preside over the reconstruction of the Somnath Temple, from where the crushing defeat, subjugation of Hinduism and the thousand-year-reign of aliens had begun. Churchill noted, during the India Debate in the House of Commons, that more casualties had been recorded during the four months of Nehru's Interim Government than in the previous nine decades of the Raj and this was only a beginning. He opposed Independence to India, or the 'Hindu reign' as he put it, on the ground that the subcontinent would be plunged into a civil war—the mother should not be allowed to deliver the child for the fear of her own death! About the Muslims, he said they numbered 90 millions and could not be described as a 'minority' or given a separate nation on that basis. But Churchill was past his prime, a cry in the wilderness. The malaise was deeper: bereft of any rejuvenating genes, unlike atheistic or polytheistic societies such as China and India, both Christianity and Islam were in the throes of exponential and unstoppable decay, trembling in the same Noah's Arc as the returning ancient infidel oceanic floods threatened to drown 'humanity' everywhere.

On 18 December 1946, Prime Minister Clement Attlee invited Lord 'Dicky' Mountbatten, the man with the 'fatal charm', to become the 19th and the Last Viceroy and perform the caesarian surgery. A day before, while returning to India, Jinnah visited Egypt to warn the Muslims at a conference there that they could be free only when Pakistan became a reality! Or else, the Hindu imperialists could annex the Middle East! The Great Leader, frail and weak, recognised the Disease and declared on 20 December: ***If India were to be ruled by the Hindu imperialists, it would be as big a menace for the future, if not bigger, as the British imperialist power has been... The whole of the Middle East would fall from frying pan into the fire...If a Hindu empire is achieved, it will mean the end of Islam in India, and even in other Muslim countries.*** No Muslim could ever be as prophetic after the Prophet! But Jinnah ignored the fact that Egypt itself was enjoying freedom from the yoke of the Caliphate that died two decades ago.

On 20 February 1947, Clement Attlee announced in the Commons his government's desire to 'transfer power into responsible Indian hands by June 1948', and appointment of Mountbatten as the last Viceroy. In the red-hot, post-Second World War era, things began to change swiftly thereafter: The very next day, under instructions from the Foreign Office, a British First Secretary informed the US State Department that Attlee's government would not redeem the pledge given earlier by Churchill at the Yalta Conference that Britain would monitor and superintend the security over the Mediterranean Sea, including allies like Greece and Turkey. This meant a huge emerging power vacuum in a Western Europe then facing the real threat of a Stalinist USSR, forcing the USA to step in: the Democrat Harry Truman enunciated the 'Truman Doctrine' in the US Congress on 12 March . . . within the next 100 days, the situation became so volatile for Britain within and without that it found the 'Jewel' heavier and hotter than the Crown itself. A fugitive Empire's Last Viceroy, on 3 June announced to *prepone* its escape from India to 15 August rather than waiting for June 1948.

Thus, the two beginnings, of decolonisation and the Cold War, took place within a 100 days' space, both accelerating the pace of deAbrahamisation across the world: the Jews were now returning to Israel, the Christians missionaries to their home countries and the Muslims to their own, wherever they could. Decolonisation and the Cold War would soon menstruate the 'Third World' and make them ready to receive the sperm of the Third Wave in the next few decades.

In India, the majority of Muslims were, like their Hindu neighbours from whom they had emerged, poor, illiterate and innocent, used by fanatics like cannon fodder. Within a week of the Attlee announcement in February 1947, the League's beasts had invaded courts and houses in Lahore to hoist their flag across the Punjab, accompanied by what they knew best—killing the infidels. They had begun to hone this acquired genetic mutation triggered by their conversion from Hinduism to Islam and would turn it upon themselves once they finished the Hindus once for all—as they do now daily in Pakistan and Afghanistan. The League's Direct Action began at a hundred places. Not that there were no saner voices amongst Muslims: Khizar Hayat Khan had to resign on 2 March for taking the League to task at Peshawar. The League had, by now, been transformed into Jinnah's own SS, a band of bandits and mass-murderers, a private army for the fulfilment of the ambitions of a private man with a private agenda. The Congress and the Akali Sikhs proclaimed 11 March as 'Anti-Pakistan Day' across the Punjab.

On 5 March, the Commons voted for the fastest politico-biotechnological surgery undertaken anywhere to deliver a mouse from the womb of an elephant. Three days later, the Congress reluctantly conceded Muslim-majority districts as 'Pakistan'. Jinnah was elated at this pyrrhic victory: reacting to it, he told journalists in Bombay on 12 March that 'We have got to stand on our own legs. We are...not only different from the Hindu organisations but are, in fact, in conflict...We have no common ground for cooperation... God willing, we shall have full Pakistan now'. Unperturbed by the continuing bloodshed led by Muslim army, civil and police officials—in March itself, several hundred lives had perished in 'Pakistan'—Jinnah had now completely forgotten that he had resigned from the Congress in 1920 because the latter was *appeasing* the Muslims; coming full circle, he was now satisfied that the Congress was appeasing the Hindus! Islam had mutated this great patriot into a pariah in his own land of birth.

It was time Muhammed (Ali Jinnah) met his match in a Madanmohan Krishna (Menon). On 13 March, this roving ambassador to Nehru suggested to Mountbatten that there should, in fact, be, not one, but two 'Pakistans'. In the Northwest, the Punjab and Sindh should both be partitioned. The charismatic Nehru, on the other hand, meeting his match in Mountbatten, for once sized up his political rival Jinnah who had, however, seen in the Mahatma his real adversary: Jawaharlal told Dicky that Jinnah had ensured that Pakistan should never be subjected to constructive criticism simply because the new 'nation' would not be able to stand to it. Islam, like the desert it had sprouted in, never had a solid foundation anyway and moved like a sand-dune, wherever the winds carried it: the 'nation' created in the guise of Islam's 'separate identity' could, therefore, never be based on reason or vision but on illusion, the mirage in the desert of mind. Pakistan will have to rid itself of this acquired genetic disorder only by mutating back into Hinduism.

Within ten days of his taking over as the Viceroy, Mountbatten met the Indian Mount not beaten by the winds of history. Gandhi, on the contrary, was returning the monsoon of history triggered by Mount Sinai and Mount Hira over the last two millennia. As if squeezing the Muslim mind to the last drop, he, *even now*, suggested that Jinnah be called to form a Cabinet! The Congress would guarantee cooperation with Mountbatten as an umpire, provided Jinnah disbanded all private armies like the 'National Guards', *worked for the Indian people as a whole,* and even prepare for Pakistan 'peacefully', with the proviso that if the Great Leader rejected the offer, the Congress be invited to take it. The Viceroy never carried this 'formula' to Jinnah but discussed it with Nehru who was shocked at the Mahatma's attempt to replace his disciple (Nehru) with his adversary! Nehru fancied himself as a 'historian' of sorts without ever trying to learn lessons from this subject; Gandhi had learnt lessons of history very well from Mother Nature and, therefore, the stocks called Jinnah and Nehru did not matter to him more than their real market capitalisation on the bourses, and net worth. The Mahatma's objective was, apparently, to prove that Islam, as it existed now, was untrustworthy tenant in any other culture and civilisation and even the most 'modern' *Muslim* would often remain true to the original meaning of this Arabic word, a *traitor*, to the host country. Nehru and other Congressmen, on the other hand, were practical, short-term politicians who had, by now, tasted enough power to reject their own Master's formula. And Gandhi knew his disciples as well as he X-rayed Jinnah to his bones; but, after 1947, Patel did successfully unite and consolidate India for the first time after Ashoka under a *central* Hindu regime.

For the first time, Mountbatten met Jinnah on 5 April. The Sick Man suggested, what else, a 'surgical operation' on India or see it balkanised; the Viceroy asked him for an 'anaesthetic' before this surgery. The Great Leader regretted that he had only one vote, that of himself, whereas the Mahatma always had three or four (his own, and that of Nehru, Patel and Azad), that Gandhi claimed to represent none but enjoyed enormous power without responsibility. Mountbatten tried to flatten Jinnah's claims of Muslims as a united nation vis-a-vis a divided 'Hindustan': by the same yard stick, the Muslims, too, would have to be divided on ethnic lines! Jinnah was perturbed, calling it an attempt to gift him a 'moth-eaten' Pakistan. On 9 and 10 April, the Viceroy found Jinnah as a 'psychopathic case' who would neither listen to any reason, nor had thought out any plans or schemes as to the future of Pakistan. 'Mr Jinnah...has not thought out one single piece of the mechanics of his own great scheme, and he will have the shock of his life when he really has to come down to earth and try and make his vague idealistic proposals work on a concrete basis...He could not provide a single feasible argument in favour of Pakistan. In fact, he offered no counter-arguments. He gave the impression that he was not listening.' The brilliant secular lawyer, who mesmerised the courts once upon a time, had, as a 'Muslim' leader, lost all reasoning power and arguments. Islam had irreparably damaged him; in retaliation, he would do the same unto the Muslims—in fact, he had no vision for Pakistan's development and had simply dumped the new 'nation' out of India from where he transported it lock, stock and barrel the way a coolie heaves a sigh of relief after unburdening himself of the alien weight. As Mountbatten noted, 'He was, whatever was said, intent on his Pakistan—which could surely only result in doing the Muslims irreparable damage'. Until he met Jinnah, Mountbatten could never believe that someone could be simply so completely devoid of any sense of logic or responsibility and could hold such a sway on power; Jinnah was like a heartless, copycat municipal worker on duty to throw out the 'encroachers' unmindful of what would they do in a hostile weather. Both Jinnah and Nehru were racing against time to enjoy the fruits of their 'labour' at least in the twilight years of their advanced ages. Unlike the 78-year-old Mahatma, the 58-year-old Nehru had aged fast mentally as he tried to position himself as a world-class 'statesman'; Drs J A L Patel and Colonel Rahman, personal physicians of Jinnah, on the other hand, kept the Great Leader's debilitating diseases and impending death a closely-guarded secret lest its exposure abort the birth of Pakistan.

That fateful year, 1947, like 711, was destined to decide the future creed of India; it was a year of political hysteria—there were no real heroes, not even Gandhi or Jinnah, nor were there any villains. For, one's hero was another's villain, one's martyr another's traitor. Partition was painful to everyone but inevitable. Jinnah was losing his mental faculties and balance along with physical strength with his persecution mania as dreadful as his sister Fatima's; she egged him on to breakaway from Hindustan as she egged him on to dissociate from his only child, the daughter Dina. The Prophet's daughter, Fatima, was a cementing bond in the First Family of Islam; here was the Great Leader's sister, also named Fatima, who had totally cut off her brother from the world of reality and relations and, on the contrary, destroyed both his family and reputation instead of being a source of strength to the lonely and sick Jinnah. Even the Pakistanis did not like this fanatical and scheming *Madar-e-Watan* (Mother of the Nation) of theirs who would be comprehensively defeated by the first military President, 'Field Marshal' Ayub Khan, in an election in the 1960s. Incidentally, Ayub Khan was the one who 'revealed' an age-old reality when he said that democracy was simply not suitable to the 'genius of Pakistan'.

After many a 'proposal' that fell by the wayside, Mountbatten informed Premier Attlee on 19 May 1947, about the inevitability of conceding Pakistan to prevent the Muslim League from directly resorting to arms; indirectly, the League hooligans, leading frenzied mobs, were already engaged in routine massacres in areas where the Hindus and Sikhs were in minority. Jinnah, who had discovered that the British were bent upon gifting him a 'moth-eaten' Pakistan by dividing the Punjab and Bengal, was now demanding an 800-mile 'corridor' cutting across North India to link the eastern and western wings of Pakistan. Realising that Jinnah would, like a government employee, put forth new demands if you concede old, Krishna Menon informed Mountbatten on 21 May that Nehru and Patel would accept the Dominion status if given that very year, 1947. Both the Prime Minister and the Viceroy were ready to accept and sought that old warhorse Churchill's Conservative help. Old and ailing, Churchill advised Jinnah, another old and ailing conservative, to accept Pakistan with 'both hands', that is its two wings in the east and west. On 2 June, finding that Jinnah was still adamant, the Viceroy had to virtually browbeat and arm-twist the Great Leader into supplication and forced him not to raise any fresh objections or demands: 'I have only one condition, and that is that when I say at the meeting in the morning, 'Mr Jinnah has given me assurances which I have accepted and which satisfy me,' *you will in no circumstances contradict that, and that when I look towards you, you will nod.*' Like an arm-twisted Gujarati businessman, that was precisely what a meek Jinnah did!

Next morning, Jinnah nodded to accept the 'moth-eaten' Pakistan: the once unputdownable lawyer had, having lost all his arguments, been forced to accept a judgment which could not be appealed against in any other court of law. Gone was all his bravado as he, his tail firmly turned, went to All-India Radio that evening to announce, along with Mountbatten, Nehru and Baldev Singh, the birth of a two-headed conjoined child, Pakistan—and even these heads, Bengal and Punjab, were ethnically divided to remain one part each in Hindustan and Pakistan. Calcutta, where the Great Game started with the Partition of Bengal in 1905, was to remain with the infidel Hindus; this triggered strong protest with the Muslims being deprived of the then financial Capital 'merely for the sake of 600,000 Hindus'. The volatile Khaksars clashed with the League at its last meeting held in India, at New Delhi, on 9 and 10 June, accusing them of betraying Islam. The Muslims had lost Delhi in 1857 and Calcutta 90 years later; the only financial consolation Pakistan had was Karachi, the port town of Jinnah; Dacca (Dhaka) was, at best, a burden due to its bulging population and poverty. The Khaksars, who had once failed to assassinate Jinnah, wanted to kill him again. The Muslims at this League meeting had tears in their swollen eyes, not because of being overwhelmed by emotions at the losses or gains of Pakistan: they had merely been tear-gassed by the police which prevented them from going after each other's throats as a rehearsal before they accelerated the massacre of Hindus and Sikhs. Chaudhary Rahmat Ali's 'Pakistan National Movement', too, came alive from woodworks to denounce Jinnah's 'compromise' as a humiliation, the 'Greatest Betrayal' and an unmitigated insult to the entire *Millat*, the International Muslim Brotherhood—as humiliating as the abolition of the Caliphate in 1924.

Gandhi had successfully enlarged and transformed the short-lived Partition of Bengal into the long-living Partition of India and was at peace with himself. Jinnah, on the other hand, was described by the League as *Shahenshah-e-Pakistan* ('Emperor of Pakistan'). Ironically, a 'nation' dominated by the Sunnis would have in its Father a heretic Muslim with an Iranian, Shia title. The last Mughal Emperor, Bahadur Shah 'Zafar' was supposedly the ruler of the 'whole' of infidel India in 1857; the first 'Muslim' Emperor of Pakistan, Jinnah, would be supposedly the ruler of the 'whole' of his new nation full of old prejudices. For the first time in history, a Gujarati had become ruler of (partitioned) part of India dominated by the Punjabis and Bengalis! And, for the first time, a Gujarati had paid Mehmood Ghaznavi's ghost in the same coin. With Jinnah began a new trend: abroad, the Gujarati businessmen would, henceforth, be known as akin to those hockey players who would refrain from scoring a goal, having set up a kiosk at the (penalty) corner awarded to them!

Nehru had a somewhat global, modern, even scientific outlook and, unlike a conservative, old-fashioned fiercely patriotic Patel who would commence rebuilding the Somnath Temple, Motilal's son would bequeath to an Independent India its democracy and science and technology. But Nehru had his own limitations at that time; not to be left behind by Jinnah, he had his own plans. Being aged, he could no longer raise a fresh family. So he settled to raise a Dynasty, the first Brahmin dynasty to rule from the political centre of India after the Shung Dynasty, launched by Pushyamitra who had assassinated the last Mauryan king Brihadritha in the second century BC. At the very first meeting of the Interim Cabinet, Nehru, who often seasoned his short-temper with short-sight, appointed his sister, Vijay Laxmi Pandit, as an Ambassador, and clashed with Liaqat Ali Khan over the latter's 'feudal' trend smacking of crass nepotism! Mountbatten had to shout down the two 'leaders' to make them fall in line.

For the first time in their history in India, the Muslim hotheads had been forced to accept a *compromise* with the infidel Hindus—non-Muslims would not understand the severe pain this would cause to the Muslim fanatic who would nurse this wound generation after generation. The League acknowledged as much in its resolution when it used this word instead of *settlement*. But the cronies' Congress, with its singular lack of knowledge of irony and humours of history, despite that 'historian' Nehru at the helms, opposed the word 'compromise' and pressed for a 'settlement'! That is, a permanent Partition of India! On 27 June, on Jinnah's suggestion, the British appointed Sir Cyril Radcliffe to chair the boundary commissions and carve out Pakistan. As he began to cut away Pakistan according to Islam's known size, rather than its exorbitant claims, 10 million people, running for shelter either under the umbrella of the Great Soul or the Great Leader, would cross the Radcliff Line, both ways, in the next few months. A mauled Islam would walk out of India trampling half-a-million of them. Mountbatten, who had delivered the two-headed Pakistan, would now have a taste of Jinnah, who insisted on becoming the Governor-General of Pakistan himself, rather than let the Last Viceroy and Independent Hindustan's first G-G become the first G-G of Pakistan as well. For, Jinnah knew he had only a few months to survive; he had been a successful lawyer but had never tasted the fruit of political power so far. He would not be a mere Premier burdened with day-to-day donkey work. Although he could not anoint himself as an old-style Emperor—he was too 'modern' for that!—he could at least become Head of the State, on par with at least Mountbatten, if not the Crown from whose government he had 'wrested' Pakistan. Moreover, if he became the PM of Pakistan, he would merely be the counterpart of Nehru, PM of Hindustan; he never saw in Jawaharlal his equal, even despised him, and always tried to be treated at par with the Mahatma and both ended up as Fathers of their respective nations. In India, on the other hand, it was a unique situation: Gandhi's first heir and father-in-law of his son, Chakravarti Rajagopalachari, would be the first and last Governor-General and his second heir, Nehru, the Prime Minister. On Friday, 18 July, King George VI approved the India Independence Bill. It was a 'family' affair on both the sides and the Crown was satisfied that the future of monarchy, with different masks, would remain as safe as in the past.

The Jinnahs, who had all but forgotten Gujarat, their homeland, and came from the mirage of Karachi, Sindh, to settle down in Mumbai, now sold off their Malabar Hill house. The story of the arrival of Islam began in Kerala where, at Kodungallur, the first-ever mosque anywhere outside Arabia, called the Cheraman Perumal Juma

Masjid, was built in the year 629 even before Muhammed conquered Mecca; the first mosque was built by the Prophet outside Medina. Interestingly, it was also in Kodungallur where St Thomas set up the first Church in 52 AD and the Jews came in 378 AD.

The containment of Islam had begun in the Malabar region of Kerala with the Adi Shankaracharya setting out to start a psychological warfare in the eighth century; Islam's return journey had begun in the same Malabar region with the Moplahs massacring thousands of Hindus in the early 1920s; in the late 1940s, there was no need for the Malabar Hill house where the exit of Islam had been plotted to clinical precision.

The Hindus regard coconut, the fruit of Malabar, as a holy offering, and value the Malabar-induced monsoon like a lifeline. The Malayalam word *Kerala* itself means coconut. Coconut's hardware protects the software inside, a la Jinnah; the Mahatma was like Arabian date, whose hardware was protected by the software *installed* outside!

Jinnah had nothing to do with those infidel symbols. Financially, he had always been a meticulous and honest man. He paid his income tax until the last date of his residence in India, 6 August 1947. Next day, he flew back from Mumbai to Karachi, the new Capital, on completion of his mission. He wanted to take a much-deserved rest. There, he revealed to his aide S M Ahsan that he never expected to see Pakistan become a reality in his lifetime—he did not know that Jinnah or no Jinnah, Islam's time was up in India. After a long time, Jinnah slept a full night, free of worries and nightmares.

But not his old adversary; he knew his work was still incomplete. The Great Soul, who had made himself strong through fasts and slows, words and silences, would be as busy as a bee. India was soaked in communal bloodshed with continuing riots and train-loads of corpses running on smoking steam engines across the new, bloody borders marked by Islam. Gandhi travelled to Noakhali in Bengal to douse the communal fires. There, the Mahatma announced to spend the rest of his life in Pakistan to look after the minorities! Who were these minorities, any way? The Hindus, of course. In India the same Mahatma was the spokesman of the majority, the Hindus; in Pakistan, he would be the spokesman of the minorities, the Hindus. But this was a pure, Mahatma-like bluff no one dare call.

Addressing the Constituent Assembly of Pakistan for the first time on 11 August 1947, Jinnah described the new nation as a 'cyclonic revolution', an 'unprecedented' phenomenon that was inevitable. And then came his innermost beliefs to the fore, even deeper than his 'roots' in Islam: '...because even as regards Muslims, you have Sunnis, Shias, Pathans, Punjabis and amongst the Hindus you have Brahmins, Khatris, Vaishnavas, also Bengalis, Madrasis etc.' These 'angularities', he hoped, will vanish. 'Indeed, if you ask me this has been the biggest hindrance in the way of India to attain her Independence and freedom and but for this we would have been free peoples long, long ago.'

Then he became emotional and spoke the way he used to do as the Ambassador of Hindu-Muslim Unity in the pre-Gandhian Congress of 1915, and spoke like a Hindu: *You are free to go to your temples... mosques or to any other place of worship in this Pakistan... You may belong to any religion of caste or creed—that has nothing to do with the business of the State... We are starting with this fundamental principle that we are all equal citizens of one State.* But, on 24 January 1948, in a speech to the Sindh Bar Association, Jinnah retracted from this much-publicised commitment to democratic citizenship and secularism made in the Pakistan Constituent Assembly. He now declared that 'Islamic law alone would be the foundation of the Pakistan Constitution' to make it a 'truly great Islamic State'.

Never was this Muhammedan dilemma—of being Islamic *as well as* democratic—so acute as in Jinnah's life. He had wrested Pakistan as a homeland for the fanatic Muslims and was now talking in their own language. Gandhi was threatening to 'invade' Pakistan, and Jinnah was threatening to follow India's Hindus. BJP leader L K Advani, a Sindhi migrant-turned-Hindu leader in India, during his 2005 'friendly' tour of Pakistan, quoted Jinnah's 'secularism' and became a Jinnah-like pariah for many Hindus; not to be left behind, another BJP leader, Major Jaswant Singh, followed suit.

This was what Gandhi always knew *will* happen, given his unfathomable knowledge of things Abrahamic—but not lesser mortals who never read beyond words. The Mahatma never revealed it to anybody for obvious reasons: Islam, being a Second Wave cult, is incompatible with modernity and science, simply incapable of midwifing the children of democracy to maturity in the Third Wave. This was what Pakistan, or any other Islamic country, was destined to become until the vagaries of Nature and their Wave Movements deIslamised them bit by bit, decade after decade and centuries after centuries, by unspooling and unknotting the Abrahamic Web.

But in that temporary reverse osmosis, Jinnah, the 'villain' of the Hindus, had even tried an image makeover on 11 August by being somewhat magnanimous: 'I think we should keep in front of us as our ideal and you will find that in course of time, Hindus would cease to be Hindus and Muslims would cease to be Muslims, not in the religious sense, because that is the personal faith of each individual, but in the political sense as citizens of the State...' On 11 August, the Father of the Muslim Nation was trying to recall his own hidden Hindu seeds, but failed on that fateful 24 January the following year when relapse occurred.

On 13 August, the day of the formal transfer of power, Jinnah received Mountbatten at Karachi airport and invited him to lunch, not knowing that it was the Muslim holy month of Ramzan! After all, Jinnah had never observed a fast. When the Great *Muslim* Leader came to know what Islam required of him, he changed the lunch to a dinner party, or *Iftaar*.

Next day, 14 August, when the Mountbattens returned to Delhi, was when the Radcliff Awards were announced, triggering mass slaughter and counter-slaughter in Lahore, Amritsar and a number of cities, towns, villages. Gandhi's fast-unto-death in Bengal, however, worked as a miracle and the blood-letting slowly subsided. The man had this magnetic, mesmeric, moral quality, despite his suspected political machinations and hypocrisy, that he could force you to create peace simply by threatening to go to war against himself! Like those immortal, recurring monsoon clouds that force the Indian Earth, year after year, to create Life simply by dashing themselves against the mountains and committing suicide, Gandhi was embodiment of a monsoon cloud. Even those who knew that the man was, at least on political issues, a wily fox, admitted his moral superiority and the ability to move mountains. He was too human to be a devil; but he was merciless enough to let things take their natural path. He considered India bitten by a monsoon bug and decided that bad, poisoned blood must be allowed to ooze out, so that the body was saved: that was how he paved the way for Islam's return journey as a moral course but opposed excessive blood-letting that could kill the patient.

But Jinnah's Pakistan was bankrupt since birth—it remained so even thereafter, depending always on doles and donations and hoaxes, the World Bank and the IMF. It was so bankrupt that it had to seek a loan of Rs 20 crore from the Nizam of Hyderabad to run day-to-day affairs in September 1947; but that did not prevent either Jinnah or his cohorts to show off their 'wealth'. A profligate Pakistan immediately purchased a house in Washington for $150,000 to serve as the impoverished nation's Chancery, an aircraft for a similar amount and a super-limousine for $6,000 for the new 'Emperor'. Nehru and Patel wanted to withhold the payment of Rs 550 million as Pakistan's share in the Reserve Bank cash balances to teach Jinnah a lesson; but Gandhi forced them to part with the money. It was not the Mahatma's magnanimity. He saw it pointless to rob a beggar; secondly, he knew that most Indians treated creation of Pakistan as a good riddance and would not like to be blamed as defaulters themselves, especially not by the impoverished and scheming enemy; thirdly, India, as a new nation, needed to be seen as honest in its dealings internationally so as to earn goodwill; fourthly, the gesture demonstrated that the foundations of the Islamic nation were, after all, cemented by the infidel money; fifthly, the Mahatma was aware that Patel was preparing to take 'police action' against Hyderabad which was scheming to join Pakistan—so, the message to go would be while the government of India was throwing the 'hell out of here' by giving away Rs 550 million to Pakistan, it would take strong action against any of the princelets who privately dared to assist Pakistan financially or otherwise from Indian soil.

The Muslim separatists were still busy against India. The Muslim Nawab of Junagarh, Gandhi's own backyard in Gujarat, too, was plotting to merge with Pakistan. Sir Shahnawaz Bhutto, the Sindhi Hindu-convert land-owner and father/grandfather of two future Prime

Ministers of Pakistan—one of them hanged by an Islamabad apparently 'annoyed' with him for pledging to fight India for a thousand years, the other assassinated in 2008 by Islamists themselves—was the main conspirator in this operation. But Patel knew how to deal with these in-house Pakistanis still resident in India: he supported anti-Nawab agitations in Junagarh and Bhopal and integrated these erstwhile 'Muslim' States having Hindu majority. There was, however, a 'Hindu' state with Muslim majority, Kashmir, that was, as Pa 'K' istan's jewel, still out of bounds. The Muslims saw no contradiction in their 'policy' of mergers with Pakistan: Hyderabad, Bhopal and Junagarh, being Hindu-majority but Muslim-ruled, should merge with Pakistan; Kashmir, Hindu-ruled but Muslim-majority, should ***also*** merge with Pakistan! Wherever there was a single Muslim, there must be a portion of Pakistan, as it were. No wonder, many Muslims found it difficult to rent a house in Hindu areas across India ever since formation of Pakistan, lest they encroached and grabbed the property.

As Gandhi celebrated his last, 78th birthday, on 2 October 1947, the Kashmir crisis cropped up with its short-sighted 'King', Sir Hari Singh, signing a 'standstill agreement' with Pakistan to prevent the Muslims in the Valley from revolting with cross-border support. India had, so far, had to deal with 'intellectuals' of the three Presidencies of Calcutta (East), Bombay (West) and Madras (South)—who thought it their birth-right to rule the riff-raff called Hindustan and Gandhi had to employ his utmost political skills to clear this scholarly mess to make the Freedom Movement a truly national one. The slot of North was still vacant, making it an incomplete (N)EWS, as incomplete as Pa(K)istan. The Kashmiri Hindus and those who converted to Islam, who, like their counterparts in the three erstwhile Presidencies, were given to treat the rest of 'India' as a subhuman settlement, now filled the slot and tightened the noose around their own neck. Unlike the three Presidencies on the Indian mainland, theirs being a border state, they could even think of remaining 'independent' of both India and Pakistan. They were, therefore, destined to remain slave to both. The 'superior' Aryan Kashmiris, who believed they were as unadulterated as their winter snow, fell victim to their overpowering ego. But their ego was pampered by certain Brahmins of Varanasi who did not allow re-conversion of the Kashmiri Muslims back to the Hindu fold in the middle of the 19th century and they, instead, became hyper-active in converting the entire Valley to Islam. The Kasmiris' Hinduism proved to be hollow. They had no capacity or will to meet the Islamic onslaught unlike the millions of Hindus in the mainland. The Kashmiri Pandits, both Hindus and Muslims (even after they converted to Islam)—there were no other dominant Hindu castes there—were merely literate, not educated, and helplessly witnessed their winter snow succumbing to the summer sands from Arabia.

The procrastinating Maharaja, who was ironically named after Lord Krishna, helplessly saw 5,000 Pakistani army men 'volunteers', dressed as Kashmiri *kabayalis* (tribals), invading the land in British vehicles, ostensibly to rescue the Muslims from 'Hindu tyranny'. Hari Singh, like Nehru, had never been accused of any political savvy whatsoever and the two fellow Kashmiris (The Nehrus, too, were Kashmiri Pandits who had settled down in Allahabad), suffering from incurable cancer of superiority complex, now set out to further mess it up. When the monarch sought help, Mountbatten despatched V K Krishna Menon to have Hari Singh sign an accession agreement; the King, too clever by half, refused. His Prime Minister, M C Mahajan, however, tried to salvage the situation by agreeing to Delhi, saying he would be forced to seek Jinnah's help in securing Srinagar if Nehru failed to provide immediate military assistance. Jawaharlal again proved myopic—many Congressmen even wondered why the Mahatma had anointed him as his successor in the first place! The reason was, perhaps, Gandhi did not have any other *Brahmin* of matching social stature and background to be groomed in the most populous North India, as a counter-balance to the Congress leaders of the three Presidencies; moreover, Nehru, with his socialist pretensions and capitalist tastes, had, admirably, set up a network of international leaders and armchair 'intellectuals' to associate with, which quality came in somewhat handy in his foreign affairs after Independence; Patel, from Gandhi's Gujarat, was a strict disciplinarian but, with his rustic intelligence, knew how to take the bull by horns. Thus, while Patel was forcing, by hook or crook, the 560-odd kings and kinglets of India to join the Union, Nehru, known for arrogance and anti-Pakistan attitude, angered Mahajan.

Patel, however, rescued two-thirds of Kashmir for India by reassuring Mahajan, roping in the Kashmiri Pandit convert, Sheikh Muhammed Abdullah, and airlifting the First Sikh Battalion from New Delhi to Srinagar. Jinnah, the Governor-General, tried to match Patel but his own acting British commander-in-chief General Sir Douglas Gracy frustrated his plot to turn the clashes into a war. The Great Leader, who wanted to secure Srinagar for Pakistan so that he could inhale fresh and fragrant air there to strengthen his tubercular lungs, now had only one last year left of his life. On 30 October, he told his audience at a public meeting in Lahore: 'Don't be afraid of death. Islam teaches us to be ever ready for death. We should face it bravely to save the honour and dignity of Islam and Pakistan. There is no better deliverance, salvation for a Muslim than the death of a martyr for a righteous cause.' Jinnah was foreseeing his own death but he was not afraid of it; he considered himself a martyr who was dying for the righteous cause of Pakistan.

But what Jinnah thought Pakistan should *be* was not the same as what the Islamic clergy thought it must *become*. On 14 and 15 December 1947, the strange assortment of mullahs, maulvis, maulanas, sheikhs, pirs etc who had increasingly begun to control the Muslim League, demanded full Islamisation of Pakistan by ejecting the remnants of infidel culture; at the same time, it also 'expressed grave concern at the rising tide of communal antagonism against the Muslim minority in the Indian Union where…Muslim life and property continue to be insecure'.

Amidst the ongoing communal riots in January 1948, even in Delhi, the Mahatma sat on a fast-unto-death to force the Nehru government to pay Rs 550 million to Pakistan to tide over its financial crisis. Angry Hindus and Sikhs protested against the Mahatma, marched with black flags, and denounced him as 'Muhammed Gandhi' shouting slogans demanding death to him; Gandhi, who had learnt to remain unperturbed in South Africa, remained calm. On 20 January, the eighth attack on the Mahatma failed as he had already finished his prayer meeting at Birla House when the bomb exploded.

Both Gandhi and Jinnah had outlived their utility to their respective nations—the irreverent had turned into irrelevant. Their role was up and curtains sliding down. They were no longer political assets to their respective peoples.

On 30 January, Nathuram Godse assassinated Gandhi, making him a political asset to the vampires' paradise that the Congress Party was beginning to putrefy into; the Mahatma, when still alive, had already become a political liability to the Congress as Nehru and Patel increasingly ignored him as an imbecile old man; with Patel's death in 1950, Nehru gradually turned the Congress into a private ranch where his Gandhi cap-donning cattle freely grazed, until they 'rebelled' and were forced to fall in line by chasing hounds of the All India Congress Committee or, later, the 'High Command'.

Like the mythological saint Dadhichi, who had donated his steeled bones to Lord Indra to assemble an ultimate weapon against the demons, Gandhi too gave a memorial—Rajghat—to the Congress, and other sundry political animals, to shed crocodile tears twice annually, and laugh their way to enhanced mental bankruptcy. India had survived even the Mahatma, but Gandhi could not survive India! After the Communal Award of 1932, he had increasingly withdrawn from Congress affairs, assured that his turnkey 'project' of deIslamisation was sprinting on an auto-pilot. He had used Nehru, Patel and others as his instruments, as he did the Ali Brothers earlier, in assembling Pakistan; he was not worried that his own creations would use him as an instrument to come to and stay in power. In his last decade, he had come to believe in his own messianic status, as did Jinnah, and became prisoner of the past in a rapidly changing world—Gandhi was no longer the great agent of Change but fossilised like the enemies he had fought so valiantly. The two Leaders were more of conjoined twins than rivals, complimenting each other: without one, the other could not be imagined.

In the end, it was Jinnah who pulled the Islamic camel-cart out of Hindustan while Gandhi pushed it from behind. Reacting to his best enemy's death, the Great Leader said: 'He was one of the greatest men produced by the Hindu community'. Jinnah was all the more dejected now. Whom would he fight with now? Even in death, the Great Soul had left the Great Leader far behind! What would he do without his adversary whom he had outlived? When the Mahatma was alive, Jinnah split India; now that Gandhi had gone, wasn't it time to sow the seeds of Pakistan's destruction as well?

Everybody who was somebody was busy gobbling the fruits of Jinnah's labour in Pakistan and Gandhi's in India, like the scavengers feasting on the big cat's kill. The Great Leader, too, like the Mahatma to the Congress in Independent India, had become a liability to his own Muslim League leaders who thought of him as another senile, old man. The yesterday's Young Radical, as always, as everywhere, had metamorphosed into an Old Conservative of today. Even though he was completely exhausted, Jinnah could still foresee the shape of things to come: that Pakistan's life-span was not interminable in the shape and size it then had. Gandhi's inclusion of Hindi in the Nehru Report (1927) as India's national language had incensed Jinnah no end; now he sought to do a Mahatma himself in Pakistan! Not knowing that Hindi was already the language of the whole of North India; and, even Urdu was mostly a language of *India*, not Pakistan.

On 21 March 1948, the Great Leader told a public meeting in Dhaka, the second 'Capital' of Pakistan, that Pakistan's state language *will* be Urdu and Urdu alone. Jinnah was sowing the wind; Pakistan would reap the whirlwind in 1971. He warned the Bengali Muslims not to be misled on this issue:'Anyone who tries to mislead you is really the enemy of Pakistan. Without one state language, no nation can remain tied up solidly together and function. Look at the history of other countries. Therefore, so far as the state language is concerned, Pakistan's state language shall be Urdu...I tell you once again, do not fall into the trap of those who are enemies of Pakistan. *Unfortunately you have fifth-columnists and I am sorry to say they are Muslims—who are financed by outsiders*...You must have patience.' Thus spake Jinnah who himself hardly knew any Urdu!

The Bengali Muslims, arrogant and consumed by the perceived 'supremacy' of their language and culture they shared with their counterpart Hindu *Bhadralok* Bengalis, were not ready to accept Urdu as their language and eventually broke away from Pakistan in 1971. Urdu, in fact, could not really become the 'state language' of Pakistan either, except formally: besides the Bengalis, the Punjabis, Sindhis, Baluchs and the Pakhtuns all slowly rejected Urdu as a 'polluted' language and continued with their own—more Indians still know this language than did the Pakistanis, ever. Why did the Pakistanis do so? Because they treated the immigrants—the *Muhajirs* (Refugees), those Muslims who migrated from India to Pakistan—and their language, Urdu, as polluted due to infidel contact! In any case, Urdu was never the state language even during the Delhi Sultanate or Mughal Empire: this status was given to Arabic/Turkish or the Persian. Urdu was, and remained, as hybrid and orphaned as the Hindus who converted to Islam and its fall from grace both in India and Pakistan was a natural corollary of the accelerating rate of deIslamisation. Gandhi saw this coming and the Mahatma, who once preferred Hindustani (a hybrid colloquial of Hindi and Urdu), later actively promoted Hindi instead, enrolling several litterateurs of the Hindi belt into the Freedom Movement; lacking official and popular patronage, Urdu, as a parasite language, declined quickly.

Jinnah's tiff with Gandhi had begun with the issue of language when the Great Leader chose to speak in English and the Great Soul in his mother tongue, Gujarati, at a function in Bombay in 1915; it ended on the same issue. The only difference was that Gandhi freely spoke the languages he knew (Gujarati, English, Hindi etc.) whereas Jinnah did not really know much of Urdu or Hindi, and pretended not to know Gujarati or Sindhi either and, as far as possible, remained slave to His Majesty's language, English.

The relations between the Father of Pakistan and the first Prime Minister, Nawabzada Liaqat Ali Khan, deteriorated rapidly after 1947, as did between the Mahatma and Nehru in India. Not only this, the Great Leader's relations with the Governors and Chief Ministers of the Pakistani provinces did not remain cordial either. He was deeply dissatisfied with their performance, especially their lack of interest in the welfare of the immigrants from India; they remained strongly provincial, even xenophobic in their outlook and Islam was no longer the force that bound them.

In June, Jinnah, accompanied by his shadow sister, Fatima, flew to Baluchitan's town Quetta to breathe the fresh air he could no longer dream of elsewhere in Pakistan after the loss of Srinagar. He flew back to Karachi for a function and returned to Quetta on 6 July, to be put up at a hill station, *Ziarat*, which literally meant 'burial tomb'! Ziarat was a quiet hill station in Baluchistan at the edge of a cliff. For Jinnah, life was like a cliff-hanger in this burial tomb. Like an eagle, he had flown from the ground-level to this height of 8,500 feet above the Arabian Sea level and perched atop this mysterious burial tomb believing it to be heaven. That was the ultimate tragedy of lunotheism: like a mirage, it lures you promising better life in heaven, only to plunge you into a hell.

On 7 August 1948, the Muslims offered special Id prayers for Jinnah's health. On 13 August, he dressed up in a new suit and a matching tie, with shining pump shoes on, and left on his final journey to Karachi on a hospital stretcher in his big car but had to halt at Quetta. Next day, he was surprised to see the Pakistan government release *his* message on the first anniversary of the 'Independence Day'. In his last days, his love for typical Gujarati delicacies *halwa and puree*, became more pronounced as he struggled against his serious illness—the still-living child Mamadbhai Jhinabhai struggling to set himself free from the old, diseased, dying cage of a body called Muhammad Ali Jinnah—but he was increasingly getting conscious of the impending death. On 29 August, he wept before his doctor, Lt Col Ilahi Bakhsh, fearing death; his famous iron will was no longer visible as he gave up the fight.

His death, like his life, took place in the strangest circumstances. On 11 September 1948, while being carried from Quetta on his way back to Karachi, his ambulance ran out of petrol and its engine, too, broke down! Imagine the vehicle of a Head of the State breaking down midway, with no immediate replacement available! His staff waited for an ambulance to arrive. He had survived the air journey from Quetta to Karachi but was dying on the highway to his home in the Capital, his home town, on both sides of which there were hutments of the Muhajirs, the fresh arrival of refugees from India, the victims of his political machinations. No one recognised Jinnah or his caravan, or that the Great Leader who had brought them there was lying in a run-down ambulance, helpless and listless. Finally, he managed to reach the Governor-General's mansion in the evening, where, after two hours of sleep, he briefly opened his eyes. 'Fati', he whispered to his sister, and closed his eyes again. His head dropped. He died at 2220 hours, 9/11/1948.

The ambitious Fatima, who had played an important role in shaping the personality of Jinnah by keeping him away from other family members and relatives, even his wife Ruttie and daughter Dina, and finally separated him from India as well, tried to cash in on the Great Leader's popularity; she had already inherited most of his wealth. The grateful Pakistanis had once titled her as the *Madar-e-Millat* ('Mother of the Muslim Nation') but she was not satisfied with this ceremonial role. She continuously clashed with Liaqat, who was assassinated in October 1951, and others who followed him in the fratricidal Pakistani politics. After being ignored for more than a decade by the Rawalpindi establishment and prodded on by the Opposition, she decided to run for Presidency against Ayub Khan in 1964-65. But she won support only in East Pakistan! In 1948 itself, Jinnah had cautioned the East on the Urdu question; by 1968, the question had assumed importance as Dhaka was pressing for preservation of Bengali culture and language. It was due to this reason that it supported Fatima. She was defeated by the Rawalpindi establishment and died on 9 July 1967, not waiting to see her brother's dream of uniting Muslims in the name of Islam being shattered in 1971 with the emergence of Bangladesh.

None from the Jinnah family or relations ever opted for Pakistan; they remained rather unknown citizens of India. They were simple people who, perhaps, realised the futility of it all. 'PakIstan' was the Last Sigh of the Muslim in the East. Jinnah's only daughter, Dina, had married a Parsi-born Christian, Neville Wadia, and visited Karachi only for her father's funeral—and, on March 24, 2004, witnessing India crush Pakistan in a One-Day International (ODI) cricket match in Lahore, as she cheered the winners from the office of Pakistan

Cricket Board Chairman Shahryar Khan. The Great Leader's two great grandchildren continued to live in Bombay and brothers and their families along the Konkan coast of Maharashtra where few knew them. It was only Mamadbhai and his sister Fati in the Lohana-Thakkar family who believed they were 'Muslims': Islam had cut them off from their roots in Gujarat, Sindh, Maharashtra, India, and even in their creation, Pakistan, where the orthodox Sunnis now treated them as heretic Ismaelis!

'PakIstan' was the creation chiefly of nine 'Muslims'. The 'new nation', built from old bricks, was an attempt to create a new lunar system with a new luno-centric mythology. Jinnah was the Moon of this system with its nine 'planets' being Sir Syed Ahmed Khan (Mercury), The Agha Khan (Venus), Allama Iqbal (Earth), Choudhary Rahmat Ali (Mars), the Ali Brothers (Jupiter and Saturn), Nawabs Mohsin-ul-Mulq and Viqar-ul-Mulk (Uranus and Neptune) and Syed Ameer Ali (Pluto). They were Muslim elite, English-speaking, highly-educated and intelligent people, the Young Radicals of their day. But, Islam was almost their tragedy, all the more pronounced in an infidel land that bred insecurity amongst them as regards the future of their faith in the land occupied by their ancestors *without assimilation* and they chose to make it retreat before it was too late. This concern for Islam made these promising youngsters backward looking, reactionary and obscurantist—for most educated Muslims, Islam is like a stake where they return in the evening after a hectic 'modernising' day. Unlike many an educated Hindu, they utilised their 'Western' knowledge not to get rid of their medieval shackles but to strengthen the Cage they had locked themselves in.

Thus, Sir Syed, who once saw the Hindus and Muslims as the two eyes of the same nation, quickly rescinded and closed the Hindu eye by forming the Muhammedan Defence Association a year after the Indian National Congress came into being (1885); Sultan Muhammed Shah, The Agha Khan III, whose forefathers had fled Persia and were rescued by the Hindus of Sindh and Gujarat seven centuries ago, tried to cut the very tree that had sheltered them—he saw no contradiction in being 'nominated' for the Nobel Peace Prize (1924) for maintaining peace between Turkey and the West and his own efforts, through the Muslim League and the Aligarh Muslim University, in sowing the seeds of discord between the Hindus and Muslims, or speaking in favour of separatist 'Pakistan', specially at a time when he, as the only Asian, was elected as President of the League of Nations in July 1937; Dr Iqbal, who once sang paeans for the 'composite' culture of India, soon found plagiarising his own old verses in favour of the new nation; Rahmat Ali, the unsuccessful student, sold his 'dream' of Pakistan first of all to his fellow Punjabi Muslims whose enmity against the Hindus and Sikhs he took with him to England; the Ali Brothers, like Leftists the world-over, were the left-over of their contemporary politics and expediencies who 'Islamised', with help from Gandhi, the Freedom Movement and became reactionary-rightists of the first order—the oxymorons saw no contradiction in being 'Muslim Comrades', believers in monotheism and atheism simultaneously; the two Nawabs who drafted the Muslim League's separatist agenda and Syed Ameer Ali had the distinction of setting up the first-ever mosque in London and the United Kingdom, making the Britons aware of Islam and tolerant of its 'demands' in India as they were tolerant of the 'demands' of the Jews in the Middle East!

No wonder Nature buried some of them in lands far away from their roots for growing up rootless: Jinnah in Karachi; The Agha Khan in Egypt; Rahmat Ali in England; Maulana Muhammed Ali Jauhar in Jerusalem; Syed Ameer Ali in Sussex, England.

But this does not mean they are dead forever.

They, like the History they made, would be undead.

Post Script: a Requiem, a Rebirth

POST-BRITISH India evolved two bridge-generations: the Nehruvian generation (1947-70) and the Indira Gandhian generation (1971-90). In both, a strong, *unlisted* Brahaminical element had inherited the baton from the British Raj and many political parties were virtually ruled by the *Dwij* or 'upper castes', led by the Brahmins. In a way, the Brahmins revived and tried to reattach their socio-political power to the pre-Muslim era by slowly reviving elements that went with 'Mother India'. The Manu-inspired, Dwij-driven socio-political applecart was, however, incongruent with democracy and science in the 20th-21st centuries that India had embraced. Henceforth, the Dwij would increasingly move to *Gyanyoga*, sciences, and the *Adwij*, 'other castes' to *Bhaktiyoga* and *Karmayoga*, the socio-political-religious firmament.

Great scientists like C V Raman, H G Khurana, Vikram Sarabhai etc had firmly and irreversibly put this Emerging India on a modern, scientific path and aligned it with the rest of the world. India was on way to a rebirth; the Old Order was to be replaced by the New. After 1990, therefore, the Dwijs' hereditary patronage system began to crumble with the arrival of the *unlisted castes*, Other Backward Castes (OBCs), who, together with the Scheduled Castes and Scheduled Tribes (SCs and STs) came to occupy socio-political metabolism. This changed the very genetic code of Indian society and politics for the first time since King Harsha. Gradually, the listed Dwijs began to lose their importance in politics. Beginning with the Sarda Act in 1930, they slowly turned monogamous and raised fewer children. Since democracy and elections are based on numbers, the listed castes politically became more important while the unlisted ones slowly shifted to the levers of resources-based economic system. The Ayodhya Movement has, basically, been a requiem for the Dwij, whose political importance, despite false starts, is fading.

Much of contemporary India is now studded with Adwij rulers across political spectrum, led by Prime Minister Narendra Modi. This India, increasingly free of Christian, Islamic and the Dwij influence, has the potential to force the alien religions to retreat further away trans-Indus. The Dwij-centric, *Manuwadi* Hindutva is being replaced by the Adwij-based Hinduism, as the cultural nation's polytheism and multiculturalism flower to fruition; recent efforts to revive non-Aryan 'demons' like Mahishasur as newer gods by the Adwij castes is a straw in the wind. Its long-term impact would, of course, be on the Adwij population that had converted to Christianity or Islam over the last millennia under foreign rule. Already, many among those who converted from Adwij Hindu castes to Islam, are under pressure due to the return of the Hindu Adwij rule across many states. With their Hindu fellow castes across the table enjoying relatively better deals and fruits of power, some of them are threatening to reconvert to Hinduism. In April 2017, some *burqa*-clad Muslim women, buffeted on issues like alimony and *triple talaq*, openly favoured this; this went viral on electronic and social media.

For the converts, their old caste could never leave them in peace even in their new faith (Christianity/Islam), a reason why they demand parity with Hindu caste fellows. The *Pasamanda* Muslims in the Hindi heartland, for instance, demand parity with and job reservations available to their fellow SCs and some Christians in Goa threaten to re-embrace Hinduism! They have a reason, too: due to *Indianisation* of Islam—read Hinduisation—the 'upper caste' Muslims, such as the Sayyeds, would not intermarry with those in the Pasamanda castes of socially-backward Muslims. Out of nearly 50 major Muslim caste groups in India, some 45 belong to the Pasamanda category which constitutes an estimated 85% of the Muslim population. This caste-composition ratio is similar to the one in the Hindu population! An influential section of those Muslims who carved Pakistan out of India belonged to the upper or intermediate castes, the Sayyeds et al; many in the upper Christian castes either migrated abroad after 1947 or their population fell due to low fertility, exogamic marriages and other reasons. Due to theo-erosion, the remaining Muslims and Christians, who stayed back or were born in India after 1947, mostly belonged to the Adwij segments; *they* are now merging back into the Hindu ocean from which their forefathers had emerged.

In Gujarat, a milder variety of Muslim converts from Hinduism, called *Mohr-e-Islam* (Stamped with Islam), or, as the Gujaratis call them, *Mole Islam*, (Diluted Muslims!), had evolved during the Muslim rule. In Rajasthan and Haryana, the *Mewati* Muslims also evolved similarly. They both silently, increasingly returned to the Hindu fold, a reason why militant Islamists of the Ahl e-Hadis variety are trying to stop this exodus and *reIslamise* them. More and more, the neo-Brahmins in India could be those who reconvert to the Hindu fold!

These too are straws in the wind.

In Pakistan, upper caste Muslims, who dominated the Islamabad Establishmnt, successfully planted the Islamic terror-bomb in their own society. They are essentially continuing India's indirect drive to push Islam further across the Durand Line in a new setting.

The hegemony of the Brahmins in the Indian society was far stronger than that of the Papacy or the Caliphate in the Christian or Muslim worlds. They were the real, even if invisible, social and psychological rulers of India until 1990. Some even weakened the anti-Manuwadi organisations from within simply by joining them. For instance, P C Joshi, E M S Namboodiripad etc in the Communist Parties, Jayalalithaa in the Dravid camp, and Satish Mishra in the Bahujan Samaj Party. Irrespective of their 'ideology', the Brahmins often supported a fellow Brahmin if s/he became a ruler (Nehru, Indira, Vajpayee, Jayalalithaa, Mamata Bannerjee etc).

While many influential upper caste Muslims migrated to Pakistan in 1947, a majority of the local Muslims in the new nation were, basically, converts from the lower castes, who were scared of remaining in India led by a Brahmin, Nehru. Pakistan's influential Muslims were mostly of Punjabi, Pathan or Central Asian origins who, too, would not play second fiddle to infidel Hindus. They formed the first generation of Pakistani power elite. After 1971, with the Bengali majority breaking away, the second generation of Pakistanis came mainly from Punjabi stock. Flush with Arab funds, they tried to prevent the country's slow melting back into pre-Islamic moorings, particularly after Islamabad 'discovered' the Harappa culture as its own! They were so scared of a further possible retreat of Islam that General Zia ul-Haq launched a fresh re-*Islamisation* drive in a country whose state religion was Islam and capital Islamabad! Ironically, Pakistan has the dubious distinction of having an organisation no other Muslim country boasts of: *Aalami Majlis Tahaffuz Khatm-e-Nubuwwat* (International Organisation for Protection of the Finality of the Prophet!). Its website says its sole aim is to unite all the Muslims of the world to safeguard the sanctity and finality of Prophethood, and refute the repudiators of the belief in the finality of the Prophethood of Muhammed! In this competitive Islam, as even Pervez Musharraf once said, more Muslims are being killed by the Muslims themselves than by non-Muslims. Clearly, Pakistan is imploding due to Islamabad!

This fate of a retreating Islam in the Indian subcontinent was apparent to many even before 1947. Gandhi and Jinnah were not the only leaders who 'discovered' the Muslims' *separateness.* Even Hindu leaders like Lala Lajpat Rai, V D Savarkar and B R Ambedkar were among those who saw Pakistan coming; but none of them could marshal the forces to make Islam retreat from Allahabad to Islamabad. In fact, the Pakistan Movement was not only the beginning of deIslamisation of the Indian subcontinent but also coincided with the unearthing of the Indus Valley Civilization/Harappa Culture in Sindh, Gujarat and the Punjab provinces: the large-scale *return* of 'Muslim' population from the Gangetic Valley towards the Indus was a virtual reversal of what had happened in the past. It was not only a rediscovery of the Indus Civiliation but resettlement of many of the descendants of 'natives' there as history turned a full circle. Hating to be called a neophyte seven-decade-old nation, Pakistan now traces its history to the polytheism of Mohenjo-Daro and Harappa but, while professing monotheism in the same breath, wants to dissociate from 'Aryan' India.

Why is Pakistan failing so spectacularly? Because it has been neither a state nor a nation: the State-seat of South Asia has mostly fluctuated like a pendulum between the empires centres around Purushpur (Peshawar) and Patna (Patliputra) over the last 2,000 years; members of the South Asian Association for Regional Cooperation (SAARC), a euphemism for pan-Hindu/Buddhist colourful carnival, have been somewhat like its cultural satellites, with their top pilgrimage centres located in mainland India, not in what is now Pakistan. Some of these 'sovereign' countries like Pakistan, Sri Lanka and Bangladesh even have their own armies. But, then, some states of India have had even private, caste, community or race-based 'armies', including the Shiv Sena, a political party. Clearly, India is the fulcrum of South Asia. And she is polytheist, multicultural, pluralist—an aggregator, not an exterminator.

Contrast this: Pakistan is essentially a miniature Mughal dinosaur revived after a British interregnum, a rag-tag ruling clique of medieval *mansabdars*, *mullahs* and mercenaries whom India could not accommodate and managed to bundle them out.

That was why the Deoband-based Islamic seminary, *Dar-ul-Ulum*, and its 'patriotic' and 'liberal' supporters, the *Ahrars*, did not want

India to be partitioned as they believed that their God-given task of converting all the Hindus of this *Dar-ul-Harb* (Land of the Infidels) into *Dar-ul-Islam* (Land of Islam) was still incomplete. So incensed was this seminary with Jinnah, who was walking away with Pakistan like a pied-piper, that it denounced him as *Qafir e-Azam* (the Great Infidel)—and the likes of Mufti Kifayatullah openly regretted that Jinnah and his Muslim League had *confined* Islam to just a corner of India.

In hindsight, Nature had, apparently, assigned this task to Gandhi and Jinnah. While the Mahatma's task of waking the Hindus up was relatively minor, Jinnah shouldered the greater responsibility of luring monotheism out of India for which the country was waiting for long. Jinnah was, therefore, the greatest Indian after The Buddha, for being the One who 'detoxified' India after the alien catalyst turned sour. Millions of Jinnah-hating Hindus never realised that the atheist 'Muslim' leader was like aperture of the tumor from which the pus of fanatic monotheism oozed out of India. He successfully reversed the process of *official monotheism* of the central government in India, which began with Muhammad bin-Qasim's invasion of Sindh in 711. Jinnah amputated a gangrened organ to save the rest of the body, which was revived by Nehru and others.

After Chanakya, it was Jinnah who taught India *real politic*, that a nation emerges from the churning of a society, and often walks out in a pool of blood after shunning fads like peace and love-for-all that have little meaning in the real, biological, competitive and evolutionary world. Jinnah was, perhaps, Father of the Indian subcontinent, who began ridding it of accretions left on its *body politic* by the 'slavery' of the last 14 centuries. With Gandhi and Jinnah, India's medieval era, which had begun in 711, came to an end.

When Muhammad bin-Qasim invaded, India was *Dar-ul-Harb* For a thousand years thereafter, it remained a *Dar-ul-Sulh* (Land of Compromise), a la the Communists' temporary 'compromise' with the bourgeoisie; when Jinnah led *his* flock out of India, it again became a *Dar-ul-Harb*. Pakistan's Sindh, from where the entire Indian subcontinent was supposed to have been won for Islam since 711, was ironically converted into *Dar-ul-Hizra* (Land of Emigrants) after 1947. Even Pakistan could never really become *Dar-ul-Islam* what with the competitive Islamism between 70-odd sects of 'Muslims' vying for space, and 'peace' that, in official Christianity and Islam, is a synonym for complete victory of the Faith over 'infidels.

As the popular Pakistani singer Ghulam Ali would sum it up: *Chupke-chupke raat-din aansoo bahana yaad hai; humko ab tak aashiki kaa woh zamana yaad hai.* (Can't get over the times when I'd cry in silence; can't forget how I loved thee those days!)

Or, as Gandhi and Jinnah would paraphrase in their native *Gujarati* language: *Kahevay nahin ke sahevay nahin* (Neither can we talk about it nor can we suffer it anymore).

India has sung its requiem and taking rebirth; Pakistan has yet to join in. But she will. For theirs is a violent love story—they cannot love each other without hating one another! In the end, they will have to sleep in the same bed!

The Yellow Men's Burden

CHINA

IF India is the land of monsoon, China represents winter and Japan spring—the life and times of these ancient nations have been tremendously influenced by these cyclical seasons since their origins. The Indians suspend work until the monsoon shower lasts, the Chinese do so in winter. Until the Opium Wars of the mid-19th century, the Chinese would cover himself with up to a dozen layers of tunics, to be shed one by one as winter waned. The world has never seen China without clothes!

The Chinese language has no alphabet or spelling, parts of speech or even grammar. Every word could be used as a noun, pronoun, verb, adverb or an adjective in accordance with its context and tone. The spoken Chinese dialects have just 400 to 800 monosyllabic vocables (word-sounds) that compress nearly 40,000 characters of the written language. Each of these vocables may have up to nine tones and its meaning differs in accordance with the manner it is spoken; each of this sound serves a number of purposes. No other language humans evolved has been as complicated, particularist, subtle and brief. That is why outsiders often take over a decade to master this difficult language. Culturally unable to share and assimilate much, the Chinese and Japanese do not easily learn another people's language either. Because of this disconnect at cultural and linguistic levels with the outside world, they could never hold on for long over the areas they conquered outside the 'Mongol borders'. In our times, China could not much do in the Information Technology revolution, centred around *English*, and Japan's economy declined when global economy came to run around information technology (IT). Thus, the languages of these Yellow Men's region were, ironically, their asset as well as liability. Brevity is a characteristic the Chinese evolved over the ages. Theirs is the oldest and most widespread surviving language in the world.

For a Chinese, each idea could be represented by a specific sign or a set of signs. One major reason why China could not be conquered or ruled by others for a long time was that *the others* could never master its language and so never knew how and what the Chinese were talking about; even the conquering Mongols, who actually catalysed the stagnant Chinese Civilisation some 800 years ago, eventually retreated, leaving the Chinese to bounce back to and retrieve *their* civilisation. It was mainly during the Mongol and Ming periods that the Chinese population multiplied manifold within to offset the losses suffered due to the aliens, particularly after the T'ang influence on Central Asian barbarians weakened when the region succumbed to Islam. The increased population of peasants eventually made the Chinese Revolution of 1949 possible as the final frontier against Christianity and Islam, the way India, too, witnessed increased population due to multiplication within in the same centuries, that would slowly overwhelm the Islamic and then Christian rulers, and then the old Brahminical order.

China's age-old foreign policy does not recognise 'sovereign' foreigners; you are either part of China or its satellite. She did not have a 'foreign ministry' as would not recognise other nations. As Mao

Zedong said: 'Those who are with us are our friends. Those not with us, are our enemies, whom we will destroy.' To manage neighbouring tributaries like Tibet, Xinjiang or Mongolia, China had a 'colonial' office. She ignored the Nuclear Non-Proliferation Treaty (NPT) by supplying nuclear secrets to Pakistan and through it to Iran, Libya and North Korea, the three 'rogue states' in the American demonology. She would also bar entry of India into the Nuclear Supply Group (NSG) to keep Pakistan on its side *until* Beijing reaches West Asia and Africa via Gwadar and One Belt, One Road (OBOR), essentially a Mongol II enterprise, unveiled in May 2017. After weathering the global recessionary storm after 2008, despite piled up debts amounting to $ 27 trillion, China again thumbed nose at the USA on the treasury bonds and Google issues, amongst others. Only China has had the guts to thwart Islam; she routinely executes Muslim terrorist intruders from a 'friendly' Pakistan in Xinjiang; in April 2017, she banned christening Muslim children after Muhammed! No other nation could forcibly marry Communist gerontocracy with capitalism as when Deng Hsiao Feng launched his Four-Pronged Modernisation Programme in the 1980s. The Shoguns' Japan took five decades to modernise and defeat Russia in 1905; China squeezed her backwardness and modernised at a breakneck speed, in just two decades. Culturally superior, civilisationally reassured, unburdened with God, the Chinese evolved a rare habit of looking for opportunity in each crisis: the then US President Richard Nixon, after reopening American dialogue with China in the 1970s, discovered that the Chinese use two brush-strokes to write the word 'crisis'. One brush-stroke stands for danger; the other for opportunity.

China has been eternally optimistic and aesthetic; this optimism comes from her atheism, the way India's chaos comes from her polytheism—in the former, god is unimportant; in the latter He is mortal. That's how China and India became the only continuous civilisations, despite the many misfortunes and disasters that came annually as man-made or natural crises, even as other monotheistic civilisations rose and fell with clock-wise precision.

China has always treated all other civilisations as 'barbarian', the way India has seen others as *mlechchhas*, or unclean. Only with India has China been relatively lenient because of Buddhism, the original 'godless religion'. Until the 1860s, Chinese official documents used the word 'barbarian' to describe the foreigner! All aliens were seen to be either paying 'tribute' to China or 'refusing' to pay. They never called their country as *China*; for them their nation was variously known as *Tien-hua* (In the Shadow of the Holy Heavens), *Sz-hai* (Littoral of the Four Seas), *Chung-kuo* (Middle Kingdom), or *Chung-hwa-kuo* (Middle Kingdom of Flowers) and finally, after the 1949 Communist Revolution, *Chun-hwa-min-kuo* (Middle Kingdom of Flowery Peoples). For 7,000 years, China, even when not a civilisation, has had a continuous culture; scores of civilisations rose from and returned to dust since at different places on the globe. China's has stood firm and continuously evolved; only India has bowed, to bounce back each time. Mortal civilisations needed immortal God; immortal China did not need Him.

The pride of China were not its Emperors but philosophers and artists, in that order—the Emperor was respected but remote, who sat in the Forbidden City while philosophers and artists rose from amongst the common people; India, too, had seen her Emperors sit at the feet of sages and philosophers. The East always valued wisdom and renunciation more than smartness and ostentation, and dismissed showmanship as frivolous, even in intellectual affairs. The Buddha was respected because his disciples crossed the Himalayas on foot; Christian and Muslim missionaries were dismissed with contempt as they came mounted on ships or horses. Buddhism survived in China because it was humble; Christianity and Islam made little impact because they sought to humble a patient China. Both India and China survived 'spiritual' assaults from the Fertile Crescent because they had their philosophers as insurance cover when their Emperors became dysfunctional. As in India, philosophers sensed the problems evolving human societies could face due to an exponential pace of Change; nowhere else were literacy and political culture as wedded as in China—if you were literate, you were a politician. Each of the nine great philosophers—Wen Wang, Lao-tze, Confucius, Mo Ti, Yang Chu, Mencius, Hsun-tze, Chuang-tze, and The Buddha—gave alternatives.

No two other neighbouring civilisations have ever been as supportive, subtle and protective of each other as China and India. Even their 'enmities' have more often been apparent than real. At the Bandung Conference (1955), India helped China end her isolation and later become a member of the UN Security Council; in turn, when India overslept after forcing both Islam and Christianity out in 1947, kicked her hard to wake up in 1962 through a quick war, *warning* the peace-intoxicated neighbour that Pakistan was yet to be defeated comprehensively! India took her lesson seriously and, in two phases (1965 and 1971) partitioned Pakistan, a 'close, all-season ally' of China! Other countries would not comprehend these silent nuances, subtlety and the deft, mature moves of two ancient and neighbourly civilisations that had realised the importance of meditation at the dawn of history. China and India survived because they thought long-range like a *Thing*, and came closest to Nature.

This harmony created by China's philosophers and kings reached its zenith when the Mongols emerged on the scene in the 13th century. They were basically Tatars, more famous as 'Mongols' (literally meaning, 'the brave'), a group of barbarian tribes welded together by a military genius, Changez Khan (Genghis Khan), into a potent force of hardy people in the north-western frontiers of China that had now become a desert. Six centuries ago, another genius, Muhammed, had similarly welded the barbarian tribes of the Arabian desert into a socio-political cult called 'Islam'. Each military success of these freshly welded groups gave them impetus to carve out vast empires on the ruins of exhausted ancient cultures and civilisations of Asia—they both moved at break-neck speeds from opposite directions until they collided with each other in Baghdad. Like Muslims before them, the Mongols suddenly came into picture and achieved such a series of stunning military success and destruction as has had no parallel in history. Much of today's Chinese population has descended from the Mongols.

The atheist Mongols came as old Asia's answer to the monotheist Muslims. There was, however, a difference: after mushrooming on the dysfunctional civilisations of Syria, Egypt, Persia and India, the Muslims settled down as a bridge between the scholarships of the Orient and Occident and, unwittingly, wrote the script of their own downfall as Europe and India slowly recovered from shock—the Mongols, devoid of scholarship, had no such pretensions. They came only as a tornado and returned as quickly after leaving behind death and destruction. It was not surprising that the West, after licking wounds in Iraq of 2004, thought of reviving the Mongol Cavalry to police the (Muslim) world!

The single-most important but negative 'achievement' of the Mongols in the Muslim Empire was that they permanently destroyed the region's traditional irrigation system that had kept the Mesopotamia prosperous and populous since the Sumerian times. The Mesopotamia turned desert despite its great rivers Euphrates and Tigris. The Mongols could not, however, penetrate Egypt whose Sultan defeated Halaqu's army in the Palestine (1260), thus finally stopping the Mongol menace. The Mongols shared three common things with the Muslims that enticed them to convert to the faith of those they had conquered: a strong leadership that justifies spiralling conquest and loot, the barbaric methods used in this expansion and changing the racial complexion of the vanquished. No wonder India and China had to evolve their own defense mechanism against both the Muslims and the Mongols, respectively. But the Mongols did not *enter* neighbouring India although they could—China, too, did not penetrate much of India in 1962—because a subtle Confucius and a silent Buddha did not challenge their valour.

But the Mongols did some 'good' to China as well: they prevented *only* the Muslims from preaching Islam at a time when the western Mongols had been won over by Islam. In fact, the Mongols, as counter-catalysts and moderators, demonstrated to the Muslims the last limits of Islam, and destroyed forever its inherent belief in the *invincibility* of their Brotherhood when they devastated the Baghdad-based Caliphate in 1258. Instead, they encouraged Taoism and Buddhism in China. This struggle at the cultural and political level continued in both India and China; but being *only catalysts*, neither the Mongols in China nor the Muslims in India could ever be fully assimilated. The Chinese and the Hindus used these alien catalysts for their own rejuvenation and then devised a counter-strategy to ward off this culturally incompatible assimilation. Both China and India shone in the Kublai Khan and Akbar regimes, respectively, but this brilliance was akin to the insectivorous Venus flytrap plant which attracts butterflies through colourful displays. The resilience of the Chinese gradually weakened the Mongol arms the way the Hindu resilience weakened the Muslim arms. The Mongols and the Mughals proved themselves better warriors than administrators and Kublai's successors were forced to restore the mandarin examination system; the British, Mughals' successors, introduced the Civil Services in India. The Chinese and the Hindus lapped up these opportunities and overthrew the conquerors whose chief weakness was their inability to understand the human mind due to the absence of philosophic traditions that trains the Mind of a society to survive in hostile climes.

Even the 'native' dynasty, the Ming ('Brilliant'), did not last long, founded as it was by a former *Buddhist* monk in 1368; cultures eventually reject alien religions and belief systems the way the human body rejects a transplanted organ not from the same blood group. That was how the truly native Chinese Manchus came on the scene; they, were akin to the original Chinese. The Manchus were followed by the Ch'ing ('Pure') Dynasty. Its second Emperor, K'ang-hsei's regime was the most peaceful, enlightened and prosperous reign in China's history at a time when his 18th century contemporaries in Mughal India, Aurangzeb, and Louis XIV in France, were readying their reigns for Revolution. The Ming Emperor, Ch'ien Lung (1736-96), more of a poet than a ruler, saw an English delegation led by Lord McCartney seeking apologies for 'importing' opium into China; the Emperor pardoned him, but refused to follow the policies that could have ushered in an Industrial Revolution in China which, he thought, would threaten the traditional Chinese achievements.

Apart from philosophy and language, the Chinese were shielded from monotheistic religions by the inventions they made *for others*. They had mastered the art of keeping the enemy off by giving away their inventions. For instance, they found that gun-powder, invented during the T'ang dynasty for use in fireworks, could be used in making hand-grenades and throwing at the enemy. The Arab Muslims, who imported what they called the 'Chinese snow', employed gun-powder not only in their imperial expansion but also during the Crusades against the Christians. Similarly, the best use of compass, another Chinese invention dating back to the times of Moses of Israel, was made by Europeans sailors who discovered the 'New World'.

Such a perfectionist and self-contented society did not need a God to pull its chestnuts out of fire—but its negative fallout was equally momentous as a pride in a great cultural tradition, much like in India, long continued to make it hard for it to recognise its own inadequacies or respect individual efforts in innovation. This made learning from foreigners, or 'barbarians', difficult. In order to gear herself up against the Abrahamic cyclones, the post-Mongol China virtually fossilised herself, just like post-Ghori India did..

No doubt even the Chinese were as superstitious as any other people but they did not seek absolutist solutions to their relativistic problems. They were sceptic, pious, rationalist, nationalist and irreligious by nature—a strange mixture of contradictions as they simultaneously believed in all that their great philosophers said and lived in a fantasy of their own *to become perfect without divine aid.* China was the only society where philosophers successfully blocked the ways of God from invading the human mind. If India survived due to her many a mortal god, China survived and re-flowered due to her many an immortal philosophers. Human beings resort to revolution or surrender when their gods fail to solve their problems; India learnt to change her gods every time a revolution loomed large whereas China refused to have any church dictate its society.

That was why neither Christianity nor Islam really succeeded in China—they already had the Buddhist Heaven and the Amitabh Buddha that Christianity and Islam, the Johnies-come-lately, offered in the form of God-Jesus and Allah-Muhammed dualism. If one had to worship these imported prophets, well, the Chinese would better worship their home-grown products like Confucius and Lao-tze! Christianity entered China in its Nestorian form in the year Muhammed died, 632 AD; the missionaries cried their hearts out for emancipation of the 'infidel' China and later the Protestants tried to implement the Nestorian dream of converting the vast land. All they achieved in a thousand years was to convert one per cent of the Chinese! Eventually, Christianity lost its mission due to a struggle between the Rome-based Jesuits who would like to incorporate the Chinese elements as part of Christianity and the recalcitrant Dominican and Franciscan Orders who believed the Chinese were under the Devil's influence and who, therefore, needed to be saved. The Chinese ensured that Christianity itself was not saved in China. Even the two million contemporary Muslims in China are not 'Chinese' but foreigners.

China frustrated this foreign invasion of her culture and civilisation through her sheer grit and stringent family rules and morals. The invisible and timeless government of China resided not in the temples or palaces but in the hearth and home where the parents passed on to their offsprimg the moral code they had inherited. Political changes and economic misfortunes did little to disrupt this balance, just like caste and the *panchayats* prevented invasion of Abrahamic religions into the heartland of India to a large extent. The way the Hindus would hanker after a son who could perform their last rites, the Chinese, too, favoured sons, for war and tending to the ancestors' graves. Celibacy was a crime against society—no wonder Buddhism (and later Christianity) could not much succeed in China for a long time. The philosophers had taught the state to leave to the family the task of maintaining social order. The Chinese home reflected the microcosm of China: it was at once the church, the nursery, the school, the factory and the state where the will of the cleric, the head master, the proprietor and the Emperor was combined in one person—the Patriarch—as in the Hindu case. This self-governed society of a vast land like China, where a self-controlled people internalised these traits, had elements of autonomy, democracy as well as aristocracy: democracy meant liberty, not licence, and the individual was 'free' as long as he was part of the whole and, as the link between ancestry and posterity, did not violate the tradition. The individual and the family were responsible for each other's acts; they preferred to be ruled by custom rather than law.

But as important as the Chinese society was the Emperor who ruled by 'divine' right as the Son of Heaven as also the Supreme Ruler of the Earth, the ultimate God-King who ruled the seasons and the Universe. But even his powers were limited by custom and law; he was not beyond reproach. An unjust or unworthy monarch could be checkmated by the 'Censor' and violently thrown out to protect the Order. For a thousand years, the state was run by mandarins, the public servants selected through stringent examination.

By the time the Crusades 'ended', the unpopular Church's influence and market declined in Europe, geographically only an extension of Asia; it tried to compensate this shortfall in numbers and faith by 'liberating' the infidel souls in the East hanging on to the coat-tails of politico-economic imperialism, investment and venture capital. The destructive energies of the Crusades had left millions dead in Europe and millions others died of epidemics like the plague, depleting manpower to work the fields. The era of Renaissance, Reconstruction and Reason witnessed an unprecedented activity in the discovery of the mechanical power and the evolution of nations, democracy and sciences. In Europe, the Church slowly became an outdated and rejected 'technology' which could now be dumped in Asia and Africa—for the Church, this imperialism was a new 'Crusade' by other means. After Jesus, Christianity had rejuvenated Greece and Rome, the way Islam rejuvenated the Middle East; subsequently, the two faiths lost their catalytic moorings, became burdensome for their own people who sought to shift this burden onto other societies.

A combination of these forces scripted history in the coming centuries. China was readying itself to deal with the emerging White Peril, product of a Europe revivifying itself parallel to the slow paralysis of the Church; the Greko-Roman past had been revivified in the post-Crusade Europe, giving it back the scientific spirit and reason it had been stripped of by the Dark Age. Shortage of cheap manpower had forced Europe to discover mechanical power and machines became mothers of more machines at an accelerating pace. The 15th century geographical discoveries opened up the seas as alternate routes to the East, as the Muslims controlled land between the East and the West. In the 16th century, the Portuguese established themselves in Macao; in the 17th, the Dutch came to control Formosa and the British virtually annexed Canton. China treated them all as unwelcome intruders and, apart from heavy taxes, tried to control them through various means.

With her control of India and Burma, Britain dominated South Asia while France controlled Indo-China and Russia entered the north of Asia from the Ural mountains to the Pacific Ocean. The 19th century saw yet another entrant to the Far East, the USA, and China's tiny neighbour, Japan. The West's object in the Far East was to open up China and Japan, virtually closed to all aliens, for commerce. The force used by the West against these two countries gave rise to the Far Eastern Question—the contemporary South China Sea imbroglio is part of this Question. In the latter half of the 19th century, the Question became further complicated when Japan quickly metamorphosed from being a victim of imperialism to an aggressor herself and began to carve out its own sphere of influence as the 'natural' imperialist force, the local West in the East. Japan was the first Yellow Man to take the Burden of the East.

Unlike previous barbarian attacks, the Chinese realised that Christianity and Islam tried to 'assimilate' the host in a reverse osmosis mode. China had seen the struggle of India against Islam; now it was the turn of China to struggle against Christianity. For more than a century after the Portuguese landing in China (1517), the Jesuits tried to convert China the way they found best: by trying to adopt the Chinese ways and culture and then remould and reboot Peking in the image of Rome. Even as the Jesuits sought to ingratiate themselves with their hosts—in the beginning, they would not even speak of the religion but work their way through by distributing medicines and opening schools, as they did in India and elsewhere—and tried to make themselves acceptable. They learnt the Chinese language and translated works, wore the Chinese clothes, and tried to become 'White Chinese' in all possible ways. Then they slowly unveiled the Cross and tried to hammer it into the 'Satanic' heart of the Chinese infidel who, however converted many of the Jesuits into Chinese ways! Since failure has no father, the Jesuits coming cropper made the Pope furious: instead of harvesting souls to the Christ, the Jesuits had taken to the infidel way of life with no returns in an age of investment capital! The Jesuits had even begun to 'Sinify' Christian teachings. Even in the 21st century, the Vatican could do little against China appointing its own 'Bishops'! To check this 'improper flexibility' the Vatican sent two papal emissaries to China. The Church discovered that the infidel souls could not be peacefully harvested for the Christ. It sought help from some European kings, who, at home, were opposed to the shrinking Church; but to buy peace with them, they agreed to help the Church abroad. That was how the missionaries tagged on to the traders, tourists and militarists. China, like India, would now have to open her trade to Europe and give 'concessions' to the emerging consortium of alien pirates and brigands.

The way Islam came to India as a 'disruptive intervention' to whip the Hindus back in action and change, Christianity came to China to stir placid waters of complacency. For the first time in more than two millennia, China would have to change in the face of the imported culture of a new wave of barbarian conquerors. While India had erected mental defences as the Islamic cyclone easily swept through the material land, China was now erecting material defences against Europe's 'spiritual' attacks that began with trade as in the Indian case. For three centuries, Europe tried to sell its spiritual scrap to China, but trade concessions infuriated the native Chinese against the foreign Manchus who found it difficult to stem the nationalist tide created by secret societies and cults against all aliens.

So, the struggle now was two-fold: the native Chinese wanted to overthrow the Manchus as well as the Europeans by shifting alliances; in contemporary India, the Sikhs and the Marathas were similarly struggling against Islam and Christianity. Poor peasants were at the core of this dual war in both the countries because they were, from the First Wave (agriculture), the repositories of tradition and culture and the most affected of the lot due to the surging Second Wave (industries). Until the native monarchs ruled, these peasants remained content in their poverty and illiteracy as they found their rich culture and tradition compensating for their materialist miseries; but when they discovered the alien rulers were now trying to deprive them even of these, they rose in revolt. In the 1770s and 1780s, China witnessed large-scale peasant revolts parallel to the decline in imperial authority. It was not merely the cyclical pattern of dynastic rise and fall as in the past. The whole gamut of Chinese life was about to undergo change as China prepared for a veritable Revolution. They discovered that the Emperor was unable to protect their culture and tradition from alien influence; that imperial expansion into Korea (1627) and to Burma (1792) had only made the nation ugly and obese, weakened the core of Chinese culture and brought in more aliens and miseries, in that order; that the cunning British, unable to penetrate anything except silver in China had only increased inflation and were now bringing in Indian opium to kill the Chinese soul at a time when Karl Marx said that religion was the opiate of the masses. Christianity had found a way to harvest the Chinese souls for Jesus simply by drugging the Chinese, something the Islamist cult of *Hashishuns* (Assassins) did in Iran earlier. Islam had spread mainly through the sword; now Christianity was expanding using the drug!

Europe had unsuccessfully tried to woo China for long and now was the time to force its entry and take revenge like a jilted lover. Britain took the lead and the East India Company pushed opium into China even as the Chinese government tried to prohibit its import by declaring it illegal in 1800. The British, dedicated believers in making every crime look legal—in fact, law-making emerged alongside readymade clothes—connived with corrupt local Chinese officials to smuggle opium in. In 1839, a Chinese special commissioner, Lin, destroyed 20,000 chests of opium, leading to the outbreak of the Opium War as the hapless China protested against the nefarious British attempt. The Opium War (1839-42), however, ended with the Treaty of Nanking by which China ceded Hong Kong to Britain and agreed to open five ports to European trade: Canton, Foochow, Ningpo, Amoy and Shanghai. China was also forced to agree to pay a large war indemnity and to treat British officials at par with their Chinese counterparts. This treaty registered a fundamental change in China's relations with the West. The Canton monopoly and the tributary status of the alien ended now. The British kicked open China for the whole of the West to barge in and indulge in the scramble of the vast nation as they were doing in contemporary Africa, too. The USA and France appeared in 1844 to share the spoils, followed, in the next decade, by Holland, Belgium, Portugal and Prussia.

China, like India, now had two enemies: the old traditions that tried to protect culture but had now fallen prey to modernity, and the new, White Barbarians—a slow realisation led to a century-long upheaval. From the 1840s, the Chinese Revolution revealed itself as a double repudiation of these two enemies. Repudiation of the foreigner increasingly fanned nationalist outrage while repudiation of outdated traditions that had failed to protect the Chinese culture and needed to be replaced led to learning of things West. Like India, and then Japan, China would defeat the alien at its own game. The gradual revolution was set to finally shatter for good a social system that had been the foundation of their life for thousands of years. The New Age called for dropping the old flab and shed the hide that had protected them so far. China and Japan did it more quickly because of their geography than history; India took time because of her history, the fact that Islam was still being elbowed out of the subcontinent, and sometimes it even returned like backwater after a tide, as in the case of Islamic terrorism now.

To start with, these Asian cultures were slow to react and respond to the Western encroachments which produced a simple, xenophobic hostility, especially in areas where traders and missionaries were active and collaborated with local traders. Unlike Adi Shankarcharya in India, few Chinese realised that the alien attack involved a deeper issue of the future, that of questioning an entire Order; the Chinese rulers, just like Indian monarchs, did not immediately sense a cultural threat, assured as they were that China had suffered defeats in the past, its culture had survived unscathed and assimilated many conquerors instead. As in the Indian case, it took the Chinese a couple of centuries to realise that the Abrahamic-European enemy was different from the Mongols; the latter did not have *extra-territorial religious loyalties*—this is what would, in the 21st century, metamorphose as 'globalisation'—and that the Abrahamites were trying to absorb China rather than the other way round. The first sign of a deeper danger was realised when, in the 1840s, the Emperor had to concede legality to the missionary activity. It was only then that the Chinese officials, steeped deep in the Confucian mind, sensed the corrosion of tradition at a faster pace and stirred up popular feeling against the Christian missionaries, leading to riots in the 1850s and 1860s. Officially, China had to apologise for these acts and the popular 'rebels' were punished. In the 19th century, China began to emerge as the main Asian country to take on Christianity, just as India was bracing herself to take on Islam, tormented as they were by these alien guests-turned-ghosts. The emboldened missionaries continued to undermine the traditional society by directly preaching individualism and egalitarianism alien to China; they acted as a magnet to converts by offering them economic and social advantages. In Europe, Christianity had harvested souls; in the Americas it had thrashed the souls; in Asia, it would now buy them outright!

This undermining of China was aided by the militarist-missionary European nations, who forced the host to yield more and more 'concessions'—it was like shopkeepers demanding discount from the customer! The undercurrents of discontent against native and foreign enemies had begun to take shape in the form of the biggest peasant revolt in human history: the First Wave variables were now revolting against the Second Wave fixations. These veritable rebellions were rooted in man's hunger for land—at a time when Christianity tried to make the Chinese think of Heaven and replace their own Son of Heaven with an alien Son of God. The Chinese would have none of it. They murdered a French missionary and 'insulted' the British Union Jack. These were pretexts enough for the British and the French to join forces again in 1856, threaten Peking and forced China to sign the double Treaties of Tientsin (1858) extracting further concessions and indemnities, and 11 more ports were forced open for trade, besides, of course, the promise of 'tolerating' Christian missionaries to rub salt in the wound. China's humiliation was complete by the grant of the right of 'extra-territoriality', that is, exemption of the aliens from the jurisdiction of the Chinese courts.

The West was prodding the sleeping Dragon, the way Dalhousie poked India.

These rebellions would start with the Taiping Rebellion (1850-1864), culminating in the Red Revolution of 1949. Unequal treaties imposed on China by Britain, the USA and France 'guaranteed' toleration of Christian missionaries and reserved jurisdiction over foreigners to consular and mixed courts; more Chinese ports were forced to open to foreign trade, sale of opium was 'legalised' and the Russians allowed themselves to build Vladivostok. For the first time in their long history, the Chinese were forced to set up a new department to deal with foreigners and their affairs in 1861 as alien wolves and native worms continued to nibble at her *Body Sinic*. The old challenge of peasant revolution was acquiring a new ideology—the imported Marxism would morph into native Maoism, but that was how China would thumb its nose at Europe. The peasant uprising had begun as a protest against Christian missionaries who wanted to forcibly convert the Chinese but it soon expanded into an attempt to overthrow the still-alien Manchu rule as well. Curiously, the rebellion was led by one Hung Hsin-Chu'an of the southern province of Kwangtung. A Protestant missionary had taught him at Canton about Jesus and his mission and tried to convert him to the new Faith. Instead of falling into this trap, the scholar decided to become a Prophet himself, began to see 'visions' inspiring him enough to found a new religion! He began to preach his new faith combining Christianity's anti-idolatry with his own 'visions'. In Kwangsi, his followers mushroomed forcing the government to persecute them even as he declared himself as the 'Heavenly King', and tried to found a new dynasty, that of T'ai P'ing, or the 'Great Peace'. He then moved northwards, his gangs fought the governmental forces, smashed idols, destroyed old libraries and left behind a trail of blood and ruin. Then they captured Nanking, their new 'capital'. Another of their band marched upon Peking but were repulsed near Tientsin. The T'ai P'ing held Nanking for 11 years (1853-64) in the course of which they devastated a considerable portion of the Yangtze delta.

Akin to the 1857 Rebellion in India, the first step or force-multiplier towards a greater revolution, and not *the* Revolution itself, the T'ai P'ing rebellion did not last long; it was only a seeding process. The Chinese, by and large, rallied to support the ever-alien Manchu dynasty, despite its unpopularity, thanks to a Confucian scholar Tseng Kuo-fan, who organised a powerful militia, defeated the rebels and recovered Nanking with the help of a British soldier, Captain

Gordon. Though saved for the time being, the Manchu dynasty was now completely exposed to the looming danger, as events of 1911 proved. The mid-19th century China was, just like contemporary India, in the fourth state of human matter: it was neither solid (monarchy), nor liquid (oligarchy) nor gaseous (democracy)—it was in the chaotic plasma state wherein all atomic particles were in a free state, without any bonds to bind them. China was, therefore, in for a major reconstruction of not its own society but that of the West and Asia—and that could include West Asia in the 21st century.

The 13-year-long rebellion prepared the way for the revolutionary movement which would sweep China thereafter. But, for now, Christianity, having discovered in Hung Hsin-Chu'an the home-grown alternative to Jesus, was in for a further shock. The most picturesque Manchu of the post-Rebellion era in the 19th century was the remarkable Empress Dowager who, upon the death of her husband, Emperor Hsien Feng in 1861, became regent to her son, who, too, died in 1875; she forced her way and elevated another infant to the throne while continuing as regent until her death in 1908. Even as the European scramble, political and economic exploitation of China continued, Japan, too, entered the fray, profoundly modifying the situation in China and complicating the Far Eastern Question. That an Asian coloniser has been born was proved by Japan which, converting to European imperialism, seized the Loochoo Islands, forced a war upon China and, through the Treaty of Shimonoseki (1895), compelled her to renounce her suzerainty over Korea, trying to annex it.

This spelled the defeat of the Russian aims in the Far East where Russia wanted to acquire an all-weather, warm-water port by controlling Manchuria and Korea, particularly Port Arthur. France and Germany, for their own reasons and to keep the new player, the non-European and non-Christian Japan, in check, supported Russia and this Three Power Intervention forced Japan to return the Liaotung Peninsula and Port Arthur back to China, of course in return for an additional indemnity which the poor Chinese had to pay. The three European 'friends' of China now forced the latter to 'reward' them for this gesture, gave loans to China to pay indemnity to Japan and got concessions in return. The Chinese, who were now discovering the real face of Christian countries, did not take it lying down; they murdered two German missionaries in Shantung (1897), only to find Germany getting even more concessions! A fresh wave of loot and scramble began in China in which the European leeches would bleed the Yellow Dragon white. Russia acquired Port Arthur and so did other Europeans enrich themselves with Chinese rags.

Interestingly, it was the USA which unwittingly saved China from dismemberment at the hands of Europe and Japan. Although the USA had actively worked in the drive to open up China, she had not yet joined the scramble for creating her own sphere of influence on Chinese soil. Having herself been a European colony a hundred years ago, the American policy was trade and commerce, not empire-building or colonisation. But when the US realised that the European spheres of influence could shut her (American) interests off, she proposed an 'open door' policy in 1899, envisaging a China with an open market for all nations.

The 1850s-1870s period also witnessed major Muslim uprisings in the North-West and South-West of China, attempted at—what else!—secession from the 'infidel' Chinese rule and carving out independent Muslim enclaves that could be Kashmirised later. China was now like a conceiving woman who had weakened considerably during her pregnancy. China, which had never formally been a colony, had, in the 19th century, almost become one, particularly with the aggressive Roman Catholic missionaries acquiring the right to buy land and raise buildings and then not only penetrating the land's economy but also its society and polity by protecting converts and thus disturbing law and order. These incidents left a lasting anti-Christian and anti-Muslim impression on the Chinese mind—that the Chinese converted to Christianity or Islam could not be trusted due to their extra-territorial loyalties. In that era of crumbling certainties, even the Chinese sphere of influence was swept away in the alien flood as the British and the French annexed Burma and Indo-China in the 1880s. Even the next-door neighbour, a resurgent Japan, did not hesitate to pitch in by annexing Formosa (Taiwan) and the Pescadores, forcing China to recognise the Korean independence. Each nation which could did encroach upon China and raped her. The New Barbarians, using electricity age weapons to reinstall their Stone Age beliefs, could not be stopped by the Old Order, just as in contemporary India.

So China would have to do as India was doing. You cannot short-circuit evolution, except through mutation in which case you must pay the price for that extra momentum. Europe had outgrown Christianity by first being in Christianity and thus processing itself into things unChristian. If India and China had to overthrow the aliens, they must first learn the intruding ideologies' mechanism that make the assault possible, as also overcome their own weaknesses that make this penetration possible. In India, social reformers like Raja Ram Mohun Roy had shown how to imbibe the enemy's strengths and shed one's own weaknesses. It was, above all, the Japanese assault of 1895 that stirred China into action; if even the tiny Japanese could do it, why couldn't the Chinese? This thought-process led to the formation of a society to study how the Chinese could strengthen themselves by learning the modern ways. This came to fruition in what came to be known as the 'Hundred Days of Reforms' in 1898, a half-hearted and, therefore, abortive attempt. But an attempt nevertheless.

This was an energiser. A prelude to the greater event that would shape up now. Just like the failed 1857 Revolt in India, that charged up the sleeping land into action, the Chinese too had their own 'Boxer Movement'. The protest against foreign encroachment and exploitation, with the realisation that the *common denominator* of all European enemies was their shared *Christianity*, took the shape in a movement led by a secret society called the Righteous Fraternity of Fist-Fighters or Boxers. It began as an organised campaign against foreign missionaries and Chinese Christians and there was a war-cry against the 'foreign devils', including the reforms on Western lines being introduced by Emperor Kwang Hsu. But the movement got support from Tzu-Hsei, the Empress Dowager, who seized the reins of power by removing the Emperor and cancelled all his reform edicts in 1898. She soon became the rallying point of all those Chinese who were anti-West and anti-Christian. Under her patronage, anti-Christian riots broke out at many places and scores of Christian missionaries were murdered in this 'war to the knife' in 1900. It climaxed with a German minister being shot down on the streets of Peking and his body being dragged by the insurgents; the Europeans took refuge in their legations but were soon hunted down by the Boxers for two months. But an 'international' force fought its way into Peking, forcing the Empress and her court to flee. Order was restored and so were extracted fresh concessions and indemnities. It was in this scenario that the US Secretary of State, John Hay, declared the 'open-door' policy in China. The break-up of China was also prevented by the Anglo-Japanese Alliance of 1902 against Russia which had, posing as a sympathetic friend of China during the Boxer Movement, demanded a military protectorate over Manchuria. Alarmed, Japan eventually forced a war upon Russia in 1904 to evacuate Manchuria; her defeat forced Russia to halt her advance in the Far East.

Realising that her old weapons were no match to the new alien powers, China began to think of mending ways, at least temporarily. The reform movement in China began after she faced a crushing defeat at the hands of a smaller neighbour like Japan. The necessity of remodelling Chinese institutions on Western lines led to the growth of a powerful 'Young China' movement under the leadership of a 'modern sage', K'ang yin-wei, who convinced the young emperor, Kwang-Hsu, of the need to Change. In 1898, the monarch issued a series of edicts ordering opening of educational institutions along Western lines. Besides, he also established a new department for translation of foreign literature and science, encouraged foreign travels, scrapped many a useless office and tried to reorganise the army and the bureaucracy. But this movement, lasting only about 100 days, quickly drew reaction from within as the Dowager Empress, who was aunt of the monarch, led an anti-reform rebellion, compelled the Emperor to surrender power to her, cancelled reforms and executed six pro-reformists. She was aided by the Boxer Movement which, too, was anti-reform and anti-foreign.

Despite this series of anti-Christian movements, China itself was not benefited so far. When the Boxers failed and the aliens marched upon Peking, they became convinced that the aliens could be met on an equal footing only by acquiring alien weapons. Even the monarchists believed that reforms alone could prevent dismemberment of the Empire that was now fully in the grip of competing viruses nibbling at the Chinese vitals. So, in 1905, the Empress abolished the antiquated system of the mandarin examination for officials, promoted Western-type education and converted many temples into schools. Thereafter, a commission was sent to Europe to study the system of post-Crusades governance; she also prohibited opium traffic. China was now promised a parliamentary constitution in 1917.

But, at home, with the failure of Hundred Days of Reforms, the weakened Chinese 'empire' now went back to its old methods of confronting the alien threat and stirred up a reactionary and xenophobic uprising against Christian missionaries and the converts, who were once again murdered in large numbers. But the Boxers were soon boxed in by the Europeans' combined armed might under a German commander—because a German minister had been killed by the Chinese. The Chinese, therefore, ended up paying a huge indemnity, just like the Indians ended up having the British Crown of Thorns on their head after the 1857 Rebellion. This back and forth movement of the Chinese society resulted in China, finally, giving in to the Western pressure and began her really hard march along a path so successfully trodden by Japan just a generation before.

The Dragon had begun to rise.

The Young China Party, dissatisfied with the slow pace of reforms and emboldened by the defeat of Russia by Japan, now began to unseat the Manchus. After death of the Dowager Empress in 1908, the leadership vacuum was, ironically, filled by a converted Christian Cantonese doctor of medicine, Dr Sun Yat-sen, who captured Nanking, made it the national Capital of a provisional Republic with himself as its President, forcing the young Last Emperor, Pu Yi, to abdicate in February 1912. China, which had fought against Christianity for so long, now had a Christian President! For the first time in 2,000 years, China did not have an Emperor because it had become a Republic.

The Manchus were alien to mainstream China but were still Asiatic; Sun Yat-sen was a Chinese but still an alien Christian. Clearly, he was only a stop-gap recruit.

Now have a look at the ongoing US-led 'War on Terror', being run by the 'Coalition of the Willing', whatever that means. It is necessary to understand how America unwittingly helped China to emerge stronger *then* and is *now* assisting India similarly. In the First World War, China had no direct interest or hand, buffeted as she was with her own problems. But, in 1915, while, for the first time and for a change, Europe was fighting it out against Europe in Europe itself and not in Asia or Africa, Japan saw its opportunity in China and presented to it a set of 21 demands asking for rights and concessions calculated to make the vast China a *Japanese* protectorate. Suddenly the US realised that her so-called 'Open-Door Policy' in China was being humbled by Japan, the Johnny-come-lately on the global chessboard. Under US pressure, Japan modified some of the demands but still wrested interests in Manchuria and Mongolia. President Yuan Shi-kai assented to these demands secretly without taking into confidence the nationalists (Kuomintang) or the Parliament at Peking. Meanwhile, Britain, France and Russia joined hands with Japan against Germany, and America, too, came on board. Emboldened, Japan further humiliated China even as the West looked West while the East boiled. Japan controlling China was like tail wagging the dog. Kuomintang strongly opposed China joining the War but pro-War lobby forced Peking to declare war on Germany and Austria in August 1917—not because it would tame the far-away Germans but because it would keep the neighbouring Japan in check. The German and Austrian yokes in China were the first ones she shook away. Her enslavement had begun to disappear and she now found a seat at the Peace Conference to discuss the Far East, particularly Japan. But when the West refused financial aid to China, she had to turn to Japan, giving the distant neighbour an opportunity to effect a fatal embrace and tighten economic hold on the Dragon.

The end of the First World War saw Japan exacting price on China by trying to annex German interests in Shantung. Japan was supported by the 'Allied' Powers who had secret agreements with it against China. An angry China, therefore, refused to sign the Treaty of Versailles and concluded a separate treaty with Germany. Versailles, close to the German heart, would create a Hitler; Versailles, far away from China, would create a Mao Zedong. For it produced a violent explosion of popular feelings in China and anti-Japanese agitation flared up. Alarmed at this slow rise of the Dragon, US President Warren G Harding called a conference of eight powers in Washington in 1921 to consider the Far Eastern Question which solemnly affirmed the independence and territorial integrity of China but continued with the Open-Door Policy. A humbled Japan promised to restore to China Kia-Chow and other German property rights in Shantung in return for a monetary compensation. The Washington Conference brought ancient China on the modern political world-stage, still dominated by *Christian* powers with the exception of Japan.

But the death of Yuan Shi-K'ai proved detrimental and confusing for the time being as the affairs of China went from bad to worse—most people thought the Dragon was in the throes of disintegration and death. The various Tuchans, or military governors of the few weeks, eliminated each other for supremacy in the phantom 'central' government of the Republic, which hardly existed in Peking, reducing it to puppetry. These selfish warlords fleeced China under the leadership of the most powerful of them, Chang tso-Lin of Manchuria, while the country struggled with widespread natural calamities like famine and starvation. Meanwhile, Sun Yat-sen, who was instrumental in China setting up a constitutional government in 1917, became its President and began to unify the country through a new Kuomintang reorganised with Russian help. He was disillusioned with the West—and Christianity—as they not only did not help China but sabotaged her efforts to regain her self-esteem. The Sovietised Russia, ostracised by the West and fighting the White Army, too had found her calling in Asia and actively took interest in the 'well-being' of fellow Chinese. Communist Russia actively made the Church *inactive*; China's own Church-lessness was one of the most important factors that united the two neighbours for a time. The Russian diplomat, Michael Borodin, transformed the Kuomintang into a highly organised party of disciplined members, united together by the common programme of action on lines of the Russian Communist Party in a pyramidal structure. Through a treaty with Russia, the latter renounced all her extra-territorial rights and other interests in China which recognised the USSR.

It was an 'Age of Principles'—whatever that meant. Woodrow Wilson had his 14 Principles for the League of Nations; in the 1950s, India would have her Five, in *Panchsheel*—each 'statesman' was counting his own and breaking these himself or encouraging others to violate these. Sun Yat-sen was content with just Three: in his *Sun Min Chu I* (Three Principles of the People), he propounded the programme and principles of his party: through the first Principle of Nationalism, he tried to transfer the people's loyalty from the family to the state; through the second Principle of Democracy, he tried to achieve democracy in three successive stages of military governance, political tutelage under Kuomintang and then a constitutional regime of a popularly elected Parliament and President through the Third Principle, he tried to ensure the people's livelihood, the transformation of peasantry through an equitable distribution of the land as the first requisite of transforming a predominantly agricultural society into an industrial one.

But he passed away in March 1925. It was a strange year indeed. So many nations were doing and undoing so many things. In Germany, for instance, a clown-like corporal named Adolf Hitler was emerging as a serious dictator; in Japan, militarists were dictating terms; in Arabia, the Saudi-Wahhabi combine was hell-bent on making Arabia a sixth century country in the 20th century; in India, after having aroused the Muslims but not providing them a receptacle to invest their energies, Gandhi was busy plotting the arousal of the Hindus—the year saw the rise of both the Hindu nationalist RSS as well as the Communist Party of India as the second and third front of India's struggle for recognition at world level. China, too, was now ready to receive the Communist bug, what with Sun Yat-sen's Three Principles providing the background for the Reds. But you first need nationalists who can really become internationalists. The government had earlier, in a bid to imitate Japan, issued several reforming decrees to put China on the road to Westernisation which had received setback due to the Boxers' Movement; but Sun Yat-sen's efforts made the Chinese youth modern in approach. It was the students who first voiced protests against the award of Shantung to Japan by the Peace Conference of Paris in 1919, setting all China ablaze with rage. Student agitations against both foreign domination and moth-eaten Chinese practices reached their tipping point in 1927 when the Communists and the Kuomintang joined hands…in 1989, it was the students, again, at Tiananmen Square in Beijing and in 2014 in Hong Kong, leading a million mutinies. China is hard to crack from outside; inside, however, it is brittle…for, it has different ancient philosophers coming alive for war and peace!

The nationalist drive received great momentum when the League of Nations failed to act against Japanese attack on Manchuria. Since 1898, universalisation of education had helped create a whole new generation of youth for national reconstruction. This generated a love for one's own language, a major factor in revivification of ancient societies. In India, Gandhi was encouraging Hindi as the national language as an integrating factor; in the USSR, Stalin did the same with Russian; in China, too, a striking feature of literary revolution was the substitution of the spoken language of the country for the ancient classical forms. This great movement for spread of the vernacular, known as *Pai Hui*, as a literary medium was launched by Hu Shih, an America-returned scholar; in 1917 itself, he had begun to write only in the spoken language. This was how a common vernacular evolved, replacing the multitude of dialects which had long been a handicap in national unity. Eventually, Pai Hui became the national language of China. This and the mass education drive of Y C Sen, who had worked out a course of study based upon 1,300 characters in most common use, integrated China like never before. The ancient Chinese family system was declining, women were gradually emancipating due to female literacy and the Dragon was discarding its old hide, having developed a new one. Rational criticism, an absence of organised religion and Church, and the zest for things new had made Confucianism and Taoism as native 'religious systems' things of the past; Buddhism was in the throes of existential crisis. Virulent opposition to Christian missionaries, as 'advance agents' of Western imperialism, forced the Cross not to cross the Chinese limits any more; Christianity's denationalising influence was kept firmly in check. No other nation had the guts to put The Vatican firmly in its place.

But this bit of external sheen was yet to translate into internal glaze.

Sun Yat-sen's successor was his son-in-law and secretary Chiang Kai-shek. Born in 1888, he was educated at Tokyo Military College and later in Russia, to emerge as Director of the Whampoa Military Academy in 1924. He tried to unite the nation under the Kuomintang aegis with Communist support. But his enemies within and Communist Party let all hell break loose in Nanking in 1927, thus inviting foreign powers and Japan's intervention. It forced him to break off relations with the Russian Communists and set up a nationalist government at Nanking which soon captured the old capital Peking, renaming it Peiping (Northern Peace); the Capital of this Unified China was transferred to Nanking. But Chiang's difficulties were gargantuan; the new regime was not yet fully master of the nation and he had to wage war both against the Kuomintang rebels as well as the Communists who were waiting in the wings, apart from the ancient warlords. Russia, too, finding an opportunity to get even, clashed with China over the control of the Chinese Eastern Railway until 1932 when peace returned on this front.

The Communist Party of China was set up at Shanghai in 1921 under the leadership of Li Li-San and Mao Zedong with the simple objectives of elimination of warlords, resistance to foreign imperialism and ushering in Chinese unity. For a time, they also joined the Kuomintang, a bourgeois party and stop-gap ladder in their view. While Sun Yat-sen was skilfully able to hold them together, Chiang did not inherit this trait and broke up with them in 1927. He began to crush the Communists in a strong drive. To their dismay, however, Chiang and Kuomintang were, essentially, urban phenomena in a predominantly rural China. Ironically, while in Europe, Communism was essentially a revenge of the agricultural labour-turned-industrial labour, the have-nots resisting pains of Change against the forces ushering in the Second Wave (industrialisation), in China, this was the revenge of the First Wave variables against itself in a struggle to become the Second Wave constants. In other words, European Communism was the product of the state's inability to shift the benefits of Industrial Revolution to the labour class that had left agriculture as their means of livelihood; in China, there was no industrial revolution so far—it was really a Great Leap Forward for an agricultural society to skip the pangs of industrialisation and attempt to parachute an entire generation directly into the post-industrial arena. The Communist struggle in China was aimed at reorganising the rural society, through agricultural reforms, into an urban, industrial one; and it was they, not the Kuomintang, who really represented the Chinese soul clamouring for emancipation—just like India, where Bhimrao Ambedkar, despite his limitations, really unveiled the majority Indians' soul, all other parties and leaders being just mainly passing urban phenomena and time-servers.

China, like India, was now discovering its underdog coming to the forefront—those hitherto invisible in villages, would now be vanguards in town.

Unable to hold their own in the cities, the Communists redoubled their struggle in rural areas even as Chiang's forces drove them into the mountains of southern Kiangsi. Mao, now Chairman of the Chinese Soviet Government, together with his Commander-in-Chief Chu Taeh, organised peasantry in Kiangsi and Fukien provinces with armed intrusion and expropriation of the landlords and rich peasants. Distribution of land among peasants, irrigation and flood-control schemes made the Communists popular in the rural areas; in the urban areas, too, they raised wages of industrial labourers and shortened working hours. Unlike European Communism, where it was aimed at establishing the proletarian dictatorship, as in Russia, the Chinese experiment aimed at peasants controlling the fate of the nation—had Marx been alive, he would have been startled at China's *industry-less* Communism! The Kuomintang's Nationalist Government, meanwhile, unsuccessfully carried out four major anti-Communist campaigns until 1933 to crush the ancient forces raising their head from under the eternal soil. Chiang flung one million men against the Communists and badly defeated the Red Army. Realising the danger of extinction, Mao and Chu led the Communists on their famous 6,000-mile (9,700-kms) Long March to join friendly forces of the North-West China in 1934, crossing 18 mountain ranges and 24 rivers, fighting all the way over a difficult terrain. Thousands of faithful Communists died on the way and what remained of the Red Army was a steeled force now ready for a string of victories—the Chinese version of an invincible,'Chosen People', the kind of mythology that keeps a people fighting adversaries ages after ages, was now ready thanks to the excellent Communist propaganda. Communism, as a socio-political-economic ideology in a state that would be strengthened more, rather than withering away in the classical Marxist sense, did not, however, change the situation much in a vast land rendered poor by centuries of agony. But China would declare itself as the 'People's Republic', rather than being the 'Celestial Empire' or the Middle Kingdom; and there would be no 'Son of Heaven' now. In this great churning, the peasantry, which was hitherto at the bottom, was surfacing, crossing all the feudal hurdles, becoming the proletariat, and launching into an industrial age. The ancient China was ready to pole-vault across the Great Wall, upon itself, upon its own shoulders.

All it needed was a pole.

Nothing brings peace like war.

Or, as the Afghans say, they are at peace only when they are at war.

This pole was provided by Japan. Few historical accidents were like this one when poison became the best rejuvenator—China would, of course, do the same to India in 1962! So, the Japanese invasion of Manchuria in 1931-32, essentially a wake-up call, temporarily united the Kuomintang and Communists against the common enemy; the full-scale invasion of the land in 1937 by this ancient neighbour-turned-new enemy again glued together the native enemies suspicious of each other's intentions more than the common enemy they were fighting against. With Japan attacking Pearl Harbour in 1941, the Allied aid came to China which had been largely cut off by Japan from the rest of the world. China fiercely resisted the Japanese aggression putting paid to the latter's ambition to dominate Asia, South-East

Asia and the Far East. For this taming of Japan, the UK and the USA signed treaties with China, relinquishing their extra-territorial rights and special privileges. China was now almost fully de-colonised; the century-old shadows of eclipse were departing. As soon as Japan's fate was sealed at the Cairo Conference (1943), the Communists and the Kuomintang—in that order, as now the order was reversed—reminded themselves that they had merely halted their civil war against each other. America tried to broker peace between the Kuomintang Army and the Communist guerrillas as the latter continued to drive the former away from one region after another. At last, the Kuomintang, which essentially represented the nation's temporary bridge with the West and Christianity, were forced to leave the mainland China and take shelter in the Island of Formosa (Taiwan), under protection from the USA.

History had turned full circle now: the USA, which had paved way for the entry of Europe and Japan in China through the Open-Door Policy, now found the doors closed on it! On 1 October 1949, the People's Republic of China was proclaimed with Mao as Chairman of the Chinese Communist Party and Chou en-Lie as Premier. The Soviet Union promptly recognised the New Government in Old China. For the first time, the USA's foreign policy had collapsed completely in the same area where Washington had launched its foreign policy in the first place, the Far East, in the mid-19th century. Collapse of Chiang Kai-shek's regime was the worst-ever snub for the Americans who had just cut their teeth on the world stage. It was also beginning of deChristianisation of the East.

Born in a relatively prosperous family, Mao Tse-tung, or Mao Zedong (1893-1976), emerged as China's principal Marxist theorist, military leader and statesman. In 1911, when the Xinhua Revolution began against the monarchy, he had joined the Revolutionary Army and the National Party, Kuomintang. Influenced by the Russian Revolution, he joined the Chinese Communist Party (1921) as a founding member. Unlike Russia, however, China was predominantly agrarian. Early on, therefore, Mao realised that a Communist Revolution in China would be led primarily by farmers.

The way his contemporary Gandhi was supporting two contradictory Movements in India, the Non-Cooperation and the Khilafat, Mao, too, found himself supporting the nationalist Kuomintang and the internationalist Communist 'revolutions'. The way Gandhi used the reactionary Khilafat drive as a force-multiplier for the progressive Non-Cooperation, Mao, too, used the *bourgeois* Kuomintang as a force-multiplier for the *proletariat* Communist movement. Sun Yat-sen was the father of the modern Republic of China but he, being a Congregational-Protestant Christian, could not become the soul of the nation, the way Jinnah and others could not become the soul of India despite their brilliance. Their role was like that of the chaff, protecting the seed until it germinated.

Like Gandhi in India, Mao in China was this seed. Sun Yat-sen's policy of active cooperation with the Chinese Communists continued from 1923 until 1927 when he was succeeded by Chiang Kai-shek. Meanwhile, Mao had adopted Leninist ideas and wanted to convert the Russian 'factory revolution' into China's agrarian Communism. Soon, Chiang purged the Communists, forcing them to flee to the mountainous Jiangxi Province where 'Chairman' Mao set up the Soviet Republic of China with a strong army of guerrilla fighters. By 1934, the Communists controlled a dozen regions in Jiangxi, forcing Chiang to despatch a million-strong government forces and surround the red stronghold. This forced the Mao-led Communists to launch their famous 'Long March' in which over 100,000 fighters and their dependents trekked the north and west across mountains. In the next 12 months, only a third of them survived across a 9,700-km-long journey, the like of which the world had never seen before.

The way China would 'kick-start' India in 1962, Japan, too, kicked-started China in 1937. When the Japanese Imperial Army invaded China, Chiang fled his capital to Nanking and sought support from in-house foe Mao to fight the external enemy. Millions of Chinese died in this civilisational shake-up in the East when Nature eliminated surplus populations and removed the scaffoldings after construction of the Edifice. Kuomintang had served its purpose and was outdated in a China where native genius was now flowering. On 1 October 1949, in Tiananmen Square, Peking (Beijing), Mao announced the establishment of the People's Republic of China. Chiang Kai-shek and his followers fled to the Island ofTaiwan, where they formed the Republic of China.

Although it all began well, floods, bad harvests and other calamities took a heavy toll on this great revolution as both agricultural and industrial productions failed. About four million people died of starvation between 1959 and 1962, one of the reasons why China tried to divert the nation's attention outside by attacking India.

China proved that a people's salvation was possible even without God, Christianity or Jesus, Islam or Muhammed. It has proved the Spanish proverb correct that the more the world changes the more it remains the same! So, China has changed a lot; and China has remained the same. Her Sons are no longer satisfied with their native Heaven; they seek out new ones in America, Europe, Australia and Japan. The Celestial Empire is now studded with earthly entertainment, decay and regeneration. The Middle Kingdom is in a corner of Asia. And has its own fault-lines in Hong Kong, Macao, Xinjiang and Taiwan, the way America has its own in Texas, California or the Hawaii Islands. These fault-lines remind us, when they get activated from time to time, the limits of human arrogance. The more China spreads itself far and thin, the more would she get exposed to this permanence of temporariness. The Chinese miracle is stupendous. The way Gandhi plotted expulsion of Islam from India, Mao too plotted the expulsion of Christianity from China. Gandhi was the product of a thousand-year-long churning of India; Mao was product of 500-years-long churning of China. They both were orthodox men using new tools imported from Abrahamic sources, to defeat Abrahamism. They fathered their New Nations from Old Seed. And disappeared, leaving their nations to pay lip-service twice a year to their heritage. Both China and India reacted very slowly against invasions of alien ideologies and cultures. But they reacted comprehensively. Like Nature.

And, they have not come full Circle. Yet.

JAPAN

SPRING is the shortest season, one that hurries up extension of Life. Few realise the onset of this season which silently marches in at the fag end of winter. New foliage. New flowers. Feasting insects. Chirping birds. A new dawn. The old dusk... Garish colours suddenly appear on the plants. Spring is the celebration of Life, its revivification. Unlike humans, plants and animals do not enjoy a round-the-year sexual drive; Nature, therefore, rushes them through the spring to procreate in this mating season.

Japan is embodiment of spring on the earth. Flowers have been a cult in Japan. Although each nation loves spring, in Japan it acquired new connotation. Like Nature miniaturising changes during spring, Japan too imbibed the art of miniaturising in all spheres of human life as a national character—from bonsai to micro-chips. This rush-through made Japan assimilate great changes within a short period, unlike other slow-moving nations including China and India. Japan emerged as the first Asian Tiger, that defeated Russia in 1904, thus inspiring a great decolonising drive in Asia and Africa single-handedly against a dozen European nations, that later included America. What other nations achieved in several generations, Japan achieved in a few. But, at the same time, this art of miniaturising also had its flip-side and limitations: for it blinded this nation towards the realities of world politics and Japan could not see the atom bombs coming down on Hiroshima and Nagasaki. But, with spring in her feet, Japan recovered within a generation from this huge calamity, jumped and skipped, scooted and scurried, absorbed democracy at a speed greater than any other nation, to regain her position in the Group of Eight (G-8) nations. Japan is the spring child of Nature.

From the 12th to the mid-19th century, Japan remained virtually cut off from the rest of the world. Some contact with Europe did begin in 1542 with the arrival of the Portuguese traders, followed by the Spanish and the Dutch, 1609. For two centuries (15th and 16th), Japan sank into a state of feudal anarchy until order was restored by three great rulers, Nobunaga, Hideyoshi and Iyeyasu, the last emerging the real Shogun remaining in power until 1867. An American fleet forcibly delivered the new Japan through a Caesarean section in 1868, something that created the modern nation. Like Gujaratis, most Japanese never bothered about philosophy or the sciences but focused on their user-friendly end-products, ie. politics and technology. They thought politics is the end of philosophy the way technology is that of the sciences. That was why Japan did not have many philosophers or theoretical scientists and managed to skip centuries of backwardness to emerge on world political scene.

Hideyoshi, a 16th century contemporary of Akbar in India and Queen Elizabeth in England, was a peasant's son. He was illiterate, ugly and monkey-faced—therefore earning the sobriquet *Sarumen Kanja*. During his time Japan would stimulate and spur up Asia against Christianity when 'Saint' Francis Xavier (1506-52) decided to force Christianity upon Japan. Fresh from setting up an Inquisition in Goa, India (1542), to massacre infidel Hindus who remained unimpressed with the passion of the Christ, this Spanish Jesuit missionary arrived on the Japanese shore (1549-51) to set up a Christian mission that would work upon the Japanese mind for the next 100 years. However, he discovered that the docile Indians were easier to prey upon than the intrepid Japanese; so he returned to India, went to China thereafter and died of fever there, assured of being canonised (1622). The fear that Roman Catholic propaganda intended as a preparation for Spanish conquest of Japan led to the expulsion of the Spanish in 1624 and the Portuguese in 1639 and, subsequently, to the almost total extermination of Christianity by persecution. In the Japanese town of *Nagasaki*, the Jesuits forced its ruler, Omura, to pressurise his population to accept the Cross and weed out Buddhism. The Great Monkey-Face, not amused at this invasion of 'spiritual' monkeys, ordered the Vice-Provincial of the Jesuits to answer five questions: (1) Why were the Jesuits forcing the Japanese subjects of the Shogun to become Christians? (2) Why were the intruders destroying the Buddhist temples and those of local deities like Hotoke and Kami? (3) Why were they persecuting the Buddhist monks? (4) Why did the Spanish and Portuguese Jesuits eat cattle like cow and ox, considered holy and useful by the Japanese and (5)Why were the invader merchants buying and selling the poor Japanese in the slave trade?

Dissatisfied with the answers, the Shogun denounced the Jesuits as the 'greatest criminals' and ordered them to leave Japan within 20 days, or face death. The Portuguese and the Spanish Jesuits, arrogant barbarians trying to sell humble Jesus to proud Japanese, laughed at him, further enraging him to stamp out Christianity. He feared that the spiritual conquest of Japan by these crafty missionaries might, as in the contemporary America, lead to its political conquest by the military. He curtly ordered the missionaries in 1587 to get out of Japan. They didn't. Hideyoshi then put more than 20,000 of them, including converts, to death in one go. This anti-foreign feeling culminated in the promulgation of two edicts in 1637 forbidding them from entering Japan on pain of death; similarly, the Japanese, too, were forbidden to leave it on the same penalty. Only a few Dutch were allowed to continue commerce under strict limitations. Thus was Japan hermetically sealed against the outside world until mid-19th century. Before he died in 1598, Hideyoshi conceived the idea of the new Japanese capital, Yedo (Tokyo), in place of Kyoto. Hideyoshi left behind a ticking atom bomb in Nagasaki, long before America dropped one in August 1945. This Nagasaki bomb against the Cross later metamorphosed into Japan's militarism against *Christian* interests in the Far East and found expression against Russia (1905) and then against many, including America (Pearl Harbour, 1941).

Unlike Hideyoshi, Shogun Iyeyasu first tolerated Christianity. But he soon discovered that the Jesuits, uncouth, intolerant and crafty, considered him a malleable fool, his lenience as a weakness and tried to exploit the situation to their advantage, as they did in other lands. In 1614, therefore, he banned the preaching as well as practice of Christianity all over Japan and ordered all remaining converts and missionaries either to leave the nation or renounce their faith. Even after his death, this anti-Christian drive continued and Christianity was virtually stamped out. In 1638, the last batch of about 40,000 Christians were massacred *en masse* on their fortified peninsula of Shimabara. Thereafter, the Japanese peeped into the world only through the Dutch window they had been left with at Nagasaki, until the King of the Netherlands, in the 1840s, warned him that Japan could no longer remain isolated and its fate will be very much like China's. But, internally, Japan was readying itself for this.

For, Iyeyasu remembered how the Christian missionaries, whatever their in-house differences, secretly worked in tandem with a single-minded devotion and ambition to bring all infidel lands under the Christ. In 1596, a Spanish galleon was pillaged by the Japanese; its pilot, Landecho, complained to Masuda, a minister, against the 'outrage'. An amused Masuda asked the complainant how had one man, the Pope, won so many lands. The arrogant Landecho boasted that the ***Christian kings first send traders and then missionaries to convert the infidel, followed by the troops who join hands with the fifth-columnist converts who, together, subjugate the whole land.*** No Christian or, for that matter, Muslim, ever blurted out such a closely-guarded ***Brotherhood secret*** anywhere in the world since the inception of Abrahamism.

The land of Samurai, who numbered more than a million out of a total of 25 million population in the 16th century, would never tolerate this self-righteous arrogance. Like the contemporary Islamic society in the Fertile Crescent, where every Muslim was a soldier-at-short-notice and every soldier was a Muslim, the new Japan came to believe that every gentleman was to be a soldier and every soldier would be a gentleman. This was in sharp contrast with the pacifist China and India where gentlemen were supposed to be those *shunning* war and embracing philosophy and spirituality—and since these dignified 'gentlemen', often impotents masquerading as celibates, considered undignified wars to be fought not *by* them but by others *for* them, both these largest of the countries continued to be enslaved by the smallest of nations. Thus, Japan preferred to model itself on Islam to take on Christianity—*minus monotheism*! In India, on the other hand, the divided Rajputs, Marathas and Sikhs emulated the Mughals to defeat the united Mughals. In Japan, sword became the soul of Samurai who, like these Indian warrior classes, followed a stern code of honour, called *Bushido* (the Noble Way), stressing virtue, shunning material benefits, dying to protect a promise, hard and frugal living, suppress emotions, suffer silently, remain courageous in all extremities, follow total asceticism and self-control—their women were taught to celebrate their martyrdom. Their only loyalty was to their master—in 1912, when Emperor Mutsuhito died, General Nogi and his wife ended their life to be with their monarch in the Heaven.

Unlike other nations in the Orient, Japan, always overcrowded due to shortage of land, would not encourage fertility, particularly in the Samurai period when the warrior would normally remain bachelor until he turned 30 and would sire not more than two children thereafter. They were only a moderately religious people, never fanatics, given more to piety and prayer rather than disputations. It was this trait that made them transform even Buddhism from being an invitation to Nirvana to a cult of protecting lovely deities, pleasant ceremonies, festivals, ikebana competitions, pilgrimages and a woolly paradise somewhere around Mount Fuji. They counted their enemies carefully and constructed 128 types of hell in which to pigeon-hole them! Even for the Japanese who embraced Christianity, the Devil continued to be non-Biblical: he was not green but did have horns and sabre-tooth, a flat-nose and claws—unlike the Bible's celibate Devil, this one would lure women to sex and men to provide him with proteins; the Japanese Devil was not a round-the-clock enemy of God as he had no time for theological disputations, kept as he was busy with men and women—the first example of how Japan adopted alien technology to suits her own needs.

On the other hand, Buddhism gave Japan a school of *Bodhisattvas*, who were ready to help those tired of the Devil's alleged machinations. These Bodhisattvas were, in Japan's bonsai parlance, those high souls who, like trees, were carefully right-sized in the pot itself to provide the original fruit. That is, they could be persuaded to *transfer, a la technology,* to the pious some of the grace they had accumulated over the many incarnations of virtuous living. Besides this imported religion, Japan had its own native ones. They worshipped Our Lady Kwannon and Jizo, a Jesus-clone, both feminine deities, and the fierce Sun Goddess, Amaterasu O Mikami. Buddhist temples also had a Shinto shrine in the same premises. There were other cults and sects, too; but the most famous were those that, like Buddhism, trained men into the art of *Zen* meditation. By the 18th century, when the Shoguns went over to either Confucianism or their successors revived Shinto, Buddhism declined in Japan—the Land of Rising Sun was now feeling the heat of Europe and would have to prepare itself for the scorching summer. The days of Buddhist pacifism in the centuries of a violent Christianity vanquishing a violent Islam, and even ejecting it from Europe's Iberian Peninsula, were now over. It was time Japan reverted to Shintoism, its native, realistic faith, rather than the exotic Buddhism.

Shinto stressed oneness with natural forces and loyalty to the reigning Meiji dynasty as descendent of the Sun Goddess. Obedience and devotion to the Emperor were, therefore, not to be questioned as they evolved an aggressive nationalistic fervour—post-1945, however, these traits were somewhat discarded as Japan was 'processed' into democracy by the USA, believing the ghost of General Hideki Tojo had thus been buried; he was Japan's General and Minister for War (1940-41), and Premier (1941-44), forced to resign in 1944 and hanged as war criminal, but remained alive in the hearts of many Japanese; because of his legacy, off and on, Japan tries to rearm itself. Officially, Emperor Hirohito disavowed his 'divinity' in 1946 and Shinto was disestablished as a state religion. Shinto, in fact, is not one religion but an umbrella under which come some 130 sects and cults. Shinto was the Chinese transliteration of the Japanese concept, or the Doctrine/Way of the Gods, called Kami-no-Michi, whose chief shrine was at Ise, near Kyoto. In this Temple of Amaterasu O Mikami, the holiest shrine of the Sun Goddess, the Japanese have reverentially preserved a mirror they believed She gave to her son, Jimmu, the First Emperor, in the seventh century BC. From Jimmu to Hirohito, each Japanese Emperor was from the same Meiji dynasty in an uninterrupted chain. No other nation loved the Sun so much!

Some philosophy, also imported from China, strengthened this Japanese fixation. Due to the Mongoloid 'pollution', the Japanese had come to look down upon the Chinese since the 13th century and, in 1552, all intercourse with the Dragon had been forbidden. Fujiwara Seigwa, a scion of the famous Japanese family, however, went to China to study the revived Sung Confucianism. After his death (1619), his pupil Hayashi Razan, found a master not in Confucius but in the first Tokugawa Shogun. Hayashi decided to cleanse Japan of both aliens, Buddhism and Christianity, declaring these religions as degenerative doctrines threatening to weaken the nation's moral fabric and fibre, which must be replaced by the truly atheistic moral code of Confucianism, much nearer home than the aliens originated in far-away lands. From the same school subsequently came philosophers like Kaibara Ekken and Nakaye Toju who stressed a muscular and masculine Japan rather than a tender and feminine nation that Buddhism and Christianity 'sought' to make them. The rebirth of Shintoism, ironically, spelled doom for the Shogunate the way the rebirth of various Hindu streams through the Bhakti Movement in the contemporary Mughal India weakened the hold of Islam. Within, Japan had become moth-eaten during the Shogunate era as the Samurai softened into complacence and comfort in two centuries of peace. Post-Iyeyasu, all Shoguns, except Yoshimune, were mediocre time-servers. Japan was waiting for the Americans the way India was waiting for the British—from the West came not only colonial exploiters but also the despised Christian missionaries and the refreshing libertarian forces—in that order.

Japan's exclusion came to an end when US President Millard Fillmore (1850-1853) summoned Naval Commodore Matthew Galbraith Perry to command an expedition that would reopen communication between Japan and the outside world after 250 years of isolation and anti-Christian crusade. The Japanese, until then used to see volcanoes bursting out of the Earth, were startled to see 'floating volcanoes' when Perry demonstrated a show of evident military and naval superiority of his four steamships; an exhibition of US technical superiority enabled him to negotiate with Japan the Treaty of Kanagawa (1854), granting the US trading rights with Japan and, of course, putting an end to the 'persecution' of Christianity—meaning total freedom to the Christian missionaries to convert the Japanese by hook or crook; meaning also that any obstacle in this conversion business would mean a 'persecution' of Christians. Only, Perry forgot that his own elder brother, named (Oliver) Hazard, had died on a similar mission to South America in 1819. America, product of a theo-fatigued deChristianising Europe, as the last post of the Christ in a corner of the Earth, was relapsing into the same faith. At home, America was fighting a Civil War ostensibly to restore equal rights to the Blacks and other 'coloured' people but racially trying to keep the Blacks away from mainstream Protestantism despite their conversion; abroad, it had begun to court the likes of brothers Matthew and Hazard—and the new Gospel that, at a time of deChristianisation of Europe, Asia needed Christianisation to keep the dying faith of and in Jesus alive.

The Shogunate of Japan, the last of whom was Keiki's in 1867, was coming to an end; but Japan would export the same junked Shogunate to the outside world in the near future, the way the West would dump its obsolete theologies in the Third World. In the 1860s, the Western cartel of the US, Britain, France, Russia and the Netherlands, won concessions like commercial privileges, diplomatic exchanges and the well-known extra-territoriality for Western residents in Japan. In all, the West had breached the secluded Japan at six ports; in turn, Japan would soon imitate the West and breach it at 60 ports.

After India and China, Japan had become a major Western playground in the East, although there were many other, smaller countries in the East and South East Asia facing the same catalytic-enemy bent upon their creative destruction; while India and China were engaged in creating a decisive response to Islam and Christianity, respectively, Japan did the unthinkable. While monarchy was racing towards extinction in China, as well as India, it was strengthening in Japan! On one hand, the weakling Japan was unable to resist the West and, on the other, two great confederacies of feudal powers, already adopting Western military techniques, were challenging the Tokugawa Shogunate. In 1868, when the West apprehended a violent anti-West and anti-Christianity revolution, disorder and anarchy, in a surprise move, the imperial court resumed its power, replacing the Shogun, in what came to be known as the 'Meiji Restoration'; the isolationist but powerful Daimios, until now subjects of the conservative Shogun, 'discovered' that the latter himself was a subject of the Emperor and that, being 'pro-West', should be shown the door—the Shogun was caught in an unenviable position between the Devil in the deep sea and the Daimios. The Daimios, incorrigible enemies of the 'European barbarians', decided to compel the Shogun to abdicate in 1867; the new 'Era of Meiji' began on January one, 1868.

They would have dethroned even the Mikado (Emperor) but two events saved him. A British squadron bombarded the Kagoshima town in retaliation of the murder of a Briton by the Samurai of the Daimio of the Satsuma clan in 1863; in another incident, a combined Western force bombarded the Shimonosheki town in 1864 to punish the Daimio of Choshu for firing upon Western vessels. The Daimios concluded that the West was extremely powerful and only a united Japanese nation, by rapid Europeanisation, could meet the alien challenge. The Shogun, being considered 'pro-West' was not the man of the hour; but the Emperor, if recharged, could unite the whole nation against the Christian challenge. That was how the Daimios decided to unseat the Shoguns and restore to the Mikado all executive powers he had been denied. While abdicating, Keiki admitted his shortcomings, incompetence and shame: 'Now I have noticed that foreign interference is becoming more pronounced by the day and unless we have a strong central authority as our government, the foundations of our state would fall to pieces.' Japan was preparing to pay the West in its own coin. It was a strange phenomenon typical of Japan: the dormant, centuries-old sleeping bud suddenly flowering back as if spring had revivified it. The middle class and overawed Japanese, who were deeply influenced by the West, were quick to learn from the nation's enemies the secrets of their strength, the way the Indians and Chinese learnt Western techniques to vanquish Western techniques. The Meiji Restoration was somewhat like Mazzini Restoration in Italy, emulated in contemporary Europe wherein nationalism rooted in a conservative view of society would destroy much of customs and traditions it was supposedly developed to defend. In Europe, nationalism ***now*** undermined Christianity but in the East, it spread the Cross! Japan saw many a Japanese convert to Christianity, even though they continued to honour their Emperor, defender of the infidel Shinto faith! The revised Shinto faith involved a propaganda to convince the masses that the restored Emperor was divine in lineage and wisdom and that his decrees must be accepted as the edicts and Will of God.

The year 1868 saw a conservative revolution opening the way to radical change: underneath layers, the Meiji Restoration was, in fact, restoration of the Sun Goddess, Amaterasu O Mikami, Mother of the Emperor. During the next 30 years, Japan de-eclipsed itself rapidly by adopting many of the Western ways, including abolishing the privileges of the feudal nobility, compulsory elementary education for boys and girls in 1872, a representative system of local government in 1879, a bi-cameral Parliament and a Constitution ten years later. Count Ito Hirobumi framed the Constitution on the model of Prussia in which the Emperor was the source of the whole national effort—clearly, Japan was inching to join Germany in a future attempt at possible world conquest. The Germans had once destroyed the Holy Roman Empire in Western Europe; the Japanese would now destroy the Holy British Empire in East Asia.

Japan was importing the West into the East and exporting the East to the West and the Rest, in the end preparing to pay a heavy spiritual cost for these excesses and successes. Unlike China and India, whose roots in philosophy had enabled them to move slowly and fashion their response to Christianity and Islam respectively, Japan, bereft of long-term philosophical traditions that mould a society's graduated response to the enemy, as food to be assimilated and faeces to be extruded, chose the fast lane and the fast food for fast answers: from the sword, the transformation to the gun was smooth. The Sunrise was welcome but too fast for comfort. Accidents were to be Japan's lot. Like the Arabs and Mongols, who too rose suddenly to stardom, the Japanese were also scripting a similar role for themselves. For five decades after Independence in 1947, India had to struggle against the caste system that had decayed from a fortress into a prison; Japan, in one go, ensured that its untouchables, Eta, were freed from their caste disabilities and all classes became theoretically equal before the law. Japan never forgot the humiliation of 1853 and pranks of Perry and ensured that, in the Constitution, the Army and the Navy were responsible only to the Emperor. The year 1853 had indicated that Japan would take revenge upon the West; she established conscription, made each school in the land a military training camp and a nursery of nationalistic ardour, the way American support to Israel over the al

Aqsa issue made each Islamic seminary a potential breeding ground for terrorism across the world.

With an amazing speed and aptitude, a strongly armed Japan was soon sitting across the High Table, talking 'peace' with aliens. The first thing Japan did after the Meiji Restoration was to plot a gradual absorption of her teacher, China—like a rabbit swallowing the python!—which the combined might of Europe and America could never achieve. With her landmark victory against Russia in 1905, which became a turning point in modern history, Japan not only ended the rule of Europe in the East, it also led the resurrection of Asia: Japan became a precursor and role-model not only for China and India, but also to a hundred other societies colonised and Abrahamised by the West and the West Asia.

Japan learnt from the West that it was not enough to be merely pacifist and civilised—in fact, a pacifist is considered impotent and idiot. One must be militarily and economically strong to be heard in the court of the West which laughed at silent prayers but heard only loud explosions. Therefore, Japan decided to shed the badge of inferiority imposed on her by 'unequal' treaties she was forced to accept by the West. Her plea in 1871 for a modification of these treaties went unheard in Europe, which was now soaking a lot of Bismarck's 'Blood and Iron Policy'. This taught Japan a lesson: you cannot make the West listen to you unless your Army, trained along European lines, beats the drums right into their ears. It was in the character of Abrahamic religions that as soon as you convert to any of these, your world-view and psychological make-up undergoes a desert-change; you become expansionist and imperialist, smelling conspiracies and, in turn, turning into conspirator, and the first thing you do would be to strike at your own root, own culture, own family, own nation—Abraham, Father of Many Nations, did spur the process of change in stagnant societies but, later, also turned out to be the biggest denationalising factor in the world. Japan proved an exception: spread of Christianity made it more conscious of its own culture and unity—but the expansionist and imperialist bug did bite it as well.

The next five decades saw Japan on a roller-coaster of politics and power-play as the softening influence of Confucianism and Buddhism waned in direct proportion to the worship of the Divine Emperor who, as the upholder of Shintoism, enjoyed utmost loyalty of the Nation, in practice even above the Constitution. Its victories of a nation of 'dwarfs' against Leviathans like China and Russia immensely increased the international prestige and fear of Japan, now called the 'Yellow Peril' which now felt free to get herself rid of 'unequal treaties' of the post-Perry era. Now the Far East meant Japan, Nippon, the Land of Rising Sun. For the world colonised by the West, Japan became a source of inspiration for all nationalist movements.

The first Russo-Japanese War was unique as an Asian and non-Christian nation won a decisive victory against an essentially European-Christian power, for the first time in a 2,000-year-long ongoing Clash of Civilisations. After Japan's bloody but decisive naval victory at Tsushima, in which each of the two rivals lost 60,000 soldiers, US President Theodore Roosevelt intervened to persuade them to sign the Treaty of Portsmouth (1905). If Trafalgar had overhauled European politics in the 19th century, Tsushima changed the face of Asian politics in the 20th. The victory of Japan effectively checked the advance of Russia in the Far East and that of Europe in Asia, in general, and of Christianity and Islam in the world and, above all, broke the myth, the spell of the 'invincibility' of the West. This sowed seeds of a hundred nationalist and anti-imperialist movements across the world. The 13th century Mongol menace had defeated Europe and the Fertile Crescent; the 20th century Japan defeated Europe. For the first time in modern history, an Asiatic power had utterly humbled a European power, the largest and supposedly very powerful; the Sun had finally started Rising in the East eclipsing the Dark Age. The immense prestige that Japan thus acquired gave her a standing of the dominant power in the Far East, stimulated her national pride and prodded her to continue the expansionist drive against China which, essentially, was a way to prod the sleeping Dragon to wake up, the way China would wake up India in 1962.

The infidel would, henceforth, remain the common denominator in world politics. China, India, Japan made it impossible for organised religions of Abrahamic lineage to convert many outside their boxes. The Abrahamites, unable to find converts among the infidels, would now discover and exterminate 'infidels' in their midst, in a no-holds-barred self-destruction in their respective fratricidal Brotherhoods—had not Abraham similarly tried to end his own life! That suicidal streak survived in the Jews, the Christians and the Muslims, and then revived whenever they found themselves trapped in the choppy infidel oceans they once thought to have dried up—after 1945, the Jews generally degenerated into uncreativity and the Christians into old-age complacency; the Muslims are now eliminating their own surplus population and fighting to stay relevant.

Like China, Japan viewed the East as its natural territory and 'strategic depth' and bigger nations there as her natural feast. Having assimilated European 'values' and militarism, after forcing Russia out, Japan annexed Korea outright (1910) and, during the First World War, consolidated her hold on Asia, particularly over China. This War, at the root of it all, was the beginning of Christianity's interminable decline. It was a natural process of decay for Abrahamic faiths. For them, missionary activity was like business: if they fail to expand outside, they start imploding within. Due to Japan's effective military action, China's strong anti-Christian moves and India's subtle anti-Islamic drive, the 'progress' of these Abrahamic religions had been stalled. Christianity was forced to outsource security of Jerusalem: the Jews were 'returning' to Israel after 2,000 years of wandering, this time tasked with securing *their* Holy City *for* the Christians *from* the hands of the Muslims. Having thus checkmated in Asia and Europe, Christianity had begun to swallow its own tail in the early 20th century, the way Islam's *Jinn* of *Jannat* (Genie of Paradise) is bottling itself up in the 21st.

The Washington Conference was successful in that it shifted the epicentre of 'world politics' from Europe to America in the West and to Japan in the East: the world was split into an America opened up by Britain on one side and, in turn, a Japan opened up by America on the other. America was extrusion of recalcitrant Christianity in its Protestant software from Europe, Japan extrusion of a pacifist Buddhism from Asia. The political democracy of America has since been struggling against spiritual dictatorship of Christianity, the way the political democracy of Japan, post-1945, would struggle against the legacy of financial Shogunates, or large corporate cartels. The contours of this future had begun to shape up in the two nations as natural corollary of the long battle between the Abrahamic religions on the one side and the 'infidels' on the other. The inter-War Japanese fervently believed the way their contemporary Nazis did: that they were a superior race, born to rule others, like the Jews, the Romans, the Greeks, the Romans, the Aryans, the Chinese, the British…the Americans…

The micro-size Japan sought to create a 'New Order' in the East, the way its alter ego, America, believed in its own 'New Deal' in the 1930s. Under this New Order, Japan was to be the Leader in a 'co-prosperity' sphere in which she, along with Manchuko and China, were, as the first three members, to be the self-reliant economic blocks from which European exploitation was to be eliminated.

To keep a check on the Communist Soviet Union, Japan even entered into an Anti-Comintern Pact with Germany. Now Japan was ready to ride the Dragon. They had not, however, factored in the resilience and patriotism of China. The ease with which they succeeded in their Manchurian venture made them believe in their own invincibility; but when they tried to encroach upon the Chinese mainland, the rival Nationalists and Communists united against the aggressor. The aggression began at Marco Polo Bridge in July 1937. The Japanese misadventure united China like never before; China had begun to open up with Marco Polo in the 14th century; she now began to flower at Marco Polo Bridge in the 20th.

America, which believed she was an open society, had not reckoned with Japan becoming so much open as to close all American options in the East. The USA branded Japan a 'wanton aggressor' and tried to control it in the Brussels Conference (1937). As soon as the Second World War broke out that year, Japan expanded her 'co-prosperity sphere' from the Far East to East Asia, while entering into a military alliance (1940) with Germany and Italy, the latest prime movers in Europe thumbing their nose at France, the UK, the USA and, later, the Soviet Union. Japan also sought to neutralise the Russians by secretly entering into an agreement by sending its Foreign Minister, Matsouka, to Berlin and Moscow. Alarmed at Tokyo joining the Berlin-Rome Axis, the USA began to tighten screws on Japan, which, having learnt the Western art of talking peace till preparations for war were over, sent a 'peace mission' to Washington and, at the same time, bombed the American naval base at Pearl Harbour on 7 December 1941.

Like the First World War, the Second, too, had begun as a war between European nations. Japan registered phenomenal successes initially in the Pacific chapter of the War, liquidating in three years the whole European empire in the East built over three centuries: from Pearl Harbour in the West to the Diamond Harbour (India) in the East, Japan effectively destroyed Christian superiority. Emboldened at the startling successes of the men China always mocked as 'dwarfs', European colonies across the world witnessed an outburst of nationalist movements against alien domination. Many nationalists, such as Subhas Chandra Bose of India, joined hands with Japan, even if temporarily. The process Japan started in 1905 was completed by 1945: Western, Christian 'superiority' and 'invincibility' became a thing of the past. Initially, Japan was seen as a liberating force by the Asiatic people and inspired other European colonies to throw away the foreign yoke. By posing as liberator and benefactor, Japan had begun to weld the Far East into a Greater East Asia Economic Zone—but, as always, the 'liberator' soon became the new master resorting to old tactics for exploitation of the colonies.

Japan being a small nation bereft of natural resources, soon began to feel the pangs of colonial project; it became more and more difficult to keep the possessions and increasingly clear that the Nippon's importance was just to remove the darkness of night and crack the dawn. Having done that, it was time for Japan to retire as a hundred nations, inspired by it, were now going to be up and back on their feet. The USA, with her enormous resources, now took the lead on behalf of the West which, under General Douglas

MacArthur, began to push Japan back into its real self. With the Philippines' fall in July 1945, the Japanese wave fully receded. The Potsdam Conference of the Allied Powers that month called upon Japan to surrender but the military government of General Tojo ignored this warning. This refusal prompted the 'morally' gargantuan Allies to drop atom bombs on Hiroshima and Nagasaki. The two famous towns in the Land of Rising Sun were destroyed by the flames of 'thousands of suns', forcing Japan to unconditionally surrender on 14 August 1945. The Japanese dream of an Empire of its own suddenly vanished in the thin year. Her entry on the stage was welcomed as an actor but its over-acting was hooted down. Japan shrunk back to the four original islands which formed the state during the Meiji Restoration in 1868.

Did Japan formally and voluntarily declare the Second World War close? That question remains open! A suspended judgement. For, in terms of conventional wars, Japan did not lose the War; it surrendered not because its Army had lost but because of the devastation caused by atom bombs.

Japan never forgot the humiliation as to how, during the Allied rule from August 1945 to April 1952, and radical reforms in land, social and educational sectors as well as the in framing of a new 'Peace Constitution' in 1946, Emperor Hirohito had to renounce his claims to divinity, as the Son of Amaterasu O Mikami, and become a powerless figurehead ruler, committing his nation to a pacifist foreign policy—within 78 years, the Shoguns had voluntarily surrendered their powers to the Emperor who, in turn, surrendered his to Parliament; no other nation had moved so fast on the time-line of evolution of human society. Japan always retained its honour: US President Barack Obama's full bow before the Emperor was demonstrative of this Pride of the Dwarf.

Post-1946, in the absence of an active Emperor, this smouldering Japan saw the emergence of new Shoguns: they were the *zaibatsu*, the powerful finance and industrial houses. They were destined to fight the ancient battles against the world through modern means. And not alone this time: they became forerunners of the Asian Tigers like

Taiwan, Singapore, Hong Kong, Malaysia, Korea—who all basked in the glory of Japan, and later in their own, briefly.

Waiting for the emergence of revived dinosaurs, India and China.

That is how India, China and Japan have risen against the West and the Fertile Crescent. Against the Abrahamic religions and all that emanated from these.

Monsoon. Winter. Spring. Cycle of Evolution.

In clockwise precision.

It is the heyday of the Infidel who has Returned for the first time after Moses.

Epilogue

The Sky-Holders

The West has often viewed the East as an enigma; the East, in turn, has seen the West as a global dogma. Does the arrival of a revivified enigma in the 21st century, reflect the departure of dogma; or, do we mean that the 'Rise of the East' could essentially correspond to the Fall of the West?

Neither.

For instance, there have been many 'predictions' about the fall of the West. So much so that the then US Vice President Joe Biden even complained of being driven crazy because so many people were betting on America's imminent demise. From Oswald Spengler's *The Decline of the West* (1918), to Arnold Toynbee's 12-volume *The Study of History (1934-1961)* to Paul Kennedy's *The Rise and Fall of the Great Powers* (1988), to the more recent Niall Ferguson's *Complexity and Collapse: Empires on the Edge of Chaos* (2010), there have been dire warnings, off and on, on why the West has been tottering—some even offering prescriptions!

While Spengler explained that he did not view the Decline as a catastrophic occurrence but a protracted one, Ferguson thought that America's fall could be as sudden as its rise was. They did not view *their* religions, or those of others, in terms of technological evolution, their incremental irrelevance, or the need to replace them. The West has not waned; it has only rejuvenated the East.

A slow decay of monotheist Christianity and Islam in the 20th century has been parallel to the rise of 'infidel' nations like

Japan, China, India, and many other countries in the East. The main reason why these countries gradually retrieved their former pride and managed to bounce back in global reckoning was their parallel movements for extrusion of ex-catalyst alien religions and intrusion of technology and democracy.

But more than the rise of these Asian nations, another important development is unfolding across the world.

Mao once said women hold up half-the-sky. Today, women make up the backbone of production-line workers in China's private, export-oriented factories and increasingly flood professions like medicine, teaching and even journalism. One-fifth of the National People's Congress parliamentarians are female, higher than the 17% of the US Congress' women members. Women now own over 20% of businesses in China, compared to the world average of 30%. The one-child policy freed many women from caring for large families.

In India, too, women are set to control 33% of the elected seats in Parliament and the State Legislative Assemblies, thanks to the Women's Reservation Bill pending in Parliament. India was the first country to grant voting rights to women who have occupied all top posts, political and others, across the spectrum of the society, at one time or the other; Indira Gandhi was said to be the 'only man' in her Cabinet! Even hybrid Pakistan and Bangladesh, which often behave like Hindu camels in the Muslim desert tent, have seen women-on-the-top. Similarly, many other countries, including Muslim, have, under pressure from the below, been slowly bringing women forward.

This is unlocking the immense potential of those holding half-the-sky in changing the face of the Earth, once again. This had happened only when the First Wave crested in Egypt and a 'Bearded Pharoah', a woman, marked it, or when Cleopatra reigned in the Land of the Pyramids. Off and on, women briefly came to power in different countries but the male pressure continued to destabilise them, leaving them only in the footnotes of history. They may now write their own page in His-Story. Our women are the fount of the emerging Fourth Wave.

We are now going to shed old diapers and sport new ones. Some would rather be forced to wear these; others would continue to wear them even while claiming to don designer wear. Few would, however, admit they continued to wear the old ones or were forced to shed and change diapers.

We should go back to the drawing board where Nature sketches the architecture of our society, weaves a world-wide web out of us human beings and matures it to rise as a Wave.

The Third Wave, now cresting globally in the 21st century, is set to demolish a number of notions and institutions of the Second Wave.

Interestingly, the rising Fourth Wave is increasingly centring upon that ancient Crucible, the Fertile Crescent: the Middle East (West Asia), where the women are seen as the most oppressed, is emerging as the zone of deep depression around which a gargantuan human cyclone is building up.

Imagine a cataclysmic end to male hegemony in the Fertile Crescent due to a possible all-out war, and the resultant, sudden unlocking of potential of some 1,500 million Muslim women? Added to non-Muslim women, the Daughters of Eve would number over 3,000 million! They would hold the entire Sky!

Those who can, would see and hear. Others would have to go back to schools for the differently-able kids to learn the sign language and other skills.

Meanwhile, there Arrives the Enigma: the East.